The Changing Economic Order:
Readings in American Business and Economic History

Under the general editorship of
JOHN MORTON BLUM
Yale University

THE CHANGING ECONOMIC ORDER: *Readings in American Business and Economic History*

edited by

ALFRED D. CHANDLER, Jr.
The Johns Hopkins University

STUART BRUCHEY
Columbia University

LOUIS GALAMBOS
Rice University

Harcourt, Brace & World, Inc.
New York / Chicago / San Francisco / Atlanta

Preface

This book of readings deals with men and institutions. The selections describe and analyze the actions of manufacturers, merchants, laborers, farmers, government officials, and others who were responsible for economic change in America. They help to explain how and why the actions of these men transformed American economic institutions and so made the American economy the most productive and most affluent in the world. The book should thus supplement textbooks in economic history that describe in broader and often more quantitative terms the overall development of the economy. It is also planned to serve as a textbook in courses in business history. In the teaching of business policy and administration in business schools the readings can provide historical

79290

depth and understanding by indicating how present business practices came into being and by showing the changing relationship of businessmen to other groups in the economy.

In order to provide a manageable set of readings covering the broad span of American economic and business history, the focus for selection had to be sharp. It seemed best to concentrate on those men and institutions that had the most important influence on the production and distribution of goods and services, including those involved in transportation and government. In this way we could provide the student with a clear picture of the basic changes that have taken place in the American economic order.

Among these changes, the most profound and far-reaching has been America's transition from an agrarian to an industrial order. A relatively simple, undifferentiated economy was replaced by a highly complex one based on a sophisticated technology and requiring careful planning to maintain a proper balance between stability and growth. This great transformation can be best understood by dividing American economic history into three chronological periods: the agrarian and commercial economy from colonial times to the middle of the nineteenth century, the industrializing economy from 1850 to World War I, and the managerial economy from World War I to the present. Such chronological divisions emphasize the real differences in economic activities in each of these different time periods and at the same time point out some of the values and institutions that have provided the essential continuity in the history of the American economy.

Although the editors of this volume together have set up its overall format, each has had the primary responsibility for selecting the readings and for writing the introduction for one of its three parts: Professor Stuart Bruchey for Part I on the agrarian and commercial economy, Professor Alfred D. Chandler, Jr., for Part II on the industrializing economy, and Professor Louis Galambos for Part III on the managerial economy. All three of us are most grateful to the authors and publishers who have permitted us to reprint their writings. We particularly wish to thank Professor Howard F. Bennett of Northwestern University for his perceptive and constructive criticism of our manuscript.

ALFRED D. CHANDLER, Jr.
STUART BRUCHEY
LOUIS GALAMBOS

Contents

PART THREE

The Managerial Economy, 1914 to the Present   357

Part One ⌣ *The Agrarian and*
                    Commercial Economy

1607 ⌣ 1850

I

Since the historian's function is to describe change, and to analyze and explain it, the longer the period with which he is concerned the more difficult his task. Part I of this book embraces the more than two centuries between the beginnings of colonial settlement and 1850. No brief commentary or restricted set of readings can reflect all the important changes that took place over so long a period. Only a representative few of the many facets of American economic life during the period can be exhibited. Selectivity is necessary, therefore, and requires no elaborate defense; but the reader should be cognizant of the grounds on which particular selections have been made.

A consideration of overriding importance is that the early American economy was primarily agrarian and commercial, rather than industrial. Most people made their living by farming or by helping move farm commodities to domestic or foreign markets by providing transport, financing, or other services. This is not to deny that the nation became increasingly urban and industrial during the later decades of the period. In 1787 Tench Coxe estimated that 90 percent of the population was engaged in agriculture. According to a recent scholarly estimate by Paul David,[1] at the beginning of the nineteenth century 83 percent of the labor force was employed in agricultural pursuits. By 1850, however, the proportion had declined to only 55 percent, with the sharpest drop occurring after 1820. During the same five decades between 1800 and 1850, the urban proportion of the population nearly tripled, rising from about 6.5 percent to 18 percent. Admittedly, brief characterizations and statistical landmarks like these provide only very rough guides to processes of change which are continuous and interconnected, but they do remind us that the American economy was indeed agrarian and commercial throughout the period, although less so in 1850 than in 1790.

Whether or not the American economy grew at a constant rate during the long colonial period (1607–1776) or, as some scholars believe, accelerated after the early decades of the eighteenth century is a problem not easily solved in the absence of statistical data. Whatever the truth may be, it is evident that fundamental forces making for change had less effect before the Civil War than after it. Professor David has found that the rate of growth of per capita real product amounted to 1.3 percent per annum between 1790 and 1860. Not till after the Civil War did the growth rate rise, to approximately 1.8 percent. Unquestionably, the accumulative, permeating effects of industrialization were responsible for the increase.

Speaking comparatively, then, fundamental change was slow during the long early years of America; and this fact is essential to understanding those years. If we associate industrialization, urbanization, rapid technological change, large-scale production geared to the demand of an integrated national market, and complexly organized units of business enterprise with the rapid economic changes of the past century, then their absence, or embryonic presence, goes far to explain the relatively slow changes of the early years. Expressed more positively, the fundamental characteristics of the early agrarian and commercial economy were its small-scale production for local or regional markets and its relatively small capital requirements for production, with the consequent ability of noncorporate forms of business enterprise to assemble the capital sums required. Partnerships and individual proprietorships were the common forms of enterprise, and relationships between employers and their workers tended to be personal. In agriculture the small family farm was everywhere typical, even in the cotton-dependent South, during ante-

[1] Paul David, "The Growth of Real Product in the United States Before 1840: New Evidence, Controlled Conjectures," *Journal of Economic History*, Vol. XXVII (June 1967), pp. 151–97.

bellum years. And in part because the capital requirements of such social overhead as turnpikes, bridges, and canals were comparatively small, they could be met by quasi-public corporations and by state and local, rather than by federal, levels of government. In comparison with later years, markets were small and the pace of business a leisured one; institutional forms and techniques of administration were relatively simple, and government was most active at levels that reflected the spatially confined requirements of domestic enterprise. To say that change was occurring is only to recognize that the subject under discussion is history. The task of Part I, then, is to display, within a context of relatively slow change, some of the principal institutions and techniques involved in the production and marketing of farms crops. Brief selections will also trace the rise of industry, an industrial labor force, and other new institutions and methods that were gradually reshaping the economy along more "modern" lines.

II

Climate and soil were the chief determinants of the crops grown in the three main regions of colonial America. Harsh winters and rocky soil limited the agricultural potential of New England; although the area was self-sufficient in the seventeenth century, it became increasingly dependent thereafter on outside sources for grain. New England was an area of small farms, the chief export products of which were livestock, salted meats, and lumber. Sales of fish, ships, and rum also contributed importantly to the region's export earnings. In the middle colonies most holdings were also small, the chief exceptions being in New York, along the Hudson River. In the middle region wheat, which at one time had also flourished in the Connecticut Valley, was the most important cereal crop; but corn, oats, barley, and rye were also raised in abundance. From the tidewater area of Maryland south lay colonies in which the large plantation was dominant. Notable for the extent to which it concentrated on a few export staples, the South also produced most of the food required for its own consumption needs. Tobacco was the great staple of colonial Maryland and Virginia, rice and indigo of South Carolina and Georgia, and tar, pitch, turpentine, and other naval stores of North Carolina. Throughout the eighteenth century the value of exports of tobacco exceeded by far that of any other colonial commodity. The available statistics for these and other exports provide good presumptive evidence of a widespread commercialized agriculture in the colonies.

Wherever possible, colonial farmers and planters grew crops for sale as well as use. They also actively engaged in the production of land values, a fact that limits the meaning of the term "self-sufficiency." It is true that farmers situated too far from either internal or coastal markets or from navigable rivers practiced self-sufficient forms of agriculture. The extent to which they did so, however, has probably been exaggerated. It is important to realize that the "apparently self-sufficient farmer in a remote valley," to cite the words of Thomas C. Cochran, "was a man sacrificing current income for future income." [2] As Percy Bidwell and John Falconer make clear in the first of the readings, the pioneer farmer of New England and the middle colonies was chiefly engaged in producing capital goods: "The income which he did not take out of his enterprise steadily accrued and was shown in the increased value of his land." And, in Cochran's judgment, this production of land values by farmer-entrepreneurs was "the most important business ingredient in colonial culture." [3]

Whether farmers and planters were businessmen to the same degree merchants, moneylenders, and manufacturers were is debatable. Evidence continues to mount in support of the thesis that the typical country dweller was market oriented. Among this evidence is the important recent work of Aubrey C. Land, whose article on economic behavior in the tobacco-planting society of the Chesapeake region in the eighteenth century is second in the readings. Land finds little trace of self-sufficient agriculture in the tidewater area. The countryside, he says, "was peopled with commercial farmers who depended on the production of a cash crop and on the market nexus." Perhaps even more surprising is his portrait of "the great planter." Far from being that of a man taking his leisure on broad estates worked by indentured servants or slave labor, the picture we see is of a many-sided entrepreneur: tobacco planter, storekeeper, moneylender, manufacturer, and land speculator. Perhaps the most spectacular success of all, Land suggests, came from speculation in real estate.

Unlike the large planters, the small farmers, whether of colonial New England or the ante-bellum West, looked to their own families for the bulk of their labor supply. Both farm and urban labor was scarce, since the population was small in relation to the supply of land. As a result, large families were desirable on the farm; from early youth children were trained to do all the necessary chores. Female members of the family worked as hard at their various tasks as the men and, when needed, helped in the fields during the harvest seasons. Nevertheless, most farmers also needed outside help during the haying, harvesting, and butchering seasons and by the middle of the nineteenth century the use of hired help for at least part of the year was a standard practice in well-established farming areas.

Even in the ante-bellum South, where cotton had assumed the leading role played by tobacco in colonial times, nearly three-fourths of all free Southern families owned no slaves at all in 1860. The typical Southerner was a nonslaveholding small farmer. A large majority of the slave-owning families, moreover, owned only a few slaves. In 1850, 89 percent of the owners had fewer than 20 slaves, 71 percent had fewer than ten, and almost 50 percent had fewer than 5. The planter aristocracy was

[2] Thomas C. Cochran and Thomas B. Brewer, eds., *Views of American Economic Growth: The Agricultural Era* (New York: McGraw-Hill, 1966), p. 11.
[3] Thomas C. Cochran, "The History of a Business Society," *Journal of American History*, Vol. LIV (June 1967), p. 9.

made up of some 10,000 families living off the labor of gangs of more than 50 slaves.

Slaveholders with small farms usually gave close personal supervision to the unspecialized labor of a few slaves. Many were obliged to work in the fields alongside their hands, although those owning as few as half a dozen slaves sought a more elevated social status by refraining from such labor. Those farmers and small planters who owned from 10 to 30 slaves did not as a rule employ overseers, although they might have had the aid of a slave foreman or driver, whose function was to urge on the slave gangs by word or whip. Agricultural units of this size usually benefited from some labor specialization. Besides the field hands and driver, there might have been a few slaves who exercised manual skills or performed domestic work. Even so, the unit was too small for full-time carpenters or cooks, so that the latter often had to work in the fields as well.

Maximum specialization was possible only for those planters who owned 30 or more slaves. Those owners almost always had overseers, who were generally retained on a year-to-year basis under a written contract that could be terminated at will by either party. There is an excellent description of the manifold managerial duties and responsibilities of overseers in the selection by William K. Scarborough, a very thorough modern student of the subject. Included in the selection is a written set of instructions or plantation rules drawn up by a planter for the guidance of his overseer. A careful reading of Scarborough's account will reveal the same entrepreneurial concern on the part of the agricultural businessman in the South that has previously been noted as an attribute of his counterpart in the eighteenth-century Chesapeake Bay area. It is only a convention that historians establish separate categories for agriculture and business.

III

Many analyses of the business opportunities prevalent before 1850 concentrate on institutions and activities generated by the marketing of agricultural commodities. These were numerous, complex, and changing; they involved both foreign and domestic commerce, and they reflected innovations in transport and changes in the flows of goods. Only a few highlights can be touched upon in a brief discussion. It is evident that distinctions must be drawn between the products of differing regions, between foreign and domestic commerce, and between the colonial and post-colonial periods.

The principal markets for the fish, lumber, wheat, and flour of the New England and middle colonies were in the West Indies. It is notable that this trade occurred between two agricultural communities; the markets for West Indian staples, particularly sugar, so widened during the eighteenth century that the island economies devoted the principal part of their resources to the cultivation of those staples and depended for their food supplies on the nearby American colonies. Some colonial commodities, most notably the grains (all of which the English lumped together under the name "corn"), competed with English agriculture and normally were excluded from the mother country by the English Corn Laws. Even without the handicap of the Corn Laws, however, geographic proximity would still have led to the dominant position of American supplies in the islands.

By a well-known multiangular commerce, the Northern and middle regions procured the specie or bills of exchange on England that permitted them to pay for imports of British manufactures. Some of the Navigation Acts and other legislation by which Great Britain sought to regulate the trade of her empire very much affected this commerce—for example, by excluding Dutch and other foreign vessels from American ports. Other laws, such as the Molasses Act of 1733, were simply not enforced during a long period of comparative neglect prior to 1764. While scholars have differed on the effects of English laws on colonial economic growth, they appear increasingly inclined to believe that those effects were minimal. Thus, the selection on foreign commerce, by Stuart Bruchey, is concerned with the more fundamental and abiding problems and techniques of conducting commerce.

Because the Bruchey selection deals with American merchants, it is pertinent in the main to the mercantile activities of the middle and New England regions in the eighteenth and early nineteenth centuries. The history of the Southern colonies and their staples is quite different, largely because indigo, naval stores, tobacco, and other goods were not only noncompetitive with British interests but were much in demand by sectors of British industry and trade. English law "enumerated" these staples—that is, placed them on lists of goods that could be shipped only to England or its colonies. Until 1673 American vessels loaded these staples and carried them directly to the continent. At that time the English Parliament closed a loophole in the law that allowed this traffic, and British merchants appear to have had the trade to themselves. They were the first of a series of factors (commission merchants) to dominate the marketing mechanism of the South prior to 1850.

In the Upper South, the Chesapeake Bay region of Maryland and Virginia that is the setting for Aubrey C. Land's article, numerous navigable streams permitted seagoing vessels to penetrate to the very wharves of the planters. Vessels dispatched from British ports unloaded their supplies on those wharves and took on board not only the planter's own crop of tobacco but also that which he had taken in trade at his store. The planter-storekeeper had himself obtained the imports on credit, the usual length of which was one year, and his consignment of tobacco enabled him to discharge part or all of his debt. Often he made the consignment to the same merchant who had sent the ship with its supplies.

As the interior began to be settled during the eighteenth century, the consignment system increasingly gave way to direct purchases by resident representatives of British firms. Agents of Scottish mercantile houses opened stores in the back country as centers for both the purchase of tobacco and the sale of imported merchandise. According to a recent investigation by James H. Soltow, these stores appear to have offered merchandise on credit to any planter from whom a yearly purchase of at least 300 hogsheads of tobacco could be made. Planters' accounts were supposed to be settled at the close of the crop year; but this policy was difficult to enforce, and some balances remained unpaid for as long as four or five years.

British merchants also played an important role in the economy of the Lower South. Since in this region the shoal channels of the inland streams made their navigation by ocean-going vessels impossible, seaports developed at the available harbors. The commercial capital of the entire region was Charleston, which acted as a funnel through which rice, indigo, and naval stores were exported to England. While the existence of a flourishing seaport created commercial opportunities for numerous colonists, most of the great merchants who handled Charleston's foreign trade in the eighteenth century were, as in the case of the Upper South, Englishmen or Scots. Thus, planters throughout the colonial South may be said to have depended on the marketing and credit facilities provided by the British.

When cotton became the great staple of the ante-bellum period there occurred a change in the cast of characters, but the plot remained the same. New England and middle-states merchants, particularly those of New York, provided the vessels, insurance, and other services, supplies on credit, and often the factors too. The latter were often Northerners who had settled in the South's leading cotton ports—New Orleans, Mobile, Savannah, and Charleston—or inland in one of the fall-line towns, which by 1860 included Fayetteville, Columbia, Augusta, Milledgeville, Macon, Atlanta, Montgomery, Nashville, Memphis, and Shreveport. Coastal factors obtained their supplies from New York on credit, supplied them to the larger planters on credit, and marketed cotton for a commission. Inland factors did much the same thing, although their business relationships were founded mainly on the needs of smaller planters, farmers, and keepers of general stores in the smaller towns and villages. A chain of middlemen often stretched from seaport to plantation, with the planter or farmer selling his cotton to a general store, the store selling it to an inland factor, and the latter ordering it to be forwarded to a Northern or a foreign market by a coastal factor. Most of the cotton was shipped directly to Europe, principally to Liverpool, from the cotton ports of the South; but between the early 1820's and the mid-1850's there was a significant amount of cotton sent to New York for transshipment. By mid-century, a third of the crop was being used by textile manufacturers in New England and in the middle states.

In sum, the role of the factor in the marketing of cotton and in plantation supply was crucial. While many plantations, especially the larger ones, sought as high a degree of self-sufficiency as possible, they were still dependent to some extent on outside sources for such articles as bagging, rope, twine, dry goods, and equipment, and often for corn and livestock as well. Furnishing these goods on credit, making cash advances, and holding a planter's funds subject to his order were all part of the factor's role as banker. Commercial banks also played an important, although indirect, part in the financing of cotton transactions. Although they seldom offered loans directly to planters or farmers, they did discount the notes of planters that had been endorsed by a factor. Factors were thus the intermediaries through which commercial-bank credit reached the plantations. They also had other functions, personal as well as economic. Naturally, such complex relationships gave rise to numerous differences between planters and factors. Nevertheless, Ralph W. Haskins, in his article on the factor, reaches the conclusion that harmony was the rule and dissension the exception.

No other product of ante-bellum America approached the importance of cotton in the export trade. For the period 1815–60 cotton alone constituted more than half the total value of domestic exports. Early in the period it had two rivals, wheat and flour (counted as one) and unmanufactured tobacco, which made up 16 percent and 15 percent, respectively, of the value of domestic exports for the years 1816–20. But these were the high points for both during the ante-bellum years. Within the country, however, wheat, corn, livestock, and other products provided the principal means by which the West reimbursed the East for manufactured goods. Indeed, the three principal regions of ante-bellum America tended to specialize—the West in foodstuffs, the South in cotton and other export staples, and the East in manufactured goods—and to develop a relationship of interdependence. The foreign demand for cotton enabled the South—the Southwest in particular—to concentrate to a significant degree on the production of that staple, using the earnings from its sale to pay the East for manufactured goods and financial and shipping services and the West for food supplies and livestock. The internal market for the goods and services of each region thus expanded in part because of the demand for cotton created by the English industrial revolution. But both the magnitude and the direction of the domestic trade that ensued also depended upon the growth of New York City as a great center for imports of foreign manufactures and upon the development of manufacturing in the Atlantic states north of Chesapeake Bay.

The settlement of the interior of the country, when conjoined with transport conditions favorable to commercial agriculture, thus created an interdependence between foreign and domestic trade, and regional specialization heightened the interdependence. As we have seen, when the cultivation of tobacco moved into the interior in the eighteenth century, direct exports to foreign markets were no longer possible. The opening of stores in the interior represented an institutional response to this changed situation. The movement of cotton planting into the interior in the early nineteenth century produced similar results; inland factors settled in fall-line towns and opened stores for the supplies of planters and farmers and warehouses for the storage of cotton. Other enterprising men followed cotton farther west and opened stores where supplies could be obtained on credit and later paid for in cotton. These stores and warehouses were by no means confined to the South. Jonathan Trumbull's store in Lebanon, Connecticut, where the future governor of that state bartered gunpowder, flints, knives, earthenware, lace, and other imports for flaxseed, hogs, oxen, turkeys, and other forms of "country pay" is typical, as is the store of Thomas and John Hancock in late eighteenth-century Boston, of the Northern response to a similar need. And so in the West too. On a trip to the Ohio country in 1789, Colonel John May was surprised to come upon "a settlement of five log huts, or cabins, and not more than fifty acres of land cleared" called Mingo Bottom. "Yet, small as the settlement is," the Colonel confided to his journal, "here is a store, with a very good assortment of goods, to the value, as I suppose, of £1000." [4]

In the pioneer West farmers with access to navigable rivers at first marketed their own goods. For example, those adjacent to the Mississippi River or its tributaries accompanied their own shipments downstream, disposing of their produce personally at some market along the river or at New Orleans. But direct marketing had its disadvantages: it was time-consuming, the farmer could not get a quick return on his crop, and markets were difficult to reach, unstable, and often glutted. The institutional response to this situation was general stores in the villages and smaller towns and, as population increased, forwarding and commission merchants in the larger centers.

Lewis E. Atherton is an authority on the stores of the South and West and on other mechanisms of internal trade in the ante-bellum period. His article shows why the Western storekeeper "was an integral part of the three-cornered trade relationship that characterized American economic life before the Civil War." As Atherton makes clear, the system of bartering store goods for produce became universal in the West, with storekeepers sometimes making cash purchases as well. Storekeepers opened accounts for farmers, then charged sales to them and credited them with payments in produce, or for services performed, such as hauling goods, cutting brush, or grinding axes. Their confreres in the South and North did the same thing.

Just as farmers had done early in the nineteenth century, storekeepers often took their produce to market in person. In time, however, in the larger towns along the Ohio and Mississippi Rivers, farmers began to use intermediaries. These forwarding and commission merchants handled grain for both farmers and storekeepers, provided storage facilities, located the most efficient transportation, and endeavored to sell at the most remunerative market. Gradually, houses dealing in the produce trade began to extend cash advances to country storekeepers, enabling the latter to offer additional credit to farmers. A recent study by John G. Clark

[4] "Journal of Col. John May of Boston. Relative to a Journey to the Ohio Country, 1789," *Pennsylvania Magazine of History and Biography*, Vol. XLV (1921), p. 144.

reports that by the early 1850's New York commission houses and grain dealers

> were flooding the rich regions of Ohio, Indiana, and Illinois with eastern bank notes advanced to packers, millers, and western grain merchants, on products to be shipped east. . . . The system of cash advances, together with improved transportation facilities, enabled farmers to market their crops soon after harvest. Grain dealers in the West were enabled to gather in produce through the winter and store it until the lakes opened up in the spring. In the days before large sums of eastern money became available to help move the produce, many dealers were forced to hurry off their shipments to New Orleans during the late fall and early winter.[5]

Obviously, important improvements in techniques of marketing Western produce took place during the ante-bellum period. Yet, the necessity of resorting to a number of forwarding and commission merchants to get Western produce to market and Eastern goods to the West was time-consuming and cumbersome. The explanation for this necessity, Atherton makes clear, is that transportation facilities were not yet organized on a national scale. Not till the advent of nationally organized railroad systems in the 1870's and 1880's was it possible to avoid the costly delays of multiple transfers and to lower the storage, insurance, and other costs of maintaining large inventories.

IV

Long before then, however, significant innovations in transportation had lessened man's dependence on the elements. While the article on foreign commerce by Stuart Bruchey questions the validity of the emphasis usually placed upon the delays and uncertainties associated with an age of sail, there can be no question that the advent of the steam engine greatly reduced the effects of wind and tide. Even so, it is not only the availability of more rapid and regular transportation but also its perceived utility and commercial organization that produce economic consequences. Bruchey's discussion of American foreign commerce suggests that even before the appearance of the steamship, improved commercial organization and increased dependability of demand in the West Indies lessened the need for island-hopping in search of a market. And studies by Robert G. Albion have shown that the port of New York's national preeminence was largely because of the establishment there of packet-line service by groups of private vessels for transatlantic commerce in 1818 and for coastal trade in 1822. Sailing on regular schedules at specified times, the packet service did much to cause the channels of European trade to flow to New York rather than to Boston or Philadelphia. The coastal packets, in turn, provided the cargoes of cotton and

[5] John G. Clark, "The Antebellum Grain Trade of New Orleans: Changing Patterns in the Relation of New Orleans with the Old Northwest," *Agricultural History*, Vol. XXXVII (July 1964), p. 137.

other Southern products that helped make profitable and eastbound trips of the ocean packets.

Within the country, the principal transport innovations of the period were turnpikes, canals, railroads, and steamboats. Indeed, economic historians often call the period 1800–30 "the turnpike era," 1825–40 "the canal era," and 1850–1915 "the railroad age." (Steamboats are no less important for not having been assigned an age or era!) The building of the Lancaster Turnpike in 1794 initiated the turnpike era; the appearance of the steamboat on Western rivers in 1817 inaugurated its domestic use; the opening of the Erie Canal in 1825 began a rage for canal construction. Although the first American railroad dates from the late 1820's, it was a large increase in mileage in the 1850's that initiated the railroad age. The economic effects of these transport innovations and the competition between them is described in the selection by George R. Taylor.

Turnpikes were mainly constructed between the larger towns or westward over the mountains. New York and Pennsylvania had the greatest turnpike mileage, and by about 1825 southern New England was crisscrossed with many main roads. In the South, however, construction lagged, and in the Lower South very few through roads were built. In the Old Northwest few roads were completed except in Ohio. Greatest of all the turnpikes was the National Road. Built by the federal government, the road reached west as far as Vandalia, Illinois, by mid-century. The turnpikes were doomed economically, however, by their inability to meet the need of an agrarian economy for a cheap means of transporting bulky products over considerable distances.

The rivers provided the only economical routes of commerce for early inland settlements. As Taylor makes clear, "the prosperity of the western states depended upon their ability to exchange the products of their farms for needed manufactures and other outside products like salt, sugar, and coffee." The steamboat provided the solution of the problem of the high cost of shipping goods to the West by way of New Orleans and the Mississippi River. First the canal and then the railroad made the 300-mile land route between the east coast and the Ohio Valley feasible.

In 1817 a total of 17 steamboats, with a combined tonnage of 3,290 tons, were recorded as operating on the western rivers; the corresponding figures for 1850 were 740 steamboats and 141,834 tons. In 1830, five years after the opening of the Erie Canal, total canal mileage, mainly in New York, Pennsylvania, and Ohio, amounted to 1,277 miles. The corresponding figure for railroads in that same year is merely 73 miles. By 1840, total canal and railroad mileage were almost exactly equal, 3,326 and 3,328 miles respectively. New York, Pennsylvania, and Ohio continued their leadership in canal mileage, the railroad leaders being New York, Pennsylvania, and Virginia. Railroad construction had taken place almost entirely east of the Appalachian Mountains. Between 1840 and 1850 less than 400 miles were added to the network of canals. Railroad mileage, in contrast, rose from 3,328 miles to 8,879 miles, and by 1860 the total was 30,636 miles. Railroad construction in New England and New York accounted for nearly 60 percent of the increase in the 1840's, but in the 1850's the most striking gains occurred in the West. The railroads did not constitute a unified, integrated system, however. In 1860 there were more than 300 independent railroad lines, with variety in gauges adding to the cost and delays of rail shipment. Speed and regularity of transport within the national market awaited the integration that is described in Part II.

What lay behind much of the extraordinary activity in the field of "internal improvements"—as contemporaries called it—was a vigorous interstate and interurban rivalry for the trade of the West. States and cities sought to make their own communities funnels through which Western produce might flow. Partly because private supplies of capital were either scarce or difficult to attract to long-term investments and partly because construction projects would bring diffused gains to the community generally, much of the rivalry took place on the public or political level. A long colonial tradition helped assure this result, for it had been common for public bodies to seek to encourage private persons, by tax exemptions or other aids, to provide utilities that would otherwise have required an allocation of scarce public funds and an unpopular increase in taxes.

Governmental participation in internal improvements projects took two forms. As the excerpt from Stuart Bruchey's article on corporations makes clear, one form was the creation of quasi-public business corporations. During the entire colonial period, only half a dozen such corporations had been authorized by the Crown or Parliament. Part of the explanation for their paucity lies in the fact that colonial businesses were generally small-scale and local and that no large supplies of capital or labor were generally in search of employment. A fuller explanation, however, requires taking into account an important political change.

Most colonial corporations were set up under charters granted by royal governors in the name of the Crown, although usually with the consent of the provincial councils. The sovereign was recognized as the source of legal authority, with parliamentary approval required after 1688 in the case of a grant of exclusive or monopoly privilege. In both royal and proprietary colonies the legal right of the assembly to incorporate was subject to the veto of the governor or higher English authority. The Revolution brought an important change in this situation. Because of the fiction that the Revolution was fought to free the colonists from the exactions of the Crown, a revulsion against executive authority was manifest in the early state constitutions, as well as in the Articles of Confederation. The power to incorporate shifted from the central to more local government and from the executive to the legislative arm— and therefore to persons more responsive to community pressures upon government to provide community services.

In consequence, in the brief 11 years between 1789 and 1800 state governments created more than 300 corporations, two-thirds of which were concerned with inland navigation, turnpikes, and toll bridges. Bruchey's article emphasizes the continued dominance of quasi-public purposes in state incorporation during the early decades of the nineteenth century and makes the point that the colonial tradition of public encouragement to induce the devotion of scarce private capital to public ends took the form of grants of monopoly rights of way, tax exemption, power of eminent domain, and other privileges.

The second form of governmental participation in internal improvements projects was more direct. Indeed, as George R. Taylor has expressed it, "in no other period of American history has the government been so active in financing and actually promoting, owning, and controlling banks and public works including turnpikes, bridges, canals, and railroads." [6] The excellent survey article by Robert A. Lively summarizes and discusses the contributions of a number of scholars whose studies during the past several decades have added appreciably to our knowledge of the role of government in American economic development. One of Lively's criticisms of this body of work is that it fails to assess the contribution to public works made by private capital. Responding to this criticism, Carter Goodrich, Julius Rubin, H. Jerome Cranmer, and Harvey H. Segal have since calculated that no less than 73.4 percent of a total investment of about $188,000,000 in canal construction in New York, Pennsylvania, Ohio, Indiana, Illinois, and Virginia between 1815 and 1860 was financed by state and municipal governments.[7] Still more recently, however, there has appeared an even more important and as yet unanswered critique by Albert Fishlow, *Railroads and the Transformation of the Antebellum Economy*. Railroads built by the states or with state aid in the 1830's, Fishlow points out, were built ahead of commercial demand for them, and in general they proved "dismal failures." Railroads built in the Midwest in the 1850's, on the other hand, were constructed in response to demand and were notable successes. In a word, the balance sheet of the public sector in American economic development is yet to be drawn up.

V

There are few readings under the final heading of industry and labor because there is comparatively little to say about both subjects until after the middle of the nineteenth century. To be sure, manufactures occupy a familiar place in colonial economic history, but for the most part market and transport limitations dictated that they be what have been called "neighborhood manufactures," dispersed local manufactures protected by high transport costs from the competition of distant producers. Shortly before the Revolution improvements were made in the application of power to milling machinery and processes, and, as will be famil-

[6] George R. Taylor, *The Transportation Revolution, 1815–1860* (New York: Rinehart, 1951), p. 383.
[7] Carter Goodrich, ed., *Canals and American Economic Development* (New York: Columbia University Press, 1961), p. 213.

iar, the period of embargo, nonintercourse, and war from 1807 to 1815 stimulated the growth of manufactures, especially cotton textiles. That industry, together with the making of iron and the production of woolen goods, carpets, paper, flint glass, lead, sugar and molasses, salt, and steam engines, grew more rapidly in the 1820's than the rate of population. The statistical researches of Robert E. Gallman indicate that between 1839 and 1859 the share of manufacturing in commodity output rose from less than 20 percent to 33 percent. Altogether, the evidence of manufacturing growth is impressive. Most of the manufacturing, however, was not done by factory methods. It was not till after 1850 that factories rose in considerable numbers; they are therefore discussed in Part II.

The techniques of the "domestic system" used before mid-century that are described in the article by Blanche Hazard may be regarded as typical of the earlier agrarian and commercial economy. In her study of the Massachusetts boot and shoe industry, which supplied shoes first to local and then to Southern and Western markets, Miss Hazard was influenced by the work of nineteenth-century German economic historians who divided the organization of industry into a number of "stages," and some of these stages into transitional "phases" of development. While many present-day economic historians believe that concepts of stages often impose too high a degree of rigidity upon the developments encompassed by them, the principal steps in the developing organization of the boot and shoe industry are clearly delineated in Hazard's essay. They are, in chronological order, the home stage, the handicraft stage, the domestic stage, and the factory stage.

Of principal interest to us here is the domestic stage (1750–1850). Under this form of organization of the industry the shoemaker, together with his apprentices and journeymen, and also, on a more irregular basis, the women and girls of his family, worked in his craft shop on materials and tools supplied in whole or part by the "capitalist-entrepreneur," or wholesale merchant. One of the most important contrasts between this "putting-out system" and the factory stage of organization that succeeded it is that under the latter the workers were gathered together under a single roof where their labor could be supervised. Another important contrast is between the use of hand tools and machinery. Until the 1840's the shoemaker had used the hand tools familiar to the trade for centuries. A variety of machines, most notably the sewing machine, soon replaced them. In order to supply the expanding demand in the 1850's, the industry required larger buildings, more capital, and larger supplies of raw materials as well as organizational changes. Essentially, the factory stage was reached after mid-century, and these were principal characteristics of the new system.

The final selection, by Foster Rhea Dulles, discusses the impact of growing industrialism upon labor, the deterioration of working conditions, the living conditions endured by immigrants in the urban slums of the East, and the resulting involvement of workers in the "hazy garrulity" of various programs for the general reform of society in America in the 1840's.

Early factory workers in the United States were unable to form strong or enduring unions. At times of serious dispute with employers temporary organizations often sprang up, but the more lasting unions were those of skilled workers, artisans, and mechanics that began to be organized in the 1820's. These unions differed from their counterparts during the colonial and early national periods in that the latter had contained not only journeymen (men paid daily wages) but master craftsmen (employers) as well. With the expansion of markets following the transportation improvements of the early nineteenth century and the subordination of older craft shops in the cities by merchant capitalists under the domestic system, journeymen shoemakers, printers, and other craftsmen in the larger American cities organized craft societies from which masters were usually excluded. Intent on improving wages and hours, these organizations of the mid-1820's represented the first beginnings of a real American labor movement.

During the period 1827–37 the movement grew in strength. It formed federations on both the local and national levels and engaged vigorously in efforts to bring about reform by means of political action. The Mechanics Union of Trade Associations, which represented a local union of 15 workingmen's societies in Philadelphia, was formed in 1827 and became the first "city central," or trades union in the United States. In 1834 the Philadelphia trades union joined with similar organizations in other cities to form the National Trades Union, the first national labor organization in the United States that brought together workers from different crafts. In 1835 and 1836 about half a dozen national unions were formed. But the national organizations, like the trades unions, were too weak to survive the economic depression that broke out in 1837 and disappeared completely. Perhaps a key to their failure, and to the period itself, is supplied by Dulles' judgment that the most important distinction between conditions in the ante-bellum period and later is that the worker did not consider himself to be a permanent employee.

There is much to support the validity of this judgment. Studies by William A. Sullivan of Philadelphia and Edward Pessen of Boston have shown that the workingmen's districts in those cities voted for Whig or well-to-do business-interest candidates, rather than those supporting Andrew Jackson. Analyzing the life histories and occupations of 850 men active in the Workingmen's political movement in New York in the early 1830's, Walter Hugins found a complete absence of factory operatives, that is, of unskilled workers. Most were skilled craftsmen, including masters as well as journeymen, with a liberal sprinkling of professionals, and even a few merchants and lawyers. In view of these findings it is perhaps not surprising to discover that the leaders of the Workingmen's parties that formed in several states in the late 1820's and early 1830's were not themselves workers but reformers, small businessmen, and ambitious politicians. Party objectives included mechanics' lien laws, a ten-hour day, abolition of imprisonment for debt, abolition of compulsory militia duty, and free public education. Most of these practices bore heavily on labor, but some were of wider social significance. That "workingmen" should have sought them is not surprising in view of Joseph Dorfman's finding that to the Age of Jackson the term "workingmen" meant "working classes," "producing classes," or "useful classes." It excluded only bankers, bartenders, and "political capitalists."

We do not really know whether or not the society and economy of the ante-bellum period justified the ideology of mobility to which so many men apparently subscribed. There is much contemporary testimony in support of the view that the doors of opportunity were open wide. Indeed, the distinguished French observer Alexis de Tocqueville believed that equality of social condition lay behind the "prodigious" commercial activity he saw in the early 1830's, including that of the farmers, for "most of them make agriculture a trade." The farmer "brings land into tillage in order to sell it again, and not to farm it. . . ." [8] De Tocqueville understood the psychological truth that men take for granted the existence of gross inequalities, but when inequalities are very small they passionately seek to remove them: "Hence the desire for equality always becomes more insatiable in proportion as equality is more complete." It was to this desire that De Tocqueville attributed the "all-pervading and restless activity," the "super-abundant force," that he found in the American people.[9] Numerous scholars, including Lee Benson, who has called the period the Age of Egalitarianism, are inclined to accept the view that social and economic mobility were marked.

Other considerations also support the belief that equal access to opportunity was widely shared, at least among white men. Much of the productive machinery of the time was light, wooden, inexpensive, and well within the capital-raising power of partnerships and proprietorships that dominated the business scene. Because heavy industry was almost entirely lacking, the economy's private capital, whether in the form of vessels, warehouses and stores, inventories, agricultural investment, or manufacturing mills, was highly liquid. Investors could quickly shift their funds from one opportunity to another. Indeed, they did so with such alacrity as to amaze another contemporary observer, Francis Grund, who commented on the agility with which men won, lost, and recouped fortunes. De Tocqueville also noted that wealth circulated "with inconceivable rapidity, and experience shows that it is rare to find two succeeding generations in the full enjoyment of it." [10] Unquestionably, it was a highly speculative period.

Not least among the speculators were small pioneer farmers in search of capital gains from rising land values. But the speculators were generally small rather than large operators. Speculation, moreover, is a

[8] Alexis de Tocqueville, *Democracy in America*, ed. by Phillips Bradley (New York: Vintage Books, 1945), Vol. II, p. 166.
[9] *Ibid.*, Vol. I, p. 261; Vol. II, p. 147.
[10] *Ibid.*, Vol. I, p. 53.

froth thrown up by the churning of most societies, and rarely if ever does it affect the deeper economic forces at work. When we focus on the latter we realize that for all the appearance of motion, the period, when compared with that which followed it, was one of slow economic change. It was a decentralized, precorporate, preindustrial age that moved within bounds set by relatively small markets, a relatively low level of technological expertise, and a relative simplicity of organization in all departments of economy and life. How great the contrast is with later periods will be clear from the readings in Part II and Part III.

One ～ *Small Farmers of the New England and Middle Colonies*

PIONEERING IN THE EIGHTEENTH CENTURY *Percy W. Bidwell and John I. Falconer*

In studying the agricultural development of New England and the Middle Colonies in the eighteenth century, we can distinguish two sharply contrasted types of farming and of rural life: (a) pioneering, the agriculture of the new settlements on the frontier, and (b) the agriculture of the older communities along the seacoast and in the river valleys.

Until recent years pioneering has been an important feature of our agricultural history at all stages of its development. The frontier with its apparently inexhaustible supply of new, cheap land and its democratic and unrestrained social life has always been present to the westward of the older settlements, drawing away from them their surplus population, the most energetic as well as the most unruly of the younger generation. If the frontier has been a safety-valve for the relief of political discontent, it has also proved, changing the metaphor, a sponge absorbing much of the best talent from the farms of the East.

REPRINTED with permission from Percy W. Bidwell and John I. Falconer, "Pioneering in the Eighteenth Century," *History of Agriculture in the United States, 1620–1860,* Washington, D.C.: The Carnegie Institution, 1925, pp. 69–83.

The Westward Progress of Settlement

The first American frontier, as Professor Turner [1] has shown, was on the Atlantic coast. Until the end of the seventeenth century the colonists had occupied only a narrow fringe of the Coastal Plain from the Penobscot River to New York City and in addition the lower valleys of the Connecticut, Hudson, and Delaware Rivers.[2] In the hundred years ending in 1763 the colonists, amid almost incessant Indian warfare, had succeeded in clearing and settling a strip of Coastal Plain about 100 miles wide. This area, intermediate between the coast settlements of the seventeenth century and the trans-Allegheny settlements of the late eighteenth century, Professor Turner had aptly termed "The Old West." In New England the frontier was found in the first half of the eighteenth century in the western counties of Massachusetts and Connecticut. In New York the population expanded along the Hudson and Mohawk Valleys into the valleys of their tributaries, the Wallkill and Cherry Valleys, and also along the sources of the Susquehanna. In Pennsylvania the trend of settlement was into the Great Valley, the fertile limestone region of the southeastern part of the State and then southward along this valley into the southern uplands.

After the Treaty of Paris (1763) had removed the French and Indian menace, a great swarming of pioneers into new land took place. From the old towns of Southern New England thousands of settlers moved into New Hampshire, Maine, and Vermont. After the Revolution, immigration continued into northern New England, until by 1812 practically all its lands available for farming had been taken up. Into New York State, meanwhile, a stream of New England settlers had been flowing via the Mohawk Valley to take up lands in the fertile Genessee Country. From the older settlements of Pennsylvania emigrants passed across the Alleghenies and into the fertile valleys of the Ohio. It is unnecessary to repeat here the story of the westward movement of our population. We are interested only in the kind of agriculture which was carried on by the pioneers of the eighteenth century, and inasmuch as the record of the expansion of agriculture into the Ohio and Mississippi Valleys belongs chiefly to the nineteenth century, we shall confine our discussion to conditions east of the Alleghenies.[3]

The Causes of Expansion on New Land

The forces which caused the movement of the agricultural population westward to the Alleghenies were varied. The soil of the old settlements

[1] *The Old West*, in Wisconsin Hist. Soc. *Proceedings*, 1908, pp. 184–233.
[2] Maps showing settlement in 1660, are to be found in Channing, *United States*, I, 510, and in Shepherd, *Historical Atlas*, 189, 191.
[3] For a full discussion of the movements of population in the eighteenth century see Turner, *The Old West*, in Wis. Hist. Soc. *Proceedings* (1908), pp. 184–233. Also Mathews, *The Expansion of New England*, chapters I to V.

soon showed the effects of an exhausting cropping system without adequate fertilization. Jared Eliot[4] wrote in 1747 from Killingworth, Connecticut, on Long Island Sound, that soil depletion was in his opinion the most important cause of the failure of the wheat crops; continuing:

> When our fore-fathers settled here, they entered a Land which probably never had been Ploughed since the Creation; the Land being new they depended upon the natural Fertility of the Ground, which served their purpose very well, and when they had worn out one piece they cleared another, without any concern to amend their Land, except a little helped by the Fold and Cart-dung. . . . Our Lands being thus worn out, I suppose to be one Reason why so many are inclined to Remove to new Places that they may raise Wheat: As also that they may have more Room, thinking that we live too thick.

As early as 1750 the declining yield of grain crops showed that the land in the neighborhood of Philadelphia was being "worn out";[5] and in the neighborhood of both New York and Boston it was evident before the end of the eighteenth century that fertility was decreasing.[6]

The Rise of Land Values
in the Older Communities

Land values in the eighteenth century reflected the increasing scarcity of good land in the older communities as contrasted with its abundance on the frontier. Price data of the eighteenth century are fragmentary[7] and unsatisfactory because of the disordered state of the colonial currencies. In the case of land values comparisons are rendered especiallly difficult by the lack of standardized units. Comment on the rise in land values around Philadelphia in 1750 is found in the report of a German traveler, who wrote:[8]

---

[4] *Field Husbandry*, 23, 24.
[5] Watson, *Philadelphia* (1830 ed.), 717.
[6] New York Society for Promotion of Useful Arts, *Transactions*, I (2d ed., 1801), 57; American Academy, *Memoirs*, I, 385.
[7] Fragmentary data are to be found in the writings of the travelers of the period. See especially Cooper, *Information Respecting America* (1794), pp. 71, 94, 107, 108; Richard Smith, *Journal* (1769), pp. 21, 32. See also Brown, *Schoharie County*, New York, 15; American Museum, VII (1790), p. 296; Washington, *Letters on Agriculture* (Knight ed.), 35–37, 107. Brown, in Mass. Hist. Soc. *Collections*, 1st series, IX, 118, 124.
[8] Mittelberger, *Journey to Pennsylvania*, 118.

The price of farms in Pennsylvania, especially round Philadelphia, is already quite high; from 30 to 50 florins are paid for an acre, only a day's journey from the city, although the ground is still uncleared forest land. If a place is desired for a homestead, which is already in a habitable and cultivated condition, containing a dwelling-house, barns and good stables, together with meadows, orchards, tilled fields and sufficient woodland, twice as much is asked for it as for uncultivated land, the price being about one hundred florins per acre. Rich Englishmen have already bought up from the Indians all the remote land far and near, where all is as yet wild and wooded, in order to sell it again to the Europeans who are coming to the country. Our German people who emigrate there do not get land enough for nothing upon which to build a cottage. The price of land is increasing from year to year, especially because the English see that so many people, anxious to own farms or plantations, are coming to the country every year.

The author of *American Husbandry* (1775)[9] commented on rising land values in New England.

Trade, navigation, fisheries, increasing population, with other causes, have operated strongly to raise the value of all the estates under cultivation, whose situation is favourable, for in proportion as the wild country is taken up good lands and convenient situations rise in value; till we see they come, near the great towns, to as high a value as in the best parts of Great Britain, for near Boston there are lands worth twenty shillings an acre.

The best summary of the situation is to be found in the report prepared by William Strickland [10] in 1794 for the English Board of Agriculture. After giving a number of figures for land values in various parts of New York State, he concludes:

Hence the average price of land, in the old settled country below Schenectady (rejecting such as being mountainous is little capable of cultivation, and such as for mercantile purposes, or from being in the vicinity of large towns, is of increased value) appears to be £3. 7s. 10d. per acre, and of the new settled country, to the west of it, 9s. 3¾d.

Regarding New Jersey and Pennsylvania, he wrote:[11]

The best land in Jersey and in that part of Pennsylvania which is east of the mountains, exclusive of the German tract, may be settled at about £4. per acre; they certainly average something more than the old part of New York, this tract not being mixed with any barren mountains, and being less rocky and broken.

The back lands of Pennsylvania sell for considerably less than those of New York: from what information I could obtain, I could not state

[9] I, 63.　　[10] *Observations*, 12.　　[11] *Ibid.*, 16.

them at more than 3s. or 4s. per acre; a great quantity was upon sale for less; the tenure of them is less satisfactory than of those of New York, the titles less to be relied upon, and the whole having less credit, many egregious frauds have been committed upon purchasers, particularly those in Europe.

Land Policy and Emigration—New England

The policy adopted in the eighteenth century by the northern colonies in the disposal of unoccupied lands favored the dispersion of population and the rapid settlement of new areas. In the older New England towns up to the early seventeenth century it had been relatively easy for a newcomer to obtain free of cost all the land he could effectively use. During the eighteenth century, as the supplies of undivided land in the town commons became diminished, the proprietors adopted a less liberal policy in land distribution.[12] About 1725 there came a change in the policy of certain New England colonies in the making of town grants. The prudent policy of distributing new land purely for the sake of settlement was abandoned, and instead both Massachusetts and Connecticut sold whole townships to grantees who intended not to settle but to resell at a profit. There followed a period (1730–1740) of speculation in "wild lands," which, although in the end it proved disastrous to those who had bought large tracts, did nevertheless stimulate pioneering.[13] A similar period of land speculation was inaugurated about 1760, when Governor Wentworth of New Hampshire sold the grants of 130 towns in Vermont, chiefly to speculators.[14] The settlers who took up these lands soon discovered that the title to the whole tract was disputed by the province of New York and violence and bloodshed resulted before the matter was adjusted.[15]

In Pennsylvania

In Pennsylvania, under the proprietary government, it was relatively easy for pioneers to acquire vacant land. The price of land when purchased from the land office fluctuated between £5 and £15 per 100 acres (i.e., between 1s. and 3s. per acre), beside a small quitrent, and sales were for cash and not on credit. However, the great majority of settlers who took up land in the back country, especially in the period of great German immigration, 1718–1732, did not trouble to acquire a title, but simply squatted on unoccupied land. During the first half of the eight-

[12] Judd, Hadley, 286.
[13] Mathews, Expansion of New England, 81–84, 92, 101.
[14] Turner, in Wisconsin Hist. Soc. Proceedings (1908), 193.
[15] Beckley, Vermont, 66.

eenth century the management of the proprietary lands was in great confusion and the practice of squatting became general. By 1726 it was estimated that there were 100,000 squatters and of 670,000 acres occupied (1732–1740) over two-thirds were settled without grants.[16]

> Squatting, though discouraged by the proprietors, as it defrauded them of quitrents, soon became the most popular and regular method of acquiring land. Squatters' rights forced their way from presumptive titles to an established position, first as personalty and finally as realty. They became the basis of land transfers through the customary alienation of improvements instead of the legal title. Toward the middle of the Eighteenth Century the proprietors were forced to recognize them in the so-called settlement rights as a legitimate mode of obtaining title to land. From this time they supplanted office rights as the general basis of the acquisition and transfer of land throughout the province.

The lands thus occupied without title had eventually to be paid for with interest, but the squatters were given the right of preemption and thus there was virtually established a credit system of land purchase in Pennsylvania which undoubtedly contributed greatly to the rapid settlement of the back country.[17] Not until 1769 were the affairs of the land office brought into a semblance of order. The township plan after that date was more effectively carried out, the size of grants was restricted, and actual settlement and improvement were required.[18]

In New York

The land system of colonial New York was less favorable to the small settler than either that of New England or Pennsylvania, and largely on that account the movement into the back country was less vigorous in that province. We have already remarked the unusual number of large land grants by the English governors at the end of the seventeenth century. The practice continued until the Revolution. A tabulation of the "more important patents," 1700–1775, shows that out of a total of 211 grants, 128, or 61 percent, were for tracts of between 1,000 and 10,000 acres, and 83 were over 10,000 acres. The largest patents granted (2) were for 100,000 acres each. The average grant was 10,400 acres.[19]

Tenant farming was in only a few cases successfully established on the so-called manors of New York, and so the large holdings remained for the most part uninhabited and uncultivated. Squatting was practiced on such tracts, and the squatters at times could vindicate their titles in court, because of conflicting grants and careless surveying, but in general

---

[16] Ballagh in American Hist. Asso. *Report* (1897), 112.
[17] Turner, *The Old West*, Wisconsin Hist. Soc. *Proceedings* (1908), p. 213.
[18] Ballagh, Am. Hist. Asso. *Report*, 1897, p. 112.
[19] French, *Gazetteer of New York*, 49–52.

the young farmers looking for new land preferred to emigrate to a colony where fee-simple grants were more readily obtained. In 1764 Lieutenant Governor Colden wrote to the Lords of Trade: [20]

> Your Lordships have been informed of several extravagant Grants of Lands in this province; three of them contain, as the proprietors claim, above a million acres each, several others above 200,000. All these were made without any previous Survey, as usual in other cases, and without mentioning any quantity of land intended to be granted. Tho' these grants contain a great part of the province, they are made on trifling acknowledgements. The far greater part of them still remain uncultivated, without any benefit to the community, and are likewise a discouragement to the settling & improving the lands in the neighbourhood of them, for from the uncertainty of their boundaries, the Patentees of these great Tracts are daily enlarging their pretensions, and by tedious & most expensive Law-suits, distress and ruin poor families who have taken out grants near them; of all which, I propose to send your Lordships particular proofs before winter.

And a year later he wrote: [21]

> The uncertainty of the Grant, both as to the quantity of the Land and boundaries of the Tract granted, which in Law invalidates the grants of the Crown, turns greatly to the advantage of the owners of these great Tracts, by the artifices they make use of to inlarge their claims perpetually. Thereby they are in continual contention with the Farmers contiguous to them, who have purchased Bona Fide, and improved the Lands; and by the expence of Law Suits many of the most industrious Farmers are ruined. . . .

In 1774 only 1,000,000 acres of the 5,000,000 acres of the province were improved, and the settlements were all east of Utica on the Mohawk, and were mainly confined to the Hudson River, Manhattan, Staten and Long Islands.[22]

Land Policy After the Revolution

After the Revolution the new States of Massachusetts, New York, and Pennsylvania all began a liberal distribution of the vacant lands which they had inherited from the previous colonial governments. In Pennsylvania, by the acts of 1780 and 1783, tracts in the northwestern part of the State, known as the Depreciation and Donation Lands, were set aside for the soldiers of the Revolutionary War and were later opened to

[20] O'Callaghan, *N.Y. Documents Relative to Colonial History*, VII, 654.
[21] *Ibid.*, VII, 795.
[22] Ballagh, *loc. cit.*, p. 110.

settlement. Western lands were at that date not greatly in demand, and many of the soldiers sold out their rights to speculators at low prices.[23] A land office was opened in 1781 and lands were sold at prices varying with the location from £3 to £30 for 100 acres.[24] In 1792 a general act was passed for opening the unsettled lands in the Commonwealth for settlement and improvement. The price of land was reduced, the maximum now being £7 10s. per 100 acres for land north and west of the Ohio and Allegheny Rivers. A limit of 400 acres was set on all grants, preemption rights on that amount being granted to settlers already in possession. Actual settlement by purchasers was made a condition for retention of title.[25]

Land Speculation in New York

In New York, also, vacant lands, the so-called Bounty Lands in the western part of the State, were distributed to Revolutionary soldiers.[26] A tract of about 1,800,000 acres was laid out in square townships of 24,000 acres which divided into 200-acre lots. Private soldiers received 600 acres and officers larger amounts in proportion to their rank. As in Pennsylvania, large amounts of the Bounty Lands got into the hands of speculators, the soldiers having sold out their rights at ridiculously low prices.[27] In 1786 an act was passed whose title significantly read "An Act for the speedy sale of the Unappropriated Lands within this state." Having provided for laying out townships of 64,000 acres, divided into lots of 640 acres each, the law fixed a minimum price of 1 shilling per acre and required one-fourth of the purchase price to be paid down and the balance within 60 days. Actual settlement within 7 years was a condition for a valid title.[28] In 1791 the act was amended so that, with certain exceptions, the State lands might be sold by the commissioners of the land office "in such parcels, on such terms, and in such manner as they shall judge most conducive to the interest of this State. . . ."[29] Thus, of course, the 1 shilling minimum price was abolished. An orgy of prodigal disposition of the state domain followed, over 5,500,000 acres being sold in a single year, the State treasury receiving only £412,173, or on an average 1s. 6d. per acre for the land. The largest single tract sold contained 3,635,200 acres and brought only 8d. per acre.[30]

23 Agnew, *Northwest Pennsylvania*, 28; Feree, *Pennsylvania*, 194–98.
24 Read, *Abridgement of the Laws of Pennsylvania* (1801), 208–19.
25 *Ibid.*, 219–24.
26 By the acts of 25 July, 1782 and 11 May, 1784. See *Laws of New York* (Cook edition), 5th Session, 1782, chap. 77, p. 521; 6th Session, 1784, chap. 63, p. 731.
27 Maude, *Visit to Niagara*, 38.
28 *Laws of New York*, 9th Session (1786), chap. 67, p. 334.
29 *Ibid.*, 14th Session, chap. 42, p. 245.
30 O'Callaghan, *Documentary History of New York*, III, 1069–83.

The Wild Lands of Maine

Massachusetts, too, attempted to replenish her empty treasury after the Revolution by land sales. The District of Maine, then a part of the State of Massachusetts, was still largely unoccupied and contained millions of acres of "wild lands." The land system in Maine, as we have seen, had differed from that of Southern New England in the greater frequency of large grants directly to individuals. Titles had become uncertain owing to the overlapping of grants, and settlement had been hindered. For this reason, and also on account of the severe losses which the exposed Maine Coast suffered during the French and Indian wars, settlement was hindered, and not until after 1763 was progress made into the back country.[31]

Beginning in 1785, however, a land office was established and a campaign of land selling was inaugurated. In the years 1785–1792 something over 600,000 acres were disposed of at an average price of 41.4 cents per acre. In 1793 a sudden fever of land speculation raised the sales for that year to over 2,000,000 acres, but the average price fell to 12½ cents per acre. Hoping to check the speculative mania, the legislature in 1795 suspended all sales. But speculation nevertheless continued, for the large tracts of land which had been liberally granted in aid of educational institutions and for internal improvements were now placed on the market in an effort to convert them into cash.[32]

Massachusetts had acquired in 1786 a 6,000,000-acre tract in Western New York in settlement of her claims in that region, and between 1787 and 1793 this entire tract was placed on the market and sold, mostly to companies organized for the purpose of resale at a profit. About 2,500,000 acres were taken in a single tract by Messrs. Gorham and Phelps and another large tract was sold to the Holland Land Company.[33]

Land Policy Summarized

In summary, it is clear that the land policy of all the colonies from 1700 to 1775, with the exception of New York, favored rapid settlement of the back country. After 1780, liberality was changed into reckless prodigality, and under the stimulus of financial necessity great tracts were thrown on the market. Much of the land was sold directly to middlemen, and other tracts came into their hands indirectly by sale from the origi-

[31] Sullivan, *Maine*, 43, 44; Lincoln, in Mass. Hist. Soc. *Collections*, 1st series, IV, 149.
[32] Greenleaf, *Survey of Maine*, 399–401, 428. Felt, in Am. Statistical Asso. *Collections*, I, 75–78.
[33] Turner, *Holland Purchase*, 325, 326, 401.

nal grantees. The temporary results were undoubtedly a great stimulus to emigration to the frontier. The land companies exerted themselves to find settlers to whom they could resell their holdings. Every settler on a new tract enhanced the value of the unsold land. To stimulate sales, the land companies extended long credits, whereas purchases directly from the States were usually for cash or on from 2 to 12 months' credit. In the long run, however, there appeared glaring evils. In the haste to dispose of lands, surveys were carelessly made and disputed boundary-lines led to uncertain titles. A particularly bad situation of this sort arose in Maine, where the settlers on the so-called Kennebec Purchase, fearing to lose their lands and improvements, were kept in a state of unrest for almost a generation, and were finally stirred to armed insurrection before the conflicting claims were quieted.[34] Absentee ownership, also, was introduced and complaints became frequent that the progress of new communities was hindered by the indifference of absent landowners to local improvements and by the existence of large tracts held out of cultivation. Finally, the system of long-time credit led to inevitable disputes between the settlers and the land companies. The pioneer's life was arduous, as we shall see, and the task of clearing absorbed so much of his energies for the first few years that he had little opportunity to raise surplus crops. When he finally had a surplus, high transportation costs often shut him off from a market. The result was that a large proportion were unable to pay their annual installments as they fell due. The threat of ejection led to violent antipathy to the land company, and in some cases to violent action on the part of the settlers for the redress of their "grievances."

Other Causes of Emigration to the Frontier

Combined with the economic motive, the demand for new soil, were undoubtedly others more psychological in nature. Some men were unable to fit into the rigid, Puritanical social and ecclesiastical systems. They emigrated in order to breathe the freer, more unconventional atmosphere of the pioneer communities. Others were simply infected by the contagious spirit; their friends had gone or were going; they too wanted to see the new country and to live its new life. Dwight takes account of these and other motives in the following passage from his *Travels:* [35]

> In the formation of Colonies, those, who are first inclined to emigrate, are usually such, as have met with difficulties at home. These are commonly

[34] Gardiner, in Maine Hist. Soc. *Collections,* 1st series, II, 288–92; Felt, in Am. Statistical Asso. *Collections,* I, 78.
[35] *Travels,* II, 458 (edition of 1821). In the succeeding pages, 458–60, one may read a description of the successive stages in the settlement of new land, from pioneering to ultimate cultivation in well-settled communities, which has attained the rank of a classic in economic history.

joined by persons, who, having large families and small farms, are induced, for the sake of settling their children comfortably, to seek for new and cheaper lands. To both are always added the discontented, the enterprising, the ambitious, and the covetous. Many of the first, and some of all these classes, are found in every new American country, within ten years after its settlement has commenced. From this period, kindred, friendship, and former neighbourhood, prompt others to follow them. Others, still, are allured by the prospect of gain, presented in every new country to the sagacious, from the purchase and sale of new lands: while not a small number are influenced by the brilliant stories, which everywhere are told concerning most tracts during the early progress of their settlement.

General Description of Pioneer Farming

A general view of the life and work of the pioneer farmers may be gained from the description by a French traveler [36] of what he saw in western Connecticut in 1780:

I saw, for the first time, what I have since observed a hundred times; for in fact, whatever mountains I have climbed, whatever forests I have traversed, whatever byepaths I have followed, I have never travelled three miles without meeting with a new settlement, either beginning to take form or already in cultivation. The following is the manner of proceeding in these improvements or new settlements. Any man who is able to procure a capital of five or six hundred livres of our money, or about twenty-five pounds sterling, and who has a strength and inclination to work, may go into the woods and purchase a portion of one hundred and fifty to two hundred acres of land, which seldom costs him more than a dollar or four shillings and sixpence an acre, a small part of which only he pays in ready money. There he conducts a cow, some pigs, or a full sow, and two indifferent horses which do not cost him more than four guineas each. To these precautions he adds that of having a provision of flour and cider. Provided with this first capital, he begins by felling all the smaller trees, and some strong branches of the large ones: these he makes use of as fences to the first field he wishes to clear; he next boldly attacks those immense oaks, or pines, which one would take for the ancient lords of the territory he is usurping; he strips them of their bark, or lays them open all round with his axe. These trees mortally wounded, are the next spring robbed of their honours; their leaves no longer spring, their branches fall, and their trunk becomes a hideous skeleton. This trunk still seems to brave the efforts of the new colonist; but where there are the smallest chinks or crevices, it is surrounded by fire, and the flames consume what the iron was unable to destroy. But it is enough for the small trees to be

[36] Chastellux, *Travels*, 34.

felled, and the great ones to lose their sap. This object completed, the ground is cleared; the air and the sun begin to operate upon that earth which is wholly formed of rotten vegetables, and teems with the latent principles of production. The grass grows rapidly; there is pasturage for the cattle the very first year; after which they are left to increase, or fresh ones are brought, and they are employed in tilling a piece of ground which yields the enormous increase of twenty or thirty fold. The next year the same course is repeated; when, at the end of two years, the planter has wherewithal to subsist, and even to send some articles to market: at the end of four or five years, he completes the payment of his land, and finds himself a comfortable planter. Then his dwelling, which at first was no better than a large hut formed by a square of the trunks of trees, placed one upon another, with the intervals filled by mud, changes into a handsome wooden house, where he contrives more convenient, and certainly much cleaner apartments than those in the greatest part of our small towns. This is the work of three weeks or a month. His first habitation, that of eight and forty hours. I shall be asked, perhaps, how one man or one family can be so quickly lodged; I answer, that in America a man is never alone, never an isolated being. The neighbours, for they are every where to be found, make it a point of hospitality to aid the new farmer. A cask of cider drank in common, and with gaiety, or a gallon of rum, are the only recompense for these services. Such are the means by which North-America, which one hundred years ago was nothing but a vast forest, is peopled with three millions of inhabitants; and such is the immense, and certain benefit of agriculture, that notwithstanding the war, it not only maintains itself where ever it has been established, but it extends to places which seem the least favourable to its introduction. Four years ago, one might have travelled ten miles in the woods I traversed, without seeing a single habitation.

Methods of Clearing

In clearing the ground the first step was to cut down, grub out, and burn the underbrush. Then the larger timber might be destroyed either by girdling or by cutting it down and burning it. It is hard to distinguish the two systems: both were used in the same localities and were sometimes combined on the same tract. Cutting down the timber was probably the prevailing method in northern New England, in fact it was sometimes called the "Yankee system," [37] but girdling was also practiced in New England.[38] In the region originally settled by the Swedes, on both sides of the Delaware River, girdling was the favored method.[39] In

[37] Lorain, in Philadelphia Agric. Soc. *Memoirs*, III (1814), p. 112.
[38] See Dwight's description, *Travels* (1821 ed.), II, 125.
[39] Acrelius, in Pennsylvania Hist. Soc. *Memoirs*, XI, 147.

Pennsylvania, the thoroughgoing German settlers in the southeast practiced the Yankee system. Dr. Rush [40] wrote:

> In clearing new land they do not girdle the trees simply, and leave them to perish in the ground, as is the custom of their English or Irish neighbors; but they generally cut them down and burn them. In destroying under-wood and bushes, they generally grub them out of the ground; by which means a field is as fit for cultivation the second year after it is cleared, as it is in twenty years afterwards.

Elsewhere in Pennsylvania and in New York both methods of clearing were practiced.[41]

Girdling was more economical of labor at the beginning, but eventually the dead trees fall and must be removed, and in falling they endangered the lives of farmers and their stock. The type of pioneer who expected to remain only a few years on the tract he had cleared, and then sell out and move farther into the wilderness, usually practiced cutting and burning instead of girdling. The ashes from his great piles of logs gave him, when converted into potash, a cash crop in the first season, whereas his neighbor who girdled his trees might have to wait several seasons before he had a salable surplus. The fact that the humus in the soil was often destroyed by his huge fires did not worry the "exploiting" pioneer who did not intend to settle permanently and cultivate the land.[42]

Pioneer Crops and Tillage

On the land thus cleared the pioneer raised chiefly grain crops. Indian corn was usually the first crop on new land, although under some circumstances wheat or rye was planted. Thus in northern Vermont and in the Mohawk Valley wheat was more usually sown on new land, probably because of favorable marketing conditions.[43] Rye was a favored crop on new land in New Hampshire. Belknap wrote: [44]

> Of all grains, winter rye thrives best on new lands, and Indian corn, or barley, on the old. Barley does not succeed well in the new land; nor is flax raised with any advantage, until the land has been cultivated for some years. The same may be said of oats and peas; but all kinds of escu-

[40] *Account of the German Inhabitants of Pennsylvania* (1789). Reprinted in Pennsylvania German Society *Proceedings and Addresses*, XIX (1910), 58.
[41] Cooper, *Information Respecting America*, 116–19; Lorain, Philadelphia Agric. Soc. *Memoirs*, III (1814), p. 112.
[42] On the whole subject of clearing, see Belknap, *New Hampshire*, III, 131–37.
[43] Richard Smith, *Journal*, 19; Miller and Wells, *Ryegate* (*Vermont*), 193; *Orleans County* (*Vermont*) Hist. Soc. *Proceedings* (1889–91), p. 39; Watson, *Essex County* (*New York*), 479.
[44] *History of New Hampshire*, III (1792), 136. See also Runnels, *Sanbornton* (*New Hampshire*), I, 59.

lent roots, are much larger and sweeter in the virgin soil, than in any other.

It was observed in the more northern districts and in the higher altitudes that Indian corn did not yield as well on the new lands as on the old, and it was claimed that the ground must first be prepared for corn by some other crop. Belknap [45] explained the matter by reference to the date of planting. In the regions where the growing-season was short, the clearing process postponed the date of planting so long that corn did not come to full maturity. Potatoes were an eighteenth century innovation among pioneer crops. Like maize, they were planted with the hoe, usually without plowing. The seeds of wheat, rye, and other grains were raked in by hand or scratched in with a harrow.[46]

Livestock, Hay, and Pasturage

A grass crop often followed two years of grains, the seed having been sown, perhaps, with rye or wheat, but the few animals which the pioneer took out with him to his new home gathered most of their nourishment from the woods and natural meadows. The supply of hay in new settlements was often insufficient for winter fodder and cows went farrow and in some cases literally starved to death.[47] The importance of livestock in pioneer agriculture increased in regions where cattle could be successfully fattened for market. In some regions of New Hampshire and Maine cattle were driven into the new tract to be pastured there in advance of settlement. Where there was but little underbrush the cattle browsed in the woodlands, and meanwhile the settlers brought their cleared lands into mowing as soon as possible. In New Hampshire many farmers in the old towns fatted cattle for market on land in new settlements which they had cleared and brought into grass.[48]

The Importance of By-Industries—Potash and Maple Sugar

The pioneer farmer was often engaged in accessory occupations which, although furnishing him an important source of income, often interfered with farming operations and hindered the development of good agricul-

[45] New Hampshire, III (1792), 136.
[46] Lorain, in Philadelphia Agric. Soc. Memoirs, III (1814), p. 112; Cooper, Information Respecting America, 113, 116–19; Notes on Lancaster (New Hampshire), in Massachusetts Hist. Soc. Collections, 2d series, III, 98, note 2; Richard Smith, Journal, 21.
[47] Runnels, Sanbornton (New Hampshire), I, 60; Smith, Rev. Thomas, Journal, 266, 267, 269.
[48] Belknap, New Hampshire, III, 135; Lincoln, in Mass. Hist. Soc. Collections, 1st series, IV, 145; Coffin, in Maine Hist. Soc. Collections, 1st series, IV, 288.

tural practice. Fishing and hunting often took up a large share of his time, and where there were suitable water courses for floating logs to the saw mills, lumbering was a favorite occupation. In districts where much lumbering was carried on, farming was generally in a bad state. Belknap [49] wrote:

> The best season for sawing logs is the spring, when the rivers are high; this is also the time for ploughing and planting. He who works in the sawmill at that time, must buy his bread and clothing, and the hay for his cattle, with his lumber; and he generally anticipates the profit of his labor. Long credit is a disadvantage to him; and the too free indulgence of spiritous liquor, to which this class of people are much addicted, hurts their health, their morals and their interest. They are always in debt, and frequently at law. Their families are ill provided with necessaries, and their children are without education or morals.

Where saw-logs could not be gotten to mills the making of potash for sale was often an important by-industry. A "potash house," to which ashes were brought by the farmers and converted into potash and pearlash, was usually found in new settlements in New England and New York, and less frequently in Pennsylvania.[50] The method of manufacturing potash as then practiced was described by La Rochefoucauld [51] as follows:

> Large tubs, with a double bottom, are filled with ashes; the uppermost bottom, which contains several holes, is covered with ashes, about ten or eleven inches deep, while the under part of the tub is filled with straw or hay. Water, being poured over the ashes, extracts the particles of salt, and discharges all the heterogeneous matter which it may yet contain on the layer of hay or straw. The lie is drawn off by means of a cock, and if it should not yet have attained a sufficient degree of strength, poured again over the ashes. The lie is deemed sufficiently strong when an egg swims on it. This lie is afterward boiled in large iron cauldrons, which are constantly filled out of other cauldrons, in which lie is likewise boiling. . . . This salt is of a black colour, and called *black potash*. Some manufacturers leave the potash in this state in the cauldron, and encrease the fire, by means of which the oil is disengaged from the salt in a thick smoke, and the black potash assumes a grey colour, in which state it is packed up in barrels for sale. . . .
>
> Pearlash is potash purified by calcination. To this end the potash is put into a kiln, constructed in an oval form, of plaster of Paris; the inside of which being made otherwise perfectly close, is horizontally intersected by an iron grate, on which the potash is placed. Under this grate a fire is

---

[49] *New Hampshire*, III, 261; see also Mass. Hist. Soc. *Collections*, 1st series, IV, 90, 149; Kendall, *Travels*, III, 72–84; Watson, *Essex County* (New York), 478.
[50] Williams, *Vermont*, II, 361; Graham, *Descriptive Sketch of Vermont*, 40; Cooper, *Information Respecting America*, 143; Campbell, *Travels*, 268, 285.
[51] *Travels*, 1799 Edition, I, 385.

made, and the heat, reverberated by the arched upper part of the kiln, compleats the calcination, and converts the potash into pearlash. . . . The process of calcination lasts about an hour.

The apparatus necessary for this manufacture was inexpensive, the largest outlay being for the purchase of the kettles in which the lye was boiled. The products, pearlash and potash, were used to some extent in the household in making soap, in scouring wool, and in bleaching and dyeing cloth. The larger part of the output was sold, partly for use in glass-making and other manufactures, and partly for export.

Maple sugar was another important by-product of pioneer agriculture. Williams [52] wrote:

> The manufacture of maple sugar is also an article of great importance to the state [Vermont]. Perhaps two thirds of the families are engaged in this business in the spring, and they make more sugar than is used among the people. Considerable quantities are carried to the shop keepers; which always find a ready sale, and good pay. The business is now carried on, under the greatest disadvantages: Without proper conveniencies, instruments, or works; solely by the exertions of private families, in the woods, and without any other conveniencies than one or two iron kettles, the largest of which will not hold more than four or five pailfulls. Under all these disadvantages, it is common for a family to make two or three hundred pounds of maple sugar in three or four weeks.

The production of maple sugar was found in the back settlements of New England and New York, and in Pennsylvania as well, though perhaps less generally.[53]

The Progress of Pioneer Communities—Hardships of Pioneering

The first years of a pioneer's life were full of exhausting toil and often marked by the most discouraging hardships. Clearing the woods was a slow process. The typical settler would clear, perhaps, on the average from 1 to 3 acres a year. Those who were exceptionally energetic or who had exceptionally large families would do considerably better. In Concord, New Hampshire, at the end of 5 years several of the settlers had as much as 12 acres cleared, fenced, and ploughed, or in mowing. One settler with 5 grown sons had broken up, cleared and mowed more than 80 acres, besides erecting "very considerable buildings." [54] At the end of

[52] Vermont, II, 363. For descriptions of the process of making maple sugar see Dwight, Travels (1821 ed.), I, 40; Belknap, New Hampshire, III, 113.
[53] Richard Smith, Journal, 26; Mittelberger, Journey to Pennsylvania, 71; Coxe, View of the United States, 65.
[54] Bouton, Concord, New Hampshire, 128–31.

the first 10 years in another New England town every settler had at least 15 acres cleared and some had 50 acres.[55] If all went well at the end of 4 or 5 years the settler might expect to be fairly comfortably fixed, at least as regards food and shelter. In the meanwhile, however, he and his family might have been facing death from starvation and exposure. Until the first corn crop was harvested grain must be brought in from outside. Of the Sandy River settlement in Maine, Allen wrote: [56]

> No corn could be had by the new settlers the first summer, nearer than Fort Western (Augusta), 40 miles; several of them had to go on foot to that place and carry a basket of corn on their backs, first to Winthrop to mill and then home to keep their families from starving; many expedients were resorted to, to allay the cravings of hunger; some lived for several days at a time on greens; some dug up their potatoes after they were planted, cut out and replanted the eyes and ate the rest. After three or four months, when green corn was fit to pick and potatoes large enough to dig, all were relieved essentially. The months of May, June and July, 1781, formed the most distressing period in the settlement of Sandy River. After the corn crop came off in the fall, almost every one had a tolerable supply; one settler raised a little wheat that summer; but then there was no mill within 40 miles, and no way to go to mill but on foot, till they could go by sledding in the winter. Several prepared large samp mortars,[57] with a spring pole by which a man could pound a bushel a day so as to make one half fit for bread; the other half made good hominy.

The situation described above is perhaps extreme, but it is abundantly evident that if the pioneers had depended on the products of their fields and on their domestic animals for food they would have had very little to eat. As it was, meat was rarely tasted, unless it were game, and the nuts and berries of the forest were welcome additions to brown bread, pea or bean porridge, and baked pumpkin.[58] As the settlement grew older less reliance was placed on the forest for food resources, except by the less thrifty and industrious, who could not settle down to the regular tasks of farming.

The house of the pioneer, the often-described log hut, was neither a comfortable nor a hygienic dwelling, Belknap wrote: [59]

> They erect a square building of poles, notched at the ends to keep them fast together. The crevices are plaistered with clay or the stiffest earth which can be had, mixed with moss or straw. The roof is either bark or

[55] Miller and Wells, *Ryegate, Vermont*, 96.
[56] In Maine Hist. Soc. *Collections*, IV, 39.
[57] The samp mortars used on Long Island are described in Furman, *Long Island Antiquities*, I, 227.
[58] Miller and Wells, *Ryegate, Vermont*, 94, 190; Leonard, *Dublin, New Hampshire*, 280, 283; Dwight, *Travels* (ed. 1821), II, 313.
[59] *New Hampshire*, III (1792), 258; see also Leonard, *Dublin, New Hampshire*, 279, 281.

split boards. The chimney a pile of stones; within which a fire is made on the ground, and a hole is left in the roof for the smoke to pass out. Another hole is made in the side of the house for a window, which is occasionally closed with a wooden shutter. . . . Ovens are built at a small distance from the houses, of the best stones which can be found, cemented and plaistered with clay or stiff earth.

In such "dark, dirty and dismal" habitations the pioneer family lived for at least the first 10 or 15 years, and often much longer. In Chester, New Hampshire, the first frame house was erected in 1732, 13 years after the first settlement;[60] in Hallowell, Maine, most of the inhabitants were still living in log huts in 1784,[61] about 25 years after the first settlement; and in Ryegate, Vermont, settled in 1775, log houses were still occupied in 1865.[62]

Summary—Pioneering a Process of Capital-Making

It would seem from the foregoing description that the economic struggle on the frontier must have been more severe than in the older-settled communities. The pioneer family undoubtedly worked harder, and for the first few years at least enjoyed less in the way of comforts and satisfactions in return for their efforts. Their houses were less comfortable, their food and clothing were more scanty, and in general their standard of living was lower. Judging by the pioneer's consumption of economic goods, we should conclude that his income was small and that on the whole there was little profit in pioneer farming.

But such a judgment would be mistaken. The pioneer did indeed take out only a meager income from his farm in the first 5 or 10 years, but the income taken out was often only a small part of the total income which accrued during that period. In his first years the pioneer was chiefly engaged in producing capital goods. There are occasional cases recorded of woodland farming with considerable initial capital, where hundreds of acres were cleared and brought into cultivation with the aid of indentured servants, negro slaves, and hired laborers.[63] But as a rule the pioneer exhausted his ready cash in the first payments on his land, and his entire stock of capital which he took to his new home consisted of an axe, a gun, a few tools, perhaps a plough, some flour, and a few head of livestock. With this meager equipment he undertook a double-task: (1) the maintenance of his family with the immediate necessities of life, or the production of consumption goods, and (2) the clearing of land, erection of buildings, and the building of roads, or, in other words, the creation of capital goods. It was because the greater part of his time

60 Bell, in New Hampshire Hist. Soc. *Collections*, VII, 347.
61 North, *Augusta, Maine*, 189.
62 Miller and Wells, *Ryegate, Vermont*, 94.
63 *American Husbandry*, I, 109–21, 191–96.

and energy were devoted to the latter kind of production that his standard of living seemed low.

The pioneer farmer may be compared to a business corporation which pursues a conservative dividend policy. Instead of paying out all of current income to the stockholders, it puts a large share back into the business, thus increasing the value of its capital. The pioneer was engaged in literally "ploughing in his profits." The income which he did not take out of his enterprise steadily accrued and was shown in the increased value of his land.

The following quotation describes, perhaps in too optimistic language, the economic position of the pioneer farmer.[64]

Amidst the hard living and hard labor, that attends the forming a new settlement, the settler has the most flattering prospects and encouragements. One hundred acres of land in a new town, does not generally cost him more than he can spare from the wages of one or two years. Besides maintaining himself, the profits of his labor will generally enable a young man, in that period of time, to procure himself such a tract of land. When he comes to apply his labor to his own land, the produce of it becomes extremely profitable. The first crop of wheat will fully pay him for all the expense he has been at, in clearing up, sowing, and fencing his land; and at the same time, increases the value of the land, eight or ten times the original cost. In this way, every day's labor spent in clearing up his land, receives high wages in the grain which it procures, and adds at the same time a quantity of improved land to the farm. An acre of land which in its natural state, cost him perhaps the half of one day's labor, is thus in one year made of that value, that it will afterwards annually produce him from fifteen to twenty five bushels of wheat; or other kinds of produce, of equal value. In this way, the profits attending labor on a new settlement, are the greatest that ever can take place in agriculture; the laborer constantly receiving double wages. He receives high wages in the produce of his corn or wheat; and he receives much higher wages of another kind, in the annual addition of a new tract of cultivated land to his farm. This double kind of wages, nature with great benevolence and design, has assigned to the man of industry, when he is first making a settlement in the uncultivated parts of America: And in two or three years, he acquires a very comfortable and independent subsistence for a family, derived from no other source but the earth, and his own industry.

[64] Williams, *History of Vermont*, II, 353.

Two ～ *The Tobacco Entrepreneurs of the*

Eighteenth-Century Chesapeake

ECONOMIC BEHAVIOR
IN A PLANTING SOCIETY:
THE EIGHTEENTH-CENTURY
CHESAPEAKE   *Aubrey C. Land*

One of the venerated books in the Western tradition contains an economic statement which it is not necessary to footnote: "The poor ye have with ye always." This maxim gets a quantitative twist at the hands of John K. Galbraith in *The Affluent Society:* "Nearly all throughout all history have been very poor." [1] This paper is not a homily on these texts, but the findings reported here assuredly illustrate them. Poverty has never been enjoyable to the subject or very interesting to the observer. But no student of the eighteenth-century Chesapeake can afford to overlook it or to fix exclusively on the successful who somehow avoided it. Poorer folk of Virginia and Maryland had economic and political roles that still, fifty years after Thomas J. Wertenbaker's research, have not had a proper recognition in descriptive accounts. [2]

[1] (Boston, 1958). 1. Documentation in this paper will be kept to the minimum required for intelligent appraisal of the argument. The detailed references, many in the form of sets of statistical tables, will appear in my forthcoming study of Chesapeake enterprise. This paper is a summary statement of the position taken in the study.

[2] Wertenbaker, *Patrician and Plebeian in Virginia, or, The Origin and Development of the Social Classes of the Old Dominion* (Charlottesville, 1910), especially Part Two, "The Middle Class"; and *The Planters of Colonial Virginia* (Princeton, 1922), particularly Chapter III, "The Virginia Yeomanry," and Chapter VI, "The Yeoman in Virginia History."

FROM Aubrey C. Land, "Economic Behavior in a Planting Society: The Eighteenth-Century Chesapeake," *Journal of Southern History,* Vol. XXXIII (November 1967). Copyright 1967 by the Southern Historical Association. Reprinted by permission of the Managing Editor.

A few hopeful signs of change have appeared in the past dozen years. By now the composition of Chesapeake society and the economic behavior of some of its people have received enough attention that students no longer stare in shocked unbelief when told the brute facts. Robert and Katherine Brown have presented a Virginia rich in variety and range of estates.[3] Louis B. Wright has provided a wholesome corrective to the planting stereotype in *The Cultural Life of the American Colonies*.[4] His portrait of the "agrarian leaders" of the Southern seaboard emphasizes prudential virtues that could have come directly from the lexicon of Benjamin Franklin himself: hard work, shrewd planning, responsible conduct, and an eye to the main chance.

Still, several tasks remain for other hands, among them three in particular which can bring the record closer to the actualities. The first of these needs is a sharper definition of planters' estates, of their worth expressed in terms of some constant measure. Without precise measurement description of the texture of life in the planting colonies is difficult and talk about economic change or progress next to impossible. Given workable sources, the task of obtaining an accurate conception of social composition is in good part technical, that is to say, statistical.[5] Beyond this analysis of crude raw materials drawn from inventories, accounts, and tax lists lie difficulties of another order. The second undertaking—a harder look at the economic activities of planters—compels the investigator to make inferences and constructions from evidence that must be rated as something less than ideal. For many of the actual individuals on whom full information would be helpful, mere scraps remain. Their letter books, which would permit detailed descriptions, and their ledgers, which would give exact measures of profits, have for the most part perished. Their trails must be followed through the public records and surviving collections, large and small, of private papers. Frequently the scent is faint, and at times it disappears altogether, leaving the tracker with the frustrating necessity of quartering a large field until he can pick up the trail again.

The greatest difficulty of all lies in the third task, putting the economic behavior of individuals in the context of the planting society as derived from the statistics. In substance, the end product of this process is a theory of the workings of the Chesapeake economy in the eighteenth century. And theoretical formulation, never an easy matter, has special difficulties for the Chesapeake of that time. The investigator must of course meet the usual historical canons, the criteria of supporting strength in his evidence for the theoretical superstructure. Besides he

---

[3] Robert E. and B. Katherine Brown, *Virginia, 1705–1786: Democracy or Aristocracy?* (East Lansing, 1964).

[4] (New York, 1957), especially Chapter I.

[5] Technical should not be equated with "easy." Statistical analysis of eighteenth-century materials has pitfalls for the unwary. A study of colonial materials similar to Sir George N. Clark's *Guide to English Commercial Statistics, 1696–1782* (London, 1938) would be a godsend to scholars and to beginning students particularly.

must wrestle with a semantic problem of speech and writing couched in the language of an agricultural community but whose reference is to business enterprise. In other words, he must in his analysis impose categories that do not grow out of the language of the speakers, who talked like planters but acted like astute businessmen. For the enterprisers of the time were hewing their procedures and rules out of the raw stuff of everyday experience and putting them to the proof by trial and error without much regard for the convenience of later researchers. Quite likely, if these men could somehow be summoned to the witness box, they could offer in explanation of their conduct little more than the platitudes frequently in the mouths of entrepreneurs. Yet faced with actual situations calling for decision in their own day, they responded with surprising sureness. Accordingly, their behavior and its bearing on Chesapeake society became concerns of first importance.

Perhaps the simplest way of making sense out of the complex realities of Chesapeake economic life is to pose two questions whose answers may lead to useful conclusions about the economy and economic behavior in the planting society. First, what was the matrix from which "the great planters" of textbook fame emerged? Second, by what process did they arrive at their positions of dominance or leadership? Neither is a simple question, and neither is easy to answer in a few words.

The first question calls for a look at the characteristics of planting society through the length and breadth of the Tidewater. Two are immediately striking. First, of subsistence farming there is hardly a trace. The countryside was peopled with commercial farmers who depended on the production of a cash crop and on the market nexus.[6] The measure of Chesapeake economic health was the tobacco exported, chiefly to Britain, a trade that grew from approximately fifteen million pounds of leaf around 1670 to some thirty millions in 1700 and finally to one hundred millions in the 1770's. Other products were by no means negligible, as

---

[6] The statistical tables, on which these and subsequent generalizations rest, are based on an analysis of the inventories of estates and on the subsequent accounts of probate which together give details of personal property holdings, number of slaves and value, debts owed and debts due, exchange rates, and, for a few counties, sizes of crops, number of children and the like. These inventories are about as nearly accurate as any evaluations one is likely to find for the colonial period. Each was made by two appraisers appointed by the county, assisted by the nearest relative (often the heir) and the largest creditor. The tabulation includes all inventories and accounts for alternate decades from 1690 to 1760; that is to say, about half of all estates brought to probate in the counties represented. The three Maryland series are the Inventories & Accounts, Vol. 1–39A; after this volume the series is divided into Accounts in one set of volumes and Inventories in another. The Virginia "inventories" and "appraisements" appear in the county court records. Comparatively, the Maryland records are better preserved. All thirteen counties were usable. Only five Virginia counties could be used: Westmoreland, Northumberland, Northampton (Eastern Shore), York, and Surry. Major groups of records for the other Virginia Tidewater counties have perished. Chance preservation has left a reasonably good geographical distribution. The Maryland materials are found in the Maryland Hall of Records, Annapolis; those for Virginia at the Virginia State Library, Richmond.

will appear. But tobacco provided Chesapeake planters with a cash crop to employ their "hands" of all descriptions. It also called for some sort of organization to handle the crop, to forward it on to the wharves of London and the outports. Small producers or great, all were bound to the tobacco market, whose workings few understood well and almost none perfectly.[7] Many honest planters regarded the marketing mechanism with suspicion and professed to see tobacco production as a kind of bondage to a shadowy, somewhat sinister group of merchants across the water.

The second characteristic is the size of the productive units. The producers who swelled these export figures were small planters. The term planter almost invariably conjures up the image of a rather large-scale operation, usually involving slaves or bond labor. To contemporaries, planter had the technical meaning of a person who planted, without much regard to the size of his crop or his economic status. John Nevil of Queen Anne's County, Maryland, whose affairs were settled in 1751, left an estate in personalty, after debts were discharged, of £931 4s. 3¼d. currency and £10 6s. 5d. sterling. The record officially designated Nevil as "planter." [8] His neighbor William Peters died in 1753, leaving for his heirs £21 11s. 2d. currency and debts of £14 15s. 11d., or a net estate of £6 15s. 3d. Peters also rated the designation planter.[9]

The Peterses always outnumbered the Nevils. A recently published paper on the northern Chesapeake divides Maryland planters into four strata according to sizes of estates. These were (1) planters with personalty appraised at £100 or less, (2) those with estates in personalty valued at £100 to £500, (3) those between £500 and £1,000, and (4) those in the bracket above £1,000. The last qualified as "great planters," and they never formed more than a fraction of the total community of planters, something like 2.5 percent in the decade 1690–99 and about 6.5 percent half a century later.[10]

These three lower brackets show a broad spectrum of conditions, both sumptuary and financial, from impoverished dirt farmers to petty slaveholders. It is difficult to bring crop sizes of producers in these three groups to a simple statement, as, for example, a ratio expressing weight of the crop to the value of the planter's estate. Still the figures tell something. Forty percent of the growers in four prime tobacco-producing

[7] An extraordinary case is cited by Samuel M. Rosenblatt, "The Significance of Credit in the Tobacco Consignment Trade: A Study of John Norton & Sons, 1768–1775," *William and Mary Quarterly*, 3d Ser., XIX (July 1962), 383–99. William Nelson, president of the Virginia Council, leading Norfolk merchant, and large planter, was not clear on the system of drawbacks on re-exported tobacco.

[8] Accounts, Vol. 31, folios 95–97 (Hall of Records, Annapolis).

[9] *Ibid.*, Vol. 34, folios 194–96.

[10] Aubrey C. Land, "Economic Base and Social Structure: The Northern Chesapeake in the Eighteenth Century," *Journal of Economic History*, XXV (December 1965), 639–54. This growth was anything but even. The local and temporal variations deserve further study for additional insights they give into the dynamics of the planting order. The big fact remains that the typical planter was the small producer, not a grandee like William Byrd or Charles Carroll.

countries of southern Maryland in the decade 1750–59 marketed crops of less than 2,000 pounds, amounting to four hogsheads or less. Another 40 percent had crops ranging from 2,000 to 5,000 pounds, or between four and ten hogsheads. These were the small producers, altogether 80 percent of the planters in these counties.[11] Individual returns from such crops came to £30 sterling or less, comprising for most of these planters their entire cash income.

At the other end of the spectrum the largest producers, planters who made crops of 10,000 pounds of tobacco or more, were a small percentage of the whole—2 percent in this sample, to be exact. During the decade crops of these growers ranged from 11,171 to 16,098 pounds of tobacco, or twenty-two to thirty-two hogsheads. Net returns for such crops at prevailing tobacco prices ran between £66 and £96 sterling.[12] Such incomes do not lead to riches; yet all these largest producers were men of great estates.

The contrast in numbers and productive capacities between the great-planter element and the ubiquitous small producers is clear enough from these data. Like most statistics these describe rather than explain. Yet questions press forward insistently for answers. How did the wealthy attain their riches Why did small producers remain attached to an unrewarding husbandry? Ultimately satisfying answers are not likely until the economic historian joins forces with the sociologist and social psychologist.

Until that time the prosaic explanations of economic history must be offered for the behavior of small planters, particularly for their attachment to tobacco culture. The statute books contain dozens of acts encouraging, by one device or another, alternative crops—hemp, flax, grain, and the like. For those accustomed to the life and station of the small planter, tobacco offered the optimum crop, one requiring relatively small capital outlays and at the same time easy to raise. At any rate, the

---

[11] For some local reason the appraisers of estates in the adjacent counties of St. Mary's, Calvert, Charles, and Prince George's began the practice of entering crop sizes in the inventories. In other counties of Maryland and Virginia similar entries appear occasionally, but without the uniformity required for a reliable statistical compilation. The happy custom of the four lower counties of the Maryland Western Shore has supplied a unique statistical series. For the decade 1750–1759 crop sizes in the counties ran as follows:

1 to 2,000 pounds	40 per cent of all producers
2,001 to 5,000 pounds	40 " " " " "
5,001 to 10,000 pounds	18 " " " " "
Above 10,000 pounds	2 " " " " "

These are weights produced, not weights shipped. Some of the larger producers shipped several times the amount they raised. The difference represents tobacco acquired by any of several nonplanting activities.

[12] These figures err on the side of generosity. They have been calculated at the rates for 1759, the best year of the decade for planters. Prices in that year were highest (range 12s. 6d. to 36s. 6d. per hundredweight of tobacco; mode 20s. 6d.) and sterling exchange most favorable (range 1.65 to 1.50; median 1.575).

small planter behaved as though determined to give an example of how not to get rich. Year after year he produced his cash crop, raised his meat and cereal foods, made many or most articles of daily use by hand out of local materials, and bred his own increase. A harsh commentator might describe his existence as squalid; it seems more proper to call it rude, an adjective that also aptly applied to many of his other activities including such amusements as gander-pulling, cudgeling, and eye-gouging, then accepted by small-planter society.

Small planters and their ways must be given prominence in any balanced account of society and the economy of the Chesapeake. They had the numbers that counted heavily in politics and production. Their manners and standards won the approval of Thomas Jefferson himself, who evidently referred to this type in his description of an ideal citizenry. In the historical record they have remained the invisible people of the Chesapeake. Yet for these thousands, man after man, exist biographical sketches of the most reliable kind. These are not in the format of the *Dictionary of American Biography,* and they require some practice to read easily. But after the first few dozen the reader penetrates these "Accounts," concise to the point of density, to enter the world of the small planter in his surroundings of house and goods, his relatives and friends, his creditors and debtors, his crops and cattle, his sports, and occasionally even his farewell appearance at the grave. The sheer pleasure of sightseeing in this unfamiliar society can make the student forget that such sources yield best to the humdrum exercise of statistical compilation. For before him stands a body of materials that can be worked to give magnitudes—how much and how many—so difficult to ascertain for the colonial period. These magnitudes are wanted for the small planters of the tobacco colonies because their existence made possible the glittering personages who figure as stars in the golden age of Virginia and Maryland. Men of bolder vision and broader talents, these "great planters" gained their pre-eminence and wealth in organizing the tobacco trade and providing the services demanded by a pioneer economy.[13]

In its outlines the economy of the Chesapeake conforms closely to the classic model of the pioneer economy. On the essential movement of staple exports and capital imports the well-being of the whole region depended, subject to all the hazards of demand for tobacco in European markets. In prosperous seasons heavy staple exports and high capital imports created a circular or spiral motion in these colonies: a high investment rate, full employment in spite of heavy immigration, profit inflation, and rising prices. The spiral had its fluctuations, periods of slowdown or recession which brought cries of hardship from market-sensitive planters. These were the economic crises that set provincials to consider-

---

[13] The literature on various aspects of underdeveloped countries is substantial, and models are far from simple for these nations. One of the best examples of historical application of the model is in W. A. Mackintosh, "Some Aspects of a Pioneer Economy," *Canadian Journal of Economics and Political Science,* II (November 1936), 457–63.

ing alternatives to the staple. In the press, in legislative halls, in private correspondence, even in occasional verse, planters bemoaned their plight and put their minds to ways of breaking the grip of the staple, the "dead palsie," as one put it. But as often as good times succeeded the bad most planters fell back on the old ways.

In this pioneer economy the great planters had roles different in kind from those of the small producers. They were not, in other words, small planters writ large. Run the family tree of this elite back to its rise —back to the time when some ancestor, not very remote, worked in his shirt sleeves and osnaburgs—and you discover an individual who behaved like anything but a planter of the genteel tradition. His most constructive and rewarding activities fall more appropriately into a classification other than planting.

Except for the graceless term "entrepreneur," no designation quite fits this Chesapeake type. "Merchant" suggests too much the counting-house and blue-water commerce. Yet the handful of men who came to the top of the economic pile in Maryland and Virginia during the last eight decades of the old empire won their wealth in ways quite like their mercantile counterparts to the north and by exercise of the same talents. But always, too, they had a foot in tobacco production, and as their planting catches the eye, other activities are screened off by this picturesque role. Even their own sons escaped the grubby ways of the trader for the seductive routine of gentleman planter, often to the detriment of the family fortune. Whatever the term describing their twofold commitment, these men of enterprise took advantage of the investment-price-profit spiral as they provided the Chesapeake some of the needed commercial services. In the common speech of a later day they would be called simply "businessmen," and perhaps that description, vague as it is, best applies. Their activities show them as men of affairs; their attitudes and outlook identify them with the tradition of business enterprise in American life.

Many of them began as petty merchants and tobacco factors, buying crops of the local small producers, who could not maintain accounts with the great consignment houses of the mother country, and selling them the few commodities needed about small farmsteads. The actual process closely resembled the crop-lien system of the post-bellum South: credit during the year for the small planter's purchases with his tobacco crop wholly or partially liquidating the indebtedness in the winter. Of course, not every person who kept store made a killing. Most of them did not. Most remained small operators, and some died near the edge of bankruptcy. In the probate papers of these estates, the phrases "run away" and "left the province" beside the names of debtors tell a story of a kind of mobility in the lowest economic strata that made the business of the petty merchant risky. But some did well, particularly those few who expanded their operations beyond the country store to include handling slave cargoes and supplying credit on a larger scale than usual.

The merchant-planter Edward Dixon of Hanover County, Virginia, obviously did well, far better than the average planter who kept store. By a happy accident a set of his account books has survived. The first volume, Ledger F of the series, records his sales for the years 1743–47.[14] By that time Dixon had climbed out of the class of petty store-keepers. His books carried accounts for 462 customers, rich and poor, with particulars of the sales to each itemized. A few larger customers made purchases that came near £100 Virginia currency a year: sugar, rum, wine, textiles, hardware, mirrors, ribbons, millinery, spices, household utensils, harness, shoes, powder, shot, and occasionally a wig. But the great majority of the accounts show customers with slender pocket-books and modest tastes: three-quarters of them took less than £10 currency in goods each year.[15] Individually small, these accounts when taken together make an imposing element of Dixon's total sales, which came to some £3,000 currency a year.

The size of Dixon's turnover tells only vaguely what kind of net return he realized when all accounts were settled. If his markup was the usual 50 percent, his gross profit comes to £1,000 currency. Doubtless he had the usual overhead costs of building and equipment, bad debts, and sundry losses from water, fire, theft, and vermin. Yet after all these are allowed, Dixon must have appeared affluent in a community where a majority of families counted on an annual income of £100 or less. Beside his store Dixon had two plantations worked by his slaves under overseers.

Accounts of estates drawn from the public records lack the rich detail of Dixon's ledgers, but they tell a similar story of consumer buying habits. The executors of John Ballard, merchant in York County, Virginia, collected 160 debts on his books, most of them between £2 and £10 currency.[16] William Fishwick of Dorchester County, Maryland, had 162 debtors, obligated in the amount of £412 15s. 3d. currency and 5,853¾ pounds of tobacco, an average of just over £3.[17] One hundred twenty-three debtors of John Connor, merchant in Kent County, Maryland, owed a total of £508 17s. 6½d. currency, or just under £5 on the average.[18] In Surry County, Virginia, the administrators of William Harris tell no more quantitatively than the total value of his inventory, £162 4s. 5d. currency and that he had in addition 230 gallons of rum and 250 pounds of sugar. They do mention among other assets a list of debts due and on his books but do not particularize.[19] Altogether his operation as pictured was small. Equally small was the business of James Goodwin of

[14] Edward Dixon Collection (Manuscript Division, Library of Congress). If Ledgers A to E cover time spans approximately equal to that of Ledger F, Dixon must have gone into business around 1730.
[15] To be precise, 98 accounts were £2 or less (21 per cent of all accounts); the next 251 were between £2 and £10 (54.3 per cent). Altogether these 349 amounted to 75.3 per cent of all accounts.
[16] York County, Wills and Inventories, No. 20, 1745–1759, folios 235–41.
[17] Accounts, Vol. 43, folio 172.
[18] Ibid., Vol. 36, folios 392–98.
[19] Surry County, Deeds and Wills, Unnumbered, Part 2, 1715–1730, folio 308.

York County, Virginia. His appraisers tell us that the total amount of debts due came to £434 8s. 11d. currency but do not say how many.[20] The debts due the estate of John Potter of Northampton County, Virginia, run to a list of 152 names, the greatest debtor among them owing £20, the smallest 6d.[21]

Such data, though far from ideal, abound in the accounts of estates, and the mass gives a consistent picture of the operations of small merchants. Most of them, whether large or small, sold on credit. Small planters could buy on no other terms. Some of the largest merchants went beyond selling their stock on credit to something resembling a loan business. Edward Dixon paid the freedom dues to indentured servants who had served their time for some of his well-to-do clients. Dozens of inventories of country merchants list notes of hand and bonds for repayment of sums borrowed by planters when they were short of cash.

To call these creditors "moneylenders" creates a misleading image. The terminology, it is true, comes from contemporary usage: men spoke of lending money or having money out at interest. Not much cash actually changed hands in these transactions, certainly no large sums. Many affluent planters had currency or gold and silver "in the house," but the sums rarely ran beyond a few dozen pounds, hardly a base broad enough to carry on an over-the-counter loan business. What, then, was the character of the credit mechanism embraced by the contemporary term "moneylending"? The question is worth investigation for an insight into the expedients of a society chronically starved for capital and plagued by tight money.[22]

Of the two most prevalent types of credit arrangements, that which rested on the English base is the least and simplest. Put schematically, A, the English merchant or investor, extended credit to B, a colonial storekeeper or planter, who further gave credit to X, Y, and Z in his neighborhood.[23] In this arrangement B became a middleman, restricted in the credit he could offer or the loans he could make to the sum extended by the English principal. This credit mechanism, resting on an English base, could never have supported Chesapeake debt. The result would have resembled a pyramid standing on its apex.

The larger and more complex tissue of debt resulted from local processes that made colonials themselves the capitalists. The lenders, men of some substance and boundless enterprise in the counties of the Chesapeake, established credit for the borrower and received the borrower's obligation to repay the loan in one of several forms—mortgage, bond,

[20] York County, Wills and Inventories, No. 20, 1745–1759, folios 518–19.
[21] Northampton County, Wills and Inventories, No. 18, 1733–1740, Part 1, folios 120–21.
[22] Extended analysis of this subject would run beyond the limits of editorial toleration. This sketch offers an outline which is amplified in my forthcoming study.
[23] A variation of this arrangement is presented in Rosenblatt, "The Significance of Credit in the Tobacco Consignment Trade," 383–99. The colonial middleman, B, was Norton's son in this case.

note of hand. This instrument in the hands of the lender became an asset, money due with interest at some future date on such and such security. It could be sold, and sometimes was; it could be offered as security, and was on occasion. Thus was woven the tissue of debt so striking to investigators who look into the inventories and accounts or into the proceedings of the county courts.[24] In the records it appears that everyone owed everyone else—and that was not far from the case.

Records of the most authentic sort—the administrations of estates—set at rest the question of who held the Chesapeake debt. The great bulk was held by provincial capitalists. These locally held debts get little attention as a rule. Like the submerged part of an iceberg they are not seen, while the debts due British merchants, a fraction of the whole, show clear and sparkling. But for the provincial holders they were solid assets, as reliable as those held by the British, and not mere paper values. They represented in the final analysis the created capital—the houses, barns, wharves, fences, orchards, ships, gristmills, sawmills—of a century when the rate of capital formation was high.[25]

To be brief, planter creditors should not be thought of as *rentiers*, men with liquid capital which they invested in securities at the rate of 6 percent allowed by law. They were more nearly creative capitalists, entrepreneurs whose fortunes grew in rough equivalence to the economic growth of the Chesapeake. If many of them profited handsomely, they also made essential contributions: they provided banking services to the community, and they took the risks. Quite naturally some became casualties on the battlefield of business enterprise. The survivors accumulated estates that after death would endow their heirs but that in their lives enabled them to enlarge the scope of their enterprises.[26]

Specifically the planter-entrepreneur, a few of them at least, found in manufacturing another kind of investment that yielded possibly the highest nonspeculative returns in the whole region. The Chesapeake fell far below New England in wood products—pipe staves and lumber—and well below the Carolinas in naval stores. Still, some merchants met their balance of payments shipping these commodities, and some entrepreneurs made money producing them. But in iron the Chesapeake cap-

[24] In some counties suits for the recovery of debts came to more than 90 percent of all cases tried.

[25] The kind of study made by Martin L. Primack, "Farm Capital Formation as a Use of Farm Labor in the United States, 1850–1910," *Journal of Economic History*, XXVI (September 1966), 348–62, would be of great use to students of the Chesapeake. Lacking the ready statistics available for this later period, I have based my estimates on the differential value of escheat and special warrants, which reflects in a crude way the value added by improvements. Hugh Jones makes some useful observations on capital formation in *The Present State of Virginia*, ed. by Richard L. Morton (Chapel Hill, 1956), 137–38.

[26] The list of persons of first fortune who had "money out at interest," as they put it, is long. Some of the best-known Maryland examples include Charles Carroll of Carrollton, Richard Bennet, Osburn Sprigg, Samuel Chew, Sr., and Amos Garrett. The Virginia records do not yield this information as easily. Known examples include Robert Carter of Nomini Hall and William Fitzhugh.

italists developed works that surpassed any others in the colonies and measured up to European standards for pig and bar production. At least six native capitalists who rose to top wealth owed part of their success to investment in ironworks.[27]

Perhaps the most spectacular successes of all came to those planters who also became land speculators.[28] Their tracks in the Chesapeake country have not been carefully followed through the last years of the seventeenth and early eighteenth centuries. They should be, because in land speculation the Chesapeake enterprisers were innovators. As merchants, moneylenders, and manufacturers they departed from planting pure and simple, but in all these they followed ancient practice and employed instruments familiar to modern capitalism. As land speculators they broke new ground. The idea of treating land as a commodity for wholesale turnover at a profit had no roots in England. There, improved lands were likely to be family estates, either your own or, for newly rich purchasers, someone else's, in either case too cherished for ordinary traffic. Wild lands to be reclaimed from a state of nature were simply nonexistent save in the fen country. To those Englishmen transplanted to the Chesapeake, land seemed a good, an end or object in itself. Like Greek in Dr. Samuel Johnson's aphorism, a man got as much of it as he could. The earliest landed magnates in the colonies of Virginia and Maryland thought in traditional rather than capitalistic terms: of large holdings as a permanent estate and as a badge of station.[29] But by the early eighteenth century the notion of amassing land beyond the conceivable family needs of endowing heirs and providing against soil exhaustion began to appear in the rent rolls and debt books. First tens of thousands, then hundreds of thousands of acres of wild land were set down against the names that became the first families.[30]

Somewhere in these decades the idea of land speculation was born; the amateur planter-speculator became the professional. The social costs and benefits resulting from this transformation have hardly been touched

[27] Some Chesapeake iron was exploited by English iron masters, notably at Principio, at the Nottingham Furnace, and at the Lancashire Works, all in Maryland. The chief native syndicate is discussed in Keach Johnson, "The Baltimore Company Seeks English Markets: A Study of the Anglo-American Iron Trade, 1731–1755," *William and Mary Quarterly*, 3d Ser., XVI (January 1959), 37–60.

[28] Like "moneylender," the term "land speculator" is easily misconstrued. Ray A. Billington, "Origins of the Land Speculator as a Frontier Type," *Agricultural History*, XIX (October 1945), 204–12, indicates some of the varieties and functions of men in this traffic.

[29] A few looked to the remote past of feudalism and attempted to establish manors in Maryland, without much success, however.

[30] The Virginia records show about 400 estates of 1,000 acres or more in 1704, but of this total only 121 were above the 2,000-acre mark, and only 17 came to 5,000 acres or more. These are hardly huge speculative holdings. Landed estates of 10,000 acres or over can be counted on the fingers of one hand. Rent Roll of 1704 (Virginia State Library). But the race was beginning: of forty-six patents signed in April 1706, a quarter were for 1,000 acres or more, two of them around the 5,000-acre mark. *Calendar of State Papers, Colonial Series* (43 vols. to date, London, 1860–   ), XXIII, 210–11.

realistically in historical literature. Some, and not the least, of the speculators combined development with their land operations.[31] Their con-
veyances frequently carried provisions binding the occupant to make
specified improvements: he must build a house of stated dimensions, he
must plant so many apple trees, or clear and fence a certain number of
acres. In other words, the landed men enforced capital formation on
properties they leased or sold.[32]

Unquestionably the most lucrative practice of speculators, sales on
credit, opened the door to profit inflation of a degree never before
known in the planting society. Speculators who obtained their land at
slightly more than a penny an acre found buyers without ready money
willing to purchase farmsteads at prices that ranged from five shillings
an acre up to a pound, giving a mortage in lieu of cash. In effect, the
speculator created a loan secured by the land he sold, a property that
was bound to increase in value by large annual increments as the holder
improved it by clearing, fencing, building houses and barns, and planting orchards. Many of the debts held by the Carrolls, Dulanys, and Car-
ters—their money out at interest—originated in land deals of this kind.
Profits of fiftyfold to a hundredfold were common, of two hundredfold
were not rare. Understandably, the speculative-minded limited entrance
to their club to the politically significant and to men of substance who
could not be disbarred.

It is fair to say that those who rose to the very top of the economic
ladder came up by gains from activities other than planting. Fraction-
ally, this element was small. Case studies of its members become almost
monotonous in their uniformity. Somewhere near the roots of the family
tree an enterprising type appears, not always a man of refinement but
invariably one who was energetic and sometimes ruthless. Beyond planting, his energies spilled over into merchandising, land speculation,
moneylending, or manufacturing, and occasionally into all. All these
called for ability beyond that required for successful planting on a small
scale. William Fitzhugh of Virginia and Thomas Bordley of Maryland
were scarcely more representative of Chesapeake planters than was
Andrew Carnegie of American businessmen of his day. Yet they were
also planters, not a class set above but an integral part of planting society, sharing its prejudices, experiencing its misfortunes, and receiving
its rewards as planters in good seasons. Probably never since in American history has top wealth enjoyed a more harmonious relationship with
the rest of society.

The sense of community between wealthy planter and small pro-

[31] The kind of activity that accompanied speculative selling is suggested in Aubrey
C. Land, "A Land Speculator in the Opening of Western Maryland," *Maryland
Historical Magazine*, XLVIII (September 1953), 191–203.
[32] Not all speculators sold land outright. The practice of leasing, with improvements
specified in the lease, had real advantages, as well as shortcomings. Willard F. Bliss,
"The Rise of Tenancy in Virginia," *Virginia Magazine of History and Biography*,
LVIII (October 1950), 427–41. The findings of Bliss are congruent with results I
have obtained for earlier years of the century.

ducer was sufficiently durable to withstand the greatest of strains—that of the creditor-debtor relationship between them. Many, possibly a majority, of the planters in the highest bracket of wealth were creditors. They held the mortgages, notes, and book debts of small producers, who were almost to a man debtors. The totals of locally held debt are staggering, many times the amounts owed by Jefferson's "certain great families" to British houses.[33] Jefferson's famous observation has had the mischievous effect (for historical accuracy) of persuasively simplifying a complex matter. But in directing attention to a single facet Jefferson followed the mystique of planting society, which held the wicked British merchant community to account for ills of the economy—for unsatisfactory tobacco prices, for the prevalence of debt, and other evils. Chesapeake creditors never became targets for the wrath of their debtors.[34] Quite the contrary, small producer and great planter made common cause.

Common cause in politics shows strikingly in the voter support of the planting elite by the numerous small-planter element. A prominent family name did not automatically get their votes, as Landon Carter learned to his cost when he failed to "familiarize" with them. George Washington instinctively adjusted to the realities of politics when he took to "swilling the planters with bumbo." He meant the small producers specifically, for they were the electorate of his district. He would have committed political suicide by setting himself off as a member of an economically favored class.

The faith representatives kept with their constituents runs like a familiar refrain through the legislative journals. Public works from lighthouses to buildings for safeguarding public records came under the sharpest scrutiny from delegates who would not have missed the few

[33] This complicated subject needs further study. The figures compiled *ex parte* by British merchants were described by the British ambassador as "grossly exaggerated." When finally compounded in the Convention of 1802, the sum paid was about one-eighth the amount the merchants claimed due. Samuel Flagg Bemis, *Jay's Treaty: A Study in Commerce and Diplomacy* (New York, 1923), 439. Emory G. Evans, "Planter Indebtedness and the Coming of the Revolution in Virginia," *William and Mary Quarterly*, 3d Ser., XIX (October 1962), 511–33, deals mainly with the motivation of planters rather than the authenticity of the stated debt.

[34] A considerable number of Maryland and Virginia planters who were creditors in their own provinces actually had sterling balances with British merchant houses. Such cases appear early in the eighteenth century. A few selected from a dozen or more estates probated around 1720 will illustrate the point. Edward Cole, St. Mary's County, Maryland, had a sterling balance of £350 10s. 10d. with the house of John Hyde, London; Accounts, Vol. 3, folios 57–59. Richard Harrison, Calvert County, Maryland, had sterling balances as follows: £944 19s. 5d. with John Hyde, £583 13s. 5d. with Jonathan Scarth, £362 13s. 5¼d with Joseph Jackson, and £60 14s. 3d. with Gilbert Higginson for a total of £1952 14s. 0¼d.; Accounts, Vol. 3, folios 11–14. William Harris, Surry County, Virginia, had a sterling balance with his English correspondent, which unfortunately is not separated from the total of £750 currency due him; Surry County, Deeds and Wills, Unnumbered, Part 2, 1715–1730. Similar illustrations could be drawn for each subsequent decade down to the War for Independence.

shillings added to their taxes for these facilities. But for the planter of petty estate and annual cash income of twenty or thirty pounds, even a few shillings was a drain. Consequently, investment in the public domain was minimal.

The poverty that meets the eye throughout the eighteenth-century Chesapeake calls for brief comment on planter experimentation with alternate crops, or rather the comparative lack of such experiments. There was considerable talk about other crops and some official encouragement from England to broaden the base of the economy. Except for one area the results came to little. In the first place, tobacco prices were never consistently low enough to threaten the Chesapeake with ruin. Hard years, sometimes two or three in a row, brought provincial legislatures to serious discussion of crop limitations or led desperate small planters to such direct methods as tobacco-cutting riots. After the 1720's European demand raised prices, and economic growth proceeded at a steady pace.[35] In the second place, experiments had cost tags beyond the resources of the small producer, both in time and capital outlay. Moreover, his habits and skills as a tobacco planter did not easily adapt to radical changes in husbandry.

One interesting group, blessed with ampler capital and greater flexibility, proved the exception. Its members comprised prosperous planters with estates valued at £500 to £1,000, not men of first rank in fortune but those obviously above the usual cares of the poor. Some tried hemp or flax and won prizes for their efforts. Others grew crops of indigo. One indigo venture, "the St. Domingo Scheme" of young Kensey Johns and Brian Philpot, Jr., produced a net profit of slightly over 50 percent.[36] None of these crops caught on permanently. The sketchy evidence available indicates that planters in this intermediate class led the way in the transition to grain culture on the Eastern Shore of Maryland, the only successful breakaway from the tobacco staple in the Tidewater. If this surmise is correct, does it not indicate that planters in this group were in a position to withstand economic pressures that bound smaller fry to the cycle of tobacco?

This paper has attempted neither to raise all questions that could be asked about economic behavior in the tobacco colonies nor to develop fully the implications of those selected for discussion. Short of the complete analysis that is bound to be the work of many hands and minds, it has seemed reasonable to choose a few questions for which answers are suggested by evidence from contemporary court records and other economic materials. These records speak unambiguously as to the broad spectrum of planters' estates, running from the pinched circumstances of the host of small producers to the opulence of the fortunate few. These

[35] Jacob M. Price, "The Economic Growth of the Chesapeake and the European Market, 1697–1775," *Journal of Economic History*, XXIV (December 1964), 496–511.
[36] Brian Philpot, Jr., to Kensey Johns, December 2, 1756; August 28, 1757, in Johns Papers (Maryland Hall of Records).

few rose to dominant positions by types of enterprise more often associated with a business community than with the leisured routine of the field crop. In a nutshell, they provided services for an agrarian society as merchants, moneylenders, and land dealers. And as manufacturers and processors they supplied some consumer goods. Clearly, they saw in the community needs an economic opportunity, and their estates show the consequences of their perception. They possessed the chattels and adornments of the good life, and they owned the obligations—the paper—of a debtor society. Yet neither their activities as businessmen nor their wealth divorced them from their social milieu, the vast body of the poor and the moderately endowed. They simply became "the great planters," and in their political roles they expressed the imperatives of a planting society which had struck deep roots in the Chesapeake.

Three ⌣ *The Management of an Ante-Bellum Cotton Plantation*

MANAGERIAL DUTIES AND RESPONSIBILITIES William K. Scarborough

Multitudinous duties and exacting responsibilities were associated with the management of southern plantations. Among the major responsibilities of the overseer were the welfare and discipline of the slaves, the care of livestock and agricultural implements, and the production of staple and subsistence crops. He assigned gangs to work, apportioned tasks, and supervised the labor of slaves in the field. He was expected to be sufficiently acquainted with contemporary medical practices to determine whether ailing Negroes needed professional attention and to treat minor complaints without outside help. To the overseer was given the responsibility for insuring that the slaves were properly fed and reasonably clean. He was obliged to make periodic inspections of slave cabins and was responsible for the distribution of Negro clothing. Finally, upon the overseer depended, "to a large extent, the security of the whites against

REPRINTED with permission from William K. Scarborough, "Managerial Duties and Responsibilities," *The Overseer: Plantation Management in the Old South,* Baton Rouge, La.: Louisiana State University Press, 1966, pp. 67–90.

uprisings of slaves."[1] It is apparent that the life of a conscientious and energetic overseer was an arduous one.

Upon the assumption of his post, the overseer was usually given a set of written instructions which outlined his duties and detailed the wishes of his employer regarding the care and punishment of Negroes, apportionment of work, methods of cultivation, and other points respecting the management of the estate. The plantation rules for Andrew Flynn's "Green Valley" plantation, located in the Yazoo-Mississippi Delta just south of Memphis, illustrate the nature of these instructions. "Green Valley" was a relatively small cotton plantation with a slave force of just under forty. The following is a detailed exposition of rules for the government of the plantation as set forth in 1840:

1st   A good crop means one that is good taking into consideration every thing   hands, breeding women, children, mules, Stocks, provisions, farming utensils of all Sorts & keeping up land, ditches, fences & C & C. The object therefore must be not to make a given number of bags of cotton but as many as can be made without losing as much or nearly as much in these particulars as is gained in cotton.

2nd   The overseer will never be expected to work in the field. but he must always be with the hands when not otherwise engaged in the Employer's business & must do every thing that is required of him, provided it is directly or indirectly connected with the planting or other pecuniary interest of the Employer at Green Valley Plantation.

3rd   He must never, on any account be absent a single night or an entire day, from the plantation without permission previously obtained. Whenever he goes to Church or elsewhere he must return without fail, before Sundown.

4th   He must keep all the keys carefully & where no one can have access to them but himself   He must never allow any one to unlock the Smoke House or corn crib except himself under any circumstances. He must lock the Stables every night. open them every morning & see personally that the mules are cleaned & fed twice a day at least & watered as often as necessary.

5th   He must visit the negro houses every morning by daylight. Once a week at least he must visit every negro house after horn blow at night.

6th   He must attend particularly to all experiments instituted by the Employer, conduct them faithfully, & report regularly & correctly. Some overseers defeat important experiments by carelessness or Wilfulness.

7th   He will be expected to give his opinions on all matters connected with planting & plantation affairs   the reasons for them, but if they are not adopted by the Employer, he must obey the instructions given, implicitly, thoroughly, & with a sincere desire to produce the best result.

[1] Moody, "Slavery on Louisiana Sugar Plantations," 209.

Employed must be collected at once & put away carefully in their proper

8th   He will be expected to give minute information of every thing going on at the plantation or elsewhere that may be Known to him which may affect in any way the Employer's views or interests without being asked & of course, on all occassions [*sic*] to be very accurate in his Statements & sincere in his conjectures

9th   He is particularly charged to take care of the Stock, to obey all instructions whatever to them, to count them all at least once a month & to have them fed, salted & C. Every care must be taken of the mules

10th   The horn will be blowed by the Driver in the morning just before daylight & again just after daylight. At the latter the negroes will go to work   If it is very cold or rainy or if the Season is sickly the hands should not go out before Sunrise & not then if the rain continues. At night the horn will blow, in Summer at 9 & in winter at 8 o'clock after which no negro must be allowed to be out of his house on any pretence.

11th   The negroes must be Kept as much as possible out of the rain   It is much better to lose some time than to run the risk of Sickness & death. The Overseer must see that they have good fires after rains & of winter nights—

12th   They must be flogged as seldom as possible yet always when necessary. A good manager who is with the hands as much as he Should be can encourage them on with very little punishment. Violent threats must never be used & the Overseer is strictly enjoined never to kick a negro or strike one with his hand or a stick or the butt end of his whip. These things will not be tolerated. No unusual punishments must be resorted to without the Employers approbation

13th   The sick must be visited at least three times a day & at night when necessary & treated with every possible attention. Unless it is a clear case of imposition a negro had better be allowed a day's rest when he lays up. A little rest often saves much by preventing serious illness. Medicine must be given carefully & sparingly & when there is doubt what to give, let nothing be given. Never administer Calomal or Castor oil unless they are prescribed & insisted on by a Physician.

14th   The children must be very particularly attended to, for rearing them is not only a Duty, but also the most profitable part of plantation business. They must be kept clean, dry & warm, & wellfed & seldom [illeg.]. Plain food is necessary for them: bread, hominy or mush, Soupes, Sugar & a little meat: molasses for those two or three years old, but not for those younger. Vegetables in general not proper for them.

15th   Pregnant women & sucklers must be treated with great tenderness, worked near home & lightly. Pregnant women should not plow or lift; but must be kept at moderate work until the last hour if possible. Sucklers must be allowed time to suckle their children from twice to three times a day according to their ages. At twelve months old children must be weaned.

16th   When any kind of business is done with, all the utensils places. Waggons & carts must always be repaired & put under the shelter ready for use. So also with [illeg.] ploughs, spades   & C & C.

17th   The following is the order in which offenses must be estimated & punished. 1st Running Away   2nd Getting Drunk or having spirits   3rd Stealing Hogs. 4th Stealing. 5th Leaving Plantation without permission   6th Absence after Horn blows. 7th Unclean house or Person. 8th Neglect of work   The highest punishment must not exceed Fifty lashes in one Day.[2]

The above rules are typical of those drawn up for the government of plantation establishments throughout the South.[3]

Theoretically, most planters were in general agreement regarding the relative order of importance of the various functions performed by the overseer. This order was delineated in the introductory pages of Thomas Affleck's widely used *Cotton Plantation Record and Account Book*. The following paragraph from that source indicates the ideal criteria by which the planter judged the performance of his overseer:

In conclusion,—Bear in mind that a *fine crop* consists, first, in an increase in the number, and a marked improvement in the condition and value of the negroes; second, an abundance of provision of all sorts for man and beast, carefully saved and properly housed; third, both summer and winter clothing made at home; also, leather tanned, and shoes and harness made when practicable; fourth, an improvement in the productive qualities of the land, and in the general condition of the plantation; fifth, the team and stock generally, with the farming implements and the buildings, in fine order at the close of the year; and young hogs more than enough for next year's killing; *then*—as heavy a crop of cotton, sugar or rice, as could possibly be made under the circumstances, sent to market in good season and of prime quality. The time has passed when the Overseer was valued solely for the number of bales of cotton, hogsheads of sugar, or tierces of rice he had made, without reference to his other qualifications.[4]

In actual practice, however, many proprietors ascribed a great deal more importance to the production of staples than Affleck indicated. This emphasis upon crop results at the expense of long-range improvements re-

---

[2] Andrew Flynn Plantation Book (Microfilm copy in Southern Historical Collection, University of North Carolina, Chapel Hill), 1840.
[3] Other outstanding, detailed sets of instructions include the following: (1) "Rules for Overseers," *Farmers' Register*, VIII (April, 1840), 230–31; (2) Rules and Directions for Alexander Telfair's "Thorn Island" Plantation, in Phillips (ed.), *Plantation and Frontier*, I, 126–29; (3) Rules on the Rice Estate of P. C. Weston, in Phillips (ed.), *Plantation and Frontier*, I, 116–22; also printed in *De Bow's Review*, XXII (January, 1857), 38–44; (4) Rules and Regulations for the Government of the William J. Minor Plantations, in Minor Plantation Diaries (William J. Minor and Family Papers), XXXIII (1861–65), XXXIV (1861–68); and (5) John Hartwell Cocke, "Standing Rules for the Government of Slaves on a Virginia Plantation," in Cocke Papers (Southern Historical Collection).
[4] Thomas Affleck, "The Duties of an Overseer," in *Cotton Plantation Record and Account Book* (7th ed.; New Orleans: B. M. Norman, 1857); also printed in *De Bow's Review*, XVIII (March, 1855), 345.

mained dominant among most planters in the cotton belt until the end of the antebellum period.[5]

Despite differing views regarding the importance of staple production, there was universal agreement among planters that the welfare of their slaves was the paramount managerial consideration. This responsibility received the greatest emphasis in instructions to overseers throughout the South. It may be noted that six of the seventeen rules relating to the administration of "Green Valley" plantation were concerned exclusively with this subject. It is hardly surprising that the planter, who had a substantial investment in every slave on his plantation, should be interested in keeping them healthy and contented. The principal task of the overseer was to insure that these conditions were maintained among the Negroes under his supervision. Thus, P. C. Weston, a South Carolina rice planter, directed his overseer "most distinctly to understand that his first object is to be, under all circumstances, the care and well being of the negroes."[6] Similarly, Louisiana planter Maunsel White, distressed to learn of an outbreak of measles on one of his absentee cotton plantations, declared in a letter to his overseer: "I regret exceedingly to hear that my people are troubled with the measles—I feel confident you will take good care of them *let what may happen to the crop.*"[7]

A duty of many overseers, especially on larger plantations, was the maintenance of various record and account books. The fact that countless overseers were able to discharge such a function adequately reinforces the contention, expressed earlier, that the vast majority of plantation superintendents were at least literate. The type of information which the overseer was required to enter in the plantation book is illustrated by the following rule of a Mississippi cotton planter:

> The overseer shall keep a plantation book, in which he shall register the birth and name of each negro that is born; the name of each negro that died, and specify the disease that killed him. He shall also keep in it the weights of the daily picking of each hand; the mark, number and weight of each bale of cotton, and the time of sending the same to market; and all other such occurrences, relating to the crop, the weather, and all other matters pertaining to the plantation, that he may deem advisable.[8]

In addition to a plantation book, William J. Minor required his overseers to keep a separate record of slave births and deaths, a wood book, and a "receipt & forwarding book in which all articles received at the place or sent or shipped from the place are to be entered with the date of each transaction, prices & name of vessel or boat when known."[9]

[5] See pages of this [Scarborough's] book.
[6] Phillips (ed.), *Plantation and Frontier*, I, 116.
[7] Maunsel White to James N. Bracewell, May 17, 1848, Maunsel White Lettercopy Book, in Maunsel White Papers and Books; italics by author.
[8] *De Bow's Review*, X (June, 1851), 626.
[9] Rules and Regulations for the Government of the William J. Minor Plantations, in Minor Plantation Diaries (William J. Minor and Family Papers), XXXIII (1861–65), XXXIV (1861–68).

The maintenance of plantation record books was especially important to an absentee owner as a supplement to the reports received from his overseer. Thomas Affleck contended that the use of his plantation book had promoted improvement in managerial practices. For example, recording the daily amounts of cotton picked by each hand compelled the overseer to institute an invariable and uniform system in the harvesting of that crop. In addition, said Affleck, the maintenance of the plantation book aided the overseer by providing evidence that the orders of his employer were being executed.[10]

There was considerable difference between the status of an overseer on an absentee estate and that of one on a resident plantation. The latter was often subjected to rigorous supervision by the master, and his duties might be confined to the daily execution of orders relating to supervision of the slaves in the fields and in their quarters. On the other hand, absentee owners frequently operated with comparative freedom of action. One authority expressed the view that under absentee ownership "the opportunities for abuses and misunderstandings increased." [11] Although there can be no quarrel with the argument that opportunities for abuses were greater on absentee units, it is certainly debatable whether misunderstandings between proprietor and overseer were more frequent on such plantations. Indeed, it seems more probable that friction between the two was reduced by their physical separation.

Most planters were painfully aware of the degree of power exercised by managers of absentee properties. James H. Ruffin, North Carolina lawyer and planter, displayed his knowledge of the powerful position occupied by his absentee overseer when he lamented: ". . . this man Dobbs will *ruin* and *beggar* me if he is not more closely watched than he has heretofore been. He is a man in my opinion totally devoid of principle and without the smallest regard to my interest when his own is not also consulted. He has under his management and control every thing I am worth to use or to abuse it according to his own will and pleasure." [12] The apprehension with which many planters regarded the installation of a new overseer upon their absentee property, and the most common abuses which occurred under absentee overseerships are clearly revealed in the following oft-quoted instructions from George Washington to one of his absentee managers:

I do in explicit terms, enjoin it upon you to remain constantly at home, unless called off by unavoidable business, or to attend divine worship, and to be constantly with your people when there. There is no other sure way of getting work well done, and quietly, by negroes; for when an overlooker's back is turned, the most of them will slight their work, or be idle altogether; in which case correction cannot retrieve either, but often produces evils which are worse than the disease. Nor is there any other

10 Thomas Affleck, in *Southern Cultivator*, XIII (March, 1855), 75–76.
11 Phillips, *American Negro Slavery*, 280.
12 Cornelius Oliver Cathey, *Agricultural Developments in North Carolina, 1783–1860* (Chapel Hill: University of North Carolina Press, 1956), 59.

mode than this to prevent thieving and other disorders, the consequence of opportunities. You will recollect that your time is paid for by me, and if I am deprived of it, it is worse even than robbing my purse, because it is also a breach of trust, which every honest man ought to hold most sacred. You have found me, faithful to my part of the agreement which was made with you, while you are attentive to your part; but it is to be remembered that a breach on one side relieves the obligation on the other. If therefore it shall be found by me, that you are absenting yourself from either the farm or the people without just cause, I shall hold myself no more bound to pay the wages, than you do to attend strictly to the charge which is entrusted to you.

There is another thing I must caution you against, not knowing whether there be cause to charge you with it or not, and that is, not to retain any of my negroes, who are able and fit to work in the crop or elsewhere, in or about your own house for your own purposes. This I do not allow any overseer to do. A small boy or girl for the purpose of fetching wood or water, tending a child, or such like things, I do not object to; but so soon as they are able to work out, I expect to reap the benefit of their labor myself.[13]

The overseer of an absentee estate was usually obliged to discharge additional responsibilities not required of resident managers. In addition to the normal obligations associated with crop production and slave management, he was frequently burdened with financial and logistical responsibilities inherent in the operation of a commercial agricultural enterprise. He might be called upon to institute law suits against debtors of the estate, order supplies from the commission merchant, negotiate loans, collect delinquent accounts, and, in general, to act for his employer in any matter involving the plantation under his cognizance. Moreover, the absentee manager was obliged to transmit, at frequent intervals, detailed reports covering every aspect of plantation operations. Alexander Telfair directed the overseer of his "Thorn Island," Georgia, plantation to "write me the last day of every month to Savannah, unless otherwise directed. When writing have the Journal before you, and set down in the Letter every thing that has been done, or occurred on the Plantation during the month." [14] Clearly, the post of overseer on an absentee plantation called for a man of uncommon ability.

The planter community was not reticent about offering advice to the overseer concerning the managerial practices he should pursue in the execution of his manifold duties. Most of this advice was focused upon the vital problem of Negro management. Those points most frequently stressed by proprietors in relation to this subject are illustrated by the

[13] *Plantation and Farm Instruction, Regulation, Record, Inventory and Account Book* (Richmond: J. W. Randolph, 1852), 4. Also printed in *De Bow's Review,* XVIII (March, 1855), 339–40.
[14] Phillips (ed.), *Plantation and Frontier,* I, 128.

following directions, drawn up by John Hartwell Cocke for the guidance of inexperienced overseers on his Virginia estate:

> . . . never permit any order you give to be disobeyed, or disregarded, without a strict inquiry into it, & punish the offender if necessary.
>
> Set the first example of strict attention to your duties & you may with the more justice, & propriety, inflict punishment upon others for the neglect of theirs.
> Therefore never make an order without Punctually attending to it for if you make a rule & forget it yourself with what face could you punish others for neglecting it also?
> If you punish only according to justice & reason, with uniformity, you can never be too severe, & will be the more respected for it, even by those who suffer.
>
> Arrangement & regularity form the great secret of doing things well, you must therefore as far as possible have every thing done according to a fixed rule [15]

The two principles of slave management universally emphasized by southern planters in their directions to overseers were a firm discipline, tempered with kindness, and a uniform, impartially-administered system of justice. "No person," declared P. C. Weston, "should ever be allowed to break a law without being punished, or any person punished who has not broken a well known law. Every person should be made perfectly to understand what they are punished for, and should be made to perceive that they are not punished in anger or through caprice." Moreover, the South Carolina planter warned against the use of abusive language or violence of demeanor as "they reduce the man who uses them to a level with the negro, and are hardly ever forgotten by those to whom they are addressed." [16]

Overseers were also cautioned against indulging in too much familiarity with Negroes under their control. Joseph Johnson advised the new overseer of his Warren County, Mississippi, plantation: "Your experience & good sense has taught you, that, familiarity with slaves will not do, an Overseer ought to have but little Conversation with negroes under his care & that only to tell them what to do & then to see that he is obeyed." [17]

There were differing views within the planter class concerning the degree of severity necessary to establish and maintain the overseer in an unassailable position of authority over the slaves. Thomas Ruffin of North Carolina thought it desirable for a new overseer to instill within

[15] John Hartwell Cocke, "Standing Rules for the Government of Slaves on a Virginia Plantation," in Cocke Papers (Southern Historical Collection).
[16] Phillips (ed.), *Plantation and Frontier*, I, 122.
[17] Moore (ed.), "Two Documents Relating to Plantation Overseers of the Vicksburg Region," 35, quoting Joseph Johnson to George Comer, December 23, 1831, in Benjamin L. C. Wailes Collection, Mississippi Department of Archives and History, Jackson.

the Negroes a fear of himself at the outset of his adminitsration. Slaves, contended Ruffin, developed no respect for their overseer "unless he makes them fear him at the beginning." [18] Another observer, however, stressed the importance of a display of kindness toward the Negroes by their overseer. "Kindness, and even gentleness," he declared, "is not inconsistent with firmness and inexorable discipline." [19] This view was echoed by Virginia planter Hill Carter, who advised his "friends, the Virginia overseers, to use a little flattery sometimes instead of stripes." [20]

Although overseers were repeatedly cautioned against undue familiarity with the Negroes, some slave managers apparently failed to interpret this injunction as a prohibition against cohabitation with sirens of the slave quarter. There has been much speculation, but little concrete evidence, concerning the degree of miscegenation which occurred in the Old South. With regard to relations between white overseers and female slaves, the preponderance of evidence indicates that such unions were formed but that they were almost universally discouraged by members of the planter community.

Illicit relations between overseers and slaves were most common on absentee estates, where both temptation and opportunity tended to be greater than on resident plantations. The gullible Fanny Kemble, during a brief stay on her husband's Georgia rice estate, found evidence that former overseer Roswell King, Jr., had fathered several illegitimate slave children during his long term as absentee manager. One slave woman horrified the actress with the following account of her experiences under King:

> She told me a miserable story of her former experience on the plantation under Mr. K____'s overseership. It seems that Jem Valiant . . . was her first born, the son of Mr. K____, who forced her, flogged her severely for having resisted him, and then sent her off, as a further punishment, to Five Pound—a horrible swamp in a remote corner of the estate, to which the slaves are sometimes banished for such offences as are not sufficiently atoned for by the lash.[21]

Although Miss Kemble's intense antislavery bias seriously distorted her general account of affairs at Butler's Island, there seems little reason to doubt the veracity of her statements regarding King's conduct with the female slaves on that plantation. King and his father had operated the estate without any direction or interference from the owners for more than thirty years.

On his visit to John Burnside's Louisiana sugar holdings in 1861,

---

[18] Phillips, *Life and Labor in the Old South*, 325.
[19] *De Bow's Review*, XXI (September, 1856), 278.
[20] Hill Carter, "On the Management of Negroes; Addressed to the Farmers and Overseers of Virginia," *Farmers' Register*, I (February, 1834), 565.
[21] Kemble, *Journal of a Residence on a Georgian Plantation*, 253. For a critical appraisal of Miss Kemble's narrative, see Margaret Davis Cate, "Mistakes in Fanny Kemble's Georgia Journal," *Georgia Historical Quarterly*, XLIV (March, 1960).

William Howard Russell reported seeing a number of fair-complexioned slave children whose presence was attributed to the activities of previous overseers. It did not seem to the present manager, observed Russell, "that there was any particular turpitude in the white man who had left his offspring as slaves on the plantation." [22]

Extant plantation manuscripts contain few references to the problem of overseer-slave sex relations. A notable exception is afforded by the correspondence of Rachel O'Connor, who, perhaps because she was a woman and therefore sensitive to such relationships, had a great deal to say upon the subject. Mrs. O'Connor, who operated a plantation near St. Francisville, Louisiana, was driven nearly to distraction in the early 1830's by the disposition of her overseers to fraternize with the female slaves. In a series of letters to her brother and sister-in-law, David and Mary Weeks, she recounted the amorous exploits of overseers Patrick and Mulkey. Of the former, whom she regarded as "one of the best of farmers," Mrs. O'Connor remarked in one such missive: "Patrick behaves too mean to be a white man. His tracts are often found where he has been sneaking about after those negro girls." [23]

Accordingly, in the summer of 1832, Patrick was replaced by Mulkey, a married man with three grown sons, who made a good beginning, and for a time enjoyed the confidence of his employer. Shortly after engaging Mulkey for a second year, Mrs. O'Connor confided to her brother that "he dont appear to wish to abuse the negroes nor to have Wives amongst them, so far." [24] By the following fall, however, it became apparent that Mulkey too had developed a more-than-passing interest in the dark-skinned ladies on the place. In an irate letter to her brother, the proprietress charged that he was "a shameless being, nearly as bad as Patrick in the same way. if it was not for that he could oversee very well. but as it is, he has too many ladies to please." [25] As Mulkey's indiscretions became more flagrant, relations between employer and overseer deteriorated rapidly, culminating in the latter's enforced departure at the end of November. "Bad as Patrick acted," concluded the plantation mistress, "he was not one half as bad as this vilian, and his sons are as mean as himself." [26] Happily, the distraught proprietress had better luck with her next overseer, named Germany, who managed the plantation in splendid fashion for at least four years. After observing her new manager for more than two years, Mrs. O'Connor declared herself "perfectly satisfied with his management." He had refrained from "puting himself on a footing with those under his charge," and he had "no favorite misses to fight and abuse the boys about." But Germany, she

[22] Russell, *My Diary North and South*, 274.
[23] Rachel O'Connor to Mrs. Mary C. Weeks, June 4, 1832; O'Connor to David Weeks, July 8, 1832, Weeks Hall Collection.
[24] O'Connor to David Weeks, November 6, 1832, Weeks Hall Collection.
[25] *Ibid.*, October 23, 1833.
[26] *Ibid.*, November 20, 1833.

concluded, was the only overseer she had ever employed who was entirely "clear of that meanness." [27]

Although such instances of overseer liaisons with female slaves were not isolated, they were certainly not typical. On many plantations such conduct resulted in the immediate discharge of the overseer. Alabama planter James Tait, plagued by difficulties resulting from interference with the slave women by his overseer, jotted down the following maxim: "A legacy to my children.—Never employ an overseer who will equalize himself with the negro women. Besides the morality of it, there are evils too numerous to be now mentioned." [28] Joseph A. S. Acklen, proprietor of one of the largest estates in Louisiana, imposed the following prohibition upon his overseers: "Having connection with any of my female servants will most certainly be visited with a dismissal from my employment, and no excuse can or will be taken." [29] Such restrictions undoubtedly had an effect in limiting nocturnal encounters between white overseers and slave women.

The lack of community of interest between overseer and slave was emphasized in a report prepared in 1846 by a committee of three, headed by John A. Calhoun, and presented to the Barbour County, Alabama, Agricultural Society. After alluding to the community of interest which governed the relationship between planter and slave, Calhoun observed: "There is one class of our community to whom all the motives referred to, to induce us to kindness to our slaves, do not apply. Your committee refer to our overseers. As they have no property in our slaves, of course they lack the check of self-interest. As their only aim in general is the mere crop results of the year, we can readily conceive the strong inducement they have to overwork our slaves." [30]

It is doubtful whether many overseers had any humanitarian feeling for the slaves under their supervision. One writer complained that the overseer had a low idea of slavery and did not see any reason to improve the conditions of the slave.[31] Upon cold reflection, however, it is difficult to discern why any overseer would have entertained thoughts of improving slave conditions, for to elevate the slave was to make him dissatisfied with his status, thereby increasing the already-formidable problems of Negro management. Kenneth Stampp has charged, with some justification, that overseers had a decided preference for physical force in dealing with slaves. "Overseers," declared Stampp, "seldom felt any personal affection for the bondsmen they governed. Their inclination in most cases was to punish severely; if their employers prohibited severity, they ignored such instructions as often as not." [32]

[27] O'Connor to A. T. Conrad, April 12, 1835, Weeks Hall Collection.
[28] Phillips, *Life and Labor in the Old South*, 282.
[29] Phillips, *American Negro Slavery*, 273–74.
[30] John A. Calhoun, "Management of Slaves," *De Bow's Review*, XVIII (June, 1855), 715. Also printed in *Southern Cultivator*, IV (August, 1846), 113.
[31] Bassett, *Plantation Overseer*, 274.
[32] Stampp, *The Peculiar Institution*, 183.

The observations of Frederick Law Olmsted during his stay on a large absentee cotton estate in Mississippi substantiate the view that overseers were inclined toward severe physical punishments. One overseer, asked by Olmsted whether the punishment of Negroes was not a disagreeable task, responded: "Yes, it would be to those who are not used to it—but it's my business, and I think nothing of it. Why, sir, I wouldn't mind killing a nigger more than I would a dog." [33] While visiting another unit of the same estate, Olmsted observed what he termed "the severest corporeal punishment of a negro that I witnessed at the South." The flogging had been administered to a young girl whom the overseer had discovered shirking her work. The overseer justified the severity of punishment in the following fashion: "If I hadn't punished her so hard she would have done the same thing again to-morrow, and half the people on the plantation would have followed her example. Oh, you've no idea how lazy these niggers are; you northern people don't know any thing about it. They'd never do any work at all if they were not afraid of being whipped." [34]

The typical overseer attitude toward slavery and the Negro was reflected by H. M. Seale, for at least fifteen years manager of the Houmas sugar estate in Ascension Parish, Louisiana. Resting after the labors of an August day in 1853, the veteran overseer contemplated events of the past year and evaluated slave morale on his plantation in these terms: "I am Getting on very well with my bisness this year   very little trouble with the Negroes. . . . My Negros Seem to be perfectly content." [35] Eight years later, William H. Russell visited Houmas and recorded his impression of Seale in these words:

> The overseer, it is certain, had no fastidious notions about slavery; it was to him the right thing in the right place, and his *summum bonum* was a high price for sugar, a good crop, and a healthy plantation. Nay, I am sure I would not wrong him if I said he could see no impropriety in running a good cargo of regular black slaves, who might clear the great backwood and swampy undergrowth, which was now exhausting the energies of his field-hands, in the absence of Irish navvies.[36]

For his part, the slave did not ordinarily view his overseer with unconcealed admiration. Indeed, he looked upon the overseer as a symbol of all the odious features of the institution of slavery. As one writer has observed: "If a single individual of the slave regime may be singled out for the chief object of the slaves' hatred, it would be the overseer." [37] The slave recognized that his superintendent did not have the prestige of

33 Olmsted, *Back Country*, 82.
34 *Ibid.*, 87.
35 H. M. Seale Diary (MS in Louisiana State University Department of Archives, Baton Rouge), August 8, 1853.
36 Russell, *My Diary North and South*, 275.
37 Flanders, *Plantation Slavery in Georgia*, 266.

a property holder, and, as a result, the authority of the overseer "had to be maintained by fear of the lash rather than by respect." [38] The difficult position occupied by the plantation manager was rendered more precarious by the obvious conflict of interest between master and slave. An inefficient and incompetent overseer, who did not maintain strict discipline among the slaves, was often viewed with favor by the latter. On the other hand, "overseers who were vigorous in the prosecution of their duties and exacting in their demands on the slaves were the overseers who experienced the greatest difficulty in managing slaves." [39] Thus, a Tennessee proprietor who had engaged one of the latter sort was compelled to shift him to another plantation, after a term of only six months, because the "negroes . . . had such an unconquerable hatrid for the man, that I believe they would have done better without any." [40]

Slaves often went to great lengths to discredit an unpopular overseer in the eyes of his employer. One of the most common means of effecting this purpose was to go directly to the owner with tales alleging mistreatment and mismanagement by the overseer. Unfortunately, many planters declined to discourage this practice of tale-bearing and consequently undermined the authority of their managers. A more sophisticated stratagem was employed by the Negroes on John H. Cocke's "Hopewell" plantation in order to discredit their overseer, J. Walter Carter. Only the alert action of steward Richard D. Powell prevented the loss of the cotton crop at "Hopewell," an absentee plantation in Greene County, Alabama. Powell recounted the incident to his employer in the following manner:

> The negroes attempted in a very friendly way in May to make Carter loose the crop. After finding himself in the grass he took the place of his head man, or Driver, & put him to work the first row & all the other hands to follow him, & all hands slighted their work by covering up the grass lightly, & not Cutting it up when small, & he became so restless that he did not take time to see how the work was done, & had his plows runing about, & plowing a spot here, & a spot there, & where they did plow, they would let the plows run over the grass, & not plow it up. All hands found I understood all about it, & from the first of June Overseer & negroes have done well—Carter never did have such a plain talking from any man before, I reckon as I gave him & it has made [him] see plainly all his foolish ways & C—The negroes understood me fully too, & all was done in friendship, & love, with a promise of punishment when the Crop was Laid by, or a good barbacue, & one or two days rest. They had the barbacue last Saturday.[41]

[38] Moody, "Slavery on Louisiana Sugar Plantations," 210.
[39] Wall, "Ebenezer Pettigrew," 184.
[40] Chase C. Mooney, *Slavery in Tennessee* (Bloomington: University of Indiana Press, 1957), 161, quoting Lucius Polk to William Polk, May 8, 1827, in Polk-Brown-Ewell Collection, University of North Carolina, Chapel Hill.
[41] Richard D. Powell to John Hartwell Cocke, August 14, 1857, Cocke Papers.

Notwithstanding the quaint phraseology of the steward, one may readily doubt whether the Negroes were motivated by sentiments of friendship and love in their efforts to oust Carter from his post.

Two basic types of labor organization—the gang, or time-work, system and the task, or piece-work, system—were employed on southern plantations. Operations on virtually all agricultural units in the tobacco, cotton, and sugar regions were conducted under the gang system, in which field slaves worked in gangs supervised by Negro drivers for a specified time period each day. Occasionally, however, the task system was utilized in those areas to perform certain types of labor for which it was better suited than was the gang method. Thus, on F. D. Richardson's "Bayside" plantation in St. Mary Parish, Louisiana, task work was sometimes used in ditching and scraping stubble.[42]

The task system of labor, in which individual workers were assigned specific daily tasks, was employed almost universally on the rice coast. The drainage ditches, which divided rice fields into half or quarter-acre plots, offered convenient units of performance in the successive planting, cultivating, and harvesting processes. Some planters found it expedient to deviate from the task method during actual planting operations. William Butler declared that in planting, the slaves "should be always Kept in gangs or parcels & not scattered over a field in Tasks as is too generally done, for while in gangs they are more immediately under the Superintendents Eyes."[43] Rice planters also might abandon task work in an emergency, "as in the mending of breaks in the dikes, or when joint exertion was required, as in log rolling, or when threshing and pounding with machinery to set the pace."[44]

The chief advantage of the task system was the ease with which it permitted a planter or overseer to delegate many of his routine duties to a Negro driver. It also gave some stimulus to rapidity of work by its promise of leisure time to those who finished their tasks early. However, for this incentive to be effective the tasks had to be so limited that the slowest field hand could finish in time to enjoy a few hours of free time. The performance of every hand therefore tended to be standardized at the usual accomplishment of the slowest and weakest members of the group.[45]

Olmsted had praise for the task system as he found it employed on the South Carolina rice coast. He noted that the tasks assigned would not have been considered excessively difficult by a northern laborer and mentioned several instances in which energetic and industrious slaves had finished their tasks by two o'clock. Commenting upon the advantages of the system, Olmsted declared: "The slave works more rapidly,

[42] Bayside Plantation Records (Southern Historical Collection), II, April 3, 1862.
[43] William Butler's Observations on Rice Culture (Microfilm copy in Southern Historical Collection, University of North Carolina, Chapel Hill), 1786.
[44] Phillips, *American Negro Slavery*, 259.
[45] *Ibid.*, 247.

energetically, and, within narrow limits, with much greater use of discretion, or skill, than he is often found to do elsewhere." [46]

The calculation of proper tasks for his Negroes called for a considerable amount of judgment on the part of the master or overseer. It was not desirable for any hand to be put in a task which he could not reasonably be expected to finish, for it was manifestly subversive of discipline to leave tasks unfinished and grossly unfair to punish for what could not be done. In general, the ordinary winter task in the rice belt was eight to nine hours, and the usual summer task required about ten hours to complete.[47] One proprietor, in an instruction to his overseer, defined a task as "as much work as the meanest full hand can do in nine hours, working industriously." [48] Alexander Telfair was more general in his definition, requiring simply "a reasonable days work, well done—the task to be regulated by the state of the ground and the strength of the negro." [49] It was not uncommon for the more active and industrious Negroes to assist the slower ones in the completion of their daily tasks.[50]

The determination of a proper work load for each slave was a vitally important function of the overseer on all plantations, regardless of whether the task or gang system was utilized. Although the proprietor might issue general instructions, a final judgment concerning what could reasonably be required of individual slaves could be made only by their immediate supervisor—the overseer. John H. Cocke issued the following directive to his overseers: "You are expected to have learned by your own experience what is a days work for a hand in every variety of Plantation Business, & daily compair [sic] what your people do with what they ought to do & thus perfect your judgment in such matters, enabling you to calculate beforehand what can be performed." [51]

Negro drivers were utilized on most southern plantations to assist the overseer in the execution of routine duties. Where drivers were not appointed, as on Telfair's "Thorn Island" plantation, the problems of Negro management were increased immeasurably. Telfair's policy was enunciated in the following instruction to his overseers: "I have no Driver. You are to task the negroes yourself, and each negro is responsible to you for his own work, and nobodys else." [52]

The maintenance of good relations between driver and overseer was essential to the proper functioning of plantation management. If proper slave discipline were to be maintained, it was imperative that the overseer support the authority of his driver. A Santee River, South Carolina, manager always required his Negro driver to dress better than the other

[46] Olmsted, Seaboard Slave States, II, 64, 112.
[47] Easterby (ed.), The South Carolina Rice Plantation, 346.
[48] Phillips (ed.), Plantation and Frontier, I, 117.
[49] Ibid., I, 126.
[50] Easterby (ed.), The South Carolina Rice Plantation, 346.
[51] John Hartwell Cocke, "Standing Rules for the Government of Slaves on a Virginia Plantation," in Cocke Papers (Southern Historical Collection).
[52] Phillips (ed.), Plantation and Frontier, I, 129.

slaves. The sagacious superintendent explained: "This caused him to maintain a pride of character before them, which was highly beneficial. Indeed, I constantly endeavored to do nothing which would cause them to lose their respect for him." [53] The driver was always reprimanded privately. He was required to report to his overseer every night in order to report the work of the day just ended and to learn what undertakings were scheduled for the following day. This practice "gave the driver a habit of regularity, and prepared him for a proper discharge of his duties should I be sick," declared the Santee overseer.[54]

The esteem in which an outstanding driver might be held by his overseer is reflected by the following notation of overseer Robert P. Ford in the plantation journal of Louisiana sugar magnate R. R. Barrow:

Andrew The Driver Died

The Residence has met with a great loss in the death of this valuable man, in the loss of Andrew I suppose the Plantation will materially suffer as his servises as a driver cannot be replaced   he was about 60 years old   he was well liked by all who knew him   he was a negro of uncommon good mind and I have regarded him one who possess good Judgement about Plantation work   he was Buried this evening and all the negroes on the Residence & Mertle Grove attended his funeral   he was aware of his approaching death and expressed an entire willingness to die   he conversed freely an hour before his death with many of his fellow servants and expressed a hope that he would meet them all in heaven—he was certain that he would go to heaven—before his death he bid all an affectionate farewell and died about 7 oclock in the morning triumphantly and thanked his god that he should soon be in heaven   his loss was generally and universally regretted and deep sorrow was depicted on the countenance of evry one who knew him   both white & Black   he was buried tonight [55]

The punishment of a driver by his overseer was obviously a matter which called for the exercise of considerable judgment and discretion. One planter issued the following directive to his managers: "The overseer must not punish the driver except on some extraordinary emergency that will not allow of delay, until the employer is consulted. Of this rule, the driver is, however, to be kept in entire ignorance." [56] If a driver's offense was sufficiently serious to warrant punishment, he was usually demoted and a more trustworthy slave elevated to take his place.

The hazards of arousing the hostility of Negro drivers are seen in the outstanding example of general demoralization which resulted from conflict between an overseer and his drivers on Ebenezer Pettigrew's North Carolina plantation. In the absence of his employer, then in Wash-

[53] *Farmers' Register*, IV (June, 1836), 115.
[54] *Ibid.*
[55] R. R. Barrow Residence Journal (Southern Historical Collection), April 21, 1858.
[56] *Farmers' Register*, VIII (April, 1840), 231.

ington serving a term in Congress, Pettigrew's aggressive overseer Doctrine W. Davenport attempted to strip certain faithful and trusted slaves of special privileges previously accorded them by their master. The result was a swelling tide of discontent among the Negroes, beginning shortly after Christmas, 1835. While Davenport was absent on business, two old and trusted drivers led the Negroes in a great frolic. The Pettigrew Negroes gave a splendid feast for slaves from neighboring plantations, rode their master's horse about the countryside, and generally misbehaved. Upon his return, Davenport administered one hundred lashes to one slave for his part in the affair and placed three others in irons. The weary overseer continued to experience difficulty with the rebellious slaves throughout 1836, and his troubles did not finally subside until Pettigrew's return to North Carolina in February of the following year.[57]

As has previously been noted, slave medical care was a primary responsibility of the plantation overseer. Despite the fact that the best available medical care was provided for ailing Negroes on most plantations, the health problem was a serious one throughout the South. Many proprietors had their slave forces decimated by epidemics of cholera, yellow fever, malaria, measles, and other diseases which swept relentlessly from one plantation to another.

The problem of slave health was particularly acute on the rice coast. One visitor to that area noted that "the negroes do not enjoy as good health on rice plantations as elsewhere; and the greater difficulty with which their lives are preserved, through infancy especially, shows that the subtle poison of the miasma is not innocuous to them." [58] Nevertheless, one rice planter visited by this observer boasted a steady annual increase in his Negro force of 5 percent—better than was averaged on many interior plantations.[59]

On many plantations in the rice belt the death rate exceeded the birth rate, and it was necessary to purchase additional slaves periodically in order to maintain a full complement of Negroes. The mortality rate of infants under two years of age on the "Comingtee" and "Stoke" plantations of John Ball, Jr., during the period 1803–34, was an alarming 33 percent for the former and 36.5 percent for the latter.[60] Slave lists for James B. Heyward's "Rotterdam," "Copenhagen," and "Hamburg" plantations during the period 1805–61 reveal a steady decrease in the total number of slaves on the three units from 394 to 332.[61] An identical trend was noted in the slave lists for Charles Manigault's "Gowrie" plantation during the years 1833–61. Particularly devastating were cholera epidemics in 1834 and 1854, which together wiped out thirty Negroes

57 Wall, "Ebenezer Pettigrew," 116–18, 208–09.
58 Olmsted, Seaboard Slave States, II, 45–46.
59 Ibid.
60 John and Keating S. Ball Books (MSS in Southern Historical Collection, University of North Carolina, Chapel Hill), II.
61 Slave Lists for Rotterdam, Copenhagen, and Hamburg Plantations, in Heyward-Ferguson Papers and Books (Microfilm copy in Southern Historical Collection, University of North Carolina, Chapel Hill), 1850–61.

owned by Manigault. The latter was obliged to purchase additional slaves frequently in order to keep pace with the death rate on his plantations.[62]

The slave mortality rate in Louisiana was so striking that antislavery zealots accused sugar planters of deliberately working their Negroes to death. On the plantations of R. R. Barrow the natural increase of slave population lagged far behind the death rate, obliging Barrow to procure new slaves frequently. During the period from July, 1857, to March, 1858, he purchased no fewer than sixty-eight Negroes in three separate lots.[63] Louisiana planters lived in constant fear of cholera epidemics. That dreaded disease took the lives of twenty-eight slaves and the overseer on Lavinia Erwin's Iberville Parish plantation in the summer of 1835.[64] In May, 1854, twenty-six fatal cases were recorded on the Lapice plantation in St. James Parish.[65] Although he had no scarcity of cases, Effingham Lawrence was more fortunate than the proprietors cited above. After weathering successive epidemics of measles, whooping cough, and diphtheria with little loss of life on his "Magnolia" plantation, Lawrence entered the following comment in his journal: "We have had during the Past 18 months over 150 cases of measles and numerous cases of Whooping Cough and then the Diptheria all of which we have gone through with So far with But little Loss Save in the Whooping Cough when we lost Some 12 Children   We have otherwise enjoyed most excellent Health." [66]

To combat such outbreaks and to prescribe for minor ailments were important duties of the overseer. George Washington averred that "it should be made one of the *primary* duties of every Overseer to attend closely, and particularly to those under his care who really are, or pretend to be, sick." [67] Similarly, James R. Sparkman, a South Carolina physician and planter, declared that "on every well regulated rice plantation, the *sick* receive the *first* and if necessary the undivided attention of the overseer." [68] To enable the overseer to meet his medical responsibilities, the editor of a plantation and account book in the Upper South advised proprietors to supply their overseers with several medical books and the following medicines: "Calomel, Castor Oil, Epsom Salts, Spirits Camphor, Spirits Nitre, Spirits Hartshorn, Rhubarb, Ipecac, Jalap, Hive

[62] Slave Lists for Gowrie Plantation, in Manigault Plantation Records (Southern Historical Collection), 1833–61.
[63] R. R. Barrow Residence Journal (Southern Historical Collection), July 10, 1857; February 28, 1858; March 12, 1858.
[64] Alice Pemble White, "The Plantation Experience of Joseph and Lavinia Erwin, 1807–1836," *Louisiana Historical Quarterly*, XXVII (April, 1944), 393.
[65] Valcour Aime, *Plantation Diary* (New Orleans: Clark and Hofeline, 1878), 170.
[66] Magnolia Plantation Journals (Henry Clay Warmoth Papers and Books), October 4, 1860.
[67] Washington to Pearce, March 22, 1795, in Conway (ed.), *George Washington and Mount Vernon*, 175–76.
[68] James R. Sparkman, "Description of Life Among the Slaves, 1858," in Easterby (ed.), *The South Carolina Rice Plantation*, 349.

Syrup, Dover's Powder, Magnesia, Paregoric, Laudanum, Opium, Blister Plaster, Scales and Weights, Spatula and Mortar, 1 Thumb Lancet, 1 Gum Lancet, 1 pint Injection Syringe." [69] With such an assortment of supplies, it is a wonder that the overseer did not set up his own practice.

Moore Rawls, the outstanding overseer of Lewis Thompson's absentee sugar plantation, took his medical obligations seriously. In the following letter to his employer, Rawls outlines the precautions he has taken to prevent his Negroes from contracting the fever: "I have done every thing I possible could to prevent fever. The negros had around everry house, old troughs & Bbls to catch & keep water in.   I at last Dug a weel in the quater and even then they did not want to clean up around their houses. I think there must have been 200 vessels of one kind or other with water in them." [70] On another occasion Rawls gave Thompson the following account of an unorthodox, but apparently effective, treatment he had administered to an injured slave: "I have got Phill out wagoning   I commence on his foot in July. never let it be wet at all, applyed nothing but an ointment made of bacon rine & fat   light wood burnt together, mixt with burnt Leather. hope it may remain well." [71] Another Louisiana manager, plagued by numerous cases of the "Bowel complaint," reported to his employer: "I have given camphor and Laudnum and followed with calomel and rhuburb   I find it the best medcine I can give for that complaint." [72]

Such quaint remedies did not always benefit those to whom they were administered. Summoned to combat a cholera epidemic on a Concordia Parish plantation, a Louisiana physician discovered that two Negroes treated by the overseer had already succumbed. [73] Some professional practitioners sharply criticized what a New Orleans physician, Dr. D. Warren Brickell, termed "the almost universal practice on the part of owners and overseers, of tampering with their sick negroes for one, two or more days before applying for medical aid. This practice may be in some measure excusable in the more common acute diseases of negroes, but during the existence of a malignant epidemic it is wholly unpardonable. . . ." [74] Although not entirely without merit, such a protest ignores the paucity of trained physicians—especially in the rural South—and the primitive nature of medicine in the early nineteenth century. Notwithstanding the infelicitous treatments prescribed by overseers and masters, the available evidence indicates that the health status of plantation

[69] *Plantation and Farm Instruction, Regulation, Record, Inventory and Account Book,* 11.
[70] Rawls to Lewis Thompson, October 10, 1857, Lewis Thompson Papers.
[71] Rawls to Lewis Thompson, October 28, 1860, Lewis Thompson Papers.
[72] Jesse L. Ward to Jacob Bieller, August 23, 1835, Alonzo Snyder Papers.
[73] William Dosite Postell, *The Health of Slaves on Southern Plantations* (Baton Rouge: Louisiana State University Press, 1951), 105.
[74] *Ibid.,* quoting D. Warren Brickell, "Epidemic Typhoid Pneumonia Amongst Negroes," *New Orleans Medical News and Hospital Gazette,* II (1856), 546.

slaves in the Old South was comparable to that enjoyed by the populace as a whole during that period.[75]

It was clearly in the interest of the overseer to keep his hands in the best possible physical condition. A general outbreak of sickness could have a profound effect upon the crop results if it occurred at a critical time. The harried overseer of Colonel J. B. Lamar's Georgia plantation penned the following account of his vicissitudes during a siege of illness, which reached its peak just as the cotton attained full maturity:

> I hav bin Sick Since you left hear myself twice about too weeks but was only confined on the bed for 4 days   I am up at presant but not much acount   The Negrowes on this place Is verry Sickly & hav bin all the while since you Left us & the d[is]eases Is growin wors all the while as well as the attacks more numorous   18 on the Sick list today   16 of that nombr Field hands   too out of the croud Billous fever & very Bad caises   the Ballance chils & Fevers. Those that are out some of them unwell & unable to doo much   all of them has Bin Sick & some of them has Bin sick twice & Several of them down the third time   I hav so much Rain that It Is a hard mater to get one of them well   As Soon as one Gets out It Rains on him or he Is In a large due or in a mud hole & Back he comes again   this Is the way I'm getting on & I call this Rather Bad luck   At least Getting on Slowley   I hav used 2½ Gallons caster oile & ½ Gallon Sprts turpentine & 4 ounces quinine up to the presant   I am doin the best I can with them   Barron [a doctor?] has Bin hear 15 times . . . yours Truly,   Jonas Smith
>
> P.S.   Since I commenced Riting 4 hands hav come to the house with fever   makes 20 field hands down. I nearly hav a chill my Self.[76]

The experience apparently proved too much for the overseer, Jonas Smith, for, in October of the same year, he requested his employer to inform him of any proprietor in the vicinity of Macon "that wold hire to Go on ther plantation & Gave a Good price & a heathy place." [77]

Overseers often experienced great difficulty in determining whether a slave was really sick, or whether he was merely feigning illness in an effort to avoid work. The practice of "laying up" in order to enjoy the benefits of a unscheduled vacation was apparently common among southern Negroes. George Washington, who kept a close watch on affairs at his Mount Vernon estate even during his presidential terms, frequently questioned whether Negroes reported out for extended periods of time were actually sick. His thoughts on the subject are summarized

---

[75] William D. Postell, *Health of Slaves*, 164.
[76] Jonas Smith to John B. Lamar, August 25, 1852, in Phillips (ed.), *Plantation and Frontier*, I, 310.
[77] Smith to Lamar, October 5, 1852, in Phillips (ed.), *Plantation and Frontier*, I, 311.

in the following letter of March, 1795, addressed to Mount Vernon steward William Pearce:

> I observe what you say of Betty Davis & c^t—but I never found so much difficulty as you seem to apprehend, in distinguishing between *real* and *feigned* sickness;—or when a person is *much* afflicted with pain.—Nobody can be very sick without having a fever, nor will a fever or any other disorder continue long upon any one without reducing them:—Pain, also, if it be such as to yield entirely to its force, week after week, will appear by its effects; but my people (many of them) will lay up a month, at the end of which no visible change in their countenance, nor the loss of an oz of flesh, is discoverable; and their allowance of provision is going on as if nothing ailed them.—There cannot, surely, be any *real* sickness under such circumstances as I have described; nor ought such people to be improperly endulged.[78]

Those suspected of "laying up" without cause were usually "cured" by a few judicious applications of the lash. The steward of a Mississippi estate, explaining why he had ordered to the field a Negro girl believed to be feigning illness, told Olmsted: *"We have to be sharp with them; if we were not, every negro on the estate would be abed."* [79] Moore Rawls gave one Negro, who had "been pretending to be Sick several weeks," what Rawls described as "a genteel whiping." The overseer expressed the view to his employer, Lewis Thompson, that the punishment had "done him more good than all medicne could have been given to him." [80] In like manner, Doctrine W. Davenport reported to Ebenezer Pettigrew that four of the latter's Negroes had attempted to feign illness. "I courd the hole four in fiftene minits," asserted Davenport, "and they have not been sicke since." [81] On Maunsel White's "Deer Range" plantation, a Negro was placed "in the stocks for feigning illness when not so." [82] Such punishments undoubtedly discouraged many slaves from taking advantage of their owners and overseers by pretending to be sick.

Running away was the most serious common offense charged to slaves on southern plantations. Although runaways occurred with monotonous regularity, they never ceased to evoke expressions of amazement from planters and overseers, to whom the reason for running away was usually a complete mystery. For example, a puzzled Mississippi overseer complained: "Lundy left no knowing Where nor what for." [83]

[78] Washington to Pearce, March 22, 1795, in Conway (ed.), *George Washington and Mount Vernon*, 175. See also Phillips, *American Negro Slavery*, 285.
[79] Olmsted, *Back Country*, 79.
[80] Rawls to Lewis Thompson, July 27, 1857, Lewis Thompson Papers.
[81] Wall, "Ebenezer Pettigrew," 116, quoting Doctrine W. Davenport to Ebenezer Pettigrew, June 12, 1836.
[82] Deer Range Plantation Journal (Maunsel White Papers and Books), August 16, 1860.
[83] Doro Plantation Account Book (Charles Clark and Family Papers), VIII, September 30, 1853.

Typical also was this terse entry in the diary of a Louisiana manager: "Calvin Ran off this morning for nothing." [84] In point of fact, however, the flight of plantation slaves was attributable to a variety of reasons— dislike of the overseer, fear of punishment, the desire to escape difficult or unpleasant work, reunion with another member of one's family.

Perhaps the most common cause was that revealed in a letter from Stephen Brown, overseer of George Austin's Peedee, South Carolina, estate, to Josiah Smith, Jr., Austin's Charleston agent. Brown reported that three Negroes had absconded early in December, 1773, "for being a little chastis'd on Account of not finishing their Task of Thrashing in due time." [85] Brown did not disclose the nature of the chastisement. Two Louisiana Negroes, Edmund and Peter, were apparently motivated by their desire to escape a similar correction when they decamped "without a word or a blow" in the summer of 1845. The only cause which the proprietor's son could "assign for their going off" was that "Peter was two days chopping behind: and Edm. 1½ days behind." He concluded, however, that both were "natural runaways and are just playing one of their favorite games." [86]

Occasionally, a particularly incompetent or severe overseer provoked the Negroes under his charge to depart *en masse*. Such a situation developed in the summer of 1844 on Levin Covington's Mississippi plantation, where the harassed overseer reported the departure of no fewer than eleven slaves within a period of less than two months.[87] The mass exodus of slaves from a small Jefferson County, Georgia, plantation is recounted in the following letter from overseer I. E. H. Harvey to his employer, H. C. Flournoy of Athens, Georgia:

> Sir: I write you a few lines in order to let you know that six of your hands has left the plantation—every man but Jack. They displeased me with their worke and I give some of them a few lashes, Tom with the rest. On Wednesday morning they were missing. I think they are lying out until they can see you or your uncle Jack, as he is expected daily. They may be gone off, or they may be lying round in this neighbourhood, but I don't know. I blame Tom for the whole. I don't think the rest would of left the plantation if Tom had not of persuaded them of for some design. I give Tom but a few licks, but if I ever get him in my power I will have satisfaction. There was a part of them had no cause for leaving, only they thought if they would all go it would injure me moore. They are as independent a set for running of as I have ever seen, and I think the cause is they have been treated too well. They want more whipping and no protecter; but if our country is so that negroes can quit

[84] Seale Diary (Louisiana State University Department of Archives), May 30, 1853.
[85] Josiah Smith, Jr., to George Austin, January 31, 1774, in Josiah Smith, Jr., Letter-copy Book, Southern Historical Collection, University of North Carolina, Chapel Hill.
[86] George Marsh to John Craig Marsh, August 25, 1845, Avery Family Papers.
[87] Phillips, *Life and Labor in the Old South*, 208.

their homes and run of when they please without being taken they will have the advantage of us. If they should come in I will write to you immediately and let you know.[88]

.   .   .

[88] Phillips, *American Negro Slavery*, 303, quoting I. E. H. Harvey to H. C. Flournoy, April 16, 1837.

Section 2 ∽ Business in the Agrarian and Commercial Economy

Four ∽ The Merchant in Foreign Trade

SUCCESS AND FAILURE FACTORS: AMERICAN MERCHANTS IN FOREIGN TRADE IN THE EIGHTEENTH AND EARLY NINETEENTH CENTURIES *Stuart Bruchey*

Why one man succeeds in business and another man fails is a difficult problem at any time. The difficulty lies not so much in our ignorance of the general factors involved as in tracing their complex interaction. Intelligence and good luck, for example, are certainly fundamental: but can we say with confidence where the one ends and the other begins? What of other elements of success, such as prudence, persistency in will, good housekeeping habits, and the aids of the business community? Can we be sure of the part played by each of these factors in particular business decisions? If so, are sufficient case histories of businessmen available to warrant general conclusions?

I believe the answers to these questions are very largely negative. For one thing, far more records of success than of failure have survived

REPRINTED with permission from Stuart Bruchey, "Success and Failure Factors: American Merchants in Foreign Trade in the Eighteenth and Early Nineteenth Centuries," *Business History Review*, Vol. XXXII (Autumn 1958), pp. 272–92. Copyright 1958 by The President and Fellows of Harvard College.

the attrition of history. Even the success stories have their limitations. The bookkeeping records of foreign traders, for example, do not as a rule permit correlation between a specific investment decision and a specific gain or loss, for merchants did not usually compute the results of particular shipments.[1] We know well, however, that some men made only a living, while others made fortunes. Still others, such as the New York merchant Victor duPont, went bankrupt.[2] Most of the Jacksons and Lees of Massachusetts "at some time or other [in the eighteenth century] either failed in business or came to the very brink of such a disaster."[3] In March, 1803, Robert Oliver, merchant of Baltimore, noted that "upwards of 100 failures have . . . taken place in this City in the last three years. . . ."[4] An increasing number of studies of American merchants illuminate some of the areas of difference between them which have led to these varying results. Many of the studies also show that the merchants themselves had definite ideas concerning the qualities making for success.

Let us first consider the factor of prudence. It is undeniable that the same man sometimes plunges and sometimes reins in. On the other hand, some men appear temperamentally disposed to caution, others to an easier trust that things will come right. James B. Hedges clearly sets forth the difference between the merchant John Brown of Providence and his brothers, Moses and Nicholas. John was eager to reinvest each year's profits in an expanding business. But Nicholas, "cautious, [and] conservative by nature," probably approved the terms in which Moses rejected the plan: " 'who Ever plays any Game the Rubbers, or plays the last for the Value of the whole gain of the Preceding many, will Sooner or Later Loose the Whole at one Throw.' "[5] Miss Virginia D. Harrington has written that the proportion between speculative and revenue-producing holdings of real estate in the hands of the colonial merchants of New York depended partly "on the temper of the individual."[6] Miss Elva Tooker concludes of the Philadelphia merchant Nathan Trotter: "Nothing is clearer throughout Trotter's business career than his prudence, caution, and moderation."[7] Prudence lay near the center of the

[1] Richard Pares, *Yankees and Creoles* (Cambridge, 1956), p. 139. Pares finds this "strange." But except for the necessity of dividing profits with joint investors no such calculations were required: merchants based their investment decisions not upon records of past gain or loss but upon fresh market information; S. Bruchey, *Robert Oliver, Merchant of Baltimore, 1783–1819* (Baltimore, 1956), pp. 135–41.
[2] In 1805. For this and other information about the duPonts, I wish to express my gratitude to Dr. Norman B. Wilkinson, Research Associate of the Eleutherian Mills-Hagley Foundation in Wilmington, Delaware.
[3] Kenneth W. Porter, *The Jacksons and the Lees* (Cambridge, 1937), Vol. 1, p. 4.
[4] Oliver Record Book (hereafter ORB) 5, pp. 42–44, to P. Godeffroy Sons & Co., et al., March 22, 1803 (Maryland Historical Society—hereafter Md. Hist. Soc.).
[5] James B. Hedges, *The Browns of Providence Plantations* (Cambridge, 1952), p. 16.
[6] Virginia D. Harrington, *The New York Merchant on the Eve of the Revolution* (New York, 1935), p. 133.
[7] Elva Tooker, *Nathan Trotter, Philadelphia Merchant, 1787–1853* (Cambridge, 1955), p. 57.

business values of Robert Oliver & Brothers. They "desired to have an accurate knowledge of the length and breadth of their obligations," a contemporary merchant later wrote about the most extensive operation in which the Olivers ever participated, "before the scheme could be set in motion." [8] Oliver repeatedly showed his concern for security as well as profit-potentiality. By curtailing his investments in trade and by choosing not to send "a large amount in any one Vessel" he twice enabled his house to survive deflationary shock waves that toppled many of his Baltimore confrères.

To Oliver, the opposite of prudence was a "sanguine speculative disposition." ". . . before you can expect much business in the Commission line," he once advised an apparent beginner in trade, "you must establish a reputation for real industry & prudence & quit visionary Schemes." He thought Richard Caton of Baltimore "too sanguine," "too speculative." [9] Caton surely resembled John Brown of Providence, who had an "inclination toward undue risk-taking." [10] According to Oliver, Aquila Brown, Jr., of Baltimore, lost "upwards of 140,000 Dollars in two years by bad debts on the Sale of Linens." [11] But no doubt an ability to draw learning from loss has proved an important factor in the final success of some men. John Jacob Astor, according to his biographer, partly owed his fortune to that ability.[12]

Probably most men who have entered business have desired to succeed. But some men have hitched their wills to the traces of a single-minded drive. The records of Robert Oliver supply evidence of an extraordinary attentiveness to the life of trade. "You can hardly fail to succeed," he once advised a younger man, "if you will abandon Politicks, *think only of your business,* follow it with unremitting industry and depend on yourself instead of others." He found John F. Kennedy "very irregular in his business," told a Secretary of War (James McHenry) that he paid "little attention" to his "private concerns," and wrote that a Mr. Holmes was "the most inattentive Man to his business we ever met with and he has suffered much by negligence." Oliver once used the occasion of a visit to Philadelphia, presumably made for the purpose of attending the funeral of the man to whom he owed most, to purchase ninety boxes of Havana sugars. On a later trip to New York, again for unstated purposes, he bought over $160,000 worth of nankeens.[13] The man from whom he bought them, John Jacob Astor, undoubtedly exemplifies even more clearly than Oliver a single-minded devotion to the goal of success.

[8] Vincent Nolte, *Fifty Years in Both Hemispheres or, Reminiscences of the Life of a Former Merchant* (New York, 1854), p. 97.
[9] Bruchey, *op. cit.,* pp. 364–65.
[10] Hedges, *op. cit.,* p. 11.
[11] ORB 5, pp. 42–44, to P. Godeffroy Sons & Co., et al., March 22, 1803 (Md. Hist. Soc.).
[12] Kenneth W. Porter, *John Jacob Astor, Business Man* (Cambridge, 1931), Vol. II, p. 621.
[13] Bruchey, *op. cit.,* pp. 363–64.

"Astor's life," to use the words of Miss Henrietta Larson, "was business, and he had a passion for profits and an abhorrence of waste or loss."[14] A contemporary merchant, Vincent Nolte, once remarked of Astor: "His mind was incessantly busied with the increase of his resources, and had no other direction."[15]

We know from Kenneth W. Porter's careful study that Nolte's characterization exaggerates, and that Astor found time for family, friends, and a variety of cultural interests.[16] Yet it is clear that Astor's business schemes sometimes incubated during nonbusiness hours, while riding around Manhattan on his horse, for example. Perhaps this explains why he reputedly " 'did not bestow at his countinghouse more than half the time most merchants feel compelled to give their concerns.' " But no doubt for the majority the countinghouse represented "a chance to think, to plan, to work out policies, to arrange for others to do the detailed work."[17]

Yet it must be admitted that we have little satisfactory evidence of the length of time spent by merchants in their countinghouses. The natural assumption, that it depended upon the volume of trade, would appear from Astor's instance not always to hold. Samuel Eliot Morison has supplied additional reason for questioning the dependence: despite a considerably increased volume of trade the merchant patriciate of Federalist Boston can hardly have spent more than three hours a day in their places of business.[18] We know that the "busiest years" of Colonel William Pepperrell of Piscataqua and of his son lay in the decade following the Peace of Utrecht, which was "one of expanding trade," but the evidence does not permit a situating of the Colonel in his countinghouse any specified number of daily hours.[19] Neither does it in the case of Robert Oliver for such a year as 1807, during which the Baltimore merchant dispatched vessels twenty-six times to Vera Cruz, Lisbon, Barcelona, Amsterdam, Trieste, and New Providence.[20] In other instances, oblique evidence provides support for the possibility of sizable stretches of time in the countinghouse. Business, for Thomas Hancock, was "his one engrossing interest." During 1771–1772, at least, his nephew John was "spending less and less time in the countinghouse, and more and more in bed or the general assembly." The biographer of Gerard G. Beekman, a New York merchant whose trade at least touched "four continents," reports that Beekman "abstained from such pleasures [as hunt-

---

[14] N. S. B. Gras and Henrietta M. Larson, *Casebook in American Business History* (New York, 1939), p. 78.
[15] Nolte, *op. cit.*, p. 143.
[16] Porter, *Astor*, Vol. II, Chap. 23.
[17] Gras and Larson, *op. cit.*, pp. 78, 6.
[18] Samuel Eliot Morison, *The Maritime History of Massachusetts* (Boston, 1921), pp. 130–31.
[19] Byron Fairchild, *Messrs. William Pepperrell: Merchants at Piscataqua* (Ithaca, 1954), pp. 47, 49.
[20] See list of sailings in front of ORB 6 (Md. Hist. Soc.).

ing] in his early years, preferring to devote his energies to trade." [21] Similarly, Elias Hasket Derby of late eighteenth-century Salem is said to have had "his commercial affairs at all times during his early life directly under his eye." [22] By the mid-nineteenth century, at any rate, the merchants of New York, according to Scoville, spent considerable, if leisurely stretches of time in the "throne-room" of their enterprises.[23]

In that throne-room lay the bookkeeping records which made it possible for all the strings of diverse enterprise to be controlled by the hand of the resident merchant. "Considerable judgment was needed," as Miss Harrington has said, "to juggle remittances, returns and investments successfully." [24] Accounts informed that judgment, at least for men with good housekeeping habits. How carefully did eighteenth-century merchants keep their accounts? W. T. Baxter believes that colonial bookkeeping was in general "dilatory" and that a leading reason for this was the "tiny scale of business." [25] The association between care in recordkeeping and scale of business seems to me persuasive. But I believe Baxter's generalization has two weaknesses: (a) it appears to rest largely upon an examination of the records of small-scale firms whose proprietors were primarily storekeepers rather than merchants and (b) does not take into account changes in the scale of business which occurred as the eighteenth century advanced.[26] Of course, even in the late eighteenth (and early nineteenth) centuries many firms were in business in a small way, so that it is not surprising to find, as Margaret E. Martin has found in examining the records of Connecticut River Valley merchants, that

---

[21] W. T. Baxter, *The House of Hancock, Business in Boston, 1724–1775* (Cambridge, 1945), pp. 146, 281–82; Philip L. White, *The Beekmans of New York in Politics and Commerce, 1647–1877* (New York, 1956), p. 218.

[22] James D. Phillips, *Salem and the Indies* (Boston, 1947), p. 78.

[23] Cited by Robert G. Albion, *The Rise of New York Port* (New York, 1939), p. 264. The word "throne-room" is Miss Larson's (*op. cit.*, p. 6).

[24] Harrington, *op. cit.*, p. 116.

[25] W. T. Baxter, "Accounting in Colonial America," in A. C. Littleton and B. S. Yamey, *Studies in the History of Accounting* (Homewood, Ill., 1956), p. 280. Baxter believes that " 'colonial accounting' " lasted well into the 19th century. "By say 1820, the modern look is beginning to creep in: cash appears more often, debtors can sometimes be distinguished from creditors, and the double-entry structure is less incomplete." (Pp. 286–87.)

[26] Baxter cites not only the records of a "general store," but also those of an innkeeper and blacksmith (pp. 275, 278, 280). It is true that a merchant was also a storekeeper, but I disagree with Baxter's conception of the storekeeping function as the focal point of the merchant's business activity, an activity in which ventures in foreign trade are regarded as "sidelines to his principal business" (p. 280). Baxter first elaborated this conception in his interpretation of Thomas Hancock as driven to engage in a variety of trading enterprises by the necessity for obtaining sterling exchange with which to pay for the goods he imported from London for sale in his store. In my opinion, it is infelicitous to envisage Hancock's "little bookshop" as the "nerve-center of a complex and far-flung business," which included shipowning, mining and paper mill projects. (Baxter, *House of Hancock*, pp. 45–48, 62.) I believe Hancock to have been a typical 18th-century merchant in the sense that he sought profits from investments in diverse enterprises.

their daybooks "were usually kept in the most informal manner." [27] In England itself at the end of the eighteenth century "double entry was practised . . . mainly by merchants engaged in wholesale trade, and by no means by all of them." [28] Miss Martin adds, significantly: "No account books of *important* Hartford merchants who might have kept their books in a more careful manner have been discovered." [29]

There is reason to believe that as the volume of trade increased, earlier eighteenth-century laxness in record-keeping often gave way to a careful practice of double entry. In this respect as in others, furthermore, the evidence is clear that one merchant differed from another. The beginnings of change appear to have accompanied an early increase in trade volume between 1720 and 1740, and they have been described as follows by Carl Bridenbaugh: [30]

> In every colonial port this period brought a marked advance in the methods and extent of trade. The increased sums of money and larger number of items handled made it necessary for merchants to maintain staffs of clerks in their counting houses. Bookkeeping by "Double Entry, Dr. and Cr., the best Method," came into wide use everywhere except at Newport by 1733, and schools gave instruction in shorthand and the Italian method of keeping books. Accountants offered their services in all the larger towns. . . .

Obadiah Brown of Providence reflects this new emphasis on careful record-keeping for in the early 1730's, and "probably at the insistence of his older brother," Obadiah "taught himself accounting methods, using for this purpose *A Guide to Book Keepers according to the Italian Manner* [i.e., double-entry] published in London in 1729." [31] Probably the next generation of Browns also kept its accounts with care, for a year's end calculation of gain or loss is implicit in the proposal of John Brown "'of Augmenting our Business Annually as our proffits may be or the Contrary Lessening as we Loose. . . .'" [32]

On the other hand, accounts might inform the judgment of an uncle but not of his nephew: "Thomas [Hancock] knew as much about his own affairs from an accounting standpoint as was possible in mercantile capitalism, while John was generally hopelessly swamped." [33] Or one cousin and not the other: "James [Beekman] was as meticulous in keep-

[27] Margaret E. Martin, *Merchants and Trade of the Connecticut River Valley, 1750–1820* (Smith College Studies in History, Vol. XXIV, No. 1, 1938–1939), p. 144. Daybooks, however, are books of first, rough entry and can be expected to have been kept with less formality than journals.
[28] A. C. Littleton and B. S. Yamey, *Studies in the History of Accounting* (Homewood, Ill., 1956), p. 11 (Introduction by B. S. Yamey).
[29] Martin, *op. cit.*, p. 144. (My italics.)
[30] Carl Bridenbaugh, *Cities in the Wilderness* (New York, 1938), p. 359.
[31] Hedges, *op. cit.*, pp. 5–6.
[32] *Ibid.*, p. 16.
[33] Editor's preface (N. S. B. Gras), in Baxter, *House of Hancock* p. xxii.

ing records as Gerard was careless." [34] "Mr. Freelands' Books," a fellow merchant in Baltimore once complained, "have been so irregularly kept that there is no finding out those that have been indebted to him." An "ignorance of business [and] confused accts" had led another Baltimore merchant astray.[35]

Miss Harrington finds that "most" New York wholesale houses on the eve of the Revolution appear to have used double-entry bookkeeping, and that a "fairly high level of proficiency must have been maintained." The ledger and wastebook of the Livingstons, for example, are "models of the double-entry books": [36]

> The ledger contains impersonal accounts as well as those of individual customers: adventures, bills of exchange, bonds and notes, merchandize general, vendue account, invoice accounts, bills receivable, bills payable, interest account, suspense account, profit and loss, and also accounts for special articles such as pig iron, sugar and the "Ship Commerce."

In Maryland, the Ridgely Account Books, which embrace most of the eighteenth century and continue into the nineteenth, are kept by double entry. The combined Daybook and Journal (1788–1795) of the Baltimore merchant William Wilson shows, like the Ridgely volumes, use of Profit & Loss, adventure, and other impersonal accounts. But no Maryland accounting records, to my knowledge, compare in richness with those of Robert Oliver & Brothers of Baltimore. Some notion of how meticulously the Olivers kept their books is provided by a credit to the Profit & Loss account for 6 cents, which is offset by a charge to the account of ship captain William Robinson "to make his account on the Books agree with the one furnished this day, which arises from charging him a half cent too little on sundry Premiums of insurance—." [37]

Just as merchants differed in respect to prudence, will, and housekeeping habits they differed also in intelligence. It is, of course, impossible to exhibit this difference except in terms of varying reactions to similar situations. And it hardly need be said that variety in reaction itself depends not only on intelligence, but also upon knowledge, and upon such other factors, as capital or credit status, liquidity and knowledge of the extent of it provided by orderly accounts, prudence, force of will, and so forth. Furthermore, the situations themselves are very numerous, far too numerous for consideration here. In changing contexts provided by government action or inaction and by rising and falling markets in peacetime and war, merchants had to decide such questions as what commodities to invest in and where to buy them, where and when to ship them and in what assortments, whether to consign their goods to ship captain, supercargo, or resident merchant, whether to invest in

[34] White, *op. cit.*, p. 656. But James was certainly not a meticulous bookkeeper all his business life (cf. p. 352 with pp. 469, 490, and 492).
[35] Bruchey, *op. cit.*, p. 364.
[36] Harrington, *op. cit.*, p. 96.
[37] In Md. Hist. Soc., Baltimore. The Oliver entry is in ORB 10, p. 225.

vessels or freight space, what goods to have purchased as returns, whether to invest part of the proceeds of the outward cargo in bills of exchange, where to dispose of return cargoes: by reshipment or by sale in the local market, and, if the latter, what credit terms to give and what men to trust; and finally, how to employ the proceeds of business: i.e., how to balance investments between ships or ship-shares, commodities, warehouses, bonds or notes, real estate, and, later, stocks.

Numerous as were the decisions to be made, almost all of them called for the exercise of judgments with respect to foreign markets. Residing in one port as they did, and not accompanying their wares to market, all merchants depended considerably upon other members of a wide mercantile community, upon ship captains and supercargoes (especially in the East Indian trade), and upon other merchants resident in foreign (and often domestic) ports. The interdependence of resident merchants throughout the commercial world rested upon a mutual need for services almost indispensable to the conduct of trade. Resident merchants not only supplied each other with the information upon which investment decisions often rested, but performed other services, such as advancing part of the value of goods prior to their sale and holding them for better times. "Information was exchanged," Miss Martin makes clear, "regarding prices and the probable course of trade . . . and . . . advice [was] given to agents or friends. . . ." That information was as important in coastal as in foreign trade is suggested by the admonition sent in 1784 by Johnson, Johonnot & Company of Baltimore to its resident agent in Boston: "I can only say this that if we do not pay strict attention in writing & answering our Letters p every post. we had better leave writing. at all. [sic] and trust all to Chance—"

Hedges found in the Brown Papers "many illustrations of the care with which [the Browns] gathered all possible information before embarking upon a new venture." [38] As the case of Gerard G. Beekman illustrates, a merchant might seek information from another American city: "In the season of 1753–54 Gerard began to exchange information with a resident correspondent of Philadelphia, Townsend White." [39] Or he might seek it abroad. Robert Oliver in 1807 went so far as to propose (successfully) to an English house giving him keen competition in trade to Vera Cruz that the two firms exchange information in regard to the nature and value of their shipments, the number of vessels and voyages made, the nature of exports from the United States, and the condition of the Vera Cruz market! [40] Far more typical was the routine exchange of price and market information between two merchants residing in different ports. Acting on the basis of such information every merchant was at one moment principal, at another commission agent.

Agency relationships typified eighteenth-century commerce between

[38] Martin, op. cit., p. 124; Hedges, op. cit., p. 330; to Francis Johonnot, Feb. 15, 1784 (Letter Book, Johnson, Johonnot & Co., 1783–1785, Md. Hist. Soc.).
[39] White, op. cit., p. 243.
[40] Bruchey, op. cit., p. 317.

Europe and America, as well as between many of the ports of Europe itself. Accoring to Sombart and Max Weber the growth of consignment trading "was the outstanding feature of eighteenth century trading." The commission agent, says Charles Wilson, was the "real representative" of the trade between Amsterdam and the ports of England, Spain, and other countries. W. T. Baxter finds the agent to have been "the keystone of New England's foreign trade." "The London commission merchants with whom the Trotters [of Philadelphia] did business," Miss Tooker observes, "were in effect their representatives abroad." [41]

The ship captain-agent, however, dominated colonial trade with the West Indies. According to Kenneth W. Porter, "Participation by local merchants in the sale and purchase of cargoes in the West India trade is not conspicuous." Hedges reaches a similar conclusion, for "only occasionally were factors employed to assume part of the burden of buying and selling." In the West Indies, Miss Harrington has noted, "the market, though steady, varied from island to island." John Hancock's "instructions to captains show that it was often undesirable to draw up rigid plans regarding the route to be followed. . . ." Instead, as Christopher C. Crittenden has observed, the master might be instructed to proceed to a particular island, such as Martinique, and upon arrival "to inquire concerning the condition of the markets both there and in other islands to the leeward, and . . . to sell where, everything considered, the greatest profit could be reaped." Or he might, Hedge's emphasizes, enjoy even greater leeway by embarking on "a huckstering voyage with cargo to be sold wherever he could find a market." Richard Pares believes that the majority of colonial West Indian shipments were consigned to captains.[42] Such consignments, by no means came to an end with the colonial period. In July, 1794, for example, the Baltimore merchant Samuel Smith ordered a ship captain to Fort Dauphin "where you will enquire the state of the market, and either sell there or proceed elsewhere, as you shall find most to our Interest." [43]

This widespread reliance upon ship captains in the West Indian trade is attributable to a variety of circumstances. Miss Martin has pointed out that many merchants "had received their early mercantile training as captains of vessels engaged in that trade and were well-acquainted with market conditions both in the West Indies and in adjacent Central and South American ports." Only a limited number of commodities were imported—principally sugar, rum, molasses, and coffee—and these were "much simpler to select and appraise" than European manufactured goods would have been. Furthermore, goods were often

[41] For Sombart and Weber, see Harrington, op. cit., p. 68; Charles Wilson, Anglo-Dutch Commerce & Finance in the Eighteenth Century (Cambridge, 1941), p. 11; Baxter, House of Hancock, p. 197ff., 300ff.; Tooker, op. cit., p. 75.
[42] Porter, Jacksons and Lees, Vol. I, p. 48; Hedges, op. cit., p. 27; Harrington, op. cit., p. 91; Baxter, House of Hancock, p. 56; Christopher C. Crittenden, The Commerce of North Carolina, 1763–1789 (New Haven, 1936), p. 109; Hedges, op. cit., p. 9; Pares, op. cit., p. 77.
[43] Ltr. to Capt. Thomas O'Bryan, July 30, 1794. Smith Letter Book, III (1794–1818), Md. Hist. Soc.

bartered against goods, "which eliminated the necessity of a commission merchant to provide short-term credit." In addition, as Pares reminds us, except for lumber nearly every article of North American produce was perishable in the tropics, and hence could not be stored for long to await an upturn in the market. Advances by agents, although sometimes made pending the sale of an outward cargo, were therefore not as important as they would otherwise have been. An even more basic reason for consignments to captains was the necessity for giving them leave to take their cargoes in search of markets that were not glutted. "Only three ports— Bridgetown in Barbados, Kingston in Jamaica, and above all the Dutch island of St. Eustatius, were markets of conspicuous size or wide commercial connections. The capitals of the lesser islands were glutted by a very few cargoes—still more so the smaller towns like Spikestown, Barbados." Certainly in the earlier colonial years probably few merchants did sufficient business with any one port to permit active relations with an agent there. Much less did volume justify relations with agents at several markets. This I think is the reason why, to use the language of Pares once again, "hardly any North American merchant had such wide connections as to possess a settled correspondent in every likely West Indian port." [44]

To be sure, not all North American merchants consigned their West Indian cargoes to ship captains. "Most" of the Pepperrells' shipments to the islands during the middle colonial years, and to Spain and Portugal as well, "were consigned to their correspondents." Pares finds that some Philadelphians, at least, "seem to have done half their business, or more, through resident factors [i.e., agents]." Philip L. White's study of the Beekmans of New York reveals that while Gerard (1717–1797), in his "scattered, sporadic, speculative" Caribbean ventures, "quite often" entrusted his cargoes to ship captains, James (1732–1807) participated in an agency relationship with a merchant of Barbados which conformed to the "general pattern of much colonial trade." [45] Trade statistics for the period are notoriously meager and unreliable but it is highly probable that the volume of West Indian trade increased in the advancing eighteenth century,[46] bringing with it an increase in consignments to resident

---

[44] Martin, *op. cit.*, p. 133; Pares, *op. cit.*, pp. 84, 78. It is my conclusion, rather than Pares', that advances were therefore not as important as they would otherwise have been.

[45] Fairchild (Pepperrells), *op. cit.*, p. 156; Pares, *op. cit.*, p. 77; White, *op. cit.*, pp. 307, 339.

[46] For West Indian trade expansion in the case of *New York,* see Harrington, *op. cit.*, App. D and G; for *Philadelphia,* see Robert G. Albion, "Colonial Commerce and Commercial Regulation," in Harold F. Williamson, ed., *The Growth of the American Economy* (New York, 1951), p. 53; for *Baltimore,* see Clarence P. Gould, "The Economic Causes of the Rise of Baltimore," in *Essays in Colonial History Presented to Charles McLean Andrews by his Students* (New Haven, 1931); for *the Connecticut Valley region* (general trade expansion), see Martin, *op. cit.*, pp. 19–20, 52–53; for *Newport,* see Bridenbaugh, *op. cit.*, pp. 331, 362; for *Charles Town,* see Bridenbaugh, *op. cit.*, p. 332; for *the British West Indies,* see F. W. Pitman, *The Development of the British West Indies, 1700–1763* (New Haven, 1917), pp. 190, 202–03.

agents. Miss Harrington finds that New York merchants on the eve of the Revolution "commonly had agents resident in the West Indies." The Baltimore firm of Oliver & Thompson, established soon after the end of the Revolution, nearly always made its consignments to agents during the years 1785–1790.[47]

In the 1790's an increase in variety was added to the increased volume of goods exported to the West Indies. During most of the colonial period articles of domestic produce or manufacture had made up the list of exports, e.g., the timber and fish of Piscataqua, the bread and flour of New York, the candles turned out by the " 'Spermacetic Works' " of Obadiah Brown of Providence, or various goods picked up in coasting voyages by Rhode Islanders lacking in a tributary back country. After the outbreak of the Continental Wars in 1793 had seen a superior British fleet wipe enemy shipping from the high seas, American merchants began to import such goods as nankeens (from China) and German linens (especially from Hamburg and Bremen) not only to supply domestic American markets but also to provide, via neutral shipping, for the total needs, and not merely part of the provisioning needs, of the Caribbean islands. The Olivers of Baltimore reveal some of the effects of the new demand. "One cargo of German linens," they wrote in 1800, "was formerly a large supply for a year's consumption and we have now a demand for more than fifty cargoes. The consumption of East India Goods has also increased astonishingly." A few months before they had made clear that the reason for much of this greatly increased demand was "Our West India trade on which we chiefly depend for the Sale of Linens. . . ."[48]

Rising demand must have made more and more possible the services of resident commission agents in the West Indies. Let us consider why this should be so. News of need for an article in the islands often took three or three-and-a-half weeks to arrive in Baltimore, and even if a merchant there had a supply of the article on hand and a vessel outfitted and ready for sea it required another three or three-and-a-half weeks for it to reach market. In earlier colonial times these six or seven weeks would have permitted some huckstering, island-hopping ship captain or two, dispatched to the West Indies with cargoes of familiar commodities suited to an habitual commerce, to stumble luckily upon the demand and fill it. But would not this situation have occurred more readily in 1750 than in 1800, and in 1700 than 1750? In the later years was it not increasingly possible for a resident merchant to say to his agent, as Samuel Smith of Baltimore said to one of his in 1788: "We hope your next [letter] may encourage the return of our Brig[an]t[ine] to you"?[49] In the later years, in short, even if an agent informed correspondents in several North American ports of high prices in his market, it seems quite possi-

[47] Harrington, *op. cit.*, p. 193; Bruchey, *op. cit.*, p. 148.
[48] Bruchey, *op. cit.* pp. 80, 190, 194–95.
[49] Ltr. to Messrs. P. Burling & Co., Nov. 6, 1788 (Smith Ltr. Bk., II, in Md. Hist. Soc.)

ble that those prices were supported by a demand of sufficient depth to accommodate without loss more cargoes than in the earlier years. Could not merchants increasingly, therefore, avoid the wasteful and time-consuming ventures of their huckstering ship captains and base their investment decisions on price information from a number of alternative markets? If so, it became increasingly important for men like the Olivers to place their business "in the hands of Men of Stability, *good information* & undoubted integrity." [50] For there can be no question that the larger profits "depended on having first knowledge of a market and arriving before the crowd." [51]

The preceding discussion seems to me to suggest the possibility that the eighteenth-century merchant became more and more able by forethought to narrow down the area of impotency ruled by luck. This interpretation must, however, meet a widely held view that slow and unsure means of communication placed a heavy discount upon the value of planning. "Despite the merits of the agency system," says Baxter, "it involved very weak control by a merchant over his foreign trade. He had perforce to trust his agents blindly." Not only was "skill at bookkeeping and auditing so rare that he had little check on their transactions" (a point which we have seen is open to question), but his messages to them traveled "at a snail's pace." Hedges also emphasizes "the leisurely pace of commerce in the eighteenth century," and the "guesswork and uncertainty involved in transacting business at such a distance" as that between Providence and Surinam. When a vessel arrived, Byron Fairchild concludes, was "chiefly a matter of wind and weather." [52]

It is my opinion that far too much emphasis has been placed upon the irregularity and uncertainty of communications. It is true that copies of letters and bills of exchange were sometimes sent in triplicate, or even in quadruplicate. But these acts of insurance attest only to the possibility that important documents might miscarry: in themselves they shed little light on the question of how great was that possibility. Similarly, one might cite many examples of long passages and delayed arrivals. But their typicality must await adequate statistical evidence of sailing times, and it may be that definite answers are impossible to attain. Lacking adequate data, one may incline toward Carl C. Cutler's thesis of the "fitful, changeable character of the North Atlantic gales," or subscribe to the less romantic view of Herbert Heaton: "Much has been said about the 'maddening uncertainty' of sailing ship movements. Yet the dates of arrivals of vessels [from England to American ports] do not vary greatly from year to year." [53]

[50] ORB 4, pp. 29–31, to J. & F. Baring & Co., July 22, 1800. (My italics.) (Md. Hist. Soc.)
[51] Harrington, *op. cit.*, p. 87.
[52] Baxter, *House of Hancock*, p. 302; Hedges, *op. cit.*, p. 28; Fairchild, *op. cit.*, p. 51.
[53] Carl C. Cutler, *Five Hundred Sailing Records of American Built Ships* (Mystic, Conn., 1952), p. 22; Herbert Heaton, "The American Trade," in *Trade Winds*, C. N. Parkinson, ed. (London, 1948), p. 200.

William Pepperrell does not appear to have been at the mercy of the elements: he "seems to have counted on Barbados sugar, molasses, and rum being ready in March, since four of his seven spring sailings between 1717 and 1724 arrived in Barbados during that month." The other three arrived in February or earlier. It was not uncertainty with regard to the elements, but with regard to the market, together with William's "positive assurance that he could depend upon Thomas Kerby, his correspondent at Antigua, to accept goods whenever available and hold them for the arrival of one of William's vessels," that explain the "irregularity of his Antigua sailings." [54] A voyage from Baltimore "to the West Indies and back," the Olivers remarked in 1797, "is *often performed* in 6 or 7 weeks." In 1808 the Baltimore firm observed that its schooners "generally completed their voyages [to Vera Cruz and back] in 60 days." That this is close to the truth is indicated by the available evidence: The average time required for 20 such voyages undertaken in the years 1805–1807 was 62½ days. On the other hand, in August of 1802 the Olivers reported that one of their vessels "had forty nine days passage to St. Croix which *should not have* exceeded 15. . . ." [55]

The fact that these Baltimore merchants could say that voyages were "often performed" in a specified time, or that a voyage "should not have" exceeded a given number of days, seems to me to point to the distinct possibility that regularity in communications was the rule and not the exception. It would therefore seem to me justifiable to place less stress upon wind and weather and more on the intent of the merchant shipper, less on fortuity and more on forethought. If there was relatively little forethought in early colonial times and more dependence upon lucky strikes by wandering ship captains was it not possibly because the volume and nature of the West Indian demand rather than the elements blunted the point of planning?

Since forethought depended so much on fresh information from many market centers I suspect that it became increasingly important in the advancing eighteenth century to acquire and retain good agents—and not by any means for West Indian trade alone. Merchants themselves often solicited agency business, as did Carter Braxton of Virginia in 1763 and James Beekman of New York after 1783.[56] Sometimes agents were sought out: "perhaps it may suit you in future to Transact similar business for the House of S. S. & B & Buchanan Spear & Co—in both which our S. S is interested," Samuel Smith of Baltimore suggested to a Martinique merchant in 1794.[57] From time to time representatives of foreign houses came in droves to the cities of America to drum up business for their principals. Agents for British houses swarmed in Boston in 1785. In

[54] Fairchild, *op. cit.*, p. 52.
[55] Bruchey, *op. cit.*, pp. 144, 300. (My italics.)
[56] Hedges, *op. cit.*, pp. 72–73 (Baxter); White, *op. cit.*, p. 541 (Beekman).
[57] Ltr. to John Gay, July 30, 1794. (Smith Ltr. Bk., III, Md. Hist. Soc.) Col. Wm. Pepperrell tried in 1727 to obtain the services of an agent in Carolina to avoid the delays of ship captains (Fairchild, *op. cit.*, pp. 94–95).

1799 Oliver referred to the "many agents" of Dutch houses then in Baltimore. To make new American connections was among the purposes of Alexander Baring's trip from England in 1795, and Oliver was among his acquisitions. At different times Oliver dispatched his two younger brothers to Europe partly for the purpose of acquiring additional agents.[58]

Because of the key role they played in eighteenth-century commerce, ability to manage one's agents with skill often affected the outcome of investments. As is to be expected, merchants displayed varying abilities in this regard. The Pepperrells' biographer concludes that "an important element" in the success of the Piscataqua merchants "was their ability to maintain satisfactory relations with their correspondents." But that luck cannot be ruled out as a factor in that success is evident from the fact that when William Pepperrell's agent at Antigua complained that the sale of lumber cargoes was tedious, Pepperrell "agreed with what the latter had to say . . . thanked him for not giving up his business, and then went on sending more lumber." Thomas Hancock "did not scruple" to send his London supplier "a rival correspondent's prices, demanding a rebate." If "all was not sweetness and light" in the relations between James Beekman and his correspondents, neither was it between the Olivers and theirs.[59] The Olivers could bristle at affronts to their credit reputation, complain about poor sales, or quarrel about rates of commission. But when they found a correspondent who was "*Solid, Liberal & Active* qualities which we consider absolutely necessary for an agent" they endeavoured to hold on to him. A new firm in Liverpool once solicited their business; they wished it well but stated that they "could not change from a House with whom we have been long connected." To a warmly recommended house in Amsterdam they wrote: "you cannot expect that we would quit Men with whom we have been long connected without being first assured of some advantage." They were highly reluctant to change correspondents, and almost always did so only after long and repeated efforts to accommodate differences. "We have wrote you at least twenty Letters, since we received any from you," they told a Martinique merchant in 1800. "Surely we have not given you any just cause of offence, and if we had, it was your Duty to let us know it—." They showed their appreciation of good men not only by thanking them for jobs well done, but by inducing other Baltimore merchants to consign shipments to them, thus enabling them to earn commissions.[60] And, like Gerard G. Beekman of New York, who rarely used captains or supercargoes in his trade with Rhode Island, "probably [because of] the desire not to offend his correspondents," [61] the Olivers' apologies are by no means uncommon when they addressed their shipments to captains or supercargoes. ". . . Nothing but the Uncertainty of your residence pre-

[58] Bruchey, *op. cit.*, pp. 149–51.
[59] Fairchild, *op. cit.*, pp. 164, 54–55 (Pepperrells); Baxter, *House of Hancock*, p. 201 (Hancock); White, *op. cit.*, p. 350 (Beekman).
[60] Bruchey, *op. cit.*, pp. 149–51, 159, 142, 156–57.
[61] White, *op. cit.*, p. 298.

vented a direct consignment both this voyage and her last," they told a Martinique correspondent in 1796.[62] To one agent they paid $4,600 "for the purpose of dispatching the Brig Isabella from Jeremie . . . ," while to another they gave a bonus of $20,000 as "an additional Compensation . . . for your faithful Services at Vera Cruz." [63]

Orders for goods that were accompanied by specifications too precise and confined seem to indicate quite clearly an uninspired management. Gerard G. Beekman's specifications were so cautious in the period after 1770 as to leave his biographer in doubt whether his orders were possible of fulfillment. James Beekman "seemed congenitally unable to recognize that the constant wartime trend was upward. Consequently he frequently spelled out in his orders price specifications which bore little relation to the actual state of the British market into which his orders came." In ordering goods from London during the period from 1803 to 1822 the Trotters of Philadelphia "often . . . left so little discretion to their agents that the latter were prevented from taking action when opportunities arose quite unforeseen." To a merchant of Venice who had sent them "so particular" an order that they preferred not to fill it, the Olivers of Baltimore wrote: [64]

> we have no desire to do commission business unless we can give perfect satisfaction and if you should hereafter think proper to give us any orders, we advise you to state your views and expectations and leave us to Judge of the propriety of carrying them into effect.

At the opposite extreme was imprecision. James Beekman had a "remarkable talent for vagueness and ambiguity." One supplier threw up his hands: " 'We cannot tell what you mean by yard wide Cotton Strips at 12½ per Ell neither could our Agent in Manchester. . . . we wish you would send us a pattern of it.' " In one instance at least there appeared in Colonel William Pepperrell's instructions to his ship captain "a certain amount of ambiguity and confusion" which led to an unintended trip from Barbados to London and, from the viewpoint of profit, "an unsatisfactory voyage." [65]

But this was far from typical, for when the Pepperrells "sent their captains on a 'trading voyage,' " they "attempted to provide for every contingency" by means of their "thorough, detailed letters of instruction." The Browns of Providence "might give [to their ship captains] reasonably specific instructions or they might grant substantial measures of discretion." Gerard Beekman "frequently . . . employed his own discretion in contravening his instructions when he deemed it was in his customer's interest to do so." The British correspondents of James Beekman "usu-

[62] Bruchey, op. cit., pp. 150–51.
[63] ORB 18, p. 46, entry of Feb. 15, 1806; ORB 6, p. 411, to J. G. Villaneuva, Sept. 13, 1808 (Md. Hist. Soc.).
[64] White, op. cit., p. 290 (Gerard Beekman), p. 387 (James Beekman); Tooker, op. cit., p. 75 (Trotters); Bruchey, op. cit., p. 143.
[65] White, op. cit., p. 387 (James Beekman); Fairchild, op. cit., pp. 66–67.

ally . . . exercised their own discretion in deciding how far above his [price] maximum they could go with safety." John Jacob Astor was in the habit of giving "detailed instructions . . . to his captains and agents" but he could do so "without . . . stifling his agents' initiative." On the whole, the relations between the Olivers and their agents were more characterized by elasticity than by rigidity: they appear as a rule to have preferred an informed judgment to meticulous obedience to instructions. They once expressed their regret that a Dutch house had complied with their preference for an immediate sale: "We always prefer an early Sale, but we do not By any means wish you to part with our goods when the Market is depress'd by large arrivals and especially when so many circumstances combine to induce a belief that a favourable change will soon take place—." When on another occasion a cargo did not do as well as they had hoped, the Olivers attributed it to the failure of a Hamburg agent to comply with "our positive orders . . . to sell immediately." Yet they concluded that "your intentions were no doubt very good and we must rest satisfied." Sometimes the Olivers expressly authorized an agent to send their vessel to a second port. Yet they would not deny his discretionary power to do so, even if they considered it "contrary to positive instructions." They once criticized a Leghorn agent not because he had ordered their vessel to Genoa, but because "if it was consider'd expedient to send her to a second Port, Genoa was not the proper place." [66]

The wide discretion practiced and expected by the Olivers was thus subject to criticism after the event, so to speak. *Ex post facto* criticism must itself have provided valuable guidance to agents who would receive many other consignments in the future. Interchanges of complaint and rebuttal must themselves, therefore, have narrowed the area of uncertainty in continued relations between merchant and agent. But it should be emphasized that even the first in a series of shipments to an agent saw the merchant make the "controlling decisions," i.e., the investment-initiating decisions which sent a cargo of a certain kind to a particular port (this was certainly the rule) at a particular time. And when he dispatched a cargo only to a general market area, addressing it to captain or supercargo on board to give him power to take it to the most promising port, he was far from impotent if he had intelligence and knowledge enough to restrict discretion with prearrangements and preferences, and if he had resident agents in a number of ports to supply guidance and aid on the spot. Fairchild makes clear that resident merchant, captains and agents formed for the Pepperrells an intelligently managed team,[67] but I should like once again to make use of the rich Oliver materials to illustrate the nature of teamwork.

In September, 1803, the Olivers contemplated a voyage of their Schooner *Ann* to Europe, a sale there of her outcargo of sugar and

[66] Fairchild, *op. cit.*, p. 163 (Pepperrells); Hedges, *op. cit.*, p. 27 (Browns); White, *op. cit.*, pp. 253, 387 (Beekmans); Porter, *Astor*, Vol. I, pp. 533, 536; Bruchey, *op. cit.*, pp. 142–143 (Olivers).
[67] Fairchild, *op. cit.*, pp. 156, 163.

coffee, purchase of a cargo suitable for the West Indies, and remittance of the proceeds in bills to either London or Amsterdam, depending on exchange rates. Appointing a supercargo, Lowry, they addressed him thus:

> We hope and expect you will be able to procure at <u>Leghorn</u> a correct state of the different Markets in that quarter which will enable you to determine where the cargo will answer best. We have already informed you that <u>Trieste</u> is the Port we have in view, but you are at liberty to proceed to any other where you think her cargo will answer better. . . . If the Blocade of <u>Hamburg</u> and <u>Bremen</u> is continued Sugar and Coffee will probably be very high at Trieste and German Linens low, in which case you will of course proceed there and load the Ann with such articles as you may think most likely to answer here, preferring Linens calculated for the Spanish Colonys provided you find that Nation are at War with England.

The Olivers also sent letters to houses in Trieste, Venice, Leghorn, London, and St. Thomas. They asked the Leghorn house to give Lowry "any information in your power . . . respecting the value of Sugar and Coffee at Trieste and other Markets in your neighborhood." In the event the proceeds of the sugar and coffee were insufficient for the purchase of the homeward cargo, the Barings of London were asked to furnish aid in this manner: "If you have any friend there [in Trieste] in whom you can confide we wish you would send an introduction to our Super Cargo who will value [i.e., draw] on them." From the house in St. Thomas, the Olivers requested information on the "State of your Market" for German linens, in case Lowry purchased returns in Trieste, and for Castile soap, oil, red wine "and such articles as are generally imported from the Straits." By July of 1804 the Olivers were able to inform the same house that the *Ann* had arrived in Trieste "about the 20 March," and they expressed the hope she was then at St. Thomas, for the Captain "is instructed to place his Cargo in your hands provided you can sell it at certain limits and to bring it here in case these limits cannot be obtained." The *Ann's* cargo, purchased in Trieste, was unloaded in Baltimore after calling at St. Thomas in vain for a market.[68]

In sum, as the case of the *Ann* illustrates, an eighteenth-century merchant might do much to influence the outcome of his investments in foreign trade. To do so, he necessarily relied on the aid of his agents, chosen and managed with varying degrees of skill. Indeed, if it be true, as seems quite possible, that an increased West Indian trade was accompanied by an increased use of agents, the area of business amenable to control widened during the course of the eighteenth century. To be sure, communications were slow, they were sometimes irregular, and decisions once taken might later appear mistaken in the light of changed conditions, or of factors previously unknown. Yet when such a situation developed we often find an Oliver, a Beekman, an Astor, or a Brown dispatch-

---

[68] Bruchey, *op. cit.*, pp. 146–47.

ing follow-up letters in the wake of a departed ship captain.[69] There must be few such letters so poignant as the one addressed in August, 1794, by Samuel Smith of Baltimore to Captain Thomas O'Bryan: [70]

> Since your departure from hence—we have certain accounts—that F Dauphin [Fort Dauphin] was taken by the Brigands. and every white person, whether on shore or on board the vessell—was put to Death—So that it will be perfectly unsafe for you to go there—

Sometimes follow-up letters failed to arrive in time.[71] When all is said and done, the difficulties under which he labored, as Hedges has well observed, "demanded that the successful eighteenth century businessman use continuously every ounce of wit, imagination, patience, and perseverance which he possessed." [72]

Some merchants, as I trust the preceding pages have made clear, had more wit and perseverance, more prudence and better housekeeping habits than others. In general and in the long run possession of these qualities must have played significant if imponderable roles in the achievement of business success. But having said this I would reaffirm my sense of the impossibility of demarcating between these factors themselves, or between all of them, on the one hand, and, on the other, luck. The luck (it is not always this, of course) of having the right relatives is a case in point. Gerard Beekman "profited in many ways from the assistance of his relatives in getting started," and for his cousin James "the family tie was [also] beneficial." Porter has extensively discussed "Kinship and Business" as a "conspicuous feature of business in early Massachusetts [that appeared] in all its aspects." I agree with Robert K. Lamb's thesis that the "extended kinship family" must be emphasized as a factor in the success of entrepreneurs. Certainly no one familiar with the story of Robert Oliver would be inclined to minimize the role of luck. Two nearly incredible sets of brother-in-law relationships gave him an opportunity to make from trade to Vera Cruz in 1806–1807 a nearly incredible net profit of $775,000 in 18 months. But no reader of the record of those months can fail to be impressed with the intelligence and vigor (and also occasional unscrupulousness) with which Oliver proceeded to make the most of his opportunity, or with the extent of his dependence upon a faithful agent.[73] Here, as elsewhere, it is a case of the man and the moment, and while, with an ear to what a poet once said about the outcome of the best laid plans, I would give luck its due, I would also give man his, especially, in this narrow case, the business community of man.

[69] ORB 3, pp. 81–82, to Hall & McIntosh, Aug. 16, 1797 (Oliver); White, *op. cit.*, Vol. I, p. 272, to John Bennit, Jan. 28, 1756; Porter, *Astor*, Vol. I, p. 431; Hedges, *op. cit.*, pp. 78–80.
[70] Smith Ltr. Bk., III, 1794–1818 (Md. Hist. Soc.).
[71] Pares, *op. cit.*, p. 85.
[72] Hedges, *op. cit.*, p. 29.
[73] White, *op. cit.*, pp. 534 (Gerard Beekman), 347 (James Beekman); Porter, *Jacksons and Lees*, Vol. I, p. 88; Robert K. Lamb, "The Entrepreneur and the Community," in *Men in Business*, W. Miller, ed. (Cambridge, 1952), p. 93; Bruchey, *op. cit.*, Chap. 6 (Oliver).

PLANTER AND COTTON FACTOR
IN THE OLD SOUTH: SOME AREAS
OF FRICTION *Ralph W. Haskins*

Amid the financial chaos of the late Jacksonian period, a Mobile cotton factor wrote reflectively: "Commerce must regulate it[s] Self . . . the Planter Should Carefully and Closely attend to his Interest: and the merchant do the Same. thereby a ballancing power would be exerted— and both parties will be equally bennifitted." [1] The proposition was sound in theory but difficult in practice. For the factor had touched upon one of the fundamental problems of American economy—how to reconcile the interests of producer and middleman. Historically, this relationship has been marked by strife in varying degree, and the Old South was no exception. That the grievances were not all on one side is equally apparent. This study is not concerned with efforts to solve the mutual problems of factor and planter; rather, it is an analysis of some of the outstanding differences, partly as contemporaries saw them and partly as they appear in the light of research. Dissension did not outweigh harmony, for the latter was the rule and the former the exception. However, this paper is concerned with the points at which friction did occur.

To say that the cotton factorage system exerted a profound influence on the ante-bellum South does not necessarily identify one with the "moonlight and magnolia" school.[2] If the factor had comparatively few ties with thousands of rural southerners in the smaller income group, he

[1] Duke Goodman to Richard Singleton, Mobile, September 4, 1841, Singleton Papers, University of North Carolina Library, Chapel Hill.

[2] Cf. John K. Bettersworth's review of Lewis E. Atherton's *The Southern Country Store, 1800–1860* (Baton Rouge, 1949), *Journal of Southern History*, 16: 84–86 (February, 1950). Though the influence of the factorage system has probably been overemphasized, a really critical judgment would seem to await a detailed study of factorage.

REPRINTED with permission from Ralph W. Haskins, "Planter and Cotton Factor in the Old South: Some Areas of Friction," *Agricultural History*, Vol. XXIX (January 1955), pp. 1–14.

played a prominent role in urban life; and, above all, his was a key position in the plantation system. The commercial practices known collectively as factorage were the products of a slow evolutionary growth which dated back to the work of joint-stock companies, continued through the colonial period, and were characteristic of ante-bellum times.[3]

Marketing the cotton crop was probably the most important of the factor's varied services. As agent for the planter or interior merchant, he watched the fluctuations of the market, offered timely advice in this connection, and gauged the most favorable opportunity for disposal. His responsibility did not end with the sale; accountable to the shipper for the proceeds, he was indirectly liable to the consumer for the quality of the cotton. Scarcely less significant was the factor's role as supply agent for the plantation. To a certain extent, he took the place of the retail merchant as a provider of goods for the planter, although he did not dominate this field. His buying function was twofold: in addition to his capacity as supply agent, the factor sometimes purchased cotton either independently or for others. Not only did he supply the plantation, but he shouldered much of the burden of financing this enterprise. He held the planter's funds subject to order, extended credit through a system of advances, procured bills of exchange, discounted notes, and remitted specie. Finally, contemporary records show conclusively that he was not only a banker but a personal agent as well—investment counsel, stockbroker, collector, real estate operator, and jack-of-all-trades. In short, he rendered a multitude of services so diverse in nature that he was a veritable "planter's factotum."

Though the community of interest between planter and factor centered around the plantation, the cotton crop, and the system of advances, it was further promoted by common origins, by blood ties, by an overlapping of professions, and by reciprocal services of various kinds. In the main, the relationship was a cordial one. "I cannot close this Communication without expressing my *entire satisfaction* with you, as my Cotton

[3] The usages of that day render it very difficult to distinguish between "factors" and "commission merchants." In theory, there was a differentiation of function: the former was an agent employed to market produce for a principal, in this case the planter; the commission merchant secured supplies of various kinds for his customers. One circular announced Duke Goodman's location in Mobile, "as a seller of Cotton and other produce of the country, better known as a (factor)—Also of purchasing the Planters' supplies, and of receiving and forwarding country Merchants' and Planter's goods, and executing all orders from Merchants and Planters." Goodman Circular, Mobile, June 7, 1832, Singleton Papers. Goodman was thus identifiable as factor, as commission and forwarding merchant, and even as general merchant. In each of these capacities, a compensation, or commission, was usually forthcoming. In practice the "factor" and "commission merchant" were practically synonymous and the two functions shaded off into each other. Though directories issued after 1800 by southern cities indicate an increasing specialization, the factor often continued to perform a variety of services characteristic of a general merchant. Southern laws and southern courts seem to have made no distinction; indeed, the terms were used interchangeably and indiscriminately.

Factors," [4] wrote a Tennessee planter. A Charleston factor in desperate straits expressed with picturesque language his gratitude "for your unsought for Act of profound friendship in Risquing my Character . . . from an Unfeeling and unprincipald Wretch, for the Paltry Sum of Twenty three dollars—woud of damd me for ever." [5] Granted that much sentiment was strictly commercial—in the interests of bigger and better business—plantation and mercantile records nevertheless contain many expressions of friendship and confidence. Perhaps the ante-bellum planter and factor came as near to achieving harmony as did any combination of merchant and agrarian. But neither in individual cases nor in the wider sphere of group interests were the relations of factor and planter entirely free from discord. Producer and middleman wrangled over the manifold problems connected with marketing, purchasing, banking, and general agency.

Since selling the crop was the factor's most important function, it was but natural that friction should be greatest in the field of marketing —as regards forecasting, quality of cotton, transportation, the selling process itself, and in the various assessments levied by the factor.

Even before the crop was on its way to market, many planters came to question the accuracy of crop forecasts and cotton statistics issued periodically by factors. There were obvious defects. Communication prior to the telegraph was slow, a fact amply illustrated by the exchange of market reports. For instance, Liverpool accounts of May 25, 1825, reached a Petersburg house 39 days later. On May 3 of the following year, the same firm had quotations issued 41 days before.[6] A more pointed though unproven accusation was voiced in 1852 during the course of a movement by cotton planters to obtain more accurate statistics on the growing crop. Spokesmen for this project attributed much of the sudden price fluctuations to the tardiness with which the amount of the American crop was ascertained. "It is in the power of all parties interested," they added, "to magnify or diminish the estimate as best suits their interest for purchasing from the planter, or selling any stocks they may have on hand." [7]

More specific were disputes over the quality of cotton itself. Much of this controversy centered around "false-packing," which took several forms and was sometimes accidental but often deliberate. One method involved the use of thin strips of prime cotton on the two sides of the bale usually sampled. The inside was composed wholly of inferior material. At other times, there were layers of various grades, each of poorer quality as one penetrated toward the center.[8] A widely-used technique con-

[4] Wm. F. Reed to Heard & Simpson, Memphis, April 26, 1859, Heard Papers, University of North Carolina Library.
[5] Goodman to Richard Singleton, Charleston, November 24, 1825, Singleton Papers.
[6] Robert Hamilton & Company to Duncan Cameron, Petersburg, July 2, 1825, and May 3, 1826, Cameron Papers, University of North Carolina Library.
[7] DeBow's Review, 13:294 (September, 1852).
[8] James E. Boyle, Cotton and the New Orleans Cotton Exchange: A Century of Commercial Evolution (Garden City, New York, 1934), 53–54.

sisted of labeling inferior varieties as "prime" or some other high grade: low-quality Alabama, billed as Mississippi or Louisiana cotton, was sold on the New Orleans market.[9] Less ingenious shippers placed stones, dirt, trash, or water inside the bale to increase the weight. Georgia petitioners, addressing the legislature in 1823, observed with rare insight that the poor showing of the state's cotton could be attributed to the presence of rocks within the bales.[10]

It was sometimes difficult to fix the responsibility for false-packing within the plantation force. Some planters were not overly scrupulous, but a share of the blame lay with others. When overseers or slaves received a percentage from the sale, they were occasionally tempted to "load" the cotton.[11]

Factors, either to enhance their profits or to protect their reputations as dealers in high-grade cotton, occasionally resorted to substituting one quality for another. According to the Liverpool American Chamber of Commerce, a large proportion of shipments arriving in Liverpool in the 'fifties contained falsely or irregularly-packed bundles, and now and then whole parcels of 20, 50, or even 100 bales were mixed or "plated." [12] "Round," or repacked bales, drew additional criticism.[13] A curious letter from an upstate Georgia firm to an Augusta commission house sheds further light on usages in the trade: "you must crowd our lots with others that are better, in selling, and make Gus weigh our Cotton, so as to gain, or in other words, not let him take off so much for wet." [14]

Not all such cases could be attributed to dishonesty—a number were due to carelessness in picking, ginning, and packing, to exposure to damp weather, or to damage en route. Under these circumstances, the term "false" or "irregular" packing might also mean less merchantable cotton. Many planters did not closely supervise the raising of their crop and its preparation for market; with essentially unskilled labor involved,

[9] Mobile *Commercial Register*, May 18, 1824, cited in Charles Davis, *The Cotton Kingdom in Alabama* (Montgomery, 1939), 144.

[10] Charles G. Cordle, "Henry Shultz and the Founding of Hamburg, South Carolina," James C. Bonner and Lucien E. Roberts, eds., *Studies in Georgia History and Government* (Athens, Ga., 1940), 88–89.

[11] James Harvey Merritt to John Singleton, Charleston, April 29, 1820, Singleton Papers; see also Savannah *Daily Morning News*, February 28, 1860.

[12] *Hunt's Merchants' Magazine*, 36:352 (March, 1857). For other instances of alleged substitution by factors, see *Pattison v. Moore*, Porter, *Alabama Reports*, 3:270–78 (1836) and *Austill & Marshall v. Crawford, Alabama Reports*, 7:335–43 (1845).

[13] "Round" bales, in this context, meant cotton repacked at market, with the inference that inferior grades were mixed at random. Prior to the development and widespread use of superior methods of compression, "round" represented a regular classification. Planters of sea-island cotton did not generally pack their cotton in "square" bales; instead, they preferred it packed in bags. Lewis C. Gray, *History of Agriculture in the Southern United States to 1860* (2 vols., Washington, 1933), 2:736.

[14] Benson & Rosamond to Heard & Simpson, West Point, Georgia, November 22, 1858, Heard Papers.

it was not surprising that a bale might contain several grades.[15] Not uncommonly the product defied classification. "The fact is—it was not exactly cotton—nor trash—But a conglomeration of moats—& frostbitten Stuff resembling—rats nests—made of nankeen." [16] Extensive damage resulted from exposure to the weather prior to arrival at market. The correspondence of Mrs. James K. Polk with her New Orleans factors affords a graphic picture of losses from carelessness, mishaps in transit, and destruction by fire.[17] The Indiana farmer Solon Robinson, visiting the South in 1850, declared that the handling of cotton was "one continued waste" all along the line from producer to consumer. Landing and exposure to the elements, the method of sampling, and other practices contributed to reduce the quality.[18] Robinson may have exaggerated, but southerners were slow to adopt habits of economy in production and marketing.

Losses in weight—the difference between plantation and market figures—elicited much controversy. In the 'forties, an Alabama planter shipped to a New Orleans house 51 bales which she claimed amounted to approximately 24,500 pounds, and received a sales account which credited her with nearly 4000 pounds less. "Common courtesy tells us to treat your communication . . . with respect, yet the writer of the same deserves no consideration from us," remarked the factors in rejecting a demand for remuneration; "and [we] are somewhat surprised that after transacting the business of your husband & self for so many years . . . the writer should insinuate that we had willingly wronged you out of a cent." [19] In a somewhat similar way, evidence cited in a Georgia court case of 1859 showed a difference of some 6000 pounds between the shipping-point and Liverpool.[20] To assess responsibility for these discrepan-

[15] Franklin Robinson to Samuel Pickens, Mobile, April 18, 1831, Samuel Pickens Papers, Alabama Department of Archives and History, Montgomery; Byrne, Vance & Company to James Sheppard, New Orleans, February [28], 1857, James Sheppard Papers, Duke University Library, Durham, North Carolina; Richard Nugent & Company to C. D. Hamilton, New Orleans, September 21, 1859, C. D. Hamilton Papers, Mississippi Department of Archives and History, Jackson. Depositions in a South Carolina court case illustrate the way in which false-packing might be accidental. In eight bales of sea-island cotton, the product was found to be mixed with hair one or two inches in length, in the proportion of a pound or a handful to each bale, or of one or two hundred hairs to each handful of cotton. Untanned hides had been used as bands for the machine in which the cotton was ginned. *Carnochan v. Gould*, Bailey, *South Carolina Law Reports*, 1:179–81 (1829).

[16] N. Scudder to St. John R. Liddell, New Orleans, April 23, 1856, Liddell (Moses, St. John R., and family) Papers, Department of Archives, Louisiana State University, Baton Rouge.

[17] These letters are scattered through the Polk Papers (Mrs. Polk), Library of Congress; some of them were printed in John Spencer Bassett, *The Southern Plantation Overseer as Revealed in His Letters* (Northampton, Mass., 1925), passim.

[18] *Hunt's Merchants' Magazine*, 22:350–51 (February, 1850).

[19] Mary Coffee to Maunsel White & Company, Florence [Alabama], April 13, 1851, and Maunsel White & Company to Mrs. Coffee, New Orleans, April 23, 1841, John Coffee Papers, Alabama Department of Archives and History.

[20] *Cloud & Shackelford v. Hartridge & Hartridge, Adm'rs.*, Georgia Reports, 28:272–76 (1859).

cies is difficult, if not impossible. In a sense, it is beside the point. No matter whether the fault lay with the planter and his force, the carrier, the factor, the weigher, other intermediaries, or even the elements, it often occasioned bitter dispute, in a cycle which ran the gamut from agency to agency, from destination back to origin.

Moreover, there were numerous quarrels over sales. Aside from the unpredictability of the market, inadequate returns could be traced to various influences operating singly or in combination: ill-luck, poor handling, and the violation of contract or instructions. One such experience might well render the producer wary. It is not difficult to imagine a Louisiana planter's reaction when, after he complained of a meager return, his factor explained the loss as an unwise tactical move. "The lot . . . was unfortunately sold two days too Soon. . . . I requested my partner not to offer . . . until The following monday. . . . instead of waiting . . . he Sold on Saturday, Thereby not participating at all in The mark[ed] improvement in prices, which Commenced on the following monday." [21] Breaches of contract brought ready complaint. Written or verbal contracts were not a fixed custom, but the planter generally gave directions for the disposal of his crop.[22] In the spring of 1847 a South Carolina grower and his Charleston merchant agreed that the latter was to sell upon receipt of written instructions. These were given in July; nevertheless, the factor dallied for several months and finally obtained the year's lowest price. "I regret that truth and candour compels me to say," wrote the irate planter, "neither your management of this part of my business, nor apology for its mismanagement is by any means satisfactory." [23] Parties to verbal contracts or "understandings" found to their sorrow that these agreements were susceptible to varying interpretation.

Still other disagreements stemmed from the terms of sale, particularly when the extension of credit to the purchaser was followed by difficulty in securing payment for the cotton. That this widespread practice led to considerable abuse is suggested by the comment of a Louisiana jurist in 1825. In New Orleans, said John Slidell, it was quite too common to repose confidence in the buyer—confidence to such a degree that the latter obtained control of the merchandise before the price was paid. Speculators, without real means but enjoying an undeserved credit, thus made large-scale operations in the market. Such laxity was a prolific source of fraud and litigation.[24] Perhaps the fact that they received comparatively small consignments from individual planters but often sold in wholesale lots to buyers may have influenced some factors to overextend themselves in dispensing credit to consumers' representatives.

Incidental costs of marketing contributed further to the differences between planter and factor. The situation was scarcely overstated by the southern correspondent of a New York newspaper: "The steamer charges

[21] M. Gillis to St. John R. Liddell, New Orleans, November 1, 1860, Liddell Papers.
[22] While this was true in the main, it varied with individual cases.
[23] E. K. Anderson to William Law, Charleston, December 6, 1847, and Law to Anderson, Darlington [South Carolina], December [n.d.], 1847, William Law Papers, Duke University Library.
[24] *Campbell & Rickarby v. Penn, Louisiana Annual Reports*, 7:376 (1852).

a dollar a bale. The sampler, weigher, drayman, piccory, warehouse and pressmen and brokers, all have a snug per cent. The factor has on an average a dollar a bale for selling . . . and all that comes out of your pocket and mine, and all but the great unshirted." [25] Far from acquiescing in these levies, growers frequently and emphatically registered their disapproval of assessments for drayage, storage, labor, insurance, compression, and sales commissions. There were probably few planters of the Old South who did not at one time or another complain of such exactions.

The significance here does not lie in charges alone; more subtle were the growth of custom and the inertia of routine, through which certain practices gained such wide acceptance that they are almost totally disregarded in contemporary records. One example was the "average account." In 1845, Austill & Marshall of Mobile sold an upstate planter's crop as part of a larger lot, which averaged 13 cents per pound. But the factors paid the planter only 12 cents, the relative value of his cotton. Austill & Marshall maintained that this procedure was according to "usages of trade," but their appeal was denied by the Alabama Supreme Court.[26] A similar case arose from a charge of 45 cents per bale for drayage, storage, labor, weighing, and insurance. Here again the factors invoked the "sanction of custom," but nothing in their testimony indicated how they had reached the precise calculation of 45 cents. On the other hand, there was no information as to the proportionate value of money or scrip to which the planter's insurance policy entitled him.[27]

In the same category were tendencies to maintain fees at unnecessarily high levels or to charge for services that had not been rendered. Though they continued in the 'fifties to assess planters for drayage, storage, and labor at the old rate of four dollars, certain New Orleans factors obtained the same accommodation for one dollar through contracts with local cotton presses. The savings represented were not being passed on to the producer. One innovator proposed to cut these costs by one-third: "as it [one dollar] is all I pay, therefore, it is all I have a right to charge. Whilst Most of the larger houses here actually pay less than this—and Still retain the old charge of 4/. But upon what ground I am unable to learn." [28] A South Carolina planter, examining some sales accounts, discovered that he had been billed twice for insurance he had not required.[29] Considering the fact that many planters were careless in their

[25] "Cotton Factors and Commission Merchants," *The Soil of the South,* 3:677 (October, 1853).
[26] *Austill & Marshal v. Crawford,* Alabama Reports, 7:335–42 (1845). This case suggests a further query: suppose the relative value of the planter's cotton had been fourteen cents? Would the factors have relied on relative value or average price?
[27] *Brander, William & Company v. Lum,* Louisiana Annual Reports, 11:217–19 (1856).
[28] N. Scudder to St. John R. Liddell, New Orleans, November 10, 1855, Liddell Papers.
[29] *Huguenin v. Legare & Colcock,* Richardson, *South Carolina Law Reports,* 11:204–16 (1858).

bookkeeping, it is a moot question whether such charges appeared by accident or by design.

As supply agent for the planter, the factor furnished the necessities for day to day existence on the plantation, as well as the luxuries. Less often he obtained slaves. Upon numerous occasions he lent credit through the acceptance of drafts or settled the planter's bills rendered by others. Finally, as the planter's personal agent, the factor received and forwarded goods to their destination. The problems connected with plantation supply provided an additional source of friction.

High prices drew their share of criticism. In December 1834, an Alabama planter complained of an excessive charge for supplies. This was denied by his Mobile factor who demanded a retraction in order to protect his standing.[30] Controversy often resulted from the leeway allowed the factor in the selection of goods. In filling a Carolinian's order for three sacks of ground salt, a Petersburg house bought from another firm at $2.75, instead of drawing from stock at $2.50. Though the factors explained that superior quality and quantity really made the salt cheaper than their own, the substitution was not acceptable, and the 25 cents in question was refunded.[31]

A notable trend in the period from 1800 to 1860 was the shift from cash to credit sales. Planters who were "under advance" from their factors often found this accommodation a mixed blessing which brought with it the inconvenience of credit prices. For example, a New Orleans factor's "bill of sundries" furnished to a Mississippi planter under date of May 24, 1828, carried the additional statement "Due in cash on 24th Sept. next. after which I shall charge you at the rate of 10 PCent Interest until this amount is paid." [32] A later writer observed that debtors were being forced to pay 20 cents per pound for bacon, when the cash price was but 12. With the average credit about four months, interest thus accumulated at the rate of nearly 200 per cent per annum.[33]

The most significant feature of commissions and other expenses was the factor's adherence to accepted standards. Southern chambers of commerce regulated such fees in the major ports. Yet there were violations of these "tariffs of charges." Some factors charged more than 2½ per cent for purchasing; some assessed commissions at times and at other times omitted them; and a number required no commissions at all. The journal of a Savannah house shows that not only did it invariably levy this fee but in their case, it was seldom less than three per cent.[34] Such proceed-

[30] Davis, *Cotton Kingdom,* 148.
[31] A. & P. Hamilton & Kevan to Duncan Cameron, Petersburg, August 1, 1829, Cameron Papers.
[32] Maunsel White & Company Invoice, New Orleans, May 24, 1858, Zachariah Walker Papers, Mississippi Department of Archives and History.
[33] D. A. Tompkins, "Money in Cotton Growing," *Southern States,* [n.v., n.p.] (July, 1897), cited in Norman Sidney Buck, *The Development of the Organisation of Anglo-American Trade 1800–1850* (New Haven, 1925), 70.
[34] Tison & Gordon Journal, July and September, 1856, 1857, and 1859, Gordon & Company Papers, Baker Library, Harvard Graduate School of Business Administration, Boston.

ings suggest that, depending upon the circumstances, it might at times have been a matter of how far one could go. Whereas factors as a group spoke piously of "tariffs of charges" and "usages of trade," some individual merchants had little hesitation in departing from the "norm." "Custom," or general mercantile practice, might occasionally mean nothing more than the policy of a particular firm.

Factors also bought cotton on a limited scale, either for others or on their own account. This procedure seems to have been customary at the beginning of the nineteenth century, when the factor was more apt to be a jack-of-all-trades than a specialist, and often purchased the planter's entire crop for resale or consignment elsewhere.[35] As the cotton traffic grew increasingly intricate, contemporary opinion became more and more opposed to a factor or commission merchant acting as both buyer and seller of cotton. In this business, where a respectable fortune could conceivably be made by a few timely or lucky maneuvers, factors must have found it hard to withstand the temptation to plunge. Probably most factors were conservative in this respect, and with good reason: not only were they concerned with their standing in the mercantile community, but news of speculation and other untoward practices eventually reached their customers. Some planters were not above speculation, but they did not condone such tactics in their agents. Nevertheless, some cotton transactions were purely for speculative ends. According to testimony in a South Carolina court case of the 'twenties, factors of every description often sold for themselves, and "selling rice and cotton it is often that they are the planters, and may be speculators in the produce too." [36] A contributor to *Farmer and Planter* sounded a warning in 1858:

> As it is strongly suspected that many cotton factors are also cotton *Speculators,* having interests directly opposed to the interests of the planters and interior shippers, it behooves the latter to scan with a suspicious eye, the singular and improbable statements and estimates of the supply of cotton, put forth by the former.[37]

When a Charleston merchant declared that no factor could sell and at the same time buy cotton because the two functions militated against each other, he was merely voicing the opinion of the majority of producers.[38]

---

[35] Almy & Brown to Wheeler & Warren, Providence, May 5 [n.d.], to Adams & Lathrop, Providence, February 28, 1803, and to Ogie & Maxwell, Providence, November 16, 1804, Almy & Brown Papers, Rhode Island Historical Society, Providence; Hary Grant to Pierce Butler, Charleston, March 31, 1796, Pierce Butler Papers, Southern Estates, Pennsylvania Historical Society, Philadelphia.
[36] *Davenport v. Riley,* McCord, *South Carolina Law Reports,* 2:200 (1822).
[37] Quoted in Gray, *Agriculture in the Southern United States,* 2:711.
[38] Frederic W. Sollee to Richard Singleton, Charleston, December 4, 1824, Singleton Papers. An outstanding exception was James Adger of Charleston, apparently both factor and cotton buyer, as well as agent for Brown Brothers & Company. See *H. W. Conner & Co. v. Robinson,* Hill, *South Carolina Law Reports,* 2:360 (1834), and John Crosby Brown, *A Hundred Years of Merchant Banking: A History of Brown*

Despite the essential nature of the factor's services as banker and personal agent for the planter, these services frequently caused much bickering. Though dishonesty was occasional on both sides, there were more fundamental differences. With the planter it was the "vicious cycle" of indebtedness, and the burden of interest and other charges; with the factor it was the liquidation of old accounts, the misappropriation of loans, and the loss from overadvances.

The character of the cotton trade and the methods of transaction lent themselves to chicanery. The factorage business, with its relatively small initial capital investment, its constantly fluctuating personnel, its keen competition, and its expansion to inland trade areas, gave ample opportunity for unscrupulous individuals. Cotton planters and cotton factors were not always a select group.[39] At times, too, policies followed by some factors demonstrated that there was a very thin line between honesty, expediency, and bad faith.[40] Not a few producers would have accepted at face value the pointed jocularity of a Louisianan newly embarked in the factorage and commission business—"depend on it we are Smart fellows—& very honest—for Merchants." [41]

Nor were planters above reproach. A Charleston concern, furnishing a client with 800 dollars for a trip to the springs, was astonished to find him apparently requesting a duplicate advance. It developed that the forgery had been attempted by a man who had once before swindled the factors.[42] And a Kentuckian, posing as a wealthy planter with a large cotton crop to market, utilized a forged letter from a New Orleans factorage house to mulct Brown Brothers & Company out of a considerable sum.[43]

The system of advances, which had prevailed since colonial times, was a major source of controversy. Long before the Revolution, southern planters had fallen into chronic indebtedness, and the habit continued with the rise of the Cotton Kingdom. "A disposition to contract debts is one of the vices of the Carolinians," declared an early nineteenth century historian. "When crops are anticipated by engagements founded on them

---

Brothers & Company, Brown, Shipley & Company, and the Allied Firms (New York, 1909), 256, 262–64.

[39] One New Orleans factor was described privately as "a great scoundrel," who rendered false accounting of cotton proceeds. Journal of Thomas F. Pleasants, New Orleans, June 25, 1815, Pennsylvania Historical Society.

[40] For example, a partner in a Charleston firm was accused of undervaluing a debtor's property and thus favoring the latter's brother over several planter creditors. See William Law to Robinson & Caldwell, Darlington, November 23, 1841, and Deposition of Creditors of James Law, Sumter District, South Carolina, January [n.d.], 1842, William Law Papers.

[41] James Sterrett to Nathaniel Evans, New Orleans, December 5, 1805, Evans (J.N. and family) Papers, Department of Archives, Louisiana State University.

[42] A. H. Boykin to Robinson & Caldwell, Warm Springs [Georgia], August 2, 1837, and Robinson & Caldwell to Boykin, Charleston, August 2 and October 9, 1837, Boykin Papers, Duke University Library.

[43] Beginning with the letter from "H. S. Hill" to Maunsel White, the correspondence in regard to this episode is quoted at some length in Brown, A Hundred Years of Merchant Banking, 206–07, and note 1, passim.

before they are made, ruin is often the consequence, and much oftener since the Revolution than before." [44] A half-century later, it was charged that factors were advancing money as required during the summer, thus carrying over engagements into the cotton season—an arrangement beneficial to one side only, according to the writer, since it placed planters under obligation to continue their business in the hands of the factors.[45]

From the planter's standpoint, one particularly objectionable feature of the system was its tendency to give the factor a measure of control over the cotton crop. Despite all that has been written about southern credit based on word of honor and little else, the factor was a business man; and sound business dictated that a liberal credit policy rest on security wherever possible. Many factors were loath to extend loans on the casual basis of a conversation, an "understanding," or even a letter, and imposed conditions of all kinds. Some expected to receive a planter's crop in time to meet his drafts at maturity; others premised the acceptance of any drafts upon the receipt of the crop or the producer's valuation of the cotton to be shipped. A few declined such services during the inactive season of the year.[46] Some refused to advance unless they were allowed to sell at their own discretion; others expected the proceeds of the sale to cover the advance; and a smaller number withheld any accommodations unless the whole crop were shipped to them.[47] By the latter restriction, a sample lot of 100 bales went in its entirety to the factor, although the debt may have been equivalent in value to only 50 bales. A Florida planter's mortgage reads: "I promise and agree to ship and consign at my own risk . . . the whole of my said cotton crop that I grow during the said year." [48] Historians have long stressed the heavy burden imposed by the penalty commission, which bound the planter to cultivate so many acres of cotton, and to forfeit a certain sum per bale for each bale by which the crop fell short of the stipulated amount. It is likely, however, that this practice was more prevalent after 1865. If the penalty commission had been employed on an extensive scale, one might expect it to be the subject of litigation in southern supreme courts, as were most of the difficulties between planter and factor.[49]

[44] David Ramsay, *The History of South Carolina, from its first Settlement in 1670, to the Year 1808* (2 vols., Charleston, 1809), 2:222, 224.
[45] *DeBow's Review*, 25:714 (December, 1858).
[46] Flower & Faulkner to John M. Pintard, New Orleans, August 26, 1809, Pintard Papers, Department of Archives, Louisiana State University.
[47] For examples of such qualifications, see *Hancock v. Tanner & Evans*, Stewart & Porter, *Alabama Reports*, 4:264 (1833); *Powell v. Aiken & Gwinn, et al.*, *Louisiana Reports*, 18:330 (1841); E. L. Andrew & Company to Samuel Pickens, Mobile, October 26, 1841, Samuel Pickens Papers; M. P. Holloway & Company to James Sheppard, Grand Gulf [Mississippi], November 16, 1846, James Sheppard Papers.
[48] Kathryn Abbey, ed., "Documents relating to El Destino and Chemonie Plantations, Middle Florida, 1826–1868," *Florida Historical Society Quarterly*, 7:192 (January and April, 1929).
[49] Cf. Clement Eaton, *The Old South* (New York, 1949), 399, citing A. H. Stone, "The Cotton Factorage System of the Southern States," *American Historical Review*, 20: 557–65 (April, 1915), and Weymouth T. Jordan, *Hugh Davis and His Alabama*

Equally controversial were the "customary" fees—charges for interest and commissions for advancing, negotiating, and carrying over unpaid accounts. It is not enough to say that commissions were fixed by law or standardized by locale at from two and one half to five per cent. An observer noted with a considerable degree of truth that "he lends the planter money, on which he gets interest you may be sure; sometimes what the law 'allows,' and sometimes 'what money will bring.' "[50] Factors often circumvented legal restriction by written contracts which authorized excessive interest rates and commissions.[51] At times these fees were highly complex in their ramifications. A South Carolina plaintiff alleged that commissions had been charged upon each item in the account, upon the factor's balance, and three times upon the principal. Not only had interest been deducted on each bill from the day of purchase rather than the day of payment, but interest had itself accumulated interest.[52] When factors' accounts were vague as to the use of funds, it was sometimes difficult for customers to grasp financial technicalities. Sometimes it was a matter of open discrimination. A Charleston house adopted a temporary policy of subtracting interest in its own favor, while refusing the same privilege when a balance was due the planter. "The money is of no use to us, as it is Subject to *Call* at any moment," argued one of the partners. "You ought not to be surprized if you loose some of your customers," replied a kinsman.[53]

Much depended upon the alertness of the planter. Few were as vigilant as the Alabamian who checked all accounts and noted characteristically on one, "This Act [account] paid but not rected. To be taken to Mobile when I go." [54] Of a different stamp was the Louisianan who said that he was satisfied with the usual "reservation of errors" and had "no curiosity to look into it, until a final settlement." [55] In quite another category were those who detected discrepancies but failed to register protests. Such failure was generally tantamount to accepting the statement as correct.[56] Considering the laxity of planters in general, it might well

Plantation (University, Ala., 1948), Chs. 6–7. But Stone was discussing the system as it existed in both the Old and the New South and did not say definitely that the penalty commission was employed in the former; nor did Jordan refer specifically to the practice. There appears to be little information on this particular subject, either in plantation records or in state supreme court decisions.

50 "Cotton Factors and Commission Merchants," 677.

51 *Barret v. Chaler, Syndic, Louisiana Annual Reports,* 2:874–76 (1847); *Thompson v. Milne, ibid.,* 4:210 (1849).

52 *Walters & Walker v. McGirt, Meekins & Son,* Richardson, *South Carolina Law Reports,* 8:288–90 (1855).

53 J. K. Robinson to James M. Nelson, Charleston, January 15, 1851, and Nelson to Robinson, Cuddoe [South Carolina], January 24, 1851, James M. Nelson Papers, Duke University Library.

54 See James A. Tait's comment on Norris & Boykin Account Current, Mobile, December 17, 1839, Charles and James A. Tait Papers, Alabama Department of Archives and History.

55 *Dunbar et al. v. Bullard, Louisiana Annual Reports,* 2:812 (1847).

56 *Freeman v. Howell, ibid.,* 4:197–98 (1849); *Boyce v. Smith,* Dudley, *South Carolina Law Reports,* 248–49 (1838).

be assumed that many travesties committed in the name of "usages of trade" or "clerical errors" went unnoticed or unchallenged. The system had its possibilities for the arbitrary use of funds.

Such devices for control, together with credit prices, tended to mire the planter in a debtor-creditor relationship. With all its exactions, this routine was continued despite the warnings of such reformers as M. W. Philips of Mississippi: "Draw bills! This bill business is the very thing that ruins us. *Keep out of debt and control your cotton.*" [57] Even after 1865 former planters complained of "long years of bondage" in which Charleston factors held sea-island growers.[58]

It was commonplace to speak of "years of bondage," of "endless shackles of debt," and of "planters harnessed to the factor's plow." But the system of advances did not favor one side exclusively. If many planters found it well-nigh impossible to escape indebtedness, creditors had their own problems. The papers of William Bostwick, a Connecticut Yankee in Augusta, reveal the difficulties factors encountered in the collection of debts. After some years as a warehouse and commission merchant, Bostwick shifted in the early 'thirties to groceries and dry-goods, and spent almost two decades in this trade, while cajoling, threatening, and suing planters. Even after his departure in the late 'forties, there remained many outstanding accounts.[59] A Mobile factor, in advance to a client, finally sent his clerk upstate to obtain cotton, money, or negotiable paper.[60] And in the midst of financial issues created by the formation of the Confederacy, an old New Orleans factor, who was reputed to have made and lost a fortune, commented cynically: "Extend credit indeed to the Planters; who Knows them better than I do. & who has Suffered more. . . . they would swamp any Government on Earth & themselves along with it." [61] When a planter owed several creditors, the problem was infinitely more complex. Here the factor had to consider prior liens—"debts of superior dignity."

No less irritating were difficulties attending overadvances, the misuse of borrowed funds, and breaches of contract. In large part, the factor's dilemma stemmed from the peculiarities of the southern system, an economy of a colonial type: the presence of a planter class, with its demand for agricultural credit on an extensive basis, and the reliance upon paper rather than specie—upon bills of exchange, notes, orders, receipts, or drafts. Far from being self-sufficient, the factor himself depended almost entirely upon the credit system. His strength often lay not so much

[57] *DeBow's Review*, 7:411 (November, 1849).
[58] Guion Griffis Johnson, *A Social History of the Sea Islands, with Special Reference to St. Helena Island, South Carolina* (Chapel Hill, 1930), 70.
[59] Bostwick to George Scott, Augusta, May 29, 1834; to Charles A. Read, Augusta, March 3, 1838; to James A. Merriwether, Augusta, October 22, 1842; and to T. P. Pease, New Haven, March 25, 1847, William Bostwick Papers, Yale University Library.
[60] *Kirksey, et al. v. Bates, Alabama Reports*, 1:304–05 (1840).
[61] Maunsel White to J. D. B. DeBow, Deer Range [Louisiana], November 9, 1861, J. D. B. DeBow Papers, Duke University Library.

in his own means as in his *access* to various sources of capital. The financial state of many houses was somewhat nebulous, with a comparatively small investment in capital, a large backlog of acceptances, and no little stake in optimism. In 1826 the low price of cotton had occasioned a great many overdrafts, and a New Orleans commission merchant resolved on a radical change of policy: for "in the way we have gone on we were a perfect convenience to all the country & at the end of the season we have not a Dollar left." [62] He spoke with palpable exaggeration; nevertheless, it is surprising how often factors were hard-pressed to raise even a small sum of money. The factor had his time of troubles, a critical period in which he was under the necessity of meeting the planter's bills at maturity and frequently lacked the funds or produce to do so. Small wonder that he sometimes despaired of the future, when debtor prodigality could elicit such commentaries as the following, distorted though it is:

> The long credit which merchants and traders . . . are obliged to give the planters, is the subject of universal complaint among the former; and whatever credit the Carolinians may deserve for their "unaffected hospitality, affability, ease of manners, and address" . . . yet the payment of their debts can never be reckoned among their virtues. . . . When they receive money in advance, for their crops of cotton or rice, it is immediately squandered away in the luxuries of fashion, good eating and drinking, or an excursion to the northern states, where, after dashing about for a month or two with *tandems, curricles, livery servants,* and *outriders,* they frequently return home in the *stage coach,* with scarcely dollars enough in their pocket to pay their expenses on the road.[63]

It was particularly galling to advance money or accept drafts and then fail ro receive the expected consignment of produce. Planters solicited loans and later shipped their crops wholly or in part to other merchants.[64] There were numerous instances where the factor financed the planter in anticipation of consignment, only to find that the returns were not sufficient to cover the loan.[65] Seldom were producers as conservative as the Georgian who contracted with his factors to advance nine cents per pound on the crop prior to sale, but declared that he expected no more than the value of the cotton, *"as he wanted no anteing back on him."* [66] The court records indicate that factors often found it necessary to "ante-back" because of overadvances. Literally thousands of these credits were based on a mere "understanding" or conversation. Such mu-

[62] Wilkins & Linton to Josiah Stoddard Johnston, New Orleans, June 13, 1826, Josiah Stoddard Johnston Papers, Pennsylvania Historical Society.
[63] John Lambert, *Travels through Lower Canada, and the United States of North America, in the Years, 1806, 1807, and 1808* (3 vols., London, 1810), 2:381–82.
[64] *Lyons v. Lallande, Louisiana Annual Reports,* 9:601–02 (1854).
[65] *Jones v. Somerville,* Porter, *Alabama Reports,* 1:437–38 (1835); *Jernigan, Lawrence & Company v. Wimberly, Georgia Reports,* 1:220–21 (1846); *Fleming v. Hammond, ibid.,* 19:146 (1855).
[66] *Hardeman & Hamilton v. Ford, Georgia Reports,* 12:206 (1852).

tual confidence was highly laudable but not always prudent; in the absence of written agreement, it was difficult to prove the existence of a contract—a frequent avenue of escape for delinquent debtors. Though well-nigh indispensable to the plantation, this complex system of agricultural credit had its shortcomings.

Friction between planter and factor revolved chiefly about marketing, supplying, and banking, but other practices provoked mutual distrust. Planters who were themselves careless refused to tolerate these qualities in their factors. Absentee planters were one thing; a factor off the job was something else again. One Virginian wrote skeptically of a Petersburg commission merchant: "I understand Bowe is still in Richmond. I do not understand what he is at there. I don't think it looks well for him to be absent at this busy season from his Business." [67] Negligence in forwarding accounts or answering correspondence generally brought strong reaction and might result in a change of factors.[68] Less frequently it was sheer incompetence. A Louisianan who had moved to the North and left his affairs in the hands of a local firm was incensed by the lack of cooperation—no sales accounts, no rent returns, and belongings either unshipped or lost. "Although I have repeatedly written on urgent business none of my communications have been answered." Planters should exercise discretion in trusting the management of their property to such negligent people. "The man is lazy and does not possess one grain of common gratitude." [69] Upon occasion a few skeptics came to question the ability of factors in general.

The factor had other grounds for dissatisfaction. Writers of the past and present have emphasized the fundamental nature of the services rendered by factor to planter. Yet the assistance of planter to factor was also highly significant. It is well to remember that this relationship involved in many cases a mutual exchange of favors in the form of loans, endorsements or guarantees, negotiable notes, and in general, a reciprocal use of credit. When a New Orleans factor expressed his appreciation for a token of confidence, "coming as it does . . . from a native Country Man—whose good Standing, in the planting Community & even *Kind* feelings toward me—*without any patronage*—would be of importance to my character & Stand before the Community," [70] he was merely observing that the support of prominent planters might well mean the difference between success and failure. Lack of such support or the withdrawal of credit facilities could bring disaster. Thus the reaction of a factor when a planter relative failed to furnish the blank signatures deemed necessary for the transaction of certain business: "Is it from want of con-

[67] Jos. M. Sheppard to James Sheppard, Glencairn, Hanover County, [Virginia], November 21, 1840, James Sheppard Papers.

[68] Simon Magwood to Frances Butler, Charleston, December 12, 1826, Pierce Butler Papers.

[69] O. H. Spencer to Nathaniel Evans, E[lizabeth] Town, [New Jersey], April 16, 1817, Evans Papers.

[70] N. Scudder to St. John R. Liddell, New Orleans, March 26, 1856, Liddell Papers.

fidence [or] are you afraid to trust such documents in my hands?" [71]

Of course, it was irritating enough for a patron to change factors without explanation. Still more harmful was the effect of "talk" among planters—of facts or rumors regarding incompetency, insolvency, speculation, or dishonesty. The incidence of such unfavorable publicity is shown by a pathetic plea from a Mobile factor:

> I have been striving to get through with all my immediate liabilities or in fact all but my bank dbts this season and find that I have a sufficiency of means which can be relied on during this spring to do it. . . . I could have worked through without any discredit, had not Genl [John] Pickens become so much enraged and spoke freely of it to different individuals who have spoken I presume of it here, I learned yesterday he was on his way here determined to have his money and I am now looking for him. I recd. a very severe letter from him on Sunday. . . . I hoped you would prevent the Genl. from saying anything as it would only be calculated to injure me, and not benefit him, but make my chances of paying my debts even worse. . . . you know the family I have to support, they are dependant on my exertions, and I hope I will not be charged with dishonesty. I will never defraud any one out of a dollar. . . .[72]

The result was to threaten the factor's standing among his planter customers or perhaps to cause a "run on the bank." Likewise, it injured the merchant's reputation in the city and might well affect his credit facilities at home and elsewhere. It is only natural that factors thus victimized went to great lengths to clear away the clouds of suspicion.[73]

Controversies involving individuals were sometimes accompanied by a diversity in viewpoint between planters and factors in general, a difference in outlook which may have reflected something of the historic distrust between producer and middleman. Often members of the one group tended to "see eye-to-eye" against the other. In this respect the planter's irritation from specific grievances may have influenced, and in turn been influenced by stereotypes. What manner of man was this factor? A cock-of-the-walk, if one can credit an Englishman's picture of New Orleans cotton merchants who "wore striped jackets, cocked their hats on one side with an air of defiance, and swung a sword stick between their extended legs." [74] An outlander, said others; often a veritable bird of passage, who lived in the South only during the cotton season. Was it true that New Englanders had by 1820 monopolized the Charleston fac-

---

[71] Will. Flower to Chas. L. Mathews, New Orleans, October 27, 1849, Mathews (Charles L., and family) Papers, Department of Archives, Louisiana State University.

[72] J. Simpson to Samuel Pickens, Mobile, April 13, 1842, Samuel Pickens Papers.

[73] Byrne, Vance & Company to James Sheppard, New Orleans, February [28], 1847 James Sheppard Papers; *Donnell v. Jones, et al., Alabama Reports*, 13:490–99 (1848); Davis, *Cotton Kingdom*, 148.

[74] J. E. Alexander, *Transatlantic Sketches, Comprising Visits to the Most Interesting Scenes in North and South America, and the West Indies* (2 vols., London, 1833), 2:16–17.

torage business—Yankees who, having replaced the "native merchants, enlightened, wealthy, and influential," now remained aloof, contented with their large fortunes? [75] D. R. Hundley pointed an accusing finger at commission merchants who were outwardly respectable, yet willing to finance the slavetrader, and thereby enjoy a snug portion of the latter's proceeds without partaking of his social stigma.[76] Birds of a like feather were "Kit Swindler and Co.," a hypothetical New Orleans house described by Lewis Atherton in *The Southern Country Store*.[77] Or was the factor in reality a conservative businessman, trusted friend and servant, loyal to the planter and southern interests? In the light of these and other descriptions, factors were a highly contradictory group. Indeed, such stereotypes represent departures from strict truth. Yet the changing opinions of contemporaries are sometimes more significant than the actuality.

Contributing to the planter's state of mind was his ignorance of the city. If by chance he held the landed aristocrat's legendary contempt for the "vulgar pursuit of trade," if he were comparatively isolated and knew relatively little about city ways in general and city cotton transactions in particular, if times were bad and cotton prices low, and above all, if his individual relationship with the commission merchant had been an unhappy one, then the planter might listen with a receptive ear to stories about citified factors, sophisticated men of Big Business. He might readily believe rumors about "syndicates" or "combinations" which threatened the freedom of navigation on the Alabama River.[78] His misgivings about the factor's specialized knowledge of the cotton trade—a field in which some planters had little more than vague notions—might give color to tales of designing middlemen leagued together to defraud the producer by means of drawbacks and other devices. Perhaps personal experience in court cases tried outside his own county or parish led him further to distrust the seaports, where mercantile influence and prestige were greater.[79] In short, even the rural South experienced something of the traditional antipathy between city and country.

At any rate, planters chafed at "systematic oppression." They believed themselves the victims of duplicity: the factor was extending the right hand of friendship, while rifling the planter's pocket with the left. In the light of available evidence, one may wonder whether some of these allegations were well-founded. There was inaccurate crop informa-

[75] Harriette Kershaw Leiding, *Charleston: Historic and Romantic* (Philadelphia, 1931), 202; E. S. Thomas, *Reminiscences of the Last Sixty-Five Years, Commencing with the Battle of Lexington* (2 vols., Hartford, 1840), 1:34, 40–41; 2:226.

[76] D. R. Hundley, *Social Relations in Our Southern States* (New York, 1860), 145–46.

[77] Opelousas *Courier*, May 13, 1854, cited in Atherton, *The Southern Country Store*, 32.

[78] Minnie Clare Boyd, *Alabama in the Fifties: A Social Study* (New York, 1931), 94–95.

[79] Robert M. Davis, *The Southern Planter, the Factor and the Banker* (New Orleans, 1871), 4.

tion, whether accidental or deliberate. Fraudulent selling was notorious. Some factors were also purchasers of cotton and hence tended toward a double standard of values. Not only was the producer saddled with various forms of open exaction; usury and more subtle practices such as average accounts, clothed in the guise of "custom," were by no means uncommon. Nevertheless, the relationship between factor and planter, considered in its entirety, suggests that these complaints were of comparatively little significance.

Factors as a group were hostile to innovation, particularly when reduced fees were contemplated. In 1855 a New Orleans factor announced the negotiation of a contract with a local cotton press: in the future, the cost of drayage, storage, and labor would be only one dollar instead of the usual four.[80] Whether this arrangement was successful is not disclosed. In one sense, it increased the risk to the producer, since the factor tended to become less responsible; seen from the mercantile standpoint, its directness implied the elimination of lucrative middleman's fees. After Georgia planters criticized the two and one half per cent sales commission charged by Savannah factors, a correspondent of the *Daily Morning News* pointed out that this increase was due largely to the extension of railroads. And who had benefited most from such developments? The planters of the state. "Then we say why not live and let live?"[81] When a Savannah firm announced its intention of handling cotton at 50 cents, a critic expressed his fear that the success of this experiment might result in forced retirement for the city's cotton sellers, thus deprived of their sole means of support.[82] Such attempts at uniformity in Savannah must have seemed the more incongruous to Georgia and South Carolina growers, when fees in Charleston ranged from two and one half per cent or even less on the bale, and at least one Augusta firm advertised at 25 cents.[83] The trade was basically conservative and such schemes met with sharp disapproval.

On the other hand, factors sometimes attributed to calculated intent certain moves on the part of planters. In general the ante-bellum commercial conventions reserved for the factor a place within the southern framework; broadly speaking, they called for the cooperation of planters and factors.[84] Yet during a convention of the 'fifties, an orator could speak disparagingly of past meetings "designed to circumvent the commission merchant of New Orleans. . . . Every planter who had a dozen

[80] N. Scudder to St. John R. Liddell, New Orleans, November 10, 1855, Liddell Papers.

[81] Savannah *Daily Morning News*, June 3, 1857.

[82] Savannah *Republican*, [n.d.], quoted in Savannah *Daily Morning News*, August 1, 1857.

[83] *Dulin v. Caldwell & Company*, Georgia Reports, 29:364 (1859); John P. Campbell, comp., *The Southern Business Directory and General Commercial Advertiser* (Charleston, 1854), 293.

[84] Herbert Wender, *Southern Commercial Conventions, 1837–1859* (Baltimore, 1930), 10–11, *passim*; William Watson Davis, "Ante-bellum Southern Commercial Conventions," Alabama Historical Society, *Transactions*, 5:153, 157, *passim* (1904).

negroes wanted a railroad running by his house and another by his kitchen." [85] Though such sentiments may reflect nothing more than city or regional rivalry, the theme of these gatherings—commercial autonomy of the South, with the elimination of middlemen through direct trade with Europe—suggests that the history of ante-bellum commercial conventions, with their lack of positive accomplishment, may warrant further investigation.

But producers took even more decided action. In the late 'thirties planter resentment against Mobile factors reached so high a pitch that the Alabama legislative session of 1837 was the scene of acrimonious debate following the introduction of a bill to remedy alleged abuses in the sale of cotton. Although the measure, which provided for the establishment of a state marketing agency, was passed after a heated debate, action did not progress beyond the planning stage.[86] A local crop-reporting agency functioned for a time in Marengo County, Alabama.[87] In 1858 a Cotton Planters' Association met at Macon, Georgia, and appointed an agent for receiving, selling, and shipping cotton for Savannah and Charleston. The group expressed its desire that "planters shipping their cotton to either of the above markets will prefer their appointed agent." [88] Such experiments in producer control were interrupted by the Civil War.

Without considering its effects on the South at large, the burden of the factorage system fell unevenly upon the planter class. Business policy was influenced by many considerations. In some cases, factors were under obligation to their principals. Through individual arrangements or for purely personal reasons, they often refrained from charging commissions on unpaid accounts, assessing interest, or collecting other fees. There were additional reasons why growers did not remain in the same state of dependence upon the factor. In contrast to the colonial period with its predominantly English market, the staple producer of ante-bellum times lived relatively nearer the shipping-point; not infrequently, though location was but one of many considerations, his degree of autonomy varied in proportion to his distance from the seacoast. Planters strategically situated might expect to keep abreast of the market, withhold shipment of their cotton (depending upon transportation costs) for favorable prices, and purchase their own provisions in town. Moreover, larger or more solvent planters, though they were apt to be at the mercy of the carriers, were perhaps less under the control of commission mer-

[85] Speech reported in DeBow's Review, 19:625 (May, 1855), and quoted in Davis, "Ante-bellum Southern Commercial Conventions," 181. For additional reference to friction between planter and merchant, though in regard to cotton planters' conventions, rather than commercial gatherings, see Weymouth T. Jordan, "Cotton Planters' Conventions in the Old South," Journal of Southern History, 19:322, passim (August, 1953).
[86] William Garrett, Reminiscences of Public Men in Alabama, for Thirty Years (Atlanta, 1872), 44–47.
[87] Gray, Agriculture in the Southern United States, 2:720.
[88] DeBow's Review, 25:217 (August, 1858).

chants. Some maintained their own transportation, obtained supplies elsewhere if they so desired, traded with several factors simultaneously, and shifted agents almost at will.[89] Whether factors discriminated against the smaller planter is a proposition exceedingly difficult of proof.

Regardless of individual relationships, planters in general chose largely, if by no means exclusively, to patronize the coast factor rather than the home merchant. That the choice was a wise one is open to question. Room for doubt lies not so much in the familiar sense of "shop at home and save," though seaport rates for supplies were not always lower or cotton prices higher. Rather, the crux of the situation seems to have been the planter's greater familiarity with things local. Given the dearth of evidence at hand, one can do no more than speculate that the city factor's gain at the producer's expense came above all in some of the highly technical and less well-known facets of this relationship: in money matters, particularly as regards exchange, with which some planters were familiar but few expert; in certain aspects of the trade with which the producer was not directly connected, especially transactions with cotton press operators, brokers, buyers, and other middlemen; and in the vagaries of double-entry bookkeeping, as expressed in "customary" fees, in "clerical errors," or in various hidden charges. That planters would have enjoyed more convenient arrangements with local merchants is problematical; at any rate, they would have been more likely to understand the local merchandising process. In the long run, the returns to the planter himself and to his own community might have been greater if his capital had circulated largely at home.[90]

To say that the information now available on the factorage system comes mainly from plantation records is to imply that the association between planter and factor has been seen primarily from the producer's viewpoint. This is not strictly true. Nevertheless, the balance has favored the producer, and anything resembling a definitive judgment must necessarily await more detailed studies of commission merchants and their operations.

A comparative lack of information does not obviate the broad conclusion that neither side realized a very definite advantage. If indeed this were a "contest," it was in the larger sense a contest without a victory. A factor once wrote concerning a dispute over damaged cotton, "Who do you blame? the pickery, the boat, or ourselves?" [91] Were he a philosopher or had he enjoyed the advantage of historical hindsight, he might

[89] Hary Grant to Pierce Butler, Charleston, March 31, 1796, W. Mein to Butler, Savannah, March 15, 1803, and factors' correspondence at random, Pierce Butler Papers; similar correspondence in Singleton Papers; and Ralph B. Flanders, "Farish Carter, a Forgotten Man of the Old South," *Georgia Historical Quarterly*, 15:148 (June, 1931).

[90] For discussion of the influence of the factorage system on southern economy, see Atherton, *Southern Country Store*, Ch. 2, and Stone, "The Cotton Factorage System of the Southern States," 557–65.

[91] Maunsel White & Company to Mrs. Mary Coffee, New Orleans, April 23, 1841, John Coffee Papers.

better have advised his correspondent to blame it on the system. There was something enervating about the ante-bellum factorage process, bulwarked by tradition and unfriendly to innovation. To say the least, it was expensive for both producer and middleman; its often loose and informal basis of credit made it doubly dangerous; and its colonial foundations rendered all the more difficult a major break in the cake of custom.

Even with its many drawbacks, would a new system or even a major change in the old have been really satisfactory? Suppose direct trade with Europe had been established. Would the producer have found the Liverpool market less mysterious than the transactions in New Orleans? Just how long would a planters' association have continued to depend upon a single agent for Charleston and Savannah? Considering the prevailing attitude toward governmental paternalism, how feasible was a state marketing agency? In the minds of many southerners such proposals for control, either through voluntary restriction or by law, had their limitations. Ideas of this kind were too far ahead of their time; they were overridden by a routine of two centuries' standing and by the incentive for individual gain. Intent on the production of a cash crop and basically hostile to regulation of any kind, most planters paid little more than lip service to these suggestions. They were alternately enthusiastic and lukewarm as their personal interests were affected. Their complaints varied with times of prosperity and depression, rising in the wake of the panics of 1837 and 1857. Among them there was too much individualism and too little unity of effort.

Indeed, a much sounder brief can be made for harmony than for discord between ante-bellum planter and factor. For all their carping and complaining, for all their differences great and small, it is doubtful whether the one could have dispensed with the other. In 1793 the suit of a South Carolina planter against a Charleston factor was tried before a jury composed equally of planters and merchants. The former stood unanimously for the plaintiff, the latter for the defendant. Since neither side would yield, the case was dissolved by mutual consent.[92] The decision was perhaps symbolic of the relationship between planter and factor in the Old South. Perhaps each really hoped, and sincerely tried, to attend carefully and closely to his own interest and in some way exert a balance, to their mutual benefit. Let change come with the passing of time.

[92] *Executors of Godfrey v. Forrest*, Bay, *South Carolina Law Reports*, 1:300–01 (1793).

THE PIONEER MERCHANT
IN MID-AMERICA   *Lewis E. Atherton*

The western merchant found it necessary to engage in the produce trade for two reasons: first, as a means of increasing sales to western farmers, and second, as a means of making payments for goods purchased in the East. In a real sense the western storekeeper was an integral part of the three cornered trade relationship that characterized American economic life before the Civil War. During that period the South alone produced cash crops suitable for export in large quantities, and these were handled by eastern merchants and commission men, who also supplied the South with merchandise. The West also relied on the East for merchandise and other manufactured products. Lacking cash crops which would command an immediate sale in European markets, the West made up for the deficiency as much as possible by serving as a source of foodstuffs, mules, and forage for the South. Credits established in the South in this manner could be transferred to eastern merchants to pay for goods purchased there. By taking the farmer's crops in exchange for merchandise the western merchant supplied the farmer with eastern goods, and by sending farm crops to the southern market was able to meet a large part of his bills to the eastward.

Even though this system was beneficial to the West, farmers and merchants alike frequently complained against the flow of cash and credits to the eastward. A citizen of Franklin, Missouri, in 1821 wrote to the editor of his paper, and commented on the hard times and scarcity of cash. He was sure, however, that there was sufficient money in the country, if only it were properly handled. The West exchanged its money for "imported finery and foreign gew-gaws" instead of developing its own factories. The four or five stores in Franklin were pointed out as horrible examples of the prevailing system. Each of these annually remitted $12,000 to $15,000 to the East, exporting cash and leaving the local com-

REPRINTED with permission from Lewis E. Atherton, "The Pioneer Merchant in Mid-America," *The University of Missouri Studies*, Columbia: University of Missouri Press, Vol. XIV, No. 2 (April 1, 1939), pp. 90–102.

munity short of currency. A system of domestic manufacture would end dependence on other sections and keep the money at home.[1]

Several years later, during the hard times in 1837, a merchant wrote to the editor of a St. Louis paper and threatened eastern wholesalers with the loss of the western market if they were too insistent on collecting accounts. He had been aroused by the announcement in a Philadelphia paper that two agents were to be sent west to collect in specie the debts due eastern wholesalers. In the writer's estimation such a course would have been reprehensible at any time, but he considered it downright villainous when the object was to remit the money to England in order to sustain banks there. The East was asked to consider that steamboats now came from New Orleans in seven and eight days. Only habit explained the practice of Cincinnati, St. Louis, Louisville, and Nashville merchants buying second hand in New York and Philadelphia instead of directly in France and England. "Let our wealthy western merchants consider such a possibility." [2] In spite of all the grumbling, however, the West found it necessary to rely on the three cornered relationship with the other sections.

The system of bartering produce for store goods was universal in the West. Merchants realized the necessity of this as a means of making sales, and mercantile account books reveal its importance. Bills very frequently were settled by the farmer bringing in produce to balance the charges against him. Thus James Aull took three barrels of whiskey from Aaron Overton at eleven dollars and thirty-three cents a barrel, and two more at a slightly higher price, the whiskey cancelling Overton's account. Another customer paid in beeswax. A third brought in a supply of tow linen for which he received credit at twenty-five cents a yard. Another account was settled by tallow and country sugar. One farmer paid his bill by hauling goods. Another brought in a load of oak planking. Cutting brush and grinding an axe was the means of settlement for one man who had nothing in the way of produce to offer. Scythe stones were the medium of payment employed by still another.[3]

The same conditions prevailed in Wisconsin. Jared Warner's account book between 1849 and 1859 indicates that few men settled their bills with cash. Moses Hicklin paid in cash, pork and flour; George Engle paid in cash; Benjamin Brown paid in wheat and flour; Sameul Rosencrants paid part of his bill in wheat and gave a note for the remainder; John Bureingame paid by working for Warner, by one coonskin, and by rafting and boating.[4] Warner's accounts exhibited more uniformity than those of many merchants in that he received a large part of his payments in pork and wheat, other storekeepers frequently being paid in a multitude of different ways.

Moses Payne at Columbia, Missouri, received much produce in exchange for goods. In 1830 Cornelius Short brought him a dozen eggs

[1] Franklin, Missouri, *Missouri Intelligencer*, April 23, 1821.
[2] St. Louis, Missouri, *Missouri Argus*, May 26, 1837.
[3] James Aull, *Ledger,* Independence, Missouri, beginning 1827.
[4] Jared Warner, *Ledger 1849–59.*

which were rated at four and a half cents. In return, Short bought a "bonnet and trimmings" at three dollars and seventy-five cents, promising to bring enough bacon to town the next week to settle the account. As bacon was accepted at the rate of four cents a pound by Payne, over ninety pounds were required to pay for the one article purchased.[5] Elisha and Gilbert Read at Chicago pursued the same course, accepting many different items in payment. Abnor Bristol paid his bill of two dollars and twelve cents with cash and a whippletree; Walter Chambers received three dollars and thirty-seven cents credit for chopping thirteen and a half cords of wood, and also applied fifteen and a half bushels of wheat on his bill. Ebenezer Ford chopped forty-two cords of wood and butchered hogs for the Reads. Walter Chambers cut saw logs and did one day's work with his team. Hamilton Dickerson made a pair of pantaloons. Simon Read brought in two hogs; John Jeffry paid in work; John Mack paid with three and a half barrels of cider; and Mr. Perry settled by bringing in two and a half bushels of pease.[6]

Merchants doing this kind of a business obviously accumulated a great deal of produce in a short time. This was often processed before being shipped to the larger cities to pay wholesale bills. Burrows at Davenport, Iowa, bought some goods in St. Louis and New Orleans. These he could pay for directly by sending flour from his mills to the two cities. James Aull at Lexington, Missouri, built up credit in the same manner. In his order for 15,000 pounds of sugar and 10,000 pounds of coffee from James Breedlove and Company at New Orleans in 1833 he explained that he hoped to pay for the whole amount from the proceeds of a shipment of bale rope. Shipments of large quantities of bagging and rope enabled him to meet many such bills without the necessity of transmitting money. Smaller shipments of honey, beeswax, furs, pork, and tobacco were conducive to the same end.

Joseph Hertzog had a lead factory at St. Louis, and the extent to which he relied on shipments from this to cut down on money remittances is evident from a letter to a New York commission house in 1811. The New York firm had a consignment of Hertzog's lead, and he was anxious to have it sold, the deprivation of the money threatening to interrupt his accustomed spring shipments to the western store. It was now March and he had expected to receive $5,000 in money from lead sales by the first of February.[7] James Wier at Lexington, Kentucky, shipped tobacco, cotton, yarn, bagging, and rope to New Orleans and the eastern cities, as his letter books between 1806 and 1824 show. Shipments from his hemp factory were especially large, and frequently were consigned to Philadelphia, New York, and Baltimore commission houses.

This double value to the merchant—increased sales to farmers through the barter system, and the use of farm crops to care for remittances to the East—caused the storekeepers of Mid-America to develop a

[5] J. M. and A. M. Payne, *Day Book 1830–31*.
[6] Elisha and Gilbert Read, *Account Book 1818–59*.
[7] Letter of Joseph Hertzog to David and Philip Gum at New York City, dated Philadelphia, March 30, 1811, *Letters from Joseph Hertzog 1811–15*.

regular system for handling the produce which they accumulated. The value of this to the farming class is indicated by a dispute which developed in Missouri in 1821. Farmers near Franklin, Missouri, became disgusted with the local merchants over their efforts to defeat state banking legislation and for their unwillingness or inability to handle the shipment of farm crops. As the farmers saw it, the merchants were unwilling for them to have either state money or the returns which their crops would bring. These two solutions were the only ones which they saw as a means of getting the funds necessary to purchase the supplies needed by them. And they were right in their analysis, even though they were doing their local merchants an injustice in assuming that they did not want to take farm crops in payment for supplies. William Lamme and R. S. Barr and Company, the largest local merchants, advertised that because of the hard times and lack of cash in the country they would take farm crops and give a receipt for them. They would also advance the cash necessary to put the produce in shape for market, pay the freight, and personally attend to selling the products. The farmers would receive pay in specie as soon as the crops were sold, being charged only the legal rate of interest for any money advanced, and a five per cent commission on the sales made.[8] Ill feeling continued, however, and the farmers decided to form a co-operative enterprise to handle exports.

This resulted in "The Missouri Exporting Company," which had its articles of incorporation ready by October, 1822. The organization was to have a capital stock of $20,000 divided into twenty-dollar shares. One dollar had to be paid in for each share purchased at the time a farmer subscribed, the balance coming due as the directors ordered, although never at a rate greater than four dollars a share every three months. The organization was a democratic farm movement, as evidenced by the provision permitting only one vote, no matter how many shares were owned. Directors were elected at a meeting in Chariton, Missouri, on the first Monday in December, each director being required to own twenty-five shares to be eligible to serve. An experienced mercantile head was to be appointed by the board of directors, no one being eligible to the post who did not own $1,000 worth of stock. Dividends were to be declared once a year. The business was to be limited to "commercial transactions generally"—a rather vague statement of its scope. In exporting crops stockholders were to receive preference over those who were not members, and produce was not to be sold at retail unless the purchaser's note had sufficient endorsers to make it safe.[9]

By December 17, 1822, the company was ready to transact business, one of its officers asking members to turn in a list of the kinds and quantities of produce they would have for export in the spring and summer. Carpenters were requested to submit bids for the construction of flatboats, as the company was expecting to need two or more on the first of each month from March to July.[10] No further notices appeared in the

[8] Franklin, Missouri, *Missouri Intelligencer,* July 16, 1821.
[9] Franklin, Missouri, *Missouri Intelligencer,* October 29, 1822.
[10] Franklin, Missouri, *Missouri Intelligencer,* December 17, 1822.

local papers, and it is probable that no marked success was achieved by the concern. Conditions in Missouri continued to improve during the twenties, serving to lessen farm animosity towards the mercantile class.

The wide range of products accepted in exchange for goods has already been indicated, with different localities doing their largest trade in produce peculiar to their area. Some merchants took farm crops solely because it was the only way they could do business in the community, and for that reason they usually exchanged goods for produce—the farmer needing to look elsewhere for the disposal of a cash crop. In almost every community of any size, however, there was at least one merchant who would buy from the farmer for part cash and part trade. David Lamme needed rags so badly for his new paper mill in Missouri that he advertised for them, offering three cents a pound for linen and cotton rags and one cent a pound for other kinds. Although he owned a store, there was no mention of barter—the operation of the new mill having immediately created a demand.[11]

L. P. Marshall at Franklin, Missouri, owned a large warehouse on the river and was in a favored position for collecting and shipping produce. To increase this business he advertised for hemp, offering half in cash and half in goods.[12] John Adams at Edwardsville, Illinois, in 1832 was offering one dollar in merchandise or eighty-seven and one-half cents in cash for good castor beans. His desire to obtain these caused him to offer goods in advance to responsible people until a crop was harvested.[13] There was no doubt that merchants preferred to pay in goods from their shelves, and used every means to accomplish this. But in many cases opportunities for profit, or immediate need, caused them to lose no time in making cash purchases when produce appeared.

As the quantities collected by individual storekeepers assumed appreciable size by the end of the year, commission firms in larger places competed for the privilege of handling the shipments. New Orleans commission companies often mailed quotations to stores in the Mississippi valley, a list of prices sent to E. D. Sappington at Jonesboro, Missouri, by Renfro, Breedlove, and Richeson of New Orleans in 1825 being typical. The statement contained a full analysis of the probable price range for all crops during the coming season. A detailed discussion of the tobacco market was repeated for bagging and twine, pork, flour, whiskey, lard, and furs. Some attention was devoted to articles like beeswax and ginseng, which seldom were shipped in large quantities. Sales of corn, beef, and pork were reported as being most extensive in the spring, at which time the planters, having realized the proceeds of their own crops, were ready to purchase foodstuffs in quantities. Exchange rates on eastern cities were also included in the report.[14]

Representative shipments of James Aull from his store at Lexington,

11 Columbia, Missouri, *Missouri Intelligencer*, January 11, 1834.
12 Fayette, Missouri, *Missouri Intelligencer*, January 22, 1830.
13 Edwardsville, Illinois, *Illinois Advocate*, June 5, 1832.
14 Circular in *John Sappington Manuscript Collection*.

Missouri, indicate the range and quantity of produce handled by merchants in the smaller towns. April 1, 1828, he shipped 1,058 muskrat, four hundred and ninety-six raccoon, sixteen otter, thirty-two mink, twenty-four wild cat and fox, and sixty deer skins to St. Louis. The next month found Aull shipping an unstated amount of beeswax to a commission firm at Philadelphia, St. Louis houses not offering as much as he thought the shipment was worth. In June he offered to send two hundred raccoon skins to a Franklin store, bearing the expense of hauling the furs to Franklin and waiting until November for his money if the Franklin merchant would pay a shilling a piece for the lot. The same month he shipped two hogsheads of tobacco to New Orleans, consigned to James Breedlove, a member of the firm which sent the circular to Sappington at Jonesboro. A letter to the commission firm of Tracy and Wahrendorff at St. Louis directed them to pay the freight to that place and oversee the transfer of the tobacco to another boat. Early in the autumn he sent nine barrels of beeswax to Franklin by wagon, whence they were shipped by keel-boat to St. Louis. Tracy and Wahrendorff handled the transfers at that city, sending the produce on to Breedlove at New Orleans. There the goods were transferred to a coastal vessel and consigned to Robert Toland in Philadelphia, to be sold and placed to Aull's credit. Aull valued the shipment at three hundred eighteen dollars and twenty cents, hoping to obtain twenty cents a pound by sending the beeswax to the eastern city.

In October he sent a barrel of honey to a Judge Tod, a Franklin firm crediting him with fifteen dollars for the service. On November 5 a wagon was dispatched to St. Louis to bring back a load of merchandise. The driver was to have three thousand pounds of freight for the trip down, and part of this consisted of eight barrels of beeswax, Aull directing Tracy and Wahrendorff to dispose of this lot in St. Louis. In April of 1829 James Breedlove at New Orleans received a shipment of nine barrels of beeswax. May found Aull shipping seventy muskrat and nine otter skins by keel boat to Tracy and Wahrendorff, who were requested to dispose of them in St. Louis.

Before starting East in 1830, Aull dispatched twenty-one barrels of beeswax to St. Louis, Tracy and Wahrendorff being requested to hold the shipment until he reached there. Four packages of the same product were sold in St. Louis the following spring. In April of that year he gave the steamboat *Trenton* a shipment of twelve bales of hemp, one barrel of tallow, and two hogsheads of tobacco. Tracy and Wahrendorff were to load the tallow and beeswax he had sent them earlier in the year, shipping the whole to New Orleans. Sixty-eight barrels and kegs of honey and eight barrels of beeswax from Lexington, and six hundred seventy-three gallons of honey and six barrels of beeswax from Liberty constituted a shipment in November. Tracy and Wahrendorff were directed to insure the beeswax and send it to New Orleans for sale. The honey constituted more of a problem. Aull was afraid it would leak out of the containers, and asked the St. Louis firm to sell as much of it as they could to the small grocers there. The rest could be shipped up the Ohio river, if freight rates were not too high. In 1831 and 1832 Aull sent raccoon, fox, otter, and deerskins to Tracy and Wahrendorff.[15]

The shipments mentioned above resulted partly from direct purchase and partly from barter for goods. The records of other storekeepers in the West vary from it only in the type of article received in the barter process. And taken collectively the records illustrate the way the West solved its problem of marketing crops. The merchant was thus the basic agent in enabling the Mississippi valley region to build up credits in southern and eastern markets to pay for merchandise. The great majority of such men considered the produce trade only as a sideline, but a few, like J. M. D. Burrows at Davenport, Iowa, finally turned to it as their principal occupation.

In the early years Burrows disposed of the produce taken in barter by selling to the trading posts up the river. Fort Snelling, Prairie du Chien, and Snake Hollow proved to be his best markets. At the latter place he exchanged bacon, flour and beans with the Indians for feathers and beeswax, which he sold in Cincinnati. In the spring of 1814 he was able to dispose of his produce in one sale, the American Fur Company at Prairie du Chien taking the whole amount.[16] Finding the produce trade profitable, Burrows enlarged his enterprises, and in the spring of 1844 tried a venture to New Orleans. Potatoes were quoted at two dollars a bushel in that market, but were selling for only fifty cents at Davenport. So Burrows loaded a flatboat with 2,500 bushels, deciding also to send another boat with a cargo of pork, bacon, beans, oats, corn, and brooms. The boats were dispatched in the care of men hired for the trip, Burrows keeping track of their progress by reports from steamboat captains who passed them coming up the river. When they were nearing the mouth of the Illinois river, he took passage on a steamer and caught up with them as they approached St. Louis. There he attempted to obtain insurance for the trip down the river, but discovered that the St. Louis companies did not write policies on flatboats. This proved an unwelcome surprise. Trading mainly with Cincinnati in the past, he had always been able to obtain insurance on such vessels. Two days of anxious negotiation ensued, and finally, through personal friendship with a director of one of the St. Louis companies, Burrows was able to obtain a policy.

The company insisted on his accompanying the boats to their destination, however, a trip he had not originally intended to make. The journey would keep him away from business for two months, but he could not afford to allow the boats to proceed without insurance—all of his available capital being tied up in the shipments. So Burrows made the journey, arriving in New Orleans after a trip of six weeks. When he reached there the city was full of potatoes, the high prices prevailing earlier in the year having attracted shipments from France. Potatoes were unsalable, and the best he could do was to trade his cargo to the captain

15 Aull letter books covering the period cited.
16 Burrows, pp. 33–41.

of a Bermuda vessel for eight cents a bushel delivered on board ship. Payment was made on coffee.[17] The loss occasioned by the venture was the result of the slow means of transportation prevailing in the West— the same factor which wrecked so many merchants in their wholesale orders.

Burrows did not desist from his operations, and the winter of 1845 found him buying breadstuffs to the limit of his capital. The commission firm of Henning and Woodruff at St. Louis had told him to buy $100,000 worth of wheat, either for himself or on their account, expecting a deficiency in the English market to cause a great increase in price. Burrows decided to employ his own money and reap the whole reward, making trips throughout the surrounding territory during the winter to buy. Before time to start shipments the Mexican War broke out and prices tumbled. Rumors that privateers were operating on the ocean caused insurance rates to rise until they equalled ten per cent of the value of the goods.

Burrows had bought flour at from four dollars to four dollars and a half a barrel and wheat at sixty cents a bushel. Some of his holdings were sold in St. Louis, the flour bringing two dollars and twenty-five cents a barrel, and the wheat forty cents a bushel. But the market there could not take all he had, the rest being shipped to New York City. The flour soured on the ocean voyage, and his sales in New York City had to be made at a dollar for flour and twenty cents for wheat. Burrows was virtually penniless as a result of the venture, and Henning and Woodruff at St. Louis were also heavily involved. Woodruff had a wealthy brother-in-law, E. K. Collins of New York City, who owned the Collins shipping line, and the latter carried the commission firm through. It in turn helped Burrows, Billings at Beardstown, Illinois, and Walker of Burlington, Iowa—all of whom had been engaged in the enterprise.

Unsettled international conditions caused prices to continue low during the summer and early winter months, and the partners all decided to buy again. This time they were able to obtain grain at very low rates, other buyers near Davenport gladly selling all their grain to Burrows. Prices advanced rapidly in the spring months, and the commission firms that had remained in the business cleared up their losses of the previous year and had a good reserve of capital besides.[18] R. M. Prettyman, Burrows' partner in the mercantile business at Davenport, decided that such violent changes from profit to loss and back again were not to his liking, and decided to sever that business connection. In the end they agreed to continue as partners in the store, with Burrows conducting the produce business on his own capital. The connection was of value to Burrows because he frequently bought grain half for cash and half in trade. This enabled him to make a double profit on the grain obtained for merchandise. The arrangement suited Prettyman, as it freed him from the risks of

[17] Burrows, pp. 58–60.
[18] Burrows, pp. 61–69.

the produce business and still gave him an easy way of disposing of produce taken in exchange for merchandise.

After 1805 Burrows was engrossed in the milling and meat packing business, a series of fires and other calamities causing him to lose his money in the sixties. He is representative of the merchants in the smaller places who gradually transferred their activity to the produce trade. Most of these men retained their stores, however, finding that the arrangement gave them a good chance to dispose of merchandise. Elisha and Gilbert Read of Chicago ran a general store in the twenties, concentrating more and more on farming, lumbering and the sale of foodstuffs in the thirties. Their Day Book shows that they did considerable mercantile business in the later period, selling goods to men who worked for them and taking produce in exchange for supplies from their stores.[19] Jared Warner's tax assessment for 1850 listed three houses, a saw mill, barn, smith shop, eighty acres of land, a store house, another mill (probably lumber also), merchandise, logs, and cash—the whole being valued at slightly more than $5,000.[20] An earlier account book indicates the way this property was probably handled, as it contains the record of his interests in lumbering and the provisions trade. Numerous men worked for him, and these received one-third of their salary in cash and two-thirds in provisions. For example, April 18, 1843, Ezra Rice was employed at fifteen dollars a month, five dollars to be in cash and the remainder in trade.[21] Later entries show that Ezra took drygoods and coffee as well as meat for his ten dollars. These supplies were drawn from Warner's store as needed.

Thus local merchants varied in the degree in which they engaged in the produce business. Some did only what was necessary to hold their customers, others went over to that line of activity completely. But all were involved to some extent—the barter system being universal. Furthermore, the economic life of the West—built, as it was, around the collecting and processing of raw products, and the exchange of these for manufactured goods in distant markets—gave rise to the development of forwarding and commission merchants in all the larger towns in the Mississippi valley.

The functions of commission and forwarding naturally went together. Merchants buying goods in distant markets had to rely on forwarding organizations to handle the transfers, freight, and insurance duties connected with bringing goods to the West. In that period transportation was not organized on a national scale, and it was impossible to ship supplies any great distance without employing several different companies in the process. Nor was there any guarantee of regularity in the schedule on which these small groups operated. Even if a merchant personally accompanied his goods, he found it a great saving in time to

19 Elisha and Gilbert Read, *Account Book 1818–59.*
20 Jared Warner, *Day Book 1849–51,* entry on last page.
21 Jared Warner, *Day Book 1830–49.*

engage the service of forwarding companies at the points of transfer, such concerns being fully acquainted with the organization of transportation in their localities. These firms also possessed warehouses in which goods consigned to their care could be stored until shipping arrangements were completed.

Furthermore, they maintained connections with similar groups in other cities. In this way a forwarding agency was much more likely to receive a share of the business passing through its own city, companies at other places consigning goods to its care, a practice which also contributed to a more efficient handling of shipments. Men having such connections were also well equipped for the commission business. Merchants were in daily contact with them and very likely to see goods or produce left for sale. They had the necessary space for storage and were acquainted with conditions in other markets. Consequently the two functions were generally found together. Many indeed carried a stock of goods on their own account and added the business of merchandising to their other functions.

No other group of business men in the West could boast of the wide trade connections developed by the commission and forwarding groups, unless it was the fur companies. Henning and Woodruff, the St. Louis company with which Burrows did business, was a branch of James E. Woodruff and Company of New York, another office being maintained in New Orleans under the title of John D. Woodruff and Company. Vairin and Reel at St. Louis maintained a branch in New Orleans under Julius Vairin, and owned a large warehouse on Water street in that city. The firm offered to make liberal advances on goods consigned to St. Louis or New Orleans for sale. In addition to this they engaged in the wholesale and retail trade in drygoods, hardware, and saddlery.[22]

Tracy and Wahrendorff carried a supply of goods for wholesale and retail. The forwarding and commission activities of this company are apparent from the business transacted with them by James Aull. In addition to this, they were agents for several insurance companies, Tracy being on the board of directors of an insurance concern which had its headquarters in St. Louis. In 1823 they had the agency for two steamboats running between Pittsburgh and St. Louis, an advertisement in that year offering freight downstream at a dollar a hundred pounds. Allen and Grant were their agents at Pittsburgh, giving them a direct connection with that city.[23] Even in the smaller towns such men frequently maintained wide connections, A. Dinsmore at Burlington, in Iowa Territory, advertising a commission and forwarding business in 1841, and giving references in St. Louis, Pittsburgh and Philadelphia.[24]

Hill and M'Gunnegle at St. Louis owned stock in local insurance

22 Advertisements of the firm appeared frequently in the *Missouri Republican* between 1832 and 1835.
23 St. Louis, Missouri, *Missouri Republican,* December 10, 1823.
24 Burlington, Iowa Territory, *Hawkeye and Iowa Patriot,* April 15, 1841.

companies and were agents for others. They advertised their "extensive warehouses" at the steamboat landing, where they conducted a commission and forwarding business. Liberal cash advances were promised on goods consigned for sale. John G. Stevenson handled their business at New Orleans, the firm offering to advance money on goods consigned to him from St. Louis, when the products were insured and non-perishable. They held the agency for a number of steamboats running to New Orleans, to Galena, Illinois, and to Louisville, Kentucky. Goods shipped on these were handled free, except for actual costs involved in making transshipments. Extensive advertisements were placed in the local papers to publicize the goods they had for sale on commission. One week's advertisements in a bi-weekly paper listed coffee and Madeira wine, one hundred and forty-four kegs of powder, coal grates, feathers and glass, flour and cider, ground alum salt, cotton yarns, New Orleans sugar, paper, whiskey, and dried peaches—each of the announcements referring to a separate consignment. The coffee and sugar came from New Orleans and the paper from the Phoenix mills in Cincinnati.[25] If a manufacturer wanted to invade the West directly he found commission firms an easy way to place his goods on sale.

These companies had a set system of rates, western and eastern Chambers of Commerce frequently publishing standard charges for their own localities. In Philadelphia and New York in the late thirties the charge for selling merchandise was two and a half per cent, the same rate prevailing for buying and shipping goods to other places. Commission houses charged two and a half per cent for buying and holding goods subject to a merchant's call, but performed this function without charge if they were supplied with funds before goods reached them and became subject to payment. The rate for obtaining insurance was one-half of one per cent, the fee rising to two and one-half per cent for adjusting and collecting insurance losses. The standard rate for receiving and forwarding goods was one-half of one per cent.[26] In the West higher charges generally prevailed for all these services. For instance, a five per cent commission was allowed for selling merchandise, just double the rate prevailing in the East.[27]

A large volume of business resulted in good profits for such companies. James L. Applegate received some excellent commissions, even though he was located on the upper Missouri river two hundred miles from St. Louis. John Atchison of Galena, Illionis, sent him 12,000 pounds of lead which he sold at five cents a pound. Atchinson received five hundred and twenty dollars for his lead, and Applegate thirty dollars for making the sale. Christy, Gentry and Company of Lexington, Missouri, consigned one hundred bales of hemp to Applegate, for which he ob-

25 St. Louis, Missouri, *St. Louis Beacon*, May 6 to May 13, 1830.
26 Foster, *Bills of Exchange*, pp. 115–16.
27 J. E. Thomas, "Commercial Summary," in St. Louis, Missouri, *Missouri Argus*, January 27, 1837.

tained $1,600. From this thirty dollars was deducted for freight, ten dollars for insurance, twenty-five dollars for drayage, and eighty dollars for Applegate's commission.

Goods coming from a distance bore much heavier charges. William T. Saunders of New Orleans sent twenty-five hogsheads of sugar, 2,000 sacks of salt, and one hundred and fifty boxes of raisins by the steamer *Alex Scott.* The goods brought $6,097.50, but were subject to charges of nine hundred forty-eight dollars and thirty-seven cents. Applegate received three hundred four dollars and eighty-seven cents as his commission. Other charges were seventy-two dollars for drayage, sixteen dollars and fifty cents for insurance, and five dollars for labor.[28] The charges totaled only about sixteen per cent of the value of the goods, a figure that compared favorably with the twenty to twenty-five per cent charged for moving goods from the seaboard to the St. Louis area. There was no escape from the enormous costs connected with shipping merchandise, no matter what procedure was employed. Commission and forwarding agents expedited shipments and relieved merchants from the necessity of personally accompanying every box of goods they moved from one place to another. In that sense they performed a real service.

[28] Sales listed in *Lisbon Applegate Manuscript Collection.* The sales are not dated. Lisbon was probably located near Chariton, Missouri, as he received some of his mail there.

Section 3 ⌐ Transportation and Government in the Agrarian and Commercial Economy

---

Seven ⌐ Ante-Bellum Forms of Transport

DOMESTIC TRADE *George R. Taylor*

Each new method of transportation had to establish itself in a bitter competitive battle against previously existing devices, and each new traffic route had to meet competition from established ones. This competitive struggle provides one of the chief characteristics of the period, and it profoundly affected the rate and nature of American industrial development.

Turnpike vs. Water and Rail Transportation

Turnpikes were chiefly built over routes where water transportation was not easily available, so that for the most part they served to supplement rather than to compete with water routes. Thus in New England they led inland in a generally east and west direction and avoided to a considerable extent paralleling the coast or the Connecticut River; in New York they radiated out from Hudson River towns, and in the Middle Atlantic states generally they ran at right angles to water routes or led westward over the mountains.

FROM "Domestic Trade," *The Transportation Revolution, 1815–1860*, by George Rogers Taylor, pp. 153–70. Copyright 1951 by George Rogers Taylor. Reprinted by permission of Holt, Rinehart and Winston, Inc.

For travelers, stagecoaches were faster, although more expensive and much less comfortable for long journeys, than sailing packets. But where coastwise journeys were very roundabout, stagecoaches secured considerable patronage. Travelers between Boston and New York who wished to avoid the tedious voyage around Cape Cod brought a brisk business to the stages between Boston and Providence. But from Providence to New York such persons usually preferred the sailing packets and later the steamships. Similarly, those going from New York to Philadelphia increasingly avoided the time-consuming sea journey by taking coaches over the much more direct turnpike routes across New Jersey.

The steamboats on their advent quickly absorbed most of the parallel turnpike traffic which had survived previous river competition. Their competition actually hurt only a few stage lines and stimulated many others, which began running so-called "accommodation" stages timed to meet the steamboats at such ports as Hartford, Connecticut; Albany and Newburgh, New York; and Richmond, Virginia. But for the transportation of goods, turnpikes could compete successfully with carriage by sea or river only under very special conditions. The large number of heavy wagons on the Boston–Providence Turnpike indicates that, for valuable freight shipments between New York and Boston, merchants often used this turnpike in order to avoid the long sea journey around Cape Cod.[1] Appreciable quantities of valuable freight also moved by wagon over the mountains from Baltimore and Philadelphia to Ohio River points, thus saving not only the tedious coastwise trip to New Orleans, but also, before steamboat carriage became important, the expensive three or four months' passage from New Orleans to the upper Ohio River.

Lead from the Galena district in southwestern Wisconsin was sent down the Mississippi and thence by sea to a market on the Atlantic coast. Not only was this route exceedingly roundabout, but steam navigation on the river between Galena and St. Louis was expensive and undependable. Unusually low water in the summer of 1839 greatly curtailed the river trade, and the successful experiment was made of shipping lead across southern Wisconsin in wagons drawn by six or eight yoke of oxen. At Milwaukee the lead was sent on to an eastern market by lake, and the wagons returned loaded with merchandise for the mining district. Once established, the trade on this overland route remained substantial during the forties despite the competition of the river route.[2]

Most turnpikes, especially those in New England and the South, were not faced with important canal competition, but where such competition did appear, results varied. At least in the case of the Middlesex Canal, the waterway won the freight business away from the teamsters only after an extended struggle. Not until the late 1820's and after re-

[1] Taylor, "The Turnpike Era in New England," pp. 236–40, 254–56; Lane, *From Indian Trail to Iron Horse,* pp. 159–60; Kistler, "The Rise of Railroads in the Connecticut River Valley," p. 24.
[2] Orin Grant Libby, "Significance of the Lead and Shot Trade in Early Wisconsin History," *Collection of the State Historical Society of Wisconsin,* XIII (1895), 313–25.

peatedly lowering its rates did this canal succeed in overcoming important turnpike competition not only in carrying raw materials and manufactured goods for the textile mills of Lowell, Massachusetts, but also for transporting such bulky country produce as ashes and grain from tributary farming areas as far as 160 miles northward in New Hampshire.[3] This struggle merits attention because it reveals the fundamental shortcomings of canals and emphasizes those factors in land transportation which later proved so advantageous for the railroads.

The one clear advantage of the canal was its lower ton-mile rates, but the superintendent of the Middlesex Canal in a report submitted in 1822 pointed out the following considerations which, unless rate differences were sufficiently great, led shippers to prefer wagon transportation:

1. Practically all goods had to be carried from the farms to the canal by wagon. The teamsters having a monopoly of this business charged very high rates. The same carriers greatly reduced their ton-mile rates when they carried goods all the way to Boston.

2. Through shipment by team permitted avoidance of truckage charges between the canal and the warehouse in Boston.

3. The country trader who personally accompanied his shipments, supervised the sale of his produce in Boston, and actually purchased his return load did not have "to wait in town after making his purchases nor at home for his goods" if he used turnpike transportation.

4. The trader who conducted his operations from his store in the country and shipped by turnpike dealt with a single teamster who made a round trip for him and who was held responsible for delays or damage to goods. If the merchant used the canal he dealt at a distance and often through intermediaries with canal agents, Boston teamsters, and merchants. This was inconvenient and frequently gave rise to difficulties in fixing responsibility for delays or damage to shipments.

5. The time of arrival of goods sent by canal was unpredictable, and country traders were often put to the expense of sending teams to secure freight at the nearest canal port only to find that their shipments had not arrived.[4]

Of course these difficulties arose in part from the lack of fast communications and from the imperfect commercial organization of the time. But they illustrate the superior flexibility and convenience of road over canal shipment.

The canals of the Middle Atlantic states promptly took away from the turnpikes most of their long-distance freight. Thus, teamsters could not compete with the Morris Canal across New Jersey nor with the Erie and the Main Line of the Pennsylvania for shipments to the West. Nevertheless, they continued to do a large local business and, until the railroads came, to operate over their old routes in the winter when ice closed the canals. In middlewestern states the periods of canal and turn-

[3] Roberts, *The Middlesex Canal, 1793–1860*, pp. 148–54, 166–70.
[4] *Ibid.*, pp. 149–51.

pike building coincided, and to a considerable extent roads were built to facilitate movement of goods to and from canals or rivers.

In the transportation of passengers, the turnpikes suffered little from canal competition. Most American canals did little or no passenger business. The Pennsylvania Main Line and the Erie were exceptional in that they carried many passengers, especially during early canal days, but this was largely new business which would not have existed but for the canals. In fact, the more successful canals like the Erie actually stimulated turnpike traffic. Impatient of the slowness of canalboats, many persons chose to travel by coach on New York turnpikes which paralleled the waterway. Turnpikes which led to the canal often became canal feeder lines, and their traffic increased with the growing population and wealth of the region.[5]

When the railroads appeared, they quickly captured the passenger business and thus took over the chief remaining turnpike traffic. Even less could the wagon lines compete effectively for freight with parallel railroad lines, though for a few years, until rail freight rates were considerably reduced, wagon routes offered occasional competition where rail lines were usually roundabout and charges high. But for freight shipment of fifteen miles or less, railroads were at a disadvantage as compared to the more flexible wagon. In most areas the railroads actually added to the business of the teamsters, for the increased demand for short haul movements more than made up for the long-distance traffic lost to the railroads.[6]

Competing Water Routes

The phenomenal growth of overland commerce between the Atlantic states and the West during the decades preceding 1860 should not be permitted to deflect attention from what was in 1816 and remained in 1860 the most important trade route in the country, that along the Atlantic coast. This coastwise shipping lane was challenged by the development of an extensive inland waterway system paralleling the coast. Roughly following Gallatin's great plan, canals connecting bays and sounds made possible, by the 1830's, continuous shipment on this sheltered passage from New London, Connecticut, to Wilmington, North Carolina.

But long-distance shipments by this inland passage did not seriously

[5] Durrenberger, *Turnpikes*, p. 142; Holmes, "The Turnpike Era," V, 270, 290–393; Lane, *From Indian Trail to Iron Horse*, pp. 161, 263; Leland D. Baldwin, *Pittsburgh: The Story of a City* (Pittsburgh: The University of Pittsburgh Press, 1937), p. 188; McKelvey, *Rochester: The Water-Power City, 1812–1854*, p. 94; Oliver W. Holmes, "The Stage-Coach Business in the Hudson Valley," New York State Historical Association, *Quarterly Journal*, XII, No. 3 (July, 1931), 246.
[6] See Kistler, "The Rise of Railroads in the Connecticut River Valley," pp. 185–89; Kirkland, *Men, Cities and Transportation*, p. 202.

rival those by sea. Naval stores from North Carolina and flour and to-bacco from the Chesapeake region continued for the most part to move to New York and New England markets by coastwise vessels, the man-ufactured products of the northern states and Europe furnishing valuable return cargoes. Nevertheless, the canals were utilized for some long-distance shipments. Thus, barges laden with coal from Richmond, Virginia, arrived in New York Harbor via the James River, the Chesapeake Bay, the Chesapeake and Delaware Canal, the Delaware Bay and River, and the Delaware and Raritan Canal, and the limited amounts of merchandise moved all the way back to the Chesapeake ports by this route. Even from far up the Susquehanna, barges descended to the Chesapeake and fol-lowed this inside route to New York, a journey of about seven hundred miles.

But it was over the shorter distances and primarily between Phila-delphia and New York that the canal system so successfully challenged the sea route that only the bulkiest products were left for coastal vessels. Of course, a little later the railroads in turn took the most valuable freight away from the canals, and the inland and sea routes were left to divide the less valuable business between them. In the late twenties, an-thracite rapidly became the great export staple of Pennsylvania. Most of the Lackawanna coal from northeastern Pennsylvania moved directly to New York over the Delaware and Hudson Canal and that from the nearby Lehigh fields reached the same market over the Morris Canal. From this latter source large quantities of anthracite also went down the Delaware Division Canal and reached New York either by way of the Delaware and Raritan Canal or by sloop around Cape May. Anthracite from the great Schuylkill area arrived at tidewater on the Delaware River via the Schuylkill Navigation or the Reading Railroad and, al-though much was sent on to New York by sea, the Delaware and Raritan Canal, by adjusting its tolls to meet coastwise competition, managed to capture an appreciable part of this business.[7]

The prosperity of the western states depended upon their ability to exchange the products of their farms for needed manufactures and other outside products like salt, sugar, and coffee. At the beginning of this pe-riod the high cost of transportation erected a wall around the states west of the Alleghenies which seriously blocked the economic development of that area. In a sense, this barrier was overcome by the spirit of a pio-neering people who, defying or ignoring difficulties, crowded into the broad western valley. Three great developments in the technique of transportation—steamboats, canals, and steam railroads—helped to raze this wall and to justify frontier optimism. The part played by steamboats and canals is here briefly summarized; the role of the railroad is exam-ined in the following section.

At the beginning of this period the transportation to and from the

[7] *Hunt's Merchants' Magazine*, VIII (1843), 546–49; Lane, *From Indian Trail to Iron Horse*, pp. 257–76; Albion, *The Rise of New York Port*, pp. 134–42; MacGill, *History of Transportation*, pp. 233–34.

Ohio River Valley moved counterclockwise in an irregular circle more than three thousand miles in circumference. Upcountry produce such as wheat, flour, butter, pork, and pork products from western Pennsylvania, Ohio, and Indiana; tobacco and hemp from Kentucky; cotton from Tennessee and lead from Missouri, Illinois, and Wisconsin—these moved southward by flatboat to New Orleans on the river arc of the circle. Transportation on this section was far from satisfactory. It was time consuming and expensive not only because the flatboats had to be sold for little or nothing at New Orleans,[8] but also because the men who manned them had, at least before steamboat days, to return home as best they could, usually by foot over the Natchez Trace, which followed the old Indian trail from Natchez through the Chickasaw country to Nashville. Also, trade moved almost exclusively in one direction. Upriver shipments were almost prohibitively expensive even for the most light and valuable merchandise.

From New Orleans, some upriver products were exported to Europe and the West Indies, but in large part they flowed around the second and longest arc of the circle, i.e., by coastwise vessels to Atlantic ports, chiefly New York, Boston, and Philadelphia. Though much the longest of the three parts of this circular route, it presented the fewest problems. Costs of ocean transportation, even on this long sea route, were, despite the danger of gulf hurricanes and the peril of storms off Cape Hatteras, remarkably low. Also, trade could move as easily in one direction as the other.

In order to overcome the delays and costs of breaking cargo at New Orleans, in the first decade of the century a considerable number of seagoing vessels had been built on the Ohio River, loaded with produce for eastern or foreign markets, floated down the river to New Orleans, and then sailed to their destination. Despite many discouragements, attempts of this kind were still being made in the years immediately following the War of 1812. Thus, the fifty-ton schooner *Maria*, built at Marietta and carrying a cargo of pork, flour, and lard, arrived at Baltimore, Maryland, in July, 1816, in forty-six days.[9] But the hazards of river navigation by seagoing vessels and the rapid development of the river steamboat soon gave the *coup de grâce* to this unique development.

Finally, the circle was closed by the routes across the Appalachian Highlands from Philadelphia and Baltimore over which the West received, in return for its downriver exports, textiles, hats, shoes, hardware, china, books, tea, and so on. This overland stretch of about three hundred miles proved the least satisfactory arc of the whole route, for transportation by wagon over this short distance cost more than shipment by sea and river all the way from Pittsburgh to Philadelphia.[10] Moreover, as on the river route, freight moved chiefly in one direction, for the cost of

[8] Baldwin, *The Keelboat Age on Western Waters*, p. 54.
[9] *Niles' Weekly Register*, X (May 11, 1816), 184, and X (May 20, 1816), 346.
[10] Berry, *Western Prices before 1861*, p. 81.

turnpike carriage eastward across the mountains effectively discouraged return loads made up of the bulky produce of the frontier.

Developments during the four and one half decades of this study greatly affected the flow of commerce on each of the three arcs of the circle described above. The introduction of fast, regularly sailing packets added materially to the speed and dependability of shipment on the coastwise sector. On the river, steamboats greatly reduced the time and cost of shipment and made upriver traffic little more expensive than downstream. And on the bottleneck arc across the Appalachians, canals and then railroads performed a similar miracle.

By making possible upriver trade and greatly reducing transport costs both up and down the river, the steamboat gave the first great impetus to western growth. An increasing flood of western products came down the rivers, while northward from New Orleans there began to move a growing stream of eastern and European merchandise—salt, sugar, coffee, and a hundred other needed items—which frontiersmen could now afford to purchase.

Chiefly because of this technological change in river transportation the terms of trade shifted sharply to the advantage of the westerners. This is strikingly shown in the behavior of prices of western exports as compared with imports. Because of the deflation of 1819–1820 the level of prices in all American markets was much lower in 1826–1830 than in 1816–1820, but the prices of western export staples declined less in the Ohio River Valley than at New Orleans and Atlantic ports, and the prices of imports into the West fell more drastically in the Ohio Valley than at seaport cities. Thus during 1816–1820 a barrel of flour averaged $2.16 higher in New Orleans than in Cincinnati. By 1826–1830 New Orleans prices were only $1.75 higher, a 19 per cent decline. For other major exports this differential was even greater. The difference between mess pork prices a barrel was $7.57 in the first five-year period, while only $2.41 in the second, a 68 per cent decline.[11]

As would be expected from the fact that upriver freight rates declined much more than did those for downriver shipments, the price difference on imports shrank even more sharply between these two five-year periods. Coffee which cost 16 cents more a pound in Cincinnati than in New Orleans in the first period cost only 2.6 cents more in the second, a decline of about 84 per cent! On sugar the difference for a hundred pounds fell from $10.33 to $2.64, or 74 per cent.[12] Some notion of what these changes meant in terms of purchasing power to the inhabitants of the Ohio Valley may be easily illustrated. In 1816–1820 an Ohio farmer could exchange a barrel of flour in Cincinnati for 27 pounds of sugar; in 1826–1830 it would bring 39 pounds. Or taking a more favorable ratio, a barrel of pork which would have exchanged in the earlier period for 30 pounds of coffee would buy about 52 pounds of coffee in

11 *Ibid.*, p. 106.
12 *Ibid.*, p. 113.

1826–1830.[13] These comparisons are, of course, in terms of wholesale prices, but there is no reason to believe the picture would be appreciably altered were retail quotations available.

No sooner had trade adjusted itself to changes wrought by the river steamboat, than canals, penetrating the barriers on the short Appalachian route, further stimulated western commerce and influenced the direction of its flow. It will be remembered that the Erie Canal was opened for through traffic in 1825, the Pennsylvania Main Line in 1834, the two canals across Ohio respectively in 1833 and 1845, and the Illinois and Michigan Canal in 1848. The first effect of these new waterways was greatly to stimulate traffic from the landlocked areas through which they passed, although before long the commerce of the whole Great Lakes area and the Ohio Valley began to feel their influence. The valuable manufactured products of the East moved in growing volume directly westward across New York and Pennsylvania. The merchants of Marietta, Cincinnati, Louisville, and even of Frankfort and Nashville secured an increasing portion of their merchandise over both northern Ohio routes and via the Pennsylvania canal system. By 1846 more than half of its manufactured imports reached the Ohio basin by this latter route. The value of goods shipped to the West by way of the Erie Canal was nearly $10,000,000 in 1836; by 1853 it was more than $94,000,000. Chicago became an important receiving and distributing point for New York merchandise and, with the opening of the Illinois and Michigan Canal in 1848, St. Louis, which had been an important distributing center for goods imported via New Orleans, began to get increasing shipments by way of the Illinois and Michigan Canal.[14]

For the first time the bulky products of the West began to flow directly eastward. By connecting with the Great Lakes, the canal system of New York had tapped the finest inland waterway in the world. The immigrants who crowded the Erie canalboats and settled first in Ohio, Indiana, and Michigan, and later in the more western lake states, soon sent back over the route they had traveled an increasing flow of flour, wheat, and other frontier products. By 1835 flour and wheat, equal to 268,000 barrels of flour, were shipped from the West to tidewater via the Erie; by 1840 shipments exceeded 1,000,000 barrels. By 1860 they totaled 4,344,000 barrels. As early as 1838 receipts at Buffalo exceeded those at the Mississippi River port. After 1848 Buffalo received wheat and flour even from faraway St. Louis via the Illinois River, the Illinois and Michigan Canal, and the Lakes.[15]

[13] Computed from tables in Cole, *Wholesale Commodity Prices in the United States, Statistical Supplement.*
[14] Switzler, *Report on the Internal Commerce of the United States*, p. 211; Emory R. Johnson and others, *History of Domestic and Foreign Commerce of the United States* (2 vols., Washington: Carnegie Institution of Washington, 1915), I, 232–35; Putnam, *The Illinois and Michigan Canal*, pp. 102–05.
[15] *Monthly Summary of Commerce and Finance* (January, 1900), p. 1969; *Eighth Census: Agriculture*, pp. cxlviii and clvi; Putnam, *The Illinois and Michigan Canal*, pp. 102–05.

In the Ohio Basin, produce, which from the first settlement of the West had gone down the river to market, now began to reverse its flow. Produce was carried to Lake Erie by either the Miami or the Ohio Canal and thence via the Erie Canal to the New York markets. Grain and flour from Pennsylvania, Kentucky, and southern Ohio and even some Kentucky tobacco moved to eastern markets by way of the Ohio Canal. As early as 1842 the value of farm products shipped from Cleveland at the head of the canal was about equal to the value of such products shipped from New Orleans. But most of these exports were the products of Ohio farmlands situated near the canals. Neither of the two canals across Ohio ever developed a large through traffic, despite the fact that low rates were instituted in order to encourage long-distance traffic. Apparently through traffic was discouraged by the large number of locks and the slow rate of movement possible. Nevertheless, in 1846 James L. Barton asserted that flour was being shipped from St. Louis via river to Cincinnati and thence by canal and lake to New York City. Though the freight cost via Cincinnati was $1.53 a barrel compared to $1.40 via New Orleans, he claimed the northern route was to be preferred because of the danger of souring and other damage to the flour on the southern route.[16]

The alternative direct route eastward—up the Ohio and over the Pennsylvania Main Line Canal—also provided an outlet for a number of western products. About 20,000 hogsheads of tobacco annually passed eastward over the Main Line Canal, and by 1850–1852 total shipments of pork and pork products by this route were almost as large as those sent down the river. But the total volume of through traffic eastward via this Pennsylvania canal, though considerable, fell well below that on the Erie. In 1844 it amounted to less than 75,000 tons, while that on the Erie for the same year totaled over 350,000 tons.[17]

A third direct water route to the East—through British North America by way of the Welland Canal, Lake Ontario, and the St. Lawrence River—constituted another outlet for the bulky products of the West. In fact, in the late fifties a number of ships carried western products directly from Chicago to Liverpool over this route, but for the most part cargoes were transshipped at Quebec. Much money was spent on digging canals and in improving navigation on the St. Lawrence River. Hopes ran high that a good deal of American trade would be attracted to this northern route, but it was never able to compete effectively with the Erie Canal–Hudson River outlet. Although the cost of shipment from

[16] *Lake Commerce,* Letter to the Hon. Robert M'Cleland (Buffalo: Jewett, Thomas and Co., 2d ed., 1846), p. 18.
[17] Ernest L. Bogart, "Early Canal Traffic and Railroad Competition in Ohio," *Journal of Political Economy,* XXI, No. 1 (January, 1913), 58–65; Johnson and others, *History of Domestic and Foreign Commerce of the United States,* I, 230–37; Berry, *Western Prices before 1861,* pp. 83–90; Switzler, *Report on the Internal Commerce of the United States,* pp. 210–11; Louis Bernard Schmidt, "The Internal Grain Trade of the United States, 1850–1860," *Iowa Journal of History and Politics,* XVIII, No. 1 (January, 1920), 94–124.

Chicago to Quebec was less than that to New York via the Erie Canal, the ocean freights from Quebec to Liverpool were much higher (nearly double in 1856) than from New York to the great English market. The port of Quebec was closed during the winter, lacked the excellent port facilities of its rival to the south, and held out scant promise for inbound cargoes.[18]

Despite the tremendous volume of commerce developed by the canal routes, the Mississippi trade showed no slackening in its growth. The rise in the value of receipts at New Orleans from the interior is shown in the accompanying table. For 1860 the value was the greatest in river history up to that time, and from 1820 to 1860 the total value of commerce at New Orleans from upriver had about doubled in each successive decade.

Value of Receipts at New Orleans from the Interior for Selected Years, 1816–1860

(In thousands of dollars)

Year	Value
1816	9,749
1820	12,637
1830	22,066
1840	49,764
1850	96,898
1860	185,211

Source: William F. Switzler, *Report on the Internal Commerce of the United States,* Part II of Commerce and Navigation, *Special Report on the Commerce of the Mississippi, Ohio, and Other Rivers, and of the Bridges Which Cross Them* (Washington: Government Printing Office, 1888), pp. 199, 209.

But it should not be concluded that river traffic was unaffected by the competition of canals, beginning in the thirties, and of the railroads in the fifties. The whole West was growing so rapidly that for the time being there was more than enough business for all channels of trade. The tremendous tonnages reaching Buffalo from the Lake region consisted largely of new production made possible by the Erie Canal. At the same time that produce was being diverted eastward from the Ohio Valley, states tributary to the upper Mississippi—Illinois, Missouri, Iowa, Wisconsin, and Minnesota—were rapidly increasing their shipments down the river. Moreover, the lower Mississippi Valley was one of the most rapidly developing sections of the country, with the result that receipts of cotton and sugar at New Orleans tremendously increased.

Although the rate of growth of commerce on the Mississippi did not slacken, major changes in its nature were taking place. New Orleans became much less important as a distributing center for the manufactured products of the East. The value of eastern products reaching the interior

[18] Samuel McKee, Jr., "Canada's Bid for the Traffic of the Middle West: A Quarter-Century of the History of the St. Lawrence Waterway, 1849–1874," *Report of the Annual Meeting of the Canadian Historical Association* (May, 1940), pp. 26–35.

in 1851 was about twice as great by the Hudson and canal as by coastwise shipment and the Mississippi. At the same time the upriver shipments of such products as West Indian coffee and Louisiana sugar and molasses grew greatly as western population increased and the canals of Illinois, Indiana, and Ohio opened up new markets for southern, Caribbean, and South American products.

Significant changes also took place in the character of the downriver trade. Though the total value of river commerce continued to increase, the major part of this growth was due to increased receipts of southern staples, chiefly cotton, sugar, and molasses. In 1819–1820 western products had constituted 58 per cent of the total value of receipts at New Orleans. By 1849–1850 they were about 41 per cent of the total. It is significant that even before 1852, when through railroad connections were made with the Ohio River at Cincinnati, shipments to New Orleans of most of the major Ohio Valley products had already begun to decline in volume. Thus tobacco receipts at New Orleans reached their peak in 1843, wheat and flour and corn in 1847, butter in 1848, and pork in 1849.[19] Though upcountry produce arriving in New Orleans increased during the fifties, it was largely consumed in local delta markets or exported to the West Indies. Coastwise shipments of western products to the East showed a marked decline. Hence by 1860 the canals and railroads had almost completely substituted direct trade across the Appalachians for the old indirect route via New Orleans and the sea.[20]

Railways vs. Waterways

Before 1840 the amount of traffic carried by American railways was negligible as compared with that moving on all inland waterways. By 1860 the total volume carried by the two methods was probably about equal, and the value of goods transported by railroad greatly exceeded that carried on the internal waterways. As the railroads were opened over new routes, they almost without exception immediately took away from competing waterways most of the passenger and light freight business. Except for the Erie Canal, which long provided cheap water passage for impecunious immigrants, passenger traffic on canals collapsed as soon as rival railroads were completed. The decline was just as sharp for other water routes, though a few long coastwise passages or shorter overnight sailings, as those between Albany, Hartford, or New London and New York, long retained a part of the passenger business because of their convenience.

Before through rail lines were completed from New York City to Lake Erie at the beginning of the fifties, the Erie Canal had developed a

[19] Berry, *Western Prices before 1861*, pp. 580–81; Switzler, *Report on the Internal Commerce of the United States*, pp. 209–15; Dixon, *A Traffic History of the Mississippi River System*, pp. 16, 24–26.
[20] Berry, *Western Prices before 1861*, pp. 90–91, 107; Dixon, *A Traffic History of the Mississippi River System*, p. 34.

tremendous business in transporting westward the manufactured goods of the East. This trade reached its peak in 1853, but as a result of railroad competition was more than cut in half by 1860.[21] Even in the carriage of the heavier and bulkier commodities the railroad proved an unexpectedly successful competitor. Confronted by railroads, such weak canals as the Middlesex and the Blackstone had collapsed before 1850. The Pennsylvania Main Line Canal, with its excessive lockage and its portage railroad, ceased to operate as an important through route soon after the Pennsylvania Railroad reached Pittsburgh in 1852. Most of the western canals rapidly lost the cream of their traffic to the railroads during the fifties.

River traffic was also adversely affected. Most of the trade on the upper Connecticut simply disappeared soon after rails paralleled the river. After 1852 the volume of goods shipped down the Ohio River to New Orleans declined because of railroad competition, but, so far as Ohio River traffic was concerned, this loss was more than compensated for by increased upriver shipments to the railheads at Pittsburgh and Wheeling, a growing traffic with St. Louis and the upper Mississippi River area, and greatly increased coal shipments.[22]

Railroads, which, beginning in 1853, were rapidly completed across Illinois and Wisconsin to the Mississippi River, had no trouble in getting all the business they could handle. The number of bushels of wheat arriving at Chicago jumped from 937,000 in 1852 to 8,768,000 in 1856, and corn from 2,999,000 bushels in the former year to 11,888,000 in the latter. But commerce on the upper Mississippi also continued to increase during this decade. At St. Louis, the great distributing center for the whole upper Mississippi area, goods were transferred from the steamboats of the lower Mississippi built to operate in four to six feet of water to steamboats of the Missouri and upper Mississippi which might navigate in thirty inches or even less. At this great center, steamboat arrivals grew from 1,721 in 1840 to 2,879 in 1850, and to 3,454 in 1860.

In the long run, the river could not retain much traffic in competition with the railroads. The difficulties of navigation on the upper Mississippi and the long journey via New Orleans on which goods were especially likely to damage and spoilage proved much more costly than that directly eastward by rail or rail and water. But during the fifties settlement was advancing so rapidly in Illinois, Wisconsin, Minnesota, and Iowa that both the rivers and the railroads were taxed to carry the growing traffic. So both increased in absolute tonnage carried, but from about 1847 and especially after 1852 the rivers transported a decreasing proportion of the total trade of the upper Mississippi area.[23]

[21] S. P. Chase, "Foreign and Domestic Commerce of the United States," *Senate Document* No. 55, 38 Cong., 1 Sess. (1864), p. 181. This document is hereinafter referred to as the *Chase Report on Foreign and Domestic Commerce, 1864.*
[22] Cf. Berry, *Western Prices before 1861,* pp. 39, 90–93; Johnson and others, *History of Domestic and Foreign Commerce of the United States,* I, 244–47; Hunter, *Steamboats on the Western Rivers,* pp. 484–88.
[23] John B. Appleton, "The Declining Significance of the Mississippi as a Commercial Highway in the Middle of the Nineteenth Century," *The Bulletin of the Geo-*

Even some of the cotton trade of New Orleans was surrendered to railroads. The Western and Atlantic Railroad, pushing westward from Augusta, made connections with Chattanooga in 1849, Nashville in 1854, and Memphis in 1857. As a result, thousands of bales of cotton, which would have gone down the Tennessee and Cumberland rivers and the Mississippi to the Crescent City, instead swelled the exports of Charleston and Savannah. Nevertheless, the whole West was developing so rapidly and cotton and sugar production in the delta region immediately tributary to New Orleans was advancing so tremendously that the river trade continued its rapid growth down to the war. Exports of cotton from New Orleans and the total volume of river trade both reached their peak for the ante-bellum period in 1860.[24]

In tonnage terms, most of the domestic commerce still moved by water in 1860. The direct trade between the West and the north Atlantic seaboard expanded so rapidly during the fifties that the railroads, the lakes, and the Erie Canal were all needed to deliver western products to the East. The tonnage carried by the Erie Canal grew tremendously despite railroad competition and did not actually reach its peak until 1880. The Great Lakes served as a gigantic extension of the Erie Canal, and during the fifties railroads, pushing westward from Chicago and Milwaukee, acted as feeders to the Great Lakes trade so that its volume, swollen by the corn of Iowa and the wheat of Illinois, Wisconsin, and Minnesota, grew from year to year in almost geometric ratio. By the end of the decade western flour (and wheat equivalent) transported to tidewater via the Erie Canal exceeded 4,000,000 barrels; of this probably about two thirds came from ports on Lake Michigan.[25]

The railroads also rapidly increased their eastward shipments. The tonnage of through freight carried eastward by the Pennsylvania, Erie, New York Central, and Baltimore and Ohio railroads was not yet quite equal to that transported by the Erie Canal. But it was much more valuable, for the rails transported practically all of the merchandise and livestock, most of the packing house products, and about two thirds of the flour. As a result, the heavier and bulkier products, such as grain and lumber, made up an increasingly large percentage of lake and canal traffic. This tendency is well illustrated by shipments from Chicago, a point from which commodities could be shipped eastward with equal facility by water or rail. Data available for 1859 show that heavy and bulky products, like corn, wheat, and lead, moved predominantly by water, whereas such items as hides, livestock, and general merchandise were carried chiefly by rail. Flour held an intermediate position, with

graphical Society of Philadelphia, XXVIII (October, 1930), 267–84; Isaac Lippincott, Internal Trade of the United States, 1700–1860 (Washington University Studies, Vol. IV, Pt. 2, No. 1, Second Study, October, 1916), p. 136.
[24] Johnson and others, History of Domestic and Foreign Commerce in the United States, I, 240–46; Dixon, A Traffic History of the Mississippi River System, pp. 32–36; Van Deusen, Economic Bases of Disunion in South Carolina, pp. 238 ff.
[25] Johnson and others, History of Domestic and Foreign Commerce in the United States, I, 231–32; Internal Waterways Commission, Preliminary Report, 1908, p. 233; Eighth Census of the United States: Agriculture, p. cl.

365,000 barrels being shipped eastward by lake and 307,000 by rail. But in terms of tons of western produce moved eastward to tidewater, the Erie Canal was still the predominant agency in 1860. In that year the tonnage reaching tidewater from the western states and Canada via the Erie Canal totaled 1,896,975. Through freight moving eastward by the New York Central, Erie, and Pennsylvania railroads appears to have been about half the canal tonnage.[26]

Railroads had little effect on the coastal trade between New England and the southern Atlantic states. Manufactured goods, lumber, and ice moved to southern markets, and cotton, tobacco, and naval stores were received in exchange. But trade with the West was appreciably altered. Textiles and other merchandise destined for the Ohio Valley had formerly been sent by coastwise vessel to Philadelphia and Baltimore and thence overland to market. With the completion of the Western Railroad to Albany in 1841 these products began to move directly westward by rail and canal and later all the way by rail. Also, with the opening of the Erie Canal much flour had moved by sloop from Albany directly to New England coastal markets. The Western Railroad gradually secured this business so that little was left of this coastwise trade by 1860.[27]

The coastwise trade between the South Atlantic and the Middle states was also largely unaffected by the coming of the railroads. Rail lines extended north from Washington, D.C., along the coast to Boston and beyond. But south from the capital city the only coastal railroad connecting with the east and west roads of the Carolinas and Georgia was the stem extending 325 miles from near Washington to Wilmington, North Carolina. Unfortunately this route was comprised of several independent railroad companies, and as late as the Civil War had three gaps, places where rolling stock could not pass from the rails of one road to those of another. One of these barriers occurred between Washington and Acquia Creek on the Potomac River in Virginia. The other two were short breaks at Petersburg, Virginia, and Weldon, North Carolina. Passengers were transported across these breaks in the line without great difficulty, and as a result the railroads were able to compete fairly effectively with the coastwise packets for the passenger business. But the cost of reshipping freight was prohibitive. Not until well after the Civil War did the railroads begin to offer important competition for seaboard shipments south of Washington.[28]

Hope had run high that the line extending northward from Mobile

[26] Johnson and others, *History of Domestic and Foreign Commerce in the United States*, I, 238; Pierce, *A History of Chicago*, II, 494; and Schmidt, "The Internal Grain Trade of the United States," pp. 94–124; *Chase Report on Foreign and Domestic Commerce*, 1864, pp. 138, 140–41; *Hunt's Merchants' Magazine*, XLIII (December, 1860), 701.
[27] Albion, *The Rise of New York Port*, pp. 128–29.
[28] Howard Douglas Dozier, "Trade and Transportation along the South Atlantic Seaboard before the Civil War," *South Atlantic Quarterly*, XVIII, No. 3 (July, 1919), 232–34.

and connecting with the Illinois Central at Cairo would promote intersectional rail traffic. In 1860 the lack of direct physical connection between these two rail routes still made necessary a twenty-mile shipment
by ferry between Columbus, Kentucky, and Cairo, Illinois, and little
through business had developed. The rail route connecting Cincinnati
and New Orleans was opened in 1859 too late to permit much traffic to
develop before war closed such intercourse. The overland movement
of cotton to northern markets was inconsequential until the very end
of the period. For the years 1852–1858 such shipments had averaged
less than 10,000 bales a year. But in 1859 and 1860 they rose rapidly,
so that in the final year they totaled nearly 109,000 bales, or one eighth
of the total shipped northward in that year for domestic consumption.
The railroad system of the South gave great assistance in moving staples
to southern seaport markets, but not until the very end of the period
were southern rail lines beginning to be sufficiently integrated with those
of the North as to encourage long-distance rail shipments between the
North and the South.[29]

The Pattern of Trade

The rapid settlement of the West, the great increase in population, and
the phenomenal improvements in transportation which have been emphasized made possible the territorial specialization upon which rested
the striking growth of American domestic commerce during the period of
this study. The direction and magnitude of this commerce was largely
determined by the growth of New York City as the great center for foreign importations, and the development of manufacturing in the Atlantic
states lying north of Chesapeake Bay. The fundamental pattern of this
trade was very similar to that which existed between Great Britain and
this country in the colonial and early national period. The South, which
in colonial days had sent its great staples directly to England and received manufactured products in return, after 1815 found a growing
market for its raw materials—cotton, tobacco, and sugar—in the manufacturing East. The West, an exporter of grain and meat, carried on a
similar direct trade with the manufacturing states, but it also provided
the South with food products, receiving in exchange drafts on the East
which were used to pay for manufactured imports. In similar manner before the Revolution, fish from New England and grain from the Middle
Atlantic states had been exported to the West Indies to help permit payment for British imports. But this earlier trade had involved only the
fringe of states along the Atlantic, whereas the domestic commerce rapidly developing during the nineteenth century presently involved a
whole continent.

. . .

[29] Pierce, *A History of Chicago*, II, 45–46; *Nimmo Report*, 1879, pp. 122, 128.

CORPORATION: HISTORICAL
DEVELOPMENT *Stuart Bruchey*

A corporation is a group of individuals authorized by law to act as a unit. It is a fictitious legal person, and as such has a corporate name, in which it may sue and be sued, and hold and transfer property. In the eyes of the law, therefore, the group has an existence which is independent of that of its individual members. It may long outlive any one of them. This continuity of existence gives the corporate form of business enterprise a clear advantage over other forms, such as partnership, which comes to an end with the death of a partner. Business corporations, that is, chartered joint-stock companies formed for the primary object of securing pecuniary gain to their members, divide their capital stock into shares. Shares are often purchased by a large number of investors, each subscribing relatively small sums. This divisibility of the share capital facilitates the accumulation of the large sums required by modern industry. Another factor facilitating capital accumulation is the limited liability of shareholders for the debts of the corporation. In the event of bankruptcy they may lose their investments but all their other property is safe from attachment.

Advantages of these kinds go far to explain the predominance of the corporate form in modern American economic life, particularly in manufacturing. But they have little relevance to the period of its origins in either Europe or America. Indeed, to understand how the business corporation came to be used in this country, and the purposes it served, requires some attention to its old world background.

Corporations existed long before their use for business purposes. Some scholars trace their origins to such groups as the family, clan, or tribe, which are found in the most primitive societies. The more complex societies of the ancient world developed towns, gilds, and colonies; church and universities appeared in medieval Europe. The notion that

REPRINTED with permission from Stuart Bruchey, "The Historical Development of the Corporation in the United States," *Encyclopedia Britannica,* Chicago: Encyclopedia Britannica, 1963, Vol. 6, pp. 525–28.

the legal authority of the state is necessary for the formation of corporate bodies is also very old. For cases where the state did not create the corporate group, or no record of its origins could be found, there arose the theory that some associations might come into existence by prescription. Both Roman and English law made use of this theory. It is safe to say, however, that prescriptive corporations were confined to forms of association older than the business corporation.

In England, the authority of the crown was essential from the first for the formation of the business corporation. After the Revolution of 1688, that of Parliament was necessary in any case involving a grant of monopoly or other special privilege. In the 16th and 17th centuries it was business corporations in the form of great trading companies which made possible the English voyages of discovery, commerce, and colonization. These culminated, in the early 17th century, in the first permanent English settlements in Virginia and New England.

To suggest that the Virginia Company or Massachusetts Bay Company was created primarily as a profit-making association would be highly misleading. The great trading and colonizing companies did seek profits. They also divided their capital into transferable shares to ease the problem of raising it. But the achievement of neither of these objectives required that a corporation be formed. These ends might have been realized by utilizing the unincorporated joint-stock company, which form of enterprise was currently in use in some branches of English overseas trade. In the eyes of the law these unincorporated companies were large partnerships, but this fact did not inhibit their amassing and management, through agents, of large capital sums. The basic reason the state granted charters of incorporation to some joint-stock companies was to encourage private capital to promote ends which it regarded as public or semipublic in nature.

The public policies of many European governments between roughly the 16th and later 18th centuries were often those of "mercantilistic" writers, advisers, and officials who sought by means of vigorous governmental action to promote the internal unity, power, and self-sufficiency of the state. Charters of incorporation which bestowed exclusive privileges upon a group of joint-stock investors were looked upon as means to these ends. Within spheres of operation defined by their charters the great trading corporations of the 16th and 17th centuries were usually granted a commercial monopoly and the power to enforce that right by means of regulations bearing the force of law. Operating in areas distant from the protective power of the state which created them they operated essentially as elongated arms of that state. These business corporations of the early modern period were therefore far more than mere instrumentalities of private profit. The charters they received bestowed upon them a semipublic status.

These conclusions, as we shall see, are fundamental to an understanding of the nature of most of the corporations created during the long colonial period of American history (1607–1783) and for nearly fifty years thereafter. As colonial plantations increased in population there sprang up in America corporations in the form of towns, boroughs, and cities. Before the end of the colonial period a large number had been created for ecclesiastical, educational, and charitable purposes. The number of business corporations created, however, were both few and relatively unimportant. These included in the 17th century the water company of Boston and William Penn's *Free Society of Traders in Pennsylvania.* During the 18th century there appeared the New London trading society, two groups of wharf proprietors (in New Haven and Boston), three small water companies in Rhode Island, and a mutual fire insurance society in Philadelphia. The local and public service character of these corporations is self-evident.

One main reason why numerous and large business corporations failed to develop in colonial America was that the spheres in which they were required were subject to the disposition of Crown and Parliament, rather than of local colonial governments. Under the unwritten constitution of the British Empire, the terms of which were to be vigorously debated during the years of crisis between 1764 and 1776, internal matters alone were subject to the essential control of colonial governments, while imperial concerns belonged to the jurisdiction of London. Colonists had therefore nothing to do with those larger interests of Empire which required for their development both a delegation of governmental powers and large capital sums. To the East India Company and other chartered joint-stock companies from which colonists were debarred (as well as Englishmen who were nonmembers) England looked for the development of imperial commercial interests. Nor did prevailing mercantilist doctrines favor the encouraging of self-sufficiency on the part of colonies. Indeed, colonies were looked to as sources of supply for raw materials which were to be manufactured into end-products in the mother country, and as markets for those end-products.

The objects of concern on the part of the colonial governments were therefore small and local in nature, requiring in few cases the provision of services or facilities beyond the tax-yielding capacities of local communities. While the size of both foreign and domestic markets expanded during the 18th century the capital required for their supply, and for shipping, was easily amassed by individual proprietors or partnerships. Unincorporated joint-stock companies raised by transferable shares the capital requirements of mining, manufacturing, and land speculation, some of them enterprises of surprising size. Commercial banks did not exist. Marine insurance was almost always obtained from English underwriters. Travel and shipping by sea blunted the need for north-south roads, while the existence of east-west rivers that were navigable to the fall line, together with British discouragement of settlement west of the Appalachians, narrowed the need for improved east-west routes of travel.

Many elements of this situation began to change soon after the achievement of independence. Between 1776 and 1800 perhaps 250,000 western migrants settled west of the mountains, or in its valleys, thus increasing sharply the need for improved routes. State governments created more than 300 business corporations between the end of the Revolution and 1801, and the provision of inland navigation, turnpikes, and toll bridges was the purpose of two-thirds of them. No longer debarred from trade with the Far East, American merchants expanded both the geographic area and volume of their foreign commerce, particularly after the outbreak of European war in 1793 opened up the commercial world to their neutral vessels. Risks of loss increased correspondingly, more especially because English underwriters were sometimes not disposed to be generous with the claims of American neutrals. The resulting need for more reliable policies was followed by an expansion in American underwriting, with the result that the states chartered a number of insurance companies between 1786 and 1800.

The expanded volume of trade created at the same time a need for the short-term credit facilities of commercial banks, with the result that no less than 34 were incorporated between 1781 and 1801 (27 of them between 1790 and 1801). Commercial expansion, by increasing the size of urban populations, also increased their needs for other public services, so that 32 corporations for the supply of water and four for the erection of docks were created in the six year interval between 1795 and 1801. The expanded need of urban communities for protection against fire losses was reflected in the organization of nearly a dozen mutual companies between 1786 and 1800. The large majority of the total number of insurance companies (32) chartered during this same period, moreover, were privileged to write either fire or marine risks.

The predominance of highway and other public service associations among the notably increased number of joint-stock companies chartered in the early national period points clearly to the expanded sphere of responsibility on the part of American political communities following the Revolution. These business corporations were no more exclusively profit-seeking associations than the chartered joint-stock companies with which the English had pioneered in the settlement of America. They were, in fact, quasi-public agencies of the state. "Be it enacted by the Senate and House of Representatives in General Court assembled," reads a Massachusetts statute of 1818, that the following named individuals "hereby are constituted a corporation *and body politic*" for the purpose of erecting a flour mill. As bodies politic these corporations, like their predecessors, were accorded certain exclusive privileges in order to encourage the devotion of scarce private capital to public ends. Among these privileges were monopoly rights of way, tax exemption, the right of eminent domain, and the right, granted to many nonbanking corporations, to facilitate the raising of needed capital by engaging in banking operations and holding lotteries.

At the same time, the incorporation of an important number of banks and insurance companies is indicative of needs created in the main by the expanding area of American business enterprise. Except for fire insurance, these institutions served in the main the business component of the community, although by no means exclusively. One bank, it should be noted, received its charter from the national government rather than from the states. The First Bank of the United States, chartered by Congress in 1791 for a period of twenty years, was a notable public service institution. While the four-fifths of its capital stock of $10,-000,000 was subscribed by private sources, and only one-fifth by the federal government, the institution served important public purposes by acting as a depository for federal funds, making short-term loans to the federal government, transferring federal funds from one part of the country to another, and helping maintain a sound and uniform banknote currency. The Bank owed much to an early developed view on the part of Alexander Hamilton that public fiscal ends were best to be promoted by enlisting private capital in their support. On the whole, however, the character of most of these early corporations reflects the very old view that charters should be issued only to those associations formed to serve the public interest.

During approximately the first third of the 19th century public service continued to dominate the purposes for which business corporations were chartered. This is evident both from the economic and other circumstances of the times and from the kinds of corporations receiving charters. In the new and underdeveloped nation capital was scarce in relation to the needs of a population that was growing rapidly in numbers, and at the same time both settling increasingly in cities and spilling westward over the mountains. The American people had numbered only about 4,000,000 when the first census was taken in 1790; by 1830 natural increase and immigration had brought the total to nearly 13,000,000. Urban centers had totalled 24 in 1790; by 1830 their number was 90. Not surprisingly, corporations to supply water, to construct bridges, to operate ferries and steamboats, and to provide insurance and banking facilities received charters in increasing numbers from state governments. It is difficult, moreover, to exclude from the category of public service the manufacturing corporations chartered in the early years of the century. During the troubled years of Embargo, Non-Intercourse, and War of 1812 the stream of imports of manufactured goods declined to a trickle. In this situation some state governments appear to have adopted the view that the chartering of domestic manufacturing associations was a matter of patriotism. Between 1808 and 1815 New York issued more charters (165) to joint-stock companies engaged in manufacturing than to all public utilities combined (164). This phenomenon appears not to have reoccurred in any other period prior to the Civil War.

The most continuing and most costly requirement of the pre-War years lay in the field known to contemporaries as that of "internal improvements." Turnpikes, canals, railroads, and other transportation facilities were required in both the settled areas of the east and in the growing west. Impelled by hard times, but more often lured by cheap land and constantly expanding urban markets for agricultural produce, settlers poured west in a torrent following the War of 1812. The resulting need to bind the newly settled areas of the west to the economy of the seaboard states became the nation's number one economic problem. Till mid-century, the passage or turning of the Appalachian Barrier was the leading object of promoters of internal improvements.

Two main obstacles impeded the realization of this objective. Despite the fact that foreign trade had made possible important accumulations of commercial capital, serving for example as the chief means of producing some half-dozen millionaires by 1815, overall supplies of capital were scarce. Perhaps equally important was the fact that local supplies of capital were meager along the lines where turnpikes, canals, and railroads were projected to run. The second main impediment lay in the developmental nature of internal improvements projects. Few could hold out the promise of quick returns on investment capital. Indeed, almost all projects looked for most of their respective returns to the settlement and economic activity which their own construction was designed to promote. Profits would necessarily be not only deferred, but also widely diffused—in the form of increased land values and such external economies as shipping facilities for agriculture and industry.

The chartering of public service corporations was one response to the existence of these obstacles and to an extraordinarily vital public spirit presiding over the area of internal improvements. State governments not only granted tax exemptions and other previously noted privileges to corporations engaged in improving transportation facilities. They also floated bond issues to raise funds with which to subscribe themselves to the stocks of the enterprises, in many cases joining with local governments in granting outright gifts of money and other aids. Not private capital alone but public as well—federal, state, and local—joined hands in a characteristically mixed enterprise to create the social overhead capital which was so essential to the development of the nation's resources.

These halcyon days were not destined to endure. As capital accumulated, the line between public interest and private advantage became more sharply visible to critics of the privileges enjoyed by corporations. It was certainly true that abuse crept easily into the prevailing system of obtaining charters. Except for New York and Connecticut, which in 1811 and 1817 respectively passed general laws permitting qualified incorporators of certain kinds of manufacturing concerns to apply to the Secretary of State for a charter, incorporation by special act of the state legislature was everywhere the rule before the late 1830's. Lobbying expenses, delay, and bribery often attended appeals to state legislatures for acts of incorporation. It was to the advantages which incorporators under this system were often able to wring from lawmakers that Andrew Jackson referred when he complained in a Presidential message of "the multitudes of corporations with exclusive privileges which they have succeeded in obtaining in the different States." Jackson, like Jefferson before him, was a man of fundamentally agrarian temperament who deplored the rapid economic and social changes which were subordinating older and simpler modes of life to urban business values.

Agrarian critics were not alone among the opponents of specially privileged corporations, particularly banking corporations. The supporters of President Jackson formed an entrepreneurial wing as well as an agrarian wing. These business critics of existing modes of procuring charters wished for an end to special privilege; they wanted the profit-making opportunities presented by the burgeoning economy opened on equal terms to all. Jackson's Secretary of the Treasury, Roger B. Taney, well typifies this entrepreneurial attitude in his remark: "There is perhaps no business which yields a profit so certain and liberal as the business of banking and exchange; and it is proper that it should be open, as far as practicable, to the most free competition and its advantages shared by all classes of society." Under President Jackson's leadership in the early 1830's men of agrarian and entrepreneurial persuasion locked causes in a successful assault on the Second Bank of the United States. Successor to the First Bank, which had passed out of existence in 1811, the Second Bank (1816–36) had affronted both rural philosophies and the urban economic interests of state banks in its successful management under President Nicholas Biddle of the nation's currency. By curtailing loan expansion on the part of state-chartered institutions Biddle had restricted their profits. With the central regulatory agency gone after 1834 (when federal deposits ceased to be made in the Bank), the number of state-chartered banks rose from 506 (in 1834) to 901 (in 1840). In the year of Ft. Sumter they numbered 1601.

It was Taney who as Attorney General had presided over the beginning of the Bank's end by removing the federal deposits from the Bank. Four years later, as Chief Justice of the Supreme Court, he struck an even more telling blow in favor of free, competitive enterprise. In the *Charles River Bridge* case (1837) Taney severely modified an earlier ruling by Chief Justice John Marshall concerning the sanctity of contract. The issue involved was the claim by a Massachusetts bridge company that its corporate charter gave its exclusive, monopolistic business rights by implication. Taney rejected the contention, holding that no corporate charter could confer implied powers beyond the specific terms of the grant. His decision thus freed new businesses from the fear of claims of monopoly on the part of older corporations with ambiguously phrased charters.

These many-faceted attacks upon enterprise restrictions had two important consequences. New York's passage of a free banking act in 1838 served as an important precedent for similar laws in other states. More than a half-dozen states, moreover, passed *general* incorporation laws prior to the Civil War. But while an increasing number of charters were taken out under general laws the lure of special advantages from special acts led most incorporators to prefer the older method till about 1875. The second important consequence was a tendency to seek charters of incorporation in expanding fields of enterprise. Paralleling this development was a shift of emphasis in the business corporation from public service to private profit.

The attacks upon enterprise restrictions coincided with the gathering strength of forces pushing the nation's economy to new levels of achievement. At the center of these forces was continued population growth, together with increases in national income which more than kept pace with growing numbers of people. In consequence, an American nation whose numbers rose from 17,000,000 in 1840, to 23,000,000 in 1850, and to 31,500,000 in 1860 constituted an effective domestic market for both agricultural and industrial goods. New miles of railroad track knit together the producing and consuming centers of expanding regional markets. To meet the rising demand required a gradual abandonment of older methods of production. Farmers first worked longer hours, then added to their output by using such mechanical aids as threshers, mowers, and reapers. Increasingly, industrial output was expanded by means of the factory system of production. Appearing first in cotton textiles, then spreading to carpet manufacture, and to the making of arms, clocks, and watches, and sewing machines, factory methods developed rapidly after 1840. The clearest indication of the rise of factories is the great increase in the rate of urban growth in the final two decades before the Civil War. The number of cities rose from 131 in 1840, to 236 in 1850, and to 392 in 1860. By 1860 the factory system was rapidly becoming important everywhere in industry.

A rapid increase in charters granted in the 1850's heralded the dawn of the age of the business corporations. Yet it was only the dawn. Industrial techniques requiring large capital investment were of recent origin in important fields and made their way but slowly among constituent firms. Not till after 1835 did textile machinery become metallic, large-scale, and expensive. Not till 1839 were the first successful coke-smelting furnaces built in the United States. As late as 1869 nearly half the mechanical power used in manufacturing was still applied directly from water wheels and turbines rather than derived from steam engines. Lateness and lag had important consequences, for it is not so much the first appearance of new techniques as it is their spread that matters in economic growth. Imitation is more important than innovation. Among the important explanations of imitative lag must be set not only the inertia of traditional and less costly methods: Ignorance also counted for much, and what abetted it was the scarcity or lack of technical journals, trained engineers, and cost accounting techniques. The gradual overcoming of these obstacles contributed in the post-Civil War years to a wider dissemination of mechanized production methods. But on the eve of that conflict not corporations but individual proprietorships and partnerships were able to amass the capital required for the control of most of the resources devoted to manufacturing.

The second half of the 19th century is marked by three principal developments in the life of the business corporation. There occurred, in the first place, a phenomenal expansion in the use of the corporate form, especially in such fields as iron and steel, nonferrous metals, textiles, chemicals, and liquor. Indeed, manufacturing corporations have constituted a large percentage of all charters granted each year since 1875. This expansion did not take place at a uniformly accelerating rate, however. The researches of G. Heberton Evans, Jr., a leading student of the business corporation, have shown a high degree of correlation between movements in incorporations and business generally. Following a rapid increase in charters granted during the Civil War, there occurred a period of readjustment during which the number of corporations ceased to grow in some states and declined in others. This period partially overlapped a major depression lasting from 1873 to 1879. From the late 1870's till the mid-1890's incorporation proceeded at an extremely rapid rate. The second principal development of the half-century was the notable growth in size of the individual unit of enterprise. Finally, there began to take place during the 1880's such remarkable changes in administrative organization as to justify the conclusion of a leading student of these developments, Alfred D. Chandler, Jr., that the decade saw the emergence of the modern corporation.

Nine ⌁ *The State and Internal Improvements*

THE AMERICAN SYSTEM:
A REVIEW ARTICLE   Robert A. Lively

The role of government in the ante-bellum American economy has been boldly redefined in a score of books and articles published during the past decade.[1] Close analysis of state and local sponsorship of enterprise, initiated and supported by the Committee on Research in Economic History,[2] has suggested a thesis that appears to invite a new view of American capitalism in its formative years. Taken together, the works here reviewed form a consistent report of economic endeavor in an almost

[1][For the list of books and articles reviewed, see pages 165–66.—SB]
[2] Arthur H. Cole, "Committee on Research in Economic History. A Description of Its Purposes, Activities, and Organization," *Journal of Economic History*, XIII (1953), 79–87.

REPRINTED with permission from Robert A. Lively, "The American System: A Review Article," *Business History Review*, Vol. XXIX (March 1955), pp. 81–96. Copyright 1955 by The President and Fellows of Harvard College.

unfamiliar land. There, the elected public official replaced the individual enterpriser as the key figure in the release of capitalist energy; the public treasury, rather than private saving, became the major source of venture capital; and community purpose outweighed personal ambition in the selection of large goals for local economies. "Mixed" enterprise was the customary organization for important innovations, and government everywhere undertook the role put on it by the people, that of planner, promoter, investor, and regulator.

No scholar has yet attempted a general description of an America so dependent on its public authorities. The several authors who have conducted the recent surveys of little known state and local functions have carefully qualified their findings, and each has confined himself to a specific area or a selected problem in his restatement of the relation of government to enterprise. The most ambitious and inclusive accounts of positive state endeavors may be found in the articles and monographs of Louis Hartz, and Oscar and Mary Handlin. Concerned primarily with what the people wanted from their governments, rather than with what they got, Hartz and the Handlins were free to let their speculations carry them to extreme views. More limited but more impelling conclusions are presented in the works of Carter Goodrich and Milton Heath: their restraint lends force to their views of the carefully defined issues they analyze. Harry Pierce, John Cadman, James Neal Primm, Earl Beard, and others avoid bold generalizations, but add essential detail to the Goodrich-Heath story. These authors are united in their belief that the activities of state and local governments were of crucial importance in the stimulation of enterprise in the United States. Their variations on this theme are so numerous that the principal concern to which all return is surprisingly familiar. Their common specific task is the rescue of the internal improvements movement from the political historian, and the inflation of this issue as primary evidence for their new view of America's economic organization. In their report of the struggle of communities and states for control of inland produce or for access to markets, they document the emergence of a sturdy tradition of public responsibility for economic growth. The tradition as they describe it, persistent to the very end of the nineteenth century, was so extensively employed that it seems expanded in no theoretical respect by its modern uses in the Tennessee Valley or in the exploitation of atomic energy.

Recent notice of the age and respectability of this tradition began with attack on what Louis Hartz called the " 'laissez faire' cliché" that "has done much to distort the traditional analysis of our early democratic thought" (Hartz, 2, xi). Historians, according to Hartz and others, have compounded this distortion by concentration on national issues, and by excessive concern with limitations put by the Constitution or by jealous sections on the Federal government. The story obscured, meanwhile, has been that of the broad uses to which the ante-bellum states put the powers reserved to them in a Federal system. In three papers read to the 1943 meeting of the Economic History Association, Oscar Handlin, Hartz, and

Milton Heath reported that the states of Massachusetts, Pennsylvania, and Georgia were in no way inhibited by laissez-faire notions. "In the realm of the practical," observed Handlin, "there never was a period in Massachusetts history when this conception was of the slightest consequence. From the very first organization of the Commonwealth in 1780, the state actively and vigorously engaged in all the economic affairs of the area, sometimes as participant, sometimes as regulator" (Handlin, 1, 55). Of Pennsylvania, Hartz later said that, "Far from being limited, the objectives of the state in the economic field were usually so broad that they were beyond its administrative power to achieve" (Hartz, 2, 292). Milton Health concurred, though with variations, when he concluded that of Georgia "it may be said that during the early decades there developed no definite philosophies defending the exclusive validity of either individual or public action" (Heath, 3, 100).

King Laissez Faire, then, was according to these reports not only dead; the hallowed report of his reign had all been a mistake. The error was one of monumental proportions, a mixture of overlooked data, interested distortion, and persistent preconception. Scholars who tried to set the story right, moreover, found the void before them yawning constantly wider. Authors of the first major books addressed to the issue met with boldness and imagination the problem of guiding readers through a land from which theoretical signposts had been removed. Oscar and Mary Handlin, and Louis Hartz, who published their full-length studies of Massachusetts and Pennsylvania in 1947 and 1948, were engaged by hypotheses that outreached their evidence, but the shock effect of their works was a useful stimulant to fresh and original thought about the role of government in early state history. It now seems evident that the Handlins and Hartz, in their enthusiasm for the demolition of laissez-faire mythology, substituted new theories almost as unsatisfactory as the ones they so adequately undermined. They were victims, in a way, of the assumptions they discovered to be false when employed in description of the ante-bellum period. Instead of eliminating the laissez-faire theme from analysis of public policy, they merely changed its chronology. Each assumed general adherence to the philosophy *after* the mid-century point at which their studies ended; and with this presupposition they gave to their account of earlier alternative policies a tone more appropriate for description of antique curiosities than for revelation of continuing themes in American economic history. They wrote as though state sponsorship of economic development had been an all or nothing proposition, a point of view that obligated them to demonstrate the total collapse and failure of the schemes and visions they had discovered.

In this respect the Handlins' work was the more portentous: they were quick to admit that the "commonwealth" policies (their name for persisting elements of mercantilist theory and practice in Massachusetts) were doomed from the start. According to their theory Massachusetts emerged from the Revolution composed of many diverse interests, but polity in the state was dominated by the "fact that transcending interests of all its constituents was the interest of society . . ." (Handlin, 3, 30). This "unity behind diversity" was to be expressed by a "government prominent in the direction and management of productive enterprise" (Handlin, 3, 261). Ambition for bold public endeavors, however, was cramped by a narrow public purse and popular fear of debt. The state therefore operated through the grant of privilege or the gift of incorporation to private groups. Rapid extension of these grants weakened the concept of common interest, and led inevitably to the growth of a body of private rights with which the government could not interfere. The state matched its original broad purpose with growing policy in only one area, that of humanitarian reform—or, as the Handlins would have it, in "police state" functions. Otherwise their analysis of policies from the Revolution to the Civil War reveals a story of shrinking public ambitions, of "transition from the Commonwealth to the police state, from mercantilism to liberalism . . ." (Handlin, 3, 262).

The Hartz analysis revealed that in Pennsylvania there was equally persistent faith in mercantilist theory; there, as in Massachusetts, the Revolution simply meant belief in the "need for utilizing that principle exclusively for colonial ends" (Hartz, 2, 6). Pennsylvania, however, implemented faith with a remarkable array of plans, controls, investments, and public works. Policies of the state affected "virtually every phase of business activity, were the constant preoccupation of politicians and entrepreneurs, and they evoked interest struggles of the first magnitude. Government assumed the job of shaping decisively the contours of economic life" (Hartz, 2, 289). Through its chartering policy it registered influential opinions on the character and shape of banking and transport enterprises, and then on an increasing variety of industrial developments. As investing partner of enterprisers, it placed public directors on the boards of over 150 "mixed" corporations by 1844. Further, by the sale of public lands, and by the investment of more than $100 million in the public works system, the state, in its "entrepreneurial function . . . assumed major proportions" (Hartz, 2, 290). Humane regulatory policy was equally extensive, from the abolition of slavery in 1785 to the limiting of child labor in the 1850's. The state, in fact, acquired such extensive responsibilities that its bureaucratic machinery broke down; a "stable and expert administrative system . . . did not develop" (Hartz, 2, 293). Administrative failure was compounded by sectional jealousies within the state; the public credit was critically threatened by the hard times of the late thirties and early forties; and in the end the theorists of public enterprise were driven from the field by their erstwhile partners, the private directors of mixed corporations. Confident, mature, and no longer dependent on the public treasury for their existence, the now "private" corporations clothed themselves in individualist theory, and launched with "messianic vigor" a successful assault on the whole theory of state participation in enterprise.

Unhappily for a critic in search of a documented hypothesis, the image of the positive state thus revealed in the Hartz and Handlin monographs is limited by the authors' intentions to the status of an engaging speculation rather than a demonstrated reality. The authors set out to describe what the people of Massachusetts and Pennsylvania conceived to be the role of their governments, rather than to outline government activity; and with this definition of their work as exercises in intellectual history, they very often relegated principal economic themes to the position of supporting detail. For the Handlins this approach permitted convenient and specific disavowal of any effort to "assess the effects of government action upon economic trends" (Handlin, 3, xii). Selection of the "commonwealth" theme permitted adequate proof for their belief that the state government was for many years expected to show formal interest in every public and private endeavor of material consequence— but from the evidence they present this concern was displayed without cash content or interested administration. Bemused with the curiosity about the Commonwealth pattern, they avoided analysis of substantial public aid to the emerging corporations whose legal form and rights they understand so well. Louis Hartz, on the other hand, was very much concerned with positive state policies, but only insofar as these policies would illustrate the half-century of debate that led on the eve of the Civil War to the emergence of a full-blown laissez-faire philosophy. Along the way he documented Pennsylvania's extraordinary excursions into state-sponsored transportation development, but the heart of his study lies not in what the state did, but in the story of how individual enterprisers and public planners alike lost control of both their theories and good works to the private corporations that supplanted them.

The Hartz-Handlin interpretation of the rise and decline of state ambition has not been adopted by students investigating related material. Scholars at work on similar themes have found that a smaller canvas and more thorough development of relevant detail brings them to conclusions quite different from those of the works just summarized. An effort to demonstrate the practice as well as the theory of state enterprise has required them to rely on more conclusive evidence than a summary of popular hopes and complaints; and they have found that achievements, as distinct from vague desires, were the products of somewhat more orthodox capitalist purpose.

The data repeatedly employed in analysis of state endeavors has been sought in study of public aids to railroads. No other public undertakings excited such extensive argument, nor attracted, in the end, so great a share of the public's capital. Careful review of causes and effects in the story of railroad aid became for Milton Heath and Carter Goodrich a means to general analysis of the role of government in ante-bellum economic development. Heath described in his 1937 Ph.D. dissertation the railroad building efforts of communities and states throughout the South. Goodrich, in six recently published articles, surveyed the hopes, methods, and achievements of officials directing government assistance at every level of public administration. Both men, writing as economists and students of planning, sought a contemporary relevance in the familiar story of "internal improvements." In the nineteenth-century American experience they hoped to find lessons that might prove useful to modern underdeveloped countries that are also faced with problems too great for the skill and capital of their private organizations. In applying the word "planning" to ante-bellum practices, they quite consciously gave the word its modern meaning—that is, the adoption by communities of "deliberate and concerted policies . . . designed to promote economic expansion or prosperity and in which positive action to provide favorable conditions for economic activity is emphasized more strongly than negative regulation or the correction of abuses" (Goodrich, 2, 16; Heath, 2, 1).

The end to which the planners aspired was neither the achievement of an all-embracing "commonwealth," after the Handlin definition, nor yet the creation of a permanent public stake in enterprise, according to the Hartz pattern. Rather, "public railroad promotion took on the character of positive planning for a freer private enterprise" (Heath, 1, 46; Goodrich, 3, 355). In the America they described there was no particular disposition to question the propriety of public enterprise, where private efforts proved inadequate to meet public needs. There was little positive preference, on the other hand, for public works as something inherently superior to private endeavors. States or localities undertook roles for which no other agency was fitted, and then waited for the time when the public might "conveniently exchange its position as proprietor for that of regulator" (Heath, 2, 43). Milton Heath's observations on the normal cycle of municipal investment revealed a chronology and a purpose that were repeated at each level of government operation:

> . . . the public function was viewed as an initial, developmental one. After enterprises became established on a profitable basis, city governments tended to transfer their investments to new projects, and so, normally, a transition from public or quasi-public to private ownership and operation took place (Heath, 1, 49).

Local and state governments assumed the "role of the primary entrepreneurs" as part of their normal functions (Heath, 1, 51). When public-spirited citizens met to discuss the need for projects of public utility, they turned naturally toward some variety of the public corporation as the agency best fitted for large efforts (Goodrich, 1, 307). The need for capital was the factor that most frequently determined government entry into the field of enterprise; only public authorities could command sufficient credit at a reasonable interest rate for works of the size demanded. Subordinate considerations were usually present, of course: glib promoters reached eagerly for public funds; hopeful administrators sought state investments so profitable that taxes could be reduced; and in a day when works of public utility were by definition regarded as monopolistic, a people suspicious of power generally were sure to insist that their governments guide these developments with a firm regulatory hand. But underlying every justification for state endeavor was the hope that by public effort businessmen of a locality would prosper, that land values would rise, and that the competitive position of the area would be improved. The whole business community was dependent on state execution of the general investment functions necessary to economic growth; it was by state endeavor that "idle resources could be brought into employment and the social income maximized" (Heath, 1, 47–48).

Discharge of these practical functions required state governments more active, if anything, than those that might have undertaken the theoretical responsibilities discussed by Hartz and the Handlins. The Goodrich and Heath hypothesis, moreover, enjoys the advantage of superior documentation by measurable facts—and contains, at the same time, a plausible explanation for most of the impulses described by the earlier reporters. Above all, the Goodrich-Heath theme is consistent with subsequent developments in the nation's economic history. After the states handed over their projects to private direction, the Federal government emerged as the chief sponsor of transcontinental enterprise, and local governments pledged their credit to the completion of the interlacing railroad net. The terms for these later grants of aid were substantially altered by the maturity and strength of the post-Civil War private corporation, but the established role of government was if anything enlarged.

However varied the explanations for public sponsorship of enterprise, the facts supporting these stories can be summarized in one generalization: the movement was virtually unlimited both as to time and place. From Missouri to Maine, from the beginning to the end of the nineteenth century, governments were deeply involved in lending, borrowing, building, and regulating. Beyond this observation summary is difficult. Accurate measure of the public's stake in enterprise, for instance, cannot be taken from the evidence here reviewed. The statistics employed by the several authors are of an illustrative rather than a conclusive sort. Diligent in their analysis of the total figures involved in public investment, they have not undertaken similar analysis of the private contribution to mixed corporations. They show a tendency to rely on reported book values in their estimates of total construction costs, and they thus ignore both the enormous discounts involved in marketing stock to private groups, and the extensive practice by which "investors" offered overvalued construction services rather than cash for their share of developments.

Milton Heath's estimate of the cost of the Southern railroad net represents an unusual effort to take these latter factors into account. According to the Census of 1860, the cost of the South's 9,211-mile system had been $245,212,229. Of this approximate cost, the public had supplied 55 per cent through its official agencies. Further refinement of this estimate, however, suggests that private investment was so often in labor and kind that public authorities actually supplied about three-fourths of the cash required (Heath, 2, 253). In contrast, Harry Pierce emphasizes the importance of state and local investment of $47,150,035.46 in New York's railroads, but he sets total construction costs at $400,000,000, a figure left uncriticized either as to type or time of investment (Pierce, 25, 5).

The bulk of references to the extent of public endeavors, however, are presented without the foregoing bases of comparison. A review of the statistics of state and local investment suggests how generally the movement was shared, and how great a burden governments undertook, but it affords no decisive measure of the government role in contrast to that of private investors. Even with their use thus qualified, the figures are impressive. Pennsylvania was probably the most active, not so much for her investment of $6,171,416 in 150-odd mixed corporations, but for her expenditure of $101,611,234 on the construction and operation of the Main Line canal and railroad system. New Jersey, on the other hand, was one of the few states that stayed almost completely out of the movement (Goodrich, 3, 357; Cadman, *passim*). In New England, Massachusetts, the only notable state investor, put $8,200,000 in eight railroads by 1860; and she had just begun the celebrated Hoosac Tunnel Project, in which she was to invest $28,856,396 by the turn of the century (Kirkland, I, 324, 432). To the West, Missouri had pledged $23,101,000 to improvements by 1860, a sum estimated by James Neal Primm at 25 times the state's average annual income (Primm, 105). These undertakings of the late forties and the fifties have hitherto been obscured by the familiar story of panic and retrenchment in states throughout the Union after 1837–1839.

The most impressive revelation in the detailed analysis of the improvement program is the degree to which local governments maintained and extended the responsibilities relinquished by many states on the eve of the Civil War. The local aid movement, authorized by 2,200 laws in 36 states, appears to have dwarfed better-known state endeavors (Goodrich, 4, 412–23). The bulk of local aid, further, was given after the Civil War; enterprise demanded and received vital support from public treasuries so long as there was a mile of American railroad track to be laid. In Maine, for instance, the legislative delegation of Aroostook County was electing public members of the Bangor and Aroostook's Board of Directors in the 1890's, and thus defending the County's new $728,000 stake in the road's future (Kirkland, I, 491).

Harry H. Pierce, in his outstanding study of the railroads of New York, 1826–1875, has taken the only satisfactory measure of the local aid movement. In an account drawn from scattered town records, railroad books and correspondence, legislative records, and court reports, Pierce found that 315 of New York's municipalities pledged $36,841,390.69 toward the construction of the state's roads. The conclusions he drew from study of hundreds of specific projects are arresting:

> . . . the importance of these subsidies lies not in their amount but in their timeliness. In practically every instance the aid was proffered at a critical moment in the company's history. It is significant that, with the exception of the city of Albany, neither the state nor any municipality

ever assisted a railroad that was already in operation. Public money in New York always pioneered the way. It took the initial risk. . . . Government aid to railroads not only facilitated the raising of money, but also greatly reduced the cost of financing them. In many cases, particularly in the building of marginal lines, public subsidies made possible the construction of roads that would not otherwise have been built. In an even greater number of instances, it permitted the completion of projects at a much earlier date than would have been possible with private capital alone (Pierce, 25).

Other students agree that local aids were very considerable, but some assert that they were given when public subsidies were of diminishing importance (Goodrich, 4, 435). E. C. Kirkland, for instance, reveals in a few pages the mixed views with which the postwar grants have been described. He concludes that New England communities were "so extravagant and so generous that the pre-war years in comparison were but a diminutive forerunner." By reference to the total capitalization of the roads, however, he minimizes the effect of the new public investments. Although Connecticut towns subscribed 60 per cent of the new railroad securities issued in the state between 1868 and 1877, the town percentage of total capitalization in 1877 "was only nine." In his general summary of New England efforts, on the other hand, he appears to credit the aids with more decisive effect; no other policy, he reports, "public or private, produced so many useless railroads" (Kirkland, II, 309–16).

Local efforts were extensive throughout the Union. Louis Hartz concluded that in Pennsylvania, state investment was at its height "of minor significance compared with investments by cities and counties" (Hartz, 2, 86). Ante-bellum southern cities and counties contributed $45,625,-512.05 out of total southern aids of $144,148,684.92 (Heath, 1, 41). James Neal Primm concluded that most of the stock "sold" in the 1850's by the state-aided railroads of Missouri was sold to the municipalities and counties through which the roads would pass (Primm, 106). The major undertakings of Baltimore are well-known; the city invested about $20 million in railroad development between 1827 and 1886 (Goodrich & Segal, 5, 2). The indications are that cities and counties to the west were increasingly lavish in their grants as the years passed. Cincinnati exceeded Baltimore in expenditures on her municipally owned road; the city of Milwaukee, with a population of 45,246 in 1860, lent $1,614,000 in 1858. Earl Beard's recent analysis of local aid in Iowa reports as an "educated guess" a total of $50 million spent there by the 1890's (Beard, 32). More than adequate figures are at hand, it seems, to support the recent conclusion by Carter Goodrich that the generally employed estimates on the extent of public aid published in 1938 by the Federal Coordinator of Transportation are far too low [3] (Goodrich, 4, 430).

[3] Federal Coordinator of Transportation, *Public Aids to Transportation,* I (Washington, 1938), 18–19.

Detailed analysis of railroad development has not been duplicated in studies of state promotion in other fields. In the four states for which general policy has been described—Massachusetts, Pennsylvania, Georgia, and Missouri—the passage rather than the administration of promotional laws has been offered as evidence of state achievement. Grant of the privilege of incorporation, with attendant alienation of certain public powers, is perhaps the only other major concern subjected to careful definition. There were laws on every conceivable subject, but without an account of enforcement machinery there is no means by which their effect can be judged.

Massachusetts, for instance, used licensing laws to grant monopoly privileges to selected entrepreneurs; the pioneer glass manufacturers of the state were promised years of freedom from competition (Handlin, 3, 81–82). Bounties were given quite freely by several states, particularly to agriculture. Maine paid out $150,000 in the year 1839 alone to wheat and corn producers; nine states subsidized silk culture (Taylor, 380); and Massachusetts aided fisheries and naval stores production (Handlin, 3, 83–84). Tax exemptions and relief of workers from poll taxes or from militia and jury duty were other means by which industries in certain states were encouraged. Pennsylvania was active for a number of years after the Revolution in fixing prices for certain goods and services (Hartz, 2, 206). Many states encouraged quality production by inspection laws, affecting in particular goods consigned to interstate commerce. Georgia maintained 30 public warehouses for the grading and marketing of tobacco by 1800 (Heath, 3, 85); and Missouri inspected virtually all tobacco exported after she constructed a $25,000 tobacco warehouse at St. Louis in 1843 (Primm, 118). Stay laws, relief laws, and public loan offices were familiar phenomena after the Panic of 1819.

The authors cited have skirted warily around one type of major undertaking comparable in scope to the internal improvements effort. Enterprise throughout the union depended heavily on the credit provided by the investment of state capital in banking operations. Recent reappraisals of the operations of the Second Bank of the United States, however, have not been followed by more than casual summaries of the way in which states put their resources behind public or mixed banking systems. A series of articles by Bray Hammond has swept away some of the mythology surrounding these state adventures, but effort to give the movement a proper place in the general story of state enterprise has been limited (Hammond, 1, 2, 3). No one, for instance, has developed the challenging conclusion offered by Guy S. Callender more than 50 years ago, to the effect that the southwestern states, in their large-scale grants of credit to commercial agriculture, maintained responsibilities comparable to the canal and railroad building efforts of the middle states (Callender, 161–62). The amount of money invested has usually been estimated, and banking as a political issue described, but the day-to-day operations and achievements of partially or wholly owned state systems remain a field for research demanding all the support now promised by the Committee on Research in Economic History.

Opinions expressed casually about forces apart from central themes developed in the subject literature seem in some cases more important than specific illustrations of state enterprise. The role of private capital, suggested in scarcely more than parenthetical references, is quite anomalous. The authors take repeated note of the "unwillingness of private investors to risk their money in railroad securities . . ." (Pierce, 4). Initiative in new adventures was left to the state, partly because of the general inadequacy of private investment funds (Heath, 1, 47–48), but just as often because individuals seeking profit are pictured as cautious to the point of timidity. Even where such a financial community as New York made available more than adequate liquid capital, the spirit of caution prevailed. William H. Aspinwall, John V. L. Pruyn, Edwin D. Morgan, Cornelius Vanderbilt, and Russell Sage moved in to form the New York Central after communities had taken the initial risks, and not before (Pierce, 10). Further, the movement of the substantial private capital that was invested before 1860 is ascribed to community spirit rather than to the hope of gain (Heath, 1, 44–46). Merchants of Baltimore, Charleston, or Savannah sponsored connections with the interior as a program of "metropolitan mercantilism" that would benefit them in a general rather than a particular way. Similarly, the farmers of Wisconsin had not turned speculators when, between 1850 and 1857, they gave nearly $5,000,000 in mortgage notes to railroad builders; they were investing in regional prosperity (Taylor, 98).

These opinions are disquieting in view of the current interest in "entrepreneurial" history. The reviewer is certain that the right hand of the Committee on Research in Economic History knows what its left hand is doing, but there is little evidence to prove it. For instance, in the most important recent contribution from the entrepreneurial school, Thomas C. Cochran's *Railroad Leaders, 1845–1890*, the author takes only incidental and inconclusive notice of public aids other than land grants.[4] This isolation of individual endeavours from public efforts seems all the more curious in view of the fact that the Goodrich-Heath hypothesis describes an American System in which state and private initiative are fully compatible. Continued separation of the themes prevents desirable refinement of both. Greater offenders in this regard are the authors reviewed here whose exclusive concern with public aspects of the mixed corporation permits them to avoid analysis of its private parts. The corporate agency for community action was so mixed an instrument that neither description from the point of view of the state nor analysis from the position of the entrepreneur can alone give a proper view of its growth. Public efforts to employ corporations for social ends deserve their overdue notice, but private contributions remain matters of consequence.

As an early American institution, to be sure, the corporation was a public school for enterprise. Its graduates were never very loyal, but they were no less obligated to it for their experience with major engi-

[4] Thomas C. Cochran, *Railroad Leaders 1845–1890. The Business Mind in Action* (Cambridge, 1953), pp. 17–18, 96–98, 184, 189–94, 200–01.

neering projects, their knowledge of managerial problems, and their skill at gathering and handling large capital. Its modern "private" form was a very late achievement:

> The attributes of peculiar economic efficiency, of limited liability, and of perpetual freedom from state interference were . . . not present at the birth of the American business corporation. Divested of these characteristics, the form assumes a new significance. At its origin in Massachusetts, the corporation was conceived an an agency of the government, endowed with public attributes, exclusive privileges, and political power, and designed to serve a social function for the State. Turnpikes, not trade, banks, not land speculation, were its province because the community, not the enterprising capitalists, marked out its sphere of activity (Handlin, 2, 22).

In Pennsylvania, of 2,333 business corporations chartered by special act, 1790–1860, 64.17 per cent were in the field of transport, 7.2 per cent in banking, 11.14 per cent in insurance, 7.72 per cent for manufacturing, 2.79 per cent for water, 3.21 per cent for gas, and 3.77 per cent in miscellaneous categories—the form, in other words, was predominantly employed for works of public utility (Hartz, 2, 38). Society, in creating agents to perform social services, attempted through the several states to keep a firm hand both on the evolving corporate agents, and on the quality of the services the agents rendered. At the very least cities and states attempted to protect their investments in transportation companies, and at most they attempted to harness and direct growing corporate power. Both the minimum and maximum attempts were on the whole failures. In the end, society sought the measure of its achievement in the intangibles of community growth and prosperity; there were no other measures, for communities lost their money and they lost control of their corporations.

The state struggle to maintain controls, however, left the issue in doubt for a very long time. In the first place the chartering power was maintained until after the Civil War as a means of potential corporate regulation. The Dartmouth College Doctrine did not break legislative power over the state's creations; it only invited more careful charter limitations (Cadman, 426, 429; Hartz, 2, 236–52; Primm, 35–52). Corporate charters included detailed specifications on the size and power of directorates, the liability of stockholders and officers, the nature of capital structures, and on the details of the operations the organizations might attempt. Regulation of corporate services was generally undertaken. Banks were restricted to collection of interest rates specified in charters, and were often required to reserve a certain part of their loans for named classes. Dividends were controlled by law, especially when specie payments had been suspended (Hartz, 2, 258; Primm, 26–28). Public utilities were subjected to rate regulation, to requirements that certain customers get preferential treatment, and to the maintenance of minimum service schedules (Hartz, 2, 258–60). Illustration of the extent of detailed control might be expanded indefinitely for there were almost as many specific regulations as there were charters.

Effective administration of these laws proved possible only when the regulating authority worked toward reasonably defined and sensibly limited ends. Pennsylvania, equipped with the most ambitious regulatory program, failed in almost all her objectives. The reporting system by which the state's auditor-general kept in touch with state investments broke down completely; state officials responsible for public shares in mixed corporations were assigned more duties than they could identify, much less discharge; and legislative investigating committees proved to be clumsy and inadequate instruments of control (Hartz, 2, 96–103, 262–67). In Virginia, on the other hand, an excellent reporting system was maintained. The Virginia Board of Public Works avoided detailed problems in the administration of mixed corporations, and concentrated on the protection of the state's financial interests, and on the provision of expert engineering services to enterprise. Even when the board controlled a majority interest in a project, it left to private hands the detailed responsibilities of management (Goodrich, 3, 378–83). In Maryland, where the state and the City of Baltimore selected a majority of the B & O directors until 1867, a similarly effective review of financial and engineering detail was maintained. Baltimore treated the road as a public institution as long as the city had a stake in it; the City Council was seeking wage raises for B & O employees as late as 1880 (Goodrich & Segal, 5, 27).

The nature of the alliance between politics and trade cannot be revealed by facts drawn only from the records of public authorities. For one thing, public directors in mixed corporations were often private stockholders in their own right: the Virginia Board, in fact, required such a display of "interest" by its agents after 1847 (Goodrich, 3, 378–79). The distinction between politician and entrepreneur was consistently vague; three mayors of Baltimore, for instance, served as presidents of railroads aided by the city. John W. Barrett, president of the B & O from 1858 to 1884, was not master of his railroad until he was master of the state of Maryland. He continued then to welcome public subscriptions to the road's development, but he preferred control to remain in private hands (Goodrich & Segal, 5, 19–20, 28–32). Harry Pierce's analysis of the battle between capitalists of Albany and Troy, New York, for control of the western trade, reveals the difficulty of judging such public endeavors as Troy's municipally owned road in the narrow context of either "public" or "private" enterprise (Pierce, 60–81).

Analysis of the intimate association of public and private officials has for the most part been avoided by the authors considered; they have tended to concentrate instead on themes demonstrating a sharp division between public and private interests. In particular they have emphasized the persistent anticorporate spirit evident throughout the nation until deep into the nineteenth century. Abundant evidence has been resurrected to demonstrate popular expression of traditional hostility to concentrated power, to the grant of privilege and monopoly, and to the mysterious or dishonest manipulations by which irresponsible corporate managers maintained themselves. Small businessmen and conservative investors feared corporations, and the public often felt misused by them. These sentiments, however, appear not to have controlled state policies; chartering programs were constantly expanded, and the form was made available to every type of business. The most distinct policy change related to the anticorporate spirit was the frequent adoption of general incorporation laws. Studies of the general incorporation movement in Massachusetts, New Jersey, Pennsylvania, and Missouri, however, reveal it to be something other than a Jacksonian extension of privilege to all comers. For enterprisers, general laws in these states were rigid and unwelcome rules written by men who wanted to restrict corporate power and growth. They were not employed by businessmen, who continued to seek and get the special charters given freely until after the Civil War. Even the Democrats, who tended to be authors of the laws, seemed to be satisfying emotional needs rather than executing serious policy; they passed general laws, and then continued in the same sessions to grant special privileges on request (Handlin, 3, 233–35; Cadman, 431–38; Hartz, 2, 38–42; Primm, 54–62).

While communities indulged their anticorporate emotions, they continued to charter, regulate, and subsidize in their search for necessary social services. The retreat from public investment came only after the railroads had been built, and usually under the pressure of major economic crises. Increasingly, though, the regulatory effort was designed for the protection of public funds, rather than for the direction of corporate behavior. Massachusetts, in fact, demonstrated no other purpose from the start (Kirkland, I, 325). State activity declined sharply in the early 1840's, and then revived for a briefer season in the 1850's. The local aid movement reached its climax after the Civil War, before the substantial reaction of the 1870's (Goodrich, 6, 145–52). The retreat from aid by the cities was accompanied by widespread effort to dishonor municipal bonds; communities were without scruple in their efforts to repudiate debts blamed on dishonest promoters, incapable builders, and venal public officials (Pierce, 84–86; Goodrich, 6, 152–55; Beard, 16).

The retreat was not universal, and the sense of having been cheated was not generally shared. Bangor and Baltimore continued to subsidize, and in the southern states the Civil War only delayed for a season the Reconstruction climax of state aid. The financial record of the southern states had been good, the roads well built, and the hope of public profit reasonable (Heath, 2, 250–52). Communities, moreover, had never staked their hopes on business balance sheets. Only one city in 25 made a profit from railroad investments in New York, but 85 per cent of the cities subsidizing got the improved transport for which they had worked. Public losses were probably no greater than those of early private investors, and the communities had more to show for their effort (Pierce, 127). Massachusetts suffered a $9,500,000 loss on her $28,856,396 Hoosac

Tunnel expenditures; profits went to the "tunnel ring" in the northwestern part of the state. But early in the twentieth century 60 per cent of Boston's exports flowed east through the "great bore" of Massachusetts politics, and all New England depended heavily on this gateway to the West (Kirkland, I, 430–32). In Virginia a committee of the Senate, balancing profit and loss on the ante-bellum effort, concluded in 1876 that state investments had been justified by the increased wealth of the whole area served (Goodrich, 3, 387). The state-owned and operated Western and Atlantic Railroad of Georgia was not only the first railroad to penetrate the Appalachian Chain; the road won for the state control of western imports into the eastern cotton belt. Georgia, whose public planners share with the builders of the Erie Canal the greatest reputations in the improvements field, has long been recognized as the executor of a "master-stroke in railway policy." [5]

Conclusions invited by summary of the 25 books and articles digested in the preceding pages tend to take the form of questions rather than assertions. The significance of the literature reviewed cannot be established until the themes suggested are tested in a more general synthesis than has been attempted by any of the authors referred to here. At present the works present an extended and more exact analysis of the spirit, policies, and achievements of the internal improvements era. This much is clear gain. The considerable influence of the newly reported theory and detail is measured by the prominence accorded government as sponsor of enterprise by George Rogers Taylor in the most recent volume of the Rinehart *Economic History of the United States*. But the most basic reappraisal of the internal improvements movement can scarcely be regarded as "new" in any bold sense; the subject is too much a staple of American economic history, and has for too long been a principal retreat for Ph.D. students seeking thesis topics. Also, more than 50 years have passed since Guy S. Callender contributed a brilliant explanation for state accumulation of $200,000,000 in capital for investment in ante-bellum industrial development, and if two more generations pass before the current version of the Callender thesis is further refined, then the recent burst of scholarly energy may not seem very significant.

One can hope for alternative developments. Taken together, the works reviewed now end on a tentative note, and leave unresolved some of the more fundamental questions they raise. Studies of the theory and practice of local aid, for instance, reveal no changes in the public mind that justify continued use of the Civil War as a convenient point to close off the story of government activity. The absence of the Federal government from the new literature is inexplicable, particularly during the 1860's and 1870's, when Washington assumed for the states so many of their services to enterprise. A fresh approach to Federal sponsorship of economic growth, undertaken in knowledge of the traditions that de-

[5] Ulrich Bonnell Phillips, *A History of Transportation in the East Cotton Belt to 1860* (New York, 1913), p. 334.

scended to national officers from the era of state aid, might give a new look to Radical Republican policy. The decade of monetary reform, tariff revolution, and resource alienation has been so rudely handled in the liberal historical tradition that the postwar era is remembered for corrupt deviations, rather than as a time for logical extension of established public procedures. Yet the story of public risk-taking and private profit-making does not appear to have been altered very much by transfer of the issues to the Federal sphere. The Goodrich-Heath explanations and chronology for government intervention and withdrawal might add as much meaning to Federal policy as they did to the lesser efforts by states and cities. A further test of the thesis certainly seems merited; controversies on the role of government seem almost interchangeable as the decades pass. The same angry words echo out of debates in widely separated eras, whether the subject is the delivery of monopoly powers to the Camden and Amboy, the sale of the Main Line System to the Pennsylvania Railroad, the alienation of the trans-Mississippi West, or, for that matter, the negotiation of the Dixon-Yates Contract. Perhaps historians, in their dismay at certain memories they report, have too long delayed resignation before a persistent theme in the nation's economic development—the incorrigible willingness of American public officials to seek the public good through private negotiations.

The detail of these negotiations should be pursued with infinite care. No one has undertaken extended or precise description of the way public and private obligations were combined by officers and public guardians of ante-bellum mixed corporations. Their compromise of sometimes contradictory duties, nonetheless, established ruling conventions for postwar economic organization. The mixed railroad corporation was not only parent to "big" business in the United States; its leaders also defined the character of business-government relationships, the duties of corporation to public, and the responsibility of manager to investor. Customary procedures and standards of behavior for managers of the modern corporation were thus conceived in ideological twilight, and had become habitual before the individual entrepreneur achieved a firm grip on the corporate form. Perhaps from the divided loyalties of the public-spirited men who planned so boldly for early community growth there emerged the ethical confusion characteristic of subsequent corporate behavior. Speculation on this point needs support from more abundant and specific fact than is yet available from the era of the mixed corporation.

To studies of the continuing association of government and enterprise should be added the equally unbroken theme of state regulatory efforts. The hiatus between stories of state control policies before and after the war becomes increasingly hard to justify, particularly after recent indictment of the view that "Granger" laws were the product of agrarian discontent.[6] Just as individual enterprisers of the forties and fif-

[6] George H. Miller, "Origins of the Iowa Granger Law," *Mississippi Valley Historical Review*, XL (1954), 657–80.

ties had joined in unsuccessful efforts to reduce corporate power, so, in the sixties and seventies, merchants and shippers maintained and strengthened control mechanisms. The considerable complexity of the postwar laws may possibly reflect long years of uninterrupted experience and concern with protection of the public interest. The only major break in regulatory policy appears to lie in the uneven assumption by the Federal government of earlier state responsibilities. Even at Washington, state patterns were repeated; controls, whatever the level of government, tended to lag about a generation behind aids.

The substantial energies of government, though, were employed more often for help than for hindrance to enterprise. The broad and well-documented theme reviewed here is that of public support for business development. Official vision and public resources have been associated so regularly with private skill and individual desire that the combination may be said to constitute a principal determinant of American economic growth. Internal improvements dominated the association in ante-bellum years, but opportunities for broader use of the alliance multiplied as controls over the economy became more centralized. Resolute Federal decision was in time revealed to be a key to remarkable productive achievement, most notably during the wars of the twentieth century. States and cities meanwhile transformed their record of debt from millions to billions as they constructed the nation's highways and public buildings, and extended their public services; B. U. Ratchford's analysis of American state debts might serve as an outline for a score of theses on the influence of Keynesian experiments, before Keynes. Rising constantly from the impulse to public-spirited undertakings, moreover, was the neomercantilism of regions and provinces of the American economy which came to replace the earlier and simpler competition of cities and states. Commercial clubs in the cities, industrial commissions in the states, and governors' conferences in the regions all joined in sponsorship of industrial expansion.[7] The story sprawls out to ungovernable proportions, to tax exemptions, police-guaranteed labor discipline, municipal power-plant construction, and on to RFC, TVA, and AEC. Even communities in Mississippi, the very oldest and deepest of the southern states, have in the past 14 years spent $29,206,000 in the construction of free factories for 92 enterprises who have agreed to locate there. From the grass roots putting up shoots before Chamber of Commerce buildings to the Office of the President's Council of Economic Advisors there can be documented the unceasing pressure for public sponsorship of economic growth.

Milton Heath, in the earliest contribution to the literature here considered, described the public aid movement of ante-bellum years as possibly the "last great associative effort on American soil" (Heath, 2, 60). In this judgment he was probably as wrong as other authors who have

[7] Robert A. Lively, "The South and Freight Rates: Political Settlement of an Economic Argument," *Journal of Southern History*, XIV (1948), 357–84.

analyzed the internal improvements effort as something unique in the American experience. The distant historical phenomenon they report proves very close at hand. Instead of the last great associative effort, they have revealed theory and practice for the first of continuing efforts to associate the massive powers of government with the skill of enterprise. Historians have been unaccountably slow in seeking the general themes of this story; they catalogue the plans of a Hamilton, a Gallatin or a Clay, but they have ignored the rapid translation of these schemes into essential elements of a lasting American System. The notable accomplishment of the authors reviewed lies in the bold step they have taken down the road that leads from Hamiltonian dreams toward the mixed economy of contemporary America. This road is not yet fully marked, but its general direction is now clear. Further studies of government's partnership with enterprise may reveal it to be one of the major routes connecting early American hopes with recent material achievements.

The following list of books and articles reviewed is arranged to serve as an index to specific data employed in the text. Review-style citation is utilized, where reference is to material in the subject literature. The several contributions of a single author are numbered to simplify identification of the work cited. E. C. Kirkland's study of New England railroads, G. R. Taylor's general history of the ante-bellum period, and G. S. Callender's seminal article are grouped with the works below so that they can be cited conveniently, but no effort is made to summarize their generally known contributions.

Earl S. Beard, "Local Aid to Railroads in Iowa," *Iowa Journal of History*, L (1952), 1–34.
John W. Cadman, Jr., *The Corporation in New Jersey. Business and Politics 1791–1875* (Cambridge, 1949).
Guy S. Callender, "The Early Transportation and Banking Enterprises of the States in Relation to the Growth of Corporations," *Quarterly Journal of Economics*, XVII (1902–1903), 111–62.
Carter Goodrich
    1. "Public Spirit and American Improvements," *Proceedings of the American Philosophical Society*, XCII (1948), 305–09.
    2. "National Planning of Internal Improvements," *Political Science Quarterly*, LXIII (1948), 16–44.
    3. "The Virginia System of Mixed Enterprise. A Study of State Planning of Internal Improvements," *Political Science Quarterly*, LXIV (1949), 355–87.
    4. "Local Planning of Internal Improvements," *Political Science Quarterly*, LXVI (1951), 411–45.
    5. With Harvey H. Segal, "Baltimore's Aid to Railroads. A Study in the Municipal Planning of Internal Improvements," *Journal of Economic History*, XIII (1953), 2–35.
    6. "The Revulsion Against Internal Improvements," *Journal of Economic History*, X (1950), 145–69.
Bray Hammond
    1. "Banking in the Early West: Monopoly, Prohibition and Laissez Faire," *Journal of Economic History*, VIII (1948), 1–25.
    2. "Jackson, Biddle, and the Bank of the United States," *Journal of Economic History*, VII (1947), 1–23.
    3. "Free Banks and Corporations: The New York Free Banking Act of 1838," *Journal of Political Economy*, XLIV (1936), 184–209.

Oscar Handlin
1. "Laissez-Faire Thought in Massachusetts, 1790–1880," *Journal of Economic History*, III, *Supplement* (1943), 55–65.
2. With Mary Flug Handlin, "Origins of the American Business Corporation," *Journal of Economic History*, V (1945), 1–23.
3. With Mary Flug Handlin, *Commonwealth: A Study of the Role of Government in the American Economy, Massachusetts, 1774–1861* (New York, 1947).

Louis Hartz
1. "Laissez Faire Thought in Pennsylvania, 1776–1860," *Journal of Economic History*, III, *Supplement* (1943), 66–77.
2. *Economic Policy and Democratic Thought: Pennsylvania, 1776–1860* (Cambridge, 1948).

Milton S. Heath
1. "Public Railroad Construction and the Development of Private Enterprise in the South before 1861," *Journal of Economic History*, X, *Supplement* (1950), 40–53.
2. "Public Co-operation in Railroad Construction in the Southern United States to 1861" (unpublished Ph.D. dissertation, Harvard University, 1937).
3. "Laissez Faire in Georgia, 1732–1860," *Journal of Economic History*, III, *Supplement* (1943), 78–100.

Frederick K. Henrich, "The Development of American Laissez Faire. A General View of the Age of Washington," *Journal of Economic History*, III, *Supplement* (1943), 51–54.

Edward Chase Kirkland, *Men, Cities, and Transportation. A Study in New England History 1820–1900* (Cambridge, 1948).

Harry H. Pierce, *Railroads of New York. A Study of Government Aid, 1826–1875* (Cambridge, 1953).

James Neal Primm, *Economic Policy in the Development of a Western State. Missouri, 1820–1860* (Cambridge, 1954).

George Rogers Taylor, *The Transportation Revolution 1815–1860*, Vol. 4, *The Economic History of the United States* (New York, 1951).

Section 4 ⌣ *Industry and Labor in the Agrarian*
and Commercial Economy

Ten ⌣ *Manufacture Under the Domestic System*

THE ORGANIZATION OF THE
BOOT AND SHOE INDUSTRY
BEFORE 1875   *Blanche E. Hazard*

The development of the boot and shoe industry of Massachusetts proves
to be an interesting and productive field for economic investigation, not
merely because its history goes back to colonial days as one of the leading industries of the states, but more especially because the evolution of
industrial organization finds here an unusually complete illustration. The
change from older stages to the modern factory stage has been comparatively recent, and survivals of earlier forms have existed within the memory of the old men of today. Sources, direct and indirect, oral and recorded, can be woven together to establish, to limit, and to illustrate
each one of these stages and the transitions of their various phases.

. . .

The information thus gathered seems on analysis to confirm induc-
tively and with definite evidence of the transitions the stages of evolution
set forth by Karl Bücher.[1] In the boot and shoe industry of Massachu-

[1] Bücher, *Die Entstehung der Volkswirtschaft,* chap. iv. In Wickett's English translation, pp. 150–84.

REPRINTED by permission of the publishers from Blanche E. Hazard, "The Organization of the Boot and Shoe Industry Before 1875," *The Quarterly Journal of
Economics,* Cambridge, Mass.: Harvard University Press, Vol. XXVII (February
1913), pp. 236–62.

167

setts before 1875 four stages of production may be definitely traced. Altho the stages are distinct as to characteristics and essential features, they are not so as to time, for overlaps and survivals occur. The household economy or home stage, for instance, characteristic of frontier conditions, was early followed by the handicraft organization which prevailed until the middle of the eighteenth century. The domestic stage of industrial organization with its successive and overlapping phases was well under way before the Revolution and lasted to the middle of the nineteenth century, giving place about 1855 to the factory system which passed into its second phase by 1875.

To characterize briefly and then to illustrate sparingly these stages and phases is all that can be done in the limits of this article, which undertakes only to give a preliminary survey of an investigation the detailed conclusion of which, with full evidence, will be later published.

Home Stage

During the Home Stage in the shoe industry in Massachusetts shoes were made only for home consumption. There was no market for them. The standard was individual, "the best you could make or have." The farmer and his older sons made up in winter around the kitchen hearth the year's supply of boots and shoes for the family, out of leather raised and tanned on his own or a neighbor's farm. Sometimes, as the community prospered, a travelling shoemaker,—the traditional itinerant cobbler,— was given jobs enough to keep him busy going from house to house, with his kit in a wheelbarrow or over his back, to help the farmers. Each boy in turn stood on a piece of paper or on the bare floor and had the length of his foot roughly marked off with chalk or charcoal. The shoemaker selected from among his meagre supply of lasts the one which came "somewhere near" that measure. There were only two styles, low shoes or brogans, and high boots.[2]

Handicraft Stage

The second or Handicraft Stage came in the Massachusetts boot and shoe industry with easier times in each village in turn. It had been foreshadowed by the itinerant cobbler. Now the real shoemaker could stay in

[2] This scene, made familiar by pictures and descriptions of colonial days in New England, has been enacted for me in pantomime by old men whose childhood was spent in Maine and New Hampshire hill-towns where the Home Stage survived nearly to the Civil War. These men were used during their boyhood to the custom, characteristic of this first stage, of farmers exchanging sole and upper leather, or getting their whole supply by tanning the leather for others. A vat established for neighborhood work was apt to prove the nucleus of shoe manufacture at the close of the second stage of production.

his own shop, working on his own or his customer's supply of leather.[3] He dealt directly with his market in the first phase of this stage and made only ordered or "bespoke" work.

The standard was higher in general in this Handicraft Stage than in the Home Stage, and necessarily higher in some communities than others. There were no gild regulations [4] throughout colonial Massachusetts attempting to keep the standards uniform. The shoemaker's craft, however, was a recognized mystery or industry, and men in Massachusetts were given the title of cordwainer in legal documents if they regularly worked at the trade.[5] The number of master workmen in any one town was comparatively small, of course, in this "direct market" or "town economy" period, dependent as they would be upon the possible orders of a single community.[6] Their journeymen went to the frontier settlements to set up in the craft for themselves, leaving the supply of apprentices to fill their places in the future.

The instruction which the shoemaker could give his apprentices [7] had sometimes the benefit of his own training in Europe, in Philadelphia, or Boston, where the best work was done.[8] One can imagine the journeyman who drifted to the frontier to become a master, as giving to his

[3] See Mass. Col. Legis. of 1648, quoted and interpreted by John C. Commons in this Journal for Nov., 1909, pp. 41–42.

[4] The gild organization was rare enough to be exceptional. Philadelphia and Boston, receiving more new European shoemakers, and being trade centers from the earliest times, developed and maintained it. Edward Johnson in his *Wonder-Working Providence of Sion's Saviour in New England* (pub. in 1654, p. 207 of Book 3) gives first hand knowledge of this. Cf. Charter of Boston Shoemakers published in full in the Records of the Mass. Bay in New England, vol. iii, p. 132.

[5] See, for instance, the Suffolk Registry of Deeds, for 21st yr. of Reign of Geo. II, No. 74, p. 145, date Dec. 31, 1747, giving deed of Benj. Hunt of Braintree, cordwainer, to Benj. Randall.

[6] In Middleboro, in the southern part of Massachusetts, Paul Hathaway, who had been the travelling cobbler of the village, decided in 1798, when he was 21 years old, to make people come to him with their leather and let him save his time. As his custom business grew he had 3 journeymen and 2 apprentices in his 15 × 20 shop on Pleasant Street in the midst of the North Middleboro settlement. The men made the pegs and the shoes in this shop while the women spun the flax thread and made the wax in the kitchens. At 30 years of age (in 1807) Paul Hathaway gave up his craft, for working on the bench hurt his stomach, tradition says, but since immediately upon returning to his farm work, he was known as one of the most progressive farmers in the region and had raised 124.5 bu. of shelled corn on 1 acre, winning a prize which is still on record, one wonders if the community didn't hold out higher remuneration to him as a farmer than as a shoemaker. By 1807 the organization of the shoe industry in that community had passed from the first to the second stage and was on the eve of the second phase of the handicraft stage, where "sale work" was appearing to endanger the profits of purely custom-made work. The competition of Hathaway's journeymen and apprentices must be reckoned with also, as cause for his decision.

[7] The form of apprentice indenture papers was given to boys at school as a part of their written exercises so that future masters and apprentices were familiar with the terms. The form is the one in current use in England in the 18th century. Cf. Ebenezer Belcher's Exercise book, 1793.

[8] Traditions of Josiah Field of Boston, who taught Randolph the first "city ways" of shoe making, are peculiarly interesting and well preserved.

apprentices, in turn, something less exact and somewhat out of touch with town standards.[9]

There were times when the more advanced apprentices or even the journeymen spoiled a pair of shoes started for a definite customer, and these remained on the master's hands to be disposed of. Then there were slack times when the apprentices might fairly be expected to "eat their own heads off," to the shoemaker's loss. In such a case the craftsman ventured to make up the stock on hand, to employ this otherwise wasting labor, and then tried to dispose of the shoes in the village grocery store.[10] Since the market was uncertain and slow for this extra work, both stock and labor may frequently have been below the standard used in the custom-made shoes. It might naturally happen that the demands would be more steady and the profits could be relatively higher for this lower cost work, even when it was all done at the direction of the same master shoemaker in the same shop and by the same workers by simply using different standards and different grades of stock. In case the shoemakers lived in villages too far from Boston to attract customers but near enough to send in their surplus product, their attention to sale work would steadily grow. A seemingly typical case, with all its local flavor, can be followed in detail in the bills, letters, account books, and oral traditions of Quincy Reed of Weymouth. He expected to be a shoemaker just as his great-grandfather William, who landed in Weymouth in 1635, and his grandfather and father had been. In 1809 the father was a master with custom work and probably some sale work for local consumption. As Quincy tells the story, "My brother Harvey began it by taking chickens to Boston. He had a pair of chaise wheels in the barn, and putting on a top piece, loaded her up and drove to town. He hung some shoes on the chaise and we sold them in Boston. We did not have a wagon then,—I can remember when there wasn't a wagon in this part of the town, and between here and East Abington there was only one pair of wheels. All the shoes (custom-order and extra "sale" shoes) before we began business were carried into Boston in saddle bags. . . . We hired a store of Uriah Cotting at 133 Broad Street and fitted it up. Then I used to keep a chest of shoes in a cellar near Dock Square and on Wednesday

[9] Asa C. Jones (b. 1829) was sent by his father, a custom shoemaker in Nantucket, to Weymouth to learn more points of the trade.

[10] The "general store" account books of Skinner and Ward of North Brookfield for 1813 to 1815 when the second stage still survived there, show Reuben Underwood making $10.90 of shoes between Dec. 21, 1813 and July 10, 1815 to put on sale. Doliver and Norwell, joining forces, worked on a larger scale. These same books show that they made $155.25 shoes "to be left" at Skinner & Ward's "on account" between July 2 and Nov. 1, 1813.

	1813			
July	2.	By shoes taken and left		$ 47.79
Aug.	9.	" " 43.54, Aug. 14, shoes 18.75		$ 62.26
Oct.	4.	" " 1.04, Oct. 16, " 13.50		$ 14.54
Oct.	27.	" " 29.62, Nov. 11, " 1.04		$ 30.66
		Total		$155.25

and Saturday would bring out the chest and sell. I got $15 and $20 a day by it in 1809. I was sixteen and my brother was eighteen years old then. We moved into the Broad Street store with two bushels of shoes. I used to cut out what would promise to be $100 worth a day. We couldn't have them made equal to that, but I could cut them. One day I cut 350 pair of boot fronts and tended store besides. Most of the shoes were made by people in South Weymouth. We had nearly every man there working for us before long. Used to bring out the sole leather swung across the horse's back in those days. We didn't have any capital to start with except father's assurance that 'the boys are all right and will pay their debts.' When we got of age Harvey paid father $1000 for his time and I paid him $3000. By then we had got up a stock of $10,000 and I have the inventory now to prove it. We were getting $2 for the best shoes and $1.25 to $1.50 for the West India shoes. . . ."

This has been quoted at length, even tho it anticipates in part the description of the development in the shoe industry, since it suggests the manner in which that very development was thought of. This was in all probability the way in which the Lynn trade in women's shoes had developed fifty years before that time, indicating how each community worked out the same problem and passed through the same stages of growth at different dates.

Domestic Stage

The close, therefore, of the second phase of the Handicraft Stage, with its growing attention to extra or "sale" work, appears so like the opening phase of the new or Domestic Stage that it is not readily distinguished, especially where the Handicraft workman changed naturally and gradually into a Domestic Worker employed by a shoe merchant who, as an entrepreneur, marketed the goods. Yet the two stages are fundamentally different. Just as the Handicraft Stage is characterized by the direct dealing of the shoemaker with his market, and his dependence upon his own skill and efforts in making as well as selling, so the Domestic Stage is characterized by the indirect dealing with the market on the part of the shoemaker, who was simply to manufacture the boots and shoes which a capitalist-entrepreneur marketed at his own risk and profit, supplying in whole or in part the tools and materials.

Three phases of the century-long Domestic Stage can be traced, defined, and illustrated. The first, coming gradually by the middle of the eighteenth century, prevailed in Massachusetts by the close of the Revolution [11] and lasted through the opening years of the nineteenth century.

[11] Randolph, which had become a large center of men's boot and shoe manufacture by 1845, was just becoming a separate town in 1793 (having been the South Precinct of Braintree since 1727), but had already passed through the Home and Handicraft Stages into the Domestic Stage by that date. Tradition says that some of

Tho apprentices and journeymen were employed, the less skilled and more irregular labor of the women and girls of the family was also utilized. The shoemaker turned over to the entrepreneur the completed shoe, often the combined labor of every member of his family besides his apprentices and journeymen, but with all the processes done in his shop under his direction. This last fact, that the domestic worker still makes a complete shoe, is to be considered the special characteristic of the first phase of the Domestic Stage.

At the outset of this phase (in some Massachusetts towns as early as 1750), the market was widening and the possibilities of profit were as good in the shoe trade as those in other ventures in the East and West Indies trade.[12] The development of the retail and wholesale trade in cities like Boston and Philadelphia tempted capital. There were already more shoemakers than could be supported by custom work or by the small ventures of extra "sale" work. The newspaper advertisements [13] show the demand for Lynn shoes and indicate the competition which makers of women's shoes in Massachusetts had to meet from imported goods. The Lynn entrepreneurs were specializing in women's and children's shoes [14] and leaving the making of men's boots and shoes almost

---

its soldiers doing duty at Castle Island during the Revolutionary War had been taught shoemaking by English Soldiers. The historical account of shoemaking in the U.S. Census of 1900 (part III, vol. ix, p. 754) says that in 1778 men's shoes were made in Reading, Braintree, and other towns of the Old Colony for the wholesale trade. They were sold to dealers in Boston, Philadelphia, Savannah, and Charleston, a considerable portion being exported to Cuba and other West India Islands. Whether the industry was new or not to this precinct of Braintree, these soldiers added that craft to farming when they returned to their homes and began to make shoes. One of them, Adonijah French, joined forces with a relative Thomas French, who also had just returned from war and taken up his trade again as tanner and currier. They appear as early entrepreneurs contemporary with Silas Alden, who had his own vat and shop and was employing many domestic workers by the close of the century.

Lynn was far ahead of Randolph in the 18th century both in organization and in standard of work. The account book is still extant of Amos Breed, an entrepreneur of Lynn, who was one of the merchants marketing the Lynn shoes on sale at Boston stores for retail trade or for shipment to the West Indies even before the Revolution.

[12] The London archives hold records for 1771 showing the shipment of 5938 pairs from North America to the British and foreign West Indies. Of these, 1500 pairs of shoes are from Philadelphia. The bulk of the shipment probably came from the other shoe center, Boston.

[13] The Boston Gazette of April 23, 1754, advertised among the imported goods at Wm. Merchant's store opposite the Golden Ball on the Town Dock, Boston, women's silk shoes, women's and children's callimanco and Morocco shoes and goloshes.

June 2, 1755, Blanchard Cobb and also Appleton of Boston were advertising women's English clogs and shoes. By the pages of the Boston Chronicle for 1768, May 23d, can be seen that along side the imported shoes they were selling at Fred Geyer's store men's boot soles . . . and *best made Lynn shoes*, by the 100 pair, dozen or single pair. Oliver Greenleaf offered beside his "just imported from London" goods some choice men's shoes. These newspapers also advertised John Dagyr "the celebrated shoemaker of Essex" who had come to Lynn in 1750.

[14] Amos Breed's account books from 1763 to 1796 are typical:—

wholly to custom work or to cruder local work. Few if any advertisements of men's shoes appear before the Revolution.

During the years of the war, however, the supply of shoes for the Continental army had to be undertaken, and all of the stock raised and tanned in this country. Accounts show that organization had developed in the shoe industry to meet these conditions by the close of the war. Southern and western Massachusetts had come to specialize in men's shoes, brogans and high boots, while Lynn kept to her older specialty of women's and children's. That the boot and shoe business was considered profitable to capitalists and important to the people at large is indicated by the Federal tariff legislation of 1789,[15] which gave protection to this

Cimbil to Amos Breed. Dr.

1763		£.	S.	p.
May 7.	To make 20 pairs of Callimanco shoes	26	0	0
" 23.	" " 1 " " " "	1	6	0
June 11.	" " 2 " " " "	2	12	0
" 25.	" " 5 " " " "	6	10	0
July 16.	" " 8 " " " "	10	8	0
Aug. 16.	" " 5 " " " "	6	10	0

Brigham to Amos Breed. Dr.

1764				
Nov. 2.	To make 21 pr. of Calla shoes	3	17	6
" 17.	" " 10 " " dito	1	16	8
" 28.	" " 1 " " "	0	3	8
Dec. 8.	" " 5 " " "	0	18	4
" 21.	" " 8 " " "	1	9	4

These men, Cimbil and Brigham, are hired to make the shoes. Amos Breed is evidently supplying the stock. He is also keeping a sort of custom retail trade at his home in Lynn.

Nathaniel Homes to Amos Breed. Dr.

1766				
Mar. 8.	To 1 pr. of Call. shoes for Poeb	2	30	0
Apr. 19.	" 1 " everlasting " " Hannah	2	40	0
"	" 1 " leather " " Lydia	1	6	0
July 12.	" 1 " silk " " self	2	8	0
" 19.	" 1 " russet " " Poeb	2	60	0

Breed not only hired shoes made and sold them for both domestic and foreign trade but he mended them.

Wm. Estes to Amos Breed. Dr.

1774				
Mar. 14.	To mend a pr. of shoes	0	4	6
Apr. 10.	" 1 pr. of shoes	1	16	0
" 26.	" 1 " " russet shoes	2	0	0
May 14.	" mend 1 pr. of shoes	0	12	0
July 15.	" make 1 pr. of shoes	1	10	0

[15] Tariff rates of July 4, 1789:—
    On boots per pair, 50 cents.
    On all shoes, slippers or goloshes made of leather per pr., 7c.
    On all shoes or slippers made of silk or stuff, 10c. per pair.
    Tariff of August 10, 1790: provisions of previous tariff kept and one added which put on leather tanned or tawed, and on manufactures of which leather was

industry. The tradition seems as well founded as it is detailed that this action was due to the shoe merchants of Massachusetts as well as Pennsylvania. Their pressure was strong enough, joined to the general current towards protection, to over-ride the specific illustration of James Madison against protecting shoes.[16]

The increase of market for boots and shoes and its assured protection did not fail to widen the ranks of capitalists and to intensify the manner of production. A new phase, outwardly marked by prosperity and volume,[17] prevailed in Massachusetts from about 1810 to 1837. The extra

---

the chief article, a 7½% ad valorem duty, but excepted raw hides and skins from the 5% ad valorem duty put on other raw products.

By the 7th of June, 1794, the tariff on boots was reduced to 20c. per pair and that on shoes and slippers, clogs and goloshes to 5c. a pr.

[16] ". . . For example, we should find no advantage in saying that every man should be obliged to furnish himself by his own labor with those accommodations which depend upon the mechanic's art, instead of employing his neighbor, who could do it for him on better terms. It would be no advantage for a shoemaker to make his own clothes in order to save the expense of the tailor's bill, nor of the tailor to make his own shoes to save the expense of procuring them from the shoemaker. . . . The same argument holds good between nation and nation." Cf. Annals of Congress, I Cong. 1834, I, pp. 109–48.

[17] The contrast is shown in the following ledger pages of Belcher's account book for 1808 and 1817.

*Ambrose Hollis * to me*

To 1 lb. of flax ½, to 1 half Bushel Corn	$00.74
" meat & butter	.36
	1.10
By making 11 pare of children shoes	1.20
To 1 peck of corn	00.27
By making 6 pare of children's shoes	1.20
	.93
By making 8 pare of children's shoes	1.60
To 1 half bush. of corn to 1 lb. of flax	.74
	.76

Entry of 1817 in same book

Ebenezer Belcher, Cr. to Bass and Turner

Mar. 7.	To making	20	pare of mens shoes	2/		6.67
" 20.	"	50	" " "	" 2/		16.67
Apr. 1.	" "	68	" " "	" 2/		22.67
" 8.	" "	5	" " "	"		1.67
	" "	20	"	"		6.67
May 27.	" "	10	"	"		3.34
June 10.	" "	20	"	" 1/6		5.00
" 24.	" "	20	"	"		5.00
July 11.	" "	40	"	"		14.00

* A journeyman, married, and living in other half of Belcher's house.

This entry of 1817 meant steadier work on the part of Ebenezer Belcher and his journeymen for he was doing as much as this for other merchants at the same date. Shoemaking could no longer be a farmer's by-employment. It also meant that specialized work had come into the industry, for by this time the term "making" included only the processes of lasting and bottoming.

capital which was tempted into the boot and shoe industry brought severer competition for orders and suggested specialization to secure rapid work, and this specialization in processes may be taken as the characteristic of the second phase of the Domestic Stage. The time factor seemed more vital than the quality, for with such big, insistent markets, a merchant could afford to lose a disgruntled customer, sure of having plenty of others. Already the producer did not have to face the consumer or have his reputation hurt by occasional bad work. The standards were therefore lowered, and the competition of employers let into the trade less skilled and almost unskilled labor to do the cheaper work on men's brogans and women's and children's shoes for the well developed trade in the West Indies and the South. A wide difference arose not only between the quality of custom and domestic work, but between the wages of "real journeymen" and shoemakers.

As the workers grew more numerous in the employ of each Massachusetts capitalist and were scattered in their shops, called "ten-footers," [18] over a wider area, in fact all through New England, from Portland, Maine, to the Island of Nantucket, the need of inspection of the finished product, as well as of saving in the cutting of stock at the central shops became vitally necessary. Previously the stock for both uppers and soles had been given out in skins and sides, leaving it to the shoemaker to cut wisely and economically. What he could save by honest or dishonest means he felt free to keep in his "cabbage" stock box under his low shoemaker's bench. Old shoemakers are found now in every locality who recall with bitterness certain individuals whose dishonesty and poor work led to the development of the central shop. They blame the open way in which scrap leather buyers went about on regular routes to buy up the accumulated "cabbage" stock, which meant loss to the capitalist, while it was a source of profit to the shoemaker and presumably to the scrapman. These old people make the complaint with little realization that the boot and shoe industry has simply followed the example of the silk and the woolen industry in experiencing, in the course of growth, the need of saving stock as well as time, and of giving to agents the power of inspection formerly exercised by the gild officials of the Middle Ages or by the master shoemaker of early colonial days.

The central shop system rapidly developed after 1820. The stock was cut there, and portioned out, ready to deliver to workers to do the "fitting," i.e. the work on the uppers, siding up of seams, binding, counter and strap stitching. When this process was completed the uppers were returned to the central shop and given out with the proper number of roughly cut soles, as well as a definite quantity of thread, to "makers" who would last and then sew the boots and shoes. The makers had to wait generally for their work to be inspected or "crowned" at the central shop. The volume of trade and the amount of specialization can be un-

[18] The name was not exact, for the size of domestic shops ranged from 10 × 10 to 14 × 14.

derstood by the study of a single month's business dealings in one firm's ledger for 1833.[19]

The capitalist had to divide his time between his Boston office and his home shop, dealing with buyers, writing letters to order stock and conclude bargains, and deciding on the manner of payment and transportation.[20] He must have been paying attention also to tariff legislation at Washington.[21] He was planning and examining ways of investing the profits of the shoe business in other directions. Many shoe merchants of Massachusetts speculated in Maine lands [22] in 1820–30 and in Western

[19] White & Whitcomb of East Randolph (now Holbrook) were employing in 1833, from Sept. 4th to Oct. 4th, 12 men and women to do fitting, 30 men to make, and 1 man to do all the cutting, pasting and blacking. Both the styles and the finish were crude, and this is about the usual proportion of labor,—that is, one central shop worker to about forty domestic workers. The large sales during that month were to the following firms:—

	Amt.	No. prs. shoes
J. C. Addington & Co.	$226.18	250
Porter & Tileston	$205.64	212
B. C. Harris	$ 57.50	50
C. W. Howes & Co.	$257.50	250
C. W. Howes & Co.	$237.40	262
N. Houghton & Co.	—	218
Wm. Tiffany	$100.00	100

[20]
PHILAD. 9th 22, 1821.

RESPECTED FRIENDS
    H. &. L. REED
Your favour of 17th inst. was recd this morning informing that you had received the box of calf-skins and am sorry that they did not give satisfaction. The price at which they were invoiced is lower than skins are now selling for and if you think proper you can return them and we will pay the freight back cheerfully. We are sorry you have been disappointed but we are certain you could not now buy calf skins of similar quality in this city or in New York at so low a price, calfskins of light kind have seen sold by tanners here last week at $27 per doz. in the rough. Very respectfully,

Your assured friend,
C. & W. ROBINSON & Co.

(Mail to Boston)

NEW YORK, Oct. 29, 1821.
MESS. H. & L. REED
    GENTLEMEN
    We herewith enclose you a Mechanics Bank Dft for Twelve hundred and eighty six 35/100 dollars the receipt of which you will please acknowledge to our mutual friends Hubbard Hayden of Richmond, Va., and oblige yours,

Very respectfully,
CUNNINGHAM & McCORMICK.

[21] In 1816, the duty on boots was advanced to $1.50 a pair. In 1824 this amount was put on laced boots or "bootees" and a tax of 25c. a pair put on prunella or other shoes and slippers. No reduction was made on these heavy protective rates until 1842.

[22] The Littlefield Bros. of East Stoughton (now Avon), who were making money in the Cuban and New Orleans trade, invested over $80,000 in Aroostook County

and Southern lands in 1830–40. Not only individual shoe-merchants were in the speculating, expanding mood; whole shoe towns were also.[23] The big fortunes and the market as well came to a sudden end in the panic years of 1837–38. The money tied up in land investments could not be got out in time to tide over the epidemic failures. Then the Massachusetts Bankruptcy Law, by relieving debtors, settled the nicely poised fate of their braver more far-sighted creditors. Ninety per cent of the shoe merchants had to fail.[24] As a rule the men who had smaller trade and smaller risks "held on" grimly, to become the back bone of a new phase of the Domestic System.

By 1840 a new trade with new markets was gradually emerging from the boot and shoe trade, but it had to be coaxed. New styles, niceties and novelties in processes required, however, greater specialization. No manufacturer could afford to lose a single customer by slip-shod work or poor stock.[25] The competition for employment gave the employers a chance to choose only the best workmen. Shoemakers who had developed a reputation for a speciality [26] were in demand. In the old days the shoemaker-turned-capitalist could keep his workers in hand by very casual inspection or a wholesome fear of it. The outsider, as capitalist, could hope at most to know the stock and did not try to master the processes. He was generally wise enough to take as partner a man who

---

land before 1836. They "pulled out before that money was lost" in the general hard times of 1837, because they needed ready money for the New Orleans trade. There the business amounted to $100,000 a year between 1828 and 1837, but in the early 40's the results of mismanagement and the general effects of the financial depression combined to bring bad debts, so that the firm had to be content to take payments in lands in Mississippi and Texas just when land was a drug on the market.

The Reeds of Weymouth, who had grown rich out of a wholesale boot and shoe trade with such distributing centers as Richmond, Savannah, New Orleans, and Havana, invested in 1833 in Maine lands. Harvey Reed bought a whole Maine township at 9 pence an acre. Quincy Reed, however, withstood the land lure and had for a side issue a grain business which kept four schooners busy in the coastwise trade and with Spain. The bills of lading show the details of this enterprise.
[23] Lynn built forty-three new streets between 1831 and 1840. North Brookfield, which in 1820 had "nothing doing, no new buildings going up, the same old dwelling houses and farms satisfying the people," had more than one hundred houses newly built by 1838 and old houses had been repaired.
[24] Cf. Eleazar Beal and Cox notes for details of some specific cases.
[25] Johnson of Lynn tells of the helter-skelter work of the previous booming days. Good grain leather uppers and best quality soles were spoiled for wearing shoes by paper stiffenings. Shoes were so badly sewed that they easily dropped to pieces, or well sewed but trimmed so close to either edge that you could not wear a pair a second time before the stiches pulled out. Shoe manufacturers say that very cheaply made shoes are a concomitant of general hard times when "anything will sell that looks well and will hold together till the purchase is made." In good times, "even mill hands won't buy them."
[26] Samuel White of Randolph (b. 1831) was known as a champion rapid pegger; spectators came from neighboring towns in the late forties to watch him work in his little ten-footer on Union Street. He has told me that his speed was gained by using both hands at once running the dink, using the awl, and hammering in pegs in quick succession, while he held the pegs in his mouth.

knew the trade and could put his brains against money.[27] Otherwise the new shoemaker had to trust entirely to expert workmen, to foremen and agents who were devoted to his interests, and let them determine the details of stock and processes while he looked out for markets and profits.

The market was already making hints if not demands as to styles instead of accepting quietly anything the shoemaker provided. The use of different shapes and widths of block lasts came in the early forties, makers no longer depending upon "instep leathers" for making "fulls" and "slims." Sole patterns gave uniformity of shape and width at ball and shank. Patterns for rounding the soles after they were stitched and irons for polishing the edges were invented and used. Heels were put on women's shoes again [28] and men began to specialize in heeling. More workers were taken into the central shops and expected to do one thing "up to the standard." They were hired to tree boots, or to finish bottoms. Not only every sole in a case must be uniformly finished, but the appearance of the shoes in all the cases sent to one customer must be the same.[29] This increasing specialization led to the entrance into the shoe trade of young men and women who learned and knew just one process, and the cessation of regular apprenticeship [30] for shoemakers.

Not only did labor have to become more specialized and efficient in this recuperating period of the forties, the third and final phase of the Domestic Stage, but it had to be economized to meet closer competition. That fact, added to the demand for standardization of product, led to the introduction of machinery into the boot and shoe industry. Up to the forties the shoemaker had used mainly tools, and just such as had been used for centuries.[31] His kit included knives to cut upper and sole

[27] A typical case was that of Eddy & Leach of Middleboro. Deacon Eddy had a general store and the postoffice and was worth $10,000 which had been made, in part, in the shovel business. George M. Leach, whom he took as partner (1852) for the new enterprise, had only $200 but was a regular shoemaker who had previously owned a ten-footer on his farm and "taken out" shoes to make.

[28] Spring heels, which took the place of high ones in 1830, had given place to no heels at all. Brogans were almost heelless, having but one lift. Cf. Johnson, Lynn Sketches, p. 340.

[29] Henry P. Crocker of Raynham, 85 years old in 1912, described one case of this transition. The finishing of soles had been done outside with little uniformity by the individual "makers" who put on the soles. When the Gilmore Factory took the process into the central shop they gave a man only 1c. a pair, however, for finishing. Several men had failed to make a living at it and Crocker hesitated at the offer in 1847, for he was getting $9 a month "making" for someone else. Soon, however, he was earning $1 a day, then $2 and sometimes $3. His "partner hand," working beside him, did the sand-papering; Crocker put on the oxalic acid to whiten the leather, polished it with a sheep's leg bone, stamped it with the firm name and gave it to another man to "dress."

[30] There seems to be no definite, or even indefinite, case in Massachusetts of a shoemaker's becoming a regular apprentice to learn to make a whole boot after 1840. This has been a point in my investigation for several years.

[31] Interesting details of similar early tools and methods of shoemaking in Germany are given in Beitrag zur Geschichte der mechanischen Schuhfabrikation, by Gewerbeassessor Dr. Rehe, Breslau, pp. 186–87.

leather, a lap stone and hammer for pounding leather, awls for pegging holes, a stirrup for holding the shoe in place on the knee, pincers to pull the leather over the last, nippers to pull out tacks, bristles for needles and hemp thread for sewing, a buffing knife or scraper for the sole leather and a shoulder-stick for polishing soles. Then there came a little skiving machine run by hand and not very satisfactory to the older men, accustomed to skiving with a regular knife. The next machines to be invented for boot and shoe work were the "stripper" for cutting up sides of sole leather, and the "sole-cutter." A leather-rolling machine came in 1845 to save both time and strength formerly used in hammering sole leather on a lap stone. Several styles of pegging machines [32] and a machine for cutting up pegs had been patented and put in general use by the time [33] the sewing machine, invented by Howe in 1846, had been adapted to upper leather work on shoes by John Brooks Nichols in 1852.[34] There was the "dry thread" machine with a shuttle and two threads for the lighter upper work, and the "wax thread" to do chain stitching for the heavy work of "siding up" bootlegs. These sewing machines even then impressed people with their significance. Instead of merely making things easier or a "bit more speedy," they produced work which could not be matched by hand in either speed or appearance.[35]

By 1855 so general had become the use of sewing machines that shoemakers who could afford it had them in their homes to use on both cloth and leather. But it was generally the manufacturer who put the machines into his central shop, or the man with some capital and genius for machinery, who bought or leased the "wax thread" and "dry thread" machines and set them up either in a stitching shop or in a central shop where space was hired. Men and young women followed the machines,

[32] Cf. Rehe, pp. 188–89, for the story of Krantz and the introduction of the pegging machine into Germany.

[33] Proofs of dates of invention are in an unsatisfactory state at present. Not only local historians and biographers, but the United States Census Reports of 1860 and 1900, give merely approximate or relative dates for many inventions and for their introduction to practical use. Only a minute study of the patent records could furnish an indisputable array of such dates.

[34] For details concerning Nichols and his adaptation of the Howe Machine, see The Sewing Machine Journal of April 25, May 25, 1904, July 10, July 25, and February 10, 1911. These are first hand reports and illustrated. They give valuable facts on the Howe-Singer-Leavitt machine controversy.

[35] In the United States Census Report of 1860 (p. 71) this significance was not only expressed but coupled with an interesting prophecy. "The crowning invention of all, which has supplanted and given value to all other kinds of machinery, in the manufacture of boots and shoes, is the *sewing machine*. It has introduced a new era in the trade. Without it, the partial use of machinery upon the bottoms of boots and shoes was attended with little economy, because the cost of *stitching and binding* the uppers, which was the larger item of expense, was not reduced in a corresponding degree. Altho of quite recent introduction in this branch of industry, its employment along with the sole-cutting machine, and other appliances, is gradually bringing about a *silent revolution* in the boot and shoe manufacture. . . . It is safe to predict that this change will go on until the little workshop of the shoemaker with its bench and kit shall become a thing of the past as is the hand card and the great and little spinning wheel."

leaving the older people to "side up" and bind shoes by hand at home.[36]
Thus a new stage of organization had come in the boot and shoe industry, bringing to an end not only the third phrase but the main life of the
Domestic Stage, where the "putting out" system had prevailed and the
entrepreneur had worked in his central shop while the domestic workers
labored in their "ten-footers." Only the "making" (*i.e.* lasting and bottoming) of sewed shoes continued to be done by domestic workers far
into the next period, until the McKay machine for sewing the soles and
finally the Goodyear welting machine put an end to this last survival of
the Domestic System.

Factory Stage

The expansion which came after 1850, associated with the Californian
and Australian gold discoveries, emphasized the increasing economy of
large scale production, and hastened the transition from the Domestic to
the Factory System. Immense orders with big profits stirred and pushed
to its very limit of production the boot and shoe industrial organization.
Forty-niners who had left shoemaking relations at home or gone out
from shoe towns, naturally saw the chances for marketing Massachusetts
boots in California. The same held true in Australia.[37] Meanwhile the

[36] The books of Howard & French of Randolph for these years and of E. Twitchell
& Co., of Brookfield, show the hand work and machine work going on side by
side, and the relative cost and volume of each. The Twitchell firm had specially
ruled and printed ledgers for record of work "put out."

Date when taken	Binders name	No. of Case	Kinds of Leather Clf.|Kip.|Buff|Split	Quality 1st. 2nd.	Sizes Wom. Miss Chil.	When Returned	Price paid

This allowed the firm to keep track of where the stock was, even if it did not secure
its speedy return.

The Twitchell order-book shows not only the prices and distribution of the
goods made in the 50's and 60's, but the means of transportation by various "young
railroads" and western despatch companies. The Howard & French books show
the order and truck payment system surviving well up to the end of this Domestic
Period. They employed Elbridge Jones and Jerome Fletcher, who were stitchers, by
the day at a uniform wage of $1.66⅔ a day, paid partly in cash, in dinners (at
the rate of 14⅔c. apiece) in stock, in butter, in hay. Howard & French had their
own general store, and seldom gave orders on other stores.

There is much evidence in such account books to confirm the accuracy of the
picture given by F. A. Walker (Wages Question, p. 136) of the methods in which
payments of wages were made in New England before the Civil War.

[37] Randolph boot manufacturers were among the firms to profit earliest by this
trade. Mr. Jonathan Wales left his home town in time to have a shoe store established in San Francisco in 1851. At first he bought his goods of the Wentworth,
the Whitcomb, and the Howard & French factories of Randolph. His business increased until he was handling the output of over twenty firms in Randolph, Stough-

southern and southwest markets held steady with growing orders. Even the crisis of 1857 did not do general damage enough to interrupt the increasing shoe trade.

Agents sent home more orders than could be filled with the old rate of speed and equipment. When the hundred or more cases were engaged to go on a certain steamer, due to leave Boston [38] for its route round "the Horn" on a certain day, duly advertised, the boots must be done on time or risk being rejected at their tardy arrival in California or Australia. The domestic worker had enjoyed all the latitude he needed or wished. He sowed his fields and cut his hay when he was ready. He locked up his "ten-footer" and went fishing when he pleased, or sat in his kitchen reading when it was too cold to work in his little shop. The agents or "freighters," [39] who came down from Maine and New Hampshire with sample shoes to show the workmanship and to take back big express wagons full of un-made boots and shoes, were never sure when washouts or snow storms might delay the return of the stock. Books show that the women who "fitted" and the men who "made" boots and shoes were irregularly employed before the late fifties, and obviously at

---

ton, and North Bridgewater. Meanwhile he had entered the firm of Newhall and Gregory of San Francisco, who sold at auction all the boots and· shoes consigned to Jonathan Wales.

Mr. Frank Maguire established himself as agent in Melbourne, Australia, and marketed almost the entire output of the Burrell and Maguire factory in Randolph. Both Mr. Wales and Mr. Maguire, as distributing agents, sent home to their employing manufacturers new orders that then seemed incredibly large, and either drafts on Boston banks or bags of gold. I have seen at the home of Mr. Wales' son and daughter some of these bags, made of white drilling and stencilled with large figures giving the amounts, sometimes as high as $20,000. A large silver salver presented to Mr. Jonathan Wales in 1856 gives the names of twenty men connected with the firms which had profited by his skill and efforts.

[38] Advertisement cards like the following were sent to manufacturers:—

Winsor's Regular Line, For San Francisco.
    From India Wharf.
To sail June 25th.   The Celebrated Extreme New York Clipper Ship Golden City
                    Capt. Leary.
This Ship has been put in the most perfect order, and is now in her berth with a part of her cargo on board. She is THE great favorite with New York shippers.
Her passages have been made in 102 and 106 days, while other clipper ships, sailing at the same time, were 120 days.
Her ventilation is perfect, and her cargoes have been delivered in the most perfect order. Shippers who wish to be sure of their goods reaching California in October, will appreciate her.
The well known favorite medium ship CROMWELL, Capt. Adams, now in her berth, and loading, will sail about the 1st of July.
    For Freight or Passage, apply to
        NATH'L WINSOR, JR. & CO.
            corner of State and Broad Sts.
                            Watson's Press, 25 Doane St.
    June 7, 1858.
[39] Cf. Spinney, Mullen, and Amasa Clarke notes.

their own request. They knew that the work must be inspected at the Central Shop before they were paid, but the pay "would keep."

The rush, then, of the California and Australia trade put a stop to this condition in every shop when it brought orders from new trade or increased those from the old. More crimping and finishing, as well as cutting, pasting, and finishing was done "under the roof." There was now a greater inducement to manufacturers to invest in sewing machines for the uppers and to have the siding up and binding done in the shop by alert younger women and men, instead of by the old women at home. Practically the whole laboring population [40] of a shoe town was employed in the shop or the factory. Even for the making of boots a "gang" [41] of four or five men frequently hired a room in the vicinity of a central shop, or in it. Thus the manufacturer, to save time and to hold markets by prompt delivery of large orders in the fifties, unconsciously completed the movement well on its way in the forties, in order to meet competition and the demands of standardizing, of having shoemaking done under one roof under supervision. This is the chief characteristic of the Factory Stage of the boot and shoe organization: it had entered the industry gradually and almost unawares.

Larger buildings, now called manufactories, more capital, larger supplies of stock were the more apparent features of the growing boot and shoe trade even in the fifties.[42] By 1860 steam power was being introduced into the larger manufactories, making the hand labor of the domestic worker seem pitifully slow in comparison with the stitching

[40] Statistics of the Massachusetts Census of 1865 show the following proofs of this:—

Town	Engaged in Manufacture		Engaged in Agriculture		In Boot & Shoe Manufacturing	
	Males	Females	Males	Females	Males	Females
Randolph	1845	281	61	0	1789	248
Stoughton	1051	254	200	0	964	184
Abington	2605	358	165	0	2479	346
North Bridgewater	1231	213	240	0	1059	208

[41] 1 lasted,
   1 pegged and tacked on soles,
   1 made fore edges,
   1 put on heels and "pared them up."
   and in the case of hand sewed shoes 2 or 3 sewers were needed to keep the rest of the gang busy.

[42] There was, for example, the new Gilmore factory built in Raynham in 1857; very different from the usual grocery store or private house, turned into a central shop. It seemed like a visible proof of big trade and profits, for it had a wide porch with Doric columns, office fitted with Venetian shades and black walnut desks and railing; an elevator and dumb waiters; speaking tubes from every room to the office; a steam whistle to summon employees, and a driveway through the lower floor for ease and expediency in receiving and shipping freight. There was a carpenter shop and a special carpenter. The large machine shop, with a forge and a machinist permanently in charge, was probably one of the chief reasons why Mr. Blake and Mr. McKay came to this factory, five years later, to try out the McKay machines. Meanwhile Mr. McKay was urging the Gilmore brothers to help finance the movement of putting the machine on the market.

done by steam driven machines. By the time the Goodyear Welt machine was put on the market in 1875 and people at large realized that the Factory System had come and the Domestic had gone [43] one whole phase of the Factory System had already passed.

The Factory System, which had come in the late fifties, was the prevailing type of organization during the Civil War. The large orders of shoes for the Union Armies, added to the scarcity of labor caused by the volunteering and drafting of soldiers, were additional important factors in the use of machinery in general and in encouraging the trial of the McKay machine. During the War the practicability of the McKay machine with steam power was demonstrated, and it was widely adopted during the late sixties. More specializing came on the part of both shoe workers and manufacturers. Some southern Massachusetts towns made shoes only, others boots. Some towns in the western part of the state made only cheap brogans for laborers, while others made a finer grade of shoe to be distributed by New York jobbers. The increased variety of styles within this classification made it necessary to dispose of stock while it was in fashion.

The "expansion tendency" of the decade after the Civil War led, as it did in the thirties, to over speculation. Shoe manufacturers put more money into railroad stock and western lands than they could steadily hold there, so that when the hard times of 1873 came, many failures were found in the shoe trade.[44] Thus the first phase of the Factory Stage, like the second phase of the Domestic Stage, closed with a sense of disaster and had again to be followed by a period of recuperation.

The history of the boot and shoe industrial organization since 1875

[43] The Massachusetts Census for 1875 (vol. ii, p. 825) gives tables showing the number and wages of women "furnished with work to do on boots and shoes at home" for the year ending May 1, 1875. A few are given here:—

Town	Number of Women	Total Yearly Wage	Yearly Average wage of each domestic worker
Amesbury	4	$700.00	$175.00
Lynn	575	82,559.00	143.58+
Haverhill	225	20,207.00	89.80+
Randolph	39	1,750.00	44.87+
Stoughton	2	150.00	75.00
Webster	35	1,200.00	34.28
No. Brookfield	6	690.00	115.00
Braintree	1	300.00	300.00

These figures show that there was a marked difference among these few domestic workers either in the amount, or regularity, or the quality of their work, and also a wide difference in the completeness with which the factory system was adopted in these old shoe manufacturing centers.

[44] The trouble caused by the St. Crispin organization in demands and strikes did not seem to make serious financial difference to the Massachusetts shoe industry. Local accounts of specific contests, while interesting and prophetic of later union trouble, do not affect this conclusion, nor put the blame for failures in the shoe trade on the shoulders of labor.

makes the story of the second phase of the Factory Stage. Its course may be simply indicated, being outside the limit set for this paper. It has been characterized chiefly by an intensive system of production, tho in common parlance its chief charactristic has been the use of the Goodyear Welting machine. Competition, which has been not only acute but world-wide, has forced economies and heightened the chance of loss on the ever-increasing variety of styles which the product must take to capture the market. The insistent discovery and use of by-products, the absorption of allied industries by some shoe manufacturing firms, and the greater reliance placed by others on highly specialized allied industries,[45] the immense increase in the size of plants and of the number of employees, have all necessitated the perfecting of the factory system. The rise of the "labor problem" with the closely contested struggles with organized labor has also especially characterized this period. This central phenomenon, however, together with the other factors of transportation, market organization, and finance, which have so profoundly modified industrial organization, must be left for later presentation.

[45] The signs seen on buildings when one approaches a shoe manufacturing center, showing where heels, rands, counters, welting, findings, patterns, lasts, dies, cartons, and boxes are made, furnish a graphic illustration of the scope of allied industries. These make possible what Marshall calls "external economies" arising from "the concentration of many small businesses of a similar character in particular localities"; the "subsidiary trades" which grow up in the locality of a large industry, "supplying it with many implements and materials, organizing its traffic, and in many ways conducing to the economy of its material." *Principles of Economics*, pp. 266–71 (6th edition).

THE IMPACT OF INDUSTRIALISM
Foster Rhea Dulles

In the course of his American tour in 1842, Charles Dickens visited Lowell, Massachusetts where the new textile manufacturers of New England had established one of the country's first factory towns. The young women and girls who made up most of the working force appeared to him as paragons of virtue—happy, contented and exemplary in their conduct. With their neat and serviceable bonnets, warm cloaks and shawls, "they were all well dressed, but not to my thinking above their station; . . . from all the crowd I saw in the different factories that day, I cannot recall or separate one face that gave me a painful impression."

The English traveler also admired the well-ordered rooms in the factories, some of them with plants growing in the windows, and the fresh air, cleanliness and comfort; he was impressed with the boarding houses where the young women lived under careful chaperonage, and he was particularly struck with what he reported as three startling facts: there were joint-stock pianos in many of the houses, nearly all of the young ladies subscribed to circulating libraries, and a magazine was published —the *Lowell Offering*—that was entirely made up of stories and articles by the factory operatives. Gazing happily upon this industrial paradise, Dickens compared it with the manufacturing centers of England and earnestly begged his countrymen "to pause and reflect upon the difference between this town and those great haunts of misery."

Although it could also have been pointed out, even in 1842, that the factory girls worked incredibly long hours, were badly overcrowded in their boarding houses, and found their lives wholly ordered and controlled by the paternalistic factory owners, the picture that the enthusiastic Dickens drew of Lowell was not wholly out of keeping with the facts. Other visitors confirmed his general impressions. They too wrote of the pleasant atmosphere, of the cultural opportunities of circulating libraries and lecture rooms, and of the gay appearance of the young

FROM Foster Rhea Dulles, "The Impact of Industrialism," *Labor in America: A History*, New York: Crowell, 1960, pp. 73–89. Copyright © 1960 by Thomas Y. Crowell Company.

ladies, not only with neat bonnets over the carefully curled ringlets of their hair, but wearing silk stockings and carrying parasols. Lowell may not have been amusing as the French traveler, Michael Chevalier, wrote, but it was "clean, decent, peaceful and sober."

In these early stages of the industrial revolution, at least some parts of the United States seemed to have escaped the more unlovely aspects of its advent in Europe. The Massachusetts capitalists who established the first textile mills wanted to prevent the oppression of the workers that had so notoriously resulted from the development of the factory system abroad. They intended to draw their labor supply from the New England farming population, to a very great extent young women and girls, and attractive conditions helped them to secure the type of workers they wanted. In the Rhode Island mills, where whole families were induced to move to town with husband, wife and children all playing their part in tending the looms and spindles, the situation was quite different. Factory hands were callously exploited. The idea behind Lowell, however, was virtually that of a female boarding school, except that the young women worked in the mills rather than at their studies.

Everything possible was done to safeguard their health, and even more particularly, their morals. They had to live in the boarding houses, where they were under strict supervision and the doors were closed at 10 P.M. They were expected to attend church. Not only was discharge an immediate consequence of immodesty, profanity or dancing, to say nothing of more serious lapses from morality, but insofar as male workers were concerned, the Lowell Manufacturing Company stated that it would not "continue to employ any person who shall be wanting in proper respect to the females employed by the company, or who shall smoke within the company's premises, or be guilty of inebriety."

The long hours of work were long but not as oppressive as they might appear. Tending the looms was not so arduous as other types of factory work were to become, and the young ladies had frequent opportunities to rest, to read, to talk among themselves, and to water the plants on the window sills. After paying for their board and lodging, they seldom had more than $2 a week left out of their wages, but for members of farm families for whom any cash income was almost unknown, even this small sum seemed like riches. It generally went into the bank and there was a time when the deposits of the Lowell girls were said to average as much as $500.

The most important distinction between conditions in this early period and later years, however, was that the workers still did not in any sense consider themselves permanently employed. Most of the young women came in from the country to work at Lowell for only the few years necessary to save up money to get married, or enough to go out to Ohio and other parts of the new west as schoolteachers. Moreover, if they did not like the work, or should be laid off in slack times, they could easily return to their farm homes. They were neither firmly attached to the mills nor wholly dependent upon them.

The relatively happy circumstances of this life did not last, however, for very long. Far-reaching changes were already well underway at the time of Dickens' visit to Lowell. As competition increased in the textile industry, the benevolent paternalism of the millowners gave way to stricter controls which had nothing to do with the well-being of the workers. Wages were reduced, the hours of work lengthened, and the equivalent of the speed-up was introduced into factory processes. For a work day from 11½ to 13 hours, making up an average week of 75 hours, the women operatives were generally earning less than $1.50 a week (exclusive of board) by the late 1840's, and they were being compelled to tend four looms whereas in the 1830's they had only taken care of two. When the manager of one mill at Holyoke, Massachusetts, found his hands "languorous" because they had breakfasted, he ordered them to come before breakfast. "I regard my work-people," an agent at another factory said, "just as I regard my machinery. So long as they can do my work for what I choose to pay them, I keep them, getting out of them all I can."

Embittered complaints began to take the place of earlier satisfaction as these conditions grew steadily worse. "These ladies have been imposed upon egregiously by the aristocratic and offensive employers, assuming to be their lords and masters," wrote the *Lynn Record*. Orestes Brownson, radical friend of labor, declared that "the great mass wear out their health, spirits and morals without becoming one whit better off." In the *Voice of Industry*, a new labor newspaper devoted to the cause of mill workers, there were frequent attacks upon the policies that the employers were following.

"Your factory system is worse by far than that of Europe," stated an open letter in this journal addressed to Abbott Lawrence. "You furnish your operatives with no more healthy sleeping-apartments than the cellars and garrets of the English poor. . . . The keepers are compelled to allow . . . but one room for six persons and generally crowd twelve and sometimes sixteen females into the same hot, ill-ventilated attic. . . . You shut up the operatives two or three hours longer a day in your factory prisons than is done in Europe. . . . You allow them but half an hour to eat their meals. . . . You compel them to stand so long at the machinery . . . that varicose veins, dropsical swelling of the feet and limbs, and prolapsus uter, diseases that end only with life, are not rare but common occurrences."

The factory girls themselves more and more resented "the yoke which has been prepared for us," and tried to combat the reductions in wages and increase in work. Even in the 1830's, . . . they had experimented with strikes, and now a decade later they pledged themselves not to accept additional looms without wage increases and called for shorter working hours. But they could make no headway, and as a consequence began to return to their farm homes. The so-called "slavers"—long, low black wagons which cruised about the countryside as far afield as Vermont and New Hampshire—could no longer recruit mill hands with promises of easy work and high wages that were known to be false. The New England farm girls were quitting the mills.

Their place was taken by a new class of workers even less able to protect their interests. A rising tide of immigration had by mid-century made available a great reservoir of Irish and German girls, and some French-Canadians, who had no other alternative than to accept work in the mills no matter what the wages or hours. Conditions grew worse rather than better under these circumstances. The infusion of cheap immigrant labor, as a committee of the Massachusetts legislature noted in 1850, was causing "an entire modification and depression of the state of society in and about manufacturing places."

While the textile trade provides a striking example of what happened to working conditions with increasing industrialization, the same thing was taking place in other trades. The Lynn shoemakers had enjoyed a high degree of independence in the 1830's with their own work shops and the opportunity to fall back on farming or fishing should trade fall off. "When the spring opened," read one perhaps too idyllic account of a worker's life, "the horizon of his hopes expanded. Less clothing and fuel were needed. The clam banks discounted more readily; haddock could be got at Swampscott so cheap that the price wasn't worth quoting. The boys could dig dandelions. . . . Then if the poor man had his little 'spring pig' that he had kept through the winter, 'pork and dandelions' were no small item in the bill of fare while 'greens' lasted." But the masters steadily tightened their control over manufacturing and wages were reduced and paid in store orders rather than cash. The shoemakers gradually found themselves forced from their own work shops, from their fishing and farming in off hours, into the new factories with whose machine processes they could no longer compete.

In the pages of The Awl, a journeymen shoemakers' paper, resentment was repeatedly expressed against manufacturers who pretended to pay the workers a living wage but "did by other means reduce them to degradation and the loss of that self-respect which had made the mechanics and laborers the pride of the world." The protesting shoemakers of Lynn called upon their fellow artisans in the larger cities to take concerted action to demonstrate "that we are not menials or the humble subjects of a foreign despot, but free, American citizens." Nothing came of this agitation. A way of life was inevitably passing, and the shoemakers as well as the textile workers were inextricably caught in the toils of the factory system.

The printers' trade was also being revolutionized by the invention of new presses and the use of steam power. These developments not only tended to throw men out of work and to depress wages, but encouraged the transfer of control over their trade from the printers themselves to outside management. A highly independent profession was transformed through the widened gulf between employer and employe. Their long record of organization helped the printers, and they were to continue to enforce union rules governing apprentices and working conditions with considerable success, but they were facing new forces that made it increasingly difficult to maintain either their wages or their general status.

Among other trades, the introduction of power looms worsened conditions for the hand-loom weavers whose weekly wages, never very high, were virtually halved by the mid-forties; the relatively well paid journeymen hatters suffered a decline in their pay, between 1835 and 1845, from about $12 to $8 a week, and the cabinetmakers found themselves compelled to work longer and longer hours to earn as much as $5 a week in the face of competition from the wholesale production of German immigrants who were said to "work rapidly, badly and for almost nothing."

The greater supply of cheap labor, indeed, was as important as the introduction of machinery in cutting wages, not only in the New England cotton mills but throughout industry. In the first half century of our national history, approximately one million immigrants entered the country, but in the single decade from 1846 to 1855, the total was almost three million. Famine in Ireland and suppression of the revolutionary uprisings on the continent accounted for a swelling stream of workers crossing the Atlantic, and there was an increasing proportion of mechanics and laborers, as contrasted with farmers, among these newcomers. They tended to settle in the east, drawn to the rapidly growing cities and manufacturing centers, and were available for all kinds of work, more often unskilled than skilled, at wages greatly reduced from anything which native artisans and mechanics considered essential for decent living conditions. Immigration, that is, was perhaps for the first time providing a labor surplus which counteracted the effect of cheap land and the frontier in drawing workers off from the eastern states. A pattern that was to become even clearer in the 1880's and 1890's, when the trend of immigration showed still greater gains and a further shift toward the ignorant, unskilled and poverty-stricken peasants of southeastern Europe, was already outlined in the 1850's.

The general conditions among workers in the seaboard cities graphically revealed the effect of such immigration. Two separate estimates of a workingman's family budget in the early 1850's, the one in the *New York Times* and the other in the *New York Tribune*, gave a minimum for essential expenditures, for rent, food, fuel, and clothing, that amounted to approximately $11 a week. "Have I made the workingman's comforts too high?" asked Horace Greeley in commenting on this budget. "Where is the money to pay for amusements, for ice-creams, his puddings, his trips on Sunday up or down the river in order to get some fresh air?" But except for those in the building trades, whose relatively high wages just about met this budget, there were few urban workers who even approached it—not the factory operatives, not the workers, men and women, employed in the clothing trades, and most assuredly not the common laborers. Shortly before publishing his budget, Greeley had actually estimated that "the average earnings of those who lived by simple labor in our city—embracing at least two thirds of our population—

scarcely, if at all, exceed one dollar per week for each person subsisting thereon."

Contemporary descriptions afford ample evidence of the part that inadequate wages played in creating the slum areas of such cities as New York, Philadelphia and Boston. Over-crowding, lack of sanitary conveniences, dirt, filth and disease already stood in stark and glaring contrast to the comfortable, spacious, well-furnished homes of the wealthy. There was in New York a cellar population, estimated to total over 18,000, crowded into damp, unlighted, ill-ventilated dens with anywhere from six to twenty persons—men, women and children—living in a single room. In the notorious Five Points, hundreds of families were squeezed into ramshackle buildings, their only sanitary conveniences outside privies. Boston had equally depressing and unhealthful slums. "This whole district," a Committee on Internal Health reported in 1849, "is a perfect hive of human beings without comforts and mostly without common necessaries: in many cases huddled together like brutes without regard to sex, age or a sense of decency, grown men and women sleeping together in the same apartment, and sometimes wife, husband, brothers and sisters in the same bed."

The situation that Thomas Jefferson had foreseen when he spoke of the mobs of great cities adding just as much to pure government "as sores do to the strength of the human body," appeared to have developed. The workers themselves began to protest against immigration as creating "a numerous poor and dependent population." The abject condition they had known in their own countries, the *Voice of Industry* declared, made such immigrants all the more helpless victims of exploitation in the United States, satisfied to work "fourteen and sixteen hours per day for what capital sees fit to give them."

The harsh effect of industrialism and the mounting tide of immigration served in large measure to prevent any reconsolidation of the ranks of labor. The workingmen did not resume on a comparable scale either the political or trade union activity that had had such dynamic drive before the panic of 1837. Baffled by the new forces let loose by industrialism, they seemed to be frantically seeking means of escape. Organization was almost forgotten. Instead, the workers became involved in the more general reform movements of the day that reflected a middle-class, humanitarian revolt against the changes being wrought in American society by machines and factories. The 1840's were pre-eminently a period of vague, idealistic, utopian reforms, each one of which was held forth by its zealous advocates as a complete panacea for all the evils of the day. Communism and land reform, abolition and feminism, temperance and vegetarianism . . . there was no end to the agitation and propaganda which marked the ferment of social change.

The reformers themselves were forever seeking to win the support of workingmen for their various causes. They descended in droves upon every meeting or convention that might be summoned to consider labor issues, and sometimes succeeded in wholly dominating it. The first formal meeting of the New England Workingmen's Association in 1844, called to inaugurate a revived ten-hour movement, had only a scattering of delegates from labor societies in comparison with the brilliant array of reformers. George Ripley, of Brook Farm; Horace Greeley and Albert Brisbane; Wendell Phillips and William Lloyd Garrison; Charles A. Dana, William H. Channing, and Robert Owen were all on hand, eagerly seeking to win new disciples. The meeting was thrown open in sweeping enthusiasm "to all those interested in the elevation of the producing classes and Industrial Reform and the extinction of slavery and servitude in all their forms." However generous the impulses behind such activity, they could not have been more vague and diffusive.

The imagination of some of the workers during this period was caught by the glowing promises of the "Associationists." Through the formation of independent, socialistic communities, all of whose members were working toward a common end, the Associationists promised an escape from the consequences of the industrial revolution and actually hoped to recreate the simpler society of an earlier day. This idea was primarily derived from the utopian socialism of Charles Fourier, with its elaborate system of phalanxes, designed both to dignify labor and increase production, which had been introduced to America by Albert Brisbane. In 1840 Brisbane published "The Social Destiny of Man," a detailed exposition of Fourier's program, but far more important in spreading the gospel of Association were his writings in the column which Horace Greeley placed at his disposal in the *New York Tribune.*

Greeley was, indeed, to do everything possible to promote this tempered form of socialism as one phase of his general support for the interests of workingmen. An idealistic Yankee, who had come to New York as a farm boy to enter the printing trade, he was a familiar figure at labor gatherings and his round moon face, with its fringe of whiskers, was known to thousands of workers. "Why should those by whose toil ALL commodities and luxuries are produced or made available," he asked, "enjoy so scanty a share of them?" He realized perhaps more than any of his contemporaries among public men the effects of the exploitation of the workingmen resulting from the industrial revolution, and he felt that any lasting betterment for society depended upon their organization. He not only opened the columns of the *Tribune* to Albert Brisbane but ran a weekly letter dealing with socialism from a European correspondent— Karl Marx.

Fourierism, in any event, won many converts through the *Tribune* and even before Brisbane laid out his own plan for a North American phalanx, a group of workingmen launched the Sylvania phalanx in western Pennsylvania. Other communities quickly followed on the heels of this experiment and even the idealistic founders of Brook Farm, whose colony represented an intellectual revolt against the spirit of the times, were persuaded to adopt the form and organization of a Fourierite community. In all, some forty phalanxes, with perhaps 8,000 members, were established during the 1840's.

They were not a success. One by one they fell by the wayside, the North American phalanx itself ceasing operations in 1854. Community living and community production did not prove practical. Nor did they in any way meet the needs of labor. In spite of the enthusiastic propaganda, the answer to industrialization did not lie in an attempt to escape from it. The hopeful dreams of the Associationists foundered on the rock of economic and social forces that could not be so easily withstood or diverted.

As the phalanxes collapsed, some attempt was made to provide a partial substitute in the interests of the workingmen by establishing both consumers' and producers' cooperatives. "The direction and profits of industry," the proponents of cooperation declared, "must be kept in the hands of the producers." In Massachusetts, in New York and in other parts of the country, protective unions were organized which undertook to set up self-employing workshops whose products were to be sold at wholesale prices for the benefit of the union's members. There were other instances of cooperatives such as the Journeymen Molders' Union Foundry, which established a plant near Cincinnati, the Boston Tailors' Associative Union, and a Shirt Sewers' Cooperative Union Depot in New York. But whether consumers' or producers' cooperatives, these early ventures were no more successful than the phalanxes. Various factors accounted for their failure, but basically the conditions of American life, perhaps the American temperament, did not provide a fertile soil for the growth of cooperation. They lent themselves rather to competition and individualistic striving to make the most of the opportunities a young and growing country afforded. Cooperation was to be revived again and again in the future and to have some limited success, but neither in the 1840's nor later could it provide any real solution to the problems confronting the laboring classes.

Another and more significant reform which won widespread labor support was a new agrarianism. The original workingmen's parties had been in part wrecked by the internal friction and external attacks resulting from their flirtation with the radical agrarian ideas of Thomas Skidmore, but the new revelation did not involve the assault upon all property which Skidmore had launched so vigorously in "The Rights of Man to Property." The agrarianism of the 1840's and 1850's was far more moderate. Its thesis was that the people as a whole had a natural right to the existing public lands, and that they should be equally distributed in farm lots of 160 acres which would be both inalienable and exempt from seizure for debt. Through such a program, it was maintained, the workingmen would be assured of his just share in the national wealth and be freed from his complete dependence on the matters of capital.

The high priest of this reform was George Henry Evans. After the dissolution of the Workingmen's Party in New York, he had retired in 1836 because of ill-health to a farm in New Jersey, and only emerged with his new message in 1844. Re-establishing the *Working Man's Advocate,* his old paper, he dedicated himself to agrarianism and in season and out demanded action by Congress to promote his program. "This is the first measure to be accomplished," he wrote in the *Advocate*," "and it is as idle to attempt any great reforms without that as it is to go to work without tools. Place the surplus mechanics on their own land in the west in Rural Townships with their large Public Square and Public Hall in the center of each, leaving full employment to those who remain in the cities. . . ." There was hardly a labor meeting at which he did not appear to present this plan, wholly disregarding the practical question of whether the workers, even if they could, would want suddenly to pull up stakes and take up farming in the distant West.

The climax of his activities was the establishment of the National Reform Association in 1845. His earlier experience had led him to distrust third party political action, and the purpose of the new organization was to demand support for his program from all candidates for public office as the condition for securing the workingmen's votes. The strategy was that which the American Federation of Labor was to adopt almost half a century later: reward your friends, punish your enemies. Evans hoped to make it effective by demonstrating that the agrarians meant business. "We, whose names are annexed, desirous of restoring to man his Natural Right to Land," the membership pledge of the National Reform Association stated, "do solemnly agree that we will not vote for any man, for any legislative office, who will not pledge himself, in writing, to use all the influence of his station, if elected, to prevent all further traffic in the Public Lands of the states and of the United States, and to cause them to be laid out in Farms and Lots for the free and exclusive use of actual settlers."

Although support for this program was by no means limited to the workingmen, their close ties with the National Reform Association were clearly revealed in the membership of the original central committee. It included four printers, two cordwainers, a chair maker, a carpenter, a blacksmith, a bookbinder, a machinist, a picture frame maker, and a clothier. Associated with Evans, moreover, were such trade union leaders of the 1830's as John Commerford, who had been president of the General Trades' Union in New York, and John Ferral, leader of the Philadelphia Trades' Union. The new labor journals, re-emerging after the panic of 1837, almost universally made land reform one of their basic demands.

The movement was strongly opposed by capitalists and employers in the eastern states. "By your policy you strike down our great manufacturing interests," one of their spokesmen declared in Congress, ". . . You turn thousands of our manufacturers and labourers out of employment. . . . You depreciate the value of real estate. You make a bid for our population, by holding out inducements for our productive labourers to leave their old homes, under the seductive promise of land for nothing, and railroads without taxes, thereby decreasing our population and consequently increasing the burden of those that remain in the old states." But farmers and other settlers in the West joined forces with the eastern workingmen in supporting the movement. With its alluring slogan of "Vote Yourself a Farm," the National Reform Association appeared to be making substantial headway.

The workingmen of the 1840's were not to profit from its program and its relevancy to their relief from industrial oppression may also be questioned. The movement instituted by Evans, however, was to lead directly to passage of the Homestead Act in 1862. While it did not provide for either inalienability or exemption from seizure for debt, it granted free land to all bona fide settlers.

Land reform was closer to the interests of the workingmen than many of the mid-century humanitarian movements, but the most immediately practical undertaking was the renewed drive for the ten-hour day. While it had been widely won for artisans and mechanics in the 1830's, factory employes, as we have seen, were not generally affected. The new movement was primarily for the relief of this new group of wage earners. Unlike the earlier drive it did not take the form of trade union activity—the factory operatives were unorganized—but of political pressure upon state legislatures to establish a ceiling on hours in private industry. The National Reform Association even unbent sufficiently to make the demand for a ten-hour day one of its subsidiary planks, and it was taken up by many other workingmen's associations formed for this specific purpose.

The most protracted struggle took place in Massachusetts where the development of the textile industry created both the greatest need for reform and the strongest opposition to it. A call for concerted action on the part of the workers, seeking to bring together various local associations, was first issued in 1844 and was responsible for formation of the New England Working Men's Association. Both Fourierites and land reformers tried to take over control of this organization, and for a time appeared to have succeeded in diverting attention from the ten-hour issue, but the agitation in favor of the latter reform nevertheless gained increasing headway. Almost swamped with petitions (one from Lowell being 130 feet long with some 4,500 signatures), the Massachusetts General Court felt compelled to make an official investigation.

Its committee reported that the average working day in the textile factories ranged from 11 hours and 24 minutes to 13 hours and 31 minutes, according to the season, and that there was no question but that shorter hours and more time for meals would benefit the workers. It also asserted the right and duty of the legislature to regulate hours whenever public morals or the well-being of society were menaced. In spite of such premises, however, it concluded, largely on the grounds that industry would be driven from the state, that no action should be taken. "The remedy is not with us," the committee stated, casually brushing aside legislative responsibility. "We look for it in the progressive improvement of art and science, in a higher appreciation of man's destiny, in a less love for money, and a more ardent love for social happiness and intellectual superiority."

The factory operatives attacked the report as clearly reflecting "a cringing servility to corporate monopolies" and renewed a struggle which now crossed state lines and aroused the workers throughout the country. New arguments and counter-arguments were advanced. Labor did not emphasize, as it had in the 1830's, the need for more time for self-education and fulfillment of the duties of citizenship. It stressed instead the improvement in the quality of work that should result from shorter hours. The employers, however, were more concerned over production costs. In combatting the workingmen's views they stated that shorter hours would have to mean a lower day's wage. At the same time they reasserted a paternalistic attitude toward the workers' welfare. "The morals of the operatives will necessarily suffer," one of them stated, "if longer absent from the wholesome discipline of factory life, and leaving them thus to their will and liberty, without a warrant that this time will be well employed."

While the debate still raged over conditions in Massachusetts, the reformers succeeded in winning at least partial victories in a number of other states. New Hampshire passed the first state ten-hour law in the nation's history in 1847; Pennsylvania adopted a bill the next year providing that no person should work more than a ten-hour day or sixty-hour week "in cotton, woolen, silk, paper, bagging and flax factories," and during the 1850's, Maine, Connecticut, Rhode Island, Ohio, California and Georgia also fell in line with some sort of ten-hour laws. There was a catch, however, in almost every case. The ten-hour provision could be circumvented by "special contracts." The employer could virtually disregard the law, that is, by refusing to hire anyone unless he were willing to accept a longer working day, and through combining with other employers he could effectively blacklist any worker who attempted to stand up for his legal rights.

The inclusion of the special contract clause was defended by employers as necessary to protect the right of a citizen to sell his services as he himself saw fit. It was an argument to be advanced even more aggressively in later years when the Fourteenth Amendment was interpreted as specifically safeguarding individual freedom of contract from any infringement by state laws. Its speciousness, although he had originally opposed hour legislation, was exposed by Horace Greeley.

"To talk of the Freedom of Labor, the policy of leaving it to make its own bargains, etc.," he wrote in the *Tribune* on September 18, 1847, "when the fact is that a man who has a family to support and a house hired for the year is told, 'If you will work thirteen hours per day, or as many as we think fit, you can stay; if not you can have your walking papers: and well you know no one else hereabout will hire you'—is it not most egregious flummery?"

The workers in Massachusetts undoubtedly thought so, and in continuing their struggle through a series of Ten-Hour Conventions, they insistently demanded effective legislation that would not mean simply a standardization of the working day but a real—and enforceable—abridgment of the hours of labor. ". . . We do declare, explicitly and frankly," it was stated in 1852, "that our purpose, and our whole purpose, is, the enactment of a law which shall prohibit, in stringent and unmistakeable terms, and under adequate penalties, the corporations, chartered by the laws of the State, from employing any person in laboring more than ten hours in any one day. This is just the law—and all the law—we want on this subject."

This straightforward demand was not realized in Massachusetts—nor in any other state. The inclusion of the special contract clause rendered such laws as were passed unenforceable, and factory workers remained subject to whatever conditions their employers chose to impose upon them. "The ten-hour law will not reduce the hours of labor," one newspaper emphatically stated in regard to the New Hampshire bill. ". . . Its authors did not intend any such result. It will also fail, we think, to humbug the working-men—the only object had in view by the demagogues who originated it."

A final effort to keep the ten-hour movement alive was undertaken through a series of industrial congresses, a further outgrowth of such organizations as the National Reform Association and the New England Working Men's Association. They were first set up on a national basis, and then in the form of state or other local conventions. Instead of furthering practical labor aims, however, they proved to be somewhat vague and ambiguous assemblages, once again attracting reformers rather than trade union delegates. They tried to influence legislation in favor of free land and cooperation as well as the ten-hour day by promising political support to those who would advocate these reforms, but no real progress was made. Moreover while it was again hoped to "eschew partyism of every description," as George Henry Evans had advocated for the National Reform Association, the politicians were soon successfully taking over. The Industrial Congress in New York, for example, originally sought to limit membership to delegates of labor organizations, but Tammany Hall was before long in almost complete control.

The old story of the workingmen's inexperience in politics and the intriguing guile of the professional politicians was being repeated. James Gordon Bennett predicted the fate of the New York Industrial Congress in 1850. "It will fall into the hands of a few wire-pullers, who will turn it to their own advantage and sell the trades to the highest bidder," he wrote prophetically in the *New York Herald*. "Then will be acted over again the farces already played in this city, in which the trades have been made the ladder of needy or ambitious politicians, who kicked them away the moment they gained the summit of their aspirations."

It was not until well into the 1850's that labor began to free itself from its absorption in the hazy garrulity of reform associations and conventions and return to straight-forward trade union activity. An improvement in economic conditions, although interrupted by another brief depression in 1857, promoted this shift from the ineffectual pursuit of vaguely humanitarian panaceas. Once again the bargaining position of the workers was strengthened and the way opened to effective action through the practical weapon of strikes. The unions of this period, however, were to reveal in one important respect a somewhat different philosophy from that held by the earlier societies of the 1830's. They were much less concerned over the solidarity of labor, and fastened their attention far more narrowly on the needs of their own individual membership. Little effort was to be made to form city centrals or any other labor federations comparable to the general trades' unions.

The unions of both periods were primarily made up of artisans and mechanics; that is, skilled craftsmen, and they were largely concentrated in the old established trades. But whereas those in the earlier period were wholly sympathetic toward the organization of unskilled workers and factory operatives, and prepared to cooperate with such societies as they might form, there was little interest in these groups of workers on the part of the trade unions of the 1850's. New lines were being drawn between skilled and unskilled workers and the former were already reluctant to link their activity in any way with the latter.

The more limited scope of the labor movement during these years resulted from a growing realization of the almost insuperable difficulties in trying to organize the mass of workers who were being drawn into factories and mills. Such hopes as there had once been that this could be done appeared to be quenched by two basic considerations. In the first place, many of these factory workers at the time were women and children who were willing and able to work at much lower wages than male employes; and in the second, the ranks of male workers were being constantly swelled by the immigrants who accepted jobs regardless of the working conditions involved. The idea of the solidarity of all labor was not entirely forgotten, and was to be revived after the Civil War. The attitude of the unions in the 1850's, however, seemed to foreshadow that of the American Federation of Labor when it placed its organizational emphasis on the development of strong unions among the skilled workers rather than the more nebulous goal of unity for all labor.

While the revived unions of the 1850's consequently stressed the maintenance of apprenticeship rules, the closed shop and higher wages and shorter hours for their own members, they did not promote with any vigor the labor movement as a whole. They lacked the dynamic drive of their predecessors. In accepting the impracticability of trying to establish by political pressure or reform the equality that had been so much the concern of the workers in the 1830's, they were perhaps realistic. They recognized, as a resolution of one society frankly stated, that under existing conditions "there exists a perpetual antagonism between Labor and Capital . . . one striving to sell their labor for as much, and the other striving to buy it for as little, as they can." But their efforts to combat capital on these grounds were not to be very successful.

. . .

1850 ~ 1914

I

The modern industrial economy was built by steam and machinery. During the nineteenth century coal supplemented and began to replace wind, water, and animal power as a primary source of energy in the western world. Steam was increasingly used to drive labor-saving machinery, and this combination of steam and machinery greatly enhanced man's ability to produce and distribute goods. As a result the volume of economic activity was vastly enlarged; the outpouring of goods and services created new patterns of economic action and new types of economic organization.

In no nation was the impact of steam and machinery greater than in the United States. The application of steam power to production and transportation began after 1850 to transform American economic organization and institutions. Steam-driven vessels, steam railroads, and coal-powered factories all played fundamental roles in the swift transformation of the United States from an agrarian, commercial, and essentially rural nation into an urban, industrial one. Steam took over river and lake transportation even before 1850 and had replaced sail on the slowest ocean-going carriers of bulk cargo by the 1880's. During the 1850's railroads far outstripped canals as means of inland transportation. By the end of that decade, during which more miles of canals were abandoned than constructed, 30,000 miles of railroad were completed to form a basic transportation network east of the Mississippi. By 1873 70,000 miles of track were in operation, and by the end of the 1880's miles operated totaled 160,000. In the 1850's, too, the ocean-going steamboat and the telegraph combined with the railroads provided a fast, regular, all-weather international communications and transportation system.

The new network encouraged the rapid spread of the factory. Before 1850 the factory, with its power-driven machinery and permanent working force whose tasks were specialized and routinized, was still a rarity outside of the textile and related industries. During the 1850's factory production came to a wide variety of industries. By 1880 four-fifths of the three million workers in mechanized industry labored in factories, more and more of which were being powered by steam. As late as 1870 1.1 out of a total of 2.3 million horsepower used in manufacturing was generated by water. By 1880 the horsepower used had increased to 3.4 million, all but 0.1 of that increase being in steam; by 1899 the horsepower used in manufacturing had risen to 10.1 million, of which water power accounted for only one-seventh. One great advantage of steam was that factories no longer had to be placed on the banks of streams and rivers but could be brought into towns and cities and so could take advantage of better transportation, wider markets, and a much larger labor supply.

The resulting expansion of production was most impressive. In the 1850's the United States' industrial output was far below that of England. By 1894 the value of American products almost equaled the value of the combined output of the United Kingdom, France, and Germany. In the next 20 years American production tripled, and by the outbreak of World War I the United States was producing more than one-third of the world's industrial goods.

Such enormous growth had to bring about fundamental changes in the structure of the American economy. The most significant was the coming of mass production and with it mass distribution. Increasingly, decisions as to price and output of goods and the coordination of their flow through the economy, as well as the allocation of the nation's economic resources, became centralized in the hands of a relatively few large industrial, transportation, and financial corporations. At the same time the techniques of production and distribution became more systematized and rationalized. By World War I "scientific management" had become a byword, in fact, almost an article of faith for many American businessmen. Through such methods and institutions the owners and managers of larger business enterprises acquired greater control over their economic environment.

Centralization and rationalization did not come to all American industries. The building and construction trades, as well as the clothing, lumber, woodworking, drugs, hardware, bituminous coal, and other industries, continued to be managed by small firms. Yet even in these small units new organizations were formed. Manufacturers and wholesalers formed local and national trade associations that attempted to exert some influence over prices and production, to standardize and systematize the processes of buying and selling, and to assure some type of control over quality. But these associations never achieved the control, nor ever rationalized their industries as effectively as did the large corporations, and in consequence a number of competitive, small-unit trades became the "sick" industries of the 1920's.

The numerically larger, and therefore less cohesive groups in the economy—the farmers and the laborers—also organized in the last quarter of the nineteenth century, but they achieved even less control over their economic destinies than did the small businessmen. Of these groups, the most successful were those workers whose trades were not yet fully mechanized or turned over to factory production and thus were not yet dominated by large corporations. In the construction and building trades, urban transportation, and shop industries, workers formed first local and then national unions, finally creating, in 1886, the American Federation of Labor. These unions grew substantially between 1897 and 1904. Yet, in these same years, workers in new mass-production and mass-distribution industries dominated by the large corporations were completely unsuccessful in forming unions of their own choosing.

The last decades of the nineteenth century also witnessed basic changes in the organization of American agriculture. New methods of large-scale distribution based on the new transportation network of the railroads, ocean-going steamships, and telegraph were developed to market the crops of the North and the West. Large, commercial, mechanized farms were built on the rich soil of the prairies. As in industry the result was overproduction. Farm prices declined, and a demand grew for organizations similar to those which helped to protect workers and manufacturers. Because they were so numerous, the farmers found it was impossible to form organizations strong and effective enough to have any real control over prices and output. Even so, through their organizations the farmers were able to exchange ideas and information on ways to improve crops and farming methods and to institute new marketing forms such as cooperatives. As prices continued to decline in the 1880's and 1890's, these organizations turned increasingly to political protest and political action to better the farmer's economic condition. The political programs, centering largely on free silver and easy credit, failed to grapple with the farmer's basic dilemma of overproduction. Then, with the rapid growth of the urban market in the first two decades of the twentieth century, agricultural prices rose and protest declined. Insofar as agricultural discontent remained, it was expressed through new organizations which focused on the problems of price and production. Effective answers to the farmer's problem, however, were not found until the federal government intervened in the 1930's.

II

The railroads set the pace in the nation's drive to industrialism during the generation after 1850. They were the hub of the new transportation network that stimulated mass production and mass distribution in American industry and significantly altered the structure of American agriculture. Because of the unprecedented size of the initial investment and the continuing high fixed costs, the railroads also pioneered in nearly all the techniques of creating and managing large private business enterprises. Modern financing, administration, competition, labor relations, and government regulation all began with the building and operation of the railroads.

By stirring the imagination of the country, the railroads further stimulated innovation and change. To Americans of the 1850's the railroads symbolized the application of steam and machinery to man's needs. As Professor Leo Marx has written: "Its attributes were such that it seemed the very embodiment of the Age of Steam: fire, iron, smoke, noise, motion, speed, power." [1] The railroad reinforced Americans' optimistic assurance of man's ability to use his mind to overcome time and distance and so to control the world about him.

The first two selections in this section deal with the railroads. Leland H. Jenks considers three facets of the railroad's role as a pacesetter in his essay. Alfred D. Chandler, Jr., and Stephen Salsbury concentrate on its contributions as an institutional innovator. Jenks begins by analyzing the railroad as an idea and its promoters as exemplifiers "of the power of steam, of the advantages of the corporate form of business, of the ability of man to master his environment." He then considers it as a construction enterprise. Here he examines the way in which the railroad created new demands by bringing unused land into economic use and providing a new market for labor and for such goods as iron and steel. Jenks's views on the last point have recently been supported by the publication in 1965 of Albert Fishlow's detailed analysis, *American Railroads and the Transformation of the Ante-Bellum Economy.* Fishlow demonstrates that, even between 1856 and 1860, when the expansion of the rail system had only just begun, railroads were already using 20 percent of America's pig-iron production. In 1880, 80 percent of American steel still went into rails. Jenks further points out how railroads became immense

[1] Leo Marx, "The Impact of the Railroad on the American Imagination, as a Possible Comparison for the Space Impact," in Bruce Mazlish, ed., *The Railroad and the Space Program, an Exploration in Historical Analogy* (Cambridge, Mass.: M.I.T Press, 1965), p. 207.

users of capital, much of it foreign. It was because of this demand that the nation's money market became centralized and institutionalized in New York City. Wall Street—the symbol of American capitalism—was one by-product of the railroads.

Jenks's third concern is for the railroads as producers of transportation service. He emphasizes that the railroads' contribution was not so much in reducing transportation costs, although recent studies indicate that they did make substantial cost savings. A more important achievement was the providing of fast, regular, all-weather transportation. Once the basic network was completed, goods could be shipped directly from the ports to the interior and vice versa, eliminating many delays at transshipment points. The through bill of lading became a normal instrument of trade, and the railroads themselves took over first the functions of merchants who had served as freight forwarders and shipping agents and then those of the newer fast-freight and express companies. The assured, regularly scheduled, uninterrupted service offered by the railroads, in combination with the telegraph and the ocean-going steamship, thus provided an essential transportation and communications base for the rapidly industrializing economy.

The article by Chandler and Salsbury traces the growth of the railroad companies as the first large business corporations in America; it describes and analyzes how they were forced to pioneer in the creation of modern business forms. The essay investigates the creation of administrative structures with clearly defined channels of authority, responsibility, and communication; the definition of line and staff functions; and the development of the continuous flow of operating data—hourly, daily, weekly, and monthly reports essential for the new type of business control through statistics.

Chandler and Salsbury follow the growth of the individual railroad companies from roads of rarely more than 500 miles in length to giant systems operating over 5,000 miles of track. Such growth came because the roads could find no other solution to the problems raised by competition between large units with high fixed costs and excess capacity. The roads first tried informal alliances. When these failed to bring stable rates, their managers set up more formal associations to pool traffic and profits. When the Eastern Trunk Line and other associations failed, the managers began to build, either by purchasing or by constructing new lines, "self-sustaining" systems that tied together the leading commercial towns and cities of a region. The executives of some of these great systems created geographically decentralized structures, but most railroad officials were less imaginative. They merely extended their existing centralized organization over their enlarged business empires.

Whether centralized or decentralized, the top commands of all the large roads remained in the hands of a group or committee, usually the executive committee. As Jenks suggests, in railroad management the group first replaced the individual in carrying out the entrepreneurial function that many economic historians have considered crucial to the growth of a capitalistic economy. During the 1930's Joseph Schumpeter predicted that such bureaucratizing of the entrepreneurial function would destroy the large firm and the system it dominated and symbolized. From the 1880's to World War I, however, the bureaucratic enterprise initially developed by the railroads spread to many other sectors of the economy; and both the giant corporation and the capitalistic economy still appear to flourish.

III

If the railroad was the pacesetter for the industrializing economy, the factory was its prime mover. Once the manufacturers were assured of a steady flow of raw and semifinished materials into their establishments and of finished goods out of them, they quickly adopted the factory system of production. The significance of improved transportation in mass production of goods in the United States is suggested by the fact that as early as 1800 Americans were acquainted with two basic methods of large-scale factory production. One was the use of coal rather than charcoal for making iron and steel. The other was the production of durable goods by the fabrication and assembling of interchangeable parts. Yet Americans made little use of these techniques for half a century. Then, as the all-weather transportation system came into being in the 1850's, the first large, integrated ironworks using coal appeared; at the same time factory production was applied to the making of such articles as guns and other small arms for nonmilitary use, locks, timepieces, sewing machines, pianos, agricultural implements, clothing, and (as has been pointed out in Part One) shoes.

The swift acceptance of the factory created new problems for the manufacturers. The resulting far greater volume of production meant that supply began to outrun demand and prices to fall. Moreover, the existing system of distribution through an intricate network of wholesalers had been created before 1850 to meet the needs of the older shop- and mill-oriented manufacturing and of a predominantly agrarian and rural market rather than the needs of mass production and of an increasingly urban market. The railroad and the rapidly growing volume of trade permitted wholesalers to become larger and more specialized. After the Civil War the Southern factor disappeared, while commission agents in both the North and South tended to become wholesale jobbers who took title to the goods they marketed. Even so, the wholesalers were not yet equipped to meet many of the requirements of high-volume distribution of a single line of products in the national market.

Falling prices pushed manufacturers into the same patterns of informal alliances, more formal associations, and finally the legal combinations and administrative consolidations that had occurred in the railroads. Where the railroads had created large "self-sustaining" systems, the manufacturers ultimately formed giant integrated firms that controlled the flow of goods from the purchase of raw materials to the sale to the final consumer. These newer enterprises thus became involved in mass distribution as well as in mass production of goods and in fact became the organization that linked the two functions together.

The pioneers in fashioning integrated enterprises were those manufacturers who found the existing distribution network of the wholesalers totally inadequate for their needs. They included the makers of those durable goods that required a demonstration to the customer before purchase and the supplying of consumer credit and facilities for repair and service—the manufacturers of sewing machines, agricultural implements, typewriters, cash registers, and electrical machinery. The processers of mass-produced perishables such as meats, beer, and bananas also had to create their own distribution networks. Then, as the manufacturers of other goods and commodities for whom the existing wholesaler had been more satisfactory found that alliances, pools, and associations failed to bring price stability, they too moved into distribution. After they had legally consolidated many factories into a single operating company, they began to build their own sales organizations and moved to integrate backwards by doing their own purchasing of supplies and by controlling sources of raw materials.

The managers of the new vertically integrated enterprises, like those of the self-contained railroad systems, had, through such a strategy of growth, achieved some control over their economic destinies. In order to lower costs and increase profits, they now began to rationalize methods of both production and distribution. At this time scientific management became popular. Besides systematizing their purchasing, production, and sales departments, these managers began to develop techniques for coordinating the flow of goods through their various departments and also for the efficient allocation of resources—men, money, and machinery—to assure the corporations' present health and future growth.

The readings trace the rise of the factory and the large industrial corporation. They also suggest the continuing concern of American manufacturers with rational systematic methods of first production and then distribution. The essay of D. L. Burn describes the coming of high-volume production during the 1850's and 1860's in industries based on the fabrication and assembling of interchangeable parts. Burn emphasizes those processes which impressed British experts of that day. He considers, but only briefly, the background for American developments, suggesting, for instance, the importance of woodworking methods to the new metalworking industries. Other forerunners of American mass production, such as the large-scale manufacture of simple agricultural implements like shovels and axes, could also have been cited. Furthermore, although inventors Samuel Colt, Cyrus McCormick, and John Deere had patented and perfected ways to mass produce the revolver, reaper, and steel plow in the 1830's, they were unable to put their plans into operation until the late 1840's. Once established, they quickly became three of the largest manufacturers in the world. Before 1850 demand was apparently too limited to permit mass production. As Burn points out, the British experts sensed the significance of increased demand, and they considered the size of the market and the relative affluence of American buyers the basis for the success of mass-production methods. As the British investigators also noted, most of the products so manufactured found a ready market in Europe.

The essay by Chandler describes the growth of the large, integrated enterprise that tied mass distribution of goods to mass production by the factory. It analyzes how and why the existing wholesalers were unable to meet the needs of the manufacturers of durable and perishable goods and so stimulated the coming of "big business." And it shows how and why industry after industry followed the example of pioneers like meat packer Gustavus Swift, sewing machine manufacturer Edward Clark, and oil refiner John D. Rockefeller.

" 'Scientific Management' in Business," written in 1912 by A. W. Shaw, one of its most ardent advocates, shows how these principles were applied to mass distribution as well as to mass production. It also reveals the sincere, if naive, faith of businessmen of that day in the possibilities of rational systematic organization of business. His enthusiastic endorsement of scientific management today seems almost a parody of the movement's aims and expectations. Nevertheless, these practices, applied in a more sophisticated way in the 1920's, became accepted procedures in the managed economy of the 1950's.

IV

By the 1880's, when railroad men and manufacturers were still searching for a legal and administrative structure that would give them some control over the uncertainties created by a rapidly industrializing economy, American laborers began to see the value of organization for a like purpose. In that decade most American workers thought for the first time of joining a labor union. They had the option at that time of becoming members in local units of two very different types of organization. They could join other workers in their own trade in the local unit of a national trade union, or they could become members of a local assembly of the Knights of Labor. This latter assembly might consist of workers of one trade, but its membership was more likely to include any worker, wage earner, or even employer in a geographical area.

By the early 1890's, however, the laboring man could join only a trade union, and he could do so only if he practiced a fairly skilled trade and could pay a relatively costly initiation fee and high annual dues. In 1886, when the trade unions joined to form the American Federation of Labor, they embarked on a determined campaign to recruit members of similar trades exclusively into their own unions. The decision meant a conflict with the Knights of Labor, which was trying to bring the same workers into its local assemblies. The conflict revealed serious weaknesses in the organization and objectives of the Knights, and its effectiveness as a national labor organization ended shortly thereafter.

American trade unions had their beginnings during the 1850's when the railroads created for the first time a national market for labor. Local unions formed national organizations so that a member could obtain employment when he moved to another town. By the same token a non-union laborer would be excluded from work on jobs where the unions had agreements with employers. As they formed their nationals, these same unions began to provide other positive advantages to their present and potential members by offering health, employment, and life insurance.

The trade unions' major function soon became that of bargaining collectively with employers for shorter hours, higher pay, and better conditions of work. Since the strike was the most effective weapon to bring an employer to terms, the more energetic nationals soon began to build up strike funds to provide support for striking workers. To insure effective use of these funds, the national unions then began to exercise increasing control over the collective bargaining plans and particularly over the strike strategy of their locals.

Although trade unions made a start toward national organization in the 1850's and 1860's, only eight nationals survived the long and severe depression of the 1870's. That depression, however, made clear the importance of organization to the workingman at a time when the supply of labor outran the demand for it, and, with the return of prosperity in the 1880's, old national unions revived and new ones appeared. By the mid-1880's the permanency of the trade union movement seemed assured.

Yet in these very same years the Knights of Labor seemed to have an even more promising future than the trade unions. The Knights, which had been founded in 1869 as a secret fraternal order and had attracted in the first decade of its existence only a small number of members, did not have organizational roots as old as its rivals. It had, however, deeper ideological ones. Its leaders inherited the intellectual and spiritual traditions of the Jacksonian labor reforms and the humanitarian crusade of the 1840's and 1850's. Its basic objective was to transform the structure of the economy and to replace the wage system with one managed through manufacturing and marketing cooperatives. Terence V. Powderly, the Grand Master of the Knights, saw the formation of cooperatives as a way to "make every man his own master, every man his own employer." [2] To achieve these goals, the Knights wanted its organization open to nearly all men and women, skilled or unskilled, white or colored. Even employers were invited to join. Such broad-based local and national organizations were not to be used for collective bargaining. The Knights decried the use of strikes since the organization aimed at reforming society, not merely at obtaining a larger share of the existing economic system's output.

Such broad social and economic goals appealed strongly to American workingmen only a generation away from the family farm, where wages were rarely used. Reform unionism, espousing these objectives,

[2] Quoted in Ida M. Tarbell, *The Nationalizing of Business, 1878–1898* (New York: Macmillan, 1936), p. 149.

found its first expression in the post–Civil War years in the short-lived National Labor Union. Its final and fullest organizational development came, however, in the astonishingly rapid growth during the 1880's of the Noble and Holy Order of the Knights of Labor.

In the first selection on labor Bernard Mandel describes how two immigrants, Samuel Gompers and Adolph Strasser, built up a powerful local union of cigar makers in New York City and then fashioned a strong national trade union. Because they were Europeans and possibly because of their socialist training, they and their associates with similar backgrounds may have been more willing than native-born leaders to work out their plans within an industrial context. Gompers developed a benefit program and strike funds and carefully planned his bargaining and strike strategy; the high dues needed to carry out his objectives were alone enough to limit membership to the more skilled workers. The second selection, by Gerald N. Grob, demonstrates why "inherent differences in ideology and structure" made conflict between the trade unions and the Knights almost certain and how these very differences gave the trade unions a decisive advantage in the struggle that was to determine the course of the labor movement in the United States for almost 50 years.

The success of the unions that made up the American Federation of Labor permitted skilled workers to exercise some control over their economic fate. The AFL, however, never acquired any significant strength in industries where production was dominated by the mechanized factory and the large, integrated corporation. Its membership was concentrated in small-unit industries—building and construction, shipbuilding, mining, some food processing—and in machine shops and foundries. When an industry became fully mechanized, as did iron, steel, and glass, semiskilled labor could do most of the work and union membership sharply declined. In the pre-1914 industrializing economy only the skilled workers in conservative trade unions were able to form successful and lasting organizations that could assure them a measure of security and bargaining power. The semiskilled and unskilled simply went without the benefits of organization.

V

In the 1880's the farmers, like the workers and businessmen, turned to organization for relief from the vicissitudes of a rapidly industrializing economy. Like the industrialists, they had been plagued with overproduction and falling prices. The coming of the new transportation network in the 1850's stimulated a flow of American foodstuffs to the urban industrial markets of Europe. By the early 1860's exports of American grain and meat, tiny before the mid-1840's, had become almost as important as cotton in Civil War diplomacy.

Methods for the large-scale distribution of these foodstuffs, quickly fashioned during the 1850's by using the railroad, telegraph, and ocean-going steamship, were more efficient and systematic than those developed earlier for the marketing of cotton. The new system, based on the grain elevator, the stockyard, the through bill of lading, and the grain and other exchanges in Chicago, Buffalo, and New York, was fully completed in the early 1860's. The only major refinement came in the 1880's with the use of the refrigerated railway car and ship. The cotton trade only began to imitate this more advanced system of marketing after the Civil War with the formation of the first cotton exchanges in New York in 1870 and in New Orleans in 1871.

The railroad further stimulated American agriculture by opening up the prairies to commercial farming. "The pioneer, as he moves forward over the prairie of the west carries with him the railroad—as necessary to his life as are the axe and the plough," wrote one commentator in 1854. "The railway keeps pace with the frontier line of settlement; so that the crop of this year's frontier farm, in the great march of civilization, has only to be held to the next, to be sent whizzing to the Eastern market at a speed of thirty miles an hour." [3] In the 1850's the frontier line of settlement was still close to the Mississippi River. A generation later the frontier had gone. The Census of 1890 officially reported its demise.

On the prairie a new kind of production unit arose. Great farms appeared, larger in acreage than most pre–Civil War plantations in the South. On them a few machines accomplished the same amount of work as had gangs of Southern slaves. When manual labor was needed, workers, often migrants, were hired and were paid cash wages. The new unit had more similarities to the industrial shop than to the traditional family farm. Although much of America's crops would long be raised by the small family farm, the "bonanza" farms of the prairie were the prototype of the highly mechanized agricultural unit that by the middle of the twentieth century would grow the largest share of American staple crops.

At the same time that vast new areas came under production and that improved methods of production and distribution brought an abundance of American agricultural products, farmers in Eastern Europe, Australia, and Argentina also embarked on large-scale production for the markets of Western Europe. Inevitably agricultural prices declined sharply and inevitably, too, price declines brought strong protests. The American farmer had other grievances which intensified his outcry. In the rapidly industrializing economy he felt that his status was declining as much as his share of the national wealth. Instead of being considered a yeoman farmer, the backbone of American society, he found himself being derisively nicknamed a "rube," a "hick," or a "hayseed." And his voice seemed to count for less in state and national legislatures.

The answer, most farmers emphatically agreed, was to organize for both political and economic ends. From the 1870's on, national farmers' organizations attracted large memberships. In the 1870's the Grange was

[3] Henry V. Poor, "Pacific Railroad," *Bulletin of the American Statistical and Geographical Society,* Vol. I (1854), Pt. III, p. 81.

the most popular; in the 1880's and 1890's the Farmers' Alliance and the Farmers' Wheel attracted the most members. Although these organizations did fill a need for association and good-fellowship, they had difficulty in achieving their economic and political goals. There were far too many producers to permit voluntary control over prices and production of crops. The farmers had too many varied interests and concerns for effective political action. Farmers from the South, the East, the old Northwest, and the prairie all had somewhat different problems and needs. So, too, did the growers of different crops within each region.

In the end the changing market, rather than the efforts of farmers' organizations, brought to an end the farmers' protests. During the first two decades of the twentieth century, as the rate of growth of the farm population and the acreage under production leveled off, that of the American urban population continued to rise rapidly. In these years the American city replaced Europe as the major market for American farm products, and the American farmer enjoyed as profitable a period as he ever had in his history. While the rural population had increased only from 45.8 million in 1890 to 50.0 million in 1910 and to 51.5 million in 1920, the urban population almost doubled between 1890 and 1910—jumping from 22.1 to 42.0 million—and rose to 54.1 million in 1920. The figures for these same years on farm and nonfarm workers are even more significant. There were 9.9 million farm workers in 1890, 11.6 million in 1910, and 13.4 million in 1920; in these same years the number of nonfarm workers was 13.4 million, 25.8 million, and 31.0 million.

The readings illustrate and analyze these developments. Morton Rothstein examines the formation of the new marketing system for the large-scale distribution of foodstuffs based on the railroad, telegraph, ocean-going steamship, grain elevators, stockyards, through bills of lading, and the commercial exchanges. The section from Fred A. Shannon, *The Farmers' Last Frontier*, tells of the spread and operation of the great prairie farms and shows how their growth affected the production of wheat, cattle, corn, and hogs. Theodore Saloutous in "The Agricultural Problem and Nineteenth-Century Industrialism" describes the farmers' inability to obtain control over price and production of crops or to halt the overexpansion of acreage under production and details their failure to develop sound investment and management procedures and to act as an effective pressure group. He notes the organizations that the farmers formed and the programs they advocated, including improved educational facilities, railroad regulation, the establishment of marketing cooperatives, and, most enthusiastically of all, cheap money through "free silver." Finally, Saloutous points to the beginnings of the concepts of production control and minimum prices that the federal government would institute when, during the years of the Great Depression, it became the regulator of the nation's economy.

By the outbreak of World War I, the United States had become an urban, industrial nation and its economy by far the most productive in the world. The railroads had long since given way as pacesetters to first electricity and then the internal combustion engine. Probably an even more important stimulus to economic growth was the impressive expansion of the cities in the years after 1880, which provided swiftly growing, varied markets for the products of the nation's farms and factories. Yet, for all its growth and for all the complexity and sophistication of its organization, the American economy was in no sense assured of continuing expansion or even stability. The leveling off of demand in the 1920's and its collapse in the 1930's demonstrated the inability of the mass-production, mass-distribution economy to maintain its momentum. The resulting sharp and severe economic depression also made clear that only the federal government was in a position to act as a regulator and pacesetter for the economy as a whole.

Section 1 ∽ *The Railroads—Pacesetters for the Industrializing Economy*

THE RAILROADS AS AN ECONOMIC FORCE IN AMERICAN DEVELOPMENT *Leland H. Jenks*

I

Any attempt to discuss the way in which railroads have promoted the rise of the American economy must assume some theory of economic evolution. The following analysis is based upon Schumpeter's theory of innovations.[1] Briefly this theory holds that economic evolution in capitalistic society is started by innovation in some production function, that is, by new combinations of the factors in the economic process. These innovations may center in new commodities or new services, new types of machinery, new forms of organization, new firms, new resources, or new

[1] Joseph A. Schumpeter, *Business Cycles* (New York and London: McGraw-Hill Book Company, 1939), Vol. I, esp. chaps. iii and vii; *idem, The Theory of Economic Development* (Cambridge: Harvard University Press, 1934), chaps. ii and vi; *idem,* "The Instability of Capitalism," *The Economic Journal,* XXXVIII (1928), 361–86. Cf. the theory of Allyn A. Young, "Increasing Returns and Economic Progress," *ibid.,* 527–42.

REPRINTED with permission from Leland H. Jenks, "The Railroads as an Economic Force in American Development," *The Journal of Economic History,* Vol. IV (May 1944), pp. 1–20. This article is an elaboration and extension of a paper delivered at the meeting of the Mississippi Valley Historical Association, Washington, D.C., December 28–31, 1938.

areas. As Schumpeter makes clear, this is not a general theory of economic, much less of social, change. Innovation is an internal factor operating within a given economic system while the system is also affected by external factors (many of them sociological) and by growth (which means, substantially, changes in population and in the sum total of savings made by individuals and firms). These sets of factors interact in economic change. "The changes in the economic process brought about by innovation, together with all their effects, and the response to them by the economic system" constitute economic evolution for Schumpeter.[2]

Railroad development has had three phases or moments which have involved innovation in distinctive ways. I shall consider (1) the railroad as an idea, (2) the railroad as a construction enterprise, and (3) the railroad as a producer of transportation services.[3]

II

By the railroad as an idea is not meant the original design of steam locomotion on rails. It pertains to the inception in particular areas of particular projects, conceived as likely to be appropriate opportunities for business enterprise. In this sense the idea of any major innovation, such as the railroad, is a potent economic force. For once railway projects have been conceived and plans for their execution elaborated, it becomes easier for other innovating ideas to be entertained.[4] On the one hand, the socio-psychological deterrents against entering upon new ways are lowered. On the other, the characteristics of the prospective future are altered; they assume an aspect more favorable to men and firms with new plans than to men and firms whose position is established. Thus early railway projects were attended by a retinue of satellite innovations.

The first railway projects emerged in the United States in the thirties in a situation in which the psychological risks had already been appreciably lowered by the general passion for internal improvements displayed in a plethora of projects for canals, turnpikes, plank roads, bridges, banks, and other enterprises.[5] The earliest railways paralleled, supplemented, or improved transport systems that were already in being.[6] The real railway revolution dates from the forties, prior to the

---

[2] *Business Cycles*, I, 86.

[3] These distinctions are hinted at but not developed in *Business Cycles*, I, 130–36. They are not to be construed precisely as stages or periods, although each was relatively more conspicuous in certain decades than in others.

[4] Three types of obstacles to innovation are distinguished in *Business Cycles*, I, 100: hostility to the new idea, absence of facilitating economic functions, and inhibitions against entering upon a relatively incalculable course. Young in *The Economic Journal*, XXXVIII (1928), 534, stresses the need to remake human material in terms of new skills and habits and in terms of redistribution of population.

[5] Carl Russell Fish, *The Rise of the Common Man* (New York: The Macmillan Company, 1927), chaps. iv and v.

[6] One thinks of the Boston & Lowell, New York & New Haven, Philadelphia & Columbia, Allegheny Portage, the original Baltimore & Ohio, and the lines connecting Albany with Buffalo.

California gold discoveries, in projects to cross the Appalachians, to link the seaboard with the interior, the Ohio Valley with the Great Lakes, and, breaking away from the contours of water transport, to unite distant points by more direct routes.[7] It was the determination to build railroads in advance of traffic that gave the "railroad idea" prolonged force in American economic life. The conviction that the railroad would run anywhere at a profit put fresh spurs to American ingenuity and opened closed paddocks of potential enterprise.

Innovations are the work of enterprisers. For the railroad as idea, the role of entrepreneurship was pretty much identical with promotion; and the promoter was rarely limited in outlook to the railroad itself. In action, he was omnicompetent and omnipresent. His imagination leaped readily from the concrete problem of securing authority for a right of way to visions of a countryside filled with nodding grain, settlements of industrious families, and other evidences of progress and civilization. Each railway project involved the sanguine judgment of enterprising individuals and groups in particular, local situations that a certain line would be of direct or indirect pecuniary advantage to themselves. It was linked to specific plans for town promotion and real-estate speculation, to combinations for contracting services and supplies or for exploitation of resources, in anticipation of the actual movement of traffic by rail. But as projects multiplied they collectively acquired a symbolic function, dramatizing broader purposes. The railway projector became an exemplification of the power of steam, of the advantages of the corporate form of business organization, of the ability of man to master his environment. The early railway promoter was not only a potential economic agent; he embodied the dream of developing communities, regions, the continent.

Thus, as the barriers to new projects were periodically lowered by the inception of new railway systems, the first moment of the railroad as an economic force was manifested in a wavelike profusion of new enterprises of many sorts. Moreover, its effects in the United States were not exhausted in a decade or so, as they were in England. The railroad idea was periodically renewed for region after region and route after route, as national development, at least facilitated by the earlier railroads, widened the horizons of enterprise.

[7] The most dynamic set of American innovations consisted in plans to build railways in anticipation of traffic. Lewis Henry Haney, *A Congressional History of Railways in the United States to 1850* (Madison: University of Wisconsin, 1908), p. 31. Congressional land grants were a factor, as in the case of the Illinois Central, the first large system built through sparsely settled territory. Paul Wallace Gates, *The Illinois Central Rail-road and Its Colonization Work* (Cambridge: Harvard University Press, 1934). Canal building had, however, in the old Northwest, anticipated the railroad less successfully in building ahead of population. Frederic L. Paxson, *History of the American Frontier 1763–1893* (Boston and New York: Houghton Mifflin Company, 1924), chap. xxx. For early systems and projects, cf. Caroline E. MacGill *et al.*, Balthasar Henry Meyer, editor, *History of Transportation in the United States Before 1860* (Washington: Carnegie Institution of Washington, 1917); J. L. Ringwalt, *Development of Transportation Systems in the United States* (Philadelphia: The Author, 1888).

III

The second moment of the railroad as an economic force came with the actual construction of new lines. The statistics of net mileage added in each year from 1837 to 1937 give a quantitative measure of this contribution of the railroad to development, as appears on the accompanying charts. Two general statements are strikingly supported by these data.[8] In the first place, railway building proceeded in an undulating pattern, paralleling closely the general contours of major business cycles until the First World War. From 1850 to the nineties, omitting the years of the Civil War, the rise and fall in new construction in fact led by a perceptible interval most other indices of business conditions.[9] In the second place, there was a long-run trend in new railway construction, which was predominantly upward in absolute figures from the late 1840's

CHART 1   MILES OF RAILROAD IN OPERATION,
1837–1937

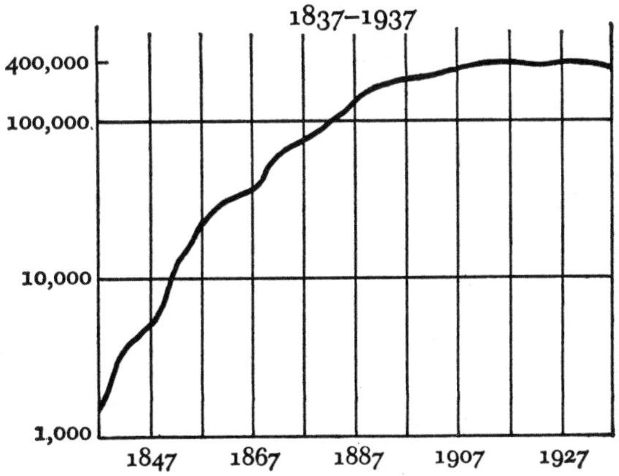

[8] The data for these charts are derived from the United States Treasury Department, Bureau of Statistics, *Statistical Abstract of the United States, 1900* (Washington: United States Government Printing Office, 1901); *ibid., 1914,* p. 637; and *ibid., 1937,* p. 379. Chart 2 is adapted from Simon S. Kuznets, *Secular Movements in Production and Prices* (Boston and New York: Houghton Mifflin Company, 1930), pp. 191, 526–27.

[9] This correlation was initially based upon inspection of the mileage data in comparison with the chart in Schumpeter, *Business Cycles,* II, 465, and the analyses of business conditions in Willard Long Thorp, *Business Annals* (New York: National Bureau of Economic Research, 1926) and National Bureau of Economic Research, *Recent Economic Changes* (New York: McGraw-Hill Book Company, 1929), II, 892. More decisive support is provided by John E. Partington, *Railroad Purchasing and the Business Cycle* (Washington: The Brookings Institution, 1929). As Partington includes orders for replacements as well as for original basic construction, he finds that orders of railway capital goods led business-cycle changes as late as 1907. Throughout this period, he finds, railway earnings followed, instead of preceded, changes in purchases.

Leland H. Jenks   **215**

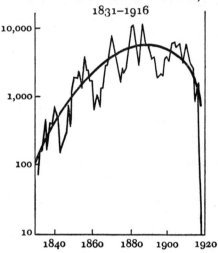

CHART 2   NET ANNUAL CHANGE IN
U.S. RAILROAD MILEAGE,
1831–1916

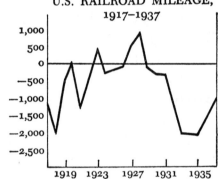

CHART 3   NET ANNUAL CHANGE IN
U.S. RAILROAD MILEAGE,
1917–1937

to about 1890. The rate of this upward trend tended to slacken with the aggregate movement approximating graphically a logistic curve, but, for the whole period, expansion of railway plant averaged about 10 per cent a year. The trend since 1890 has been irregularly downward, bearing the aspect of a reversed logistic curve. The early persistent succession of fresh waves of railway construction, arising largely in the development of new areas in the American West and South, must be regarded as one of the basic phenomena in the total economic growth of the United States, while the logistic curve of total experience presents in outline a picture of an industry passing from youth through adolescence to maturity.

But how did railway construction as such act as an economic force? How could it be a pace setter? The answer is broadly that it operated directly to create a demand for various factors of production. In response to this demand there were rises in prices or increases in supply or both. Increase of supply could come only from some sort of further innovations, such as the drawing of fresh increments of land, labor, or capital into economic uses or the transfer of such factors to move effective combinations. This process meant the periodic dislocation of the economic structure as well as the disruption of the activities of individuals and communities. At the same time it enhanced the opportunities for enterprisers having a high degree of flexibility, pioneering individuals and groups, the agents of innumerable innovating firms and procedures.

The land for railroad construction was largely new land, previously not of economic use. It cost virtually nothing to the railway companies, and not very much to anyone else.[10] Socially the land devoted to railroad purposes more than paid for itself by the increment in productivity of adjacent land. This was so obvious to everyone connected with railway building that periodic land booms came to communities even before the rails were laid. The speculative activity thus diffused in anticipation of railroad construction may have brought many creative innovations in its wake. But, by distracting labor and enterprise from productive to parasitic activities, it frequently delayed the realization of the plausible hopes upon which railroad projects were primarily based.

The demand for labor initiated a chapter in the history of immigration and colonization.[11] It also disciplined migratory and local labor power to co-operative industrial effort. But it had wider repercussions. Laborers were paid wages and the wages were spent for goods. They went to market to buy the produce of American farms and mills. Thus the demand for labor stimulated the spread of market economy and the more extensive production of goods and services for distant markets, and thereby contributed to the spread of economic specialization.

The demand for capital functioned in parallel to the demand for

---

[10] Frederick A. Cleveland and Fred Wilbur Powell, *Railroad Promotion and Capitalization in the United States* (New York: Longmans, Green and Company, 1909), pp. 199–200. "In the Southern States, and the Mississippi Valley . . . . all the real estate required for way, and for depots, stations, etc., are generally gratuity to the roads." *American Railroad Journal*, XXV (January 3, 1852), 13. Cf. James Blaine Hedges, *Henry Villard and the Railways of the Northwest* (New Haven: Yale University Press, 1930), *passim*.

[11] Gates, *The Illinois Central Rail-road*, pp. 89, 94–8. Despite its crucial importance, the subject of labor supply has been too frequently neglected by railway historians. Adequate data for labor employed in new construction are available only for a few large lines such as the Central Pacific, Union Pacific, and the Illinois Central. On each of these, upwards of 10,000 men were employed at the peak of construction. Probably a thousand men were needed for every hundred miles. Assuming that twice as many miles were in progress as were completed in any given year, the figure of 200,000 men is reached as the maximum employed at any one time in the construction of these railways. This figure was not attained until the eighties, by which time the census reported 250,000 officials and employees of railroads, presumably engaged directly or indirectly in transportation service.

labor. I am speaking of real capital, of goods, of the picks and shovels, sleepers and steel rails, engines and rolling stock and bridgework and culverts and ordinary building material, which make up the physical plant of a railroad. The construction moment of railway history brought an initial demand for these durable goods.[12] Hence there was a chance for the innovator in the lumbering industry, in quarries, in iron mills and carriage works. Indeed these industries were hard put to keep pace with railway construction. Until the later eighties, every boom period found American factories unable to meet the demand for rails, and there were heavy importations from England and Wales As late as the nineties, over one fifth of the total output of pig iron in the United States was being rolled into railroad bars.[13]

Much of this demand for durable goods turned eventually into a demand for labor in mine and quarry and mill, into wage payments to labor. And these wages too were spent for consumers' goods and meant widening markets, increased specialization, and, presumably, greater productivity.

Thus the initial impetus of investment in railway construction led in widening arcs to increments of economic activity over the entire American domain, far exceeding in their total volume the original inputs of investment capital. To this feature of modern capitalism, John Maynard Keynes and others have applied the term "multiplier." [14] It is believed that for present-day England the efficiency of the multiplier may suffice to double the impact of a new investment in construction. For nineteenth-century United States, its efficiency seems to have been considerably greater than that.

I have spoken of inputs and investment. In our economy the demand for land and labor and capital has meant another demand, a demand not for an independent factor of production, but for something equally essential, a demand for money capital.[15] In fact, without a supply of money capital there could have been no effective demand for any of the real factors, no railways, and no stimulus from them for economic development. Hence it is convenient to think of the building of railroads as an investment of money capital. To this investment there corresponded in the long run the accumulation of savings. That saving came first and investment in the railroads afterwards is a proposition for which there is little historical evidence, at least in the United States. It is true

[12] Cf. files of railway periodicals for advertisements of manufacturers and dealers in railway materials and supplies. Ringwalt, *Development of Transportation Systems in the U.S.*, pp. 132–36, 210.
[13] For details, cf. *Statistical Abstract of the U.S., 1902*, p. 380, and corresponding tables in earlier volumes.
[14] John Maynard Keynes, *The General Theory of Employment, Interest and Money* (London, 1936), chap. xi; R. F. Kahn, "The Relation of Home Investment to Unemployment," *The Economic Journal*, XLI (1931), 173–98.
[15] Admittedly "money capital" constitutes merely a vehicle or instrumentality, the means of acquiring command over the several factors of production. More commonly it is spoken of as long-term credit or capital funds. But sometimes an instrument becomes so important that it exerts influences by itself and requires consideration on its separate account.

that the practice of thrift as an individual and family responsibility was built into our social system by the Puritans. But the savings thus made in the middle of the nineteenth century went largely into land, into improvements on the farm, into the mill, the private business, and, in relatively small amounts, into public securities. Few railroads were originally financed by direct subscription of the shareholders at par in ready cash.[16]

In final analysis, the funds for railway construction came from the extension of credit by American banks and from foreign exchange supplied by European investors. This was accomplished by many devices which called into play the charitable cupidity of contractors and iron manufacturers on both sides of the Atlantic, and the lively anticipations of property owners in the area which the railroad was to develop.[17] Some of the shares were sold at a heavy discount to local residents, but more were given outright for land, for legal and legislative services, for banking accommodation, or as a bonus to promote the sale of bonds. Frequently there was a construction company, analogous to the Crédit Mobilier, which took all the securities in payment for the road and operated it pending the completion of construction. Since the books of these organizations have been conveniently mislaid, it will always be impossible to ascertain what our railroads really cost originally in money capital. The construction companies turned over whole blocks of securities to manufacturers and contractors in payment for goods and services. These enterprisers usually seem to have pledged the securities with banks for working capital in the process of supplying the goods. In New York and elsewhere, speculators and specialists in railway finance, operating also on bank loans, facilitated this inflationary process by their dealings in stocks and bonds and daily risked the credit of the railway companies in their furious contests of bulls and bears.

The American banking mechanism did not have to bear this periodic strain alone. Every burst of new railway construction, in the thirties, in the fifties, at the close of the Civil War, through the eighties, and again from 1904 to 1907, meant new investments from abroad by British, Dutch, and German capitalists.[18] Schumpeter states that the boom from

---

[16] These were chiefly railroads built in the thirties and forties. Cf. Frank Walker Stevens, *The Beginnings of the New York Central Railroad* (New York and London: G. P. Putnam's Sons, 1926). Even in these cases, as we know from accounts of the crises of 1854 and 1857, the subscribers carried their shares on bank loans. Cf. Schumpeter, *Business Cycles*, I, 325–30.

[17] Cleveland and Powell, *Railroad Promotion and Capitalization*, is still the most adequate account for aspects before 1900. Cf. William Z. Ripley, *Railroads; Finance and Organization* (New York: Longmans, Green and Company, 1915), p. 10–52; Cleveland and Powell, *Railroad Finance* (New York: D. Appleton and Company, 1912), chaps. ii–iv and the very rich bibliography; Charles F. Adams, Jr., "Railroad Inflation," *North American Review*, CVIII (1869), 138–44.

[18] This paragraph is based upon original research in London and the United States, made possible by a sabbatical from Wellesley College and a grant from the John Simon Guggenheim Memorial Foundation. An introduction to the subject is available in Cleona Lewis, *America's Stake in International Investments* (Washington: The Brookings Institution, 1938), chap. ii; Ripley, *Railroads; Finance and Organization,*

1866 to 1873, which doubled our railway mileage, was entirely financed by an estimated two billion dollars of capital imported during those years.[19] It is incorrect to suppose, as he apparently does, that any such amount of foreign money was at that time invested directly in the railways. British, Dutch, and German investors were then buying nearly half of the Civil War debt, chiefly in 5–20's and 10–40's, to the amount of more than a billion dollars par. The railroads obtained directly only about half a billion. The purchase of government bonds by foreigners, however, released savings and bank resources for railway, industrial, and commercial promotion in the United States. In no subsequent period was the impact of foreign capital as momentous; but it is easy to exaggerate its importance. Although something like one fifth of the nominal value of American railroads was foreign-owned in 1873, the whole volume of foreign claims amounted to only 6 or 7 per cent of national wealth.[20] While in the course of subsequent fluctuations foreign ownership of railroad securities may have reached the proportions of one third in 1890 and nearly as much just before 1914, yet at these later dates it constituted a smaller proportion of the total national wealth than it had in 1873. According to the estimates, foreign investments did not keep pace with the growth of the national wealth.

It would be desirable to measure more precisely the investment of money capital at successive periods. Available figures of railway capitalization are entirely unsatisfactory for historical purposes. Apart from the obscurities of early railroad finance already mentioned, tabulations and estimates do not carefully and regularly include net floating debt or exclude intercorporate securities. The pathology of early stock watering has no necessary connection with the "overcapitalization" from which most railroad systems have suffered in recent years. This overcapitalization is entirely compatible with real historical investment as large as the nominal capitalization. But the available statistics give no adequate clue, before the last few decades, when such amounts actually were invested.

Whatever the source or timing of the application of money capital, the financing of railroad construction encouraged innovations in financial enterprise: the development of stock exchanges and their techniques; the specialization of firms, old and new, in investment banking and in security brokerage; the specialization of banking institutions (especially trust companies) as trustees and registration agents for securities, and as agents for distributing capital and interest payments; the rise of legal firms specializing in corporation law and in adjusting construction activities to the intricacies of the American political system.

New financial techniques and innovations in corporate structure

pp. 1–10; and Leland H. Jenks, *The Migration of British Capital to 1875* (New York and London: Alfred A. Knopf, 1927), chap. iii and pp. 169, 255–59 and notes. Before the Civil War the share of foreign investors was smaller than it became later. In only a few cases was it an initiating factor in railroad development.
[19] Schumpeter, *Business Cycles*, I, 335.
[20] Lewis, *America's Stake in International Investments*, p. 560.

were involved when established railway companies became agents in the flow of capital. By the early fifties the Pennsylvania was using its credit to supply funds for the building of western connections which it only informally controlled.[21] With the establishment of the Pennsylvania Company in 1869, the holding company became a permanent feature of the American scene. In many cases initial construction was of the sketchiest sort and by the seventies it was an established practice, of which foreign security holders bitterly complained, for companies to invest their earnings in necessary improvements and extensions. This financing of corporate growth from within may fairly be claimed to be an American innovation in capitalistic technique, which has only recently been diffused to the British Isles.

With financial innovation came a transformation of the role of the enterpriser in connection with particular railway systems. In the initial moments of construction, the typical enterpriser was still pretty much the omnicompetent pioneer, the individual of imagination, daring, and energy. Like General W. J. Palmer of the Denver and Rio Grande, he considered himself an agent of civilization, an embodiment of collective purpose.[22] No aspect of the task of railway building was too technical for his consideration and none too petty. In looking for the enterpriser of particular lines, official titles should not deceive. There was usually one man or a small informal group of unspecialized associates who could get things done, who could deal effectively at the same time with laborers, suppliers, politicians, and the local citizenry, and could command the confidence of sources of credit. At the construction moment, administration of a large formal organization was not necessarily involved. The mechanism of subcontracting provided a pattern for the co-operation of innumerable lesser enterprisers of a similar type.

Such enterprisers were rarely able, however, to cope with recurrent financial involvements. The elaboration of the superstructure of railroad securities sooner or later compelled a more formal division of tasks and responsibilities in the continuance of construction. In some cases this involved a shift of the center of decision from the engineer-promoter to financial and legal experts either within or outside the railroad organization.[23] The financier-enterpriser assumed many guises, now entering upon new construction to win stock-exchange battles, now basing a pro-

[21] Pennsylvania Central R. R. Co., *Annual Reports, passim.*

[22] William J. Palmer, *The Westward Current of Population in the United States* (London, 1874) and Glenn Chesney Quiett, *They Built the West* (New York and London: D. Appleton-Century Company, 1934), chaps. ii-vi, throw light upon the career of this neglected enterpriser.

[23] N. S. B. Gras, *Business and Capitalism* (New York: F. S. Crofts and Company, 1939), pp. 246–59, 272–75, indicates the "normal" process by which financial capitalists became involved in industry. He is correct, I believe, in implying that the opportunity and need have not been confined to late phases of the construction moment. From the standpoint of innovation, the emergence of the financial enterpriser in the railroads is not to be identified with the rise of special departments within the organization. The latter, or their heads, may be simply parts of a formally established group functioning as management-enterpriser. See section IV below.

gram of calculated expansion upon a re-ordering of company accounts, now entering belatedly, as did William Rockefeller in Northwestern, the race for competitive bigness.[24] There was inescapably a narrowing of horizon; the financier-enterpriser could decide freely only problems stated in financial terms, and he focused his attention chiefly on relations with potential intermediaries and rivals for the supply of capital.

Thus the second moment of the railroad as an economic force came with a demand for the factors of production in new construction, accompanied by the rise of new techniques and institutions of finance, by the aggregation of capital in mobile forms, and by the gradual displacement of the omnicompetent type of enterpriser.

IV

The third moment to be surveyed is that of the railroad as a going concern, a complex of tracks and engines and cars and managers and employees engaged in the business of carrying passengers and freight. By rendering this transportation service, the railroad in operation has doubtless added directly to the real income of the United States, and indirectly to economic expansion.[25] There appears to be no satisfactory technique for giving a precise measure to the extent of this contribution. It seems that the railways carried irregularly increasing ton-miles of freight until 1929, while the aggregate of passenger-miles expanded until 1920. The quanta involved, said to be from 13 billions of freight in 1870 to 450 billions in 1929, are certainly enormous.[26] But the available figures, at least before 1890, are neither accurate nor complete. There have been important changes in the composition of traffic. As Pigou points out, any attempt to measure differences in real income between situations involving substantial variations in the use of productive factors and in the

[24] Max Lowenthal, *The Investor Pays* (New York: Alfred A. Knopf, 1933).

[25] Ringwalt, *Development of Transportation Systems in the U.S.*, pp. 382–85 and Henry V. Poor, *Influence of the Railroads of the U.S. in the Creation of its Commerce and Wealth* (New York, 1869) are representative of early discussions. "Our new railroads increase the value of farms and open new markets for their products. They lessen the time and cost of travel. They give a value to commodities otherwise almost worthless. They concentrate population, stimulate production, and raise wages by making labor more efficient. Our existing railroads are computed to create more wealth every year than is absorbed for the construction of new railroads." *Commercial and Financial Chronicle*, XVI (January 11, 1873), 41.

[26] Attempts to use railway data in connection with the study of changes in real income and "productivity" are exemplified by Arthur F. Burns, *Production Trends in the United States since 1870* (New York: National Bureau of Economic Research, 1934) and Spurgeon Bell, *Productivity, Wages, and National Income* (Washington: The Brookings Institution, 1940). A brief factual summary of the role of the railways in the economic system after the First World War is provided by the Bureau of Railway Economics, *The Railways and Economic Progress* (Miscellaneous Series No. 50, Washington, 1929). The theory there suggested that the "economic contribution" of the railways is measured by the volume of their expenditures of all kinds is, however, at variance with the premises of this paper. Incidentally, this is an unusual place to find a theory popularly associated with New Deal economics. On railroad expenditures, cf. Partington, *Railroad Purchasing and the Business Cycle*.

composition of demand is theoretically at least precarious.[27] For contemporary comparison, Holmstrom has worked out a technique by which "virtual costs" (operating and maintenance charges plus interest on replacement cost of ways and works plus depreciation and profits) are equated with "direct benefits" on the one hand and "consumer costs" plus public subsidies on the other.[28] In view of the defective character of the data and the violence of price fluctuations in the United States, there is little hope of applying these means of measurement to the historical problem.

It is commonly assumed that the great contribution of railroad transportation came from the reduction of shipping costs. As compared with pre-motorized forms of highway transportation, the advantage of the railroad has always been obvious. There is no convincing evidence, however, that railways have ever carried freight at lower costs either to shippers or to society than canals or waterways.[29] The advantages that early railways showed over canals, such as speed, flexibility of service, and special adaptability to short hauls, are analogous to those of modern highway transport over the railroad. It was far more important that the railroad brought transportation to areas that without it could have had scarcely any commercial existence at all. At a later epoch, the motor highway provides means to achieve this result, at least in British colonial areas, at lower initial social cost. But historically, the very existence of most American communities and regions, of particular farms and industrial firms and aggregates, was made possible by the railroad.

Holmstrom's study of the cost characteristics of various forms of transportation brings other considerations to the forefront of analysis. He shows that the traffic potential of the railroad per unit of installation is even now far greater than that of any other form of transportation that he considers. For colonial areas in the early 1930's, for example, he computes that human porters could carry a maximum of 1,450 ton-miles of freight per annum; heavy animals, 3,600; "horsed wagons," 118,800; tractor trains, 1,000,000; and broad-gauge railways, 3,613,500.[30] Thus an

27 A. C. Pigou, "Comparisons of Real Income," *Economica,* New Series, X (May, 1943), pp. 93–98.
28 J. Edwin Holmstrom, *Railways and Roads in Pioneer Development Overseas* (London: P. S. King and Son, 1934), chap. i. Cf. E. A. J. Johnson, "New Tools for the Economic Historian," *The Tasks of Economic History,* supplemental issue of *The Journal of Economic History,* December, 1941, pp. 30–38.
29 General treatments of the economic significance of improved transportation are also found in D. Philip Locklin, *Economics of Transportation* (Chicago: Business Publications, 1938), chap. i, and Cleveland and Powell, *Railroad Finance,* chap. i. On comparative costs of service, cf. MacGill, *History of Transportation in the U.S. Before 1860,* pp. 574–82; Haney, *Congressional History of Railways in the U.S.,* chap. iii; Charles H. Ambler, *A History of Transportation in the Ohio Valley* (Glendale, California: The Arthur H. Clark Company, 1932), pp. 358 ff.; Harold Kelso, "Waterways versus Railways," *The American Economic Review,* XXXI (1941), 537–44.
30 Holmstrom, *Railways and Roads in Pioneer Development Overseas,* p. 56. Palmer, *The Westward Current of Population in the U.S.,* relates that in 1866 the stage line

initial and continuing potential contribution of the railroad has come from the volume of traffic it has been able to carry.

The converse of this proposition is the fact that the railroad constitutes a case of increasing return, with special features that give a decisive bent to its impact upon economic structure. Its social costs per unit of traffic decrease rapidly with traffic density.[31] A familiar manifestation of this condition was the well-known shift from passengers and light traffic as principal sources of revenue in the early railroad days to bulk traffic. Any isolated railroad system would tend to expand along those lines. But as new railroads in the United States became linked to previously existing lines, and as the innovation of freight-car interchange was established after the Civil War, a principle of acceleration was manifested enabling newer lines to begin farther along the cost curve. Between 1890 and 1941 the average actual haul of each ton of freight became 50 per cent longer (increasing especially during the First World War and the 1930's); there was an increase of more than 100 per cent during the same period in the distance traveled by the average passenger. These are revealing data about the long-run function of the railroad in the economic system.[32] Such expansion is, however, not a measure of innovation; the recent increase reflects to no small degree adjustments by railroads to other innovations in the economic system. What is significant about the principle of increasing return in the railroad is that it indicates directions in which railway transportation affects the economic structure.

That the railroad tends to attract factors of production to its right of way needs no comment; this perception lay at the heart of the American railroad innovation. As Holmstrom points out, however, this supply of potential traffic does not distribute itself at random. It is polarized first about line terminals, and secondarily about traffic intersections.[33] There is a further tendency. Irrespective of rate differentials, the service of the railroad is of greatest advantage to large shippers requiring a fairly regular flow of traffic.[34] Thus railroad transportation provides a considerable addition to the external economies that firms can realize from large-scale operations. Such phenomena as the ecological structure of wholesale trade, the localization and concentration of primary processing establishments, and the vertical integration of production units in spite of their geographical separation are thus functionally related to railroad transportation service. In more concrete terms, attention may be directed

from the terminus of the Kansas Pacific in Topeka carried six passengers daily to Denver. Two years later, daily trains carried westward one hundred to five hundred passengers daily.

[31] Holmstrom, pp. 104–12.

[32] United States Interstate Commerce Commission, *Statistics of Railways in the United States, 1941* (Washington: United States Government Printing Office, 1943), pp. 159–60.

[33] Holmstrom, pp. 265–66, 273.

[34] *Ibid.*, pp. 271–72.

to the initial localization of the textile industry in New England, the development of the factory system in some other industries at points remote from water power and dependent upon rail supply of coal, the establishment of stockyards in Chicago and other terminals, the rise of assembly plants, and generally the concentration, at terminals convenient to the source of supply, of industries processing and reducing the bulk of raw materials. In all these respects, railway transportation has worked in the same direction as, but in different areas from, water transport. It has functioned differently from the realized and probable tendencies of highway traffic.

The organization of railway enterprise itself early displayed the same tendencies to differentiation that it encouraged in other industries. On the one hand, the railways transferred to other enterprises part of their business. First in individual railway lines, and gradually on a more national scale, came the innovation of express companies, specializing in the rapid transmission of small items of high value. Opportunity arose for Pullman and other specialists in high-cost passenger service. On the other hand, individual railways themselves engaged in other business activities. If their land departments developed in order to implement construction, they proved of more value in augmenting traffic density to remunerative levels. Reading and other companies acquired anthracite fields in the interest of controlling the supply of bulk traffic between terminals. A great deal of change in the internal structure of railway organizations was merely a function of their expansion, involving innovations of a highly derivative and adaptive character; but other changes involved the positive quest of increasing return. The extension of particular systems by purchase, lease, and contract did not invariably contemplate development, but often aimed at controlling for the benefit of original main lines the supply of traffic at terminal points. The consolidation movement and much resistance to it on the part of particular companies may be interpreted from this point of view.

It must be clear that to yield real income and participate in expansion are not the same as to be a force for economic development. On the economic structure, the impact of the railway as a going concern was most decisive in the early years of the expansion of each system and in many respects came from the network as a whole rather than from any particular part. In time many other forces reinforced the polarizing tendency of the railroad. Urban centers tended to generate conditions that made for their own growth into metropolises. The returns to railways from increasing density tended to increase at slackening rates. Change in the railways gradually became more a matter of adjustment to external innovations than a primary source of disturbance to the economic structure.

As early as the eighties, railway systems that had been daring ventures only a decade before found themselves embarking on extensions and improvements, not as acts of innovating faith, but to enable them to handle traffic that had been offered them or to keep somebody else from getting the business.[35] In region after region development initiated by the railroad outran the plans of the projectors. The business of the railroad came increasingly to consist not in starting something but in keeping pace with what others were doing. That the railway would carry freight at known rates and with gradual change in the quality of service came to be part of the normal expectations of every business firm, a stable part of an environment which, of course, might still be disturbed by other innovations.[36] While the real income accruing to society from railway transportation probably continued to grow until 1929, the railroad functioned decreasingly as a pace setter or as an inciting force in the expansion of which it was a part.

By the time of the financial reorganizations of the nineties, many American railways manifested signs of belonging to an industry that has reached maturity.[37] The signs became more widespread in the first decade of the present century with the completion of the last cluster of new systems. For enterprises in general, Oxenfeldt thinks "newness of economic consequence" can be assumed to have worked itself out within a year of establishment.[38] This seems too short a period for the railroad. Although the bulk of improvement in the early years of American railway systems is properly classed as "construction," the leverage of increasing return in this field involves such extensive relocation of productive forces that opportunity for major business decisions may recur for several years after "completion" of the system.[39]

That some innovations have been made by railroads since 1910 must be conceded. Both technological and organizational changes are involved in the recent rapid increase in ton-miles of freight handled per employee and per unit of capital, in the increased capacity of cars, in speed of train units, in locomotive efficiency, etc. The National Resources Planning Board, however, takes the view that potentialities in this direction are thus far more an idea than an actuality.[40]

Consolidation looms as the source of the most important innovations in the near future. In 1933 only 16 per cent of the time of a typical

[35] For instance, new financing was sought by the Grand Trunk of Canada in the seventies and the Norfolk & Western in the eighties to make it possible to handle traffic already being offered. It was not always an extension that was involved but more often double-tracks, sidings, rolling stock, and improvements in the right of way.

[36] Schumpeter, *Business Cycles*, I, chap. ii, presents a representative theoretical analysis of this "equilibrium" position to which railway enterprises have been approximating.

[37] E. G. Campbell, *The Reorganization of the American Railroad System, 1893–1900* (New York: Columbia University Press, 1938).

[38] Alfred R. Oxenfeldt, *New Firms and Free Enterprise* (Washington: American Council on Public Affairs, 1943), p. 75.

[39] The degree to which in recent decades public regulation has restricted this opportunity as far as pricing of services is concerned has been the subject of a suggestive inquiry by the National Resources Planning Board. *Transportation and National Policy* (Washington: United States Government Printing Office, 1942), esp. pp. 87–128.

[40] *Ibid.*, pp. 60–65.

freight car from shipper to consignee was consumed in hauling; 37 per cent of the time was attributable to railroad terminal movement; and a total of 84 percent was spent in terminals.[41] Co-operation among carriers could improve this condition, but changes of innovational consequence seem to wait upon government action.

But what has been the role of the entrepreneur in the railroad as a going concern? What is the source of innovation in an enterprise almost wholly concerned with rendering transportation service? The rise of a line organization with few staff features was an early aspect of railway operations, and was well established by the eighties. The Pennsylvania Central seems to have led the way in the practice of promotion from within, a practice that developed rapidly into seniority policies at all levels and the establishment of railroading as a career. For a couple of decades after the Civil War, the training thus afforded made the Pennsylvania an important source from which new companies drew top executives who often developed entrepreneurial talents as individuals. Thomas A. Scott, who rose from the ranks to the presidency of Pennsylvania, was of pioneering quality. As horizons of opportunity narrowed, however, selection from within tended to bring competent administrators of a more routine sort to top executive positions, men who had spent so many years mastering the complexities of detailed management along established lines that they had little interest in changing those procedures. This tendency has been marked in many railroad systems, and is associated with the shift to adaptive change as the principal relation of the railroads to economic expansion in recent years.

Nevertheless, some innovation has taken place, and it can occasionally be traced to pioneering leadership. Large organizations as such, however, apart from their degree of maturity, set up certain hazards to innovation. To continue operations they require the delegation of specialized authority and responsibility to a considerable number of individuals. An innovation disturbs their tasks and their relations with each other quite as much as it does economic relations and activities outside the organization. This disturbance to internal equilibrium is not adjusted through market mechanisms and bargaining transactions. It involves planning activity. Decisive importance can scarcely be allowed to attach to individuals who conceive new ideas, even when this duty is delegated to them as a specific task. The locus of decision tends to spread to a group that includes persons in a position to know and deal with prospective internal disturbances which are only partially of an economic character.[42] It is not clear that this development has explicitly

[41] *Ibid.*, p. 41.

[42] An introduction to the sociological theory of organization can be found in Chester I. Barnard, *The Functions of the Executive* (Cambridge: Harvard University Press, 1938). Cf. T. N. Whitehead, *Leadership in a Free Society* (Cambridge: Harvard University Press, 1936), chaps. vi and viii. The problem at a lower level of enterprise structure is analyzed in F. J. Roethlisberger and William J. Dickson, *Management and the Worker* (Cambridge: Harvard University Press, 1939), chaps. xxiv and xxv.

gone far in railroad organization. As an innovation in the role of entre-preneurship itself, it is emergent in some newer large-scale industries. The extent to which the management-enterpriser type, as we may call it, has actually functioned in railroads informally and without explicit rec-ognition deserves inquiry.

V

This general interpretation of the role of the railroad as an economic force suggests what might be undertaken in greater detail to apply the innovation theory to the history of particular companies and of the rail-road system as a whole. What was the impact of the railroad upon tech-nological, locational, structural, and organizational alterations in particu-lar firms, industries, and regions? Parallel inquiries could be made regarding the part played by other major innovations, such as the more re-cent rise of the electromotive industries. It is not a question of applying the facts of economic history to verify an economic theory. It is a ques-tion of using a theory as a tool to coherent understanding of the facts. Economic historians seem increasingly willing to make use of conceptual aids for this purpose. It is one of the most prominent symptoms of what may be a wider tendency to employ analytical procedures in historical studies.

For the study of long-run change, the innovation theory stresses two important aspects of historical process: (1) the distinction between in-novating (disturbing, inciting, evolutionary) change and various types of adjustment (including expansion), and (2) the distinctive role of entre-preneurship. The first of these aspects provides the framework for sys-tematic exploration of the relation between changes in several sectors of the economy, in so far as these can be interpreted in economic terms. The breakdown of the railroad innovation into three "moments" is only a convenience that may be peculiar to transportation. In any case, the dis-tinction between innovating and adaptive change is a device that should become more serviceable to the historian as it is sharpened by applica-tion to a number of particular situations. It does not necessarily require the economic historian to take into account other than economic events and processes. Indeed, its logical adequacy can only gain from rigorous limitation to the items that are considered to be a part of an economic system.

The emphasis upon entrepreneurship as the crucial factor in capital-istic evolution involves both theorist and historian in considerations that go far beyond the limits of economics. Schumpeter is explicitly aware of this fact, and insists that in his conception the economy is not isolated but functions in a larger universe which requires in the first instance so-ciological analysis for its interpretation. The theory of innovations is neither a "great man" nor a "better mousetrap" theory of history. The in-novator is a person whose traits are in some part a function of his socio-cultural environment. His innovation is a new combination of factors and elements already accessible. It relates in every phase to previously developed business and monetary habits, technological skills, and variable tastes, none of which can be regarded as functions of economic activity alone. Thus Schumpeter's theory involves the question of the sociological factors favorable to the emergence of entrepreneurship. In a recent work he has presented a partial analysis of such factors.[43] Further analysis seems to be called for, at least so far as American capitalism is concerned, analysis that will come to closer grips with the special features of American social structure and the various influences which made for a strong entrepreneurial bias in the "social character" of the nineteenth-century American.

Despite his sociological sophistication, however, Schumpeter tends to think of his entrepreneur pretty much as a deviant person—a particular individual or at most a family. This approach tends to make highly problematical the existence of any entrepreneurship in a bureaucratic enterprise such as the railway, whether under private or public ownership. It must be recognized that innovations in a socialist economy would work themselves out by mechanisms other than under capitalism. But not all of such differences would be peculiar to socialism. Practically, large-scale organization offers a new type of social resistance to innovation. At the same time, as Schumpeter himself vigorously argues, the large organization offers real support to technological change, at least, by mobilizing resources for its systematic planning.[44]

It is possible that there is a real social lag in conceptions of the entrepreneurial function. The question deserves to be considered whether policy formation by group action is an obstacle to innovation, not inherently, but only because of certain peculiarities in our culture. Is the entrepreneurial role in large organizations increasingly the function of a cooperating group? Is it true that this tendency is not absolutely new but can be discerned in earlier phases of modern industry; that it is less important in entrepreneurial studies to single out the contributions of one individual than to ascertain the personal composition of the group with which he usually interacted and the way in which the members compensated for their respective shortcomings and were adjusted to each other? In so far as there is validity in affirmative answers to these questions, a practical problem of much importance falls upon the large organizations of the present day, that of cultivating social techniques for facilitating innovations. But there would be a broader social problem, that of developing personalities whose practical imagination and responsibility for decision will be stimulated rather than frustrated by membership in policy-determining groups. This would be a task for the family and other educational institutions and for socializing processes in the wider society.

[43] Joseph A. Schumpeter, *Capitalism, Socialism, and Democracy* (New York: Harper and Brothers, 1942), chaps. xi–xiv.
[44] *Ibid.*, pp. 96–98. Schumpeter seems to regard this change as more than adaptational. In so far as it is innovational, however, it functions less to develop capitalist structure than to further its incipient transformation into something else.

Two ⌒ *The Railroads as Pioneers in*

Modern Management

THE RAILROADS: INNOVATORS
IN MODERN BUSINESS
ADMINISTRATION

Alfred D. Chandler, Jr., and Stephen Salsbury

The American entrance into the space race in 1957 created an enterprise which will in the course of time profoundly influence almost every aspect of life. Measured by any past standards space exploration is a vast undertaking. By 1970, total expenditures may reach $40,000,000,000. The manned moon expedition must conquer many difficult technological problems which require precise data from such diverse fields as biology, psychology, physics, and astronomy. Even in the embryonic stages space administrators must face a host of new and delicate problems such as the relationship of a long-term government program controlling enormous resources in money and scientific talent to the rest of the economy, the initiation and co-ordination of the complex and seemingly unrelated basic research necessary to solve the technological complexities posed by space travel, the relationship of a predominantly professional and highly educated working force to management, and many others not even imagined.

Industries which have radically altered nearly every aspect of national life are not new on the American scene. In fact space is merely the latest in a series of revolutionary enterprises—railroads, automobiles, aircraft—which have transformed the United States from Thomas Jefferson's agrarian society to today's scientific and urban economy. Thus, change and readjustment have become normal. Whole industries have grown to maturity only to fall into decline as new technology renders

FROM Alfred D. Chandler, Jr., and Stephen Salsbury, "The Railroads: Innovators in Modern Business Administration." Reprinted from *The Railroad and the Space Program* by Bruce Mazlish by permission of The M.I.T. Press, Cambridge, Massachusetts. Copyright 1965 by The American Academy of Arts and Sciences.

them obsolete. The natural question about the space effort is, therefore, what impact will it have on the economy?

New Enterprise and the Evolution of Administrative Practices: The Impact of the Railroads, 1829–1860

This chapter is concerned with the evolution of administrative structure and technique in large-scale industries. While it is too early to predict or categorize what innovations the space program will bring, a detailed understanding of changes resulting from past economic revolutions may provide a background that will prove useful in analyzing the space effort's impact upon administrative practice in the years ahead.

Although space and railroads have few technological similarities, they both involve the management of large and complex organizations, and in this sense, nineteenth-century railroads may be comparable to space in the twentieth century. Certain it is that railways forced a sharp break with traditional patterns. In three decades between their introduction in 1829 and the outbreak of the Civil War, railroads set precedents which profoundly affected every aspect of the industrial world. In truth, it is not too much to say that railroads created modern administration— that is, they moved business activity away from organizations run by entrepreneurs with the aid of personal trustees, relatives, and the like to corporations with a systematized, bureaucratic management.[1]

EARLY RAILROAD DEVELOPMENT

The coming of modern administration can best be understood by focusing on how and why America's first big businesses grew, and in what ways railroads developed methods to handle the problems arising from the size and complexity of their operations. Robert Stephenson's perfection of the steam locomotive on England's Liverpool and Manchester Railway, in 1829, immediately sparked many projects in the United States. These were of two kinds. The first was the grand enterprise meant to carry the products of the Great West to the cities on the Atlantic seaboard. In this category fell the Baltimore & Ohio, the New York and Erie, and the Western Railroad of Masachusetts. The second included the less ambitious projects, which generally ran north and south and connected well-established population centers. Of these, the Camden and Amboy, the Boston and Providence, the Philadelphia, Wilmington and Baltimore, and the Boston and Lowell were typical.

The great east-west roads soon dwarfed any previous enterprises. By the early 1850's four trunk lines connected the Atlantic with the west-

[1] H. H. Gerth and C. Wright Mills, *From Max Weber: Essays in Sociology* (New York: Oxford University Press, 1958), pp. 196–97.

ern waters: in 1851, the New York and Erie reached Dunkirk on Lake Erie; in 1853, the Baltimore & Ohio arrived at Wheeling on the Ohio River; the same year the several short lines connecting Albany with Buffalo combined to form the New York Central, and the Pennsylvania's tracks reached Pittsburgh. The 1850's witnessed an enormous railroad boom. By 1855, no less than thirteen companies operated systems that exceeded two hundred miles in length, and by 1860, that number had increased to thirty-one.[2] By the eve of the Civil War, rails had replaced canals as the leading inland transportation method, and in the north an iron network linked most important cities and towns from the Atlantic to the Mississippi River.

RAILROADS AND OTHER ENTERPRISES COMPARED

From the first, railroad managers faced unique problems. Measured in strictly financial terms, railroads quickly overshadowed all contemporary factories or other transportation ventures. The Western Railroad in Massachusetts, which in 1842 had but 160 miles of single track, cost more than $7,000,000; by 1854, the Western's capital amounted to more than $10,000,000 although it operated no greater mileage.[3] By contrast, the completed Erie Canal, more than 360 miles long, cost only $7,000,000.[4] In 1860, the New York Central, which paralleled the canal, had invested more than $30,000,000 in property, track, and rolling stock, and this was but the beginning: by 1883 the Central operated 953 miles of line with a total investment of nearly $150,000,000. And the New York Central, which owned four times the mileage that it directly operated, was not the largest system. By the time the Pennsylvania had completed its expansion program between 1869 and 1873 its total investment approached $400,000,000.[5] River steamers required much less capital than canals; in fact "the construction cost of a single mile of well-built railroad was enough to pay for a new and fully equipped river steamboat."[6] Of manufacturing concerns, textile factories were the largest, but at mid-

[2] For mileage in the years before the Civil War, see Alfred D. Chandler, Jr., *Henry Varnum Poor, Business Editor, Analyst, and Reformer* (Cambridge: Harvard University Press, 1956), pp. 267–68.
[3] *Eighth Annual Report of the Directors of the Western Railroad Corporation to the Stockholders* (Boston: Dutton and Wentworth's Printer, 1843), p. 20; *Twentieth Annual Report of the Directors of the Western Railroad Corporation to the Stockholders* (Springfield: Samuel Bowles and Co. Printers, 1855), pp. 18–19.
[4] Carter Goodrich, *Government Promotion of American Canals and Railroads 1800–1890* (New York: Columbia University Press, 1960), p. 54.
[5] Henry V. Poor, "Railroad share list, including mileage, rolling stock, etc.," *American Railroad Journal*, 29 (January 14, 1856), 24–25; Chandler, *op. cit.*, pp. 145, 320; "Statement of the Mileage, Capital, Operations, etc., of the Railroads of the U.S. for 1883," *Poor's Manual of the Railroads of the United States: 1884; Report of the Investigating Committee of the Pennsylvania Railroad Company Appointed by Resolution of the Stockholders at the Annual Meeting Held March 10, 1874* (Philadelphia: Allen, Lane and Scotts Printing House, 1874), p. 115.
[6] Lewis C. Hunter, *Steamboats on the Western Rivers* (Cambridge: Harvard University Press, 1949), p. 308.

century only the biggest mills cost as much as $500,000. In fact, in 1850 only forty-one American plants had a capitalization of $250,000 or more.[7]

Railroads differed from canals and factories in very important respects. In the 1850's even the largest manufacturing concerns confined their operations to one or two specific locations which made it possible for managers to view their entire establishments in an hour or two, or to confer with any employee within a matter of minutes. Canal managers, although they supervised works hundreds of miles long, had limited duties confined mainly to routine maintenance and toll collecting. Independently owned boats performed all actual transportation upon them.

By the 1850's many railroads operated systems hundreds of miles in length, and their managers not only supervised maintenance, but were responsible for all movement upon the line since railroads owned and operated all vehicles run upon them. No manager on the Erie or Pennsylvania railroads could inspect their domain in less than several days, and close supervision of subordinates was impossible. Despite this, railroads demanded operational precision that rivaled that of a factory mass-producing complex machinery with interchangeable parts. Safe operations could be achieved only by a strictly disciplined work force, acting in accordance with the most stringent rules. Disobedience or laxity by engineers or conductors meant possible collision, property destruction, or death.

But equally as vital, railroad managers had to make decisions based on data available to them only with detailed planning and organization. A method had to be devised to keep track of freight cars, put them at places where they were needed, and ensure that they did not accumulate in jams at terminal points or lie idle along the line. Railroads faced accounting problems of unprecedented complexity. Collecting revenues produced situations not even encountered in contemporary banking institutions, for each day large quantities of cash flowed through the hands of dozens, if not hundreds, of far-flung ticket and freight agents, passenger-train conductors, purchasing agents, and other officers.

Accounting for and ensuring the honesty of transactions involving revenue was the essence of simplicity compared to the other accounting problems. The great capital investment required to construct the systems normally resulted in a financial structure that included a substantial bonded indebtedness and a consequent large fixed cost. On Massachusetts' Western Railroad, for example, fixed costs exceeded operating expenses for several years, even after the line had been completed through to Albany.[8] Moreover, capital expenditures seldom stopped but kept growing as increased traffic necessitated more equipment, larger

---

[7] Evelyn H. Knowlton, *Pepperell's Progress, History of a Cotton Textile Company, 1844–1945* (Cambridge: Harvard University Press, 1948), p. 132.
[8] In 1842, for example, fixed costs ran $310,000; operating expenses, $266,619.30, *Eighth Annual Report of the Western Railroad Corporation to the Stockholders* (Boston: Dutton and Wentworth Printer, 1843), p. 33.

yards, bigger terminals, and double and quadruple tracking of main lines.

Bondholders and stockholders placed a premium on profitable operation. For management, however, it was not easy to differentiate between the "profitable" and "unprofitable" services. The rapid and continuing growth of the physical plant obscured the division between capital expenditures on one hand, and normal maintenance and depreciation on the other. The determination of what it cost to move each class of goods, a vital factor in shaping decisions about service, involved complex calculations. To assess a railway's ability to bid for hauling bulky seasonal commodities like grain, management had first to separate the passenger expenses from the freight, and then those for the grain (terminals, cars, engines, maintenance, capital, etc.) from those for the other freight. Setting rates soon demanded a careful analysis of both the competition and the limitations imposed by the railroad's internal economic position. And by the 1850's massive interregional freight traffic added the complications of fixing joint rates for goods traveling on two or more carriers. For all this railroad management needed precise information about maintenance costs (depreciation of track, rolling stock, depots) as well as operating costs (wood, oil, water, labor, etc.). The collection of such statistics required careful organization and routine methods for employees to record data and pass information along to the top management.

·   ·   ·

THE TRUNK LINES OF THE 1850'S REVOLUTIONIZE
ADMINISTRATIVE METHODS [9]

In the 1850's, three of the new great trunk lines, the Baltimore & Ohio, the New York and Erie, and the Pennsylvania, had managers who not only recognized the special complexities of railroad administration, but who were actively engaged in evolving new structures to meet them. The Erie's General Superintendent, Daniel C. McCallum, saw clearly that the methods that had worked on the small systems were inadequate for the large ones: "A Superintendent of a road fifty miles in length can give its business his personal attention and may be constantly on the line engaged in the direction of its details." Under such circumstances, he reasoned, any managerial method "however imperfect . . . may prove comparatively successful." In running a railroad five hundred miles long, however, McCallum maintained "any system which might be applicable to the business and extent of a short road would be found entirely inadequate. . . . I am fully convinced," he concluded, "that in the want of a system perfect in its details, properly adapted and vigilantly enforced, lies the true secret of their [the large system's] failure; and that . . . [the] disparity of cost per mile in operating long and short roads, is not

[9] Much of the following has appeared in a more detailed form in Alfred D. Chandler, Jr., "The Railroads: Pioneers in Modern Corporate Management," *Business History Review*, 39 (Spring, 1965), 17–40.

produced by a difference in length, but is in proportion to the perfection of the system adopted." [10]

McCallum represented a newly emerging group of professional managers who, as civil engineers, had built the great east-west lines, and then had turned to administering the great enterprises which they had constructed. Among the most prominent of these were Benjamin H. Latrobe, Chief Engineer of the Baltimore & Ohio, J. Edgar Thomson, the Pennsylvania's President, John B. Jervis, the Michigan Central's builder and Chief Engineer, and George B. McClellan, the Chief Engineer of the Illinois Central. Latrobe, Thomson, and Jervis had worked up the professional ladders from the late 1820's and were among the very first of the new type of professional engineer.[11] Significantly, only one, McClellan, had any connection at all with military life and he was the least innovative of the lot. These men did not borrow; they approached their brand-new problems of building an administrative structure in much the same rational and analytical way as they approached that of building a railroad or a bridge.

THE BALTIMORE & OHIO ADOPTS A FUNCTIONALLY
DEPARTMENTALIZED ADMINISTRATIVE STRUCTURE

The Baltimore & Ohio, oldest of the trunk lines, was the first to systematize its operations. Its President, Louis McLane, and its Chief Engineer, Benjamin H. Latrobe, realized that as the railroad pushed westward across the Allegheny Mountains to Wheeling it would need a "new system of management." [12] Up until the new system was adopted in 1847, the corporation operated under plans formulated in 1834, when it had completed only eighty miles of track between Baltimore and Harpers Ferry.[13] The old rules did little more than outline in scant detail the duties of the principal officers; they made no attempt to create a formal working organization, and left unclear the relationship between the various officers.

The Baltimore & Ohio's new managerial plan set forth in a manual, *Organization of the Service of the Baltimore & Ohio Railroad*, contained one basic innovation: it departmentalized the road's functions into two separate spheres, finance, and operations. Over-all fiscal responsibility

[10] *Reports of the President and the Superintendent of the New York and Erie Railroad to the Stockholders for the Year Ending September 30, 1855* (New York, n.d.), p. 34.
[11] For Jervis, Latrobe, McCallum, and McClellan see Dumas Malone, ed., *Dictionary of American Biography* (New York: Charles Scribner's Sons, 1946), Vol. X, pp. 59–61; Vol. XI, pp. 25–26, 565, 581–82; for Thomson see William B. Wilson, *History of the Pennsylvania Railroad Company* (Philadelphia, 1899), Vol. II, pp. 238–39.
[12] *Organization of the Service of the Baltimore & Ohio Railroad, under the Proposed New System of Management* (Baltimore, 1847), p. 3. The new system was accepted by the board on February 10, 1847.
[13] *Laws and Ordinances Relating to the Baltimore & Ohio Railroad* (Baltimore, 1834).

centered in the company's treasurer, who not only reviewed the internal transactions, but also handled external financing, including the routine arrangements for assigning shares of stock or bonds to merchants or bankers who had agreed to market them, assured the proper recording of the sale or other transfer of securities from one person to another, and sent out dividends and interest payments. Directly subordinate to the treasurer was the secretary, whose duties later were taken over by an an official entitled comptroller. This officer was wholly concerned with internal transactions; he inspected all passenger and freight accounts and exercised supervision of those who routinely handled the company's monies. Beneath the secretary was the chief clerk, into whose office at the corporation's Baltimore headquarters flowed required receipts and reports from all agents and conductors along the system who received or disbursed funds. The chief clerk's office compiled and checked this information, and issued "daily comparisons of the work done by the road and its earnings with the monies received therefore." [14] Daily figures were in turn summarized into monthly reports. Thus was made available the data so vital to decision making by top management, and for checking upon the honesty and efficiency of the employees. In 1847, however, there was still little attempt to break down operating expenses into their component parts or to allocate costs against the type of goods and passengers carried.

The new operating department was placed under the control of a professional engineer who had the title of general superintendent. He supervised three distinct subdepartments: maintenance of way under the master of the road, machinery (maintenance of rolling stock) under the master of machinery, and transportation under the master of transportation. Of the three subofficials the master of transportation was the most important. Everything concerned with the forwarding of passengers and freight was his responsibility, and it was his duty to employ "with the concurrence of the general superintendent and president, all officers and hands necessary" [15] for his department. This included engineers, firemen, conductors, fuel and lumber agents, and depot agents. The latter supervised six types of employees—clerks, weight masters, car regulators, laborers, watchmen, and porters.

The general superintendent was the road's key administrator. Except for the revenues, his office was the central focus of both authority and communication, and into it flowed a series of reports. Each of the operating department heads forwarded their weekly and monthly results. The master of machinery, for example, was to report on "the conditions and performance during the week of each locomotive and engine in service or under repair—and the condition of the cars, as also of the stationary machinery and workshops—and will present a monthly estimate of the probable expense of their repair during the ensuing month." [16] Besides reading reports, the senior operating executive constantly reviewed prog-

[14] *Organization of the Service of the Baltimore & Ohio Railroad*, 1847.
[15] *Ibid.*
[16] *Ibid.*

ress with department heads, inspected the road, and conferred with the president and the road's financial officers.

By the 1847 reorganization, Latrobe and McLane set up one of the very first functionally departmentalized, administrative structures for an American business enterprise. As the departments took over the day-to-day routine operating decisions, the president was able to concentrate more effectively on the long-range activities of raising and allocating funds.[17] While such a departmentalized structure would be expanded and refined as the railroads grew, it remained essentially the organization by which American railways were to be administered.

MC CALLUM'S ERIE REFINES THE BALTIMORE & OHIO'S STRUCTURE

The first refinements to Latrobe's organization came on the New York and Erie, which after it reached the Great Lakes in 1851, was the largest railroad in the United States. However, it suffered from size, and in 1853, after the railroads linking Albany and Buffalo consolidated into the New York Central, the Erie also faced formidable rail competition for the traffic of the Great West. Alarmed because the Erie's costs per mile were higher than those on the shorter roads, the company's board desired a system that would ensure a more precise accountability for expenses and a more effective appraisal of men and managers. This the directors hoped to achieve by making available "comparisons of the expenses of the various operations with those of other similar roads, with the several divisions of the road itself; and the expenses of different conductors, engine-men, etc., with each other." [18]

By the end of 1853, the directors had split the Erie into five geographic divisions, each about a hundred miles long, and they had also made the separation between operation and finance in the same manner as Latrobe's. In 1854 they picked Daniel C. McCallum, at the time superintendent of one of the new divisions, to be the general superintendent. McCallum, the inventor of an inflexible truss bridge and an able engineer, approached the Erie's management in much the same way as he designed bridges. His great strength was in sharpening lines of authority and communication, and in stimulating the flow of the minute and accurate information which top management needed for the complex decisions it was increasingly being called upon to make. Hourly, daily, and monthly reports, more detailed than those called for earlier on the Baltimore & Ohio, provided this essential information.

The hourly reports, primarily operational, gave by telegraph the

[17] Possibly one reason for the change was that President McLane had no time for day-to-day operations. For the two previous years, he had been in England raising money for his road and also acting as United States Minister, in which capacity he helped to negotiate the Oregon Treaty, *Dictionary of American Biography*, Vol. XII, p. 114.

[18] *Report of the Directors of the New York and Erie Railroad Company to the Stockholders, November 1853* (2nd ed.; New York, 1853), pp. 47–48.

location of each train and the reasons for any delays or mishaps.[19] The information thus received was tabulated, and proved vital in the elimination of bottlenecks and other trouble spots. McCallum's use of the telegraph impressed other railroad managers, because it demonstrated that wires were more than a means to make trains safe, but were also a device to improve co-ordination and better administration.

Daily reports, the real basis of the system, were required from both conductors and station agents. They covered all important matters of train operation, and the handling of freight and passengers. These reports provided information from two different sources on train movements, car loadings, damages, and misdirected freight, and acted as a valuable check on the honesty and efficiency of both conductors and agents. Engineers, too, were required to make daily reports. These were consolidated into monthly statements, giving for each engine the miles run, the operating expenses, the cost of repairs, and the work done. Such data, flowing up through the superintendent's office of each geographic division to McCallum, made it possible for him to make comparative appraisals between the different divisions, and between them and other roads. In addition, the success of experimental motive power could be easily evaluated.

Besides assisting in operations, these statistical data were essential in rate making, for only analysis of these reports could provide the information necessary to determine what were the costs of carrying an item, and whether, therefore, the charges produced a profit or not. McCallum also realized that rates depended on more than costs. The Erie had lost money because it had raised rates which it had found "unremunerative" only to discover that in so doing they had threatened to "destroy this business." [20] Higher rates by reducing traffic had cut net revenues. To guard against such a result required "an accurate knowledge of the cost of transport of the various products, for both long and short distances." Important too was knowing which way the item was moving along the line, for prices should be "fixed with reference to securing as far as possible, such a balance of traffic in both directions as to reduce the proportion of 'dead weight' carried." Unused or excess capacity on a return trip warranted lowering prices for goods going that way.

McCallum's innovations received widespread attention. Henry Varnum Poor, editor of the *American Railroad Journal*, credited McCallum with increasing efficiency while reducing the working force. The New York State Railroad commissioners described the Erie's new managerial system in its annual report. Even a popular magazine like the *Atlantic Monthly* devoted an article to the subject in 1858. In England, Douglas Galton, a leading British railroad authority, described the Erie's

[19] *Reports of the President and the Superintendent of the New York and Erie Railroad, 1855.* McCallum gives a full account of his reporting systems in this report, pp. 34–35, 51–54.
[20] This and the following two quotations are from *ibid.*, p. 79.

management in an 1857 Parliamentary report. Unquestionably McCallum's principles and procedures had a significant impact on the development of the internal organization of the large business enterprise.[21]

THE PENNSYLVANIA ADOPTS A DECENTRALIZED, DIVISIONAL
STRUCTURE WITH LINE AND STAFF OFFICERS

The Pennsylvania, rather than the Erie, tested and further rationalized McCallum's concepts of large-scale administration. Before 1860, the Erie fell into the hands of unscrupulous financiers, who like its notorious Treasurer, Daniel Drew, cared little about efficient administration. McCallum soon retired, and developed a profitable bridge-building business. On the Pennsylvania, however, engineers rather than speculators continued to run the road. J. Edgar Thomson, the builder and first operator of the Georgia Railroad, came to the Pennsylvania in 1849. In 1852 he became its president, and he continued to control its destinies until his death in 1874.

In 1857, Thomson rebuilt the Pennsylvania's managerial structure in the image of McCallum's Erie. Thomson divided his system into several geographic divisions, each managed by a superintendent who reported to a general superintendent with over-all operational responsibility for the system. His organization established solid and clear lines of authority, and ensured a steady flow of data to the top management.

The Pennsylvania's main achievement was a clarification in the relationship between the central office, and the geographic subdivisions. Both the central headquarters and the several divisions carried on at least three functional activities—transportation, maintenance of way, and maintenance of locomotives, rolling stock, and other machinery. Thomson explicitly delegated the full powers to control the road to the officers in charge of transportation—to the general superintendent in the central headquarters and to the division superintendents in the geographic subunits. The other functional officers at the headquarters set standards and procedures but could not order their subordinates in the divisions when to work and what to work on. On the Pennsylvania, therefore, the division superintendent directed the daily work of all men in his division. This meant, for example, that all the workers in the division's shops were under his control; while the master of machinery set rules and standards for "the discipline and economy of conducting the business of their [the division superintendent's] shops." [22] In short, this was the beginning in

---

[21] Chandler, *Poor*, pp. 147–48, 153; *American Railroad Journal*, 29 (May 3, 1856), 280.

[22] This quotation is from *Organization of the Pennsylvania Railroad, 1857*, p. 7. In 1857 there were only two resident engineers, each reporting to the general superintendent. After 1863 there was a resident engineer for each of the three divisions, *By-Laws and Organization for Conducting the Business of "The Pennsylvania Railroad Company,"* as revised and approved by the Board of Directors, May 13, 1863 (Philadelphia, 1863), p. 14.

industry of the line and staff system where the executives on the line of authority handled the people, and the other officers, the staff executives, handled things.

The decentralized, divisional railroad structure, with line and staff officers, that emerged on the Pennsylvania, and which became characteristic of such major systems as the Michigan Central, Illinois Central, and the Chicago, Burlington & Quincy, was neither natural nor inevitable. British railroads used a centralized "departmental" type of organization where the general superintendent did not delegate his authority to the division superintendents. Instead, each functional officer on a regional division reported directly to and received his orders directly from his functional superiors in the central office.

CENTRALIZED ADMINISTRATION EVOLVES ON THE NEW YORK CENTRAL

In the United States, the New York Central developed a centralized departmental structure. Its history differed radically from the other three great trunks lines. Unlike the Pennsylvania, the Baltimore & Ohio, or the New York and Erie, the Central was not built as a single grand enterprise, nor did its construction produce a group of able, professional engineer-managers. Instead, the Central was created from ten separate short lines by financiers and politicians.[23] The system's first senior executives, Erastus Corning, Dean Richmond, John V. L. Pruyn, and Edwin D. Worcester, were among New York's richest men, and they were powerful leaders in her Democratic Party. There was not a professional engineer among them; even the new General Superintendent, Chauncy Vibbard, had no training or apprenticeship comparable to that of the operating managers of other trunk lines.

The New York Central was one of the very first great consolidations of a number of different incorporated enterprises. Its major problems were financial and legal, and its early managers focused on these, paying relatively little attention to the development of a rational operating structure. Chauncy Vibbard, in addition to his duties as general superintendent, continued to run a profitable liquor business in New York City, and in 1861 he was elected to Congress.[24]

Vibbard did not systematize the road's structure. Although the Central had five regional divisions, each headed by an assistant or "deputy" superintendent, Vibbard delegated little authority. As late as the 1850's, he still made verbal arrangements to buy fuel wood.[25] Vibbard's many outside interests prevented him from direct supervision of all activities, and eventually strong autonomous functional departments grew up at the road's main headquarters. Under this system the division superin-

[23] The carrying out of the consolidation is described in detail in Frank W. Stevens, *The Beginnings of the New York Central Railroad* (New York: G. P. Putnam's Sons, 1926), Chapter 17.
[24] *Dictionary of American Biography*, Vol. XIX, p. 263.
[25] Alvin F. Harlow, *The Road of the Century* (New York: Creative Age Press, 1947), p. 96.

tendent's duties ended with control of train movements; and those responsible for maintenance of way and bridges continued to report to the chief engineer, the shops to a master of machinery, or a master of car repairs, and the station and freight agents to the general passenger or the freight agent. Thus, the officers at the headquarters, who on the Pennsylvania held staff advisory positions, on the Central had direct line control of and responsibility for the actions of workmen at the division level. Vibbard's structure, always haphazard, and never thought out, became formalized into an explicitly centralized departmental type when Cornelius Vanderbilt and his son William took control of the line after the Civil War. Although the Central's management structure remained different from those of other large systems, the demands of running a large railroad forced the Vanderbilts to formalize the structure and sharpen lines of authority and responsibility.

In three short decades, railroads transformed American business organization. The highly technical and complex requirements of railroad construction and operation developed a professional managerial class sharply different from the original entrepreneurs—local businessmen, bankers, or community leaders—who personally shaped and supervised small concerns. On large railroads the old managerial patterns simply would not do, and the new executives soon recognized this and set about formally to create administrative structures specifically designed to the needs of large-scale, geographically scattered, and technologically complex enterprises. The decentralized divisional structure with line and staff officers which finally emerged on the Pennsylvania was not inevitable. But the great distances on American railroads contrasted sharply with the shorter systems in Europe and in Great Britain, and thus made the centralized "departmental" type of organization, typical of English roads, less practical, as the New York Central found out. The moral of this story is that administrative problems are by no means automatically solved. Nevertheless, railroads like the Pennsylvania created the managerial skills and bureaucratic structures which, with slight modifications, made possible the administration of the new industries that in the period between the Civil War and the First World War did so much to change America from an agricultural and trading economy to a vast industrial and urban society.

The American Railroads, 1860–1900: The Growth and Management of the Nation's First Private Bureaucracies

The decade following 1865 brought enormous changes to America's railroad network. Before that time major attention focused on problems associated with building the first lines: financing, technological improvement, and operation. Prior to the Civil War, top management built an administrative structure capable of directing systems five hundred miles long.

The 1850's saw concrete recognition that railroads differed from other contemporary enterprises and that they demanded new administrative structures to meet unique problems. The line and staff organization which evolved on the Pennsylvania enabled management to increase safety, efficiency, and economy. Data flowing from each division to the general superintendent's office made possible more exact scheduling, maximum use of rolling stock, evaluation of new equipment, and provided an accurate basis for determining operating costs.

COMPETITION AMONG THE TRUNK LINES

Operational matters and construction continued to concern management after the War, but they were dwarfed by new troubles. The four great trunk systems, the Erie, the Pennsylvania, the New York Central, and the Baltimore & Ohio, entered the post-Civil War decade with compact five-hundred-mile lines that connected Atlantic port cities to terminals on the waters west of the Allegheny watershed. None reached beyond Pittsburgh, or western New York State; and all depended upon newly constructed connecting lines for the traffic which came to them from the West. From Pittsburgh, the Pennsylvania Railroad's western terminus, Chicago, was reached over the northern route of the Pittsburgh, Fort Wayne and Chicago, or a more southerly combination of railroads that included the Panhandle (from Pittsburgh to Columbus) and the Columbus, Chicago and Indiana Central (from Columbus to Chicago).[26] A series of short lines linked Buffalo and Chicago. They paralleled the southern lake shore, connecting Erie with Cleveland, Cleveland with Toledo, and Toledo with Chicago. The Atlantic and Great Western connected western New York with Dayton, Ohio. Other lines linked Buffalo with Chicago through southern Ontario and central Michigan.

Several factors profoundly affected the railroad network that stretched between New York and the Middle West. First, although no single corporation controlled trackage from the Atlantic seaboard to Chicago, a heavy freight volume did flow between these terminal points. This was the period when large quantities of grain and livestock moved eastward from Illinois, Wisconsin, Iowa, and Minnesota to Atlantic and overseas markets. And after 1865, oil shipments between the producing regions of western Pennsylvania and the East became significant. In short, through traffic between the Mississippi Valley and the coast was vitally important to the four great trunk lines, the Erie, the New York Central, the Pennsylvania, and the Baltimore & Ohio. Second, because of numerous interconnections, the western lines were not bound to a single eastern trunk but could deliver goods to any or all of the great eastern roads. Third, most of the railroads had substantial fixed costs; this

[26] Julius Grodinsky, *Jay Gould, His Business Career 1867–1892* (Philadelphia: University of Pennsylvania Press, 1957), pp. 56–58.

was especially true of the vast majority of systems outside New England, which were financed by bond issues that required large annual interest payments—which accrued regardless of the amount of traffic carried. Heavy fixed charges put a premium on high utilization, for it was only through steady and rising business that the enormous investments could be made profitable.

CONTROL OF COMPETITION THROUGH ALLIANCES

From the first days railroad managements had attempted to curb competition and rate wars through alliances both with potential competitors and with connecting railroads. As early as 1854, the Erie, the New York Central, and the Pennsylvania, together with four western railroads and several Great Lakes steamship lines, met in Buffalo and set rates between New York and all places on and west of Lake Erie.[27] But these voluntary agreements were abandoned almost as soon as they were made. Weaker lines, suffering the pressures of high fixed charges, inevitably succumbed to the lure of increasing business by lowering rates.

Alliances between connecting roads proved more enduring. The Pennsylvania was the first major system to embark on such a policy. To ensure itself a voice in the management of its western connections, it began to support certain lines financially through the purchase of their stock or bonds. In 1853, the Pennsylvania legislature passed an act permitting the railroad to "subscribe capital, or guarantee bonds of other companies, to the extent of 15 per cent of its paid up capital." [28] This act, one of the earliest laws allowing a company to hold the stock of another doing the same business, helped introduce the holding company, the legal device which became so essential to the growth of the large American business enterprise. In 1858, the Pennsylvania's President, J. Edgar Thomson, explained that his company's "policy . . . [of aiding] in the construction of Western Railways designed to facilitate trade to and from . . . [the] road" had compelled an investment of over $1,600,000 in the Pittsburgh, Fort Wayne and Chicago, the Steubenville and Indiana, and the Marietta and Cincinnati railroad companies.[29] Further, to ensure a connection between Philadelphia and New York, the Pennsylvania signed a treaty of alliance with the "Joint Companies" in New Jersey. That agreement set rates and provided for common use of facili-

[27] *Report of the Directors of the New York and Erie Railroad Company to the Stockholders, November 1853,* p. 53; also *Eighth Annual Report of the Directors of the Pennsylvania Railroad Company to the Stockholders, February 5, 1855* (Philadelphia, 1855), p. 13.
[28] Henry V. Poor, *History of the Railroads and Canals of the United States* (New York: J. H. Schultz, 1860), p. 471. This act was passed March 23, 1853.
[29] *Eleventh Annual Report of the Pennsylvania Railroad Company to the Stockholders, February 1, 1858,* p. 14; Poor, *History of the Railroads,* pp. 471, 474; *Sixth Annual Report of the Pennsylvania Railroad Company to the Stockholders, February 7, 1853,* pp. 21–26; *Seventh Annual Report of the Pennsylvania Railroad Company to the Stockholders, February 6, 1854,* pp. 6–7, 18–20.

ties.[30] By 1868, therefore, the Pennsylvania had allied itself with corporations whose tracks touched both the Atlantic and Lake Michigan. The Baltimore & Ohio followed the Pennsylvania's example, making alliances with or aiding connecting roads that ran into Parkersburg, West Virginia, and Columbus, Ohio.[31]

Although alliances with connecting roads proved more satisfactory than those with competing roads, such tactics still did not ensure stability. The Pennsylvania and the Baltimore & Ohio remained in the position of minority stockholders in their western connections; and, as events were to prove, financial strains on the western lines could easily snap alliances and raise the threat of working agreements with, or control by, hostile forces.

GOULD CHALLENGES THE ALLIANCE SYSTEM

Competition between the four eastern trunk lines had always existed, but the Civil War's traffic boom minimized problems; after 1867, however, the picture began to change. The Erie Railroad, a developmental line built through sparsely settled mountainous terrain from New York City to Dunkirk on Lake Erie, had suffered financial woes from its inception. Because of its weakness, it soon fell into the hands of Wall Street speculators. In 1867, after a spectacular stock-market war, Jay Gould emerged as the Erie's leader. Gould found himself with a railroad that had an unfavorable route, extremely high fixed costs, and a need for more capital.

Gould's first step in resuscitating his system was an attempt to control certain railroads operating between western New York and Chicago. Gould reasoned that he could not depend upon the western roads to deliver needed traffic voluntarily, and that only absolute control of connecting lines could assure a large volume of freight flowing from the Midwest to New York via the Erie. Thus, Gould leased the Atlantic and Great Western, which was in difficult financial straits because of the failure of its British backer in 1866. Next, he started buying stock in the Michigan Southern, and in the Toledo, Wabash and Western, and negotiating for control of the Indiana Central, and the Pittsburgh, Fort Wayne and Chicago. By these moves he hoped to extend his influence over lines that connected the Great Western with Chicago, and to reach out as far as possible toward St. Louis. The Indiana Central and the Fort Wayne were important freight sources for the Pennsylvania Railroad which quite naturally did not want them to pass into the grasp of the Erie.

Gould's second step was to reduce rates. Throughout most of his career he tried to attract traffic by lowering charges. He opposed limiting

[30] George H. Burgess and Miles C. Kennedy, *Centennial History of the Pennsylvania Railroad* (Philadelphia: Pennsylvania Railroad Co., 1949), pp. 236–37.
[31] Poor, *History of the Railroads*, pp. 580, 582; Edward Hungerford, *The Story of the Baltimore & Ohio Railroad, 1827–1927* (New York: G. P. Putnam's Sons, 1928), Vol. II, pp. 68, 110–11.

competition to service alone, and when he made rate agreements, he did so "only to break them." [32]

Jay Gould's attempts to seize the Indiana Central, the Pittsburgh, Fort Wayne and Chicago, and the Michigan Southern forced the Pennsylvania's J. Edgar Thomson, and the New York Central's Cornelius Vanderbilt to adopt defensive strategies. They had two clear alternatives: they could continue their attempts to protect themselves through interroad alliances, co-operation, and the negotiation of increasingly formal agreements, or they could expand their roads into large self-contained systems connecting the nation's great economic regions. Either direction involved managerial problems of a significantly different nature than those of the pre-Civil War decades.

The New York Central continued to rely on co-operation and alliances to ameliorate cutthroat competition. Cornelius Vanderbilt and his son William, who inherited his father's empire upon the Commodore's death in 1877, opposed the extension of the Central's tracks beyond New York State. Although Gould's attempt, in 1869, to control the Lake Shore and Michigan Southern, a key link for traffic flowing between Chicago and the Atlantic via the New York Central, caused the Commodore to buy a majority interest in the Lake Shore Railroad, Vanderbilt did not merge his new acquisition into the New York Central.[33] Instead, he placed the line under the separate administration of his son-in-law, Horace Clark, who also used Vanderbilt funds to purchase stock in such systems as the Cincinnati, Hamilton and Dayton, the Ohio and Mississippi, and the Michigan Central. With the exception of the Lake Shore, however, the Vanderbilts remained influential but minority shareholders in the other systems. But their stock speculations made sense strategically, for they were in corporations which provided potential allies on the routes to Cincinnati and St. Louis or in the companies which were in direct competition with the Central or the Lake Shore.

THE VANDERBILTS ENCOURAGE FEDERATION

The Vanderbilts had great faith in railroad federations which would eliminate competition by setting rates and allocating traffic. They looked backward toward the original attempt at co-operation between the trunk lines in the 1850's. The Civil War's traffic boom temporarily ended intense rivalry, which did not re-emerge until some time after 1865. Management reacted to renewed competition, both in the East and the West, by creating pools. One of the best known of these arrangements, the Iowa Pool, was formed by the Rock Island, and the Chicago and Northwestern, and the Burlington. By this unsigned, informal arrangement each company kept 45 per cent of its passenger receipts and 50 per cent of its freight revenues to cover operating expenses, and paid the balance into a

[32] Grodinsky, *op. cit.*, p. 596.
[33] *Ibid.*, p. 65.

pool which was divided equally among the three roads.[34] Such alliances generally failed, because they were difficult to modify or adjust when conditions changed, and because of the absence of enforcement devices.

Initial failures did not discourage further co-operative attempts. The panic of 1873 reduced business activity, decreased freight, and increased pressure to cut rates. That year the presidents of the New York Central, the Erie, and the Pennsylvania proposed that an association should be created to set rates, but the Baltimore & Ohio's President, John W. Garrett, who was building his own line into Chicago, blocked this by refusing to participate.[35] Competition worsened, and in 1875 Canada's Grand Trunk joined the four original eastern trunk lines as a contender for the midwestern traffic. It created a through east-west route by allying itself with the Michigan Central and the Vermont Central, and immediately cut grain rates.[36] In 1876 the situation was further complicated when the merchants of the various port cities, especially Baltimore, Philadelphia, New York, and Boston, each demanded that the railroads should set special low rates that would aid local merchants in competition for western business with those from rival ports.[37]

In 1877 the embattled railroads took steps to bring order out of chaos. In April they signed a seaboard differential agreement that gave Philadelphia and Baltimore lower prices on western traffic than it did New York and Boston. In July the roads formed the Eastern Trunk Line Association, and for its commissioner they selected Albert Fink, who had pioneered in a federation of southern lines that was started in 1875.

Fink moved quickly to set up regional committees of competing roads to meet at regularly specified times to determine local as well as interregional freight rates and classifications.[38] Simultaneously he created a large staff in New York which collected information on existing rates and traffic movements for the use of the committees in their deliberations. Fink then decided that the connecting western and New England lines must be included within his organization. In the summer of 1878, the midwestern roads formed a Western Executive Committee to set rates for and to allocate eastbound traffic. Then, in an agreement signed in December of 1878, the many roads designated a Joint Executive Committee, which would give the final approval of all rates worked out by the regional subcommittees or associations in the East and

---

[34] Julius Grodinsky, *The Iowa Pool: A Study in Railroad Competition, 1870–1884* (Chicago: University of Chicago Press, 1950), p. 17.
[35] *Twenty-Eighth Annual Report of the Pennsylvania Railroad Company to the Stockholders, March 9, 1875*, pp. 41–42; Joseph Nimmo, *Community of Interests, Method of Regulating Railroad Traffic in Its Historic Aspect* (Washington, 1901), p. 16.
[36] Edward Chase Kirkland, *Men, Cities, and Transportation* (Cambridge: Harvard University Press, 1948), Vol. I, pp. 498–500.
[37] *Ibid.*, Vol. I, pp. 508–09; D. T. Gilchrist, "Albert Fink and the Pooling System," *Business History Review*, 34 (Spring, 1960), 34; *Thirty-First Annual Report of the Pennsylvania Railroad Company to the Stockholders, March 24, 1878*, pp. 69–70.
[38] Gilchrist, "Albert Fink and the Pooling System," *op. cit.*, p. 35.

West.[39] Fink became chairman of this committee, and all cases not decided unanimously were referred to the chairman who made the final award. As a check upon Fink, a board of arbiters was created, which would be called in if a railroad refused to accept his decisions. The board of three included some of the most able and respected railroad experts of the day: Charles Francis Adams, Chairman of the Massachusetts Railroad Commission; David A. Wells, the economist; and J. A. Wright.

By the end of 1878, Fink headed a railroad federation which contained most systems north of the Ohio and east of the Mississippi. But even this organization failed. In Fink's words, "the only bond which . . . held the government together . . . was the intelligence and good faith of the parties composing it." [40] In the early 1880's, Jay Gould, who had left the Erie for greener speculative pastures beyond the Mississippi, again invaded the East and gained control over the Wabash, the Lackawanna, the Central of New Jersey, and the Boston, New York and Erie. Gould and the leaders of other weak lines soon made a shambles of Fink's organization.

By 1881 Gould's successes and Fink's failures finally caused William Vanderbilt to change his strategy. He decided that the Eastern Trunk Line Association could not adequately protect his interests. Although Vanderbilt continued to support the association, he shifted his primary energies to the course of action which the Pennsylvania had adopted to counter Gould's aggressive tactics back in 1867.

THE PENNSYLVANIA PREFERS CONSOLIDATION

The Pennsylvania's management had not opposed interrailroad co-operation, but it felt that Gould could best be checked by a grand plan of expansion that would allow the Pennsylvania on its own track to "reach all important points in the West." [41] Gould's try in 1869 to control the Indiana Central and the Pittsburgh, Fort Wayne and Chicago failed. The Pennsylvania used its superior financial power to lease the Fort Wayne and the Indiana Central. By 1873, the Pennsylvania had leased or purchased full control of a vast integrated network joining most major cities of the Midwest and the Atlantic seaboard, and the line which in 1869 had operated a main track between Philadelphia and Pittsburgh became a vast system connecting New York City with such distant points as Chicago, St. Louis, Cairo, Indianapolis, Cleveland, and Upper Michi-

[39] Ibid., pp. 36–37; Testimony of Albert Fink [before] United States Senate Committee on Labor and Education, New York, September 17, 1883, pp. 4–5.
[40] The Railroad Problem and Its Solution: Argument of Albert Fink before the Committee on Commerce of the U.S. House of Representatives, in Opposition to the Bill to Regulate Interstate Commerce, January 14, 15, and 16, 1880 (New York, 1882), p. 2.
[41] Report of the Investigating Committee of the Pennsylvania Railroad Company Appointed by Resolution of the Stockholders at the Annual Meeting Held March 10, 1874 (Philadelphia: Allen, Lane and Scotts Printing House, 1874), p. 45.

gan.[42] By such means the Pennsylvania hoped to control traffic from its point of origin to its destination, and to free itself from dependence upon other companies. For a while it went even further. In 1871 it organized the American Steamship Company to operate between Philadelphia and Liverpool.[43] This was to lessen the railroad's reliance upon the port of New York. Later, it moved into oil refining and coal mining to protect its position as a carrier of those commodities.

The Baltimore & Ohio quickly followed the Pennsylvania's lead, and by 1874 it controlled tracts reaching from Baltimore to Pittsburgh, Cincinnati, and Chicago.[44] Gould, as was said, scuttled the Erie in the early 1870's, and decided to try his hand at building a railroad empire west of the Mississippi. But Gould's temporary departure did not stop the drive toward giant self-contained systems. By 1880, the Erie had itself reached Chicago. Vanderbilt's decision, in 1881, to expand the Central merely created another great eastern system.

Meanwhile, Gould's western adventures forced railroads beyond the Mississippi to adopt tactics similar to those that had built the major eastern lines. By the late 1880's vast integrated systems linked most western cities. Among the larger railroads were the Chicago, Burlington & Quincy; the Chicago, Rock Island and Pacific; the Chicago and North-western; the Chicago, Milwaukee and St. Paul; and the Santa Fe. All, like the Pennsylvania, were consolidations of numerous smaller roads.

THE IMPACT OF COMPETITION ON ADMINISTRATION

Railroad competitive strategy profoundly shaped administration. In 1850 operating men with engineering backgrounds—the Erie's Daniel McCallum, the Baltimore & Ohio's Benjamin H. Latrobe, and the Pennsylvania's J. Edgar Thomson—created administrative patterns to run their newly built enterprises. Their structures primarily ensured safe operation and a constant flow of vital data to top management, and their ideas came to be widely accepted throughout the industry. The engineer-managers either ran their systems directly or worked closely with the promoters, usually on-line merchants and lawyers who had nominal managerial responsibilities as presidents and directors.

After 1865 the picture changed. Major entrepreneurial decisions no longer concerned promotion but involved the protection of large capital

[42] *Ibid.*, pp. 45–61; *Twenty-Third Annual Report of the Pennsylvania Railroad Company to the Stockholders, February 15, 1870*, pp. 15–20; *Twenty-Fourth Annual Report of the Pennsylvania Railroad Company to the Stockholders, February 21, 1871*, pp. 17–27; *Twenty-Fifth Annual Report of the Pennsylvania Railroad Company to the Stockholders, February 20, 1872*, pp. 14–20; and Burgess and Kennedy, *op. cit.*, pp. 195–240.
[43] *Twenty-Fifth Annual Report of the Pennsylvania Railroad Company to the Stockholders, February 20, 1872*, pp. 27–28.
[44] Henry V. Poor, *Manual of the Railroads of the United States for 1870–1871* (New York: H. V. and H. W. Poor, 1870), p. 169; Edward Hungerford, *op. cit.*, Vol. II, pp. 68, 106–08, 155, 220–27.

investments. Nor were top management's problems primarily operational, for the competitive wars which forced alliances and then the growth of self-contained systems caused energies to be concentrated upon the problems of rate making, interrailroad agreements, and consolidation. This necessitated large amounts of money. On the Pennsylvania alone capital increased from nearly $46,000,000 in 1865, to more than $400,000,000 in 1873.[45] And the vast interstate networks also demanded legal and administrative reorganizations to make possible effective control by a single management. Thus, after 1864, the engineer-manager and the part-time merchant-promoter gave way to strong financial leaders familiar with Wall Street money markets. Typical of the new men were the Baltimore & Ohio's John Garrett, the Michigan Central's James Joy, the Illinois Central's William Osborne, the Rock Island's John F. Tracy, the Chicago and Northwestern's Albert Keep, the New York Central's Cornelius and William Vanderbilt, and the Erie's Jay Gould, none of whom were engineers or operating men. Experienced railroad managers like J. Edgar Thomson of the Pennsylvania, Albert Fink of the Louisville & Nashville, and Charles Perkins of the Burlington were the exception.

THE PENNSYLVANIA PIONEERS IN NEW LEGAL
AND ADMINISTRATIVE FORMS

The holding company, a device which later provided such industrial giants as Standard Oil of New Jersey, United States Steel, and General Motors with a solid legal framework for controlling far-flung interstate industrial organizations, first emerged in full bloom as a result of railroad consolidation. J. Edgar Thomson and Thomas Scott took the lead, and in 1870 the Pennsylvania legislature at their urging created the Pennsylvania Company (as distinct from the Pennsylvania Railroad Company which was the original corporation), which came to hold the leases and stock of those railroads between Pittsburgh, St. Louis, and Chicago which the Pennsylvania Railroad Company came to control. By the end of the Pennsylvania's great period of expansion the legal ownership of the many companies that made up the system resided in the hands of three corporations. The Pennsylvania Railroad Company, the parent corporation, owned and directly administered all lines east of Pittsburgh and Erie. The parent corporation also held the stock of the Pennsylvania Company, which controlled and operated all lines running from Pittsburgh to the northwest and Chicago. And the Pennsylvania Company held the stock of a third major operating company, the Panhandle, which controlled and administered all lines from Pittsburgh southwest to St. Louis. The Pennsylvania's complex legal structure became the standard model for the other great railroad systems that emerged in its wake, and it permanently solved the knotty legal problem of how a corporation

[45] Henry V. Poor, *Manual of the Railroads of the United States, for 1868–1869* (New York: H. V. and H. W. Poor, 1868), p. 230.

chartered in one state could safely and effectively extend into other states.

But legal problems were not the only troubles faced by the Pennsylvania's management. The system had grown from a five-hundred-mile trunk in 1865 to a network of more than five thousand miles. Thomson recognized that a general administrative reorganization was necessary "to secure, by a single management . . . harmonious action throughout the entire system . . . and at the same time, to obtain the best results from the large amounts of rolling stock." [46] Thomson's new organization did not merely bring many formerly separate corporations under a single control retaining the old administrative structures; it built a new administrative form tailored to the Pennsylvania's operational needs.

Thomson created a "decentralized" managerial structure designed to facilitate control at all levels despite the corporation's enormous size. The Pennsylvania was divided into three major administrative units each of which contained an average of about seventeen hundred miles of track. These corresponded to the three great interlocking holding corporations, the Panhandle, the Pennsylvania Company, and the Pennsylvania Railroad Company, which themselves had been shaped with the idea of making them administrative as well as legal units. Each of these regional systems was placed under a "General Manager" who had full responsibility for the "*safe* and *economical* operation of the Roads committed to his charge." He directly controlled the transportation, traffic, and purchasing offices and was responsible "with the assent of the President" for the hiring, firing, and promotion of all executive and administrative personnel within his region.[47] Only the accounting and other financial and legal officers did not report directly to the general managers of the three regions. Those officials were responsible to the main office in Philadelphia.

Each of the great regional systems was further divided into administrative subdivisions. The eastern system, the Pennsylvania Railroad Company, had about five such subdivisions all of which corresponded roughly to what had been independent railroad managements before 1870; but significantly, boundaries were reshaped to meet the needs of traffic flow and administrative oversight. Each of these subdivisions, the longest of which was over five hundred miles long, or about the size of the original trunk lines before 1865, was broken into units of about a hundred miles in length.

The greatly enlarged Pennsylvania thus came to have four levels of executives. At the top were the general officers for the railroad as a whole, next the general managers who administered each of the regional

[46] *Twenty-Fifth Annual Report of the Pennsylvania Railroad Company to the Stockholders, February 20, 1872,* p. 16.
[47] *By-Laws and Organization for Conducting the Business of the Pennsylvania Railroad Company to Take Effect June 1, 1873* (Philadelphia, 1873), p. 13; *By-Laws and Organization for Conducting the Business of the Pennsylvania Railroad Company* (Philadelphia, 1881), pp. 10, 22.

systems, then came the general superintendents who handled the regional systems' larger subdivisions, and finally there were the divisional superintendents who managed the small hundred-mile-long divisions.

In effect, the Pennsylvania organization fashioned by its President, J. Edgar Thomson, was the old decentralized, divisional structure of the 1850's writ large. The general officers at the top level made the key entrepreneurial decisions—on over-all rate policies, on expansion, on meeting competition—but they relied on the data which flowed into the head office from the operating divisions. The giant Pennsylvania retained the line and staff feature of the old organization. The general officers set and enforced standards for the operating divisions, whose managers were delegated with the powers to hire, promote, and fire within their own units. The division superintendents, therefore, though their actions were in harmony with the railroad as a whole, had much of the autonomy and authority characteristic of the manager of a small railroad in the 1830's.

Although the Pennsylvania was the first interregional system to rationalize its legal and managerial structure, other railroads carried out comparable reorganizations in the 1880's after they too had expanded through purchase or construction. Among the most important of these were the Chicago, Burlington & Quincy, the Rock Island, the Baltimore & Ohio, and the Southern Pacific.[48]

While the holding company as a device for legal control of far-flung railroad empires became standard, not all companies emulated the Pennsylvania's managerial method. After all, J. Edgar Thomson was unique. He was an engineer and able operating man who also became a shrewd financier. But in the post-Civil War era financiers dominated, and as a rule they regarded administrative reform as a minor issue.

Among the managers Jay Gould probably represented an extreme. Although from time to time he controlled several groups of railroads that rivaled the Pennsylvania in size, he did nothing to reorganize them into rational administrative units. His control remained personal, and there is little doubt that lack of over-all planning, co-ordination, and appraisal

[48] The quickest method to determine whether a railroad had a decentralized structure was to check Henry V. Poor, "List of Officers of Operating Railroads in the United States and Canada, and of the Chief Railroads in Mexico," which first appeared in the 1891 edition of *Poor's Manual of the Railroads*. This gives a full list of executives on all lines and their titles. A road was considered to have a "decentralized" structure when it had at least two units each with their own general manager or superintendent who had a traffic officer directly under him, and if it had no traffic officer in the general office except for a vice president. An article in *The Railway Age, 10* (November 12, 1885), 710–11, describing and praising the Burlington structure, listed the Southern Pacific, the St. Paul, and the Union Pacific as examples of roads consolidating all lines into a single operating unit. But by 1891 the Southern Pacific had been subdivided into two autonomous units—the Pacific System (which included a large, quite autonomous Coast Division) and the Atlantic System; Henry V. Poor, *Manual of the Railroads of the United States for 1891* (New York: H. V. and H. W. Poor, 1891), pp. 916–44, 1365–69.

was a major reason why Gould's roads became a "synonym for bad management and poor equipment." [49]

Initially the Vanderbilts did little more than Gould to shape their vast holdings into a consistent framework. When Jay Gould forced Cornelius Vanderbilt into acquiring the Lake Shore and Michigan Southern Railroad in 1869, the Commodore paid no attention to its administration; he merely handed the new company over to his son-in-law, Horace Clark. Not until after Clark's death in 1873, and the consequent disclosure of the road's wretched financial condition, did the Commodore take a stronger hand. The result was a gradual movement toward the Pennsylvania's decentralized divisional structure. The Lake Shore and Michigan Southern and other railroads which the Central later acquired became major units similar to the Pennsylvania's "regional systems." When William Vanderbilt further clarified the outline of his holding, in 1883, each of the great constituent roads had professional presidents who corresponded to the Pennsylvania's general managers. At the main headquarters the executive and finance committee made many of the entrepreneurial decisions and co-ordinated policies between the constituent roads. Significantly, the accounting departments of the operating roads reported directly to the Central's head office.[50] Vanderbilt's structure never attained the highly rational form characteristic of Thomson's. The Central's component lines were not reformed with a view to developing the most efficient managerial units.

Nevertheless, Vanderbilt's methods of administration through financial control and the allocation of financial resources were particularly significant because they became a model for later empires in mining and heavy industry. J. Pierpont Morgan faithfully attended the New York Central's directors' meetings after 1879, and the financial and general office which directed the affairs of the United States Steel Corporation and other industrial combinations that Morgan helped to create bore a striking resemblance to the Central's head office. While the Pennsylvania's organization had significant similarities to Alfred Sloan's structure for General Motors in the 1920's, there was no historical relationship between these two "decentralized" structures. On the other hand, the New York Central can be said to be the administrative parent of the United States Steel Corporation and many others of the nation's first industrial giants.

Despite the decentralized divisional structure's many advantages, a quite different administrative system finally came to dominate most of America's great railroads. This was the centralized structure of which the

[49] Robert E. Riegel, *The Story of Western Railroads* (New York: The Macmillan Company, 1926), p. 161; Grodinsky, *Jay Gould*, pp. 384, 598–99.
[50] Thomas Cochran, *Railroad Leaders, 1845–1890* (Cambridge: Harvard University Press, 1953), pp. 394–95, 398, 478; *Railroad Gazette*, 17 (December 11, 1885), 785.

Illinois Central was an early example. Here, too, bankers and investors rather than trained railroad men or engineers were in charge.

THE ILLINOIS CENTRAL DEVELOPS A CENTRALIZED MANAGEMENT

The Illinois Central's history differed from many other railways: its growth was relatively unhurried, and its financing was sound. Its main line ran north and south, and it was less harassed by Gould's campaigns than the great east-west systems.[51] Even so, the company embarked on an expansion program to protect its business, and by 1888 it operated more than 2,500 miles of track. The Illinois Central's slow growth created no managerial crisis, and, as it expanded, the division superintendents, the superintendents of motive power and maintenance of way, and the traffic officers came to report directly to their department headquarters in Chicago. No one found the time or saw the need to define explicitly the duties of the different officers and the lines of communication between them.

In 1883, the road came under the control of well-established eastern investors, including the Astors, the Belmonts, and Edward H. Harriman. In 1887, a representative of this group, Stuyvesant Fish, became the road's President, and Harriman the Vice President. The two were appalled by the slipshod administrative methods and internal financial procedures, and in 1888 they set about to reform matters. For advice they relied heavily on the Illinois Central's old operating executives. The acting general manager and his subordinates in the transportation department favored moving from a centralized structure to a variation of the Pennsylvania's organization which would break the road into units of management.[52] The traffic manager, on the other hand, recommended that his department should cover the whole system and be completely independent of the transportation executives.[53] He wanted to report directly to the president and to have full authority over all traffic personnel and rate making.

The New York financiers accepted the traffic manager's recommendation, and instituted a highly centralized structure. The two key departments, traffic and transportation, remained completely separate and their managers reported directly to officials at the Chicago headquarters. The president and vice president personally co-ordinated the activities of the various departments.

The financiers preferred the centralized structure because it was less

[51] J. C. Clarke to Stuyvesant Fish, February 2, 1885, quoted in Cochran, *op. cit.*, p. 299. *Ibid.*, pp. 46–48, has a brief summary of the road's history in these years. More details can be found in Carleton J. Corliss, *Main Line of Mid-America* (New York: Creative Age Press, 1950), pp. 205–55.
[52] Minutes of the "Board" formed to write up the Illinois Central's new "classification" or organization manual, held June 21, 1889 (Illinois Central Railroad Archives, Newberry Library, Chicago).
[53] T. J. Hudson to J. C. Welling, October 5, 1889 (Illinois Central Railroad Archives, Chicago).

complex. By requiring fewer administrative personnel, it was less expensive than the system proposed by the acting general manager. Under centralization the traffic manager could quickly adjust rates and shift equipment to meet competition. But the centralized management blurred the distinction between routine operational matters and broad entrepreneurial decisions. In the long run top executives tended to get so involved in day-to-day problems that they had little time to devote to setting over-all policies and strategies. This defect, however, was not immediately apparent, and most of the railroad reorganizations supervised by J. P. Morgan in the 1890's followed the Illinois Central's example. These included the Erie, the Reading, Chesapeake and Ohio, and the Southern railroads.[54]

The events of the period from the Civil War to the beginning of the twentieth century profoundly shaped railway management. The competitive wars and the consequent formation of giant interregional railroad systems created mature managerial structures that varied only slightly from those used by present-day industrial giants. The administrative patterns erected drew heavily on the experience of the 1850's. In certain respects the structure that Thompson gave the Pennsylvania in the post-Civil War era was but a grander version of the one he fashioned for the same railroad in the 1850's. In the 1880's the New York Central formed a family of companies controlled through Vanderbilt's officers. Finally the Illinois Central carried the development of the centralized pattern to its logical conclusion.

SOME BROADER IMPLICATIONS OF THE NEW ADMINISTRATIVE FORMS

But structure alone was only part of the story. Equally as important were the changes that structure implied, many of which deeply affected American economic and social life. Within the ranks of management there developed a clear-cut separation between the top executives—the financiers who directed the competitive strategy and who made other strictly entrepreneurial decisions—and the supervisors who oversaw operating divisions, traffic departments, and the like. In both top and middle management professional experience and judgment became essential. There was little room for the part-time merchant promoter who, as late as the 1860's, played an important part in the management of many systems. This profoundly affected the railroad's stockholders and their representatives on the boards of directors, in short the owners who became increasingly dependent upon the advice of their hired managers. This led to the almost complete separation between "owners" and management which is so characteristic of the modern industrial corporation

[54] Edward G. Campbell says little about administrative reorganization in his *The Reorganization of the American Railroad System, 1893–1900* (New York: Columbia University Press, 1938), Chapter 5; but Poor's "List of Officers of Operating Railroads," in the 1898 edition of his *Manual of the Railroads,* clearly indicates the centralized structures of these systems.

where complex problems require the services of the professionally trained and experienced expert.

In a similar way the new railroad administrative structure sharpened the gulf between labor and management; in fact, the two classes became separated by barriers almost as formidable as those between the officer and the enlisted man in the military service. The expertise demanded of railroad financiers, rate makers, and other executives made it unlikely that a man without formal education who started out as a fireman or brakeman would rise to become a railroad president. The workmen themselves recognized this. Writing in 1889, Charles H. Salmons, a representative of the railroad brotherhoods, asserted that "the conditions of the trainman's life are hard. If he develops into a man of business or if he becomes a manager of great enterprises, it is in defiance of his surroundings." [55]

The painful, and at times hesitant, recognition that the traditional American Horatio Alger dream did not apply to railway labor led directly to the formation of the first really modern, national, skill or craft unions. The Brotherhood of Locomotive Engineers, oldest of the railway unions, began in 1863 when a group of Michigan Central enginemen organized to protect themselves from a "tyrannical" master mechanic.[56] By the 1870's several national brotherhoods had been formed, and were attempting to win better pay and working conditions for their men. In addition the unions provide their members with low-cost accident insurance, a necessary step because of the highly dangerous working conditions and the inadequate compensation for injured employees provided by the corporations.

Railroad administrators strongly opposed the unions. The Burlington's John N. A. Griswold saw the strike against his road in 1888 as "not a question of money, but as to who shall manage the road." [57] But despite opposition the brotherhoods grew, and by 1900 they were accepted by most railroad executives. By that time, too, Congress had passed the Erdman Act, which provided governmental machinery for mediation and, if necessary, compulsory arbitration in railroad-labor conflicts.[58] Thus, on the railroads, where modern management and modern labor unions first appeared, there also developed methods of bringing these two powerful groups together which were not used by the rest of American business for more than a generation.

[55] C. H. Salmons, *The Burlington Strike: Its Motives and Methods Including the Causes of the Strike, Remote and Direct, and the Relations to it of the Organizations of Locomotive Engineers, Locomotive Firemen Switchmen's M.A.A., etc.* (Aurora: Burnell and Ward, 1889), p. 14.

[56] Donald L. McMurry, *The Great Burlington Strike of 1888: A Case History in Labor Relations* (Cambridge: Harvard University Press, 1956), p. 29.

[57] Quoted in Cochran, *op. cit.*, p. 180.

[58] The Erdman Act, passed in 1890, provided for mediation by the Chairman of the Interstate Commerce Commission and the Commissioner of the Bureau of Labor. The Act was little used, however, until Theodore Roosevelt's second term. From 1906 through 1916 sixty-one railroad labor controversies were settled under the terms of the Act.

There can be little doubt that the impact of the railroads on American administrative practice has been great. The question inevitably arises as to whether future innovative ventures will bring similar changes or at least ones equally as dynamic. Is it possible, for example, to draw an analogy between two such diverse, but admittedly innovative efforts as railroads and space? We flatly reject the idea that historical analogies can be constructed which will predict future trends. We do believe, however, that some valid generalizations can be abstracted from the railroad experience which can be made the basis for hypotheses, and which may aid in the analysis of other innovative industries.

It appears, using the railroad experiences as a guide, that the following hypotheses can be asserted. First, that innovative industries create a need for new administrative patterns, but that these requirements do not become obvious during the first few years of the industry's existence. As a corollary, therefore, one may add that the original promoters use traditional methods to manage their new ventures. Certainly, early railroad entrepreneurs did not regard their businesses as unique. Any analysis of the space effort might start by examining the origins of its present administrative system. Was it designed to conform with current governmental and industrial standards, and do the administrators regard their enterprise as presenting unique managerial problems?

A second axiom might read that operational crises within a new industry emphasize the need for, and also shape, initial administrative reforms. It has long been a legend that the prevalence of United States Military Academy graduates in the ranks of early railroad builders and managers was especially significant. The evidence, however, clearly refutes the idea that army administrative procedures influenced railroad practice. On the Western Railroad in Massachusetts, in the 1840's, neither West Point graduate and Chief Engineer George Whistler nor George Bliss, the Springfield lawyer-president, made any attempt to reform a traditional administrative structure until the railroad suffered serious operational breakdowns. And the advanced patterns which emerged in the 1850's on the Erie, the Baltimore & Ohio, and the Pennsylvania were in direct response to the challenges presented by a railroad five hundred miles long. There can be little doubt that the Western Railroad's troubles, which received wide publicity in trade magazines such as the *American Railroad Journal,* provided the real basis for constructive thought about the management of long railroads. What kinds of operational crises, if any, will mar the space effort are still a matter of conjecture. It might be worthwhile, however, to examine failures of past space probes to determine if novel problems have occurred and, if so, whether these have exercised an effect on administrative practice.

A third hypothesis is that in the long run administrative patterns, although deeply influenced by operational and technological considerations, are also profoundly shaped by the outside environment. After

1865, forces within the American economy threw the railroads into cutthroat competition, which in turn emphasized the nonoperational problems of rate making, finance, and expansion through construction and purchase. Thus the operational managers were thrust aside and control gravitated to financiers, who were chiefly responsible for the administrative structures that evolved between 1865 and 1900. The financiers by and large neglected administration, but ultimately most railroads reorganized their management in accord with the centralized departmental concept of the Illinois Central or the decentralized divisional structure of the Pennsylvania. The experience of the late nineteenth century suggests two corollaries to the third axiom. The most obvious is that no single type of structure is inevitable. And second, that men trained in the daily operation of the unit tend to have superior administrative skills to those who have no such experience. The care and thought with which Thomson managed the Pennsylvania contrast sharply with the haphazard way in which the Illinois Central achieved its structure. The foregoing observations seem especially relevant to the space program since it is certain that outside pressure, from politics and fiscal limitations, for example, will constantly affect that program. In the years ahead space may draw its leadership from such varied fields as politics, the scientific community, and the military. Any analysis of the administrative development would do well to compare and contrast the quality of leadership arising from these various sources.

Finally, it seems evident that new administrative structures alter fundamental relationships between labor and management. The nineteenth-century railroad administrative practices created a sharp cleavage between the managerial elite and the ordinary workers. This resulted in the rise of the modern craft union and of collective bargaining. The space effort, though potentially a vast source of employment, will involve very little unskilled or semiskilled labor. This raises some interesting questions. Will a highly professional working force cause administrative reforms, and if so, what will be the role of the labor union?

The end of the nineteenth century saw the railroad network stabilize. The industry ceased to be innovative, and its management became routine. Many men who received their initial experience with the railroads went on to administer other large corporations. And bankers such as Morgan applied concepts that they learned in railroad reorganizations to other industrial ventures such as United States Steel. But the basic administrative problems which the railroads solved are still central to most large enterprises. Space, therefore, starts with advanced managerial concepts many of which have been tested and refined by large organizations since the 1850's. What alterations to present administrative practice the complex problem of space exploration will produce remain for future historians to study. It is our hope, however, that the preceding study of nineteenth-century railway managerial practices will provide helpful insights into the problem of analyzing trends in the administration of giant enterprises.

Alfred D. Chandler, Jr., and Stephen Salsbury   **257**

Section 2 ～ Business in the Industrializing Economy

Three ～ The Beginning of Mass Production

THE GENESIS OF AMERICAN ENGINEERING COMPETITION, 1850-1870 *D. L. Burn*

The view that England was industrially without a serious rival till quite late in the nineteenth century needs more qualification than it usually receives. There were directions in which the revolution of industrial method and organisation was by the middle of the century proceeding more rapidly in the United States than in England. Professional recognition of this by engineers was widespread though not universal from 1850; but it has been the subject of rediscovery by successive generations of journalists, and its early phase, between 1850 and 1870, has been neglected by English historians. In these years it was illustrated by the very frequent adoption of American methods in English industry, and to a much smaller degree by effective competition in neutral markets. The character of the American advance was brought into prominence at the Industrial Exhibitions which were fashionable from 1851, and by good fortune it was analysed in the 'fifties by several distinguished observers, notably by Joseph Whitworth.

Some of the most interesting of these early English records of Amer-

REPRINTED with permission from D. L. Burn, "The Genesis of American Engineering Competition, 1850–1870," *The Economic History Review*, Vol. II (1930–33), pp. 292–311.

ican progress come from the visits of two small Commissions to the industrial areas of the United States. Unexpected American advances were recognised at the Exhibition of 1851, and when it was decided to hold a similar exhibition at New York in 1853–4 the English Government sent distinguished commissioners to report. When they arrived they discovered that the Exhibition was not assembled at the advertised opening date, and they determined to substitute tours in the American industrial districts in place of the inspection of the new Crystal Palace. The commissioners drew up reports on their tours, and two of them, those of Joseph Whitworth and George Wallis, give a valuable sketch of New England manufactures.

A similar tour was instituted shortly afterwards by the Ordnance Department, with a view to discovering how far American methods might be adopted to increase the output of small arms. The moving spirit in this was John Anderson, Inspector of Machines in the department, who was influenced by the methods employed by Colt, the American pistol manufacturer, and by Whitworth. Anderson had recently toured England to investigate productive methods, and he was a member of the Commission sent to the States. He and his colleagues "deemed it advisable to allow as little as possible connected with the private manufactures of the country escape them, and visited many works which at first sight may seem totally irrelevant to the branches of manufacture to which their attention was more particularly directed." They subsequently presented a report which covered much the same ground as those of Whitworth and Wallis.

The three reports were drawn up by men obviously well qualified to judge the novelty and efficiency of the methods they discussed, though likely in the circumstances to describe the best practice rather than the average. In all cases the writers emphasise "the eager resort to machinery wherever it can be applied," and the extent to which industries were organised for mass production in large factories, where in England outwork and handicraft persisted. Though they often criticised the quality of machine tools where there were English parallels, they had nothing but praise for the adoption in most branches of industry of the "manufacturing principle," the production in large numbers of standardised articles on a basis of repetition in factories characterised by ample workshop room and "admirable system," designed to assist the progress of materials through the various stages of production. The principle lent itself to the use of mechanical methods, particularly to the development of automatic "special purpose" machines designed for a single operation, and dispensing largely with skilled labour. In devising machinery of this type "the Amerians showed an amount of ingenuity, combined with undaunted energy, which we would do well to imitate if we meant to hold our present position in the great markets of the world."

The commissioners gave a wealth of illustration of the tendencies they noticed. All were impressed by the woodworking industries. Whitworth discovered "many works in several towns occupied exclusively in making doors, window-frames, or staircases by means of self-acting machinery such as planing, tenoning, mortising and jointing machines," whereby builders were supplied with goods cheaper than they could produce in their own shops. Such factories were not necessarily large—one with a daily output of 100 doors employed 20 men. The same method was applied to the manufacture of furniture, everything "from sawing to sandpapering" being often performed by machinery. So too with agricultural implements—ploughs and mowing-machines. Whitworth drew attention to a factory "where all the ploughs of a given size are made to the same model, and their parts . . . are made all alike." In the manufacture of the bigger metal products less specialisation was found than in England; but frequently the American method of making smaller metal goods was the more advanced. Wood screws of a better pattern than those made in England were produced by automatic machines several of which could be supervised by one person. Files were machine-made, with one supervisor to two machines; the reduction in price more than compensated for some loss of quality, and the product was satisfactory in the view of the English commissioners; though the best files were still imported from England. Cut nails were machine-made in England at this time, but the commissioners were all impressed by the discovery in several towns of "immense nail manufactories"—one described by Whitworth employed 250 workpeople—and the scope of the machine work was in some respects novel.

In the manufacture of locks, clocks and small-arms machine methods were applied in more exacting conditions, where the accurate fitting of components was essential. One factory at Newhaven [New Haven]—not an isolated example—with 200 employees was devoted entirely to the manufacture of locks and padlocks; "special machines were applied to every part, and the parts of locks of similar description can be interchanged." The output was 2,000 per day, some of good quality being sold at 2½ d. each. Whitworth wrote that padlocks produced here were "of a superior quality to those of the same class ordinarily imported from England, and not more expensive." Jerome's clock factory in the same town, representing one of the great American industrial achievements, was also described. With a staff of 250, many being boys and girls, it had a daily output of 600 clocks, and an established reputation in English and continental export markets; and it could produce a clock for a dollar. The commissioners, however, gave most detailed attention to the manufacture of small-arms. It was found that in the production of muskets at the Springfield armoury "the parts were so exactly alike that any single part will in its place fit any musket," even if the parts were made in different years. In achieving this result there was extraordinarily little hand-work. The sixteen operations needed for the production of the wooden stock involved two and a half minutes' hand-work and twenty-nine minutes' machine-work. The metal-work was performed mainly by "circular milling tools" devoted to a single operation, and among the machines were some in which a succession of tools were brought to bear on the work one after the other (with the "most rigid accuracy"), and "edging machines," to "trace irregular figures and impart an exact outline," the form being taken from a model. Such developments of the milling machine were quite foreign to English engineering. Springfield was also distinguished for the saving of labour in moving material about the factory, lifts and carriages being employed.

The commissioners were not as pleased with the American mode of making machines as with their resourcefulness in using them. Whitworth found that the "engine tools" were "similar to those in use in England some years ago, being much lighter in construction than those now in use, and turning out less work in consequence"; though significantly enough he discovered a greater proportion of lathes with slide rests. Similarly, the Ordnance officials discovered that in the States the types of machines "usually employed by engineers and machine-makers"—lathes, and planing, shaping and drilling machines—"were generally behind those of England"; while the machinery valuable for its novelty of design was "roughly constructed (partly of wood) and would not bear comparison in stability and appearance with the highly polished iron machinery of England." Possibly an element of bias entered into these judgments, and the full significance of the contrast was not analysed.

In the years with which this article is concerned there was no other occasion which called forth such elaborate surveys of American engineering developments as those of the early 'fifties. But there were many incidental judgments, among them one of great interest passed by another of England's most celebrated machine-makers—James Nasmyth—on a factory established in England by Colt employing American automatic machinery for the manufacture of pistols. Colt's factory, established in 1851, did much to form English opinion on the desirability of introducing machine methods for small-arms manufacture. "It was impossible," Anderson told a Parliamentary Committee before his American visit, "to go through that works without coming out a better engineer." Nasmyth's praise was equally enthusiastic. He confessed himself humiliated by the experience. "The acquaintance with correct principles has been carried out in a fearless and masterly manner, and they have been pushed to their full extent; and the result is the attainment of perfection and economy such as I have never seen before." Many English mechanics knew the correct principles, "but there is a certain degree of timidity resulting from traditional notions, and attachment to old systems, even among the most talented persons, that they keep considerably behind." Nothing was more impressive than the extent to which unskilled labour could be employed. "In many cases young men mind four machines. One had been a butcher, another a tailor, another a gentleman's servant. . . . You do not depend on dexterity—all you want is intellect."

At successive international exhibitions held in Paris and London—in 1856, 1862 and 1867—the American exhibits, generally very scanty, received the applause of experts, though not, in general, of the public. Recognition was not confined to English engineers. It is possible to trace in these records some improvement in the standard of workshop machinery, and in the general level of workmanship (though in some branches this had always been high). But there was no change in the main characteristics of American productions, or in the contrasts with English work drawn by the commissioners in the reports which have been analysed.

Meantime machines developed in the United States had been frequently introduced into English industries. Sometimes the machines themselves were imported; more often they were manufactured here to American designs. "It is the custom among machine-makers in England," John Platt told a Parliamentary committee in 1867, "to purchase inventions from the Americans and adapt them to use in this country." The custom did not depend much, it appears, on English engineers visiting New England—which happened very rarely—but on the initiative of the patentees.

Two instances of American influence are so well known that it is unnecessary to dwell upon them here. The United States provided the chief influence leading to the practical success of the sewing-machine from the early 'fifties. Large numbers of machines were imported from the States, and a considerable manufacture had been established here by 1860, depending largely on the purchase of American patents. Throughout the years under discussion the main developments in these machines—such as the extension into shoemaking, and the production of devices for buttonholing—were of transatlantic origin with few exceptions. The story of the reaper is similar. Two American machines—those of Hussey and M'Cormick exhibited in 1851—provided the stimulus for the manufacture in England; though by the side of these as models there was the Scots machine of Bell. By 1862 the machines had been "improved and adapted to the circumstances of English crops, . . . and there is now no large arable district in the country where the reaping machine is not employed." It was often an imported machine.

These instances were not isolated, and the scope and importance of American influence can be shown most clearly by tracing some less well-known and individually less important instances. Among these it is perhaps natural to select first the manufacture of small-arms, which was revolutionised as a result of the visits of inspection which have been described. Anderson had introduced into Woolwich before the tours one important American invention—the Blanshard [Blanchard] copying lathe for producing irregular shapes to a pattern (such as boot lasts or "Jacobean" chair legs). The departmental commissioners were given powers to purchase machinery for small-arms manufacture and for the carriage department, and they exercised their powers with that catholicity which marked the selection of factories to visit on their tour. They appear to have purchased a complete set of the machines for the wood and metal work of musket manufacture, including the jigs and gauges, whose "continual and careful application" was fundamental in securing uniformity and interchangeability; and in addition tin-plate-working machinery, small bench tools—among them being the breast drill with bevel-geared drive—and miscellaneous woodworking machines—for planing, tenoning, mortising, sash-making and door-making. The United States also supplied the machines—or the models for the machines—in the Birmingham Small-Arms factory which was set up after the model of the Government factory at Enfield.

American influence on the use and manufacture of woodworking machinery goes back, however, before 1845 to the Great Exhibition. At this time, although some very ingenious woodworking machines had been devised in England, their scope was far smaller than that of American machines, and they were not adapted to small workshops. In 1851 a Liverpool firm imported machines from the States and exhibited them; and after some preliminary ridicule on account of the lightness of their construction and the use of wood in their framework, they were acclaimed for their success in operation. Importation continued, and within a few years several English firms had set out on the manufacture of similar machinery. They "improved" on their models, and their products were more in keeping with English canons of construction, "far above the more flimsy American products" in Anderson's eyes. But their prices were stated to be twice as high as the Americans'; and some responsible critics disliked the "needless weight, unnecessary finish and complicated movements" in their work. The States continued to be the home of novel types of machines; "we are accustomed, it was stated in *Engineering*, to look to America whenever a fresh desideratum in woodworking machinery makes itself felt in general practice"; and while perhaps this is exaggerated it is not wholly misleading. In 1867 the biggest circular saw exhibited by a British firm at Paris was of American design, and instances of the adoption of American patents by prominent English makers can easily be traced. The machines seem to have penetrated into all the main branches of woodworking industry, though it is probable that the majority of small workshops had not felt their influence by 1870.

The English hardware industry does not appear to have made much progress in the period discussed here; but where changes occurred the debt to America was big. There were three prominent instances of this. The improved methods of wood screw manufacture—producing for the first time a gimlet-ended screw—were introduced successfully by Nettlefold and Chamberlain in 1854, and were developed with such success that in the late 'fifties a very large export of screws to the States was created, to be destroyed by the raising of duties from 25 to 75 per cent. In some directions the machines were improved. By 1870 the factory was one of the biggest in the neighbourhood of Birmingham, having about 1,000 employees. A near competitor in size was the factory of the Patent Nut and Bolt Company, set up by an American inventor to develop the mass production (and therefore cheap production) of nuts and bolts of various types, which firms were accustomed to make to meet their own needs. The business had a quick success, an English firm had been established for the same object by 1862, also using American machinery. The third direction in which American influence was felt was in the manufacture of locks. The employment of automatic machines (some bringing several tools successively into operation) in lock-making was introduced into England from the States by W. Hobbs in 1851. His London factory product had lowered the price of cheap lever locks by the early 'sixties, but not enough to induce the general adoption of his methods; and in 1870 factory reports treat his works as the only one employing machinery "like that used at Enfield." The reason for this must be found partly in the expense of tools where a single article was needed in a great variety of sorts and sizes, partly in the extreme cheapness of handicraft work in the industry. It is curious that clockmaking, the third industry in America singled out by the commissioners as producing metal mechanisms with interchangeable parts, was in England unaffected by the new methods; and this applied also to watchmaking, though severe American competition in this industry had been established by 1865. . . .

Those who observed American advance in machine-making and machine-using turned naturally to try and explain its origins; and their not very systematic analysis is composed mainly of familiar features, though the conditions governing the supply of raw materials were in many respects, of course, sharply contrasted with the present position.

All explanations lay considerable emphasis on the peculiarities of the market, particularly on its size. The size of the population, growing by emigration as well as by natural increase, was such that "whether the supply of goods is derived from the home or the foreign manufacturer the demand cannot fail to be greater than the supply." The opportunity afforded by this was increased by the higher average wealth of the people. Wallis noticed how greatly the demand for ready-made clothing was added to by the fact that "all classes of the people may be said to be well dressed and the cast-off clothes of one class are never worn by another." In some respects this market was also extremely receptive; no doubt due in part to inadequate supply. Of the hardware trade it was said that "the willingness on the part of the American public to buy what is offered them, if it can in any way answer the purpose, has given a great advantage to the North American manufacturer over his European competitor, who has to contend with habits and prejudices of centuries standing, and even now almost in full vigour. . . . In the United States they overlook defects more than in Europe, and are satisfied if a machine intended to supersede domestic labour will work even imperfectly, while we insist on its being thoroughly well made and efficient." In England the public had "fixed notions of shapes, sizes and prices," and demand increased slowly enough to be supplied "in the old way, by manufacturers using skilled labour." The market of conventional consumers would not facilitate a transition to new methods, in the early years when the new methods did not greatly lower prices.

The English observers also stressed the relation between the characteristics of American industry and the peculiar difficulties which had to be overcome in order to establish it successfully. There was, in the first place, the relative dearness of some of the primary raw materials. . . .

The high price of iron was held partly responsible for the lightness of structure in machines, which was often adversely criticised in England, but which has had a lasting influence on design. (Probably it was not merely a coincidence that Whitworth within three years of his tour was advocating greater lightness in the moving parts of mechanisms.) The expense of raw materials was due partly to the high price of labour, and thus reflected the second difficulty attending American industrial advance. Among skilled artisans expense was due to scarcity; among the unskilled to the opportunity of settlement on the land. The position was regarded not merely as a constant inducement to the adoption of labour-saving devices, but as a stimulus to the inventive faculty. Wallis also laid emphasis on the influence in certain trades—probably mainly small metal industries—of difficulties which faced the immigrant skilled artisan in carrying on his industry, owing to the absence of the customary environment which had grown up in Europe. There he had been accustomed to the existence of persons carrying out complementary work; obtaining the raw material and performing the early stages of manufacture. In the new environment it was necessary to organise all stages of manufacture, hence a tendency to the integration of processes, and the adoption of a systematic factory structure. Wallis also regarded this factor as an important impulse to the adoption of machine methods.

While difficulties such as these placed the American manufacturer in the beginning at a disadvantage, there was one matter in which the Commissions of the early 'fifties found he was placed in a more fortunate position for developing factory industry than the English producer. They discovered that most of the factories were owned by corporations in which "the liabilities of partners not actively engaged in the management are limited to the proportion of the capital subscribed by each." Many such companies had been formed by incorporation even before 1800, and laws facilitating their formation had been introduced in several states in the early years of industrial growth during the first quarter of the nineteenth century. The expenses of forming such corporations were negligible, and it was obvious that the limit of risk encouraged enterprise and attracted capital from sources, many of them small, which would otherwise have remained untouched, perhaps undeveloped through the lack of sufficient facilities for investment. Though Wallis was careful to state that he saw grave dangers of inefficient management in these companies, he agreed that the laws encouraging their formation had "led to a much greater development of the industrial resources and skill of the country than, in its circumstances, could have resulted from mere private enterprise for many years to come." His evidence did not in the least illustrate the dangers of which he spoke, and the general effect of the reports must have been to add considerably to the force of the movement for a change in the English company law.

Factors of the kind discussed might affect the direction taken by American developments, but the dynamic factor, it was recognised, was to be found in the character of the people—their energy, enterprise and ingenuity. These qualities were widespread among all grades engaged in industry; and their presence among the artisans was frequently emphasized. According to Wallis, "traditional methods had little hold upon the American as compared with the English artisan, and processes holding out the least promise of improvement were quickly tested." The Ordnance Commissioners found that masters and men were convinced that labour-saving devices were for their mutual benefit, and that "every workman seems to be continually devising some new thing to assist him in his work." They were all anxious to be "posted up" in every new development. Whitworth gave the same testimony.

In some measure these facts could be explained by the partial recruitment of industrial labour by immigration. Immigrants from England, Germany and France brought the varied traditions of the leading industrial nations together; and it was possible to adopt the best elements of what had been conflicting practices. The reports of the early 'fifties illustrated one aspect of this clearly by ascribing the superiority of American castings over English to German influence. It is not improbable that immigration brought into the country persons who were enterprising beyond the average; and it was frequently remarked that once the tide of industrial advance had set in in the States, America became the Mecca of the European inventor.

A partial explanation of the energy and enterprise exhibited in American industry was also sought, in another direction, in two conditions of American industrial life which were sharply contrasted with English conditions—the absence of a fear of unemployment and the mobility between industrial employments. Whitworth explained the absence of trade unions and their restrictions on the introduction of new methods (which many English business men noticed enviously) as largely due to the relative scarcity of labour. "With a superabundant supply of hands in this country (*i.e.* in England), and therefore a proportionate difficulty in obtaining remunerative employment, the working classes have less sympathy with the progress of invention." In some respects the mobility between employments, the frequency with which men moved not only from one branch of an industry to another, but from one industry or occupation to another, might be regarded mainly as a result of the peculiar American conditions; of the growing market and opportunities, and the enterprise shown in taking openings. But it was also a cause of enterprise and improvement; partly because it averted boredom, partly, one may assume, because it helped in the circulation of ideas, since methods would spread rapidly in related trades where there were similar technical problems; and partly because the fact of extensive and as it seemed successful change provoked a straining after change, set up a fashion or ideal. "The American was a believer to an unlimited extent in progress," as Fraser said in his valuable survey of American education in 1867. "Universal movement, acting on natures peculiarly susceptible of its influence," explained to a large extent, in his view, the intelligence and versatility of the people; and while obviously this influence could not explain the beginnings of American advance, it was most likely important for its persistence.

Fraser was inclined to minimise the influence of the "only partially excellent schools," which he had surveyed elaborately. He seems to suggest that the schools were much more a reflection of characteristics than a cause. In this he was minimising an influence which several of the writers whose views have been discussed in this article rated very highly. Wallis looked upon the "sound practical education" which was common in America as fundamental in its industrial growth. The remarkable application of machinery displayed "the adaptive versatility of an educated people." Particularly in the New England states, where the industrial movement had its centre, "the skilled workmen . . . are educated alike in the simplest elements of knowledge as in the most skilful application of their ingenuity to the useful arts and the manufacturing industry of their country"; and with their "perceptive power so keenly awakened by early intellectual training" they quickly learned from other nations, and improved upon them. Whitworth similarly stressed the importance of education, and made it the subject of his peroration. He noted that it never happened in the States, as it did in England, that a man with the necessary technical skill was unable to take up a position as foreman through a lack of the primary elements of education; and he associated with education in importance the very extensive Press. "Where the humblest labourer can indulge in the luxury of a daily paper, everyone reads, and thought and intelligence penetrate through the lowest grades of society." The benefits of liberal education and a cheap Press in the United States "could hardly be over-estimated." "Wherever education and an unrestricted Press are allowed full scope to exercise their united influence," he wrote in his concluding paragraph, "progress and improvement are the certain result; and among the many benefits which arise from the point co-operation may be ranked most prominently the value they teach men to place upon intelligent contrivance; the readiness with which they cause new contrivances to be received, and the impulse which they give to that inventive spirit which is gradually emancipating man from the rude forms of labour, and making what were regarded as the luxuries of one age to be looked upon in the next as the ordinary and necessary condition of human labour." At the end of the period considered here the same view of the importance of education in the States was repeated by Field in the evidence which has already been partially quoted. "The cause of the whole difference between us is to be found in the education on the two sides of the water," he declared; and he stated the view at some length. Among other advantages he noticed that "trade unions and strikes cannot exist in that educated atmosphere."

It is probable that Whitworth and Wallis were influenced in their treatment of American education by the potential effect of their reports in matters of industrial politics. Among factors whose relative importance was difficult to weigh it would be natural to select for most emphasis those in which England's disadvantage seemed most readily removable.

The commissioners of the 1851 Exhibition had already recently drawn attention to the part played by education in the emergence of continental competition. Those countries who lacked cheap fuel or raw materials tended "to depend more on the intellectual elements of production than in this country." The Reports of 1854 gave valuable support to the people who were emphasising the industrial importance of education, though it needed the influence of three more international exhibitions to evoke a movement of real political significance.

Four ⌐ The Rise of Big Business

THE COMING OF BIG BUSINESS
Alfred D. Chandler, Jr.

Big business has become an integral part of the economies of all major industrial urban nations where means of production and distribution are in private hands. There are great private business enterprises in all but the smallest of the non-Communist countries of Western Europe, in Japan, and even in India. In the United States, however, there are more giant business enterprises than in any other national economy, and some of these are larger than the biggest businesses of other nations. In the United States, too, these great enterprises play a more significant role in the nation's economy than do similar private firms in other economies.

A few statistics reflect the dominating position which the giant business enterprises have achieved in the American economy. In 1960, 600 American corporations had annual earnings of over $10.0 million. These 600 constitute one-half of 1 percent of the total corporations in the country; yet they accounted for 53 percent of the total corporate income. The 100 largest industrials were responsible for 54 percent of all profits made in the manufacturing sector. Statistics of employment tell the same story. In 1956 approximately 220 firms had a working force of more than 10,000 workers. In the aircraft industry 10 such firms employed 94 percent of the industry's total working force. In petroleum 15 such firms employed 86 percent; in steel 13 hired 85 percent; in motor vehicles 8

REPRINTED with permission from Alfred D. Chandler, Jr., "The Coming of Big Business," in C. Vann Woodward, ed., *The Comparative Approach to American History*, New York: Basic Books, 1968, pp. 220–35.

employed 77 percent; in office machinery 4 used 71 percent; in farm machinery 3 put to work 64 percent.

Other sets of figures illustrate the same point, so let me just cite one more statistic to emphasize the scope and size of big business in the United States. In October, 1965, the New York *Times* listed the world's largest units according to gross revenue in the following order: the United States, Russia, the United Kingdom, France, then the General Motors Corporation, followed by West Germany, Japan, and Canada. General Motors' revenues of just under $20.0 billion were more than the combined revenues of Japan and Canada and were very close to the United Kingdom's $21.0 billion and France's $20.5 billion.

In the United States the big business enterprises differ from those of other nations not only in their size but also in the ways in which they are owned and managed. All the great firms are joint stock corporations. None is managed by a single man, not even by a single family. All employ senior officials who have no family relationship with the founder or his descendents and who have reached high executive position by working their way up the managerial ladder. In the United States the stock of nearly all of the large corporations is held by tens of thousands of individuals. Only rarely does a family still retain a controlling share in one of these large enterprises. As analysts of big business have repeatedly pointed out, the modern corporation in America is operated largely by professional managers who own only a tiny portion of its stock.

These professional executives have a major say in the management of the American economy. They are constantly making two sets of decisions. They determine what and how much their companies will produce and sell, and in what specific quantity, quality, and at what price. Secondly, they decide how the corporation's resources—capital, trained personnel, and machinery and equipment—will be allocated and used. In making the first set of these decisions, the managers of the giant corporations affect the pace at which the goods flow through the economy. In the second, they play a large part in determining the direction of the nation's economic growth.

In the private sectors of other economies such basic decisions are still less centralized and in their making considerations of family and kinship still play a significant role. In France, for example, family-owned companies still employ more than 70 percent of all the workers involved in manufacturing and commerce. France's distribution system is particularly specialized and localized. As Professor David Landes has pointed out: "This is a country of the family firm, the *boutique,* the artisan's shops, and the small factory." Significantly, the large enterprises in France are concentrated in the new, more technologically advanced industries such as chemical, electronics, automobile, and aeronautics. The smaller family firm predominates even more in Italy, Spain, and the Latin American countries. In Great Britain, Germany, and Scandinavia the professionally manned big business plays a larger part in the production and distribution of goods than it does in France. Nevertheless, the structure of the industries in these countries and the management of their enterprises are still in many ways more similar to France than to the United States.

In Asia the larger kinship group, rather than the individual family, continues to dominate the economy. In Japan the great business clans, the Zaibatsu, were the nation's "consciously-chosen instruments" in the revolutionary transformation of the economy in the latter part of the nineteenth century. Despite rapid industrial and technological changes, despite war and defeat, and despite American attempts to break up these groups, the great clans still dominate the economy. In India, too, private enterprises stimulating industrial change have a similar strong clan orientation. The Dalmia-Jain and the Tata groups have almost as large and diversified holdings as those of the Mitsui and the Mitsubishi in Japan.

The story of the coming of big business in the United States should, then, indicate why and how the American corporations grew to such size, why and how they came to be operated by professional managers, and why and how these managers came to make the critical economic decisions. The giant enterprises which the professional managers came to command appeared suddenly and dramatically in many of America's most important industries during the last two decades of the nineteenth century. They came as the United States was reaching the climax of its drive to industrialism which made it the world's leading manufacturing nation before 1890 and producer of one-third of the world's industrial goods by 1913.

Before the rise of the new industrial giants, that is, before the 1880's, decisions affecting the flow of goods through the economy and the allocation of its resources were even more decentralized than they were in Europe. They were made by hundreds of thousands of small personal or family firms. These firms normally handled one product or one business function. The business decisions of their owners were affected by an impersonal market over which they had relatively little control, except possibly in nearby local areas. Price tended to determine the volume of output. Price also set the pace of the flow of goods from the producer of raw materials to the factory and then to the ultimate consumer via an intricate network of wholesalers. The great shift from decentralized decision-making to centralized coordination and control of production and distribution culminated in the years between 1897 and 1902, when the first and most significant merger movement in American history took place.

An understanding of this process of centralization calls for a look back to the 1850's and to the beginning of the modern corporation in American railroads. The railroads, as the nation's first big business, came to provide the only available model for the financing and administration of the giant industrial enterprises. They became so because their promoters, financiers, and managers were among the first businessmen to build, finance, and operate private business enterprises requiring massive capital investment and calling for complex administrative arrangements.

American businessmen pioneered in the new ways more than did those of other nations, because American railroads were private rather than public enterprises and also because of the size of the system and of the individual roads themselves. By 1875 one American railroad corporation alone, the Pennsylvania, was operating a trackage equivalent to one-half the railroad mileage then in operation in France and over one-third of that in Great Britain. The only other privately built and operated railroad system, that of Great Britain, had only a little over 20,000 miles of track. By 1900 the American railroad managers were operating over 259,000 miles of track.

The financing of the American railroads required such large amounts of money that it brought into being modern Wall Street and its specialized investment bankers. The financial instruments and methods later used to capitalize large industrial enterprises were all employed earlier by the railroads. Financial requirements also forced the use of the corporate form. An individual, partnership, or family firm simply could not supply enough capital to build even a small railroad. The sale of corporate stocks and bonds was essential. The modern holding company, too, had its start in the railroads, for the management of interstate business encouraged one railroad corporation to control others in other states by purchasing and holding their stock.

The railroads were forced to pioneer in modern business administration as well as in modern corporate finance. Their managers fashioned large functional departments to handle transportation, traffic, and finance. They set up central offices to supervise and coordinate the work of the departments and the railroads as a whole. They originated line and staff distinctions in business organization. They were the first to develop a flow of operating statistics used to control movement of traffic and also to evaluate the performance of operating departments. They, too, had to meet brand new problems of modern cost accounting to make the distinctions between variable, constant, and joint costs, to differentiate between working and fixed capital, and to account for depreciation and even obsolescence.

The railroad thus provided the model for big business in industry. But the parent of the large industrial corporation was, of course, the factory. The modern factory with its power-driven machinery and its permanent working force, whose tasks were subdivided and specialized, appeared in the United States as early as 1814. Yet until the swift spread of an all-weather transportation network, including the railroad, the ocean-going steamship, and the telegraph, relatively few factories existed in the United States outside of the textile and closely related industries. Then in the late 1840's and 1850's factory production began for the first time to be significant in the making of sewing machines, clocks, watches, ploughs, reapers, shoes, suits and other ready made clothing, and guns and pistols for commercial use. The same years saw the spread of the large integrated ironworks, using coal and coke instead of charcoal for fuel. The Civil War further stimulated growth in these industries. After the war the factory spread to still others. By 1880 the Census of that year reported that of the three million people employed in industries using machines, four-fifths worked under the factory system of production. "Remarkable instances of the application of this system," the Census added, "are to be found in the manufacture of boots and shoes, of watches, musical instruments, clothing, agricultural implements, metallic goods generally, firearms, carriages and wagons, wooden goods, rubber goods, and even in the slaughtering of hogs."

In the quarter of a century following the completion of this Census, the family owned factory was transformed in many industries into a vertically integrated, multifunctional enterprise. Let me explain what I mean by these terms. In 1880 nearly all manufacturing firms only manufactured. The factory owners purchased their raw materials and sold their finished goods through wholesalers, sometimes as commission agents and at other times as jobbers who took title to the goods. By the first years of the twentieth century, however, many American industries were dominated by enterprises that had created their own distributing organizations, sometimes including even retailing outlets, and had formed their own purchasing systems. Often they had begun to control their supplies of semifinished and raw materials. The large industrial firm thus became a primary agent for large-scale distribution as well as large-scale production and, indeed, became a critical link connecting the two.

Many reasons have been suggested for this fundamental change. These include the impact of new technology, the influence of shifting overseas demand for American goods, the development of a market for industrial securities, the desire for tighter market control, the tariff, and the personal motives of bad men, the Robber Barons. I would like to propose two specific and, I believe, more significant reasons for the growth of the large industrial enterprise. One was the inability of factory owners to enforce and so maintain cartels. If the American cartels had had some kind of legal support or sanction by the government as was true of those in continental Europe, the giant corporation would surely have been slower in coming. The other reason was the inadequacy of the wholesaler network to handle the high-volume distribution of goods required by a domestic or internal market far larger than that of any industrial nation in the world.

The manufacturers who pioneered in the building of the integrated firm were those who first found the wholesaler network inadequate for their needs. They were of two types. There were the volume producers of durable goods, who discovered that the wholesaler was unable to handle the making of the initial demonstration to customers, unable to provide the necessary consumer credit, and unable to ensure continuing repair and service of goods sold. Second, there were the producers of perishable goods for the mass market, who found existing wholesalers totally inadequate for storing and distributing their products.

Among the first type were the makers of sewing machines, agricultural implements, typewriters, cash registers, carriages, bicycles, and most important of all, electrical machinery and equipment. The Mc-Cormicks in reapers, the Remingtons in typewriters, Edward Clark of Singer Sewing Machine, James Patterson in cash registers, Albert Pope in bicycles, William C. Durant in carriages, George Westinghouse and Charles Coffin in electrical machinery all pioneered in the creation of national and even international marketing organizations. Their new distributing networks usually included franchised retail dealers supported by branch offices which supplied the retailers with a flow of products, funds, spare parts and accessories, and with specialized repair and maintenance men. In order to assure supplies for the large volume of production needed to meet the demands of the new distributing system, these innovators also built large purchasing organizations, often bought or erected factories to manufacture parts and semifinished materials, and even came to own their large tracts of lumber or iron and steel works.

In these same years, the 1880's and 1890's, the volume producers of perishable goods for the mass market created comparable distributing and purchasing organizations. Among these Gustavus Swift, a new England wholesale butcher, was probably the most significant innovator. In the late 1870's Swift appreciated, as had others, that the urbanizing East was outrunning its meat supply. Swift also saw the possibilities, which only a few others appreciated, of using the refrigerated car to bring Western meat to the East. The shipment of live cattle East, which since the 1850's had been the most lucrative east-bound trade for the railroads, was inefficient and costly. Sixty percent of the animal was inedible. Cattle lost weight or died on the trip. As important, concentration of butchering in Chicago would assure high volume operations and a much lower unit cost than the current method of shipping in small lots to wholesale butchers throughout the East.

Gustavus Swift's basic innovation was the creation of a distribution network. He realized that the refrigerated car was not enough. Carloads of fresh meat could hardly be dumped in Baltimore or Boston on a hot summer's day. So in the 1880's he began to build branch houses in every major town or city in the East and in many other parts of the nation. A branch house included a refrigerated warehouse, a sales office, and men and equipment to deliver meat to retail butchers and food stores. In carrying out this plan, Swift met the most determined opposition. The railroads were startled by the prospect of losing a major business, so the Eastern Truck Line Association refused to carry his refrigerated cars. The wholesalers organized in 1886 the National Butchers Protective Association to fight "the trust."

But good meat at a low price won out. Once the market was assured, Swift then set up large packing houses in the cities along the cattle frontier and even bought into the stockyards. By the end of the 1880's wholesalers with more than ample resources realized that unless they quickly followed Swift's example they would have to remain small local enterprises. Armour, Cudahay, Morris, and the firm of Schwartzschild and Sulzberger (it became Wilson and Company in World War I) quickly built their networks and bought into stockyards. These remained the big five in the meat-packing industry until changes in transportation and refrigeration brought new challenges, particularly from supermarkets and other retail chain stores, who integrated backward to control their own wholesaling organization.

What Swift did for meat, Andrew Preston did in the same years for the mass distribution of bananas through the creation of the United Fruit Company. Also in the 1880's large brewers like Schlitz, Blatz, and Pabst in Milwaukee and Anheuser Busch in St. Louis set up similar distribution networks based on refrigeration. In the same decade James B. Duke did the same thing for a new nonrefrigerated product—the cigarette.

These pioneers in high-volume manufacturing and distribution of both perishable and relatively complex durable goods demonstrated the clear economies of scale. They provided obvious examples for manufacturers who still found the existing wholesaler network quite satisfactory. Nevertheless, the factory owners in these industries were slow to follow the example of Swift, McCormick, and the others. They had to be pushed rather than attracted into adopting a strategy of vertical integration and with it the economies of mass production and mass distribution. It was the continuing oppressive pressure of falling prices between the mid-1870's and the mid-1890's that provided this push and forced many manufacturers to organize for the mass national and increasingly urban market. The price decline, in turn, had resulted largely from the coming of the factory itself. Far more efficient than hand or shop production, the widespread adoption of the factory after 1850, and particularly after the Civil War, had led to a sharply increasing output of goods and an excess of supply over demand.

In many American industries these falling prices resulted in a similar organizational response. The pattern was the same in producers' goods like iron, steel, brass, copper, rubber products, and explosives, and in consumers' goods industries like salt, sugar, matches, biscuits, kerosene, and rubber boots and shoes. This pattern—the second route to great size—was one of combination, consolidation, and then vertical integration. To meet the threat of falling prices and profits, the factory owners formed trade associations whose primary function was to control price and production. But these associations were rarely able to maintain their cartels. If the prices became stabilized, some manufacturers would leave the association and obtain business by selling below the established price. If prices rose temporarily, the members often disbanded until the downward trend began again. The association proved to be, in the words of the first president of the Petroleum Refiners Association, John D. Rockefeller, "ropes of sand." They failed for the same reason as did the railroad cartels, which collapsed in the 1870's and 1880's. The agreements could not be enforced. They did not have the binding effect of a legal contract.

While railroad men turned unsuccessfully to persuade state and national legislatures to legalize pools or cartels, the manufacturers devised ways of acquiring firmer legal control of the factories in their industries. They initially began to purchase stock in competing companies. Then came a new device, the trust. The stocks of the various manufacturing companies were turned over to a board of trustees, with the owners of the stock receiving trust certificates in return. Less cumbersome was the holding company, whose stock could be exchanged directly for that of an operating firm and could then be bought or sold in the security markets. Once New Jersey had passed a general incorporation law for holding companies in 1889, this instrument became the standard one by which a group of manufacturers obtained legal control over a large number of factories.

Administrative control and industrial reorganization often, though not always, followed legal consolidation. The managers of a few of the new holding companies, like the owners of government-supported cartels in Europe, were satisfied with assured legal control of their operating subsidiaries. Others saw that legal control permitted them to improve their market and profit position by rationalizing the production facilities under their control. In this they were encouraged by recent antitrust legislation which discouraged the combination of companies under any legal form but did not yet penalize a single administratively consolidated firm.

So the holding company became an operating company. The factories it controlled were placed under a single manager with a specialized staff. The manager closed down the smaller, more inefficient plants and enlarged the more efficient ones. By running a much smaller number of much larger plants day and night, he quickly lowered unit costs. As a high-volume producer, the consolidated enterprise now found it could no longer rely on the fragmented distributing network of independent wholesalers. The enterprise therefore quickly moved into setting up its own wholesalers and occasionally even its own retailers and its own purchasing organization, often moving back to control of raw material.

The petroleum industry was one of the very first to combine, then to consolidate legally and administratively, and then to integrate, because it was one of the very first to overproduce for the national and international markets. In the early 1870's both refiners and producers of petroleum formed trade associations to control price and production. They were completely unsuccessful in enforcing their rulings throughout the industry. So in the mid-seventies Rockefeller, by using railroad rates as a weapon, was able to bring a large portion of the industry under the legal control of his Standard Oil Company.

However, legal control proved to be insufficient. Standard's primary market was abroad (for in the early 1870's close to 90 percent of refined petroleum went to Europe). Rockefeller therefore had to develop an efficient operating organization at home if he was to compete successfully abroad. So his company tightened up legal control through the formation of the first modern business trust. Then between 1883 and

1885 the refineries were consolidated. Where the Standard Oil trust had operated 55 plants in 1882, it had only 22 in 1886. Three-fourths of all its production was concentrated in three giant refineries. As a result, unit costs dropped dramatically. By 1884 Standard's average cost of refining a barrel was already 0.534 cents as compared to 1.5 cents for the rest of the industry. Next, the trust moved to acquire its own distributing organization in the domestic market in order to assure a continuing outlet for its massive production. This move was stimulated by the expansion of the home market resulting from the rapid growth of American industry and cities. (By the mid-1880's one-third of the illuminating oil and two-thirds of the lubricating oil products were going to the domestic market.) This creation of a distributing network meant an expensive investment in oil tanks and other storage areas, oil cars and wagons, offices, buildings, and facilities for making a wide variety of cans and other containers. Finally, in the late 1880's Standard Oil started to integrate backwards, entering for the first time into the production of crude; that is, the taking of crude oil out of the ground.

In the late 1880's and early 1890's manufacturers in other industries began to follow the example of Standard Oil, Swift, and McCormick. Before the coming of the depression of the nineties, firms in rubber, whiskey, rope, cotton and linseed oil, leather, and other industries had moved beyond a combination to consolidation. The severe depression of the mid-nineties slowed the processes. Funds were hard to find to finance the new holding companies, to help them tempt other manufacturers into the consolidation, to pay for the necessary reorganization of production and distribution facilities, and to finance the purchase of construction of factories and mines producing raw or semifinished materials. Indeed, some of the newly formed consolidations failed to survive the depression. Then as prosperity returned in 1897 and capital became easier to obtain, industry after industry came to be dominated by a handful of large integrated corporations. The promise of handsome returns from mass production and mass distribution and the harsh memory of twenty years of falling prices made the prospect of consolidation and integration difficult to resist. The result was the first great merger movement in American history.

With the merger movement big business took its modern form. Externally the new consolidated enterprises competed in an oligopolistic way; that is, competed with only a few other giants. Internally they became managed in a bureaucratic manner; that is, through a hierarchy of offices and departments. In the early years of the twentieth century the managers of America's new big businesses experimented in the new ways of oligopolistic competition in which product improvement through research and development and product differentiation through advertising, trade names, and styling became as important competitive weapons as price. Pricing became based largely on costs. With better cost accounting the companies were able to set prices in relation to a desired return on investment. The managers of the competing giants had little to gain by cutting prices below an acceptable profit margin. On the other hand, if one firm set its prices excessively high, others could increase their share of the market by selling at a lower price and still keeping the expected profit or rate of return on investment.

The managers of the great consolidations also paid close attention to developing the internal organization of their enterprises. This task involved the building of departments to handle all the different functions —production, marketing, purchasing, finance, engineering and research —and a central office to coordinate the work of the departments. Department-building often required a massive reorganization of an industry's production and distribution facilities. The creation of a central office called for the development of procedures to assure a steady and regular flow of goods and materials through the several departments and a regular and steady supply of working capital. It also required the formulation of systematic procedures to allocate the resources of the corporation as a whole.

The coordination of flow, particularly the control of inventory and working capital, came increasingly to be tied to detailed forecasts of short-term demand. The allocation of capital and the assigning of skilled personnel to existing or new ventures came to depend on a broad plan of company growth based on long-term estimates of demand. Appraising current performance as well as coordination of flow and allocating resources required the development of sophisticated cost accounting methods and of formulas for determining long- and short-term rate of return on investment.

Because these procedures and techniques involved all aspects of the industrial process, they were of more significance and had a broader application than those developed earlier by the railroads or those formulated by Frederick W. Taylor and others for the "scientific management" of factories. These methods have, in fact, become one of America's most useful exports in an age when so many nations are seeking the material benefits of a mass-production, mass-distribution economy.

The United States pioneered in the techniques of mass production and mass distribution precisely because the giant consolidated, integrated enterprise replaced the small family-owned and managed single-function firms and associations or combinations of these firms. Both economic and noneconomic differences made this change more rapid and more pronounced than in the other industrializing nations of western Europe and in Japan. The most important difference, as has so often and so rightly been stressed, was the existence of the large domestic market in the United States.

However, almost as important as its size was its newness. The existing forms of production and distribution were not as deeply entrenched in the United States as they were in Europe. The wholesale network only began to take form as the nation moved westward after the war of 1812; while the specialized wholesaling house, the key unit in the older distributing system, did not take roots west of the Appalachians and south of the Potomac until after 1850. Nor, for that matter, did the modern factory begin to move south and west until after the Civil War. Significantly the longest established factory industry in the country, the textile industry, was one of the last to accept the large integrated corporation.

In Europe the wholesalers had often existed for several generations, and factories grew out of industrial shops. So the business unit had become much more closely tied to family status and position than it was in the United States. The European preferred to remain the owner of his business, controlling price and production through a combination with other owners. By contrast, the American, having only just begun as a factory owner or as a wholesale merchant, found it easier to sell out to a proposed consolidation. He was less disturbed than his European counterpart at being transformed from an owner into a manager, particularly if the change increased his personal income.

The Europeans' preference meant that the older, more established industries—iron and steel, nonferrous metals, textiles, and agricultural processing—normally continued to be run by single function, nonintegrated family firms, while the distributing side of the economy remained fragmented in the hands of many more, even smaller, family firms. In the newer industries, such as chemicals, electronics, petroleum, automobiles, and aeronautics, technological and market requirements made easier from almost the very beginning the creation of large plants and of national and international distributing and purchasing organizations. As in the United States these same requirements forced the organizers of these firms to rely upon competent, specialized, highly trained managers. In Asia the dominance of the large clan in business enterprise has not hampered the growth of big business, but the favored position of family and clan has held back the development of carefully structured industrial enterprises administered by professional managers.

American attitudes and values may have provided an additional reason for the transformation of the cartel into a consolidated enterprise. To be effective, a cartel, in Europe or the United States, required at least tacit approval by the government. In the United States such combinations not only failed to receive governmental recognition but became explicitly illegal. The antitrust legislation reflected a powerful bias of Americans against special privilege, which had expressed itself earlier in the controversy over the Bank of the United States during the Jacksonian period.

In Europe, governmental support of special class and family interests was more acceptable. Moreover, the advocates of cartels could argue that their form of organization was essential if the nation was to compete in world markets. In any case, no other industrializing nation ever developed an antitrust movement similar to that of the United States. And, paradoxically, antitrust legislation and its interpretation by the courts, which made combinations of small units illegal but permitted the formation of large consolidated operating companies, actually encouraged the

swift growth of big business in American manufacturing and distribution.

Antitrust legislation and the newness of existing economic institutions had a significant influence on the specific time when the giant industrial enterprise took its specific form. The more underlying causes
for the coming of big business are the same as those that brought the
rapid industrializing of the nation. . . . Vast natural resources, the large
number of customers within the boundaries of a single nation, the ability
to draw on European capital and labor, the success-oriented, utilitarian,
middle-class attitudes and values of a large portion of the population all
created the basic opportunity to fashion an economy based on mass production and mass distribution and to build the great enterprises that
today carry on and link together this massive production and distribution.

Five ⌣ *System in Business*

"SCIENTIFIC MANAGEMENT"
IN BUSINESS *A. W. Shaw*

The much-discussed "Scientific Management," reduced to simple terms,
is a particular form of industrial management that develops the individual worker to the highest state of efficiency and of prosperity and at the
same time secures greater prosperity for the factory owner by getting his
product made at the lowest possible cost.

Its principles have been slowly but accurately formulated by Frederick W. Taylor, the first investigator in the field of industrial management
whose work may rightly be termed scientific.

Literally, with a stop watch, scales, and a tape, Mr. Taylor timed
the various routine operations of the workmen in the great steel plants of
Pennsylvania, in one of which he was successively laborer, foreman, chief
engineer, general manager. He measured distances that men and materials traversed, and gradually evolved the theory that a large percentage
of both labor and material was needlessly wasted,—often as high as 60
or 80 per cent in a single department,—through improper supervision

REPRINTED from A. W. Shaw, "'Scientific Management' in Business," in *Review of
Reviews*, Vol. XLIII (March 1911), pp. 327–32.

and direction. Through changes which he effected he materially reduced the time in which these operations were done. By a comparison of figures he expressed the economies which his methods effected in specific terms of minutes, cents, and ounces. Upon these terms as a basis, he constructed a plan of scientific shop management that he described in a paper which he read before the American Society of Mechanical Engineers at the June meeting of 1903.[1] That date properly marks the beginning of the present movement to establish industrial management as a profession subject to scientific laws.

. . .

Similar Principles Applied to Salesmanship

The National Cash Register Company, for instance, had reduced its selling methods to the point that it had analyzed, classified, and embodied in text-book form the theory and practice of salesmanship as applied to its particular product—the first, perhaps still the most complete codification of rules that has ever been formulated for the guidance of salesmen. Every detail of the demonstration of the company's product has been analyzed and expressed in the order and even in the phraseology that experience has proved to be the most effective. Every salesman is obliged to memorize this "selling talk," and to conduct a demonstration throughout in exactly the same words and manner as is prescribed for every other salesman; the entire process, in brief, has been standardized.

In another volume have been collected, from the practical experience of its salesmen, every objection that had been made by a prospective customer against the purchase of the product, together with the approved arguments in refutation. These arguments are studied and in many cases memorized by the salesmen.

The same methods have been employed to standardize the work of the sales department as a whole. The salesmen are divided into grades, according to their abilities. As soon as a salesman attains a specified ability as expressed in "points" (a "point" is the standard sales unit, and represents a sale of $25 in value, with additional values for the sale of special grades of goods) he is admitted to the school for salesmen, conducted by experienced instructors. Here he attends courses of lectures, recitations, and selling demonstrations extending over a period of six weeks, at the end of which oral and written examinations determine whether he is qualified for a certificate. Prizes are given for excellence in these courses, and the classes are organized and "graduated" similar to the classes in ordinary educational institutions. At stated intervals these classes are called in to pursue "post-graduate" courses of instruction, as

[1] Refers to Taylor, *Shop Management*.

the changes in the policies of the company and in its products demand.

The entire globe is divided into sales territory under district managers and their subordinates; for each district and subdistrict a sales "quota" is established each month. A "quota" is the volume of sales (as expressed in points) which, in view of the season, local conditions, and other considerations, may be reasonably expected. Thus a standard of proficiency is established for every man in the selling organization—a "bogie score" that must be equaled to maintain the record and that must be excelled in order to qualify for the numerous bonuses and prizes that are constantly held out as incentives.

So completely has this selling organization been standardized in its details and so successful has it been in maintaining an established ratio of growth, that its methods have been adopted by other organizations that are using them with equal proficiency. And when the United Cigar Stores selects locations for its shops by stationing a representative of the company on the spot for specified periods, to make an actual count of the number of people who pass that spot in the course of the day, and when in another concern an office manager, with a stop watch, times the work of every stenographer and posts each week, as a stimulus to effort, a comparative record that shows the speed, accuracy, and volume of work performed and on this record, as a basis, establishes a scale of wages, both are taking long, long steps toward Scientific Management.

Application to Business Problems in General

For these, broadly, are the steps toward Scientific Mangement:—

1. To separate from the "line organization" or to add to the line organization a staff officer or "staff organization."

2. To set up tentative standards of performance.

3. To correct these standards by working out scientifically the best methods of performance.

4. To determine the best inducement to the employee to attain these standards.

5. To equip the employee with clear, complete, and exact knowledge of the best way of doing the work.

This is not, perhaps, as Mr. Taylor would designate them, but as they might be taken by a business man who, having studied the literature of Scientific Management, would apply its principles to an individual business problem.

For Mr. Taylor's studies have been of industrial workers. And the exact systems he has devised and installed have been applications of the principles or laws that he has discovered to industrial organization. They should be introduced, in their entirety, in no factory except under the direct supervision of Mr. Taylor or of men trained by him or trained directly under his influence.

But many a false prophet will come to the business men bringing only the shell of Mr. Taylor's methods and not the principles, just as when the first general introduction of business system brought in its trail heterogeneous assortments of cards, filing cabinets, and record sheets that involved endless clerical labor to operate and which in many cases constituted useless red tape. For a period business men mistook the form for the substance; they believed that in the filling and filing of blanks they had "system," and ignored the real system of which these forms were merely the mechanical tools. The result was that this mechanical routine was either stripped of its non-essentials until it became a serviceable implement or was discarded entirely for the old-fashioned inaccurate rule-of-thumb method. A system is not a card or a filing cabinet; it is the right way of doing a thing. Similarly, Mr. Taylor's method of Scientific Management does not consist of forms or charts or of sets of rules and regulations. It is a big policy of establishing after scientific study and research a standard way of performing each industrial operation with the best possible expenditure of material, capital, and labor. The forms and rules are merely the machinery by which the policy is applied.

What Is a Full Day's Work?

Back of the Taylor principles and back of his particular method of applying them to actual workshop conditions is this affirmation of the psychologists,—that all of us, employers and employees, have but a vague conception of what constitutes a full day's work for a first class man.

Many of us confuse overwork with what is really underwork and it is only under a compelling incentive that we discover that like the runner we have a second wind.

And the problem is not merely to ascertain what is a full day's work for the workman but to ascertain what is a full day's work for the works manager, and for the office boy and the office manager, for the salesman and the sales manager, and how to induce the performance of that full day's work.

Therefore, the precise principles Mr. Taylor has formulated for industrial operations have been applied, in most cases perhaps unconsciously, to almost all forms of commercial activity.

Establishing Standards of Sales Costs

Perhaps this is best illustrated by the experience of a Chicago house whose products are sold at retail by a staff of traveling salesmen who come into personal contact with their customers.

The sales manager was additionally compensated over and above a certain salary by a percentage of the value of the sales made under his direction. His major effort, therefore, was directed to the increase in the gross amount of the sales, unconsciously irrespective of the profits to the house. That he eventually used in the conduct of his department methods that were expensive and extravagant in order to secure a large volume of sales was due to a gross but common error in the policy of the concern,—compensation based only on volume of sales. The monthly statement showed such a constantly increasing average of sales expense that finally the management issued an order that every expense requisition of the manager should be approved by an official in the financial department. Friction resulted and with it the diminution of this sales manager's most valuable characteristic,—enthusiasm. The percentage of the sales expense promptly decreased and so did the volume of the sales.

To meet this situation the management, with the sales manager and a few executives of the company who were temporarily recalled from the "line" organization and placed on the "staff" for advisory purposes, went into a careful analysis of each phase of the work of that department. Assuming for the time the viewpoint of the outsider, the committee divided each operation into its details and regarded each in its relation to the whole. Gradually it established standards for practically each operation of the department. It placed a tentative standard for the gross annual sales, based on past records and on present conditions. It established a standard percentage for the cost of making these sales. It analyzed the various expenses into their several factors. It prepared from the books of account a printed sheet, ruled and tabulated to record the daily and monthly statements in such form that they would acquaint the sales manager with the expenses that he was incurring, both in percentages and units, and in relation to the sales. It studied the methods of the individual salesmen and sales managers and prepared suggestions and directions as to the best methods to be used by both. It corrected the original tentative standards, and pointed out wasteful methods in the daily work of the salesmen and in the daily work of the sales manager.

Then the management said to that sales manager:—

Here is a codification of the methods under which our product is to be sold. Here are the exact percentages that we can afford to pay to make these sales. And here is our proposition to you. Your salary will remain as it is. On the gross amount of the sales you make we will pay you a certain percentage. If you can attain in sales that standard which we will set up and can attain the standard at a less percentage of expense than we have designated as a standard percentage, one-half of what you save will be yours to keep. You will approve your own requisitions for expense.

In seven months the sales doubled in volume and the expense had averaged below the predetermined standard and below any past record of performance.

The True Science of Business

But out of all the reverberant publicity given "Scientific Management" —the term itself has almost become standardized—what is to be gained by the average business man?

For the science of business itself, when carefully formulated, will be, after all, as Dr. Scott says, merely common sense, the wisdom of experience analyzed, formulated, codified, and all in respect to certain data.

But the data are being accumulated now. That is what business men individually and through their organizations, and business publications and educational institutions, notably the Harvard Graduate School of Business Administration, are doing to-day [1914, A. D. C.]. [They are] analyzing business the world over, picking out details, matters of routine, specific methods of management, individual plans of organization which under certain conditions have produced certain proven results—picking out, in other words, the right way of doing things, or as Mr. Taylor has expressed it, the only right way of doing things—the system.

The principles of this science of business have only just begun to be formulated. But from a study of the principles of "Scientific Management" the business man can get a new business viewpoint—a new mental attitude toward his specific business problems.

That is important. For success or failure in business depends as much upon mental attitude as upon mental aptitude. And the mental attitude that prompts one business man to make a scientific study of his own peculiar requirements and by experiment determine the most effective ways of getting the thing done—whether the task is carrying a pig of iron or selling a carload of canned corn—is the mental attitude that makes for business success.

If production costs have been high, the manager's method of attacking the problem in the past has been simply to try to lower wages or to add machinery. If selling costs have increased, he has tenaciously tried to increase selling prices. And in all of his movements he has usually been guided by accounting that was merely historic—not prophetic; by standards based on past performances—not carefully analyzing possible performances.

But a changed mental attitude suggests a new approach. If costs of production are high the business man will study the equipment that he already has. He will study workmen and ascertain scientifically just what is a full day's work for these workmen and what will help and will induce them to perform this full day's work. When selling expenses rise he will look first to the men who by words of mouth or by written words sell his product. And he will examine the standards against which these men are working and the exact methods that they use.

Result: Lower Prices

The effect upon the purchasing public of the introduction of Scientific Management will in the beginning be negligible. As long as its application is confined to occasional individual businesses, the economies that it will effect will be internal and the profit will be restricted largely to the local management. But as a scientifically managed plant, because of its lower costs of production, can eventually undersell its competitors, the same methods of management will eventually become universal and the economies will be shared by the industry generally and thus become external. The inevitable result will be a lowering of prices to the customer.

Increasing the Workman's Value to Himself

Because of the fact that scientific direction of labor is an increase in the production of the worker as a unit and of the organization as a whole, its principles have at times been opposed by various bodies of workmen who, through a misconception of their real purpose and with the knowledge of the universally recognized defects of the ordinary piece work system, have branded Scientific Management offhand as merely another effort to "speed up" the workmen. In reality the new management aims primarily not to increase the strain on the worker by forcing him into redoubled effort, but to apply his effort to greater advantage. It places at his disposal methods and machinery that have proven, by actual test, to be the most economical of his time and strength. It furnishes him with instructors (known as "functional foremen") who are more experienced in certain phases of his task than he himself, through whose supervision he is enabled to use these methods and machinery to best advantage. By a system of records, it determines the workmen's special capacities that permit him to be set at the work at which he is most proficient. And by means of a bonus system it provides for the adequate remuneration of the worker not on the basis of effort expended, but upon the more modern basis of effort practically applied and expressed in units of production. As a consequence, the workman's value to himself and to the organization is increased, as rapidly and as highly as his capabilities permit.

Six ⌐ Building a Craft Union

GOMPERS AND BUSINESS UNIONISM
Bernard Mandel

One of Samuel Gompers' major contributions to the American labor movement was his leadership in the adoption of a plan of organization known initially as the "new unionism" and later as "business unionism." He developed this scheme from a study of British unions and, even more, from his experiences in the cigarmakers' union.

The depression of 1873–79 fell with shattering force on the Cigarmakers' International Union, which had entered a period of decline in 1869. During these years the cigar mold, a tool for the shaping of cigars, was circumventing the skill of the cigarmakers, permitting the employment of women, children, and unskilled immigrants, and stimulating the transfer of the trade from factories to tenement houses. The International Union immediately prohibited its members from working in any shop where the new "machine" was used.[1]

In New York the cigarmakers struck against the use of the mold. The failure of this strike convinced them that the union must open its doors to unskilled workers. They reorganized their own locals on that basis, and in 1875 they secured an amendment to the constitution of the International which prohibited any local from rejecting members on ac-

[1] John R. Commons and others, *History of Labour in the United States,* 4 vols. (New York, 1918–1935), II, 71–74.

REPRINTED with permission from Bernard Mandel, "Gompers and Business Unionism," *Business History Review*, Vol. XXVIII (September 1954), pp. 264–75. Copyright 1954 by The President and Fellows of Harvard College.

count of sex or "system of work." [2] The New York local was then recognized by the International, receiving a charter as Local 144. Samuel Gompers was elected president of the new organization and Adolph Strasser, financial secretary. [3]

The New York cigarmakers were, at this time, one of the "strikingest" trades in the country. Strikes were undertaken without considering the state of the trade, without assessing the means needed and those available to conduct the contests, and without formulating a general strategy for the strike movement. On one occasion, Gompers and his shopmates were involved in a strike without being told the reasons for the walkout. Some strikes began when one man left a shop to protest a grievance, and the other workers merely followed him out from a sense of duty or from a fear of being called scabs. Naturally, the great majority of these strikes was lost, the treasury of the union was sapped to no avail, and members left the organization in disgust or discouragement.

Therefore strict control of strikes was a cardinal objective of the new plan of organization introduced by Gompers and his associates into Local 144, which had members in numerous small shops. In each shop with more than seven members, a shop organization met weekly. In the other shops, the members were grouped in district organizations of 200 men or less. Local authority rested with these shop and district organizations. Their delegates, together with the officers of the local, made up the Board of Administration which met weekly to transact general business. Decisions of the Board, on demand of one-third of its delegates, were submitted to referendum vote of all members of the local, as were all appropriations of $25 or more. Union officers were nominated and elected by secret ballot in shop and district meetings.

Any proposal to strike had first to be approved by members of the shop organization by secret ballot. The proposal then went to the Board of Administration. If the Board approved the strike, it appointed a strike committee to direct the struggle. First claim for support by the union went to the workers receiving the lowest wages, because the low-wage factories would not seem inviting to strikebreakers and because the other employers would not unite with their worst competitors to fight the union. "We can thus put a wedge to the lowest point of the trade, relieve greatly and effectively all those suffering by the present operation of these men, and generally establish a fair Bill of Prices, with an upward tendency," explained the secretary of the German section of Local 144. The union also proposed to set up a labor bureau to which employers and workers might send information of work opportunities. [4]

Gompers soon had an opportunity to extend the application of these

[2] *Cigar Makers' Official Journal*, I (Feb., 1876). Hereafter referred to as the *Journal*.
[3] Samuel Gompers, *Seventy Years of Life and Labor*, 2 vols. (New York, 1925), I, 110–15.
[4] M. D. Plate to George Hurst, in *Journal*, I (Nov., 1875), 2–3; Gompers, *Life and Labor*, I, 116–18.

principles to a broader field. He was first elected by Local 144 as its delegate to the Cigarmakers' International Union convention in 1877, and he represented his local in every convention from that year until his death. As the representative of the largest local, as an intimate friend and associate of Strasser, whom Gompers made president of the International Union in 1877, and as a young man with strong ideas, ardent enthusiasm for the cause of unionism, a forceful personality, and unflagging energy, it was inevitable that he should rise to a position of leadership in the International. His rapid ascent was based on his policy for reorganizing the union on an efficient foundation, one which would be sound enough and strong enough to make the union a powerful fighting organization, capable of concentrating its forces quickly and at the most strategic point. In the very process of securing a charter from the International for Local 144, he had already won acceptance for the first phase of his program of "new unionism," that is, the recognition of the mold and the opening of the doors of the union to the unskilled workers in the trade. He then set out to carry through the rest of his policy. While this program was not an exclusive invention of Gompers, he played a leading part in evolving it, and an even more important part in securing its adoption by the cigarmakers. Later, as president of the American Federation of Labor, he constantly urged the program upon the affiliated unions.

The first convention attended by Gompers met in Rochester, 30 August 1877. Only eight delegates, representing eight locals, were present; the other nine locals in the International could not afford to send representatives. Gompers introduced and campaigned vigorously for a series of constitutional amendments which provided for the support of unemployed, sick, and traveling members of the union. These proposals were defeated. Naturally, the convention also turned down his proposal for a revamped revenue system which would be needed to finance the program: an annual per capita tax of 60 cents per member, payable monthly. The only proposal from Gompers accepted by the delegates was the recommendation that each local establish a Labor Bureau to help unemployed members find work. Gompers was so dissatisfied with the work of the convention that he voted against the constitution.[5]

Local 144 had already inaugurated a partial system of benefits. In 1876 it exempted its members from dues payments while they were unemployed due to sickness, and members in good standing were entitled to out-of-work assistance for a period of three weeks.[6] Gompers was convinced that unless such a system of benefits was extended and made universal, the trade union movement had slight chance of permanence. He had seen the depression of the 1870's nearly wipe out the labor unions of the country, and he believed that this was in large measure due to the fact that, when the union was not able to protect wage stan-

[5] *Journal,* III (Oct., 1877), 3-4.
[6] *Ibid.,* I (Sept., 1876), 1.

dards, its members had no impulsion to remain in it. The "fraternal system" would provide the incentive to retain membership during a depression; thus the unions would be prepared to resume the movement for improved conditions as soon as business revived.[7]

Granting that workers joined unions mainly to protect themselves against the "fearful effects of our competitive system," and that the first task of the unions was to increase wages and reduce hours, Gompers maintained that an out-of-work benefit would be instrumental in accomplishing these purposes. He pointed out that those unions having benevolent features were less subject to fluctuations in membership and consequently the working conditions of their members were less affected by dull industrial conditions. Almost any union, he stated, could protect its members during busy seasons; it was far more important to the welfare and progress of the workers to maintain their conditions during hard times. "The very fact that the workers remain organized, ostensibly only for the 'benefits,' is all important, inasmuch as their organization is always a lever to protect them from all the wrong and injustice successfully practiced upon the unorganized."[8] A secondary reason for Gompers' advocacy of the protective system was that it would provide the workers with insurance against the vicissitudes of a chaotic economic system cheaper than such insurance could be obtained from private companies. He was always very hostile to private insurance companies, believing that they were parasites which took financial advantage of the workingmen's distress. He therefore believed that the unions should provide insurance, at least until the government would undertake to furnish it on a voluntary basis.[9]

Gompers' defeat at the 1877 convention did not discourage him— discouragement was a quality foreign to his nature. He was called many things during his lifetime, but everyone agreed that his make-up included large ingredients of dogged persistence and endless patience. He talked to his associates, wrote letters, prepared lectures, working with the zeal of a crusader to win the cigarmakers to his views. His most important early convert to business unionism was Strasser. The two men corresponded on the subject, and discussed it over beer and wine far into the night after meetings. At the next convention in Buffalo in 1879, Gompers' position was fortified by the report of President Strasser, who recommended the adoption of the benefit features. Gompers again presented resolutions for sick, unemployed, and traveling payments, and this time the 11 delegates present approved the proposals. However, they rejected a constitutional amendment to increase dues to 25 cents a week. The Committee on Constitution, of which Gompers was a member, reported that the benefit system could not be financed by the present low dues,

[7] Interview reported in the *Iowa State Register* (Des Moines), 3 May 1899; Gompers, Annual Report, *Proceedings of the 13th Annual Convention of the American Federation of Labor,* 1893, p. 12.
[8] *Journal,* XIII (Sept., 1888), 7–8.
[9] Gompers, *Life and Labor,* I, 167.

and recommended that the question be discussed by the locals in preparation for a decision at the next convention.[10]

Gompers went to the Chicago convention the following year prepared to seal his victory. He was appointed secretary of the Committee on Constitution, which was instructed to draft a law for sick benefits, to be submitted to the locals for approval. The committee proposed that members in good standing be entitled to $3.00 per week for a period of eight weeks, and an indeterminate sum for another eight weeks, with a limit of 16 weeks in a year. Pregnancy was not to constitute a claim for benefits. This plan was approved by the convention, with a clause providing for an increase of dues to 15 cents a week if the plan was adopted. The convention likewise adopted for submission to the locals a resolution offered by Gompers to pay a $25 death benefit to the nearest of kin of deceased members.[11] In order to be eligible, however, the member must have been in good standing for one year prior to his death; this was designed to keep the members "faithful and steady."[12] Both amendments were ratified by the membership.

Gompers claimed that the phenomenal increase in the membership of Local 144 was due to the introduction of these benefits. It had less than 300 members at the beginning of 1881, and over 3,000 by September. At the convention that year, the local so far overshadowed the others that Gompers, one of 53 delegates, held one-third of all the votes.[13]

Strengthened by this voting power and by its victory on the issue of sick benefits, Local 144 later set out to secure jobless benefits. In 1888 it proposed a constitutional amendment providing that each member who had paid dues for a year should be entitled to receive $3.00 during the first week of unemployment and 50 cents per day thereafter, up to $72 a year. But no payment was to be made to members who lost their jobs due to intoxication, disorderly conduct (meaning the contraction of venereal disease), dishonesty, or flagrantly poor workmanship. This was to be accompanied by an increase in dues to 25 cents a week.[14] The membership defeated these amendments by a narrow margin, but in 1889 Gompers reintroduced the proposals and this time they were adopted by the convention and ratified by referendum.[15]

As president of the AFL after 1886, Gompers usually urged in his annual reports that the affiliated organizations adopt a system of benefits; thus those who saw no other value in unionism could be induced to

---

[10] *Journal*, IV (Aug., 1879), 2; *ibid.*, V (Oct., 1879), 2–3.
[11] *Ibid.*, VI (Oct., 1880), 5–7.
[12] *Ibid.*, VI (Dec., 1880), 1.
[13] *Ibid.*, VII (Sept., 1881), 5.
[14] *Ibid.*, XIII (July, 1888), 7–8.
[15] *Proceedings*, 18th Session, Cigarmakers' International Union, 16 Sept. 1889, p. 17 (in archives of Cigarmakers' International Union); *Journal*, XIV (Nov., 1888), 11; *ibid.*, XV (Oct., 1889), 9; *ibid.*, XV (Dec., 1889), 11.

retain their membership.[16] In 1901, he summed up his experience by stating that he was [17]

> convinced beyond the peradventure of a doubt that there are no means so potent to the permanency of organization; to constant betterment in the condition of the workers; to the maintenance of industrial peace . . . and yet with all the gradual economic, social, political and moral improvements of the whole wage-working class; to instill the spirit of fraternity and solidarity among them; as to demand the payment of higher dues in the unions, coupled with the protective and benevolent features of which they admit and of which they are a corollary.
>
> Indeed, there is no factor so calculated to maintain organization during industrial stagnations, crises, or to survive even defeat in contest, as is the possession of a substantial fund raised by the membership *prior* to the stagnation or conflict.

The third major phase of Gompers' business unionism, along with the benefit system and high dues, was the mechanism for centralized control of strikes which had been introduced in Local 144 in the mid-1870's. From this beginning, the local made the control even more strict and worked to extend it to the entire union. The New York cigarmakers provided that, in any strike which did not have prior approval from the union, the local itself should send other members to man the shop. The union went even further in 1883 by providing that, if an unauthorized strike was not called off at the demand of the union president, he should advertise for nonunion men to fill the places of the strikers, and any member continuing to picket the shop would be fined, suspended, or expelled at the discretion of the union.[18]

In 1879, Local 144 proposed an amendment to the constitution of the International Union to guarantee financial support to members on strike at the rate of $6.00 per week, providing the strike was approved by the Executive Board and the Board of Appeals. The president would then issue a circular appeal for assistance and a weekly assessment on each local in proportion to its membership, sufficient to secure the necessary funds for strike relief. If the Board did not approve the strike, the applicants might appeal to a general vote of all locals. Every strike involving more than ten members would be submitted to a vote of the locals, and those involving demands for wage increases would have to receive a two-thirds vote to be eligible for assistance. Finally, each local would be required to retain in its treasury a sum of 15 cents per member to be used as a strike fund.

Gompers was appointed chairman of a committee of Local 144 to

[16] See Gompers, Annual Report, *Proceedings of the 3rd* [8th] *Annual Convention of the American Federation of Labor*, 1888, p. 12.

[17] Gompers, Annual Report, *Proceedings of the 21st Annual Convention of the American Federation of Labor*, 1901, pp. 14–15.

[18] *Journal*, VIII (Aug., 1883), 6.

explain the purpose of the proposal, and in pursuit of this assignment he wrote a long letter to the *Cigar Makers' Official Journal*. He pointed out that the system of sporadic assessments then in use caused sudden strains on almost empty treasuries and pockets, and that it was not always a reliable source of revenue. The periodic publication of the state of the strike fund would have another advantage: members would be more cautious in sanctioning strikes if they knew the fund was low and they themselves might be liable for further assessments. Referring to the large number of strikers being forced to return to work from lack of assistance in their struggles, he asserted that it was necessary in time of peace to prepare for war.

> Experience has demonstrated that heretofore some of the unions have been backward in forwarding their assessment in aid of a strike, whether in consequence of a theory or a lack of discipline is not for our consideration, but the fact remains, that a union, failing to act in accordance with the laws of an organization it is allied with, must be compelled to obey the laws or quit the organization. It is not sufficient (our union holds) for any Union to shelter itself behind a theory that they are opposed to strikes and will not support them. We are aware that notwithstanding opposition from whatever quarter, strikes will occur; that they cannot be argued out of existence; we know that strikes are but preliminary skirmishes to the great battle of labor, and will occur wherever low wages, long hours, and oppressive rules are the conditions under which workingmen toil. While we would urge toilers to avoid strikes otherwise than as a last resort, yet in view of the foregoing facts we hold ourselves in duty bound to array ourselves on the side of labor, and rendering them our hearty and effectual support. . . .

Gompers' arguments must have been persuasive, for the amendment was adopted by a two to one vote.[19] The following year, the convention ruled that strikes resulting from attempted wage reductions, from payment of wages in anything but money, or from lockouts, must be approved and strike benefits paid.[20] In 1881, the International Union adopted the policy of prohibiting all strikes, except against lockouts, wage cuts, and the truck system, from November to April; during that period strike funds would be accumulated.[21] In 1883, the Committee on Strikes recommended that any local assisting another local in an unauthorized strike be considered guilty of a misdemeanor and subject to the discipline of the Executive Board. Gompers proposed that the union countenancing the outlaw strike incur the same penalty, and the amended resolution was adopted.[22]

In 1883 President Strasser reported that during the previous two years there had been 218 applications for strikes, nearly all for wage in-

---

[19] *Ibid.*, IV (April, 1879), 2; *ibid.*, IV (May, 1879), 1.
[20] *Ibid.*, VI (Oct., 1880), 8.
[21] *Ibid.*, VII (Oct., 1881), 3 ff.
[22] *Ibid.*, VIII (Sept., 1883), Supplement.

creases; that 194 of them had been approved; and that about three-fourths of these had been won. At a cost of $77,000, wage increases of nearly $2,000,000 had been gained, besides another $500,000 saved by preventing reductions.[23] But during the next two years, the union's record was not so good, only half of the strikes being successful. This was a fairly remarkable showing for those years of depression, but Gompers was not satisfied. He decided that still more stringent regulations were needed.

In 1885 he was appointed secretary of the Committee on Strikes at the Cincinnati convention, and he took the opportunity in his report to urge the necessity of "deliberate, yet determined action, to prevent the use of a weapon which may prove disastrous to us unless handled and directed with the greatest caution." He explained:

> The question then arises, is it to the best interests of our organization and trade to at all times strike, even when the employer possesses the vantage ground, or is it not better to act like a well-drilled and disciplined army that is directed to reach a certain position, under the very fire of the enemy, with orders *not to shoot,* even amidst the greatest provocation? Certainly some men are shot down and lost; but the ranks are closed up again, and the march is onward until the position is gained, when a volley is fired in return with telling effect. . . . It is not wise nor practical, to *at all times strike, even against a reduction of wages.* The first and main object should be, if a reduction of wages cannot be successfully resisted, accept it; but maintain your organization, for by that means, and that means only, can we at the earliest possible time regain our lost ground, and even something more. . . .

Gompers concluded his report by recommending that all strikes (rather than only those for wage increases) require a two-thirds vote of approval by the membership of the International before being eligible for assistance, and that after a strike had been in progress for three months, and again every month thereafter, another vote be taken on whether aid should be continued or not. He further suggested that when a strike involving over 50 members had lasted eight weeks, the president should appoint a representative of the International to proceed to the locality of the strike, attend all meetings of the local strike committee, make regular reports to the president, and if necessary examine the books and papers of the union. These proposals were all adopted by the delegates, except the one pertaining to periodical votes on the continuance of strike relief, and subsequently ratified by the membership.[24]

Thus the Cigarmakers' International Union, largely through the prodding of the young delegate from New York, perfected one of the most rigid plans of strike control and strike assistance practiced by any

[23] Proceedings of Cigarmakers' International Union, 20 Sept. 1883, in *ibid.,* VIII (Sept., 1883).
[24] Proceedings of Cigarmakers' International Union, September, 1885, in *ibid.,* XI (Oct., 1885).

union in the country. And Gompers steadfastly defended this policy against the inevitable complaints of locals who were restrained from laying down their tools whenever they wanted to. During the depression of the 1890's, he and the other members of the Executive Board invariably turned down applications to strike for wage increases, feeling that they would be abortive and that the Union would do well to hold its own. If every local could strike at will, "and could draw upon the funds of the International Union *ad libitum*," wrote Gompers, "we might witness the day when nearly all our members in the various localities would be out on strike, drawing upon the funds at one and the same time and leaving our International Union a wreck, to be buffeted and kicked by all, workingmen and employers alike." Under those conditions, he said, the approval of a strike would be merely granting "Sympathy without relief, mustard without beef." The centralized control of strikes had been a major factor in building up the union, and its retention was the only way to maintain the strength of the organization against undisciplined and rash action by the members and attacks by employers.[25]

The program of union benefits and strike assistance obviously necessitated a financial system capable of supporting it. While pushing his plan of business unionism through the International, Gompers also succeeded in having the union adopt a uniform initiation fee of $1.00 for all locals and uniform dues of 10 cents a week (these were increased to $2.00 and 20 cents, respectively, in 1881), the strike fund and assessment system, and a sinking fund of $2.00 per member (Gompers succeeded in getting it raised to $5.00 in 1883). He also secured the adoption by the cigarmakers of the equalization system, a plan widely used in British unions but unusual in the United States. This provided that if the funds of any local became exhausted through legitimate expenditures, it had the right to the funds of the other locals. In other words, the treasuries of the various locals virtually became common property, and every three months they were redistributed on the basis of membership and financial status.[26]

Gompers was a perennial foe of what he called "Cheap John Unionism." In his reports to the AFL, in the *American Federationist,* in his correspondence, and in his addresses to international unions, he drove home the necessity of high dues (in 1907 he urged that $1.00 per month should be the minimum) and high initiation fees (when the Federation formed the national union of tile layers in 1897, its initiation fee was fixed at $99 with the approval of the AFL). "There is not a dollar which the working man and woman pays into an organization of labor," he declared, "which does not come back a hundred fold." He had ready answers to all objections. Wages are low? True, he replied, but if the unions were not sustained on an effective financial foundation, then wages would be cut even further, and "The money you refused to pay

[25] Gompers to the Editor of the *Journal,* 30 Oct. 1895, in *ibid.,* XXI (Nov., 1895), 4.
[26] *Ibid.,* V (Oct., 1879), 2–3.

into your union as dues will go into the coffers of the employers." High dues will keep out new members? When the workers see that the union provides a stone wall of protection for their interests, they will soon come within the walls for protection.[27]

Thousands of strikes, Gompers argued, would be averted and the concessions demanded by the workers secured, if it were not that the employers often knew that the union would soon be compelled to succumb because of its small treasury.[28]

> It may be generally stated as a truism that low dues, low wages, long hours and servility are natural allies and the result of disorganization or organization on the basis of low dues; while, on the other hand, organizations based on high dues, secure for the workers the highest wages, the shortest number of hours of labor, self-respect and respect of others, independence and manhood. . . .
>
> There is no trade union on earth, which has inaugurated the system of high dues and benefits, which has not lived through all the stormy times of industrial, financial and commercial panics and crises. There is no trade union on earth, based upon high dues and benefits, which has failed to keep the promises made to its members. There is no trade union, based upon high dues and benefits, which has not secured the highest and best conditions of labor as compared to other workers. There is no trade union on earth, based upon high dues and benefits, which does not perform the functions of government more honorably, more cheaply and at a lesser cost than any insurance or charitable organization on earth. There is no organization anywhere which gives to its members anything like the returns as do the trade unions.

Gompers' conception of the "new unionism" was compounded of several other ingredients besides the benevolent system, centralized strike control, and a consolidated financial system based on high dues. It included a more efficient plan of local organization, which had already been initiated by Local 144 in 1876 when it directed that each factory select a shop director to collect dues weekly and deliver them to the Board of Administration, to participate in the meetings of the Board and report on subjects of interest occurring in their factories, and to call shop meetings when necessary or on request of one-sixth of the members.[29] Some years later Gompers secured the authorization of the International Union to set up a Greater New York district organization composed of delegates from the New York, Brooklyn, Hoboken, Williamsburg, and Jersey City locals. This joint committee was to meet regularly and to decide on all questions brought before it, subject to appeal to the International Executive Board.[30] The new unionism meant to Gompers the active sup-

---

[27] Gompers, Address to convention of United Textile Workers, Washington, D.C., 18 Nov. 1901, in *American Federationist*, VIII (Dec., 1901), 546.
[28] Gompers, "High Dues are Necessary to Success," *ibid.*, III (Sept., 1896), 141–42.
[29] *Journal*, I (Sept., 1876), 1.
[30] *Ibid.*, VII (Nov., 1881), 5.

port of the official journal as a means whereby grievances could be made known to fellow members, opinions mutually exchanged, and, above all, "as a means of promulgating the principles of Trades Unionism and as an agitator for the organization of the working classes. . . ." [31] The new unionism meant the negotiation of trade agreements and their faithful fulfillment. It meant co-operation with other organizations in a national labor federation, and with the cigarmakers' organizations in other countries. In short, it meant whatever was necessary "to develop power adequate to secure better working conditions." [32] It was a "practical" program to secure immediate results through discipline, centralized control, and businesslike methods.

There can be little doubt that more efficient organization was a vital necessity for the weak unions of the 1870's and 1880's, and one of Gompers' principal achievements was his vital role in achieving this organization. But he was sometimes criticized for placing the sanctity of contracts above the solidarity of the working class and for emphasizing the immediate needs of the craft rather than the long-range interests of all wage earners. Gompers denied that the idealism of the unions was incompatible with the adoption of practical and businesslike methods of operation. He answered such criticisms from Jane Addams:[33]

> To make contracts and stick to them, even when they limit or take away the right of striking out of sympathy, is not to sacrifice idealism. To consult actual conditions and the dictates of reasonable expediency before striking or making demands upon employers is not to abandon any ideal ever proposed by intelligent unionists.
>
> The "idealism" of the labor movement consists primarily in this, that the organized workmen in striking to better their own condition and to secure for themselves more equitable treatment are really battling for social and industrial progress.
>
> When the workers raise the standard of living they raise it for all. . . .
>
> The unions are doing the work of society; in Miss Addams' words they are intrusted with the task of social amelioration. Their methods must be governed by circumstances, but no method which really promotes the welfare of union labor can possibly injure any other class.

[31] Gompers to the Editor of the *Journal*, I (Feb., 1877), 4.
[32] Gompers, *Life and Labor*, I, 144.
[33] *American Federationist*, XI (Oct., 1904), reprinted in Gompers, *Labor and the Common Welfare* (New York, 1919), 154–55.

THE KNIGHTS OF LABOR AND THE TRADE UNIONS, 1878-1886   *Gerald N. Grob*

I

The year 1886 was destined to be a crucial one in the history of the American labor movement. The eight-hour crusade, the numerous strikes, the Haymarket bomb, the entrance of workingmen into the political arena at the state and national levels, and the mushroom growth of labor organizations all contributed to the agitation and excitement of the year. Yet the importance of these events was overshadowed by a development that was to have such far-reaching implications that it would determine the future of the labor movement for the succeeding half century. That development was the declaration of war by the trade unions against the reform unionism of the Knights of Labor.

The struggle between the Knights and the other unions represented a clash of two fundamentally opposing ideologies. The Knights of Labor, on the one hand, grew out of the reform and humanitarian movements of ante-bellum America, and was the direct descendent, through the National Labor Union, of the labor reform tradition of the Jacksonian era. Banking on the leveling influence of technological change, its leaders sought to organize the entire producing class into a single irresistible coalition that would work toward the abolition of the wage system and the establishment of a new society. "We do not believe," a high official of the Knights remarked, "that the emancipation of labor will come with increased wages and a reduction in the hours of labor; we must go deeper than that, and this matter will not be settled until the wage system is abolished." [1] The leaders of the Knights therefore emphasized education and co-operation, and they bitterly opposed their constituents' participation in such affairs as the Southwest and stockyards strikes of 1886, as well as the very popular eight-hour movement of that same year.

[1] *The Laster*, IV (Nov. 15, 1891), 3.

REPRINTED with permission from Gerald N. Grob, "The Knights of Labor and the Trade Unions, 1878–1886," *Journal of Economic History*, Vol. XVIII (June 1958), pp. 176–92.

The reform ideology of the Knights, in turn, had an important impact upon the development of its structure, which followed a heterogeneous rather than a homogeneous pattern. Minimizing the utility of organization along trade lines, the Order emphasized instead the grouping of all workers, regardless of craft, into a single body.[2] Highest priority therefore was given to the mixed local assembly, which included all workers irrespective of their trade or degree of skill. Neither a trade, plant, nor industrial union, the mixed assembly could never be more than a study or debating group. Including many diverse elements (even employers), it could not adapt itself to meet the problems of a specific industry or trade. The mixed assembly might agitate for reform or participate in politics, but it could never become the collective bargaining representative of its members.

Given the predominance of the mixed over the trade local, the structure of the Knights inevitably developed along geographical rather than jurisdictional lines, and the district assembly, which included mixed as well as trade locals, became the most characteristic form of organization. The highest governmental body of the Knights—the General Assembly —was not intended as a medium for collective bargaining. Indeed, its very inclusiveness precluded such a possibility.

The trade unions, on the other hand, rejected the broad reform goals of the Knights, emphasizing instead higher wages, shorter hours, and job control. Such objectives were clearly incompatible with an organizational structure such as that developed by the Knights. Eschewing the multitrade local that had been so prevalent during the 1860's and was being perpetuated by the Order, the trade unions began to stress the craft-industrial form of organization both at the local and national levels. A relative scarcity of labor, together with a rapidly expanding economy, had created a favorable environment for the trade unions. Gambling on the hope that the rise of a national market made organization along trade rather than geographical lines more effective, union leaders chose to concentrate upon the task of organizing the workers along trade lines into unions designed for collective bargaining rather than social reform.[3]

Therefore, given the inherent differences in ideology and structure, the conflict between the Knights and the trade unions was, if not inevitable, certainly not an unexpected or surprising development.[4] Un-

[2] For the antitrade unionism of the national leadership of the Knights see the *Journal of United Labor,* I (June 15, 1880), 21 (hereinafter cited as *JUL*); Knights of Labor, *Proceedings of the General Assembly,* 1880, p. 169; 1884, pp. 716–17; 1897, p. 37 (hereinafter cited as K. of L., *GA Proc.*); Terence V. Powderly, *Thirty Years of Labor: 1859 to 1889* (Columbus: Excelsior Publishing House, 1889), pp. 155–56; Powderly Letter Books, Catholic University of America, Washington, D.C.; Powderly to James Rogers, Dec. 19, 1892; Gerald N. Grob, "Terence V. Powderly and the Knights of Labor," *Mid-America,* XXXIX (January 1957), 41–42.
[3] See Lloyd Ulman, *The Rise of the National Trade Union* (Cambridge: Harvard University Press, 1955), pp. 348–77.
[4] See Carroll D. Wright, "An Historical Sketch of the Knights of Labor," *Quarterly Journal of Economics,* I (Jan. 1887), 155; *Cigar Makers' Official Journal,* XI (June 1886), 6; *The Carpenter,* VI (Feb. 1886), 4 (Apr. 1886), 4.

doubtedly the antagonistic personalities of partisans on both sides has-tened an open rift.[5] Yet the hostilities between the Knights and the trade unions cannot be explained solely in terms of personalities, for the con-flict was not simply a struggle for power between two rivals. It was a clash between two fundamentally different ideologies—with the future of the labor movement at stake.

II

The contest between trade unionists and reformers for control of the labor movement developed on two planes. Commencing first as an in-ternal struggle within the Knights, it eventually expanded and soon in-volved the national unions. Within the Knights the struggle revolved around the unresolved question as to which form of organization best met working-class necessities. On the surface the issue of mixed versus trade locals was simply a structural problem. In reality, however, the differences between the two forms indicated the existence of a funda-mental cleavage in ultimate objectives, for the mixed assembly could be utilized only for reform or political purposes, while the trade assembly was generally a collective bargaining organization.

Although the national leadership of the Knights regarded the mixed assembly as the ideal type of unit, a large proportion of its local assem-blies were trade rather than mixed. The first local, composed of garment cutters, was strictly craft, and remained so to the end. Most of the other locals that followed were also trade assemblies.[6] On January 1, 1882, ac-cording to the *Journal of United Labor,* there were 27 working districts and over 400 local assemblies. Of the latter, 318 were trade and only 116 were mixed. Thirteen additional districts, not functioning, had 53 trade and 87 mixed locals, attesting to the relative instability of the mixed form of organization. Of the 135 locals attached directly to the General As-sembly, 67 were trade and 68 were mixed.[7]

Despite the wide latitude given them to organize trade local assem-blies, the trade element within the Knights nevertheless found it difficult to function efficiently. Local trade assemblies, no matter how inclusive in their particular area, were often ineffective when operating in a market that was regional or national rather than local in character. So long as employers could find a ready supply of nonunion labor elsewhere, efforts at collective bargaining by locals would be ineffective. The only solution lay in national organization, and the trade exponents within the Knights pressed for national and regional trade districts that would transcend the limited geographical area normally encompassed by the local or district assembly.

[5] Norman J. Ware emphasized the importance of conflicting personalities. Ware, *The Labor Movement in the United States, 1860–1895* (New York: D. Appleton and Company, 1929), pp. 162–63, *et passim.*
[6] See Wright, "An Historical Sketch: Knights of Labor," p. 146.
[7] Ware, *Labor Movement,* p. 158. The statistics on trade locals in the Knights are unsatisfactory and misleading, since many of them admitted workers belonging to different trades.

The General Assembly, therefore, meeting in January 1879, authorized the establishment of autonomous national trade districts within the framework of the Knights. But only nine months later the Assembly completely reversed itself by declaring that trade locals were "contrary to the spirit and genius of the Order," and it returned exclusive jurisdiction over all locals to the district assembly of their area.[8]

In December 1881, however, the Federation of Organized Trades and Labor Unions, predecessor of the American Federation of Labor (A.F. of L.), held its first convention. Of the 107 delegates present, no less than 50 came from the Knights.[9]

The following September the General Assembly heard the secretary of the Knights warn that trade sentiment was growing rapidly. "Many Trades Unions have also written me," he remarked, "stating that they were seriously meditating the propriety of coming over to us in a body, freely expressing the opinion that their proper place was in our Order." [10] To prevent any mass exodus from the Order to the rival Federation, and also to recruit members from the trade unions, the General Assembly enacted legislation authorizing and encouraging the formation of national and regional trade districts. This move was reaffirmed and even extended at the meetings of the General Assembly in 1884 and 1886.[11]

While permissible, at least in theory, the establishment of trade districts was not a simple matter. The basic philosophy of the Knights militated against organization along craft lines, and the establishment of autonomous trade units within the framework of the Order aroused strong opposition. "I do not favor the establishment of any more National Trade Districts," Terence V. Powderly, head of the Knights from 1879 to 1893, told the General Assembly in 1885, "they are a step backward." [12] Other reform unionists, echoing Powderly's sentiments, charged that trade districts violated the fundamental principles of the Knights.[13] Holding tenaciously to their reform concepts, the leaders of the Knights were insistent in their demands that organization should not proceed along trade lines.

Applicants for trade districts therefore could not always be certain that charters would be granted them, even though they had met all the formal requirements. In some cases charters were granted without any questions. Window Glass Workers' Local Assembly (L.A.) 300 was chartered as a national trade district at a time when such districts were contrary to the laws of the Knights, and the telegraphers were organized nationally in 1882 as District Assembly (D.A.) 45. For a while these two were the only national districts, although before 1886 there were two dis-

[8] K. of L., *GA Proc.*, Jan. 1879, pp. 69–70, 72; Sept. 1879, pp. 98, 129.
[9] Federation of Organized Trades, *Proceedings*, 1881, pp. 7–9 (1905 reprinting).
[10] K. of L., *GA Proc.*, 1882, pp. 296–98. See also the statement of the General Executive Board in *ibid.*, p. 334.
[11] *Ibid.*, pp. 364, 368; 1884, pp. 705–07, 776; 1886, pp. 265–66.
[12] *Ibid.*, 1885, p. 25.
[13] See the *JUL*, VII (June 25, 1886), 2100; *John Swinton's Paper*, Sept. 6, 1885; K. of L., *GA Proc.*, 1884, pp. 716–17.

trict assemblies composed of miners, five of shoemakers, three of railroad employees, and one each of printers, plumbers, leather workers, government employees, and streetcar employees. Between 1883 and 1885 the General Assembly went on record as favoring the establishment of trade districts of shoemakers, plate-glass workers, and plumbers.[14] On the other hand, after sanctioning the formation of builders' districts in 1882, it refused the following year to permit these districts to be represented on the General Executive Board.[15] Even while passing legislation authorizing trade districts, the General Assembly refused to allow woodworkers, cigarmakers, and carpenters to organize trade districts. Furthermore, it passed a resolution stating that no charter for a trade district would be granted unless the applicants could demonstrate to the satisfaction of the General Executive Board that the craft could not be effectively organized under the system of mixed or territorial districts.[16] The attitude of the board, however, was often conditioned by the antitrade unionism of its officers. In 1886, for example, it refused to sanction the request of five building trade locals that they be permitted to withdraw from D.A. 66 and organize their own district. At the same time it empowered a New Hampshire local to change from a trade to a mixed assembly.[17]

Trade units, generally speaking, were authorized usually in efforts to attract workers to join the Knights. Thus the International Trunkmakers' Union came into the Order as a trade district.[18] Once inside, however, workers found it considerably more difficult to secure trade charters. After affiliating in 1882, to cite one case, the plumbers later left the Knights when they encountered difficulty in obtaining a charter for a national trade district, and they established the International Association of Journeymen Plumbers, Steam Fitters, and Gas Fitters.[19]

The hostility of the national leadership of the Knights was not the sole obstacle to the formation of trade units. Mixed and territorial districts, which were first in the field and were already established as functioning organizations, were also antagonistic toward trade districts. If the latter were formed, not only would a mixed district suffer a loss of membership to a trade district, but it would also surrender its absolute jurisdiction over a given territorial area, since the autonomous trade district would exercise control over the entire craft in that area.

The General Assembly and the General Executive Board often supported the mixed and territorial districts in disputes with trade districts. Frequently the district's consent was a prerequisite to secession and the

[14] K. of L., GA Proc., 1883, pp. 438, 443, 502; 1884, p. 787; 1885, pp. 127, 133; JUL, V (Dec. 10, 1884), 856.
[15] K. of L., GA Proc., 1882, pp. 325, 347; 1883, pp. 445, 498.
[16] Ibid., 1882, pp. 311, 351; 1883, pp. 439-40, 498, 502.
[17] Ibid., 1886, pp. 126-27.
[18] Ibid., 1883, p. 506; 1884, p. 619. This was also the case in the affiliation of the harness workers. JUL, IV (June 1883), 511; (July 1883), 520-21. The Knights also aided the barbers, horse railway men, miners, railway men, and ax makers in attempts to get them to join.
[19] New York Bureau of Labor Statistics, Annual Report, V (1887), 202-03.

establishment of a trade district. This consent was not easily obtained. In 1886 D.A. 30 of Massachusetts turned down an application by four of its locals for permission to withdraw and form a national trade assembly of rubber workers.[20] While the General Assembly supported a district court decision that members of trade locals could not be compelled to join mixed locals, the General Executive Board refused to force trade members of mixed locals to transfer to trade assemblies.[21]

Even after obtaining a charter, trade districts encountered difficulties with the mixed district in their areas. Dual jurisdiction often led to friction, though in theory the system of mixed and trade districts appeared perfectly harmonious and compatible. For example, D.A. 64 of New York City, composed of workers in the printing and publishing business, became embroiled in a rivalry with D.A. 49 (mixed). In 1883 D.A. 64 failed to get exclusive jurisdiction over all workers in the trade. Soon afterward D.A. 49 charged that the printers were accepting locals not of their trade, and that these locals had also withdrawn from D.A. 49 without permission. An investigation by the secretary of the General Executive Board disclosed that D.A. 64 had been initiating lithographers, typefounders, pressmen, and feeders in order to strengthen itself as a bargaining unit, and that it had not engaged in raiding forays against D.A. 49. Although the Board upheld D.A. 64, the decision did not resolve the rivalry, and the two districts continued their feud.[22]

With the single exception of L.A. 300, trade districts did not enjoy any appreciable measure of success between 1878 and 1885.[23] The far-reaching reform goals of the Knights and its structural inclusiveness left the advocates of trade organization in the position of a perpetual minority. The expansion of the Knights into the more sparsely populated regions of the South and West, moreover, further diminished trade influence, since the mixed assembly was dominant in rural areas. Lacking a majority, the trade members were unable to establish a central strike fund or concentrate on collective bargaining, and they found that their immediate goals were being subordinated to and sacrificed for more utopian objectives.

III

The struggle between trade unionists and reformers within the Knights, however, was completely overshadowed by the rupture of relations in 1886 between the Knights and the national unions. The latter,

---

[20] *Quarterly Report of District Assembly No. 30 . . . July . . . 1886* (Boston, 1886), p. 69. For a somewhat similar case see New York Bureau of Labor Statistics, *Annual Report*, V (1887), 202–04.

[21] K. of L., *GA Proc.*, 1885, pp. 102–03, 140; 1886, p. 130.

[22] *Ibid.*, 1883, pp. 467, 508; 1884, p. 617; 1885, pp. 125, 135; 1887, pp. 1714, 1757.

[23] Even the successful career of L.A. 300 cannot be attributed to the Knights. It was due primarily to the skilled nature of the trade which permitted the window glass workers to organize thoroughly, restrict output, and regulate apprenticeship requirements. See Pearce Davis, *The Development of the American Glass Industry* (Cambridge: Harvard University Press, 1949), pp. 126–30.

stronger and more cohesive than the trade districts of the Order, were better able to take the lead in the conflict between reform and trade unionism. Disillusioned with labor reformism, the trade unions acted upon the premise that the traditional programs of the past were no longer suitable to the changing environment, and they led the assault against the Knights of Labor in 1886.

During the early 1880's, however, it was by no means evident that the Knights and the national unions were predestined to clash. The Federation of Organized Trades and Labor Unions permitted district assemblies of the Knights to be represented at its annual conventions,[24] and many trade union leaders also belonged to the Order.[25] Local unions and assemblies often co-operated in joint boycotts, and expressions of friendliness by the national unions toward Powderly and other officials of the Knights were not uncommon.[26] The International Typographical Union expressed appreciation in 1882 for the aid given it by the Knights in a number of cities, and then went on to adopt resolutions recommending co-operation with other labor organizations and permitting its members to join any body that would further the interests of the craft in their particular locality.[27] In other words, the national unions regarded the Knights as a valuable economic ally.

In turn, the Knights vehemently denied having any hostile designs upon the trade unions, and in a number of prominent cases before 1885 it acted accordingly.[28] Nevertheless, with its structural inclusiveness and reform ideology, it was perhaps inevitable that the Order, in its efforts to bring all workingmen into a single organization, would undercut trade union organizational efforts. Thus the General Assembly authorized a committee in 1883 to confer with union representatives in the hope of incorporating all the trade unions within the Knights.[29]

In the absence of any national or international union, the absorption of local unions by the Knights in the form of trade assemblies created no friction. Indeed, isolated local unions were eager to affiliate with such a powerful national organization.[30] By 1886, therefore, the Knights claimed nearly eleven hundred local assemblies, many of which undoubtedly represented local trade unions having no parent national union.

[24] Federation of Organized Trades, *Proceedings,* 1882, pp. 5, 16, 20, 23.
[25] For a partial list of trade union leaders belonging to the Knights see *The Painter,* II (Feb. 1888), 3.
[26] See *Iron Molders' Journal,* XIX (June 30, 1883), 9; XX (June 30, 1884), 10; XXI (Nov. 30, 1885), 14; Amalgamated Association of Iron and Steel Workers, *Proceedings,* 1882, p. 955; *The Craftsman,* II (Jan. 17, 1885), 2 (Aug. 15, 1885), 2.
[27] International Typographical Union, *Proceedings,* 1882, pp. 43, 58, 62, 78, 83, 87.
[28] See K. of L., *GA Proc.,* 1882, p. 270; 1884, pp. 707, 787; 1885, pp. 73, 138.
[29] *Ibid.,* 1883, pp. 460, 467, 505–06. See also Powderly Letter Books, Powderly to J. P. McDonnell, Sept. 24, 1882.
[30] Ohio Bureau of Labor Statistics, *Annual Report,* IX (1885), 28; Grace H. Stimson, *Rise of the Labor Movement in Los Angeles* (Berkeley: University of California Press, 1955), p. 45.

When, however, the Knights began to organize workingmen in trades already having national organizations, friction was quick to arise. The trouble that followed the Order's expansion into the realm of the trade unions was not simply a jurisdictional rivalry between similar organizations. As discussed above, the Order and the national unions had opposing conceptions of the legitimate functions of the labor movement, which in turn had led to different structural forms. The expansion of the Order's mixed units thus served to undermine the economic functions of the trade unions, since the heterogeneous character of the former prevented them from exercising any appreciable degree of economic power. Furthermore, the structural diversity of the Knights caused trouble when its trade assemblies sought to perform tasks that logically fell within the purview of the trade unions.[31] The national unions, moreover, took the position that geographical trade assemblies were inadequate to meet the challenge of a nationalized economy, and in fact were little better than mixed district assemblies. In defense, union officials generally refused to consent to a mutual recognition of working cards,[32] and they demanded that the Knights cease interfering in trade affairs.[33]

The Knights, however, did not heed the warnings of the national unions, and its organizers continued their sporadic work in trades having national unions. "Every week," John Swinton reported in 1885, "Trades Unions are turned into Local Assemblies, or Assemblies are organized out of Trade Unions." [34] As early as 1881 a district leader attempted to capture a typographical union local, and by 1884 there were over forty local assemblies of printers in the Knights.[35] The overzealous activities of the Order's organizers also led to trouble with the Bricklayers and Masons International Union.[36]

The trade unions continuously charged that the Order had accepted scabs and unfair workers.[37] It is probable that the unions greatly exaggerated this grievance, but there is little doubt that the existence of two labor organizations, each purporting to accomplish different ends, cre-

[31] Differences over wages, hours, and working conditions frequently ensued between trade assemblies and local and national unions, especially since no formal coordinating bodies existed. For an example of such a disagreement see K. of L., GA Proc., 1884, pp. 703, 764, 768.
[32] Iron Molders' International Union, Proceedings, 1882, pp. 15, 54–55.
[33] See the National Labor Tribune, July 7, 1883, cited in John R. Commons, ed., History of Labour in the United States (4 vols: New York: Macmillan Company, 1918–1935), II, 353. "With other trade unionists," Gompers recalled, "I joined the Knights of Labor for the purpose of confining that organization to theoretical educational work and to see that the Trade Unions were protected from being undermined or disrupted." Gompers Letter Books, A.F. of L.–C.I.O. Building, Washington, D.C., Gompers to N. E. Mathewson, Oct. 10, 1890.
[34] John Swinton's Paper, Apr. 12, 1885.
[35] JUL, II (Sept.–Oct. 1881), 158; John Swinton's Paper, Mar. 2, 1884.
[36] Bricklayers and Masons International Union, Proceedings, 1884, p. 9; Powderly Papers, Henry O. Cole to Powderly, Mar. 9, Apr. 28, 1883.
[37] The Carpenter, III (Feb. 1883), 3; International Typographical Union, Proceedings, 1884, p. 12.

ated a disciplinary problem. Intraunion disagreements frequently concluded with one party seceding and joining the Order as a local assembly. Thus the trade unions found that the Knights were attracting dissidents who normally might have remained in the union.[38]

Despite the proselytizing activities of the Knights, there was no general conflict with the other unions before July 1885. At this time the membership of the Order was slightly over 100,000, and examples of clashes with the trade union were generally the exception rather than the rule. When differences did arise, the trade unions often made conciliatory efforts at peaceful adjustment. Thus the convention of the International Typographical Union agreed in 1884 to its president's suggestion that he confer with Powderly in order to iron out existing grievances, although it refused to sanction a proposed amalgamation with the Order.[39]

In only one major case—that involving the Cigar Makers International Union—did the differences between a national union and the Knights erupt in open hostilities before 1886. Historians, placing much emphasis upon this particular conflict, have credited Adolph Strasser and Samuel Gompers, the leaders of the Cigar Makers, with the dual responsibility of helping to precipitate the internecine war between the national unions and the Knights, and then founding the A.F. of L. as a rival national federation.[40]

While the national unions generally supported the Cigar Makers in its struggle with the Knights,[41] it is improbable that sympathy for the Cigar Makers would have led to a fight with the Order. Undoubtedly Strasser and Gompers exerted great efforts to induce the unions to lend them support. The fact is also incontrovertible that both were determined, forceful, and sometimes ruthless men. Nevertheless, their efforts would have been useless unless a solid basis of discontent had already existed. In other words, for the unions to break with the Knights, there must have been more compelling reasons than simply the activities of two individuals.

IV

To understand the conflict that split the labor movement, the rapid growth of the Knights after 1885 must be examined. In the twelve months between July 1885 and June 1886 the Order's membership increased from 100,000 to over 700,000. This growth, at least in part, came

[38] For typical examples see *The Carpenter*, III (Oct. 1883), 2; VI (Mar. 1886), 4; VIII (Feb. 15, 1888), 1; Robert A. Christie, *Empire in Wood: A History of the Carpenters' Union* (Ithaca: Cornell University Press, 1956), pp. 50–51; *John Swinton's Paper*, Feb. 1, 8, 1885; K. of L., *GA Proc.*, 1885, pp. 106, 109, 140.
[39] International Typographical Union, *Proceedings*, 1884, pp. 12, 65–66, 70, 72, 102.
[40] See especially Ware, *Labor Movement*, pp. 258–79, 285, *et passim*, and Commons, *History of Labour*, II, 401–02.
[41] *Iron Molders' Journal*, XXII (Mar. 31, 1886), 14; *The Craftsman*, III (Aug. 7, 1886), 2.

about at the expense of the other unions. In many cases workers abandoned their trade unions to join the Knights. The Journeymen Tailors National Union found that many of its locals had transferred to the Knights, resulting in a considerable loss of membership. A vice-president of the Amalgamated Association of Iron and Steel Workers complained in 1886 that some sublodges in his area had been disbanded because of inroads by the Order.[42] Further difficulty was caused by overzealous organizers who made determined efforts to transform trade unions into local assemblies. In February 1886 the secretary of the Journeymen Bakers National Union protested against such activities. "We never knew," responded the secretary-treasurer of the Knights, "that the K. of L. was proscribed from bringing into its fold all branches of honorable toil." [43]

The Knights, in other words, had adopted an organizational policy diametrically different from that of the trade unions. The traditional concept of organization held by the A.F. of L. (the representative of the trade unions) required that federal labor unions (local units including workers of all trades having no separate unions of their own) be splintered into separate homogeneous craft units as soon as there were enough workers in that locality to form such bodies. The aim of such a policy was to develop the collective bargaining potentialities of the various trades. The Knights, on the other hand, sought to reverse this strategy and proceed in the opposite direction, and it encouraged the combining of trade units into mixed assemblies, which at most were reform or political units. Beneath the structural and organizational differences of the two groups, therefore, lay opposing goals.

To what extent did the Knights encroach upon the domain of the trade unions? Peter J. McGuire of the Carpenters claimed that between 150 and 160 trade unions, including the Molders, Boiler-Makers, Bakers, Miners, Typographical, and Granite Cutters, had grievances against the Order.[44] Only in the case of the Bricklayers and Masons International Union, however, is the evidence fairly complete. In response to a survey conducted in the summer of 1886, the union's secretary received eighty-seven replies. Eight locals reported the existence of bricklayers and masons assemblies within their jurisdiction, four claimed the Knights were working for subunion wages, and three asserted the Knights were working longer hours. "But there are a large number of such men scattered throughout the country who belong to mixed assemblies," the secretary reported—and herein lay the union's major grievance.[45] The complaints of the Bricklayers and Masons were echoed by most of the other major national unions.[46]

[42] John B. Lennon, "Journeymen Tailors," *American Federationist*, IX (Sept. 1902), 599; Amalgamated Association of Iron and Steel Workers, *Proceedings*, 1886, p. 1793.
[43] New Haven *Workmen's Advocate*, Dec. 10, 1887.
[44] K. of L., *GA Proc.*, 1886 special session, pp. 50–51.
[45] Bricklayers and Masons International Union, *Proceedings*, 1887, pp. 70–75.
[46] *Iron Molders' Journal*, XXII (Feb. 28, 1886), 10, 14, (Apr. 30, 1886), 8 (Aug.

In general, the national unions were fearful of the Knights for two closely related reasons. The mixed assembly, in the first place, was incompatible with trade union goals. In theory both structural forms could exist side by side, each pursuing its own ends. Thus the mixed assembly could concentrate on reform and politics, while the trade unions could develop their collective bargaining functions. This *modus vivendi,* however, presupposed that workers could belong simultaneously to both trade unions and mixed assemblies. At a time when the labor movement's primary problem was to organize and stay organized, such an assumption was unwarranted, and trade union leaders recognized the mutual hostility of the mixed assembly and trade union.

In the second place, trade union officials opposed the chartering of trade assemblies within the Knights for the reason that these units had proved incapable of developing collective bargaining and other union institutions. Furthermore, the geographical and regional organization of the Knights meant that there was little hope for the mature evolution of the national trade assembly. Since local trade assemblies were often ineffective when operating in an environment marked by a nationalized economy and the geographical mobility of labor, trade unions leaders argued that these units were attempting to perform functions that logically belonged to the national unions, and in the long run tended to undermine the standards of membership and employment that the unions had struggled so fiercely to establish.[47]

By the spring of 1886 relations between the trade unions and the Knights had so deteriorated that a collision appeared imminent.[48] Five prominent unionists therefore called for a meeting of union leaders to arrange a settlement of differences, while at the same time Powlerly summoned the General Assembly in a special session to consider, among other things, the troubles with the trade unions. The conference of trade union officials then appointed a committee of five to draw up a plan of settlement. Under the moderating influence of McGuire, who played the leading role, the committee drew up a "treaty," which it submitted to the General Executive Board of the Knights on May 25, 1886.[49]

By the terms of this treaty the Knights would refrain from organizing any trade having a national organization, and also would revoke

---

31, 1886), 6; XXIII (Dec. 31, 1886), 7; *The Craftsman,* III (May 15, 1886), 3; *Granite Cutters' Journal,* X (Apr. 1886), 3; *The Carpenter,* VI (May 1886), 2; *Cigar Makers' Official Journal,* XI (Apr. 1886), 6; *Printers' Circular,* XXI (June 1886), 66; International Typographical Union, *Proceedings,* 1886, pp. 90, 93–94; Iron Molders International Union, *Proceedings,* 1886, pp. 16, 25, 31.

[47] See *The Craftsman,* III (Feb. 6, 1886), 2 (Mar. 20, 1886), 1; *The Carpenter,* XXIV (Dec. 1904), 5.

[48] *John Swinton's Paper,* Mar. 21, 1886; Illinois Bureau of Labor Statistics, *Biennial Report,* IV (1886), 160–61.

[49] Bricklayers and Masons International Union, *Proceedings,* 1887, pp. 63–66; *The Carpenter,* VI (May 1886), 2 (June 1886), 3; *Cigar Makers' Official Journal,* XI (June 1886), 7; K. of L., *GA Proc.,* 1886 special session, pp. 1–2; Powderly Letter Books, Powderly to P. J. McGuire and Adolph Strasser, May 11, 1886.

the charter of any existing trade assembly having a parent union. In the second place, any workers guilty of ignoring trade union wage scales, scabbing, or any other offense against a union, would be ineligible for membership in the Order. Third, any organizer who tampered with or interfered in the internal affairs of trade unions would have his commission revoked. Finally, local and district assemblies were not to interfere while trade unions engaged in strikes or lockouts, and the Knights would not be permitted to issue any label or trade-mark where a national union had already done so.[50]

On the surface it appears surprising that the trade unions, which claimed to represent about 350,000 workers (although their actual membership was about 160,000), would present such a document to an organization having 700,000 members. Yet the treaty was neither a bargaining offer nor a declaration of war.[51] It was rather the logical outcome of the duality that had pervaded the labor movement since the Civil War. Under its terms the labor movement would be divided into two separate and distinct compartments. The Knights of Labor, on the one hand, would continue its efforts to abolish the wage system, reform society, and educate the working class. The national unions, on the other hand, would be left paramount in the economic field, and the Order would no longer be permitted to exercise any control over wages, hours, working conditions, or the process of collective bargaining. In other words, trade unionism and reform unionism had come to a parting of the ways.

In one sense the treaty was an expression of the fear of the skilled workers that they were being subordinated to the interests of the unskilled.[52] Yet the polarization implied in such an intepretation should not be exaggerated, for it cannot be said that the Knights themselves represented the unskilled workers. The Order was not an industrial union, nor did it emphasize collective bargaining. It was rather a heterogeneous mass that subordinated the economic functions of labor organizations to its primary goal of reforming society. The mixed assembly, while including workers of all trades and callings, was in no sense an industrial union, since it was not organized either by industry or factory. Moreover, the trade unions had never excluded the unskilled from the labor movement; they simply maintained that organization along craft lines was historically correct. "In truth," remarked Gompers, "the trade union is nothing more or less than the organization of wage earners engaged in a given employment, whether skilled or unskilled, for the purpose of at-

[50] A.F. of L., *Proceedings*, 1886, p. 16 (1905–06 reprinting).
[51] Cf. Ware, *Labor Movement*, p. 284.
[52] Perlman has interpreted the conflict between the Knights and unions largely as one between skilled and unskilled workers. Commons, *History of Labour*, II, 396–97. Undoubtedly the skilled workers feared the Knights. The Knights, however, was not necessarily an organization of unskilled workers, as the large number of trade assemblies would indicate. While the unions jealously guarded their autonomy and independence, the conflict that developed in 1886 was more than simply a struggle between the skilled and unskilled, although this aspect was an important element.

taining the best possible reward, [and] the best attainable conditions for the workers in that trade or calling." [53]

The General Assembly of the Knights, in turn, submitted its own proposals to the union committee. Its terms included protection against unfair workers, a mutual exchange of working cards, and the holding of a joint conference before either organization presented wages and hours demands to employers.[54] Clearly the Assembly's position was in fundamental disagreement with that of the trade unions. The latter had demanded unitary control over the economic field, while the Knights had demanded equal jurisdiction over membership and working standards. Thus neither side evinced willingness to compromise over basic issues.

Although failing to conclude a settlement with the trade unions, the special session of the General Assembly did not close the door to further negotiations. For the time being, therefore, the conflict remained in abeyance. While matters were pending, however, the Knights made a determined effort to end friction by intensifying its campaign to bring the national unions under its control. The national unions, however, recognized that the structure of the Knights was incompatible with trade union objectives, and the policy of the Order was only partially successful. Some of the smaller unions, including the Seamen's Benevolent Union, the Eastern Glass Bottle Blowers' League, and the Western Green Bottle Blowers' Association, joined the Knights.[55] The American Flint Glass Workers Union, on the other hand, refused to go along with the other glassworkers because of an earlier dispute with the Order.[56] In New York City the Knights made a determined but unsuccessful attempt to capture the German shoemakers and the Associated Jewelers.[57] Most of the larger and more important unions emphatically rejected the Order's overtures. The members of the Amalgamated Association of Iron and Steel Workers overwhelmingly defeated a referendum on the subject, while a similar poll conducted by the secretary of the Bricklayers and Masons resulted in the same conclusion. The Iron Molders' convention turned down the merger proposal by a vote of 114 to 27.[58] Furthermore,

[53] Gompers Letter Books, Gompers to George H. Daggett, Jan. 4, 1896. See also Gompers to Albert C. Stevens, Nov. 1, 1889; Gompers to Frank D. Hamlin, May 6, 1890; Gompers to Charles W. Nelson, Apr. 29, 1892.
[54] K. of L., *GA Proc.*, 1886 special session, pp. 53, 55, 67.
[55] *JUL*, VIII (Aug. 20, 1887), 2476; K. of L., *GA Proc.*, 1887, p. 1334; *John Swinton's Paper*, July 25, 1886; David A. McCabe, *The Standard Rate in American Trade Unions* (Baltimore: The Johns Hopkins Press, 1912), pp. 155–56. The glassworkers probably joined the Order in the hope of emulating the success of L.A. 300.
[56] *Iron Molders' Journal*, XXII (Feb. 28, 1886), 10; *Cigar Makers' Official Journal*, XI (Aug. 1886), 6; Secretary of Internal Affairs of the Commonwealth of Pennsylvania, *Annual Report*, XVI (1888), Pt. III, Section F, pp. 18–19.
[57] *The Carpenter*, VI (Oct. 1886), 1.
[58] Amalgamated Association of Iron and Steel Workers, *Proceedings*, 1886, pp. 1807–08, 1818–19, 1846; 1887, pp. 1959–62; Bricklayers and Masons International

the Typographical Union, the Carpenters, the Plumbers and Gas Fitters, the coal miners, and the Stationary Engineers all rejected the invitation to join the Knights.[59]

At the regular meeting of the General Assembly in October 1886 further negotiations between the trade unions and the Knights again ended in failure. The action by the Assembly in ordering all workers holding cards in both the Knights and the Cigar Makers International Union to leave the latter under pain of expulsion [60] was interpreted by both sides as constituting a final break and an open declaration of war.[61] The trade union committee therefore issued a call on November 10, 1886, for all unions to send representatives to a convention in Columbus, Ohio, on December 8, to form an "American Federation or Alliance of all National and International Trade Unions." Out of this meeting came the A.F. of L. Completely dominated by the national unions, the December convention excluded assemblies of the Knights from membership, and then proceeded to establish the new organization on a firm foundation.[62]

Thus by the end of 1886 the die had been cast, and the Knights and national unions prepared for war. Why had all negotiations failed? Undoubtedly the intractability of leaders on both sides contributed to the difficulties, but there were also those who had made sincere efforts to head off the impending conflict. The trade unions, furthermore, had encountered jurisdictional rivalries with the Knights, but this has been an endemic problem of the labor movement, and one which has not always had an unhappy ending.

The conflict between the Knights and the trade unions, then, had a much broader significance than the negotiations between them indicated, and represented the culmination of decades of historical development. The Knights, growing out of the humanitarian and reform crusades of ante-bellum America, emphasized the abolition of the wage system and the reorganization of society. To achieve this purpose it insisted on the prime importance of the mixed assembly, which would serve as the nucleus of an organization dedicated to reform. The trade unions, on the other hand, accepted their environment, and sought to take advantage of the relative scarcity of labor and the rising scale of production. Hence they emphasized the collective bargaining functions of labor organizations, thus tacitly accepting the workers' wage status.

Perhaps grounds for compromise did exist, but neither side was

---

Union, *Proceedings*, 1887, pp. 71, 76; Iron Molders International Union, *Proceedings*, 1886, pp. 17–20.

[59] *John Swinton's Paper*, June 20, 1886; *The Carpenter*, VI (Oct. 1886), 1. See also *Locomotive Firemen's Magazine*, X (Mar. 1886), 141.

[60] K. of L., *GA Proc.*, 1886, pp. 200, 282.

[61] See Joseph R. Buchanan, *The Story of a Labor Agitator* (New York: The Outlook Company, 1903), p. 314.

[62] Bricklayers and Masons International Union, *Proceedings*, 1887, pp. 79–80; A.F. of L., *Proceedings*, 1886, pp. 13–15. A committee from the Knights was also present at the trade union convention in December 1886 but no agreement was reached. See A.F. of L., *Proceedings*, 1886, pp. 17–18; K. of L., *GA Proc.*, 1887, pp. 1445–47.

prone to make any concessions. The national unions, by insisting upon strict trade autonomy as a *sine qua non* of settlement, were in effect demanding that the Knights should virtually abandon any pretense at being a bona fide labor organization. It is true that the unions could have organized as national autonomous trade districts if the Knights had been ready to grant permission. The leaders of the Knights, however, were unwilling to permit their organization to be transformed into what the A.F. of L. ultimately became. Indeed, after 1886 many national trade districts left the Order because of their inability to function within the framework of that body.[63] The national unions, moreover, were not encouraged by the experiences of trade districts within the Knights before 1886. Finally, there was the simple element of power, and both the trade unions and the Knights, as established organizations, were adamant in their refusal to surrender any part of it.

Between reform and trade unionism, therefore, existed a gulf that the leaders of the 1880's were unable to bridge. By 1886 this chasm had widened to such a degree that co-operation between the two seemed virtually impossible and war seemed to be the only solution. Reform and trade unionism had at last come to a parting of the ways, and upon the outcome of the ensuing struggle hinged the destiny of the American labor movement.

[63] The shoemakers, miners, machinists, garmentworkers, carriage and wagonworkers, and potters all seceded from the Knights after 1886 because of their inability to function efficiently within the existing framework of the Order. For evidence on this point see the following: *The Laster*, I (Mar. 15, 1889), 1; *Shoe Workers' Journal*, XI (July 1910), 11; United Mine Workers of America, *Proceedings*, 1911, I, 581; *JUL*, VIII (May 19, 1888), 1; *Journal of the International Association of Machinists*, VII (July 1895), 238; *Garment Worker*, III (Sept. 1896), 4; *Carriage and Wagon Workers Journal*, II (Jan. 1, 1901), 113; United States Industrial Commission, *Report of the Industrial Commission* (19 vols.: Washington, D.C., 1900–02), XVII, 59, 209; Theodore W. Glocker, *The Government of American Trade Unions* (Baltimore: The Johns Hopkins Press, 1913), p. 54.

Section 4 ～ *Agriculture in the*
Industrializing Economy

Eight ～ *The Mass Marketing of Agricultural Products*

THE INTERNATIONAL MARKET
FOR AGRICULTURAL COMMODITIES,
1850-1873   *Morton Rothstein*

Many economic historians have greeted the idea of a "take-off" period for industrialization with noticeably restrained enthusiasm, and have raised some penetrating questions about the process by which a nation enters such a stage in its development. There is more general agreement that if such a period exists, the United States had entered it by the 1850's. In his engaging and provocative work, Douglass North has stressed the role of agricultural exports in providing the launching pad and the original thrust for the American "take-off." [1] Adopting his schema, we can say that primary exports—particularly agricultural commodities—were crucial for the survival and slow growth of the colonies in the seventeenth and eighteenth centuries, basic for the economic penetration beyond the Atlantic seaboard into the continental land mass during the first half of the nineteenth century, and of diminishing importance after the mid-century point. From that date, foreign trade accounted for a stable pro-

[1] North, *Economic Growth of the United States.*

REPRINTED with permission from Morton Rothstein, "The International Market for Agricultural Commodities, 1850–1873," in D. T. Gilchrist and W. D. Lewis, eds., *Economic Change in the Civil War Era*, Greenville, Del.: Eleutherian Mills-Hagley Foundation, 1966, pp. 62–72.

portion of gross national product and the economy was capable of internally generating its own growth. But if exports were no longer the *sine qua non* of American economic development, they nevertheless attained impressive dimensions from 1850 to the turn of the century. Agricultural commodities comprised between 73 and 83 per cent of the exports in that period, and the rapid increases in shipments of farm products were the major factors in the achievement of a steadily favorable balance of trade by the mid-1870's.[2] This large-scale participation in the international commodity markets acted as an additional "booster" to the flight of the American Gospel-ship of Wealth.

In 1850, American agriculture was on the threshold of its greatest and most rapid expansion. The Mexican War had virtually completed the acquisition of easily exploitable new territories. The settlement process gained additional momentum as it broke into the prairie and plains regions and left behind the requirement of a lifetime's toil to make a farm. Technological innovations in the form of farm implements and machines, as well as railroads and other features of the "Communications Revolution," were beginning the further transformation of farming by increasing productivity and tightening the commercial network. Finally, the repeal of the Corn Laws, and the world-wide tendency toward free trade which it symbolized, promised unlimited foreign markets for the new surpluses created by the mounting agricultural output.

For the next [quarter of a century] American farmers, processors, and merchants found themselves compelled to adjust to the shifting requirements and disciplines imposed by the emerging international economy.

There can be little doubt that the Civil War directly and indirectly contributed to these changes. It is more difficult to judge whether it merely speeded some developments and slowed others, or was itself a basic causal factor. Historians have usually dealt with this subject by reheating old chestnuts about "King Cotton" and "King Wheat" in connection with British neutrality during the conflict.[3] Given the enormous increase in both these crops during the 1850's, and the size of their shipments abroad then and later, there is ample reason to agree with those who claim that the foreign market was the real "king" and that the commodities were the dependent subjects. But the discussion does highlight the shift among the components of agricultural exports. In 1850 cotton was the unchallenged leader, accounting for roughly two-thirds of the value of American agricultural exports. It put on its most dazzling performance during the next decade, when it more than doubled in volume. Grain, both in bulk and as flour, animal products, and tobacco followed

[2] Robert E. Lipsey, *Price and Quantity Trends in the Foreign Trade of the United States* (Princeton, 1963), pp. 45–52.
[3] For the most recent articles on this controversy, with many references to past battles, see Eugene A. Brady, "A Reconsideration of the Lancashire 'Cotton Famine,'" *Agricultural History*, XXXVII (July 1963), 156–62; Robert H. Jones, "Long Live the King?" *ibid.*, 166–69. I have followed the conclusions in Eli Ginzberg, "The Economics of British Neutrality during the Civil War," *Agricultural History*, X (Oct. 1936), 147–56.

well behind, growing at a more moderate pace. But in 1873 cotton shipments had still not recovered their prewar high levels, while exports of grain and animal products more than made up for this loss and were on the eve of their most spectacular growth.[4] Moreover, northern agriculture had also found outlets in Europe for its increasing volume of such perishable commodities as cheese and cattle.[5] This trend would take an additional spurt after the introduction of refrigerated railroad cars and ships in the late 1870's. By that time farmers in all sections of the nation —not just the South—had come to rely upon the international market.

Britain was by far the most important customer and the great center of world trade. Increasingly, consumer preferences in that country were of paramount concern for American processers. Meeting the demands of the "fastidious Britisher" meant that flour millers placed greater emphasis on whiteness and gluten content; hog-packers selected higher grades of the animals they turned into lard, salt pork, and bacon; and cheesemakers strove for a compact product of acceptable color.[6] As the trade in these products grew in volume, a host of other difficulties appeared. It was not only necessary to improve quality in these products, but even more urgent was the need to establish acceptable grades and standards for all agricultural exports so that uniformity of quality could be reasonably assured. These pressures began to mount at a time when improvements in transportation and communication were changing the entire character of both national and international trade. As a result, merchants on both sides of the water adopted new techniques, organized new institutions, and established new relationships to meet these challenges. During the 1850-to-1873 period, an integrated marketing system evolved in the meat and grain trades which helped the Midwestern farmers respond more quickly and efficiently to demand from abroad.

There had been little change in the methods of trading in agricultural products in the century preceding 1850. British merchant shippers dealt through their "correspondents" in the American Atlantic and Gulf ports, placing orders, accepting consignments, and supplying the bulk of commercial credit. In turn, their American counterparts performed similar functions for the merchants and dealers in the hinterland. With the westward push of the agricultural frontier, the number of intermediaries between the farmer and the importer increased. In the grain trade, for example, a New York commission merchant firm like Grinnell, Minturn & Company, agents for Baring Brothers, purchased flour and wheat from New York City dealers or directly from the interior in Albany and Buf-

[4] Lipsey, *Price and Quantity Trends in the Foreign Trade of the U.S.*, pp. 45–52.
[5] Eric E. Lampard, *The Rise of the Dairy Industry in Wisconsin, 1820–1920* (Madison, 1963), pp. 121–26; W. D. Zimmerman, "Live Cattle Export Trade between the United States and Great Britain, 1868–1885," *Agricultural History*, XXXVI (Jan. 1962), 46–52.
[6] John Storck and Walter D. Teague, *Flour for Man's Bread* (Minneapolis, 1952), pp. 197–200, 303–05; Rudolf A. Clemen, *The American Livestock and Meat Industry* (New York, 1923), pp. 95–98, 116–17, 269–70; Lampard, *Rise of the Dairy Industry*, pp. 61–64.

falo, where the local commission merchants received goods from their correspondents in the lake ports of Cleveland, Toledo, or Chicago. In turn, the western merchants bought their produce from local dealers who received goods from other dealers operating in the tributary river and canal towns.[7] In the cotton trade, the same kind of web was spun. Ogden, Ferguson & Company of New York, which dealt with several leading British importers, had correspondents not only in the major ports of New Orleans, Mobile, and Savannah, but also carried on a fairly heavy business with dealers in the interior river towns of the "cotton kingdom." [8] They in turn dealt with the local receivers of cotton at the smaller gathering points in the countryside. At each juncture along its journey to market the bale of cotton, barrel of flour, or bushel of wheat represented one or two additional commissions and handling charges.

The major seaboard merchants, in direct contact with Britain, rarely specialized in individual commodities. Baring Brothers and their agents at various ports dealt in furs, tobacco, and cotton, and in the 1830's added flour and grain to their interests. From 1815 to their demise in 1850, Ogden, Ferguson & Company were heavy importers of iron, chemicals, and other British manufactures, while exporting cotton, grain, and flour. But specialization appeared in the inland cities by 1850, and among the domestic commission merchants of New York during the following decade. A community of cotton merchants had emerged at the major Atlantic ports, along with smaller cadres of grain and flour receivers.[9] Increasingly, the established general merchants confined their activity in the grain trade to periods of high prices and heavy demand.

The achievements of the cotton men in attracting southern cotton to New York has been ably chronicled by Professor Albion.[10] Less appreciated is the work of the grain men in helping to divert western produce from the Mississippi River route to the Great Lakes–Erie Canal outlet. Leading New Yorkers such as David Dows and Jesse Hoyt extended credit to country dealers, warehousemen, and flour millers throughout the Old Northwest. The advances which they provided gave western merchants working capital to handle the growing volume of business without straining their own resources. By the 1870's, Dows and Hoyt had also built warehouses in New York harbor, elevator-warehouses at the major lake ports, and were deeply involved in organizing elevator line companies into the new spring-wheat region.[11] These men were incipi-

[7] Ralph W. Hidy, *The House of Baring in American Trade and Finance*, pp. 105–06, 356–58, 402–03; Thomas D. Odle, "The American Grain Trade of the Great Lakes, 1825–1873," *Inland Seas*, VII (1952), 23–27, 252–54; IX (1953), 53–55.

[8] Ogden, Ferguson & Company Collection, New York Historical Society. This is a recently discovered collection of company and family letters. My general observations here and later in this paper are based on an examination of the incoming correspondence of the firm for the 1840's.

[9] Fred M. Jones, *Middlemen in the Domestic Trade of the United States, 1800–1860* (Urbana, 1937), pp. 303–04.

[10] Robert G. Albion, *The Rise of New York Port* (New York, 1939).

[11] New York Assembly, Special Committee on Railroads [Hepburn Committee], *Pro-*

ent "fobbers," engaged in rationalizing and financing the grain trade with their own resources at every step from the country dealer to the New York ship side. In the same way, the evolution of a railroad network in the 1860's quickly permitted some of the leading western merchants in the grain and provisions trade to bypass the way stations between the western lake ports and the export center at New York. Evidently the profitability of the trade in the forties and fifties had made it possible for these men to accumulate sufficient capital resources to free themselves from the chain of credit typical of the earlier consignment trade. Unlike the export economies of the less advanced nations—and of the South—control of the domestic phase of the trade was completely in the hands of native merchants.[12]

Forces stronger than entrepreneurial leadership also contributed to innovations in grain marketing. With the widening scope of trade in the 1850's and 1860's, the introduction of the telegraph and through bill of lading, and the spread of the elevator system, the old methods of doing business were quickly outmoded. The merchant exchanges of the western commercial centers, founded and dominated for the most part by grain and provision merchants, took the lead in making needed adjustments. For example, the new grain elevators were equipped with highly accurate scales that made the system of measuring grain by sealed half-bushels an absurdity. In the 1850's the western grain trade organizations, led by the Buffalo Merchants' Exchange, put pressure on the newly formed New York Corn Exchange, as well as traders in other Atlantic ports, and forced the acceptance of a new system of measurement by weight. Standardization of quality came next, but it took much longer for this notion to gain acceptance by easterners. Not until 1874 did the New York Produce Exchange agree to a system of grading and inspection, western style.[13] These innovations were important in making the language of business transactions clearer, less subject to costly arbitration, and applicable to much larger shipments of produce. Some progress along this line

---

ceedings . . . (8 vols.; New York, 1879–80), III, 3113–14; information on both these men has been very difficult to acquire, although I have had more success with Dows than with Hoyt. Some information on Dows' activities was gleaned from the *Northwestern Miller*, July 9, 1880, June 3, 1881, July 14 and Sept. 22, 1882, and from his obituary in the *New York Produce Exchange Reporter*, Apr. 5, 1890. In addition to activities as a grain merchant, Dows helped organize the Fourth National Bank during the Civil War, held large investments in New York real estate, served as a director of the Rock Island, Union Pacific and Delaware & Hudson railroads. His relation with western grain merchants and speculators is revealed to some degree in Dorothy J. Ernst, "Wheat Speculation in the Civil War Era: Daniel Wells and the Grain Trade," *Wisconsin Magazine of History*, XLVII (Winter, 1963–64), 125–35.

[12] There is a more extended discussion of these points in my unpublished doctoral dissertation, "American Wheat and the British Market, 1860–1905" (Cornell University, 1960), Chaps. II, VII.

[13] New York Produce Exchange, *Annual Report, 1874*, pp. 32–33; *Annual Report, 1875*, pp. 37–38; *Annual Report, 1876*, pp. 27–28; Guy A. Lee, "History of the Chicago Grain Elevator Industry, 1840–1890" (unpublished Ph.D. dissertation, Harvard University, 1938), pp. 60–65.

also took place in the cotton trade, but in this case it was slower and came as a result of standards established in Liverpool.[14] It is significant that while grain and provision exchanges were thoroughly entrenched by the Civil War, the New York Cotton Exchange was not formed until 1870, followed by one in New Orleans a year later.[15].

Perhaps a more fundamental change was wrought by the introduction of futures trading on western grain exchanges. The custom of selling goods "to arrive" had been prevalent in many branches of commerce for years, indeed centuries. In some cases such sales were made to minimize the risks of price change between the time the contract was made and the moment of delivery; they probably represented speculative motives just as often. A form of futures trading emerged among the leading British grain importers in the 1840's and 1850's. The introduction of regular mail service on fast boats made it possible to send ahead samples of a commodity accompanied by bills of lading and other documents that covered the shipment of a cargo. As a result, merchants on the floor of London's famed Baltic Exchange bought and sold cargoes of grain that were still in transit. Such transactions in cargoes of grain "afloat" added considerably to the frantic speculation of 1846–47 and to the ensuing commercial crisis. Greek merchants, several of whom were very prominent in the British grain and cotton importing business after 1840, initiated this technique in the Mediterranean grain trade.[16] A similar form of futures trading in cotton cargoes dates from at least 1851 in New York, which had the advantage of access to fast, regular delivery of market news. By 1857 traders in the Liverpool market had begun to speculate in cotton cargoes "to arrive" from India.[17]

But none of this involved trading in "future contracts," the hallmark of the modern commercial exchange. That innovation appeared almost simultaneously in the British iron trade and in the Midwestern grain business during the late 1850's. One wishes the possible connection could be explored further, since several merchant shippers in Britain and America dealt extensively in both commodities.[18]

---

[14] Stanley Dumbell, "The Cotton Market in 1799," *Economic History*, I (1926–29), 141–48; James E. Boyle, *Cotton and the New Orleans Cotton Exchange* (Garden City, N.Y., 1934), pp. 86–88.
[15] Boyle, *Cotton and the New Orleans Cotton Exchange*, pp. 65–72.
[16] James A. Findlay, *The Baltic Exchange* (London, 1927), pp. 12–17; Susan Fairlie, *The Anglo-Russian Grain Trade, 1815–1861* (unpublished Ph.D. dissertation, London School of Economics, 1959), Chaps. II, V; Sydney W. Dowling, *The Exchanges of London* (London, 1929), pp. 148–51.
[17] Stanley Dumbell, "The Origin of Cotton Futures," *Economic History*, I (1926–29), 259–61.
[18] Ogden, Ferguson & Company had been involved in both branches of the trade before the 1850's, and several references in their correspondence indicate that other firms in both England and the United States were "interested" in both iron and grain. Daniel Wells, a leading Wisconsin entrepreneur, visited England on business in the mid-1850's and dabbled in both wheat and iron transactions then and for a time after his return to the United States. See Daniel Wells Papers, Milwaukee County Historical Society, Milwaukee, Wis.

Futures trading in the Midwestern grain market grew out of the grading and elevator system. Previously, the elevator warehouses had issued receipts for the actual grain delivered, so the identity of each lot was preserved. By the 1850's warehouse receipts simply indicated the amount stored and its grade, and these general documents had become negotiable. In the meantime, forward sales grew rapidly in all the Midwestern markets. But with the use of general elevator receipts, an exchange market also emerged in which merchants made forward contracts for sales of grain which they did not possess at the time of the transaction. Such a trader could purchase warehouse receipts for the stated type and grade immediately after his sale if he anticipated a price rise before he had to make delivery, or he could wait until just before the delivery date if he expected prices to fall. This device was just a few steps short of the modern futures contract—a much more standardized type of transaction.[19]

The coming of war in 1861 intensified the risks and opportunities always present in commodity markets and was a powerful impetus to the wider use of futures contracts, particularly for pork, lard, grain, and cotton. The exploits of P. D. Armour in pork futures captured national attention. The Liverpool and New York cotton markets adopted a form of this device and were afire with speculative activity during most of the War period. The experience gained in this way helped in the formation of British and American cotton exchanges when the trade recovered after the War.[20] Informal transactions in grain futures outside the Chicago Board of Trade finally gained respectability among the majority of hitherto chary commission merchants, and in 1865 the business was permitted inside the hallowed halls of that institution. It quickly took root and grew into the marvelously intricate "pit" trading that so fascinated Frank Norris. Many contemporary critics were suspicious of a form of business in which one man sold what he did not own to another who did not want it, but in spite of many abuses, real benefits accrued from this innovation, especially after the perfection and wider use of "hedging" techniques in the 1870's.[21] By that time eastern exporters were using futures contracts to protect their transactions in the wheat trade. If no facilities existed on the local exchange, they made their "hedge" on another market. Until they formed their own "pits" in the late 1870's, New York

[19] Charles H. Taylor, ed., *History of the Board of Trade of the City of Chicago* (3 vols.; Chicago, 1917), I, 146–47, 192–93, 331–32; Henry C. Emery, *Speculation on the Stock and Produce Exchanges of the United States* (Columbia University Studies in History, Economics and Public Law, Vol. VII, No. 2 [New York, 1896]), 37–38. A clear discussion of the character of futures contracts is contained in Julius B. Baer and Olin G. Saxon, *Commodity Exchanges and Futures Trading: Principles and Operating Methods* (New York, 1949), pp. 126–63.
[20] William O. Henderson, *The Lancashire Cotton Famine, 1861–1865* (Manchester, 1934), pp. 14–18; Thomas Ellison, *Gleanings and Reminiscences* (Liverpool, 1905), pp. 315–42.
[21] George W. Hoffman, *Hedging by Dealing in Grain Futures* (Philadelphia, 1925), pp. 11–25.

grain exporters and Liverpool importers used the Chicago Board of Trade.[22] In the cotton trade, on the other hand, the more knowledgeable New York and New Orleans merchants looked to Liverpool in the immediate postwar years.[23]

Yet New Yorkers were relatively slow in adopting these changes. Perhaps this was due to the confidence that comes with pride, for the War had added to New York's domain as the nation's leading export center. Secession cut off the Mississippi River route and New Orleans for a relatively short time, but it was long enough to shift much of the southbound grain and provision trade eastward to the Empire City. In the 1860's, New York's export of these commodities reached as high as 90 per cent of the total.[24] The War also destroyed the tobacco trade of Richmond and Petersburg, the previous market centers for foreign sales. Financial stringency in the tobacco region led to the adoption of the auction sales system for the domestic market, while the bulk of export tobacco went to New York on coastal vessels throughout the following generation.[25] Even in the cotton trade, where old relations had been disrupted by the War and southern ports had forged direct business ties with Europe in the aftermath, the loss was smaller than it had seemed. Much of the upland cotton of South Carolina and Georgia made its way north by rail toward the end of the War, and New York merchants quickly recovered the business of supplying New England mills. By the 1870's they had also recaptured an impressive modicum of the export trade—second only to New Orleans in the number of bales sent abroad in 1874-75.[26]

But many factors were already at work to destroy this transitory glory. The trunk-line railroads serving rival ports were reaching into the Midwest by the end of the War and began to divert some of the foreign-bound commodities. By the early 1870's Boston, Baltimore, and Philadelphia had snared a large part of the flour, grain, and provisions destined for export. In retaliation, New Yorkers opened an acrimonious debate over the Atlantic port differentials in the freight rate structure which lasted well into the twentieth century with no loss of passion.[27] But beneath this furor it was apparent that railroads and transatlantic cables and through bills of lading presented in themselves the major threat to New York's monopoly position. A growing number of "fobbers" and "cif"

[22] *American Elevator and Grain Trade* (Dec. 1887; Nov. 1888); André E. Sayous, "Le Marché à terme en grain à Londres," *Journal des Économistes*, Ser. 5, XXXVIII (Apr.–June 1899), 78–84.
[23] Dumbell, "Origin of Cotton Futures."
[24] David M. Ellis, "New York and the Western Trade, 1850–1910," *New York History*, XXXIII (Oct. 1952), 379–83.
[25] Nannie May Tilley, *The Bright-Tobacco Industry, 1860–1929* (Chapel Hill, 1948), pp. 201–02, 341–42.
[26] *First Annual Report on the Internal Commerce of the United States*, 44th Cong., 2d Sess., House Ex. Doc. 46, 1877, Part 2, pp. 166–84.
[27] John B. Daish, ed., *The Atlantic Port Differentials* (Washington, D.C., 1918), *passim*.

traders in the western terminal markets established direct contact with European importers in the ten years following the War and, by so doing, bypassed all the seaboard merchants. Immediately after the War several leading English grain importers set up branch offices in New York rather than relying on correspondents any longer. These offices were in direct contact with western suppliers, had superior knowledge of the shipping market, and greater authority to make the quick decisions demanded by the highly charged competitive markets.[28] In part, this was also a response to changes in the English market, for the cable and improved shipping facilities had also broken the oligopolistic structure of the British import trade and made entry into the business easier for smaller dealers. Mercantile competition assumed even greater ferocity when the "Great Depression" set in after 1873, and older merchants in both Europe and America looked back to the 1850's and 1860's as the palmy days of international trade.[29]

The developments sketched here are but a few of the manifold changes related to the commodity export trade. Some of them were undoubtedly speeded and redirected by the Civil War, although merchants themselves were more likely to attribute them to "steam and electricity" —their euphemism for railroads, cable, and telegraph—rather than price fluctuations, changes in monetary policy, or other short-term factors. Certainly the War was instrumental in the failure of the cotton and tobacco trades to create the advanced marketing system achieved by merchants in the grain and provisions business. Conversely, it was not only Europe's hunger in the 1870's and 1880's which drew heavy shipments abroad of western foodstuffs, overshadowing the foreign trade of the South, the region so much closer to the sea and so much more dependent on export markets. Other nations might well have contributed more heavily to European imports of meat and bread. Much of the credit—or blame—must be given to the marketing innovations of the Civil War era, which sensitized even further the already highly commercialized setting of American agriculture, and thus helped to bring unquestioned supremacy in food exports for the rest of the century.

[28] Hepburn Committee, *Proceedings*, I, 664, 686; New York Commerce Commission, *Report . . .* (2 vols.; Albany, 1900), I, 963–64.
[29] George J. S. Broomhall and John H. Hubback, *Corn Trade Memories, Recent and Remote* (Liverpool, 1930), pp. 26–27; *Beerbohm's Evening Corn Trade List* (London), Feb. 20, 1888, p. 620; Hepburn Committee, *Proceedings*, III, 3112–15.

THE EXPANSION OF PRAIRIE
AGRICULTURE   *Fred A. Shannon*

To a remarkable degree the major agricultural developments of 1861–
1897 centered in or grew out of the Prairie states. Not only did those
states become the most highly mechanized, but their citizens wrought
most of the significant inventions, and Prairie-state factories manufactured the bulk of the machines. From the eastern apex of the Prairies,
near Chicago, railroads radiated in fan-shaped formation out to the Mississippi, to the northward bend of the Missouri, then ran in a more parallel fashion westward to the Great Plains and beyond. The cities along
the southwestern shore of Lake Michigan and on the middle stretches of
the Mississippi River, particularly in Illinois, were excellently located for
serving the demands of farmers farther west, and their supremacy in
machine output was not the only feature of their trade.

Frontier Conditions

The Chicago stockyards, meat-packing industry, and wheat pit were famous as well as infamous before 1900. Rock Island and Moline, in Illinois, and Davenport, just across the river in Iowa, comprised an industrial center second only to Chicago in the production of implements.
Milwaukee was an early rival in the packing industry—later overshadowed by East St. Louis, Illinois, and by Kansas City, Kansas, and
Omaha. Minneapolis achieved supremacy in the Western Hemisphere in
the flour-milling industry. These and numerous intermediate centers
helped build Prairie agriculture, and were nourished by it. While the
Prairies did not include much east of the Mississippi River, and though a
great deal even of Missouri and Minnesota were outside the limits, there

FROM "The Expansion of Prairie Agriculture," *The Farmer's Last Frontier: Agriculture 1860–1897* by Fred A. Shannon. Copyright 1945 by Fred A. Shannon.
Reprinted by permission of Holt, Rinehart and Winston, Inc.

was enough similarity in the problems of all twelve of the states of the North Central division to lump them together in this discussion. This does not mean that the lessons of pioneering learned in Ohio would apply accurately in eastern Iowa, or that the Iowa experiences would serve aptly in the more westerly Prairies of North Dakota or Kansas.

· · ·

Bonanza Farms

It was in this region that the bonanza farms sprang up in the late 1870's, flourished through the early eighties, and disintegrated in the hard nineties. The romantic ideas regarding the western gold fields had entered the Prairies, and yellow bonanzas, far more lucrative than the new ore strikes of the Black Hills, were to be panned out with the plow and self-binder. The land monopolists, fostered by the federal land laws, imbibing the new spirit of bigness hubbling up in the great transportation and industrial corporations of the East, and inspired by the availability of the new machinery, decided that the practices of big business could be emulated successfully on the farm. A succession of wet years furnished all the additional incentive that was needed. Weather conditions, it was felt, were undergoing a permanent change; moreover the railroads had already come, to care for transportation needs. Hence by 1880, Eastern readers began to learn about the farm managed by Oliver Dalrymple in the Red River Valley of the present North Dakota, where thirteen thousand acres of wheat comprised a single field. "You are in a sea of wheat," one article declared. "The railroad train rolls through an ocean of grain. . . . We encounter a squadron of war chariots . . . doing the work of human hands. . . . There are twenty-five of them in this one brigade of the grand army of 115, under the marshalship of this Dakota farmer." [1] Such metaphorical description was suitable to this new development.

It was the type of organization and management, not the mere size of the holdings, that astounded the reporter. For years before the Civil War, the people had the opportunity of knowing about the huge land-holdings of the Prairie cattle kings. Theirs was an enthralling story, too little emphasized in history,[2] but it was a tale of a different kind. Great landholdings, devoted to grazing, left idle, or sublet to tenants, had been known from time immemorial, and had been found in America since early colonial days. In 1860, there were 501 farms of more than a thousand acres each in nine of the North Central states and territories, ranging from 194 in Illinois and 112 in Ohio to one each in Kansas and Ne-

[1] C. C. Coffin, "Dakota Wheat Fields," *Harper's New Monthly Magazine*, LX, No. 358 (March, 1880), 529–35, quotation from p. 534.
[2] But see Paul Wallace Gates, *The Farmer's Age: Agriculture, 1815–1860* (New York, 1960).

braska. But Georgia alone had 902 and California 262.[3] By 1870 the number in the Prairie group had grown to 635, nearly all the gain being in Illinois, but the California list had increased to 713.[4] The Census of 1880 showed the new trend. In the two preceding counts, only a fifth and a fourth of the thousand-and-more-acre holdings of the North Central states had been west of the Mississippi River. Now, of the 2,990, and in spite of the fact that there had been a striking growth in number in the eastern group, 1,621 were in the western section. Missouri led, with 685, followed by Illinois, Iowa, Ohio, and Kansas. But Minnesota had sprung from 2 to 145 and Dakota Territory from none to 74, and these represented the true bonanza farms of the period. Yet, it must be noted that Georgia had 3,491 and California 2,531 of the larger estates of the same year.[5]

Years before the celebrated bonanza farms of Dakota and Minnesota, some of the Prairie cattle kings had set a precedent for large-scale farming, in connection with their feeding of livestock. Shortly after the Civil War John T. Alexander bought the Broadlands estate of Michael L. Sullivant, located in Champaign County, Illinois. It covered 23,000 acres (as part of an 80,000-acre estate . . .), and at one time had 1,800 acres in corn alone. With livestock, grain, hay, and farm implements, it was said to have cost Alexander nearly half a million dollars. Before this purchase he already owned some 80,000 acres on which he fed 32,000 head of cattle and 15,000 hogs, besides devoting 16,000 acres to corn. In the next three years he added 26,500 acres for another stock farm. Sullivant, meanwhile, developed 40,000 acres in Ford and Livingston counties, and in "five years he had 18,000 acres in corn, and 5,000 in other crops." His corn yield alone in one year was 450,000 bushels. Most of the work on the farm was done with the newest types of implements, including 150 "steel plows, 75 breaking plows, 142 cultivators, 45 corn planters, 25 gang harrows, a ditching plow operated by 68 oxen and 8 men, an upright mower to clip the hedges. . . .", and a great number of power-driven corn shellers.[6] In Atchison County, Missouri, David Rankin, over a fifty-years period, built up a 23,000-acre estate so magnificent that it could be described only in superlatives.[7]

The number of these excessive holdings in the eastern Prairies was always small in proportion to all farms in the states. In 1880, when Illinois had 649 superfarms and Champaign County alone had 27, the average-sized holding (tenant- as well as owner-operated) for both state

[3] *Eighth Census: Agriculture,* p. 221.
[4] *Ninth Census: Industry and Wealth,* pp. 345–66.
[5] *Tenth Census: Agriculture,* bottom folio, pp. 68–100.
[6] Arthur Charles Cole, *The Era of the Civil War, 1848–1870* (Vol. III of *The Centennial History of Illinois,* Clarence Walworth Alvord, ed. in chief, Springfield: Illinois Centennial Commission, 1919), pp. 382–83; quotations from Paul Wallace Gates, "Large-Scale Farming in Illinois, 1850–1870," *Agricultural History,* VI, No. 1 (January, 1932), 18.
[7] Donald Angus, "Breaking up the Biggest Farm," *The Country Gentleman,* LXXXIV, No. 45 (November 8, 1919), 6–7, 49.

and county was 124 acres. From that time on, great estates in Ohio, Indiana, and Illinois decreased in number, while there were only slight gains in Michigan and Wisconsin. But the movement was only getting a good start in the western tier of the Prairie states. Minnesota showed a steady increase in large holdings, to 365 in 1900; Iowa remained relatively steady and Missouri declined somewhat. But North Dakota rose steadily to 1,346 in 1900, South Dakota to 2,041, Nebraska to 2,364, and Kansas to 3,559.[8] In 1890, the twelve states had 4,468 farms ranging upward from a thousand acres, about seven tenths of them west of the Mississippi.[9] By 1900, over eight tenths of the 11,560 such holdings were in the tier from Kansas to North Dakota. By the same date, the California total had risen to 4,753, while Georgia had dropped to 1,858, and New York had 248.[10] These figures illustrate the trend.

By 1880, the era of the cattle kings in the eastern Prairies was passing. As population became denser the rise in value of land compelled a change to more intensive farming practices. The cattle business was moving out on the Plains, and the big farms in the older region were gradually broken up or let to tenants. But the western Prairies had become the new farmers' frontier, and there ensued a renewal of grand-scale farming. When the Panic of 1873 halted the construction of the Northern Pacific railroad, Bismarck, Dakota Territory, which was west of the Prairies, had already been reached. The railroad company then took the leadership in the establishment of bonanza farms.

James B. Power, land agent of the reorganized company, induced George W. Cass and Benjamin P. Cheney, president and director of the corporation, to exchange some of their almost worthless railroad bonds for eighteen sections of Red River Valley land in (North) Dakota, the ultimate purpose being to encourage land sales by demonstrating the productivity of the region.[11] The partners then employed Oliver Dalrymple, an expert wheat grower from Minnesota, to manage the business. The proprietors furnished all the capital for the venture, and when the returns had repaid all this, with interest, Dalrymple was to get "half of each farm, with its stock and improvements." [12] This arrangement was made in 1875. In the first summer, two full sections of sod were broken, and the first season's crop yielded twenty-three bushels to the acre. These results were widely advertised, and the Dakota boom was on. Capitalists bought up the depreciated railroad bonds to trade for land, and independent farmers swarmed in to get what they could of the rest, and

[8] *Tenth Census: Agriculture,* bottom folio, p. 78; *Twelfth Census: Agriculture,* I, 186–204 *passim.*
[9] *Eleventh Census: Agriculture,* p. 118.
[10] *Twelfth Census: Agriculture,* I, 186–204 *passim.*
[11] Harold E. Briggs, "Early Bonanza Farming in the Red River Valley of the North," *Agricultural History,* VI, No. 1 (January, 1932), 26–27.
[12] "The Bonanza Farms of the West," *Atlantic Monthly,* XLV, No. 267 (January, 1880), 37–38.

of the unmonopolized parts of the government land, in the same region.[13]

The Red River Valley wheat lands reached back from ten to twenty miles on both sides of the river, for a three-hundred-mile strip in Minnesota and Dakota, and up to Lake Winnipeg in Manitoba—but there was no bonanza farming north of the United States. As a Minnesota observer described the Red River Valley, "The surface of the land is nearly level, with but sufficient undulation to afford good drainage; the soil a rich, friable, black alluvial mold some thirty inches deep, resting upon a retentive clay subsoil. . . . and almost every acre can be put under the plow in unbroken furrows from one end to the other." [14] Early settlers had been discouraged from diversified farming by grasshopper plagues, destructively cold winters, and horse influenza, but specialization in wheat was less hazardous. Only the spring variety could be grown, and, before 1870, this yielded a dark, inferior flour. Then, in 1870, Edmund N. La Croix, a French miller settled at Minneapolis, developed the middlings purifier, which, with the new roller process of grinding, removed all previous objections to the product.[15] The Dalrymple experiment could not have been started at a better time.

In the second season, 1877, Dalrymple got a twenty-five bushel average from 4,500 acres, and imitators made a start. In the preceding year the Grandin brothers of Tidioute, Pennsylvania, exchanged Northern Pacific securities for nearly a hundred sections of land, and got Dalrymple to manage as much of that area as was in the Red River wheat region. The total cost of making a crop on the Grandin bonanza in 1878, including interest on the permanent investment, was $9.50 an acre, and the yield was from twenty to twenty-four bushels, while the price was about 90¢. It was estimated that the Grandin holdings, of 61,100 acres of wheat lands, were five times the area of Manhattan Island. The Dalrymple interests were about 100,000 acres. Other bonanzas of note in North Dakota included the Hillsboro Farm, 40,000 acres; the Cooper Farms, 34,000; the Amenia and Sharon Land Co., 28,350; the Spiritwood Farms, 19,700; the Mosher Farms, 19,000; and the Antelope Farm, 17,300. The average of all was probably 7,000 acres, and the smaller holdings of two or three sections were not classed as bonanzas at all. Some of the estates were so broad that crews working on one side did not see members oc-

13 John Lee Coulter, "Industrial History of the Valley of the Red River of the North," State Historical Society of North Dakota, Collections, III (Bismarck: Tribune, State Printers and Binders, 1910), 570–71; George N. Lamphere, "History of Wheat Raising in the Red River Valley," Minnesota Historical Society, Collections, X, Pt. I (St. Paul: Published by the Society, 1905), 21.

14 The Cultivator & Country Gentleman, XLII, No. 1,268 (May 17, 1877), 317.

15 Edward Van Dyke Robinson, Early Economic Conditions and the Development of Agriculture in Minnesota (University of Minnesota Studies in the Social Sciences, No. 3, Minneapolis: Bulletin of the University of Minnesota, 1915), pp. 76–78; William Allen White, "The Business of a Wheat Farmer," Scribner's Magazine, XXII, No. 5 (November, 1897), 531–48 for farming details.

cupied on another portion during the entire season. Quite often, the owners lived in the East, and seldom were they the actual managers. By 1885 nearly all of the greater establishments had begun operations, and the valley up to the Canadian border was pretty thoroughly dominated by absentee landlords.[16]

The form of organization on the Dalrymple units may be taken as fairly representative of the system. "They had in crop in 1880 about 25,000 acres, conducted in farms of about 6,000 acres each of plowed land. To each of these farms there is a superintendent. These farms are again divided into divisions of about 2,000 acres each of plowed land, and each subdivision has its own farm buildings, boarding-houses, stables, blacksmith-shop, and so on, this size being considered there the most convenient, and as large enough for systematic management, while, if larger, the men might have to travel too far to and from their work." [17]

Following the first cost of land and equipment, the largest expense on the bonanza farms was for labor. This was highly seasonal and done by migratory workers. Harvesting crews started out in Kansas and followed the ripening wheat northward till they wound up in North Dakota and Minnesota, some even going on into Canada. They paid no railroad fares, and the chambers of commerce and newspapers liked to refer to them as tramps. Nevertheless, the critics recognized that these migrants were a necessity. Many of the workers were farmers released by a slack season in other parts, and some were lumberjacks seeking employment during the off season in their camps.[18] Harvesting is hard work, as anyone who has tried it can attest, and many a blacksmith turning from the sledge hammer to the pitchfork, with heavily calloused hands, has returned from the first day in the harvest field his hands so blistered that he was almost unfit for work for the next day or two. The harvest crew worked thirteen hours a day for from nine to twelve dollars a week, plus bed and board. The meals cost the management about thirty cents a day for each man, and the bedding was often a shakedown in the haymow. A few laborers had to be kept on throughout the year, and these got from fifteen to eighteen dollars a month. The Grandin bonanza used 10 men during the five colder months; 150 for April plowing; about 20 from May 1 to July 15; 100 during the rest of July; 250 in August and the first half of September (the harvest season); then about 75 till the end of October. One account mentions 400 men during harvest.[19]

The breaking of the soil was done by two-plow, riding gangs with

---

[16] Briggs, "Early Bonanza Farming," p. 29; Coulter, "Industrial History of the Valley of the Red River," pp. 574–75, 580–81; White, "Business of a Wheat Farmer," p. 534; William Godwin Moody, *Land and Labor in the United States* (New York: Charles Scribner's Sons, 1883), p. 52; Alva H. Benton, "Large Land Holdings in North Dakota," *The Journal of Land & Public Utility Economics*, I, No. 4 (October, 1925), 408.
[17] *Tenth Census: Agriculture*, bottom folio, p. 454.
[18] Coulter, "Industrial History of the Valley of the Red River," pp. 577–78.
[19] *Ibid.*, p. 577; White, "Business of a Wheat Farmer," p. 545; "Bonanza Farms of the West," p. 39.

four horses each, from four to five acres being turned by a unit in a day. Number one Scotch Fife wheat was sowed, about eighty pounds to the acre, harrows preceding and following the seeders. Dalrymple used 200 pairs of harrows and 125 broadcast seeders. Next, the feed crops of oats and barley were sowed, and some of the smaller operators planted flax, buckwheat, and turnips. During the harvest, Dalrymple used 155 binders, each handling fourteen acres a day and operated in groups of twelve or more. Each squad had an overseer and shockers. As soon as the approximately ten-day harvest was over, threshing began, with 26 steam threshers turning out an average of nine hundred bushels a day each. It took about twenty-five men and twenty horses for each unit to haul from the shock, run the machine, and transport the grain to the railroad station a few miles away.[20]

Before 1883, the yield of wheat was good, and prices were high. Bonanza managers could supply nearly all of their material needs at wholesale prices, and, if doing a big business, got rebates from the railroads on their wheat shipments. But, from 1885 to 1890, the seasons became drier, crops declined, prices dropped, and taxes mounted. In the next decade, the large-scale grower found it hard to compete with the smaller farmers who diversified their crops and cultivated their land more intensively. Hence, many of the larger bonanzas disintegrated, including the Dalrymple interests in 1896. The corporation farms of the 1920's were largely a renewal of the idea on a new wheat frontier farther west.[21] Though the Dakota boom and the bonanza farms hastened the settlement of the region, the results were far from being uniformly good. Thousands of families were tempted to take up farms where, even if the land was fertile, there was no assurance of enough good seasons to offset the bad. The best farming lands were monopolized, and, when the system broke down, the holdings were let out to tenants instead of being subdivided into freeholdings. But when the movement was at its height, few words were heard except in praise. William Godwin Moody was the rare exception of the individual strong enough to brave the disapproval of the chambers of commerce and the newspapers they influenced.[22]

A long discussion of this subject would seem out of place, considering the small number of bonanza farms in proportion to the total of all landholdings in the West, were it not that the movement so accurately exemplifies the spirit of the times. In hope of riches for themselves, farm-

[20] *Tenth Census: Agriculture,* bottom folio, p. 455; Coulter, "Industrial History of the Valley of the Red River," pp. 571–73.
[21] Charles B. Spahr, "America's Working People," *The Outlook,* LXIII, No. 10 (November 4, 1899), 565; *Tenth Census: Agriculture,* bottom folio, p. 455; Coulter, "Industrial History of the Valley of the Red River," pp. 576–77; Malcolm C. Cutting, "Big Doings in Montana," *Country Gentleman,* XCIV, No. 5 (May, 1929), 22–23, 130–31.
[22] Briggs, "Early Bonanza Farming," pp. 35–37; W. B. Hazen, "The Great Middle Region of the United States, and Its Limited Space of Arable Land," *The North American Review,* CXX, No. 246 (January, 1875), 24; Gates, "Recent Land Policies," pp. 64–65; Moody, *Land and Labor, passim.*

ers of sub-bonanza caliber emulated the bigger rivals and copied their methods as far as they were able. They tried the big commercial game, not realizing that their lack of rebates, and favors of a similar order, worked against them, and that something nearer to a subsistence basis was better suited to their need. Also, the bonanza farms called further attention to land monopolization and the growth of tenancy elsewhere in the West. There were big wheat operations in the Pacific states at the same time, and often more highly mechanized than in the Red River Valley. Also, attention should be called again to the great number of immense landholdings from Kansas to South Dakota, where states of tenant farmers were being created. In 1886, a Congressional committee provided data on the number of American land monopolies controlled from foreign countries, by listing twenty-nine that totaled 20,747,000 acres, and including an English holding of 3,000,000 acres in Texas, as well as the Holland Company's 4,500,000 acres in New Mexico.[23] In the same year, a magazine article condemned the monopolistic system as being detrimental to the political and economic structure.[24] As Gates has said, the bonanza farms were "an amazing commentary upon . . . [a] so-called democratic land system." [25] But, lastly, the bonanza farms also illustrate how farming was done on the western Prairies, even though it was generally followed on a lesser scale.

The Movement of Cereal Crop Production

The bonanza farms also exemplify the magnetic attraction of the cheaper and more fertile frontier soils for wheat growers. From early Colonial days, wherever there were rivers to transport the grain to the coast, wheat followed the frontier, and remained close to the unplowed cattle range. And so the practice continued till the aridity of the farther West repelled all efforts to keep up the advance. Before 1860, the center of wheat production had pushed out into the North Central states, which in 1859 grew nearly 55 per cent of the nation's total, while 46 per cent was in the five states of the group that lies east of the Mississippi River. Some wheat was still grown in small patches, mainly for local consumption, but, in general, the industry was thoroughly commercialized. By 1869, the movement into the West North Central states had already become pronounced, that area yielding 23.4 per cent of the national crop, as compared with 44.3 per cent for the East North Central. In the next decade the shift was not great, the eastern subsection merely holding its own, while the western group increased the total for all by 4 per cent, thus giving the whole section 71.6 per cent of the crop of the United States.

[23] "Ownership of Real Estate in the Territories," House Report No. 3,455, 49 Cong., 1 Sess., p. 2.
[24] A. J. Desmond, "America's Land Question," The North American Review, CXLII, No. 351 (February, 1886), 153–58.
[25] Gates, "Recent Land Policies," p. 65.

Then, in the 1880's, the western seven states achieved the ascendancy they were to make permanent, and by 1899 they alone grew 46.6 per cent of the total crop, while all twelve accounted for 67.1 per cent. By 1909 the West North Central states increased their lead by another 10 points, after which the competition of the Mountain and Pacific states became more telling.

Thus far, there is a misleading element in the figures. The westward movement of the production center does not mean that the older wheat-growing regions of the Atlantic seaboard were all declining in their total output, but merely that they were making no substantial gains. An exception might be made for the South Central states, which, in the 1890's, temporarily regained virtually their percentage standing of 1859. This was mainly on account of the opening of the wheat lands of Oklahoma and northern Texas; and, after all, this was just a southward extension of what was happening in the whole western tier of the Central states. On the other hand, there were some Eastern states that showed an actual decline in wheat growing. But what the westward movement essentially means is that the East, in terms of its rapidly growing population, was supplying a diminishing proportion of its own demand, and that the West was taking over this market as well as the export trade. For that matter, the Mountain and Pacific states increased their percentage of the nation's crop (over the forty years) from 4.4 per cent to 13.7, the volume for 1899 being over ninety million bushels, or nearly as much as the North Central states had grown in 1859. By 1909, the same Far Western states, though their crop had declined a little, barely exceeded all the rest of the Union except the North Central states. But this is a big exception, for the latter alone grew 73.9 per cent of all. The leadership by states can best be presented by a table. By the end of the century, Minnesota was already slipping, and, thirty years later, was to be fifteenth

The Six Leading Wheat States (and Percentages) by Decades, 1859–1899

1859 56.4%	1869 55.7%	1879 53.4%	1889 50.2%	1899 49%
Illinois	Illinois	Illinois	Minnesota	Minnesota
Indiana	Iowa	Indiana	California	North Dakota
Wisconsin	Ohio	Ohio	Illinois	Ohio
Ohio	Indiana	Michigan	Indiana	South Dakota
Virginia	Wisconsin	Minnesota	Ohio	Kansas
Pennsylvania	Pennsylvania	Iowa	Kansas	California

in rank, while Kansas, with a crop seven times as large, reached ascendancy in a rather permanently fixed wheat belt.[26] The sudden rise and

[26] The figures are collected from Louis Bernard Schmidt, "The Internal Grain Trade of the United States, 1860–1900," *The Iowa Journal of History and Politics*, XIX,

almost equally rapid decline in some states, such as Iowa and California, are largely the result of unusually good crops in those states in years when the leaders were not far apart in the race.

While the geographic center of wheat production was shifting from central Indiana to west central Iowa, in these four decades, the center of corn growing moved only from the southern tip of Indiana to a point in Illinois about fifty miles north of St. Louis. There it had remained almost stationary for ten years, and was just about permanently established.[27] The slow and gradual nature of the movement can most conveniently be shown in parallel columns of the leading states in the order of their productiveness. The striking feature of the picture is the substitution of Kansas, Nebraska, Texas, and Oklahoma for the old Southern leaders: Tennessee, Virginia, Alabama, and Georgia (table below).

The Ten Leading Corn States (and Percentages) by Decades, 1859–1899

1859 70.8%	1869 72%	1879 78.9%	1889 80.7%	1899 75.5%
Illinois	Illinois	Illinois	Iowa	Illinois
Ohio	Iowa	Iowa	Illinois	Iowa
Missouri	Ohio	Missouri	Kansas	Kansas
Indiana	Missouri	Indiana	Nebraska	Nebraska
Kentucky	Indiana	Ohio	Missouri	Missouri
Tennessee	Kentucky	Kansas	Ohio	Indiana
Iowa	Tennessee	Kentucky	Indiana	Ohio
Virginia	Pennsylvania	Nebraska	Kentucky	Texas
Alabama	Texas	Tennessee	Texas	Kentucky
Georgia	Alabama	Pennsylvania	Tennessee	Oklahoma

This can partially be explained by the growth of the one-crop specialization in the cotton belt, but still more important were the special advantages of the North Central states. Corn needs at least a five-month season, with enough but not too much rainfall, and hot weather during the period of growth. But it also needs cooler weather toward the last, so as to check the development of fodder to the advantage of the maturing ear. This last advantage was not to be found in Alabama and Georgia, except in the plateau country. The five North Central states leading in the 1869 Census grew half of America's corn, and seven of the same group ac-

No. 2 (April, 1921), 196–245, as revised and extended in Louis Bernard Schmidt and Earle Dudley Ross, eds., *Readings in the Economic History of American Agriculture* (New York: The Macmillan Company, 1925), pp. 370–80; supplementary data from Fred Albert Shannon, *Economic History of the People of the United States* (New York: The Macmillan Company, 1934), p. 450. All figures were checked with the Census reports.

[27] Schmidt and Ross, eds., *Economic History of American Agriculture*, pp. 378, 383, 387.

counted for 68.5, 70.7, and 66 per cent in 1879, 1889, and 1899. By 1880, these seven states were the world's greatest corn belt. In some years, the four that were west of the Mississippi River grew nearly twice as much as the three to the east, but a Western drouth in the late nineties moderated this ratio as well as reduced the national percentage for the whole seven.[28]

This ascendancy in the leading cereals does not mean that the North Central states were lagging in other respects. In 1899, they produced 77 per cent of the oats, 57 per cent of the barley, 52 per cent of the rye, 58 per cent of the hay, and 53 per cent of the potatoes grown in the United States. Furthermore, they had 44 per cent of the beef cattle, 52 per cent of the milk cows, 26 per cent of the sheep, 52 per cent of the horses, 23 per cent of the mules, and 61 per cent of the hogs. Some states led any of the Prairie group for certain commodities, such as California in barley, Pennsylvania and New York in rye, New York in potatoes, Texas in horses, mules, and beef cattle, New York in dairy cows, Montana, Wyoming, and New Mexico in sheep. But, except for sheep and mules, no one other section, and in most cases not all the other sections combined, could equal the records for the North Central states. In a line not ordinarily to be expected, Iowa had more beef cattle than any of the Great Plains states and westward, except Texas; Missouri and Illinois each exceeded Colorado. Montana, New Mexico, and Wyoming were the only states that had more sheep each than Ohio, and Wyoming's margin was only five hundred in nearly three million.[29]

The Corn-Hog Cycle

The bulk of America's corn crop has always been fed to hogs, and most of the corn has been consumed locally, it being more economical to take the profit from both kinds of production on the same farm. Consequently, the Middle Western supremacy in pork was a natural result of the leadership in corn. Even cattle feeders preferred to keep a drove of swine, for it was found that four cattle would waste enough corn to feed one hog, and the pork secured in this way was all clear gain. In 1874, Joseph G. McCoy was chiding the Great Plains cattlemen for not emulating the feeders of central Illinois in this respect.[30] It was also noted that a bushel of corn would make ten or twelve pounds of pig,[31] hence it became an empiric rule that hogs at five dollars a hundred pounds could be

[28] Ibid., pp. 381–87.
[29] Calculated from Agricultural Yearbook, 1899, pp. 767–70, 819–21; Statistical Abstract of the United States, 1926, pp. 608–09.
[30] Joseph G[eiting] McCoy, Historic Sketches of the Cattle Trade of the West and Southwest (new ed., Washington: The Rare Book Shop, 1932), pp. 167–68 et circa, paged as in edition of 1874.
[31] U.S. Commissioner of Agriculture, Report, 1863 (Washington: Government Printing Office, 1863), p. 203.

grown profitably on corn at fifty cents a bushel, or eight-dollar hogs on eighty-cent corn, and so on. If the price of the animals rose much above this ratio, little corn would be thrown on the market and the farmers would do their utmost to increase the size of their droves. But this tended to enhance the price of corn, and, when the overproduction of pork brought its price down past the rising value of corn, the hogs would be sold, regardless of their state of maturity, till the conditions were reversed again. But this, in turn, reacted unfavorably on the corn market, thus again hastening the movement to revive swine production. So the amount that the public was able and willing to pay for pork determined, in a large degree, the price both for corn and for hogs; and this affected the corn acreage of the following year, though not according to any scientific or mathematical formula.[32]

As may be noted on [a] graph, . . . the corn-hog cycle—from peak to peak—was from four to six years' duration. This is explained on the basis of the corn-hog ratio of prices. In 1876, and for two years following, the price of corn was very low, and on the down grade. So the farmers began producing more hogs, and in 1879 was the peak of pork production. But too many hogs were raised, and the price reached bottom levels in the same year. An advance in corn prices from 1879 to 1881 was followed by diminished hog raising and by correspondingly higher prices. Corn prices began falling again in 1882, but hog prices trended upward for another year, as production diminished. Then, in 1883, hog prices started downward. After about two years, the corn-hog ratio began having its effect on the number slaughtered. The reason was that, in those days, slow-maturing swine were the rule, and it required about eighteen months or more to prepare them for the market. Before 1900, as will be seen, the trend was toward more rapidly developing breeds. The corn-hog ratio in 1887 was 13.5—which means that a hundred pounds of hog were worth 13.5 bushels of corn. Since 10 was the acceptable ratio, the price of hogs in that year was remarkably favorable.

The corn crop in 1860 was about 839,000,000 bushels, but it dropped as low as 398,000,000 in 1863, largely because the Confederacy was not included in the reckoning and was not buying. The old level was surpassed in 1866 and 1868, and always afterward. There were numerous fluctuations, sometimes hundreds of millions of bushels in a year, as between 1872 and 1875 and again in the late eighties and the nineties. But, with each recovery, new records were usually set, until the two-billion mark was exceeded five times between 1889 and 1899. The average farm price declined from 57 cents (greenbacks), in 1867, to 31.7 cents (on virtually a gold basis), in 1878. Then it advanced to 63.6 cents in the bad year of 1881, but dropped immediately afterward and got as low as 32.8 cents in 1885 and 28.3 in 1889. But the lowest of all was at the depth of

[32] Alva Wilfred Craver, "Factors Which Tend to Cause Fluctuations in the Price of Live Hogs and Pork Products" (manuscript thesis in University of Illinois Library).

CHART 1   Average Price of Hogs, Compared with the Total Production of
Hog Products per Capita and with the Price of Corn [33]

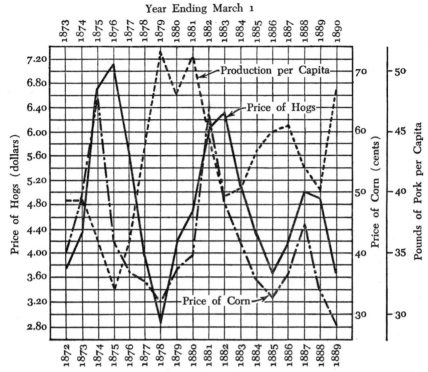

Year Ending March 1

Price of Corn December 1, Preceding End of Fiscal Year

the depression in 1896, when the price was 21.5 cents.[34] It should be borne in mind that average prices, even on the farm, mean that some producers got far less. Freight charges were so high in the western part of the corn belt that Kansas farmers, confronted with offers of seven or eight cents a bushel for their corn, found it more profitable to burn it in their stoves, thus saving largely on the cost of fuel.

A scale of corn and hog prices for the years 1880–1899 shows more than a fair degree of correlation, with only three years (1881, 1887, and 1889) when the hog growers definitely lost on the basis of corn prices. But in some years the profit was quite handsome, particularly in 1893 when it amounted, on the customary basis of reckoning, to about 100 per

[33] Adapted from U.S. Department of Agriculture, Bureau of Animal Industry, *Sixth and Seventh Annual Reports*, 1889–1890 (Washington: Government Printing Office, 1891), p. 88, with adjustments to show the relation between each dime in the price of corn and dollar in the price of hogs.

[34] *Agricultural Yearbook*, 1899, p. 759; Fred J. Guetter and Albert E. McKinley, *Statistical Tables Relating to the Economic Growth of the United States* (Philadelphia: McKinley Publishing Company, 1924), pp. 29–30.

Fred A. Shannon   333

cent. But quite often the only real profit went to the man who bought corn to feed his swine. In 1896, with hog prices at $2.90, such a buyer could make a gain, but the corn grower, whether he sold his grain or fed it, could take nothing but a loss. . . .

From early years, there was no lack of good advice on the selection of breeding stock for special purposes and the methods of feeding that would bring the quickest results. Berkshires were recommended for bacon, Poland-Chinas for lard, Duroc Jerseys for general purposes, Chester Whites for bulk, and the like. Agricultural journals constantly warned against the keeping of breeds that matured slowly, and the state and county fairs laid emphasis on quick and easy fattening. Practical demonstrations of results made quick converts of all alert farmers, so much so that the pigs they could market at two hundred pounds' weight at ages of from six to eight months came to be known as "mortgage lifters."[35] Some overly zealous raisers even insisted, with a straight face, that the young pigs' tails should be cut off to save the expense of fattening a useless appendage. But if enthusiasm ran to extremes in some directions, there was a positive and great benefit derived from the improvement of breeds. Yet, only the pig fanciers could afford to grow pedigreed animals. These required too much care, propagated lightly, and were subject to ailments that seldom bothered the old razorback or "hazel splitter." A little strain of the rangy woods animal eliminated much of this trouble, permitting litters of ten or a dozen instead of four or five, and yet producing pigs only slightly less worthy in a practical way than the delicately nurtured prize stock.[36] Between 1880 and 1899, the number of hogs in the United States increased only from 34,000,000 to 39,000,000, and the valuation from $146,000,000 to $170,000,000; but 50,000,000 at $291,000,000 in 1889, 52,000,000 at $241,000,000 in 1892, and 46,000,000 at $295,000,000 in 1893 show what better prices could do for the industry. The number in 1892 and the value in 1893 were records for the period.[37]

. . .

[35] Joseph Schafer, *The Social History of American Agriculture* (New York: The Macmillan Company, 1936), pp. 127–30.
[36] Commissioner of Agriculture, *Report*, 1863, pp. 198–203.
[37] *Agricultural Yearbook*, 1899, p. 818.

Ten ⌣ *The Farmers' Response to Industrialism*

THE AGRICULTURAL PROBLEM
AND NINETEENTH-CENTURY
INDUSTRIALISM   *Theodore Saloutos*

Perhaps no development of the nineteenth century brought greater disappointment to the American farmers than did their failure to realize the prosperity that they had expected from industrialism.[1] In fact, the results were anticlimactic. The innumerable forces, unleashed by the transformation of the national economy from an agricultural to an industrial base, made farming far more dependent, if not subservient, to the rest of the economy than most farmers suspected. Still, all the while agriculture was undergoing the most trying experiences in attempting to adapt itself to capitalistic methods of production and distribution, the farmers, through their spokesmen, proclaimed that their prosperity was fundamental to that of the Nation.[2]

Naturally, the transition from an agricultural to an industrial economy was hardly a tranquil process. For one thing, the advocates of manufactures had to make an aggressive bid for the support of the agriculturists who comprised the bulk of the population.[3] Most of the wealth in the beginning was invested in agriculture, the agrarian tradition was strong, and the thought of an industrial society haunted many.[4] That the

[1] This article was presented at the meeting of the Agricultural History Society with the American Historical Association in New York City on Dec. 30, 1946.

In its broadest sense the term *industrialism* as used in this study encompasses manufactures, commerce, transportation, and allied interests, exclusive of farming.

[2] One of the richest sources of data on the agricultural problem that remains relatively untapped by historians is the U. S. Industrial Commission's *Report . . . on Agriculture and Agricultural Labor*, vol. 10 (Washington, 1901).

[3] U.S. Bureau of the Census, *A Century of Population Growth* (Washington, 1909), 26.

[4] On the distribution of wealth C. F. Emerick, "An Analysis of Agricultural Discontent in the United States," *Political Science Quarterly*, 11:439 (Sept. 1896),

REPRINTED with permission from Theodore Saloutos, "The Agricultural Problem and Nineteenth-Century Industrialism," *Agricultural History*, Vol. XXIII (July 1948), pp. 156, 160–65, 167–74.

advocates of industrialism, a numerically inferior, strong-willed, better-disciplined, and well-financed group, should provide the framework for a system that engulfed and dislodged agriculture as the dominant segment of the Nation's economy was a tribute to their organizing genius, the potency of their agruments and the irresistible force of industrialism.

.   .   .

Obviously, any comparative analysis between farm and nonfarm endeavors should be made subject to certain qualifications. For one thing, there were vast differences between farming and nonfarming pursuits; in fact, there were wide differences and conflicting interests within agriculture itself, not to mention the divergencies within the commercial and industrial groups.[5] Likewise, one should guard against assuming that everyone entering into farming was a failure or for that matter that everyone entering industry or commerce was a financial success.[6] Caution should be exercised against reading into the past what has become obvious only recently. Also to be kept in mind is the fact that the farmers, judging from their organizations, and not those of business, commercial, and financial groups, had explanations to offer for their difficulties which varied from period to period, from organization to organization, from region to region, and from commodity to commodity.[7]

The effort to explain how the farm problem came about in terms of its relationship to the rest of the economy, however, has certain compensations. It does make more apparent the growing interdependence be-

is suggestive. Hereafter this article is cited: Emerick, in *Political Science Quarterly*. See also the U.S. Department of Commerce and Labor, *Statistical Abstract of the United States, 1904*, 552–55.

[5] Farming, compared with industrial and commercial enterprises, was essentially a family enterprise; it was affected more by climatic conditions than were the latter; a longer time was required for a turnover in the investment of the farmer; and agriculture had a more difficult time effecting economies in periods of low prices and had credit problems that differentiated it from other enterprises.

See Arthur F. Burns, *Production Trends in the United States Since 1870* (New York, 1934), 212–13, for a brief description of the competition among the various farm commodities. The Conference on Unemployment, Washington, D.C., 1921, Committee on Recent Economic Changes, *Recent Economic Changes in the United States* (New York, 1929), 1:82–83, presents in a brief but suggestive form the heterogeneity of industry. In *ibid.*, 2:549–50, Edwin G. Nourse said: "There is always danger of talking about 'the farmer' and 'American agriculture' as a unit. In a large and diversified country, differences in type, activity, and situations are numerous and extreme—so much so, in fact, that a properly special account of the several branches of our agricultural industry involves a diversity of details quite unmanageable in a discussion of the present scope. We must content ourselves with the broad outlines of major factors which apply somewhat generally over the country."

[6] U.S. Treasury Department, *Statistical Abstract of the United States, 1902*, 428.

[7] Frank M. Drew, "The Present Farmers' Movement," *Political Science Quarterly*, 6:290 (June 1891); W. F. Mappin, "Farm Mortgages and the Small Farmer," *ibid.*, 4:449 (Sept. 1889); C. Wood Davis, "Why the Farmer is Not Prosperous," *Forum*, 9:241 (April 1890); Patrons of Husbandry, National Grange, *Journal of Proceedings*, 1894, 14–24.

tween agriculture and industry and emphasizes the vast differences in the production and distribution policies, which had much to do with profits and losses. Perhaps it was a great mistake for the farmers, on the whole, to think that their special "way of life" was adaptable to capitalistic methods of production and distribution, yet the fact is that they did believe so and actually made the effort.

Ostensibly, the land policies were intended to benefit agriculture, but history bespeaks the fact that they were geared to meet the interests of the railroads, the speculators, the politicians, and others, which in the final analysis worked irreparable damage to farming.[8] The protective tariff, regardless of the industrial and commercial groups it benefited or harmed, affected the rank-and-file farmer adversely.[9] The fact that industrialists and businessmen represented a keener and more select group than did the farmers was no mean point in the quest for profits; [10] they were more influential in shaping the complexion of the modern economy than were the farmers who were repeatedly heralded as the backbone of the Nation and the guardians of its liberties.[11] The cheap raw materials of agriculture were as indispensable to low production costs for industry as was unrestricted immigrant labor.[12] Unwise investments were often made.[13] Agriculture had nothing comparable to the production and pricing policies of the manufacturers.[14] The antiquated tax structure weighed heavily and unjustly on it.[15] Producers of wheat and cotton were extremely vulnerable to the forces of world supply and demand.[16] The raw products of agriculture did not command the premiums that the finished products of industry did, nor for that matter did the labors of farmers command the rewards that those of industry and business did.[17] Obviously, a combination of complex and interrelated forces, defying solution, which varied from farm to farm, from commodity to commodity,

---

[8] Benjamin Horace Hibbard, "Land Grants," *Encyclopaedia of the Social Sciences,* 9:32–36 (New York, 1933), and his *A History of the Public Land Policies* (New York, 1924), especially 539–46 on "Effects of the Land Policies on Agriculture." See also Paul Wallace Gates, "Land Policy and Tenancy in the Prairie States," *Journal of Economic History,* 1:60–82 (May 1941).

[9] National Grange, *Journal of Proceedings,* 1894, 15; Henry J. Fletcher, "The Drift of Population to Cities: Remedies," *Forum,* 19:745 (Aug. 1895). According to a New Englander, "The Farmers' Grievance," *Nation,* 17:112 (Aug. 14, 1873), the tariff crippled about 380 out of the 390 manufacturing and industrial occupations listed in the census.

[10] Emerick, in *Political Science Quarterly,* 11:447.

[11] For a typical farmer attitude on this point, see the *California Patron,* 4(12):5 (San Francisco, May 24, 1879).

[12] Raguet, *The Principles of Free Trade,* 19, 150.

[13] J. Laurence Laughlin, "Causes of Agricultural Unrest," *Atlantic Monthly,* 78:583–84 (Nov. 1896).

[14] *California Patron,* 4(5):6 (Feb. 1, 1879).

[15] Emerick, in *Political Science Quarterly,* 11:632–39 (Dec. 1896).

[16] U.S. Industrial Commission, *Report,* 19:146 (Washington, 1902).

[17] Emerick, in *Political Science Quarterly,* 12:111 (March 1897). On this point Adam Smith was quoted in "To the Farmers of America," *American Review,* 15:191 (March 1852).

and from period to period, but in direct relation with the rest of the economy, contributed to make farming less profitable, if not downright unprofitable.

Part of the answer for the unprofitableness for farming is to be found in the rapid territorial expansion—the land-grant, immigration, and irrigation policies that encouraged people to take to the land without regard for the fact that they accelerated agricultural production beyond all reasonable market demands.[18] Land was far more indispensable to agricultural production than it was to any other industry, and the farmers should have been entitled to a strong voice in its disposition and the future policies that were adopted with respect to it.[19] But agriculture, which had a great stake in the land policies adopted, as a unit was either indifferent, ignored, forced, or misled into policies that in the long run proved ruinous. The railroads, the real estate speculator, and financial, industrial, and manufacturing interests which stood to profit from the rising land values, the new opportunities for investment and markets for manufactured goods, and the availability of large quantities of raw materials, were consulted and their counsels often prevailed.[20] The net result was the overexpansion of an already overexpanded agriculture. A New Englander who had looked upon the western areas as the resources for future generations rightly labelled as "all-wrong" their being thrown open as rapidly as they were to an exhaustive system of husbandry.[21] In similar vein the *Nation* said: "The great depreciator of agricultural credit in this country is the Government, which lets a man have a farm for a song." [22]

One must not confuse an agricultural producer with a landowner. It mattered little whether the producers were the real or the nominal owners of the land, tenants or share croppers; the fact was that it was possible for all of them to raise crops for market in any of the mentioned capacities, and there was little that could be done to check them. Easy access to land, provided of course that economic considerations were met satisfactorily, was a part of the American heritage and the placing of restrictions upon such entries would have militated against one of the Nation's most cherished traditions. One could lose his land, farm house,

[18] Erwin Graue, "Agriculture Versus Urban Enterprise," *Journal of Farm Economics*, 11:619–20 (Oct. 1929); "The Farmers' Grievance," *Nation*, 17:112 (Aug. 14, 1873); Frank W. Taussig, *The Silver Situation in the United States* (New York and London, 1893). 104. Charles Abrams, *Revolution in Land* (New York and London, 1939), 15, states that "At no time in our history was the relation of agricultural productive capacity to probable demand ever seriously considered as an element of land grant policy." According to the U.S. Commissioner of Patents, *Report, 1852, Part 2, Agriculture*, 4, "Productiveness of crops and destructiveness of soil are the two most prominent features of American agriculture."
[19] Thomas Nixon Carver, *Principles of Rural Economics* (Boston, 1911), 117.
[20] Gates, "Land Policy and Tenancy in the Prairie States."
[21] *Report of the Tariff Commission* (47 Congress, 2 session, *House Miscellaneous Documents*, serial 2117, Washington, 1882), 2:1498; hereafter this document is cited as *Report of the Tariff Commission . . . 1882.*
[22] *Nation*, 21:157 (Sept. 9, 1875).

livestock, implements, machinery, and supplies, but still turn around and become a tenant holding from a bank, an insurance company, a mortgage firm, or a farmer, and continue to produce crops for the market as he did when he owned his farm. This happened time and time again. Capital needs and managerial experience, especially among cotton and grain growers, were hardly the deterrents to producing for market that they were among manufacturers and industrialists.[23] Farming also was one of those very few occupations where people of "mediocre ability and lack of thrift can manage to eke out an existence" and "contribute to the world's food supply." Perhaps this would not have been as bad as it actually was because such production had an injurious effect on "the better-directed labors of men" who possessed "more than average skill and intelligence" and who consequently were "less amply rewarded than those . . . of the same ability in other walks of life."[24]

The application of farm machinery to agricultural production aggravated the effects of this uncalled for expansion. Agriculture lost nearly 3,500,000 workers from 1870 to 1900, but in no sense was the efficiency of the farm worker impaired. In 1900, the farmer was 86 percent more efficient as a producer than he was in 1870. From 1830 to 1895, production in the nine leading crop-producing States increased nearly 500 percent. Barley production, for instance, increased 2,244 percent.[25] The capacities to produce foodstuffs, contrary to the predictions of Malthus, greatly outstripped the capacities to consume them.[26]

This overexpansion was aggravated by the fact that the farmers represented millions of small-unit producers who were incapable of applying the mass production and distribution methods of industry.[27] Farming, in general, was unlike other enterprises in that the cost of production did not necessarily decrease as the size of the operating unit increased.[28] It was true that insurance companies, mortgage houses, and financial in-

[23] U.S. Industrial Commission, *Report*, 10:xv–xvii.
[24] Emerick, in *Political Science Quarterly*, 11:446–47.
[25] Hadley W. Quaintance, "The Influence of Machinery on the Economic and Social Conditions of the Agricultural People," in L. H. Bailey, ed., *Cyclopedia of American Agriculture* (New York, 1909), 4:109.
[26] Emerick, in *Political Science Quarterly*, 11:436.
[27] *Statistical Abstract of the United States, 1904*, 509, provides the following data:

Year	Number of Farms	Average Number of Acres to a Farm
1850	1,449,073	202.6
1860	2,044,077	199.2
1870	2,659,985	153.3
1880	4,008,907	133.7
1890	4,564,641	136.5
1900	5,737,372	146.2

[28] Charles Whiting Baker, *Monopolies and the People* (New York and London, 1889), 127.

stitutions had gained title to an increasing number of farms and that tenancy and absentee landownership had increased, but at best there was only a remote chance [of] a General Motors, a Henry Ford, or a United States Steel of American agriculture coming into being to bring to the average farmer the advantages that generally followed in the wake of combinations and consolidations in industry.[29]

It was dead wrong for the farmers to produce for the market without taking into account what other farmers were doing, but the fact was that many, if not most, farmers farmed after this fashion. The prices received depended upon what all farmers, not on what the individual, produced; but even if they realized this fact it was difficult, if not impossible, for them to thin out competition; the result was that there developed a mad scramble among millions of atomistic units of production to increase their output, as a result of which the individual producers hoped to increase their share of the total farm income. This was hardly a tolerated practice among manufacturers, and one observer urged that it was to the interest of the farmer "to supply the actual demands of the market, at prices that will give him a fair renumeration [sic] for his labor, and capital invested." If, by a stretch of the imagination, the manufacturers were to place on the market "an unlimited supply of their products, and allow the purchasers to fix the prices upon their reapers, separators, plows, wagons, etc., the dullest of business intellects would exclaim, that it was only a question of time, before they would become bankrupts." But this was the very thing that the farmers had been doing, and the curbing of such practices appeared remote indeed. One agrarian posed the question: "Can farmers conduct business successfully, except on business principles? Can they continue to force their products upon the market in excess of its requirements, and succeed?" [30]

Many farmers had overexpanded their operations not only beyond their means but also beyond what might well have been considered reasonable expectations for profit. If the findings of one researcher are accepted, some 83 percent of the mortgage debts contracted during 1880–1890 had been incurred "to enable debtors to buy lands, erect buildings and make other improvements, and that more than ninety-four per cent of it represents durable property." This growing indebtedness was confined mostly to the wealthier, not the poorer, farming districts which, in large measure, reflected an optimistic outlook. There appeared no plausible explanation for these new investments other than hope and confidence in the future of farming, but for which there was no substantial basis. Certainly the period from the Civil War to 1897 was not profitable, at least from the standpoint of remunerative farm operations.[31] Much of this indebtedness, it seems, had been encouraged by eastern creditors who had "sent unlimited sums, with reckless confidence, to be loaned on

[29] American Farm Bureau Federation, *Democracy Demands United Action* (a leaflet, n.p., n.d.); U.S. Industrial Commission, *Report*, 10:clx.
[30] *California Patron*, 4(5):6 (Feb. 1, 1879).
[31] Emerick in *Political Science Quarterly*, 11:601–02, 626–28.

Western farm mortgages." They exercised little discrimination in lending. Many farmers "were led into plans for expenditure without fully realizing the risks of farming, the operations of world-causes upon agricultural prices, or the difficulties of repaying loans after they were spent." The rates of interest charged, to be sure, were high, still they did not necessarily impede the obtaining of loans, the majority of which were made for additional farm properties. If interest rates were lower, this conceivably could have encouraged additional unwarranted expansion and speculation among farmers. There were, no doubt, legitimate credit needs and especially where opportunities prevailed, but a good deal of the money borrowed was invested in additional lands which were held for advances in price or in further unprofitable farming operations.[32] Altogether too many farmers ignored the simple economic rule of "Whoever invests unwisely, or produces too dearly, is ruined." [33]

For the farmers to curtail production after the fashion of industry during slack seasons, and hereby effect savings, was exceedingly difficult, if not impossible. Manufacturing was carried on by a comparatively smaller group of producers, as against the millions of farm operators in the United States and the untold millions of farmers in other parts of the world who produced cheaply and competed with one another recklessly.[34] Industry, as a rule, faced a drop in production during slack years, while agriculture, especially in the face of distress in urban areas, could readily serve as a place of refuge for unemployed city workers. Depressions have brought back-to-the-land movements. By taking to the land, people at least had the opportunity of raising some food for sustenance, whereas no such opportunities prevailed in the cities. This added rather than detracted from the total production.[35] Another thing, the average farmer depended upon the labor of his family, except perhaps at harvest time when additional help had to be employed; hence, there was no point to his laying off members of the family to effect savings.[36] The farmer had to support his family whether it worked or not; besides, there was no telling what would happen by harvest time. It appeared sensible, and just as cheap, to produce more as it did to produce less. The tragedy was that, while production was maintained and the operating costs remained the same, the returns to the farmer dwindled while his interest payments, his mortgage, taxes, and other debts, loomed larger than ever.

[32] Laughlin, "Causes of Agricultural Unrest," 579, 582–83. In 1900, 50.6 percent of the land in farms was unimproved, according to *Statistical Abstract of the United States, 1902*, 506.
[33] Ludwig von Mises, *Socialism* (New York, 1932), 438.
[34] Baker, *Monopolies and the People*, 126–29; *California Patron*, 4(5):6, (11):7 (Feb. 1, May 10, 1879).
[35] George McHenry, *The Cotton Trade* (London, 1863), 135, states that "The panic of 1837 caused the people to return to their regular occupations as farmers. . . ." This shift was evident during the depression years 1929–1933. See also Frederic W. Speirs, Samuel McCune Lindsay, and Franklin B. Kirkbride, "Vacant-Lot Cultivation," *Charities Review*, 8:74–107 (April 1898).
[36] Emerick, in *Political Science Quarterly*, 12:113.

The want of managerial talent among farmers was an additional cause for the unprofitableness of farming.[37] This was no mean point in view of the fact that the normal profits in farming were modest, even for the most skilled entrepreneurs. Commercial farming, for one thing, laid bare the want of managerial talent among farmers. Farming was a complicated business, ever in need of managers capable of directing their land, capital, and labor in a profitable manner.[38] The bulk of the farmers kept no records of their costs,[39] and the marketing side was neglected for the most part. People with capital and abilities normally found more profitable fields for investment than farming.[40] It was suggested that one could invest his money in government bonds and make just as much, if not more, than he could in farming and without assuming the responsibilities that farming normally entailed. Even the most cursory examination leaves little doubt but that the more competent managers, the type required to provide farming with a margin of profit, shunned agriculture and went into industry and business.[41]

One of the most pronounced evidences of this superiority in personnel was found in the fact that the industrialists, businessmen, or their representatives were, more likely than not, to be on the long end of the bargaining counter, whether they matched wits with the farmers in the market place or in the halls of Congress. The former, besides being more cosmopolitan and enterprising, were also freed from the dead weight of custom and tradition; they were better-equipped financially and psychologically; they represented a dynamic industrialism, were alive and thriving, were in a better position to exchange ideas with the most diverse elements in society, had a better knowledge of market conditions, finance, weights and measures, geography, law, insurance, legislative wirepulling, and likewise possessed a keener appreciation of the need for organization and discipline.[42] This simply substantiated the conclusion that the most progressive elements in the modern economics were found among the general industrial interests and "the least so, [among] the extractive or raw material industries. . . ."[43] These superior capacities enabled them

[37] U.S. Industrial Commission, *Report*, 10:lxxxv.

[38] Edward F. Adams, *The Modern Farmer in His Business Relations* (San Francisco, 1899), is a good treatment of the problems of the commercial farmer.

[39] Andrew Boss, "Forty Years of Farm Cost Accounting Records," *Journal of Farm Economics*, 27:1–17 (Feb. 1945).

[40] U.S. Industrial Commission, *Report*, 10:xiii.

[41] The Granger publication, *California Patron*, 4(12):5 (May 24, 1879), summed up the situation thus: "This, then, is the whole story. The mass of farmers do not have in their ranks as good timber, as regards availability, as they ought in all sincerity, to have. It is not honesty or industry which they lack. But, in a large degree, the farmers and the farming community need more strict training in business habits and business modes of thought. . . . The truly successful and honored farmers, a class increasing every year, conduct their affairs on the same exact principles which regulate banking, or the Japan tea trade, or any other solvent business."

[42] Charles Edwards, "What Constitutes a Merchant," *Hunt's Merchants' Magazine*, 1:289–95 (Oct. 1839).

[43] Edward D. Jones, "The Manufacturer and the Domestic Market," in International Congress of Arts and Science, St. Louis, 1904, *Congress of Arts and Science, Uni-*

to discharge heavy responsibilities and provide against contingencies, to outsmart and outmaneuver the farmers any time they chose to do so. If they, themselves, did not have the brains to do all these things, they, at least, had the money with which to hire them. This superiority was displayed repeatedly in the fields of production and distribution, and especially in the latter which was so important in an exchange economy.[44]

· · ·

Whereas the protective tariff shielded domestic manufacturers from foreign competition and enabled them to keep prices up, the American farmers suffered from the twin effects of a diminished foreign market and the payment of high prices for the goods they purchased.[45] An effective device to protect the cotton and wheat growers, especially from foreign competition, could not be worked out; the prices for such staples depended heavily on foreign and domestic demand; scarcity abroad enhanced domestic price levels, and an abundance depressed them.[46]

· · ·

The railroads and transportation costs invariably figured prominently in the plight of the farmers. When the farmers failed to realize the returns that they had expected to follow in the wake of an expanding transportation system, they blamed the roads for many of their difficulties. The failure to attain the profits that had been anticipated came as a sort of anticlimax; in fact, their disappointments were exceeded only by their anticipations. They had expected the railroads to work miraculous powers on agriculture; the railroads were to bring "the city into the country," provide commercial, cultural, and educational opportunities, attract a choicer class of immigrants, cheapen transportation costs, encourage agricultural production, and "double, treble, quadruple, and quintuple the worth of grain lands near where they run" as had been "the case in Ohio, Michigan, Indiana, Illinois, Wisconsin, and Canada." [47] Most of these things did happen, except for the all-important bettering of the economic position of the farmer. The roads did bring the advantages of the city to the farm; they did bring about lower freight rates and enhanced the value of the land; still the farmers were no better off than they had been before. As long as land values rose, it was possible for many farmers to show some net gains, but not necessarily be-

versal Exposition, St. Louis, 1904, ed. by Howard J. Rogers, 7:116 (Boston and New York, 1906).

[44] William J. Ashley, *Surveys Historic and Economic* (New York and Bombay, 1900), 418, says "It is a commonplace to say that while in Germany the government gets most of the best brains, and industry and commerce relatively few, in America it is industry and commerce that are most attractive."

[45] In the *Report of the Tariff Commission . . . 1882,* 2:1494, one farmer pointedly asked: "Why this favoritism, this domination of one interest to the prejudice of all others, and this is a minor interest?"

[46] U.S. Industrial Commission, *Report,* 19:146.

[47] *Hunt's Merchants' Magazine,* 31:508 (Oct. 1854).

cause of profitable farming operations, especially on the part of those who had purchased their land cheaply. Certainly, those who bought land at high prices had a hard time showing a profit unless they possessed rare managerial and business abilities and had a high degree of good fortune.

A point in need of greater emphasis was that the railroads scattered farmers over vast stretches of territory that were far removed from important marketing centers and sources of supplies.[48] This diffusion was a concomitant part of agriculture, both in its pioneer and more settled stages, and the farmers by a combination of circumstances and sheer ignorance became its victims. If farming was to be a successful business enterprise, as many had expected, it was incumbent upon the farmers as producers and purchasers to give first consideration to the proximity of their principal points of distribution and purchasing. The industrialists had learned that the localization of their establishments was of tremendous importance;[49] but the farmers, generally speaking, could hardly be as selective because of the very nature of their business.

Historians have repeatedly attributed the plight of the farmers, at least in part, to high freight rates, yet available figures show conclusively that the rates dropped drastically during the last half of the nineteenth century, while the farmers' returns failed to show anything commensurate with the drop in rates.[50] Many farmers attributed the sagging prices to these alleged extortionate rates, but by so doing they overlooked the fact that it was these lower rates that had made it possible for them to reach markets which formerly were considered incredible.[51] In 1886, for instance, cattle were shipped 2,000 miles and more, and wheat and other grains worth half as much per ton were sent in immense quantities 1,500 to 1,800 miles, because of rates that in many other countries would have been considered incredibly low.[52]

This was the argument of Charles F. Adams, Jr., who asserted that farmers had little to gain from low rates because they would have the effect of extending the areas from which supplies could be drawn and thus bring millions of more producers and acres into competition. Many farmers, who for unexplained reasons had expected their products to be carried unreasonably long distances and still be entitled to a profit, never grasped the significance of this argument. After all, there was a point beyond which the freight charges would eat up the entire worth of the transported article, especially if it was bulky and of small intrinsic value. Adams took the case of corn as an example: that of ordinary value, for

[48] "Another Aspect of the Farmers' Movement," *Nation*, 17:68–69 (July 31, 1873); and "The Farmers' Grievance," *ibid.*, 17:112 (Aug. 14, 1873).
[49] U.S. Industrial Commission, *Report*, 10:ccxcvii–ccci; and especially John D. Black, *Introduction to Production Economics* (New York, 1926), 252–541.
[50] U.S. Industrial Commission, *Report*, 10:ccci–ccciv.
[51] C. F. Adams, "The Granger Movement," *North American Review*, 120:422 (April 1875).
[52] *Encyclopaedia Britannica*, 20:254 (ed. 9, 1886).

instance, in the past had been shipped over a common earth road for a distance of only 165 miles before its money value was consumed by the cost of transportation, whereas by rail it could be carried some 1,650 miles.[53] This illustration could be applied to other commodities. If the arguments of Adams are accepted, and had mismanagement, corruption, and price discriminations been kept at a minimum, the resulting even lower rates simply would have served to increase the acreage by that much more, bring additional foreign and domestic producers into competition, and thereby depress farm price levels even more.

Besides the lower freight rates which contributed to this ruinous competition, the evidence is that the farmers became the victims of a system of taxation that was far more suitable for the first half of the nineteenth century than it was for the second. When a uniform tax was introduced on all property, "the wealth of the country consisted almost exclusively of real property, and of such personal property . . . which could not readily be concealed. Cattle, horses, and farming implements . . . comprised a large portion of the personal property." It was comparatively easy then "to assess to each man all his property, and to tax all in proportion to ability to pay taxes. This was then easier for landed property than now, as owing to its comparatively small value and uniformity, it answered practical purposes fairly well to divide it into a few classes and to tax each one at one uniform rate." But during the nineteenth century, the number of banks, railroads, and manufacturing, commercial, and industrial concerns had increased, as did the quantity and the value of the stock they issued. The more personal property increased in value, the more readily did it evade taxation. The bulk of this personal property was located in cities, which, in effect, meant that its owners bore a proportionately smaller share than did the agriculturists who could not easily hide their belongings from tax assessors.[54]

Agriculture suffered from heavy taxation in other respects. Early in the history of the Nation, the responsibility for schools and the building and maintenance of roads fell heavily on the rural communities. Farmers were also taxed for roads used by others who did not pay for them in the proportion in which they used them.[55]

Professor Edwin R. A. Seligman summarized the position of the farmers correctly when he wrote: "Those who own no real estate are in most cases not taxed at all; those who possess realty bear the taxes for both. The weight of taxation really rests on the farmer because in the rural districts the assessors add the personalty, which is generally visible and tangible, to the realty, and impose the tax on both. . . . What is

[53] Adams, "The Granger Movement," 414.
[54] Charles J. Bullock, Selected Readings in Public Finance (Boston, 1906), 208–12; and U.S. Industrial Commission, Report, 10:lix, ccclxxxvii, ccclxxxix, 247, 248, 278, 811.
[55] Benjamin Horace Hibbard, "Taxes a Cause of Agricultural Distress," Journal of Farm Economics, 15:9–10 (Jan. 1933).

practically a real property tax in the remainder of the state becomes a general property tax in rural regions. The farmer bears not only his share, but also that of the other classes of society." [56]

Farming, in effect, was unprofitable, despite the multiplication of factories, the enactment of tariff legislation, and the building of railroads. This unprofitableness was brought about by overexpansion and high production costs (labor, fertilizer, interest, transportation costs, taxes, etc.), a dwindling foreign market, discriminatory tariff legislation, a ruinous competition, cheap transportation rates, the neglect of the marketing side of farming, and inequitable tax burdens. The evidence appears strong that rising land values and the prospects for speculating in lands had encouraged many to attempt to supplement their dwindling incomes by making additional purchases, to invest unwisely in making impovements, and to buy too much machinery. Low prices, high costs, debts piled up from unwarranted investments, and crop failures aggravated their condition. This combination of forces contributed in large measure to reduce the net returns of farming, forced many agriculturists further into debt if not bankruptcy, made it more difficult for them to rise from the tenant into the landowning class, compelled many to migrate to the city, and brought forth a series of demands. [57]

The tardiness of the farmers to organize to promote and defend their interests was hardly to be attributed solely to sheer ignorance and indifference on their part. The fact that they felt the twin effects of the industrial and agricultural revolutions later partly contributed to this. This, in itself, had enabled industry for instance, with some degree of success, to organize first, while the farmers, for the most part, lacking the advantages of concentration, remained scattered and isolated. [58] Labor, though unsuccessful for the most part, also struck out to defend itself through the medium of organization before the farmers had started to stir. [59]

But it was the major nonfarming interests, other than the wage earners, who got the head start and pursued policies that either resisted or checkmated the demands of the farmers, if not to steer them into dubious channels. Industry, sensitive to the benefits of organization, obtained more than adequate representation in the major political parties and in the councils of government; it exercised influence on the press, educational institutions, and other agencies which molded public opinion; the abilities of industrial groups to obtain a high protective tariff and evade assuming a fair share of the tax load was attributable partly to the potency of their arguments, the effectiveness of their pressure

[56] Edwin R. A. Seligman, *Essays in Taxation* (ed. 8, London, 1913), 25.
[57] Emerick, in *Political Science Quarterly*, 12:114–15.
[58] For instances of early organizations in industry, see Clark, *History of Manufactures in the United States*, 280–81, 455, and 458.
[59] Benjamin Horace Hibbard, *Marketing Agricultural Products* (New York, 1921), 188–90.

group activities, and the confusion and maladjustments created by the transition from an agricultural to an industrial economy.[60] Cheap raw materials from agriculture were as indispensable to low production costs for industry as was a cheap labor supply; hence, the more effectively organized the various industrial interests became, the assumption is, the greater became their resistance to demands for higher farm prices and lower industrial tariffs. Perhaps what ensued was a form of domestic imperialism. Perhaps the anti-protectionist argument of the first half of the nineteenth century was not too far wrong when it envisaged that industrialism and the protective tariff would result in restrictions, prohibitions, and curbs on agriculture similar to those which the English had inflicted, or attempted to inflict, on the Thirteen Colonies with a questionable degree of success.[61]

Again, the fact that the farmers' organizations failed to assume national dimensions until after the Civil War neither precluded the existence of such bodies, nor necessarily implied that the farmers and their spokesmen were exactly unaware of the problems created.[62] There were organizations prior to that time, but they were local and state-wide in character, concerned largely with production, and for the most part ineffective.[63] In 1858, according to the annual report of the Commissioner of Patents, there were in existence some 912 organizations of various types: 799 were classified as agricultural, 43 as horticultural, and 70 as agricultural and mechanical.[64] There also was a considerable awareness

[60] This sentiment was expressed in the *Report of the Tariff Commission . . . 1882*, 2:1494, as follows: "It is an undisputable fact, demonstrated by its fruits, that this class have aggregated to themselves more than their share of the national wealth; they are in the ascendant in government, a privileged class, fortified in their position by dominant political fallacies, and appeals to the laboring classes."

For an 1845 version, see *Report from the Secretary of the Treasury . . . 1845*, 12–13.

[61] A. M. Simons, *Social Forces in American History* (New York, 1920), 87–88; and H. C. Carey, *Letters to the President, on the Foreign and Domestic Policy of the Union . . .* (Philadelphia, 1858), 120–22.

[62] By the 1850s, the southern planters had started to think in terms of what many American farmers were thinking of, or doing, during the last half of the nineteenth century and the early decades of the twentieth. See the following articles in *De Bow's Review*: "Cotton, and Its Cost of Production," 10:568–71 (May 1851); "Cotton and Its Prospects," 11:307–13 (Sept. 1851); "Cotton Planters' Remedy for Low Prices," 12:73–74 (Jan. 1852); "Crop and Supply of Cotton," 12:76–81; "Cotton Planters' Convention," 12:110–11; "The Macon Cotton Planters' Convention," 12:121–26 (Feb. 1852); "The Cotton Trade," 12:185–92; "Organization of Cotton Planters for Obtaining Statistics of Growing Crops," 13:294 (Sept. 1852); and "What It Costs To Get the Cotton Crop from the Plantation into the European Market," 13:301–02. See also U.S. Census Office, 8th Census, 1860, *Agriculture of the United States in 1860*, xli–xliv.

[63] It was rightfully stated in the Illinois State Agricultural Society, *Transactions*, 1856–57, 4, that "their true mission is to draw public attention to great improvements in the art of production, and excite special interest rather than supply special wants."

[64] U.S. Commissioner of Patents, *Report, 1858, Agriculture*, 90–91.

on the part of many of the relationship to agriculture of such matters as overproduction,[65] the tariff,[66] currency [67] and marketing problems,[68] transportation rates,[69] the surplus,[70] soil destruction,[71] the foreign market,[72] and the competition of newer areas.[73] Crop controls, for example, were about as American as any proposal for the relief of agriculture, having been espoused and attempted as early as the seventeenth century by the tobacco producers,[74] and again during the ante-bellum period by certain cotton-producing elements.[75]

An analysis of the causes for agrarian discontent as seen through the eyes of the farmer and nonfarmer elements presents an interesting study in contrasts. Someone suggested that one had to "pitch manure" like the farmers did in order to grasp the farm problem, but if the experiences of the farmers is any criterion "pitching manure" is more an evidence of physical labor than a guarantee that one has grasped the main aspects of the problem. It was neither the absence of farming experience nor of rural background, for that matter, that was at fault; it was the failure to see the farm problem in its proper relation to the rest of the economy. As one observer noted as late as 1914: "The farmer has . . . been ill-informed or, worse still, misinformed about the intricate difficult subjects of value, price, money, banking and credit; about the machinery and minutiae of distribution, channels of trade, and market methods; about the factors, agencies and influences involved in the retention as well as the production of farm wealth." The farmer found himself in "what Milton called 'confusion worse confounded'. . . ." [76]

The causes of the farmers' difficulties, as seen through their organizations, often appear to have been based on "contradictory theories,"

[65] Report from the Secretary of the Treasury . . . 1845, 755, 757–58.
[66] Ibid., 8, 12–13, 249, 312. For illustrations of Pennsylvania farmers in 1718 and 1830 seeking "to prohibit the importation into Philadelphia of the meats, vegetables and fruits of Jersey," see Raguet, The Principles of Free Trade, 113–14. See also William Hill, "Colonial Tariffs," Quarterly Journal of Economics, 7:80–82 (Oct. 1892).
[67] Report from the Secretary of the Treasury . . . 1845, 295–96; De Bow's Review, 13:74–76 (July 1852).
[68] Hunt's Merchants' Magazine, 27:266 (Aug. 1852).
[69] Ibid., 31:508 (Oct. 1854).
[70] Report from the Secretary of the Treasury . . . 1845, 755, 757; L. C. Gray, "The Market Surplus Problems of Colonial Tobacco," Agricultural History, 2:1–34 (Jan. 1928).
[71] U.S. Commissioner of Patents, Report, 1852, Part 2, Agriculture, 7–8.
[72] Report from the Secretary of the Treasury . . . 1845, 754–55.
[73] "The European Grain Market," American Review, 5:643 (June 1847); "The Tariff of 1846," American Whig Review, 12:302–03 (Sept. 1850); U.S. Commissioner of Patents, Report, 1858, Agriculture, 216–17.
[74] Theodore Saloutos, "Efforts at Crop Control in Seventeenth Century America," Journal of Southern History, 12:45–66 (Feb. 1946).
[75] James C. Bonner, "Genesis of Agricultural Reform in the Cotton Belt," Journal of Southern History, 9:485–86 (Nov. 1943).
[76] Wisconsin State Board of Public Affairs, Report Upon the Survey of the University of Wisconsin (Madison, 1914), 945.

varying from organization to organization, from decade to decade, and from commodity to commodity. There was no consistency in the explanations offered, unless it was in the sense of their being consistently inconsistent. Among the reasons advanced were: "mono-metallism, deficient or defective circulating medium, protective tariffs, trusts, dressed-beef combinations, speculation in farm products, over-greedy middlemen, and exorbitant transportation rates." [77] Some admitted the acquiring of more land than they could properly cultivate. References were made to the low prices, high interest rates, poor crops, poor management, the monopolistic practices of industry, extravagance, lack of organization, heavy mortgage indebtedness, and "too liberal use of their credit." [78] Another observer, though correct in part, put it too simply when he said "there are altogether too many farms, too many cattle and swine, too many bushels of corn, wheat, rye, oats, barley, buckwheat, and potatoes, too many tons of hay, and too great a production of nearly all other farm products for the number of consumers." [79] In 1894, the Master of the National Grange realistically noted, but upheld, the existing radical differences of opinion within the order on these matters: "Each one is encouraged to investigate, think and decide questions in accordance with his own best judgment." [80] E. L. Godkin, no doubt, correctly pointed to one difficulty the farmer and his spokesmen were prone to overlook: "Of the world outside he knows and cares nothing. 'America is good enough for him.'" [81]

Once the farmers became organization conscious, an endless procession of organizations followed. From 1867 to 1902, there were organized the Patrons of Husbandry, the Agricultural Wheel, the Brothers of Freedom, the Farmers' Mutual Benefit Association, the Farmers' Alliance and its political offshoot, the Populist Party.[82] This endless procession of organizations, their regional character, and the changing emphasis in their demands were evidence that the farmers had failed to find a program capable of creating the unity and cohesion that was a condition precedent to an effective tackling of the farm problem.

The Grange was foremost among the farmer organizations because it was the first to be organized and likewise the longest lived; it created a pattern that influenced contemporary organizations. The Grange, however, could claim little in its platform that was original. Its demands were a crystallization of the antimonopoly crusade that already was in progress,[83] including the agitations of the local farmers' clubs of Illinois and the campaigns of the woolgrowers' associations and the cotton plant-

---

[77] Davis, "Why the Farmer Is Not Prosperous," 232. See also Drew, "The Present Farmers' Movement," 290; and U.S. Industrial Commission, *Report*, 19:146.
[78] Mappin, "Farm Mortgages and the Small Farmer," 449; National Grange, *Journal of Proceedings*, 1894, 14–24.
[79] Davis, "Why the Farmer Is Not Prosperous," 241.
[80] National Grange, *Journal of Proceedings*, 1894, 24.
[81] "The Farmer as a Business Man," *Nation*, 63:322 (Oct. 29, 1896).
[82] U.S. Industrial Commission, *Report*, 10:ccclxii–ccclxvii.
[83] Solon J. Buck, *The Granger Movement* (Cambridge, Mass., 1914), 53.

ers of the ante-bellum period.[84] These developments, along with the in-effectiveness of the local agricultural societies of the first half of the nineteenth century, helped emphasize the need for the aggressive program that was adopted by the Grange.[85]

Oliver Hudson Kelley, the man appointed to investigate the agricultural conditions of the South, was more impressed by the lack of social, cultural, and educational opportunities among the southern farmers than he was by any other single factor. Kelley, being a Mason and having sensed the influence that body had exerted in promoting sectional friendship, envisaged the creation of some similar rural organization to cater to farmers' needs and to bring to them some of the advantages enjoyed by city people.[86]

But the Grange, like the contemporary labor organizations whose existence was threatened by depression, in search for some speedy formula for farm relief from low prices and heavy indebtedness, cast aside its social and cultural cloak and launched a double-barreled crusade for reform along the political and economic fronts. It was the panic of 1873 more than any other single factor that brought pressure on the organization to force it to adopt the political and economic program for which it is best known.[87]

During the seventies and eighties the Grange focused attention on the need for cheaper and more uniform railroad rates, the curbing of middlemen's profits and malpractices, and the obtaining of cheaper credit facilities, especially for the southern farmers.[88] These three de-

[84] Ibid., 74–75; A. C. Cole, The Era of the Civil War, 1848–1870 (Springfield, Ill., 1919), 384–85; "History of Our Rural Organizations," U.S. Department of Agriculture, Report, 1875, 437–68; Rufus Nutting, "Farmers' Clubs," ibid., 1867, 236–47; "The Florida Cotton Plan Again," De Bow's Review, 13:291–92 (Sept. 1852).

[85] There were some notes of discontent before the Civil War, but they were reflective of a small minority. For example, J. B. Turner, in the Illinois State Agricultural Society, Transactions, 1856–57, 420–21, said: ". . . while the government of the United States has expended millions of money for the comparatively meagre interests of commerce and manufactures, either directly or indirectly, it has not spent two hundred thousand dollars . . . all told, for the great interest of general agriculture since the origin of the government. . . . In my humble opinion the fifteen million of farmers of the Union have sucked the dry teat of indirect aid long enough to claim a quaff or two at the full breast of 'bona fide' direct aid."

The common objectives of the local agricultural societies were to raise better crops and livestock, to present papers on fruit culture, stress the need for industrial universities, and make awards for prize cattle, horses, sheep, swine, poultry, and fruits of various types. See footnote 63.

[86] Oliver H. Kelley, Origin and Progress of the Order of the Patrons of Husbandry (Philadelphia, 1875), 11–20.

[87] The American Annual Cyclopaedia, 1873 (New York, 1874), 625–26, gives the number of granges established during 1868–1873 as follows: 1868, 11; 1869, 39; 1870, 38; 1871, 125; 1872, 1,105; 1873, 8,400.

[88] Clark, The Problem of Monopoly, 91; Commercial and Financial Chronicle, 16: 464 (Apr. 5, 1873); C. W. Howard, "Conditions of Agriculture in the Cotton States," U.S. Department of Agriculture, Report, 1874, 219–20; Charles W. Pierson, "The Rise of the Granger Movement," Popular Science Monthly, 32:199–208 (Dec. 1887).

mands did not preclude the existence of others like taxation, farm labor, and the tariff.[89] Attention was called to the need for gathering statistics; isolated efforts were made to influence prices by encouraging farmers to limit the cotton crop,[90] and withhold wheat and hogs from market.[91] The Grange staged loud and vigorous protests over the conduct of agricultural education and demanded autonomy for those colleges connected with institutions receiving land-grant funds; investigations were made of agricultural education at home and abroad; college administrations and their curricula were probed in Ohio, California, and other States, and during the first flush of enthusiasm, Granger schools were organized in a number of States.[92]

Government regulation of railroads was high on the agenda of the Grange. This campaign was "no war against railroads as such," John Bates Clark observed, but "against the corporations as they were conducted." The roads were entitled to "honest returns for genuine investments" but not on watered stock which forced farmers to pay higher rates.[93] "The railroad companies must submit to legislative control, the people can tolerate no divided sovereignty with corporations of their own creation." The Master of the National Grange exclaimed "that the same government which can take my land for the public good and fix the price thereof, can say to the railroad, 'The public good demands that you carry freight and persons at reasonable rates, which you henceforth must do, and we will decide what those rates shall be.'"[94]

The Grangers, beginning about the middle seventies, shifted some emphasis away from the cheaper transportation issue to the establishment of cooperative stores and marketing associations. The consumers' stores sought to supplant the purchasing-agent system that had been organized to lessen retail margins.[95] Short-lived cooperative grain elevators, livestock shipping associations, and cheese factories helped decrease marketing costs. Perhaps more permanent and prosperous were the farmers' mutual life insurance companies which enjoyed remarkable success

[89] Charles W. Pierson, "The Outcome of the Granger Movement," *Popular Science Monthly*, 32:372–73 (Jan. 1888); Buck, *The Granger Movement*, 105; National Grange, *Journal of Proceedings*, 1882, 83; *ibid.*, 1883, 20–22; *ibid.*, 1894, 26.
[90] Buck, *The Granger Movement*, 294–96.
[91] *Nation*, 17:282 (Oct. 30, 1873); Jonathan Periam, *The Groundswell; A History of the Origins, Aims, and Progress of the Farmers' Movement* (Cincinnati and Chicago, 1874), 361; Herman Steen, *Cooperative Marketing: The Golden Rule in Agriculture* (Garden City, N.Y., 1923), 212.
[92] International Institute of Agriculture, *Monthly Bulletin of Economic and Social Intelligence*, 58(10):6 (Oct. 1915); Earle D. Ross, *Democracy's College* (Ames, Iowa, 1942), 79–85; and National Grange, *Journal of Proceedings*, 1892, 88–101; *ibid.*, 1901, 12–17.
[93] Clark, *The Problem of Monopoly*, 90–91.
[94] Quoted in Thomas Clark Atkeson, *Semi-Centennial History of the Patrons of Husbandry* (New York, 1916), 62.
[95] Periam, *The Groundswell*, 200–01; National Grange, *Journal of Proceedings*, 1879, 13–19.

from the start. Less successful were the Granger efforts to manufacture cooperatively farm machinery and implements, sewing machines, wagons, and other needs.[96]

The Grange had some influence on contemporary farmer groups like the Farmers' Alliance and the Agricultural Wheel.[97] Farmer organizations, like individuals, presumably learned by imitating others. The Farmers' Alliance, of the newer organizations, carried on the campaign for remedial legislation and cooperative marketing and purchasing; whereas the Populist Party, chiefly a political offshoot of the Alliance, carried on more dramatically the campaign for the direct election of United States Senators, the direct primary, woman suffrage, the initiative and referendum, better credit facilities, railroad regulation, and an inflated currency. Monopoly, or what was generally believed to have been monopoly, had to cease; railroads were to be publicly owned; the principle of representative government had to be extended; and free silver was to meet the expanding monetary needs of the country. "One can not avoid a sense of pride in the courageous and political spirit of these derided farmers who, with all their mistakes, carried on the tradition of American self-government." [98]

During the nineties, the free-silver campaign occupied the agrarian spotlight. Free silver had mustered support among the Alliancemen, some Grangers, the Knights of Labor, the Greenbackers, and lesser reform groups. After the admission of half a dozen new western States into the Union in 1889 and 1890, the free-silverites received the support of the powerful silver mining interest of the West. The silver interests were guided largely by selfish motives in subsidizing this crusade; yet it was the farmers' case that was given the most publicity. Hundreds of thousands of farmers were taught to believe that free silver was the remedy they had been searching for all the while. There was an inadequate supply of money in circulation because the Government and the monied interests had discriminated against the greenbacks and silver; the discriminatory monetary policies of the Government was the chief explanation for low farm prices. The free and unlimited coinage of silver would remedy this; the expanding monetary needs of the Nation would be met; prices would rise; interest rates would be forced down; debts would be paid off; and a metallic security would be provided.[99] As long as farm prices were high, the farmer had little to worry about in the way of

[96] Arthur H. Hirsch, "Efforts of the Grange in the Middle West to Control the Price of Farm Machinery, 1870–1880," *Mississippi Valley Historical Review*, 15: 473–74 (March 1929); National Grange, *Journal of Proceedings*, 1897, 95; U.S. Federal Farm Board, *Statistics of Farmers' Selling and Buying Association, United States, 1863–1931* (*Bulletin 9*, Washington, 1932), 2; and Henry H. Bakken and Marvin A. Schaars, *The Economics of Cooperative Marketing* (New York, 1937), 49–56.
[97] Theodore Saloutos, "The Agricultural Wheel in Arkansas," *Arkansas Historical Quarterly*, 2:127–40 (June 1943).
[98] Edward R. Lewis, *A History of American Political Thought from the Civil War to the World War* (New York, 1937), 304.
[99] The best study is John D. Hicks, *The Populist Revolt* (Minneapolis, 1931).

debts; whether justified or not, this at least was the reasoning of many. American experience with monetary problems and the relationship of the Government to prices, wages, and debts, especially since 1933, suggests that the arguments of the Populists were not as absurd as their critics made them out as being.

The peak of the free-silver campaign was reached in 1896 from which point it retrogressed steadily. Free silver had too many obstacles to overcome. The Republican tradition was still strong in the agrarian West, and the Republican Party felt that protection for industry was more important than free silver. Then, too, shipping, banking, and commercial interests, and those in general who had international affiliations were "opposed to a silver currency at a time when virtually all European currencies were on a gold basis." Beginning in 1897 farm prices began to rise, thus relieving agricultural distress and simultaneously eliminating the very force which had been largely responsible for giving the agrarian elements a degree of cohesiveness. In 1900, legislation liberalized the laws pertaining to the establishment of national banks in rural areas with note-issuing powers. The free-silver argument might have lost its potency as a result of these developments, but this hardly meant that silver was to decline in importance. To the contrary, silver "was retained as a considerable element in the American currency system"; it merely lost its appeal as a social and political issue.[100]

Another farm relief program, and one which attracted slight attention, because of the greater appeal of free silver, was the Lubin plan. Named for its author, David Lubin, who later founded the International Institute of Agriculture in Rome, it attracted the support of the California State Grange and possibly a few other State granges as well as the endorsement of the chambers of commerce in San Francisco, Portland, Seattle, and other Pacific coast cities; but it never was endorsed by the National Grange.[101] The Lubin plan, inspired by the bounty proposal of Alexander Hamilton, proposed "to restore protection unjustly deprived" the farmers by having the Federal Government pay bounties to exporters of "agricultural staples." This export bounty was to be " 'equal to the cost of ocean transportation to Liverpool.' " Liverpool was selected, according to its protagonists, because it was on the Liverpool market that the prices of such staples as wheat and cotton were determined. By this process they were to provide some form of protection, at least, for the producers and exporters of "agricultural staples." [102]

Back in 1890 the National Grange had muttered "Protection for all or free trade for all," [103] but for the Lubinites during the mid-nineties it

100 Harold L. Reed, "Free Silver," *Encyclopaedia of the Social Sciences*, 6:440 (New York, 1931); U.S. Industrial Commission, *Report*, 19:101, 148–49.
101 California State Grange, *Journal of Proceedings*, 1894, 93; National Grange, *Journal of Proceedings*, 1894, 168–76, 178–79, 192–93; Thomas Clark Atkeson, *Outlines of Grange History* (Washington, 1928), 23–24, and his *Semi-Centennial History*, 180–82; "Protection and Farmers," *Social Economist*, 9(2):10–18 (Aug. 1895).
102 *Social Economist*, 9(2):12 (Aug. 1895).
103 Atkeson, *Semi-Centennial History*, 158.

was protection or nothing. "'For the farmers say that they will not longer submit to this injustice. Free trade they do not want and will not have, except as a last resort.'"[104] The limited attention that the Lubin plan received practically vanished by the turn of the century, but the principle of paying bounties to exporters of agricultural products survived to hound the Coolidge and Hoover administrations during the 1920s.[105] This principle, after experiencing certain facial and physiognomic alterations, emerged as the export debenture plan, fathered by Professor Charles L. Stewart of the University of Illinois, and was adopted by the National Grange.

Another less emphasized relief program called for the establishment of farmers' trusts and holding companies, the thought being that "if trusts and combines are to be the order of the future, the farmer may as well enjoy whatever benefits can be derived from them; that many lines of the farmer's production might well come into combination to the farmer's advantage. . . ."[106] Withholding crops from market gained a minimum amount of attention during the seventies and eighties, but it increased during the nineties to the point of prompting the statistician of the United States Department of Agriculture to warn against the fallacy of such a program.[107] By the turn of the century, the general idea gained converts among the grain, cotton, and tobacco producers.

This, in substance, was the reaction of the farmers during the last three decades of the nineteenth century. Lower transportation rates, corporate regulation, cooperative marketing and purchasing associations, inflation of the currency, cheaper credit facilities, the payment of bounties, the granting of autonomy to agricultural colleges and their emphasis upon the more practical aspects of farm life, likewise the establishment of agricultural counter-trusts as a means for out-trusting the trusts, were included in their growing list of demands. Many critics received these and other demands with cynicism, indifference, ridicule, or outright opposition. Much of this might have been merited, but more important was the fact that the farmers had evolved no agricultural policy to cope with the farm problem. Part of the blame perhaps lay with the Federal Government which, rightfully or wrongfully refused to recognize the existence of a farm problem, and partly with the farmers themselves because of their inability to agree on the diagnosis and remedy to be administered. Each organization, baffled by the ramifications of the farm problem and the desire to preserve its individuality, laid emphasis on some particular formula with which it became identified. During the seventies and eighties it was chiefly railroad regulation and cooperatives which oc-

[104] Social Economist, 9(2):12 (Aug. 1895).
[105] This came up in the export debenture plan. See Joseph Stancliffe Davis, The Farm Export Debenture Plan (Stanford University, 1929), 1–41.
[106] J. R. Elliot, American Farms: Their Condition and Future (New York, 1890), 125.
[107] J. T. Horner, "The United States Governmental Activities in the Field of Agricultural Economics Prior to 1913," Journal of Farm Economics, 10:451–52 (Oct. 1928); and Steen, Cooperative Marketing (New York, 1923), 212.

cupied the spotlight; during the nineties, it was chiefly free silver; by the turn of the century, it was minimum prices combined with crop restrictions and withholding crops from market; during the second and third decades of the twentieth century the emphasis fell chiefly on cooperative marketing and purchasing associations, more liberal credit facilities, and the equalization-fee principle.

Many farmers, with some degree of understanding, realized that forces outside the territorial confines of their respective farms affected their fortunes, but whether they fully understood the nature of these forces, their relationship to one another and, more important, to the rest of the economy is a different matter. The institutions of higher learning were hardly in a position to guide them, even though they began to realize, after much pressure, that modern rural life required something more than the classics and other equally impractical subject matter. It appears unlikely that the farmers, as a group, realized that the more industrialism advanced, the more did the fortunes of an agricultural America become affected by forces beyond its control. The expansion of industry failed to free agriculture from the vicissitudes of the foreign market as many had predicted; in fact, agriculture became far more dependent upon the prosperity of industry than most farmers had suspected, which was in direct contrast to the manifestoes of agrarian spokesmen who had proclaimed, with unstinted ardor, that the prosperity of agriculture was fundamental to the prosperity of the Nation. The farmers were hardly as naive as many of their critics made them out as being; still the fact is that they, through their organizations, often stressed one curative to the point of minimizing and obscuring, if not completely overlooking, a multiplicity of factors that contributed materially to the plight of agriculture. The evidence of history is that the agricultural problem was the culmination of a variety of complex factors, for which there was no single simple cure and that the diagnoses of the agricultural ailments, as well as the prescriptions for their relief, are hardly to be considered as something separate and distinct from the rest of the economy.

1914 to the Present

I

America's modern industrial economy has been reshaped by a managerial revolution. In the nineteenth century steam and machinery created an industrial revolution; organizations, the men who manage them, and the complex techniques of group action have worked a similar transformation in the recent past. Within the government an obvious change has taken place. Political organizations are now the pacesetters for the economy. Although the federal government is frequently unable to achieve the rate of growth, the level of employment, or the rate of technological progress that it desires, most Americans have come to accept these objectives as appropriate political goals. In the private sector of the economy, large-scale organizations dominate most of our major industries. The family firm and the bourgeois owner have almost everywhere given way to the corporation and the professional manager. The modern corporation operates in an environment filled with other powerful organizations: labor unions once weak now match the strength of big business; farmers once disorganized now speak through potent groups. Agri-businesses are replacing the traditional family farm. In no other nation has the impact of the new organizations and management been more profound.

The managerial revolution has produced new patterns of behavior in public as well as private economic institutions. For example, there is a growing emphasis upon systematic control of the economic environment. The managers set specific goals and also control or at least attempt to control the process of achieving these goals. The techniques pioneered by the first generation of managers described in Part Two have spread throughout the economy. The rule of thumb no longer holds. Channels of authority are carefully defined, and power is allocated in a relatively rationalistic manner within the new bureaucratic structures. Activity within these organizations is managed with a precision that would have been unbelievable to most nineteenth-century Americans. Clerks of that century could be certain that no one knew to the third decimal place how many seconds it took to copy a letter. Modern managers do know, and they try to use such knowledge to improve the efficiency of their organizations. They also seek efficiency by controlling with care the flow of communications within the organization and between the organization and its environment. They reduce much of this information to statistical form, so that performances can be measured and compared. As a consequence, managerial authority is rather impersonal; it stresses achievement, usually in materialistic terms.

Managerial values pervade our economy. The managerial society is oriented toward economic rationalism, toward materialistic achievement, and toward the group as the basic determinant of behavior. Its standards are ordinarily universal and not particular to any one person or group within the society. The individual and individualistic values are increasingly subordinated to the group and to what sociologist David Riesman has called "other-directed" concepts. The managers are responsible for the efficient interaction of large numbers of persons, and they achieve their goals in part because Americans are willing to subordinate self-interest to the interests of the group. These emerging patterns of thought are reflected in all sectors of the economy, particularly in the economic activity of the national government.

By 1914 the role that the government would play in the economy had already been charted by agrarian and progressive reformers. Rapid industrialization and the expansion of American agriculture had created great wealth but had left many citizens dissatisfied with their society. Whether their concerns were cultural, political, or economic, whether their objectives were rooted in self-interest or visions of social betterment, the reformers all had come to the same conclusion: the government had to play a more active role in the economy. Concern about the economic power of big business, particularly the railroads, and about the political power of businessmen in general led to a number of changes in state and federal governments. Regulatory agencies such as the Interstate Commerce Commission, established in 1877, had been created in an effort to curb the power of the corporations. Reform groups had promoted a variety of state laws to improve working conditions in factories. Hoping to open the political process to public scrutiny and democratic control, liberal reformers had sponsored a number of measures, including the direct election of senators and the use of open congressional hearings on important matters such as the tariff. By 1914 the reform movements had already brought about significant changes in the structure and functions of government in the United States.

America's entry into World War I in 1917 climaxed this period of change. Suddenly, the nation had to coordinate the operations of its complex industrial system. Competing railroads were forced to cooperate to achieve national objectives. Labor and capital had to work together. In an effort to achieve the nation's wartime goals, governmental agencies such as the War Industries Board, established in 1917, controlled the prices and production of thousands of goods and services. A Director General managed the country's railroads as a single transportation network. America's first experience with national direction of the industrial economy was filled with blunders and crises; neither business nor government was really prepared to meet the challenges of mobilization. By 1918, however, the government had worked out a reasonably efficient system of controls, and in later years, at the time of the Great Depression, many Americans looked back upon the government's programs during World War I as a guide for future action.

Although the wartime agencies were dismantled after the Armistice and though the progressive reform movement had subsided, American government did not lapse into laissez faire during the 1920's. The basic governmental structure created before the war remained intact. National responsibilities were frequently reinterpreted during the twenties but were not abandoned, and in some cases the government actually began to play a more active role in the economy. The Department of Commerce became an important agency of change, promoting standardization of industrial products and simplification of processes. With Secretary Herbert Hoover's guidance, business associations and governmental agencies worked together in an effort to improve the efficiency of the national economy. In effect, the government and the associations were attempting to achieve objectives which formerly had been left to the control of an impersonal market mechanism. This same view of government as a partner with business was reflected in Hoover's responses to the Great Depression, which began shortly after he took office as President in 1929. Hoover tried unsuccessfully to use such agencies as the Reconstruction Finance Corporation and the Federal Farm Board to encourage economic recovery. Although his policies failed, this failure did not derive from a dedication to the principle of laissez faire.

The Roosevelt administrations committed far greater resources of money and talent to the struggle for economic recovery. When Franklin D. Roosevelt took office in 1933, millions were unemployed, private banking and industrial institutions were collapsing, and the capitalistic system itself seemed threatened. It is little wonder that under these conditions so many Americans turned to their federal government for a "new deal." In response, the Roosevelt administrations gave the country a number of new and powerful government agencies: the Securities and Exchange Commission, for instance, was empowered to oversee the nation's stock exchanges; the National Labor Relations Board supervised many aspects of labor-management relations; the Merchant Marine Act of 1936 created a new Maritime Commission. Many existing agencies—the Interstate Commerce Commission, the Federal Power Commission, the Federal Reserve System—were strengthened. Important welfare measures such as social security were at last established. In almost every sector of the economy, the impact of new governmental institutions, powers, and programs was felt. By 1940 the most significant structural and ideological change in the history of American government was completed. The central government now had the tools and the philosophy that would enable it to set the pace for the managerial economy.

Even though the New Deal programs were never very successful in dealing with the problems of unemployment and the economy's slow rate of growth, by the 1940's it was obvious that these issues were responsibilities of the government. Americans simply assumed that the federal government would and should manage things that had formerly been left to chance or to state or local governments.

The new managerial philosophy and the new governmental structure were tested and strengthened during World War II. During the forties, price and production controls were far more complete; manpower was controlled and allocated more systematically than it had been before. Shortly after the war it became clear that American involvement in world affairs was to continue—and this new situation would force many citizens to sacrifice their individual interests in order to achieve national goals.

The new assumptions about the government's managerial role in the national economy were crystallized in the Employment Act of 1946, the subject of Arthur F. Burns' article. Burns was Chairman of the Council of Economic Advisers during the first administration of Dwight D. Eisenhower (1953–57) and his remarks are all the more important because they indicate that the ideas expressed in the Employment Act have become the common property of both major political parties. Republicans and Democrats alike have acknowledged that goals such as an adequate level of employment, price stability, a satisfactory rate of economic growth, and "the management of national prosperity" are appropriate objectives for the Federal government. Neither Republicans nor Democrats could ignore the fact that our international obligations made the achievement of such national economic objectives even more essential. Debate centered about which of several objectives would be considered most vital. Would, for instance, the nation seek full employment at the risk of inflation. Or would anti-inflationary policies be followed even if they resulted in a higher unemployment rate. Burns makes clear, however, that the question of whether the national government should indeed be making these decisions—should, in other words, be the pacesetter for the economy—was no longer considered worthy of debate.

Nothing illustrates the new position of the government in our economy more clearly than the operations of the National Science Foundation. As Leland J. Haworth, director of the NSF, points out, the federal government has assumed a new role as sponsor of the nation's scientific and technological development. By the mid-1960's, federal expenditures in support of research and development (through the NSF and other agencies) totaled more than 16 billion dollars a year. In the industrializing economy, this function was performed primarily by private businesses, by universities, or by individuals working on their own. In the managerial economy the rate of scientific and technological progress can no longer be left entirely in private hands. The process of innovation has become a national concern. The National Science Foundation attempts to manage the nation's scientific resources and supply of scientific manpower. Furthermore, the NSF is only one of several government agencies that have performed the economic function of innovation. The Tennessee Valley Authority promoted and financed the development of an entire region. Its activities were remarkably similar to those of various railroad companies in the preceding century; the Great Northern and the Illinois Central had promoted agricultural development and guided settlement along their lines in much the same way as did the TVA. In the industrializing economy the function of innovation was, for the most part, left in private hands; in the managerial economy innovation has become increasingly a public function and concern.

Research and development, both public and private, have become significant determinants of the growth rate and stability of our economy. No longer is technological research left to chance. Research or, to use Sumner H. Slichter's phrase, "the industry of discovery" is highly organized; technological progress is managed in the new economy. Slichter points out some of the economic effects of research and development today and calls upon government policy-makers to increase investments in research.

In addition to promoting research, the government regulates many industries "in the public interest." This regulatory process has, however, not worked in exactly the manner envisioned when most of the original legislation was passed. In some industries the businesses that were supposed to be regulated have dominated the regulatory commissions. Competition between different firms and interests was not ended by regulation; the competition was simply shifted from the marketplace to the commission hearings. The techniques of legal and political action replaced the traditional forms of market competition. Furthermore, the elaboration and implementation of the public interest has proven to be a particularly difficult task. Some of the complexities of governmental regulation in the managerial economy are illustrated in Ralph K. Huitt's article, "Federal Regulation of the Uses of Natural Gas." As Huitt shows, the commission provides a forum in which contesting groups meet and express their positions on matters involving a wide variety of economic and noneconomic problems. The creation of a new governmental agency or commission does not, by itself, solve the problems of protecting the public interest. At its very worst, however, it does expose issues for public discussion, an aspect of the managerial economy that contrasts sharply with the secrecy that characterized economic decision-making in the nineteenth century.

Today government regulates, innovates, and guides the progress of the economy. Government sets the pace of our economic development as surely as the railroad did in the early years of the industrializing economy. While vigorous debate over the proper goals of national policy continues, few Americans question the government's role as pace-setter.

II

Despite the increasing importance of the government, the private sector continues to make a vital contribution to the managerial economy. Within the business system itself, a significant share of the goods and services are produced by industries that are dominated by giant corporations. This, of course, was already true on the eve of World War I. A wave of mergers at the turn of the century had left control in most industries highly concentrated. Oligopoly—the dominance of the few—and not monopoly became customary. Rationalization through the development of systematic controls within a highly centralized firm was one of the most outstanding aspects of this new industrial order. The efficiency and power of these business behemoths caused widespread concern during the early years of the twentieth century; many feared that the movement toward concentration would not stop until most of the nation's wealth was controlled by a few corporate leaders. Even federal and state antitrust policies seemed powerless to stop the growth of big business.

Subsequent developments belayed some of these fears. During the late 1920's, favorable conditions in the stock market helped to bring about a second wave of corporate mergers, which had a particularly significant impact upon banking and the utilities industries. But since that time the level of concentration in the economy has not changed appreciably. Big businesses have continued to grow, and present-day firms such as the American Telephone and Telegraph Company or General Motors dwarf the so-called big businesses of the late nineteenth century. Nevertheless, the national economy has grown faster than big business, and the service and distribution industries—traditional strongholds of the small company—have grown especially fast.

Still, the bulk of our output of industrial goods and services comes from relatively large corporations, and the effects of big business upon the economy are of vital importance. It is evident that most big businesses are able to prevent price competition of the sort that characterized the early industrializing economy. Prices and production in the modern economy are administered, managed; they are not determined in the short run by an impersonal market mechanism. In the oligopolistic industries, various forms of nonprice competition are important: advertising is an especially significant although, to many observers, objectionable competitive weapon. Competition to provide better service and to improve products and processes through research and development have also achieved new importance in the managerial economy.

In the years since 1914 one of the most far-reaching changes in the business system has taken place within the firm. The new corporate strategy of diversification has called forth a new type of organization, the decentralized firm. Leaders in the development of this new form of organization were the DuPont Company and General Motors. Since 1940, companies in many different industries have copied the strategy of diversification and decentralization.

In modern corporations, research and development have assumed an all-important role. Considerable debate has resulted over the precise effect of big business on the nation's technological progress; Edith Tilton Penrose's study of the Hercules Powder Company strongly suggests that in that case at least, technological progress was built into the very structure of the firm. The Hercules Powder Company is certainly representative of a genre of technologically oriented firms which has become very common in American industry since World War II. In this type of business the traditional concept of expansion within a particular industry no longer limits the growth of the firm. The company expands along lines determined by its technological and market capabilities. One of the most important factors influencing growth is the pace at which the firm's managerial structure can be adapted to new conditions and expanded as a coordinated unit. While the firm responds to the pressure of competition, this is primarily the competition of new products, of substitutes for the products that it makes. According to Penrose's analysis, this form of big business has spurred the research and development that have been key elements in our nation's continued economic growth.

The giant firm has had an even more obvious effect upon the development of systematic managerial techniques and controls. Alfred D. Chandler's study of General Motors shows how one of the nation's leading companies developed and implemented its imposing communications, accounting, and administrative structure. The forecasting system that GM created illustrates the fact that the company's prices were no longer responsive to short-run market pressures. Even without this form of price competition, however, GM's management was obviously under considerable competitive pressure as they struggled to gain a larger share of the automobile market. Management remained alert to the need for change. The forecasting system itself was a major administrative innovation; it was adopted by other firms in a variety of industries and was even used by government agencies during World War II. Like many other administrative innovations associated with the growth of big business, the forecasting system extended management's power over the environment both within and without the firm.

John Kenneth Galbraith's essay on countervailing power discusses another form of competition that keeps big business in the managerial economy from reaping monopolistic profits or from suffering for too long the blight of bureaucratic ineptitude. In place of a struggle between units making the same product, Galbraith finds that the new competition involves firms which face each other across the marketplace as supplier and purchaser. The competition that he feels preserves the vitality of the managerial economy is the competition between the giant rubber companies that produce tires and the giant automobile companies that purchase them. The consumer is protected by competition between equally powerful sellers and buyers.

All of these selections suggest that private business in the managerial economy has thus far escaped the stultifying effects of bureaucratization that Joseph A. Schumpeter felt would necessarily destroy the capitalistic system from within. There can be no question that modern management has stimulated further bureaucratization. The modern American corporation, with its emphasis upon communication, its careful allocation of power commensurate with responsibility, and its elaborate system of explicit regulations, epitomizes the bureaucratic structure of authority. These same corporations, however, maintain a devotion to technological change. The decentralized and diversified firm was itself a major administrative innovation; by freeing top managers of day-to-day operating responsibilities, it has enabled them to devote more attention to long-range entrepreneurial decisions. In this way, the modern firm has undoubtedly overcome some of the problems that Schumpeter foresaw.

Plenty of other problems remain, of course. Private decisions made by top management in firms such as General Motors obviously have important social, political, and economic consequences. No longer can Americans pretend that these decisions are made by the invisible hand of the market. While the government insures that some of these decisions will be made in socially acceptable ways, this alone does not allay the fears of those who contemplate the fact that General Motors now has a larger annual net revenue than most of the nations of the world. Whatever the ultimate solution to this problem may be, for the present there can be little doubt that the public interest is best served by having such private corporations surrounded by other powerful organizations in business, politics, and labor.

III

Labor unions in the managerial economy have also enjoyed a remarkable development. In 1914 the labor movement was still weak, with most of the strong unions concentrated in industries that were not introducing new, mass-production methods. Despite progressive reforms, the political environment was still hostile to the labor union, even to the conservative craft unions that made up the American Federation of Labor. In the early years of the twentieth century, many employers' associations had been formed or reorganized in an effort to counter whatever power these unions had acquired. On the national level, the leaders of the National Association of Manufacturers led the fight against union organizations.

During World War I, organized labor's position was considerably strengthened. The demand for labor was high. The unions, like the business associations, found friendly support from government agencies created to carry out national mobilization. Legislation such as the Adamson Act, which established an eight-hour day for the railroad workers, reflected the support that labor received from the national government. As a result, by 1920 the unions claimed over five million members.

In the twenties and the early thirties, many of these gains were wiped away. Business organizations mounted a strong offensive under the so-called American Plan, which supported the open shop (in reality this was an anti-union shop). In 1919 bitter strikes in the steel and coal industries were won by management. Union membership began to decline even though the country was prosperous and the demand for labor was high. By 1929 membership was less than three and a half million. These lean years were capped by the Great Depression, which almost destroyed a number of the nation's leading craft unions. With millions unemployed, management could well afford to root out union sympathizers and to reject union demands. From the vantage point of 1932, it was not at all clear that the labor movement would ever be able to match the power of big business in the nation's leading industries.

If any Americans got a "new deal" from the Roosevelt administrations, however, it was surely the laboringmen. At first this did not appear to be true. While the National Recovery Act of 1933 seemed to guarantee the worker's right to join a union of his own choosing, the administration of the NRA was dominated by employers and their trade associations. What the law gave to the unions, the employers and the National Recovery Administration took away. It was not until the passage of the Wagner National Labor Relations Act of 1935 that organized labor actually received the protection and support that had been promised in 1933. By creating a National Labor Relations Board to oversee labor-management relations and by specifically guaranteeing union rights and restricting the activities of employers, the Wagner Act placed the government's support solidly behind the labor movement.

One result of the new political environment was a tremendous increase in union membership. By 1940 there were almost nine million union members in America; ten years later, membership had soared to about 15 million. Furthermore, the unions were now successfully established in mass-production industries such as steel and automobiles, industries in which the older craft unions had failed to win support.

The mass-production industries were organized because of the development of a new form of union and new patterns of militant action. One does not usually think of unions as innovators, but during the 1930's changes in the political situation brought forth a new union strategy and structure. The AFL's managers hesitated to exploit the opportunities created by the New Deal; they had been forced to follow cautious policies too long and they were afraid to move too fast, to endanger their established craft organizations. Aggressive leaders such as John L. Lewis of the United Mine Workers were not so timid, however; they organized the Committee for Industrial Organization in 1935 and abandoned the craft principle of unionization. CIO leaders flirted with radical ideas and experimented with new methods of dealing with the employers. In 1937, it was primarily the CIO unions which tried the production slowdowns and the illegal but effective sit-down strikes. Walter Galenson's selection on the automobile workers shows that the new organizations and new techniques worked amazingly well so long as the unions had widespread public and governmental support. Their struggle was bitter. Lives were lost and property was destroyed. But by the end of the 1930's, management in most of our major, mass-production industries had accepted the new laws and the unions.

During the late forties and through the fifties, the government's position in regard to the labor movement changed considerably. With strong unions established, public concern developed about corruption among union leaders and about the protection of employers' rights. The Taft-Hartley Act was passed in 1947 in an effort to protect employers' rights and to insure that the public interest would not be injured by major strikes. The Landrum-Griffin Act of 1959 attempted to root out labor corruption and to protect union members from unreasonable actions by their own leaders.

Despite the negative image cast by these two important laws, it is evident that the stronger unions of the post-1935 years have on balance functioned effectively, protecting their members' rights without seriously endangering the national economy. In fact, labor-management relations in the post–New Deal era have been characterized more by peaceful relations than by headline-making strikes. Peaceful collective bargaining is not very exciting, not very newsworthy. To make the front page the union needs to engage in a long and bitter strike. Even historians find more interest in periods of upheaval than in peaceful collective bargaining. Fortunately, Gordon W. Bertram and Sherman J. Maisel's "Industrial Relations in the Construction Industry" describes and analyzes one relatively peaceful experience in industrial relations. Some aspects of labor-management relations in the northern California construction industry are unique, but others are common to many small-unit, competitive industries, where the AFL craft unions have long predominated. The regional organization, covering 46 counties, for instance, illustrates a common tendency for unions to spread over wider geographical areas and to bargain jointly with large numbers of employers. Both the employees and employers want to reduce uncertainty through specific union-management agreements. Industry-wide bargaining is normal in many of our leading industries. Similarly, the author's conclusion that the most favorable situation results when neither labor nor management has overwhelming power could be applied to most, if not all, American industries.

In construction and in most other industries an accommodation between labor and management has been reached in the years since World War II. In the last three decades, truly outstanding changes have taken place in labor organizations and in labor-management relations. This has left the managerial economy with some new, unsolved problems—particularly those of protecting the public interest in price stability and of preventing debilitating struggles in such major industries as transportation and iron and steel. But clearly a balance between corporate and labor power has been established through the active and continued intervention of the federal government.

IV

Other groups in our society have made a similar adjustment to twentieth-century conditions, to the era of large-scale organizations. American agriculture is one of these groups. During the early years of the twentieth century, the basic nature of the organizations through which farmers expressed their views began to change. A cooperative movement of formidable proportions got underway. Unlike the radical agrarian groups of the preceding century, the cooperatives espoused business methods and managerial objectives. Most other farm organizations also avoided the seemingly radical doctrines which had proved so disastrous to the agrarian movement in the 1890's. Third-party political organizations gave way to effective, nonpartisan lobbies managed by skillful leaders.

During the early twenties, the farmers sought to achieve their political objectives through the farm bloc in Congress. The bloc was a nonpartisan, independent coalition of congressmen from the agricultural areas of the country. They collaborated to push measures for agricultural relief through Congress. While it was impossible for some of the most important of the farm-supported legislation to get past presidential vetoes, the passage of new measures to regulate the packers and stockyards, to extend the War Finance Corporation, and to control the nation's grain exchanges indicated how effective the bloc was.

Necessity had something to do with this effectiveness, of course. During most of the 1920's, agriculture was depressed while the rest of the nation prospered. Wartime overproduction caused prices of major commodities to slump in 1920 and they never fully recovered before the Great Depression. Foreclosures of farm mortgages mounted; farm tenancy increased. In the Midwest and the South, throughout the nation's major agricultural regions, farm income remained low. After 1929 the situation became even worse, and by 1932 some farmers were apparently convinced that peaceful measures would no longer suffice. The short-lived Farmers' Holiday Association fell back upon violent methods in an unsuccessful effort to push prices up by keeping goods from reaching the market.

More representative of the type of farm organization that came to power in the 1920's and 1930's was the American Farm Bureau Federation. Like most of the modern farm organizations, the Farm Bureau avoided such panaceas as free silver or government ownership of railroad and telegraph companies. Its managers focused the farmers' attention on the central problems of price and production. They sought to unify all farmers under its banner and to achieve through systematic political action the power that would insure government help in dealing with overproduction.

The Farm Bureau reached its peak of political influence during the 1930's. Grant McConnell's selection tells how the organization functioned in Washington and how it sought to establish its programs. It was extremely important for the Farm Bureau to maintain a large membership and to join forces whenever possible with other farm groups because political leverage could only be achieved by an organization that spoke for the many, not the few. Skillful leadership was a vital element in the Farm Bureau's success; it had the type of managers and resources that could only be achieved by a large-scale organization. The unorganized farmer had no voice; for that matter, the unorganized citizen in any occupation frequently has no voice in the managerial society. This was shown quite clearly by the manner in which the New Deal agricultural programs favored the Southern planters, who were organized; the Southern tenant farmers were by-passed by the New Deal programs because their voices were simply not heard in Washington. By 1938 the Farm Bureau had reached the peak of its power. The Bureau's officers practically drafted the farm legislation of that year. The contrast between the Populists' failures during the depression of the 1890's and the Farm Bureau's accomplishments during the depression of the 1930's provides one measure of the farmers' successful accommodation to the political environment of the managerial society.

The New Deal programs brought the government into agriculture to curb falling prices. Through research and educational work the government had for many years been helping the farmers to produce more. Both types of programs remain with us today. Price supports and production controls devised during a period of severe agricultural depression have carried over into the years since 1940 although the economic condition of the farmer has changed markedly.

Discussion of the farm problem—which usually means the commodity programs—frequently masks the fact that in the years since World War II American agriculture has experienced a revolution. By exploiting a backlog of existing technological knowledge, American farmers have achieved dramatic increases in production. The very nature of the farm itself has changed. While the small family farm remains numerically important, a good part of the nation's agricultural commodities are produced on a new kind of farm: the relatively large agri-business. These new business units are capital intensive—that is, by buying machinery to do every possible task they replace labor with capital. The new farms are technologically advanced. They use fertilizers and plant sprays to produce the largest and the best possible crops.

In some branches of farming, large corporations—similar to those which the farmers of the 1890's attacked so bitterly—have come to dominate the market. As Edward Higbee shows, only these units can afford the machinery or the organization necessary to achieve maximum efficiency; the prices that these companies set leave the old-fashioned farmer with a choice between moving to the city or farming part-time while he holds a regular job in town. The small farmers continue to be a problem, but they no longer exert a major influence on the prices or production of the nation's chief commodities.

As a result of the new modes of organization and the new technology, American farm productivity has enjoyed a remarkable increase in the postwar years. In agriculture as a whole, one index for net output per man-hour shows a figure of 100 for 1929, 134.0 for 1944, and 307.4 for 1960. Whereas in 1930 one farm worker supplied the products for 9.8 persons, by the early 1960's each farm worker supplied products for over 27 persons. American agriculture's success in the twentieth century seems all the more startling in light of the millions of undernourished throughout the world today.

The new type of farm, the new farmer, the new style of farm organization—all these represent successful accommodations to the managerial economy. In an age which pours billions into science and technology, the managers of the new business-oriented farms have learned to harness the chemistry of fertilizers and the genetics of selective breeding. In an age of large-scale government, business, and union organizations, the farmer too has learned to organize.

V

By the 1960's, America had developed a new economic system, one which did not fit comfortably the old categories of "capitalism" or "socialism." In every corner of the economy the processes of combination, of organizational growth, and of administrative consolidation had made themselves felt. Activities within the industrial system were highly rationalized to bring them under the systematic control of professional administrators. The government set goals, influenced the pace of growth, and regulated procedures throughout the economy. In science, in business, in the labor market, and in agriculture, organizations rationalized the very process of change and sought increased efficiency through systematic controls.

The adjustment to this new system has created many problems. It is important to keep in mind that many Americans today can recall a nation in which the automobile, let alone General Motors, did not exist. Americans accustomed to thinking in terms of individual action had had to accept the restraints of highly organized group functions. New roles have been created in the managerial economy; new values have developed to meet the demands of a rationalized, organized society. For many, the result has been psychological strain. Changes in values have lagged far behind the changes in organizational size and technique.

The managerial economy has nevertheless compiled a good record in achieving the material objectives of our society. We are blessed with high standards of productivity, high levels of income, and greater measures of security than Americans have ever before experienced. During the 1920's and 1930's, the growth of our economy was relatively slow; but since 1940 the American system has sustained a substantial rate of growth. This has been done, furthermore, without encountering the type of major depression that shook the economy in the 1870's, 1890's, and 1930's. Our new blend of governmental and private organizations appears to be less vulnerable to economic fluctuations than was the industrializing economy. While the nation faces many economic problems, they are the difficulties that inevitably come with power, prosperity, and economic maturity. They can only be dealt with by educated citizens who understand the new managerial economy. Through these readings we hope to further that understanding.

Section 1 ⌣ The Government—Pacesetter
for the Managerial Economy

One ⌣ The Government as Planner

SOME REFLECTIONS ON THE
EMPLOYMENT ACT   *Arthur F. Burns*

The Employment Act of 1946 was originally designed to cope with the problem of minimizing unemployment. However, with the passage of time, it has acquired something of the force of an economic constitution. The President, his Council of Economic Advisers, the Congress, in some degree the entire executive and administrative establishment of the federal government, including the Federal Reserve Board, now function under this "constitution" when major economic policies are developed. Governmental activities in behalf of the national economy, especially when they involve new tools, have always been a matter of interest to our Association.[1] It may therefore be useful on this occasion to take a broad look at the machinery for economic policy-making established by the Employment Act and to reflect on some ways of strengthening this machinery.

I

Let me begin by recalling the early history of the Employment Act. As World War II drew to a close, many public-minded citizens became

[1] Address delivered at the Annual Meeting of the American Statistical Association, Minneapolis, Minnesota, on September 7, 1962.

FROM Arthur F. Burns, "Some Reflections on the Employment Act." Reprinted with permission from *The Political Science Quarterly*, Vol. LXXVII, No. 4 (December 1962), pp. 481–90, 498–500.

fearful that the return of peace would bring a return of mass unemployment such as existed during the 1930's. Gradually, the thought emerged that just as unemployment was eliminated during the war, so the resources of government could be used to avoid sizable unemployment under peacetime conditions. To give expression to this thought, Senator James E. Murray in January, 1945, introduced a bill called "The Full Employment Act of 1945."

In its declaration of policy, the Murray bill stated that "all Americans able to work and seeking work have the right to useful, remunerative, regular, and full-time employment," and that "it is essential that continuing full employment be maintained in the United States." Accordingly, the bill laid down the requirement that the President transmit to the Congress at the beginning of each regular session a "national production and employment budget." This budget was to cover an interval starting six months later and ending not less than eighteen months later.

For this interval in the future the "national budget" was to set forth, first of all, an estimate of the size of the labor force. Next, an estimate of the gross national product corresponding to full employment was to be presented—that is, the dollar value of the output of commodities and services that would "provide employment opportunities" for the entire labor force. A third requirement was an estimate of what the gross national product would be in the absence of new governmental programs or policies. Fourth, in the event that this prospective output fell short of the amount required to assure full employment, the President was to recommend to the Congress measures for stimulating private expenditures. Fifth, if these measures were still deemed insufficient to remove the deficiency in the "national budget," the President was to recommend federal expenditures to close the budgetary gap—in other words, federal spending was to be increased in the amount needed to bring total output to a full-employment level. Finally, in case the "national budget" indicated a prospective output which exceeded the required full-employment output, the President was to recommend to the Congress "a program for preventing inflationary economic dislocations."

This bill and its highly novel national budget aroused a great deal of public discussion. Some men viewed it as a practical mechanism for attending systematically and with forethought to the problem of protecting the nation against the ravages of depression and unemployment. Others, while favorably impressed with the aims of the bill, doubted whether economic knowledge had reached sufficient precision to make the law workable. Still others saw the bill as a device for turning America into a regimented, socialistic economy. Such fears were entertained by a large section of the House of Representatives. The House therefore proceeded with a bill that was more to its liking.

Since the bills passed by the Senate and House differed, they went to a Conference Committee which devoted eleven days to hammering out a compromise. The bill that finally emerged made no reference either to full employment or to inflation. It made no reference to a national production and employment budget, or to numerical goals or targets of any kind. It made no reference to any obligation of the federal government to fill a gap between prospective output and a full-employment output. It said nothing about the specific means to be used for stimulating economic activity. It did, however, carry a sweeping and historic declaration of policy—namely, that it is the continuing responsibility of the federal government to foster "conditions under which there will be afforded useful employment opportunities. . . . for those able, willing, and seeking to work, and to promote maximum employment, production, and purchasing power."

Other portions of the Conference bill dealt with procedures. An Economic Report by the President was required, to be presented to the Congress at an early stage of each regular session and to be supplemented, as need might arise, at other times. The purpose of this Report was to review the condition and prospects of the nation's economy, to appraise existing federal activities that bear on production and employment, and to present a program for carrying out the objectives of the proposed law. In performing these duties the President was to be assisted by a new agency, the Council of Economic Advisers. Also, a Committee drawn from both the Senate and the House was to be established to advise the Congress with regard to the recommendations of the Economic Report and to make such additional findings as it might from time to time deem desirable.

This Conference bill, which became law in February, 1946, was hailed by the liberals of the Senate as a victory for their side, just as it was hailed by the conservatives of the House as a victory for theirs. Both groups were able to do this because the only way of breaking the deadlock in the Conference was to use language that was general enough to admit of more than one interpretation.

II

Whether because or in spite of its massive ambiguities, the Employment Act has proved a useful framework for the management of our national prosperity. With few and only minor changes, the machinery for economic policy-making laid down by the Act has persisted to the present time. There have been critics who at times have wanted to scrap or drastically alter this machinery, and they came close to doing so early in 1953. But the number of critics or sceptics has diminished with the years, and the Employment Act is now looked upon with favor by nearly every articulate group in our nation.

To be sure, there is still a wide range of opinion about the precise contribution of the Employment Act to our national life, just as there is a range of opinion about the manner in which the Act has been administered by successive Presidents. I believe, however, there is broad agreement that the Act has introduced elements of order and planning in economic policy-making that previously did not exist; that the Act has served to raise the standards that we commonly apply to our nation's economic performance; that the Act has stimulated useful analytical work by economists and fact-finding by statisticians; and that the machinery of the Act has helped high government officials to think about production, employment, consumption, investment, and finances in terms of the operation of the whole economy, not merely this or that of its parts. It will also be generally acknowledged, I think, that the Act has played its part in changing the character of the business cycle—that is, in making its downward phase both shorter and milder, in limiting the incidence of unemployment, and in blunting the effects of recessions on the lives and fortunes of individuals.

These are significant achievements by any reasonable yardstick. And yet I dare say that if the Employment Act were legislated anew, it would have a different emphasis from the law that we have. Many Americans are nowadays seriously concerned about the discrepancy between our nation's rate of economic growth and that of Russia, Germany, France, Japan, and other countries. There are many reasons for this concern, not the least being an uneasy feeling that our nation's prestige and even its security may suffer as a consequence of the lagging growth rate. Theories of economic growth have of late been proliferating and clashing. Although little agreement has as yet emerged, one broad principle is beyond question—namely, that a nation's economic growth depends ultimately on how much work people do and how efficiently they do it. Yet the Employment Act nowhere expresses concern about industrial waste or the need for its avoidance. Indeed, you will look in vain among its provisions even for the word "efficiency."

The same applies to inflation. Since 1945, the price level of the commodities and services produced in our country has risen, year after year, virtually without interruption. The index stood at 75 in 1946, at 100 in 1954, at 111 in 1958, and at 117 earlier this year. This persistent rise of the price level has worked hardships on many people, it has distorted the financial accounts of business firms, and it has reduced our nation's ability to sell in foreign markets at a time when a huge export surplus is required to finance military expenditures abroad and the foreign aid programs. Yet you will look in vain in the Employment Act for any reference to the importance of maintaining stability in the general level of prices, or even for any mention of "inflation" or the "price level."

Of late, many Americans have gained fresh awareness of a fact which fortune had permitted us to slight over a long generation, namely, that our nation is not self-sufficient. We are now relearning the lesson that, in order to manage our economic affairs successfully, we must be mindful of the needs and trading policies of other nations, of the size of our gold stocks and the short-term balances that foreign governments and citizens hold here, and of the levels of labor costs, interest rates, and prices in our country relative to those in other nations. Yet you will look in vain in the Employment Act for any mention of the outside world, or of the need to conduct economic policies, both domestic and foreign, so as to enable us to discharge the political, economic, and military responsibilities that history has thrust upon us.

The reasons for these reticences of the Employment Act are not far to seek. In 1946 Americans still had vivid memories of the great depression of the 1930's when the unemployment rate, even in a relatively good year like 1937, averaged over fourteen per cent. Many citizens feared that the years ahead would be darkened by depression, while few foresaw that we were on the threshold of a great inflation. In 1946 the extraordinary performance of American industry during the war was so fresh in people's minds that it was natural to take rapid improvements of efficiency for granted. In 1946 the United States alone possessed the atom bomb, much of Russia was a ruin, and we had no clear warning of the territorial, military, and economic expansion of communism that has occurred since then. In 1946 the nations of Western Europe and Japan were near collapse and in urgent need of our help. We did not foresee how quickly they would rebuild, modernize, enlarge, and diversify their manufacturing capacity, or that their businessmen would soon challenge ours, often with substantial success, in world markets and even in our own market. In 1946 the entire world accepted the dollar as the supreme symbol of safety, strength, and stability. Few, if any, economists anticipated the uncertainty that has lately arisen about our ability to bring the balance of international payments into equilibrium.

Clearly, both the international scene and our own have changed profoundly since World War II, and so too have some of our economic problems. However well suited the Employment Act was to a time when public thought was so largely focused on the problem of unemployment, it can fit the needs of our own time only by a free interpretation of its provisions or by formal amendment. The broad language of the Act, as well as precedent and tradition, favor the former approach. After all, while the Act declares that it is the policy of the federal government "to promote maximum employment, production, and purchasing power," it also states that the methods used are to be consistent with the "needs and obligations" of the government, with "other essential considerations of national policy," and with the "general welfare." In view of these omnibus provisions, no President has ever felt seriously inhibited in emphasizing whatever economic problems he chose, provided the nation's employment needs also received due attention. For example, the latest Economic Report is addressed not only to the goal of maximum employment, production and purchasing power, but also to the goal of general price stability, to the goal of faster economic growth, to the goal of equal opportunity, and to the goal of basic balance in international payments. Clearly, this Report, far from being confined to the problem of achieving full employment, is concerned with the major economic issues of our time. As much can be said, I think, of most of the earlier Reports.

In view of the typically wide scope of Presidential pronouncements under the Employment Act, it may seem pointless to argue that anything is to be gained by amending the Act so as to broaden its explicit objectives. Yet that is precisely what I wish to argue. My thesis is simple. The Employment Act was designed to focus national policy on the alleviation, and, if possible, on the prevention of unemployment. In the meantime, other goals of national policy have been articulated with a sense of urgency, especially the achievement of reasonable stability in the general price level, the achievement of a higher rate of economic growth, and the strengthening of the international foundations of our prosperity and security. These goals are interrelated. Preoccupation with one may lead to injury to the others, and thereby also militate against full realization of the first. Federal economic policy has to address itself to each of our national goals and to their mutual accommodation. The fact that one or another Economic Report has done so admirably is not a sufficient basis for expecting that this will happen with sufficient regularity in the future. Not only do Presidents have their shortcomings, but so also do their economic advisers, and the best of men sooner or later tire or retire. If certain requirements are explicitly laid down by statute, there is a better chance that they will be respected than if the matter is left to personal discretion. In addition, amendment of the Employment Act would enhance public awareness of both the tasks and the complexity of national economic policy.

There is some historical justification for taking this position. Since the end of World War II, whenever the forces of recession have begun to gather strength, the federal government has moved fairly quickly to try to curb the decline. Not only does the Employment Act call for such action, but there are always people around to remind the Executive of the government's responsibilities. There is nothing in the law, however, that requires the government to promote efficiency or a stable price level or a liberal commercial policy or equilibrium in the balance of payments. By and large, the pressures for corrective action in these areas have been much smaller.

For example, during the course of the recession of 1953–54, the Cabinet discussed every week, at the President's insistent request, economic developments, economic prospects, and the governmental actions that appeared to be necessary or desirable to bolster the economy. Every week the Chairman of the Council of Economic Advisers reported on these matters to the President and again to the Cabinet. And nearly every week some action was taken to check the recession. But when economic recovery finally got under way and signs of renewed inflation began emerging, the great sense of urgency that had previously ruled was no longer present. To be sure, inflationary developments were carefully noted and some actions were taken to contain them. To be sure, the Chairman of the Council still made his reports weekly to the President, but he did so less frequently at Cabinet meetings. Neither the President nor his advisers felt as much pressure for energetic action as before, nor did they in turn exert as much pressure on others. It would not be difficult to supply other and perhaps more striking illustrations of the tendency of governmental authorities to be more actively concerned with minimizing current unemployment than with preventing inflation or enhancing efficiency or accelerating economic growth in the future. Because of this tendency, I think that the expansion of employment itself has suffered.

I would not argue that the mere passage of an amendment broadening the objectives of the Employment Act will necessarily make much difference in the management of national prosperity. With or without such an amendment, some government officials will continue to urge new import quotas or a higher minimum wage as a cure for unemployment, some will continue to argue for higher price supports to solve the problem of agricultural surpluses, some will continue to thunder against monopoly and yet refuse to allow railroads that want to compete on a price basis from doing so, and many will remain discreetly silent about the deliberate waste in which millions of workers and their managers have acquired a vested interest. All that I claim is that amendment of the Employment Act would favor deeper and more balanced thinking on economic issues, thereby helping to create an environment in which economic policies can be better adapted to national needs.

III

I have allowed myself to speculate that if the Employment Act were being written anew, it would have a different emphasis from the law that we have. I do not mean by this that full employment would be subordinated to other goals. On the contrary, I believe that the American people are more firmly committed to the ideal of full employment than they were a generation ago. If the Employment Act were recast today, it might even be christened "The Full Employment Act," as was the original Murray bill. Experience during the postwar period has demonstrated that the monetary and fiscal policies of government can have a powerful influence on the course of the economy without subjecting specific activities to regulation. In view of this experience, the goal of full employment has gained wide acceptance in business and financial circles as well as in other parts of our society. What we characteristically debate nowadays, therefore, is not the need for full employment, but the scale, timing, and character of economic programs for moving towards this and other generally accepted goals.

The Employment Act itself gives very little guidance on these matters. To be sure, the Act stresses the importance of promoting employment and production "in a manner calculated to foster . . . free competitive enterprise," but this constraint merely reaffirms our nation's commitment to the principle of freedom. Practically speaking, the means for dealing with recession and unemployment are left entirely to later judgment concerning the needs of the individual case. There can be no doubt that this element of flexibility has proved helpful to the government officials charged with administering the Employment Act. Indeed, economic life is so full of surprises that the Act might not have survived if the Congress had prescribed some formula, whether the one adumbrated by the Murray bill or any other, for dealing with the business cycle.

Nevertheless, not a few students of economics and politics have become dissatisfied with the way in which the federal government has been discharging its responsibilities under the Employment Act. There seems to be a growing feeling that anti-recession policies are sometimes capricious, that they are often developed or implemented in a mood of complacency, and that speedy if not automatic procedures are therefore needed to strengthen our defenses against recession. The latest Economic Report of the President has crystallized this interest in more vigorous stabilization policy by urging a stand-by tax reduction authority, besides a stand-by public works authority and a stronger unemployment insurance system. In the opinion of the Council of Economic Advisers, the enactment of these measures "would be the most significant step forward in policy for economic stabilization since the Employment Act itself."

.   .   .

There are still other ways in which the machinery for economic policy-making may be improved. One of the formidable difficulties in shaping and articulating national economic policy is the wide diffusion of power within the federal establishment. Economic policy, it is well to remember, is in large part made, and in fact made continuously, through administrative decisions and the manner of their implementation. Since the policies of individual departments or agencies of our far-flung government have ramifications that may not be recognized by their chiefs, and since what is done in the domestic sphere can have repercussions on our international relations, there is a clear need for coordination of economic policies. Traditionally, this problem has been handled by the Bureau of the Budget, the Council of Economic Advisers, interagency committees, the Cabinet, the White House staff, and in still other ways. All these devices have proved their usefulness. The fact remains, nevertheless, that they have not infrequently failed to cope successfully with the tendency of individual units of government to cling tenaciously to what they regard as being, or what may in law actually be, their exclusive prerogative.

In view of the vital role that economic policy has come to play in our times, it may therefore be helpful to establish an Economic Policy Board that would bring to economic matters the authority and prestige which the National Security Council brings to matters of defense. This Board might include, besides the President and the Vice President, the heads of the departments of State, Treasury, Commerce, Labor, Agriculture, and Health, Education and Welfare, as well as the heads of the Federal Reserve Board, the Bureau of the Budget, and the Council of Economic Advisers.

.   .   .

An Economic Policy Board thus constituted may well prove a useful experiment in government. True, the Board would impose a new demand on the President who is already overburdened. It might turn out, however, that the time spent by the President on the Board meetings was more than offset by the reduced need to discuss economic issues with department heads and other officials individually. In any event, the Economic Policy Board should provide a maximum of opportunity for balanced judgment on economic issues, thereby facilitating the development of consistent policies and the early correction of any that are found wanting.

This Board could also be helpful in the implementation of policies, which is never easy in the large establishment of government. An illustration may perhaps clarify this function. Early in 1955 it became evident that the threat of inflation was growing. By mid-year modest steps had already been taken to restrain the general expansion of credit, as well as the expansion of credit in several specific areas—housing, the stock market, and consumer instalment buying. However, nothing was done about federal spending until August, 1955, when, after extensive debate at a Cabinet meeting, the President decided to bring federal expenditures about two billion dollars below the projected estimate for the fiscal year. But in September the President had a heart attack and this impaired for a time his ability to keep the forces of government under close control. The decision to reduce federal spending temporarily, which was right and important at the time, was never carried out. Instead, federal expenditures increased and added to the inflationary pressures that were being rapidly generated by the private sector of the economy.

Of course, one cannot be entirely sure whether the decision to reduce spending would have been implemented if the President's health had been unimpaired. In view of the President's grave illness, it is also uncertain whether better governmental machinery would have made a significant difference. Nevertheless, I believe that if an Economic Policy Board, such as I have sketched, had existed at the time, the chances of implementing the President's decision would have remained good. In view of the President's disability, the chairmanship of the Board would have passed as a matter of course to the Vice President. The Board would have continued to meet on schedule. Hence, the Director of the Budget and the Chairman of the Council would have had an opportunity to report on how well the decision on spending was being carried out. As it was, the decision was forgotten amidst the anxiety and confusion that followed the President's heart attack.

This illustration has implications for governmental practice that I cannot stop to pursue. My present aim is simply to emphasize the need of better machinery for economic policy-making. It is not enough to bring good men to posts of authority within the government. The forces of economic understanding both within and outside the government need also to be mobilized in an efficient manner. This practical problem of government deserves more study than economists or political scientists have been devoting to it.

THE NATIONAL SCIENCE
FOUNDATION: THE DIRECTOR'S
STATEMENT   Leland J. Haworth

Creation of the National Science Foundation as a unique agency of the Federal Government was the result of two factors directly related to the massive impact of World War II. The first of these was the explosive technological development that accompanied the war, and irrevocably altered for all time the tone and fabric of the American social structure. Second was the fact that the national store of unexploited fundamental scientific knowledge was virtually bankrupt as a result of technological pressure, a condition made even more parlous by the enforced interruption of the education of young scientists and engineers.

J. Robert Oppenheimer, wartime director of the Los Alamos Scientific Laboratory, later testified that "we learned a lot during the war," and his words might well have been echoed by many others. "But," he continued, "the things we learned (were) not very important. The real things were learned in 1890 and 1905 and 1920, in every year leading up to the war, and we took this tree with a lot of ripe fruit on it and shook it hard and out came radar and atomic bombs. . . . The whole spirit was one of frantic and rather ruthless exploitation of the known; it was not that of the sober, modest attempt to penetrate the unknown." Thus it may be said in a sense that technology was treading on the heels of science when the war ended.

Many of the dramatic technological developments of the war were the result of "crash" programs conducted in an atmosphere of urgency at some of our major universities, and as hostilities neared an end the implications for science and technology in the years of peace ahead were visible, if yet undefined.

In late 1944, President Roosevelt addressed a request to Dr. Van-

REPRINTED from Leland J. Haworth, "The Director's Statement," in *National Science Foundation: Fifteenth Annual Report for the Fiscal Year Ended June 30, 1965,* pp. vii–x, xiv–xx, xxv–xxvi.

nevar Bush, director of the wartime Office of Scientific Research and Development, for advice as to how the lessons learned in war could be applied to the pursuits of peace. With the help and recommendations of four committees of scientists and other scholars, Dr. Bush set forth in clear and specific terms what he felt the relationships of government to science should be, and how they should be sustained. His imaginative and stimulating report, *Science, the Endless Frontier,* was to have a profound and lasting impact on the future of American science.

The Bush report pointed out that there was at the time no national policy with respect to science. Government interest in and patronage of the sciences date back to the earliest days of the Republic, with varying degrees of emphasis in accordance with circumstances or requirements of the moment. But the war and its consequences brought both opportunity and responsibility for the Federal Government to utilize science in promoting the national welfare on a scale never before envisioned. "Science," wrote Dr. Bush, "has been in the wings. It should be brought to the center of the stage—for in it lies much of our hope for the future."

This call for a place in the sun for science was inspired by vision of the great potential for the future, and not in deprecation of the accomplishments of American science in the past. Rather it articulated a coming of age for science in this country, and a fuller appreciation of science as a viable and dynamic social force.

One of the most important recommendations of the Bush report was that there be established within the Government a unique agency to serve as a focal point for the support of scientific research and science education, but resembling in many respects some of the private foundations and organized in such a way as to be sensitively responsive to the general scientific community. This was the conceptual origin of the National Science Foundation, as described by Dr. Bush.

A Broad Congressional Mandate

Public Law 507, the implementing legislation passed by the 81st Congress in 1950, was described as an "act to promote the progress of science; to advance the national health, prosperity, and welfare; to secure the national defense; and for other purposes."

Specifically the act authorized and directed the Foundation to:

develop and encourage the pursuit of a national policy for the promotion of basic research and education in the sciences;

initiate and support basic scientific research in the mathematical, physical, medical, biological, engineering, and other sciences, by making contracts or other arrangements (including grants, loans, and other forms of assistance) for the conduct of such basic scientific research and to appraise the impact of research upon industrial development and upon the general welfare;

at the request of the Secretary of Defense, to initiate and support specific scientific research activities in connection with matters related to the national defense . . . ;

to award scholarships and graduate fellowships . . . ;

to foster the interchange of scientific information among scientists in the United States and foreign countries;

to evaluate scientific research programs undertaken by agencies of the Federal Government, and to correlate the Foundation's scientific research programs with those undertaken by individuals and by public and private research groups;

establish special commissions . . . necessary for the purposes of this Act;

to maintain a register of scientific and technical personnel and in other ways provide a central clearing house for information covering all scientific and technical personnel in the United States . . . .

Although some amendments to the legislation of 1950 have subsequently been enacted, notably in the policy-making area, the broad responsibilities and functions outlined in the original act have provided the framework within which the Foundation has developed to its current status. I believe that a statement made by Dr. James B. Conant, first chairman of the National Science Board, and published in the first annual report of the Foundation, is worthy of review from the distance of 15 years. It spells out a philosophical departure point, and establishes a sense of direction for operational doctrine of the Foundation which remains substantially valid to the present.

"Both types of research (basic and applied) are of the utmost importance—important for advancing industry, public health, national defense, and extending the boundaries of knowledge, but today in the United States it is the uncommitted investigator who stands in the greatest need of public support. He needs not only more money for his equipment and for helping hands but more public recognition for the significance of his work, for he is the scientific pioneer, the man who turns the unexpected corner, the laboratory man whose experiments mark the opening of a new era or the theorist whose ideas are so fruitful as to be revolutionary. By and large the United States has not yet produced its share of such scientific pioneers compared with Europe. One of the purposes of the National Science Foundation is surely to right this balance and provide in every section of the country educational and research facilities which will assist the development of such men.

"In the advance of science and its application to many practical problems there is no substitute for first-class men. Ten second-rate scientists or engineers cannot do the work of one who is in the first rank. Therefore, if the aims of Congress as set forth in the National Science Foundation Act are to be fulfilled, there must be all over the United States intensive effort to discover latent scientific talent and provide for its adequate development. This means strengthening many institutions which have not yet developed their full potentialities as scientific centers, it means assisting promising young men and women who have completed their college education but require postgraduate training in order to become leaders in science and engineering. . . . Given time, the expenditure of public funds in this enterprise, I feel certain, will prove to have been a most advantageous investment by the American people."

.　.　.

Foundation Support of Basic Research

Although establishment of the National Science Foundation in 1950 constituted Federal recognition of the need to support basic research in the sciences, initial funding provided for the Foundation by Congress was modest. Six years had passed between publication of the report *Science, the Endless Frontier* and the Foundation's first year of activity, bringing with them a change in circumstances that could not have been foreseen by Bush and his associates. Partly because of the exigencies of the quickening Cold War and the conflict in Korea, a number of Federal agencies were already engaged during the early 1950's in substantial programs of support for scientific research, including basic research, and for improvement of science resources.

Even the agencies with rather specific technological objectives rightly justified their support of basic research in recognition of the general need to replenish the reservoir of unexploited basic knowledge. Thus, while the Government was proceeding in the direction of goals envisioned by Bush and Conant, such agencies as the Department of Defense and the Atomic Energy Commission were important vehicles through which Federal funds found their way to science. It was during this period too that the National Institutes of Health began to assume prominence as a source of support outside its own research institutes.

This pattern of pluralistic support for basic research has endured, and has been found to contain a number of advantages. It is favored by the colleges and universities. It has always been endorsed and fostered by the Foundation as sound and appropriate.

The Foundation placed emphasis from the beginning on support for the highest quality of basic research. In fiscal year 1952, the first year in which funds for the purpose were available, the Foundation awarded 96 grants for project research at 59 institutions located in 33 States, the District of Columbia, and Hawaii. The direct grant was chosen from the outset as the most appropriate type of instrument for supporting basic research on the basis that it would provide maximum latitude and academic freedom to qualified investigators, while entailing a minimum of administrative involvement for the institution.

A significant advance in support of research took place in 1956 when the Foundation for the first time provided major assistance for procurement of science facilities, with one grant awarded for construction of a nuclear reactor, and the first five grants in a series providing support for computers at universities.

The year 1956 also saw the preliminary steps which led to establishment of the National Radio Astronomy Observatory at Green Bank,
W. Va., and the Kitt Peak National Observatory in Arizona, both now
operated for the Foundation by consortia of universities. A study initiated in the same year by the National Academy of Sciences on the gap
between performance and potential in the atmospheric sciences led to establishment in 1960 of a third national research center: the National
Center for Atmospheric Research at Boulder, Colorado—also operated
by an association of universities. These national centers now provide
modern facilities for use by significant numbers of visiting university scientists and graduate students, and thus constitute effective extensions of
university research activities.

Support for the scientific aspects of *Vanguard,* America's first artificial satellite, and participation by the United States in the International
Geophysical Year (IGY) made 1957 a year of notable expansion for the
Foundation. The IGY, a comprehensive worldwide scientific undertaking, was the first "national" research program in which the Foundation
shared, and was the precursor of a number of others. As the Federal
agency uniquely concerned with basic research, the Foundation has
come to be regarded as the most appropriate executive agent for coordination and, in some cases, financial management of broad scientific
programs in which a number of departments and agencies of the Federal
Government participate, along with nongovernmental entities, and often
in cooperation with other nations on an international basis.

National research programs are usually undertaken at the initiative
of the scientific community, which may request support from the Federal
Government after the desirability of U.S. participation has been established. The National Academy of Sciences has been an important inter-
mediary between the scientific community and the Federal Government
in such matters, and usually provides continuing advisory services to the
Foundation after a national research program has been initiated. Authority to participate in national research programs may arise from the
Foundation's organic legislation, by specific legislative acts covering a
particular program, or by executive order (which is usually the case with
reference to international programs).

Foundation responsibility for national research programs covers two
general categories:

1. Programs in which the United States participates as a component
of an international group under the auspices of intergovernmental or
multinational science organizations. Examples of these are the Antarctic
Research Program and the United States-Japan Cooperative Science Program, for both of which the Foundation bears complete United States
responsibility including funding; and the International Indian Ocean Ex-
pedition and the International Years of the Quiet Sun, for which the
Foundation is the coordinating agency.

2. Programs which are entirely domestic and which involve basic research, such as Project Mohole, ocean sediment coring, and weather
modification.

Foundation responsibility for weather modification is defined in Public Law 85–510 of 1958 which amended the original National Science Foundation Act to add: "to initiate and support a program of study, research, and evaluation in the field of weather modification, giving particular attention to areas that have experienced floods, drought, hail, lightning, fog, tornadoes, hurricanes, or other weather phenomena, and to report annually to the President and the Congress thereon."

There is a third category of national research programs that should be mentioned. These are designated by the Federal Council for Science and Technology and embrace scientific fields that depend substantially on Federal support but in which the responsibility is not so sharply focused in any one agency. Among this category are included the atmospheric sciences, materials research, oceanography, and water resources research. The Foundation participates in all these programs, but only as one of several agencies having an interest in the various fields.

Other programs of support for research added gradually by the Foundation over the years were devised to provide support for major items of equipment such as nuclear accelerators, and specialized facilities such as oceanographic research vessels and environmental laboratories for biological research. Funds have also been provided on a matching basis for construction or renovation of graduate laboratories in a large number of academic institutions.

Support of Science Education

Like the support provided for basic research, Foundation activity in the field of science education dates back to the first full year of operation. Statutory authority for the Foundation to support science education arose from the need to develop an adequate national supply of scientific and technical manpower rather than support for education per se. Foundation policy, however—as in the case of research—placed emphasis from the outset on quality rather than quantity, and support of graduate education became a first priority concern.

The initial program of graduate fellowships for the academic year 1952–53 provided awards at both the predoctoral and postdoctoral levels to 624 candidates selected on the basis of national competition. This emphasis on academic excellence endures as a cornerstone of Foundation policy, and the graduate fellowship program is regarded as one of the Foundation's most effective mechanisms in support of science education. In addition to quantitative expansion of the traditional fellowship program, the Foundation has added specialized variations, notably two postdoctoral programs which provide advanced training for exceptionally able individuals who wish to become even more effective in their fields, and science faculty fellowships for college and university science teachers with the primary aim of enhancing their capability as teachers of undergraduate students.

The Foundation early recognized that the acute shortage of scientific and technical manpower in the early 1950's had deep roots in the educational, social, and economic structure of the Nation, and that correction would require long-range efforts aimed at the basic problem areas. Thus Foundation interest in science education was expanded as rapidly as possible to touch on every level of the education process from primary school to the highest level of postdoctoral study.

New programs have been developed by the Foundation over the years in a continuing effort to discharge its responsibility for science education more fully. Generally speaking, the programs in support of science education have three broad objectives: (a) to assist qualified individuals in obtaining additional advanced training, (b) to improve the quality of curricular material and the methods used in science teaching, (c) to improve the level of knowledge and other qualifications of science teachers.

·   ·   ·

Science Information Service

Acceleration in all avenues of scientific activity in the latter years of the 1950's brought with it new recognition of the need for better coordination in the dissemination of science information. While the Foundation from its inception expressed interest in this general problem area by supporting a number of science information activities, this participation by the Foundation was voluntary and permissive under the broad mandate of the original authorizing legislation rather than as the discharge of a specific statutory responsibility.

The Congress in 1958 moved to strengthen and expand the Foundation's information function by incorporating into the National Defense Education Act a provision for establishment of an Office of Science Information Service within the Foundation (Title IX, NDEA). The act also called for establishment of a Science Information Council to be appointed from nongovernmental authorities in such fields as librarianship, scientific documentation, and communications, and having as its purpose to serve in an advisory capacity to the Office of Science Information Service.

As it is now constituted, the Office of Science Information Service is responsible for providing leadership among non-Federal science information services, and in developing appropriate relationships between Federal and non-Federal activities. The function of coordinating scientific and technical information services within and among the Federal agencies rests with the Office of Science and Technology and a committee of the Federal Council for Science and Technology. Thus the objective of the Foundation's Office of Science Information Service is to supplement internal Federal information activities, and insure that scientists and other users have ready availability to the world's current and past output of significant scientific and technical literature.

CHART 1   MECHANISMS OF SUPPORT, NATIONAL SCIENCE FOUNDATION

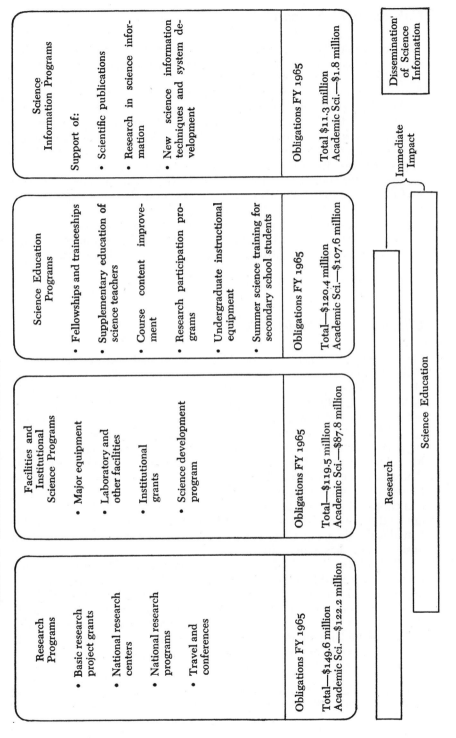

Categories of Support

The complex of support mechanisms now employed by the Foundation at the conclusion of 15 years of evolution is illustrated by Chart 1. For administrative convenience, the various activities are here arranged in four main categories, but this of course is an oversimplification in terms of the purpose and impact of the various programs. Many programs, notably those listed as Facilities and Institutional Science Programs, have a duality of purpose because of the interlocking nature of research and education, especially at the graduate level where the two are virtually indistinguishable. Even the dissemination of science information is a form of support for research on the one hand, while it unquestionably has a usefulness in promoting advanced education on the other. And just as the various activities generally have an impact on both research and education, so the allotment of funding among the four categories is somewhat arbitrary, assignments being made in terms of the primary purpose of the program although it may very well have multiple effects.

.   .   .

Climate of the Mid-1960's

Since the war, science has enjoyed unprecedented and rapidly growing Federal support. Initially this support was primarily directed at immediate exploitation of the practical fruits of science in pursuit of national objectives in such fields as military defense, public health, conservation of natural resources, and industrial development. Federal agencies with responsibilities in these and other technological areas were motivated to support basic research as the source of underlying knowledge necessary for achievement of these goals. Increasingly it has become recognized that continuance and growth of the fruits of science can occur only if the tree that bears them—science itself—is helped to grow and flourish. Federal support for research and development as a whole has approximately doubled since 1960—from $8.1 billion to $16.1 billion—but it is notable that the development share has less than doubled while the support for basic research has more than tripled.

This change in attitude toward the importance of basic research has been accompanied by other changes which have emerged at an accelerating pace, and the concept of Federal support has now been broadened across a wider range of intellectual activity without any diminution in the objectives of science and science education. There is increasing discussion of Federal support for the arts and humanities,[1] and after long hesitation the concept of Federal support for education in general is now wholly accepted.

[1] The act establishing a National Foundation for the Arts and Humanities was signed by the President on Sept. 29, 1965, after the period covered by this report.

The most dramatic and progressive of these changes in the national attitude is, of course, Federal support for education at all levels. Appropriations for the Office of Education have increased about sevenfold in the years from 1960 to the present, and legislation pending at the end of fiscal year 1965 can be expected to bring even further increases. Two impelling motives are at the base of these changes. The first results from recognition that a highly educated people makes the Nation strong in a composite sense; that for our national well-being we must develop the highest competence in all fields of human endeavor; and that to achieve this we must have high quality education at every level.

Secondly, and importantly, Federal policy has evolved in the direction of stronger emphasis on the democratic principle that every citizen is entitled to an opportunity for the best education he has the capacity to absorb effectively, and in the field he finds best suited to his talents.

There is nothing new in principle in these developments, so far as national philosophy is concerned. Public support of education for both of these motives goes back to colonial times. What is new is that in the structure of modern society the Federal Government must share responsibility for attainment of the goals.

This trend is accompanied, though as yet in less full and evident fashion, by an increasing acceptance of the value of scholarship and intellectual activity, not only for potential material rewards, but for its role in fulfillment of the human personality and development of human intellect for their own sake.

Clearly there is a pervasive mood in all parts of the country to improve education at every level, and the general interest extends higher up the educational ladder than ever before. It is my view that there is no reason to believe that science will suffer by sharing the spotlight of Federal support with other branches of scholarship. Rather science can be expected to prosper all the more as a climate more favorable to scholarship in general is developed. Government is committed to the continued support of academic science, and while there may be shifts of emphasis or modifications in levels of support of this type, I see no reason to anticipate any change in basic policy. Support of science for its own sake will, I believe, increase—in absolute amount at least, and probably also as a fraction of the Nation's total investment in science and technology.

The scientific community has played an important role in bringing about the growing interest in all areas of cultural activity and the current intensive popular interest in improving education. The attainments of science, visible for all to see, have demonstrated the public and individual benefits deriving from intellectual accomplishment and higher education. The example set by Federal support for education in the name of science has been a great source of public enlightenment and has opened the way for understanding of the positive and important contributions Federal support can make to education in general without impairing any of the cherished traditional prerogatives. Our reward will be a better intellectual and scholarly climate in the country as a whole, a climate in which science itself can flourish even more.

Leland J. Haworth   389

TECHNOLOGICAL RESEARCH AS RELATED TO THE GROWTH AND STABILITY OF THE ECONOMY

Sumner H. Slichter

The best way to indicate the significance of technological research for the growth and stability of the economy is to point out that technological research had developed sufficiently by 1937 to make Keynes' theory of employment obsolete on the day of its publication—in spite of invaluable concepts and tools of analysis contained in the work. The reason why his theory of employment itself was out of date on the day of its publication was that Keynes ignored completely the impact of technological research upon the economy. Hence, his theory of employment rested upon a theory of consumption and upon a theory of investment that were seriously in error. In addition, Keynes was led to the mistaken practical conclusion that economic progress inevitably creates a chronic deficiency of demand.

Today it is unthinkable that anyone should attempt to construct a theory of employment or a theory of growth without taking into account technological research. Within the last thirty years technological research has become a large activity that introduces fundamental changes into the operation of the economy. Measured in terms of the number of scientists and engineers devoting full time to technological research, this activity is more than five times as large as it was in 1930, and measured by the ratio of research expenditures to the gross national product, it is about thirteen times as large. In 1956, the annual budget of technological research, according to estimates of the National Science Foundation, was about $9 billion a year. Research is growing right through the recession

REPRINTED from Sumner H. Slichter, "Technological Research as Related to the Growth and Stability of the Economy," in National Science Foundation, *Proceedings of a Conference on Research and Development and Its Impact on the Economy* (1958), pp. 107–14, 117.

(as it grew steadily during the much deeper depression of the thirties), and in 1958 research outlays will undoubtedly be well above $10 billion.

. . .

Economic Significance of Research

Technological research has three characteristics that give it far-reaching economic significance. The first of these characteristics is that it greatly increases the capacity of the economy to raise the demand for goods. It is obvious that technological research increases the capacity of the economy to raise productivity. Less obvious and indeed generally overlooked is the fact that research gives the economy the capacity to bring about planned increases in the demand for goods—both by creating new demands for consumption goods and by creating new investment opportunities. . . .

A second characteristic that gives technological research far-reaching significance is the fact that much of it is a profitable activity as well as a useful activity. There are, of course, research areas of the greatest usefulness that cannot be carried on for profit, and that must be done either by nonprofit institutions or by the government or by private industry under government contract. Within the last half century, however, the fund of technological understanding has become sufficient so that many projects, particularly at the development level, can be pursued for gain. This means that many research programs can be determined by the economic calculus—by the balancing of expected gains against expected costs. The importance of this fact is that it draws into research far greater resources than would otherwise be available for it.

The part of technological research that can be carried on for profit should be regarded as an industry—*the industry of discovery.* Its product is knowledge. Slightly more than half of the research and development work now being conducted in private laboratories is financed by private funds for the purpose of making a profit. Thus, the National Science Foundation estimates that in 1956 $3.4 billion of the $6.5 (billion) research budget of private laboratories was financed by industry's own funds, and $3.1 billion by the Federal government.

A third significant characteristic of research is the fact that an increase in its output does not tend to reduce the marginal value of its product; on the contrary, it tends to increase the marginal value. Hence, the greater the output of research, the stronger tends to be the demand for still more output.

This peculiarity of research is a result of the fact that its output is knowledge. One may think of knowledge as consisting of a body of tested propositions. When two things are known, there is a possibility of seeing significant relationships between them which will yield practical applications. The larger the number of tested propositions, the more numerous are the cases in which the addition of a new tested proposition to old propositions will yield new useful applications and, in addition, will suggest hypotheses useful in adding still more tested propositions to the body of knowledge. Thus, the greater the body of existing knowledge, the greater is likely to be the value of the new discoveries.

All of this is particularly important for that part of research that is pursued for profit—the industry of discovery. Unlike other industries, the industry of discovery produces against a rising schedule of marginal utility, not a diminishing schedule.

Research and the Demand for Consumer Goods

The most important effects of technological research upon the capacity of the economy to grow stem from its effects upon the demand for goods, not from its effects upon the capacity of the economy to produce goods, though the latter effects are obviously of great importance. Once demand exists, efforts to raise output will be stepped up. In the absence of sufficient demand, however, efforts to raise capacity will be limited. Hence, it is better on the whole that demand have a slight tendency to outrun productive capacity than that productive capacity tend to outrun demand.

Technological research affects both the demand for consumer goods and the demand for capital goods. It affects the demand for consumer goods by developing new kinds and varieties of consumer goods that people want to incorporate into their standard of consumption. People acquire these additional goods by going into debt, by drawing on accumulated savings, or simply by saving a smaller proportion out of any given income. As a result, rising per capita incomes in the United States have not produced a drop in the ratio of incomes that have been saved. In the American economy personal consumption expenditures have always been an important income-determining influence—in contrast with the theory of Keynes, who held that consumption expenditures are a stable function of real per capita national income. If the view of Keynes were correct, consumption expenditures would be merely income-determined; not income-determining.

It would be a mistake to ascribe dynamic standards of consumption solely to the attractive products made possible by technological research —though in recent years this source of dynamic consumption standards has been growing rapidly. But specialized technological research, as I have pointed out, had very limited importance until about twenty-five years ago, and consumers have been a dynamic influence in the United States since time immemorial. Most of the population has been motivated by strong desires to get ahead, and this ambition has made all aspects of life in the United States, including consumption, strongly competitive. Various features of the American environment have stimulated ambition and competition—the absence of tradition and social stratification, the rapid growth of population (especially up until the end of the nineteenth century), and the abundance of economic opportunities created by the immense resources awaiting development. But, as the rate of population growth has dropped and as natural resources have become more fully developed, technological change has become a more important source of opportunity, keeping vigorous the strong ambitious and competitive spirit of early days.

A little more than half a century ago, there was widespread belief that, with the filling up of the continent and with the passing of the frontier, the United States would become like Europe a stratified society in which a class struggle would emerge. But this has not happened, largely because of the accelerating rate of technological change beginning about the middle of the nineteenth century. Of course, the accelerating rate of technological change did not depend to a large extent upon full-time specialized research workers until about the second quarter of the twentieth century. In earlier days much important research was done by brilliant self-trained men ("inventors") and more important work was done by technically trained men, but they were, for the most part, operating men interested in research problems rather than full-time research men. The recent development of full-time specialized research must be regarded simply as a far more efficient method of doing what industry had previously been doing on a fairly substantial scale.

. . .

No one, of course, knows what would have happened had technological progress added many fewer products for people to buy. Suppose that the automobile, the radio, television, a host of household electrical appliances, home movie cameras, and other things had not been invented and developed. Everyday living would obviously have been very different from what it is now. Perhaps we should have had a civilization superior to our present one—one in which men would be more interested in ideas and less interested in things. An attempt to argue the pros and cons of such issues would take me far afield. It is reasonable to suppose, however, that a much smaller variety of things to buy and to use would have led men to be more interested in leisure and less interested in income than they are today. The working week would have fallen faster. The present eager desire for more income comes largely from the fact that industry, through technological research, is able to offer the people a much wider variety of goods than they are able to purchase.

Thus, technological research has had two offsetting effects on the length of the working week. By developing efficient machinery, it has tended to reduce the value of goods relative to leisure and to bring about a reduction in the length of the working week. By increasing the variety of goods, it has tended to raise the value of goods relative to leisure and to retard the drop in the length of the working week. Between 1929 and 1956, the proportion of disposable income spent on user-operated transportation, household appliances, boats, pleasure craft, sporting equipment, radio and television receivers, and radio and television repairs increased from 9.13 to 12.7 percent. Much of the success of these parts of industry in getting a larger share of incomes after taxes must be explained by the development of products and services for which specialized technological research is responsible. Thus, technological development has helped to hold down savings in the face of rising per capita real incomes.

Research and the Demand for Capital Funds

Technological research affects the demand for capital goods in two ways—partly by developing new consumer goods that require new plants and equipment for their manufacture, and partly by the development of new processes and new equipment that represent investment opportunities.

. . .

At this point we must consider the significance of the part of technological research that I have called the industry of discovery. I have described the product of the industry as knowledge. But let us be more specific about this. The product of the industry consists in large part of investment opportunities. In other words, here we have a large and rapidly growing industry which is devoted largely to discovering or creating investment opportunities. Obviously from now on, economists in constructing a theory of investment must put the industry of discovery at the top of the list of investment determinants. In an age of research, the capacity of the economy to discover investment opportunities depends in the main (1) upon the fund of knowledge that has been accumulated and that is available to be drawn upon, and (2) upon the volume of resources devoted to the industry of discovery.

. . .

Research and Economic Stability

How will the rise of specialized technological research affect the stability of the economy? In general, technological research will contribute to stability, though it cannot be depended upon alone to produce stability.

The growth of specialized technological research will promote stability in two principal ways. In the first place, research tends to introduce into many parts of industry the sort of technology that must be financed by long-range plans which ignore the business cycle. In the second place, technological research greatly increases the number of industries in the economy and this in itself is a stabilizing influence. It is difficult, if not impossible, to eliminate fluctuations in the spending of individual industries on plant, equipment, and inventories. Hence, each industry has cycles more or less of its own, depending upon the value of the accelerator and the multiplier in the particular industry and upon the sensitivity of the investment plans of the industry to outside events. The important point is that no two industries have the same cyclical patterns or the same sensitivity to outside events. The larger the number of industries in the economy, the greater is the chance that the upward and downward movements of the economy will be sluggish resultants of averages derived from the nonsynchronized cycles of the many industries in the economy. Hence, by adding to the number of industries, technological research tends to moderate the cyclical movements of the economy as a whole.

* * *

Outside the field of military research, the Government support of research is only a small fraction of the amount that would yield enormous returns to the community. Indeed, it is safe to say that there is no field where larger Government expenditures would produce as rich a return as greater outlays on research—and also on the necessary foundations for research, the education of talented people. Perhaps it is unreasonable to expect the Members of Congress and the members of legislatures to see this fact clearly without assistance from the scientists themselves. To help the Government policymakers appreciate the Nation's need for greatly enlarged Government research outlays outside the military field is one of the responsibilities of the National Science Foundation. It is a great national asset that the country has this Foundation to help the country make wise use of its resources.

Three ⌐ *The Government as Regulator*

FEDERAL REGULATION OF THE
USES OF NATURAL GAS   *Ralph K. Huitt*

The Natural Gas Act of 1938, as amended in 1942, requires natural-gas companies subject to the act to obtain certificates of public convenience and necessity from the Federal Power Commission before transporting or selling natural gas in interstate commerce, as well as before acquiring, constructing, or extending facilities for those purposes. The issuance of such certificates is a conventional function of public-utility regulatory bodies, and the Commission has administered it in a conventional manner. The tests developed by the Commission to determine the "public convenience and necessity," relating primarily to the adequacy of natural gas reserves, physical facilities, financial resources, and market demand,[1] are commonplace standards, framed in the public-utility tradition to fit the economic and physical characteristics of the natural-gas industry. The real importance of the certificate power under the Natural Gas Act lies in the fact that issues raised in proceedings pursuant to it have transcended the scope of these standards, involving no less than an attempt to redefine in the broadest terms the public interest in respect to natural gas.

With parties in interest allowed by the Commission to intervene extensively, certificate cases became the battleground upon which coal, labor, and railroad interests sought to stay the invasion by natural gas of coal-burning market areas. Their case for restricting the growth of the natural-gas industry rested on the basic fact that, while both coal and

---

[1] The Commission first made a comprehensive statement of these standards in *Kansas Pipe Line and Gas Co. et al.*, 2 F.P.C. 29 (1939), and they are the criteria still relied upon. See *Twenty-Eighth Annual Report of the Federal Power Commission* (1948), p. 57. For an analysis of the problems arising under the certificate power prior to 1946, see Carl J. Wheat, "Administration by the Federal Power Commission of the Certificate Provisions of the Natural Gas Act," *George Washington Law Review*, Vol. 14, p. 194 (Dec., 1945).

REPRINTED with permission from Ralph K. Huitt, "Federal Regulation of the Uses of Natural Gas," *The American Political Science Review*, Vol. XLVI, No. 2 (June 1952), pp. 455–69.

gas are exhaustible resources, gas reserves are estimated in decades and coal reserves in centuries. From this premise, three arguments were made:

1. The coal and railroad industries are large-scale employers of skilled labor; natural-gas pipe-lines are not. Miners and railroad workers displaced by the substitution of gas for coal cannot be replaced when the gas is gone. Therefore, natural gas should be kept out of markets adequately supplied by coal.

2. Industrialization of the major producing states in the South and Southwest, based on natural gas as a fuel, would help to decentralize industry, foster regional development, and balance the economies of those sections. Therefore, the industrial needs of producing states should be considered in certificate cases.

3. Natural gas is a "luxury" commodity, having great value as a fuel for domestic consumption and as a raw material for the chemical industries, and perhaps for conversion into a liquid fuel. It is economic waste to burn vast quantities at low prices as boiler fuel. Therefore, the certificate power should be used for the selective control of end uses of gas.

These contentions clearly go beyond anything the Congress had in mind when it passed the Natural Gas Act.[2] Recognizing that these and other broad policy-questions could not be answered without more comprehensive factual data than could be developed from a case-by-case approach, the Federal Power Commission in 1945 and 1946 conducted a "stock-taking" investigation, giving all interested persons and groups an opportunity to be heard.[3] All aspects of the regulation of natural gas were covered, but much of the testimony had to do with the proper scope and exercise of the certificate power granted to the Commission.

Most of the parties in interest who appeared were in the happy position of arguing from easily defined self-interest. The natural-gas industry wanted as much freedom as it could get to take natural gas anywhere and in whatever quantity it should believe to be profitable. The coal and railroad interests, both management and labor, wanted to be relieved of the competition of natural gas to the largest extent possible. States which were not then being served with natural gas wanted it. States which already consumed gas wanted more of it, with dependable service and

[2] Cf. *Hearing before a subcommittee on H.R. 11662* (Natural Gas Act), U.S. House of Representatives, Committee on Interstate and Foreign Commerce, 74th Cong., 2d sess. (Washington, 1936), and *Hearing on H.R. 4008* (Natural Gas Act), *ibid.*, 75th Cong., 1st sess. (Washington, 1937).

[3] Natural Gas Investigation, Docket No. G–580. The transcript of the hearings will be cited as "Tr." Two reports were made by the Commission to Congress in 1948, one signed by Commissioners Nelson Lee Smith and Harrington Wimberly (cited hereafter as *Smith-Wimberly Report*), and the other by Commissioners Leland Olds and Claude L. Draper (cited as *Olds-Draper Report*). The *Smith-Wimberly Report* of 498 pages has numerous tables and charts, and includes the eleven staff reports summarizing and analyzing the testimony and exhibits presented in the hearings. The *Olds-Draper Report* is a 158-page presentation of their interpretations and conclusions regarding the investigation.

supply. Only in the case of the gas-producing states was self-interest not clear. The officials of each of them knew the advantages of industrialization and a balanced economy, the dangers inherent in an extractive economy. The arguments for trying to keep their natural gas at home were strong, but not conclusive. Could industries really be induced to move to the producing states? Should landowners be required to wait many years for a return on their gas? What if future developments in a dynamic technology made natural gas a relatively valueless energy source? And what if the proposed expansion in the scope of national regulatory power should lead to another and another, until the states no longer controlled their raw materials at all?

Before the public forum of the Natural Gas Investigation, powerful groups clashed over the propositions summarily stated above, rationalizing their particular requirements in terms of the public weal, talking to the administrators but loudly enough for the Congress to overhear. Through conflicting testimony the Federal Power Commission, circumscribed by federalism, uncertain of the dimensions of its authority, and divided in its sympathies, groped for solutions which might in a changing economy be rendered obsolete the day after tomorrow.

Interfuel Competition

Some of the testimony of the consuming states and of the industries adversely affected by the competition of natural gas should be noted briefly. The natural-gas-consuming areas of the United States may be divided roughly into two regions: 1) the region west of the Mississippi, extending from Texas and Louisiana to Minnesota and the Dakotas, and 2) the region east of the Mississippi.[4] The region west of the Mississippi has neither coal nor water power adequate to maintain an industrial economy, but it has in its southern part the nation's greatest concentration of natural gas and petroleum. The region east of the Mississippi has abundant coal and water power in its northern portion, and until recently it had a large supply of natural gas. It also is the heavily industrialized section of the country. The argument of the consuming states west of the Mississippi therefore is that they need natural gas to "remove some of the economic disadvantages which we do possess as residents of that area of the United States."[5] The heavily industrialized region to the east of the river presents the obverse of this view: the maintenance of their great industrial capacity makes it necessary for the states of this area to replace their dwindling reserves with ever-increasing quantities of southwestern gas.

[4] *Olds-Draper Report,* p. 85. See the discussion of the testimony presented by the consuming areas in Sec. VIII of this report.
[5] Testimony of James W. Clark, executive director of the Minnesota Resources Commission, Tr., p. 5335.

Scores of community and business leaders went to the witness stand for the consuming states and told of the importance of natural gas to their economic future. Many recognized the need for the conservation of natural gas; and, generally speaking, where there was another fuel source available, there was more amenability to some control of the use of gas as an industrial fuel. But where there was no other fuel to be had except after a long and expensive haul, putting the region in a disadvantageous position relative to other regions, citizens expressed the opinion that natural gas should be freely used to support industrialization.

Railroad, coal, and labor groups vigorously opposed the extension of natural-gas service in coal-burning territory. For example, the Association of American Railroads, in a statement filed with the Commission after the close of the investigation, pointed to the grave effects upon the railroads of the increasing competition of natural gas with coal. The statement said that coal traffic furnished almost 24 per cent of the total freight revenue of railroads in depression years and 20 per cent in normal nonwar years. Fuel oil traffic likewise was said to be important. The Association did not ask for specific relief under the certificate power, however. It suspected, although it could not furnish proof, that natural gas in unregulated direct sales to industrial users was being sold at less than the cost of its transportation in markets where it competed with coal. The Association therefore wanted the Act amended to give the Commission jurisdiction over direct industrial sales and to confer upon it the power to fix minimum rates and to permit the intervention in rate cases of parties already eligible to intervene in certificate cases.

A longer and more comprehensive statement was filed collectively by two coal associations and three labor groups.[6] It pointed out that there are approximately 500,000 mine workers engaged in the production of anthracite and bituminous coal in the United States. In the anthracite industry, which is located in a relatively few counties in northern Pennsylvania, "whole communities of substantial size rely almost wholly upon the industry for their continued existence." Natural gas already had made tremendous inroads into the employment of mine workers, it was claimed. Furthermore, several million people were said to rely directly or indirectly upon the coal-mining industry for their livelihoods. The applications of natural gas-companies for certificates of public convenience and necessity on May 31, 1946, "represented the potential displacement of close to 50 million tons of coal, or the equivalent of 31,000 mine workers' jobs. For every ton of coal displaced by competitive fuels, the equivalent of one job is lost when consideration is given to the fact that the mining industry creates jobs not only for miners but for railroad men and those who prepare and manufacture mine supplies."[7] Another great

6 *Statement of National Coal Association, United Mine Workers of America, Railway Labor Executives Association, Brotherhood of Locomotive Engineers, American Retail Coal Association.* Statements of a similar character were filed by the Anthracite Institute and the Operators of Coal Docks on Lake Michigan and Lake Superior.
7 *Ibid.,* p. 27; Exhibit 360.

social cost was seen in the fact that coal mining is largely a mechanized process requiring skilled labor, the displacement of which would leave the country in a handicapped position if it should be necessary in a national emergency to step up coal production.

The statement, referring to an exhibit presented by the Railway Labor Executives Association purporting to show the effect of the building of long-distance pipe lines into certain states, which had an adequate supply of coal at reasonable prices, in the period from 1930 to 1943, asserted that "approximately 7½ trillion cubic feet of natural gas were sold for commercial and industrial purposes. This is the equivalent of 304,-419,000 tons of coal. This would make an aggregate loss of railroad freight revenue of $681,898,560, of which $289,124,989 represented railroad wages. Applying the average annual compensation per railroad employee during the same period, it is shown that the wage loss meant the equivalent of approximately 11,304 railroad jobs a year." [8] With the same basis for calculation, the conclusion was reached that if all the applications for certificates pending on May 31, 1946, were granted, an annual wage loss of approximately $45,000,000 per year, or the equivalent of 16,592 railroad jobs, would result. By way of contrast, it was claimed that "the natural gas industry is virtually a laborless industry, as compared with those which produce, transport and distribute solid fuels." [9]

Public Officials as Industry Spokesmen

The natural-gas-producing states, with the exception of Louisiana (whose position will be discussed later), opposed any restrictions, through the use of the certificate power, on the growth of the natural-gas industry. The attitudes of the officials of the State of Texas are suitable for illustrative purposes, both because of the elaborate presentation made by them and because of their complete cooperation with industry officials.

The State of Texas did not formulate a policy: it adopted and supported the policy of the oil and gas industry. A committee appointed by Governor Coke Stevenson to recommend what action the State should take in regard to the investigation, was composed entirely of oil and gas men except for its chairman, Olin Culberson, who also was chairman of the Railroad Commission (which regulates gas in Texas). This committee met in Washington with the Petroleum Industry War Council and other representatives of the natural-gas industry to coordinate state and national industry policy.[10] The committee then recommended to the Governor that the State should appear at the investigation and support as state policy a statement of principles, containing sixteen numbered

[8] *Ibid.*, p. 28; Exhibit 464.
[9] *Ibid.*, p. 29.
[10] Testimony of Olin Culberson, Tr., pp. 3534–35 .

points, which was almost verbatim a copy of a statement of principles formulated by the Petroleum Industry War Council and endorsed by all of the important industry groups.[11] Principle Number 14, which declared that "the end use of natural gas should not be regulated" and that "the whole field is best left to the determinations set up by relative prices in a free competitive economy," was, in fact, identical with Number 13 in the statement of principles drafted by the Petroleum Industry War Council. A second committee, appointed by the Governor to prepare and direct the Texas presentation, also was made up of oil and gas men except for its chairman, Commissioner Culberson.

State officials in Texas made no attempt to solicit the opinions of manufacturers' associations, chambers of commerce, railroads, employees' groups, or representatives of other natural-resource industries.[12] The only public statement that a policy was being formulated was made in a regular statewide hearing of the Railroad Commission, attended almost exclusively by oil and gas-industry people.[13] No legislative committee or group was consulted, and the legislature appropriated no money for the cost of the committee's appearance before the hearing. In answer to a question, Governor Stevenson said that he knew nothing of the cost of the presentation nor by whom it was financed.[14] No attempt was made to obtain the services of the Attorney General's department, and the Attorney General, who made a brief statement, took no part in the preparation of the presentation.[15] Charles I. Francis of Houston, the counsel for the Governor's Committee who also directed the State's presentation, replied, in answer to a question, that he got his "funds from the funds raised by the oil and gas industry." [16] Francis also represented the American Petroleum Institute before the hearing.

.   .   .

The hegemony of the oil and gas industry in official circles was not limited to Texas. On the same afternoon that Commissioner E. O. Thompson read into the record, in his prepared statement, the principles espoused by the Texas Governor's Committee, there appeared one R. R. Spurrier, who read into the record a letter from Governor John J. Dempsey of New Mexico and an attached "Statement of Policy of the State of New Mexico." The numbered principles were substantially the same as, and in most cases identical with, those of Texas. Upon being questioned, Spurrier said that he did not know who wrote the statement nor how the identical statements came to be made, and that he could not speak for the Governor.[17]

11 For a list of the industry groups, see the testimony of E. H. Poe, Tr., pp. 12408–13.
12 Testimony of Stevenson, Tr., p. 3333; Culberson, Tr., pp. 3538–39.
13 Testimony of Culberson, Tr., pp. 3604–05, 3624–25.
14 Tr., p. 3334.
15 Testimony of Culberson, Tr., p. 3605.
16 Tr., p. 3537.
17 Tr., pp. 3449–50.

Two weeks later at Biloxi, Mississippi, there was read into the record for Governor Thomas L. Bailey a statement of principles and objectives for the State of Mississippi. The statement had been prepared by a special committee of forty-three members, designated an Advisory Committee to the State Oil and Gas Board. Seven of its members were state officials; of the remainder, twenty-three were independent operators or royalty-owners, eight represented large companies, and the other five (four of whom were lawyers) were said to be interested in oil and gas. Twelve members were definitely identified as nonresidents of Mississippi.[18] The statement which they "prepared" corresponded almost word-for-word to that of Texas and New Mexico.[19] Once again the order of items was modified; the statement on end uses, which was Number 13 for the Petroleum Industry War Council, Number 14 for Texas, and Number 10 for New Mexico, here was firmly numbered 11.

The "Free Trade" Policy

Of all the witnesses who appeared in support of the Texas policy, the most important were the four officials most directly concerned with the problems of the oil and gas industry—the Governor and the three members of the Railroad Commission. Their testimony revealed by what different roads unanimity can be reached.

Governor Stevenson's attitude stemmed from his concern for the State's financial stake in the oil and gas industry and his fear of the federal government. According to him, "Fifty-three per cent of the State's revenue comes from this industry. Any legislation or regulation that reduces the State's earnings and income from privately owned lands or devalues such property, or decreases the revenues collected by it from the oil and gas industry or the property used in connection therewith is strenuously opposed by us." [20] Stevenson made it clear that he regarded the national government as an alien thing, whose actions were to be viewed with "fear" and "alarm" and "apprehension." . . .

The question likewise was simple for Commissioner E. O. Thompson. Price was for him the great regulator. "The free play of competitive forces as between various uses of gas, and in its competition with coal or oil, will determine its value" through the price mechanism, and the best use of gas is that which brings the highest price.[21] He held no reservations about the exportation of gas—"we are sellers of gas in Texas." As for the problem of reserves, Thompson said: "We rejoice and give a bar-

---

[18] Tr., pp. 5140–44, 5226–28; Exhibit 231.
[19] The identical portions of the statements are found in that of Commissioner Thompson at pp. 3382–85, in that of Governor Dempsey at pp. 3444–49, and in that of Governor Bailey at pp. 5071–74.
[20] Tr., p. 3324.
[21] Tr., pp. 3371–72.

becue when a pipe line is built into an oil field and our oil will last less long than the present gas at the present rate of production." [22]

The other two commissioners did have misgivings about the exportation of gas from Texas. For Commissioner Beauford Jester, price and the extent of reserves were the key questions. He had opposed exportation because he felt that it was an "economic crime" to sell it at prices so low, compared with coal and oil. But if the price of gas could be made comparable to that of coal and other fuels, "economic factors and price would determine end use and federal regulation thereof would be unnecessary." And how was this higher price to be achieved? Jester firmly believed "that if left alone to economic forces," the price of gas would eventually settle on a reasonably competitive basis.[23] Inasmuch as he had come to feel better assured than formerly that the reserves of natural gas in Texas were adequate to maintain the current rate of exportation, Jester was able to support the policy adopted by the State.

The testimony of Commission Chairman Culberson was confused and contradictory. At one point he was opposed to regulation *per se,* including that which he enforced. Thus, although the Railroad Commission grants certificates of public convenience to trucks and buses, Culberson did not agree "with the philosophy or doctrine of public convenience and necessity."

. . .

In their testimony the state officials indicated an awareness of perplexities not acknowledged in the single-minded and unequivocal statement of the oil and gas industry which was made the official policy of the State. The common answer which emerges, nevertheless, is support of what some witnesses called the "free-trade" policy—a policy which means leaving the solution to whatever forces can organize and control the economy.

Natural Gas and Regional Development

The only producing state to appear before the Natural Gas Investigation to urge that the Federal Power Commission consider in certificate cases the needs of the producing states was Louisiana. The policy of this State was established by its legislature, partially in response to the *Twentieth Annual Report* of the Federal Power Commission (for the year 1940). This report had expressed concern over the increasing rate of withdrawals from the fields of the Southwest, questioned the economic wisdom of unrestricted withdrawals of gas for transportation over great distances as a substitute for coal, and expressed apprehension as to the ultimate effect of such withdrawals on potentially recoverable petroleum

22 Tr., p. 3680.
23 Tr., p. 3414.

reserves. The seriousness with which Louisiana took these comments resulted in the legislature's passing, in 1942, a concurrent resolution which on the one hand approved the Federal Power Commission's policy of inquiring into the consequences of the construction of additional pipe lines to coal-burning areas and, on the other hand, directed the State's Department of Conservation and Public Service Commission to support the State's policy in all certificate cases affecting Louisiana. It was pursuant to this resolution that the Louisiana presentation in the Natural Gas Investigation was made.

Many witnesses appeared to present the case for the Louisiana policy. Governor Jimmie Davis recounted the history of the destruction of Louisiana's resources, and especially her forests, by predatory private interests. Forests might be renewed by reforestation, he said, but "when our natural gas is gone it is gone forever," and with it the chance to bring industry to Louisiana. H. R. Bodemuller, industrial engineer for the State's Department of Commerce and Industry, analyzed the industrial potentialities of the State and the crucial role which gas, as the only readily available fuel, must play if they were to be realized. Among the others who testified in the same vein were the two Senators from Louisiana, Overton and Ellender, the former by telegram and the latter in person. But the chief burden of the State's argument was borne by Sam Jones, who had been Governor of Louisiana when the natural-gas policy was adopted.

Sam Jones' thesis was that natural gas was vital, as a fuel and as a raw material, to the development of a balanced economy in the South, and that the questions of who should get it and for what purposes should be decided in the light of that need. Early in his term as Governor, Jones had become convinced that "nearly all the South's problems sprang from the poverty that is a by-product of a raw materials and agricultural economy," and that these problems could be solved only by developing an economy balanced between agriculture and industry. This same problem was involved, Jones believed, in the Southern Governors Railroad Class Rate Case before the Interstate Commerce Commission, "a proceeding that affected the fundamental economics of three-fourths of the Nation in the South and West." An early exhaustion of Louisiana's natural-gas reserves would preclude the possibility of a balanced economy; and the time involved was not that required for depletion of the reserves, but the relatively short time needed to contract for their exportation.[24]

[24] The Louisiana argument may have been hurt by the fact that much wastage of natural gas was occurring in Louisiana, as in other producing states, despite the State's clear jurisdiction over production and distribution of gas. Louisiana in effect was asking the federal government to curtail the flow of Louisiana gas to other states, while Louisiana itself failed to implement adequately its own conservation policy. But the problem posed here by Jones is a separate (though related) one; the quantities of gas saved from physical wastage still could be contracted for exportation without hindrance from the State. For analysis of the complex problems of conservation, see *Smith-Wimberly Report,* pp. 65–154; *Olds-Draper Report,* pp. 75–84.

Moreover, the immediate problems which beset the State made urgent the need for progress on the long-run program of industrialization. War veterans were returning, war plants were shutting down, and the mechanization of the farms was working a revolution and creating widespread unemployment. The economic plight of the Louisiana farmer always had been bad: Jones cited figures to show that in 1929 the average southern farmer had an annual cash income of $186 and the average southern tenant farmer or sharecropper one of $73, while the per capita income for all the people of the South in that year was $350. Now it seemed that these desperately poor people were to lose out on the farms. The rural Negroes would be especially hard-hit. Cotton farming absorbed 75 per cent of them, sugar-cane growing 20 per cent, and rice farming 3 per cent. In cotton farming, one man with machinery would soon do the work of 12 to 15 families. Mechanization in sugar-cane growing would change a ratio of one man to 10 acres to a ratio of one man to 100 acres. And combines in the rice industry would make it possible for two men to do work formerly performed by 25. Jones pointed out that the displaced persons would be untrained and illiterate, and that they would constitute a national problem in that they would migrate. In all, Jones believed the revolution in progress in the State's economy to be as momentous as the invention of the cotton gin, which fixed the slave economy on the South, and the reconstruction period after the Civil War. He estimated that the State would have to provide 5,000,000 new non-farm jobs by the middle of the next decade. With industrialization, it could move a great step forward; without industrialization its fate would be tragic. And to obtain this rapid industrialization, the conservation by the State of its uncommitted natural-gas reserves was an essential prerequisite.[25]

Jones recognized that Louisiana itself was helpless to prevent the draining away of its reserves to the industrial Northeast. He therefore wanted the Federal Power Commission to refuse to grant certificates to increase the rate of exportation of Louisiana gas for industrial uses to areas that were rich in other fuels. This power he believed the Commission already possessed under the certificate provision; but if this interpretation were not acceptable, then he wanted the Natural Gas Act amended to ensure it.[26] What Jones desired was not an arbitrary classification of states or regions, but a case-by-case approach by the Commission to the fuel needs of the sections to which it was proposed to pipe gas. Louisiana was "asking the United States government to decide how the natural gas resources of the country shall be distributed" by providing a tribunal to which interested parties could go and present their cases.[27] Jones was not worried about the increased exertion of national authority. Although an avowed states' rights Democrat, he declared: "I do not believe in destroying the economy of my state when the only agency which can save it is the Federal government." [28]

[25] Tr., pp. 2108–29.
[26] Tr., p. 2278.
[27] Tr., pp. 2276, 2305, 2341.
[28] Tr., p. 2154.

Jones did not wish to disturb existing contracts; neither would he restrict the use of gas anywhere for domestic purposes, or the free flow of gas to areas where there were no alternative industrial fuels. Moreover, he was opposed to federal regulation of end uses, believing it to be economically justifiable to burn natural gas under boilers where it was the only fuel available; and he was opposed to the formulation of a national fuel policy, arguing that the case for close controls over natural gas rested on its scarcity and exhaustibility, and on the present technological impossibility of importing it.[29]

Upon being questioned about the association of interest groups with the position espoused by Louisiana, Jones replied that the State's representatives were working in close contact with "the National Coal Association, with some of the railroads, with some of the labor groups, simply because our idea fits in with their idea." Jones stated at the time of the hearing that he was employed as a railroad attorney. He was not employed by the coal group, although he suspected "that some of the coal companies indirectly probably have brought about my employment." He asserted that he would have accepted employment by the labor groups if they had asked him, but that he had declined legitimate employment offered him by natural-gas companies because to accept it would not have been consistent with his attitude.[30]

. . .

State Control of End Use in Interstate Commerce

The proposition which drew the least support from producer-state officials was that of end-use control. One public official who did endorse it was Redford Bond, Chairman of the Corporation Commission of Oklahoma; but he proposed that the producing state, rather than an agency of the national government, could and should be responsible for carrying it out.

Using his own state for illustrative purposes, Bond pointed out that the Corporation Commission had very broad statutory powers to prevent waste of natural gas, either in its production or in its utilization. He believed that they included the power to determine the character of a wasteful utilization. . . .

Bond gave some hypothetical examples to show how state control of end uses would work. If the Oklahoma commission were informed that gas transported from Oklahoma to Pittsburgh was being consumed there in an uneconomic use, and upon investigation found the charge to be true, it could prohibit the production of gas for that use in Pennsylvania. Again, if a railroad workers' organization in Pennsylvania believed that gas from Oklahoma threatened to deprive them of their jobs, they could

[29] Tr., pp. 2319, 2328–31.
[30] Tr., pp. 2283–84.

bring their case before the Oklahoma commission. If, after a hearing, the Oklahoma commission determined that the producer was violating Oklahoma laws, or the rules and regulations of the commission, it could shut down or limit his production. In each case, control over the producer would provide the leverage for control over the end use.

Bond believed that the national government could reenforce the authority of the states by a law, similar to the Connally "Hot Oil" Act, which would make it illegal to transport gas in interstate commerce when such gas had been produced in violation of state law. He agreed that the Federal Power Commission might also supplement a producing state's efforts by refusing to grant a certificate of public convenience and necessity for a new pipe line (or for increasing the capacity of an old one) to be used for the transportation of natural gas for uses which the state had declared to be uneconomic and for which it had prohibited production. But in the case of a disagreement between the Federal Power Commission and the state, the Oklahoma commissioner believed that "every state ought to control its natural resources." [31]

The Recommendations of the Commission

Because of differences of opinion on numerous policy questions among the commissioners, two reports were made to the Congress by the Federal Power Commission in 1948. One was subscribed to by Commissioners Leland Olds and Claude L. Draper, the other by Commissioners Nelson Lee Smith and Harrington Wimberly. Basil Manly had resigned in September, 1945, and Richard Sachse, who succeeded him, resigned in June, 1947.

The commissioners divided on certificate questions, as well as on others. Commissioners Olds and Draper subscribed, at least in part, to all three of the propositions, favoring increased regulation, considered above. They recommended that the Commission give "increased consideration to the conservation aspects in the delivery of natural gas" from gas-producing states to coal-producing regions. This consideration would include the interest of the producing states in reserving enough of their natural gas resources for their own industrial development, the needs of the "essentially consuming states" for adequate and dependable service, and the end uses to which gas from the southwestern states could be put.[32] Commissioners Smith and Wimberly confined themselves to counseling the producing states and the industry to cooperate in increased efforts to conserve natural gas, and the industry to develop alternative supplies of gas fuel to replace natural gas, as and when natural gas reserves decline.[33]

[31] Tr., pp. 1673–83.
[32] *Olds-Draper Report,* pp. 12–13.
[33] *Smith-Wimberly Report,* p. 28.

The Testimony Considered

The four points of view expressed by the Texas officials represent common responses to the question of whether some regulatory power, such as the certificate provision, should be consciously employed in the furtherance of broad social goals. One response is that it enlarges national power and therefore is bad. Another is that the public interest, whatever it is, will best be served if business is good; it is all "a matter of selling." For those who hold either of these convictions, life is made simple because complexities are assumed away and bad results of their policy are attributed to other causes. But there are troubled persons. Perceiving the need for public action, they still encounter the problem of ways and means, which is especially acute when the perceiver is a state official and the means appears to be national action. One way out then is to make an affirmation of faith that natural processes, which have not hitherto worked to bring about the desired end, will in the long run surely do so. Another answer, though not a way out, is to be confused and admit it. An assumption underlying all of these viewpoints is that when the natural gas is gone, some substitute will appear.

It is obvious that there are no "right" answers to the questions discussed in this paper. It seems safe to say, however, that two of them—whether the "economic waste" of natural gas should be eliminated through selective control of uses, and whether the certificate power should be used to adjust the clashing economic interests of various groups—are national questions which must be answered by agencies of the national government. Commissioner Bond of Oklahoma was led by his fear of an increase in national authority to make a proposal against which his experience as a regulator surely should have warned him. Leaving aside entirely the question of whether a state legally may make such determinations as Bond suggested, we may well ask what would be the consequences of an effort by Oklahoma to control end uses in Pennsylvania.

First, it would make the Oklahoma commission, and every other regulatory body willing to undertake such considerations, a tribunal for the kind of protracted interest-group conflicts which by 1945 had become an almost intolerable drag upon contested certificate proceedings before the Federal Power Commission. . . .

Worse still, the burden would be shouldered in vain, for the Oklahoma commission could not give relief. Clearly it could not prevent the importation into a coal-burning area of gas from other states. But neither, for that matter, could it stop the flow of Oklahoma gas. Interstate pipe-line systems are complex constructions. Gas ordinarily is purchased in several producing states and often from other interstate pipe-line systems; then the gas from all these sources is commingled. In fact, the requirement that gas sold to the consumer be of uniform composition and heat content makes it mandatory that natural gas be processed, and the blending of gas from numerous fields is frequently efficacious for technical reasons. It would obviously not be possible to segregate Oklahoma gas in such a system.

Finally, the experiences of the states in other aspects of regulation should have made it clear that no state can regulate effectively what goes on a thousand miles from its borders. There is no reason to believe that regulation would be more successful if it were tried from the producing end than it has been when tried on the consuming end. Under our federal system the cooperation of states and national authorities is necessary to successful regulation. . . .

The question of what the national government should do about end-use control actually is indeterminate; the answer turns upon the extent of natural-gas reserves and the data is inconclusive. There are defects in present methods of making estimates, and there is no way to be sure either of the future rate of consumption or of the future rate of discovery.[34] Much testimony was presented at the Natural Gas Investigation concerning the extent of reserves; but even when figures were close together, there was disagreement as to whether they should be the basis for optimism or pessimism. One difficulty stems from the fact that while the rate of consumption has risen steadily, the rate of discoveries has risen faster, with each year showing a net addition to reserves.

Returning to the argument of Sam Jones that natural gas should be conserved to promote a balanced economy in the producer states, it will be recalled that Jones did not argue that the United States will run out of gas, or that the nation might not be able to find an adequate substitute. He did say that Louisiana can run out of gas and that the State has no satisfactory substitute fuel. This position seems unassailable; natural-gas-producing areas do become exhausted. The fine fields in the Appalachian area and in California already must augment their dwindling supply with Texas gas. Jones' point is plain: industries which move to Louisiana for gas may stay after it is gone, but industries which burn up Louisiana gas elsewhere will not then move to Louisiana.

. . .

Actually natural gas is not unique in the problems it raises, and one might have wished that Jones had gone further. If the national government is to consider how a fuel resource may be made to serve the public interest, why should it stop with natural gas? The estimated life of oil reserves is about half that of gas, and coal has been a sick industry for two decades. It would seem only a logical extension of the argument to urge a program for the intelligent utilization of all of our energy resources.[35] If natural gas is to be used as a tool to reconstruct the economy of the South, how can other comparable tools be rejected? And if the efforts of Louisiana, based on her natural gas, should fail, the needs of her people must be met in some other way; the nation's interest in the problem can-

[34] There is a good analysis of the problem in *Smith-Wimberly Report*, pp. 31–61.
[35] Cf. Natural Resources Committee, *Energy Resources and National Policy* (Washington, 1939).

not be foreclosed. Once the terms of reference have been broadened to include the welfare of the people of a great section, it is difficult to restrict the discussion of ways and means.

Conclusion

The experiences of war and depression in this century may well indicate that the United States must look to its resources, human and material, with a view to maximizing their usefulness. Such a view could not abstract the interstate pipe-line from the integrated business of producing, transporting, and distributing natural gas; nor natural gas from the complex of energy sources which it complements and with which it competes; nor any or all of them from the lives of the people they serve. It would require a fresh look at the industries affected and a frank admission that a free people can plan for the future. If it should turn out, as some predict, that in a quarter-century or less our present fuels are obsolete and we are propelled into the future by the masterless atom, would we not be more secure for having learned to manage our resources with skill and foresight?

The decisive answers to such questions are for the Congress, not the Federal Power Commission. That a commission does and must make policy in carrying out the legislative mandate is a truism. But when the issues raised before it go beyond anything considered by the Congress in enacting the statute and when they involve decisions of far-reaching importance to the future of the nation, it is time for the Congress to restate its position. The Federal Power Commission performed its appropriate function in conducting the Natural Gas Investigation. It furnished a public platform for the contending groups, collected and analyzed the relevant data, and in its two reports made available to the Congress and the public the factual material necessary for a reconsideration of the problems of the industry. If in the political climate of the postwar years the Congress has declined the proffered invitation, the responsibility cannot fairly be placed at the door of the Commission.

Section 2 ⌒ The Business Firm in the Managerial Economy

Four ⌒ The Business Firm as Innovator

THE GROWTH OF THE FIRM —A CASE STUDY: THE HERCULES POWDER COMPANY Edith T. Penrose

A firm is both an administrative organization and a pool of productive resources. In planning expansion it considers two groups of resources; its own previously acquired or "inherited" resources, and those it must obtain from the market in order to carry out its program. All expansion must draw on some services of the firm's existing management and consequently the services available from such management set a fundamental limit to the amount of expansion that can be either planned or executed even if all other resources are obtainable in the market. This is as true for expansion through acquisition as it is for internal expansion, although acquisition permits a faster rate of growth and often facilitates diversification. A firm is not confined to "given" products, but the kind of activity it moves into is usually related in some way to its existing resources, for there is a close relationship between the various kinds of resources with which a firm works and the development of the ideas, experience, and knowledge of its managers and entrepreneurs. Furthermore, changing experience and knowledge of management affect not only the productive services available from resources, but also the "demand" which the firm considers relevant for its activities.

At all times there exist, within every firm, pools of unused productive services and these, together with the changing knowledge of management, create a productive opportunity which is unique for each firm. Unused productive services are, for the enterprising firm, at the same time a challenge to innovate, an incentive to expand, and a source of competitive advantage. It is largely because such unused services are related to existing resources and partly because of the pressures of competition that firms tend to specialize in broad technological or marketing areas, which I have called technological or market "bases." In a sense, the final products being produced by a firm at any given time merely represent one of several ways in which the firm could be using its resources, an incident in the development of its basic potentialities. Over the years the products change, and there are numerous firms today that produce few or none of the products on which their early reputation and success were based. Their basic strength has been developed above or below the end-product level as it were—in technology of specialized kinds and in market positions. Within the limits set by the rate at which the administrative structure of the firm can be adapted and adjusted to larger and larger scales of operation, there is nothing inherent in the nature of the firm or of its economic function to prevent the indefinite expansion of its activities as time passes.

Entrepreneurial services are as much productive services as are the services of management, labor, or even machines. Entrepreneurial incompetence, or general cautiousness, including a conservative attitude toward financing, should be looked on not as a failure to "maximize" profits, whatever that may mean, but as a limitation on the supply of productive services to the firm.

In the explanation of the course of expansion of a particular firm and of the limits on its rate of expansion, it is illuminating to put the chief emphasis on the firm's "inherited" resources and productive services, including its accumulated experience and knowledge, for a firm's productive opportunity is shaped and limited by its ability to use what it already has. Not only is the actual expansion of a firm related to its resources, experience, and knowledge, but also, and most important, the kinds of opportunity it investigates when it considers expansion. Moreover, once a firm has made its choice and has embarked on an expansion program, its expectations may not be confirmed by events. The reactions of the firm to disappointment—the alteration it makes in its plans and activities and the way in which it adapts (or fails to adapt)—are again to be explained with reference to its resources.

These relationships are portrayed in the chronology of the changing productive opportunity of the Hercules Powder Company. The history of this company illustrates the nature and significance of the areas of specialization of a firm—its technological and market bases—as well as some of the difficulties encountered when an attempt is made to move to new bases markedly different from the old. The outlines of the company's diversification are presented in Chart 1. The following story elaborates, explains, and discusses the significance of the movements implied therein.

In 1912 a large United States firm, E. I. Dupont de Nemours, then looked upon as dangerously close to monopoly in the explosives business, was broken into three parts by action of the federal courts as a result of an antitrust suit initiated by the federal government in 1907. One of the two "new" firms thus created was the Hercules Powder Company. At the time of its formal organization in 1913 Hercules had a thousand employees and nine plants; it produced explosives only: black powder and dynamites.

During the next forty-odd years this amputated piece of DuPont, like a cutting from a plant, continued to grow.[1] It, like DuPont, has over the years branched out in numerous directions in response to external opportunities and internal developments. The parent and its involuntary offspring have not grown in the same directions, and in only a few fields are they in direct competition with each other. Hercules is not only completely independent of DuPont, but has acquired its own personality and its own position in the industrial world quite unrelated to DuPont's position. By 1956 it had 11,365 employees, 22 domestic plants, and total assets of nearly $170 million, making it the 165th largest industrial company in the United States measured by total assets.[2]

The company's rate of growth has been modest (something over 5 per cent per year in terms of fixed assets) but fairly steady. Its financing has been conservative, virtually all of its growth having been financed with internally generated funds. It has engaged in little acquisition, only eight small companies with total assets at the time of acquisition of less than 10 per cent of the company's present net worth having been acquired in its entire lifetime. Its "entrepreneurship" has been what I have called "product-minded," reasonably venturesome and imaginative, but concentrating on "workmanship" and product development rather than on expansion for its own sake or for quick profits.

The original technological base of the Hercules firm was explosives and for the first few years of its existence it was kept busy with the expansion of this field. Two new plants were acquired and improvements were made in existing plants and in the processes of production of dynamite, smokeless powder, and cordite. One of the innovations—the pro-

---

[1] The story of Hercules also illustrates the point that the splitting up of large companies will often not have an adverse effect on efficiency if the advantages they have in expansion are economies of growth and not economies of size. For a discussion of these two types of economies and their significance see Penrose, *The Theory of the Growth of the Firm*, Chap. VI.

[2] This rank is the one given in the *Fortune Directory* of the 500 largest United States industrial corporations. Supplement to *Fortune* (July, 1957). In addition to the above, Hercules had three plants in wholly owned subsidiaries abroad and employed some 6,000 workers in government owned Hercules-operated ordinance facilities.

CHART 1
DIRECTION OF EXPANSION

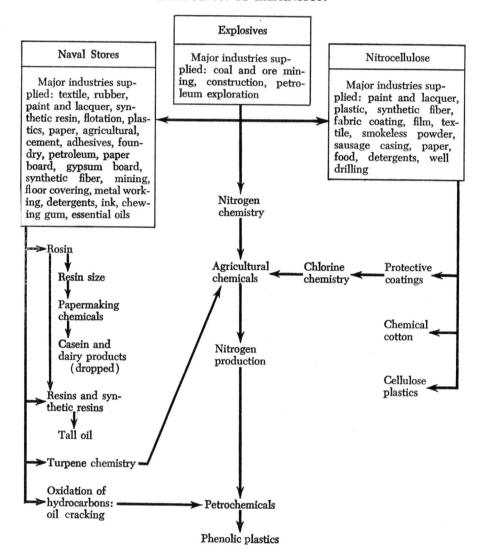

Explosives

Major industries supplied: coal and ore mining, construction, petroleum exploration

Naval Stores

Major industries supplied: textile, rubber, paint and lacquer, synthetic resin, flotation, plastics, paper, agricultural, cement, adhesives, foundry, petroleum, paper board, gypsum board, synthetic fiber, mining, floor covering, metal working, detergents, ink, chewing gum, essential oils

Nitrocellulose

Major industries supplied: paint and lacquer, plastic, synthetic fiber, fabric coating, film, textile, smokeless powder, sausage casing, paper, food, detergents, well drilling

Nitrogen chemistry

Rosin

Resin size

Papermaking chemicals

Casein and dairy products (dropped)

Resins and synthetic resins

Tall oil

Turpene chemistry

Oxidation of hydrocarbons: oil cracking

Agricultural chemicals ← Chlorine chemistry ← Protective coatings ←

Chemical cotton ←

Nitrogen production

Cellulose plastics ←

Petrochemicals

Phenolic plastics

duction of acetone (a solvent used in the manufacture of cordite) and other products from the giant kelp found on the Pacific Coast—involved an extension of the firm's knowledge and experience in a type of organic chemistry which was to become significant in its subsequent diversification.

The manufacture of explosives is still of considerable importance for

Hercules (accounting for 18 per cent of sales in 1951) and at times has been its most profitable operation, providing funds for the extension of activities in other directions. Substantial innovations have been made in the field of semigelatin explosives, smokeless powder, packaging of explosives, and explosive supplies. Some diversification into the production of chemicals used in explosives production, notably nitric acid, anhydrous ammonia, and other nitrogenous compounds, has been made, and this development has contributed in recent years to Hercules' position in the agricultural chemicals industry.

In spite of the innovations and enlarged activity, however, the explosives business was not one to permit extensive growth and development of the firm. In particular, it provided little opportunity for the use of the experience in the field of organic chemistry that had been developed by Hercules men in the course of the firm's operations. Furthermore, at the end of the First World War the plant, organization, and accumulated funds of the firm were much greater than could be used in explosives in view of the drastic decline in demand after the war. In the immediate postwar period numerous opportunities for profitable investment were open on all sides in the expanding, changing economy. But which of them would furnish opportunities for the growth of a still relatively small and specialized explosives company?

NITROCELLULOSE AND NEW AREAS OF SPECIALIZATION

Nitrocellulose is one of the most important basic raw materials in the production of explosives. In 1915 Hercules had bought the Union Powder Company, which had a plant for the nitration of cotton linters (the "fuzz" on cotton seeds and a by-product of cotton production) into nitrocellulose, then used primarily for smokeless powder, but also for celluloid and collodion ("new skin"). Already by 1917 the company was experimenting with the production of nitrocellulose for industries other than explosives, for if it could produce a suitable soluble nitrocellulose it felt sure of a large market supplying the needs of the lacquer, film, and protective coatings industries generally. It succeeded in developing an appropriate product, and by 1923 was firmly established in the field. Between 1918 and 1944 Hercules' production of soluble nitrocellulose increased from 100,000 pounds annually to 28,000,000 pounds and the price was lowered from 75 to 33 cents a pound.

So efficient was Hercules' production and quality control and so well-developed its control of explosive hazards in the manufacture of the basic product and also in its use by customers, that a number of companies withdrew from the field. Some of these were integrated companies, producing for their own use, who found it more economical to buy their requirements from Hercules; others simply withdrew in the face of Hercules' competition. The automobile industry turned out to be the biggest consumer, using nitrocellulose in its lacquers. In consequence, Hercules was in a position to profit from the rapid growth of this then relatively new industry. Nevertheless, here, as in other fields, continual attention to the development of new products and new methods to meet or surpass competitive developments has been required. For example, the advent of baked enamel for automobile finishes, which reduced the labor time required for finishing, was a serious threat to lacquer; and Hercules developed new lacquers which could be sprayed on hot and meet the new competition in cost.

Successful development of nitrocellulose for nonexplosive uses provided for Hercules an extensive technological base as well as an important market area of specialization. The development of the technological base led to expansion in still other markets; the development of the market base furthered expansion into still other branches of chemistry. Broadly speaking, the technological base was that of cellulose chemistry; the market base, supplier to the protective coatings industry.

CELLULOSE CHEMISTRY

Hercules' base in cellulose chemistry enabled it to take advantage of the growing markets in the artificial fiber and plastics industries. Cellulose acetate, an important raw material in the rayon industry and used for the production of some grades of plastics, soon became, for the firm's Cellulose Products Department, an important product in quantity, though disappointing in profitability.

The cellulose acetate market is highly competitive, and, in this as well as in most of its other products, one of the firm's biggest competitive problems arises from the ever-present possibility that its customers will integrate vertically and start producing their own requirements. In the long run Hercules can prevent this only by producing a high-quality product and selling it at a price that makes integration unprofitable for customers. Hence a relatively low sales margin is earned and continual research and experimentation are carried on. (Hercules has even experimented with the spinning of fibers in order to acquire knowledge which might be of use to its customers. As we shall see, "technical service" is one of the "utilities" Hercules sells with all of its products in order to maintain its market position.)

With the development of synthetic rubber during the Second World War came a new petrochemical base for cheap plastics (polystyrene) which soon began to displace cellulose acetate in molding powders, the basic material from which molded plastics can be made. Petrochemicals, however, involved a branch of chemistry in which Hercules had only limited experience at the time. Many of the companies producing the new plastic material had developed extensive experience during the war which gave them a new "base" in petrochemicals. Hercules' wartime activities were in very different areas. The firm's lack of an adequate technological base was sufficient to prevent it from taking up the production of polystyrene and similar petrochemical products. Consequently the company attempted to reach new markets with its own cellulose acetate by taking up the production of molding powders.

The extensive knowledge of cellulose chemistry possessed by Hercules has provided a continuous inducement to the firm to search for new ways of using it. For example, during the war Hercules, in an attempt to replace a lubricant no longer available, took up the production of an extraordinary versatile cellulose gum—sodium carboxymethy-cellulose (CMC). The firm was much impressed with the properties of this chemical composition, but was not sure to what use American industry could put it. Perhaps CMC could be used in the sizing of textiles (Hercules already produced some types of fabric coating). No one knew; nevertheless, advertisements were placed in trade papers describing the qualities of the product and inquiring "What do you see in CMC?"

The product caught on. Here, surely, is an almost perfect example of the creation of consumer demand as a consequence of entrepreneurial desire to find a use for available productive resources. The biggest uses for CMC, initially, turned out to be as a stabilizer in foods, ice cream, lotions, drugs, and cosmetics. CMC also proved to have an industrial application in oil-well drilling mud—an outlet the firm had not anticipated.

.   .   .

DEVELOPING A NEW BASE—NAVAL STORES

Broadly speaking, as can be seen in Chart I, the operations of the Hercules Powder Company, apart from explosives, can be divided into two large chemical branches, with a third becoming clearly evident in recent years. They all overlap in the markets they serve, and each leads in its later stages into new areas of chemistry which may well provide new technological bases for further diversification. The movement into new aspects of cellulose chemistry, just described, was an obvious entrepreneurial response to the postwar decline of nitrocellulose markets in the explosives field. The subsequent branching out of the company was the logical (though not inevitable) effect of its continually increasing knowledge of cellulose chemistry as well as of its developing position in its various market areas. Later we shall discuss the interaction between the technological and market bases of the firm; for the present we are concerned primarily with the technological aspects of its diversification, although clearly technological developments are of use only if profitable markets can be found.

Important as the opportunities were in the field of cellulose chemistry, however, they did not appear to the firm to promise sufficient scope for the entrepreneurial, managerial, labor, and technical services available to it at the end of the First World War. In 1919 the company had created an industrial research department for the express purpose of investigating products Hercules could profitably produce. This department decided that the firm could go into the production of wood naval stores (rosin, turpentine, and pine oil) obtained from the stumps of the long-leaf southern pine—like linters, a waste product of another industry.

Naval stores production was not as obvious an opportunity for Hercules as was cellulose chemistry, but again it was expected to provide openings for the use of the existing resources of the firm. Hercules believed that it could use its knowledge of organic chemistry to produce a purified wood rosin good enough to compete with the gum rosin when gum prices were high; incidentally, the naval stores operation would also provide a use for dynamite in the blasting out of the stumps. . . . Wood rosin could not compete [however] with gum when gum prices were low, and the naval stores business of Hercules went into the red for many years. Notwithstanding its heavy investment in rosin chemistry research, Hercules came close to withdrawing from the business.

ROSIN AND TERPENE CHEMISTRY

But research paid off; unable to sell rosin in its existing forms in competition with gum, Hercules learned how to modify the product by hydrogenation, disproportionation, and polymerization and thus to convert it into various kinds of rosins for which many new uses could be found. Rosin is essentially abietic acid; when esterified with various polyols it makes hard resins valuable in the manufacture of paints and varnishes, and Hercules already had a position in the protective coatings field. Customers could be found for hard resins and rosin esters, and these, together with a variety of specialty resins as well as straight esters, were developed into an important outlet for rosin production. The naval stores operation became the equal of cellulose chemistry as a central technological base of the firm and in 1928 was organized as a separate department. In 1936 still another department was created, charged with the task of developing new uses and new outlets for resin-based products. . . .

But rosin is only one of the three joint products of the pine stump, and markets had to be found both for turpentine and for pine oil, a relatively new industrial product in the 1920's, derived only from the wood operation. Fractional distillation methods were perfected which permitted the production of higher grades of turpentine and pine oil. In 1929 pine oil outlets were not developing fast enough to keep pace with production, and Hercules intensified its research into pine oil chemistry looking for derivative products. Thanite was developed, a terpene thiocyanoacetate providing a toxicant for insecticides, and later toxaphene, a chlorinated camphene. These products put Hercules firmly in the field of agricultural insecticides which in turn stimulated research into agricultural chemicals generally. At times the demand for pinene has exceeded the company's output and it has had to buy crude products from pulp mills for refining. As was the case in cellulose chemistry, a large variety of chemical products and processes has been developed in the field of terpene chemistry. One of the latest processes bids fair to give Hercules a more established base in petrochemicals, a field which, as was noted above, had up to recently been outside Hercules' major fields of specializations, thereby handicapping the firm in its ability to meet competitive developments.

In several of its manufacturing processes Hercules has always been involved in petrochemical operations. Although the manufacture of explosives is not in itself a chemical process, the production of the essential ammonia is. Nitric acid used for making explosives is obtained from ammonia, and the process used by Hercules to produce ammonia involves the cracking of natural gas. Furthermore, some of the processes in the rosin and terpene operations of its naval stores activities are similar in nature to the cracking of oil. Indeed, some of them can be and are used in oil cracking. Finally, in experimenting with the chemistry of terpenes and with the oxidation of the hydrocarbon by-products of naval stores, Hercules developed a reaction that utilized benzol and propolene and that resulted in a new process for making phenol. These developments opened up two new branches of chemistry for the firm: air oxidation processes and petrochemicals; new plants have been built for operation in both areas. The phenol plant, established near an oil refinery, uses a by-product of the refinery. Among the important uses of phenol is the manufacture of synthetic resins for phenolic plastics; it is also used in the manufacture of varnishes, enamels, herbicides, and pharmaceuticals. Lack of any raw material "base" in petrochemicals had prevented Hercules from participating fully in the rising markets for rubber-base paints and for phenolic plastics. One of the primary hopes of management in establishing the phenol plant was to open the way for the acquisition of further knowledge in order to provide a base for expansion in this wide field of chemistry, as well as to put the company in a position to keep up with competitive developments arising in petrochemistry and affecting the market for some of its major products.

Finally, Hercules in 1955 took up the production of polyethylene for plastics. The technology was based on the work of German scientists who had discovered in experimenting with new types of catalysts that ethylene could be polymerized at low pressures to give a new type of high molecular weight polyethylene. This not only further extends Hercules' activities in plastics, but also takes it further into catalytic chemistry, which may, in time, lead into still further technological areas.

Interaction Between Technological and Market Bases

Hercules is a producer of chemical products for other industries; it does not manufacture final products for the nonindustrial consumer. To obtain knowledge of the "demand" for its products, one of its principal tasks is to watch industrial developments in all relevant sectors of the economy in order to discover where its products might be made to supply the requirements of industrial consumers as well as or better than existing products. It is a conscious policy of the firm systematically to review its resources with an eye on external developments, asking the question, "What have we got to offer?"

Because of the nature of its market, Hercules stresses "technical service" to customers; salesmen are for the most part technically trained men. In selling their products the salesmen are expected to take an active interest in the production and market problems of their customers. This permits them to acquire an intimate knowledge of the customers' businesses and not only to demonstrate the uses of their own products and to suggest to customers new ways of doing things, but also to adapt their products to customers' requirements and learn what kinds of new products can be used. It is standard practice in the development of new products to get customers to try them out on a "pilot plant" basis and thus to assist Hercules in the necessary research and experimentation.

Obviously, it is in those areas where Hercules' personnel have the greatest experience and the most extensive relationships with customers that the opportunities for the sale of existing products and for the promotion of new products will be widest. Hence, in spite of the enormous variety of possible end uses of Hercules' chemical products, the firm nevertheless remains in a relatively few broad "areas of specialization." Approximately 40 per cent of the total value of sales are accounted for by three industry groups: protective coatings, paper, and mining and quarrying, and an additional 40 per cent by six others: synthetic fibers, plastics, agricultural chemicals, petroleum, rubber, and identifiable military uses (the last including fees obtained from the operation of government owned ordnance plants).

The interaction between the market opportunities of the firm and the productive services available from its own resources can be seen in the development of almost any field we examine. A few examples will illustrate.

PAPER-MAKING CHEMICALS

The biggest customer of rosin is the paper-making industry which uses rosin largely in the form of rosin size, a sodium soap of rosin. As a result of the close association with the paper industry consequent upon its entry into naval stores production, Hercules in 1931 acquired the Paper Makers Chemical Corporation, a diversified, loosely organized company producing a variety of industrial chemicals. On acquiring the corporation, Hercules reorganized its productive activities, consolidating production in the more efficient plants and getting rid of others; it eliminated alum production and the jobbing activities of the old company. Eventually a separate department, called the Paper Makers Chemical Department, was created to take over the remaining collection of activities.

Although the basic reason for the acquisition of the old PMC was the outlet it provided for rosin and the possibilities for growth that Hercules saw in the rosin-size business, the activities of the new department in Hercules rapidly extended not only to many other chemicals useful in the paper-making industry but also to other industries using the same or similar chemicals. Thus, with the advent of synthetic rubber production, Hercules looked into the possibilities of using rosin soap as an emulsifier in the production of synthetic rubber, and now sells a very large proportion of its rosin soap to the synthetic rubber industry.

This in turn stimulated interest in the general field of synthetic rubber production, now one of the more important areas of Hercules' research. Hercules' interest in the paper industry, arising from rosin sizes, has in recent years been substantially reinforced by the growing uses of chemical cotton in paper making. Much research has gone into the characteristics imparted to paper when chemical cotton is substituted for other raw materials. As a result, Hercules has been able to establish its raw material for many uses in paper making.

Among the activities of the old Paper Makers Chemical Corporation when it was acquired by Hercules was the production and sale of casein, a milk product used in the paper industry. Hercules retained this business for some twenty years and attempted to develop the field. For a while the operation was profitable, but owing to rising support prices of dairy products, imported casein became so much cheaper than the domestic product that it was no longer profitable to produce it. . . .

PROTECTIVE COATINGS

Protective coatings is a broad term including paints, lacquers, and other forms of providing a "coating" to protect wood, metal, cement, textiles, and other materials. Hercules' market position in this field goes back to its early production of soluble nitrocellulose for the lacquer industry; it was subsequently extended as the firm developed rosin products, also valuable in the paint and lacquer industry. The interest in the general market area of protective coatings imparted by these important uses of its basic raw materials led to developments within the firm which took it into the production of other products from other raw materials, but products that served the same types of customers and involved similar types of technological processes.

One of the early successful innovations in the field was the development of Parlon, a chlorinated rubber, valuable as an ingredient in paints for chemical plants and in other places where resistance to alkalies and acids is important. . . .

Development of the general field of protective coatings and of plasticizers also led the Synthetics Department beyond its original specialty of finding outlets for rosin in various forms, into research with chemical materials, unrelated to rosin, for the manufacture of new ingredients for protective coatings, new types of plasticizers, polyols used in rosins, and raw materials for synthetic fibers. By 1951, substantially more than 50 per cent of the sales of this department were of nonrosin-based products.

AGRICULTURAL CHEMICALS

All three of the major technological fields of Hercules have combined to give it an interest in the field of agricultural chemicals. The fact that nitrogen chemistry, in particular ammonia, is important in the manufacture of explosives and also one of the major bases of commercial fertilizers early gave Hercules a connection with agriculture. With the progressive development of chlorine and terpene chemistry and the introduction of the new insecticides, Thanite and toxaphene, mentioned above, this interest broadened. Although the original stimulus to the entry of Hercules into agricultural chemicals stemmed directly from the types of resources it possessed, once the firm had entered the field in a major way and created a technical and sales force to serve this market, the market possibilities became the primary stimulus. Extensive research activities were undertaken to develop further the firm's position in the field. A new laboratory for research into agricultural chemicals was opened in 1952, and in 1954 Hercules, together with the Alabama By-Products Corporation, set up the Ketona Chemical Corporation to produce anhydrous ammonia using by-product coke-oven gas as a raw material, the first ammonia plant to use this process in the United States. The plant produces for agricultural and industrial nitrogen users in southeast United States.

PLASTICS

Celluloid, which is virtually nothing but nitrocellulose and camphor, was the forerunner of modern plastic materials (and, incidentally, is still important in many uses). This product was produced by Hercules from the very beginning; the development of cellulose acetate further committed the firm to the plastics industry. The various kinds of chemical plastics, which in a broad sense can often be regarded as the same "product," are made by substantially different chemical processes. Hence, the widening of Hercules' position in the plastics field stems from different types of chemical technology, the development of which has itself been stimulated by the firm's attempt to maintain and improve its position as a supplier to manufacturers of plastic products. . . .

Many of the technological developments discussed above, such as the development of phenolic chemistry, were to a large extent stimulated by a desire to take full advantage of the growing opportunities in plastics.

·   ·   ·

FOOD INDUSTRIES

Finally, the latest venture of Hercules again illustrates the constantly changing and cumulative process involved in the interaction between the resources and markets of a firm. In 1956 Hercules acquired the Huron Milling Company, a small firm processing wheat flour to produce amino acids, food supplements, and wheat-based food flavoring, including monosodium glutamate. At first sight this acquisition looked rather far afield, although Hercules did have earlier connections with the food business through its CMC, discussed above, as well as chewing gum (a rosin derivative) and antioxidants for food products. Hence, although food chemistry and food markets had not been of primary concern to the firm, they were not completely alien to its experience. Nevertheless, the primary incentive for this particular acquisition and for the choice of this specific direction of expansion was somewhat different.

It will be recalled that Hercules produces its own chemical cotton from cotton linters. Production is carried on in the Virginia cellulose plant and the scale of activity depends not only on the demand for the product but on the supply of linters, which is a function of the size of the cotton crop. The supply of linters has not been sufficient in recent years to employ fully the services of the personnel connected with the Virginia cellulose operation, and the firm has been looking for some suitable activity to absorb these "unused services." The Huron Milling Company was on the market. It was a family firm whose owners wanted to get out and retire from business and also to put their assets in a different form. (Estate tax considerations may well have had something to do with their desire to sell.) At the same time, the firm's activities were of such a nature that Hercules saw an opportunity to extend its knowledge in the food field, especially in the chemistry of amino acids, and to use the personnel of the Virginia cellulose plant. The Huron Milling Company was accordingly purchased with an exchange of shares and is now operated as the Huron Milling Division of the Virginia Cellulose Department. Whether a new base will develop for Hercules remains to be seen, but a start has been made which, if it fits in well with the general nature of Hercules' activities, may not only mean new markets for the firm, but new technology as well.

The Changing Productive Opportunity of the Firm

The diversification of the Hercules Powder Company, while unique in its details, is by no means unique in its general pattern and will be found repeated in greater or less degree in the story of any number of long-established successful firms. The company's history illustrates the impossibility of separating "demand" and "supply" as independent factors explaining the growth and diversification of a firm. The Hercules story illustrates the crucial role of changing knowledge about its own resources in the determination of a firm's course of expansion; at the same time it illustrates the restraining influence of a firm's existing areas of specialization, in particular its technological bases. Whether or not the appearance of new industries, of new "demand," in the economy as a whole will provide profitable opportunities for the expansion of a particular firm depends largely on whether that firm has, or can obtain, an adequate "base" in the relevant field.

Although no single group of industries served by Hercules accounts for more than around 16 per cent of Hercules' sales, two of its primary technological bases, cellulose chemistry and rosin and terpene chemistry, have until recently accounted for over three quarters of its business, with nitrogen chemistry a third important base. Within these bases new products and new markets are continually being created; at the same time petrochemicals have become a leading activity and the emergence of new bases for future operations can already be discerned. By 1926, a bare thirteen years after the firm's creation, new product lines accounted for 35 per cent of total sales; by 1952, 40 per cent of its sales consisted of products that had originated from the firm's research activities after 1930.

The market-creating activities of Hercules are of two kinds; we have discussed one, its extensive reliance on "technical service" to its customers. The other lies in extensive promotion activities related to its customers' products and only indirectly to its own products. For example, Hercules does not manufacture hot lacquers, but it devotes considerable effort to developing the market for these lacquers; only if the end product is extensively used will the demand for the components made by Hercules be high. The firm even goes as far as to promote the sale of aerosol lacquers (lacquers packaged in aerosol cans under pressure), although it produces neither the lacquers nor the cans.

.   .   .

THE RATE OF GROWTH OF THE FIRM

The discussion so far has been concerned exclusively with the direction of expansion. What about the rate of growth of the firm? Hercules has not grown so fast as some other firms in related fields of activity, but it has grown faster than industry as a whole. Can one identify a basic factor limiting the firm's rate of growth? Here, of course, we can only speculate, draw inferences from the course of events, and attempt to interpret statements made by the officials of the firm.

Practically all of the growth of Hercules has been financed with internally generated funds. There has been some criticism within the firm of its conservative financing, and the allegation is made by many, particularly by junior executives who feel that their opportunities have been unnecessarily limited on this account, that the firm's growth has been restricted by its preference for internal financing and its insistence on a strong "cash position." On the other hand, one of the older executives, long a senior official in the firm, asserted categorically that it was not finance but rather the availability of profitable opportunities for expansion which controlled the firm's rate of expansion. He said that if Hercules found new opportunities for profitable investment exceeding its own financial resources it would borrow the money (or preferably raise it from existing stockholders) to take advantage of them.

The same executive stated that neither was expansion held back by the ability of the firm's personnel. He felt that the war record of the firm showed that if the opportunities were there it could do a great deal more than it was doing. In contrast, another senior executive took a different view: "Give us the men," he said, "and we will do the job."

These appear to be conflicting explanations of the limits on the rate of expansion of the firm. Although it is obvious that an insistence on financing all expansion from retained earnings would limit the firm's growth, it is unsafe to assume that this has provided the effective limit on expansion merely because little outside capital has in fact been raised. On the other hand, it is undoubtedly true that from a purely managerial point of view the administrative organization of Hercules could have been expanded much more rapidly than it was. In other words, it is probable that the managerial services available from the administrative and technical staff of the firm have rarely been fully used. Under these circumstances we must examine the nature of the firm's "entrepreneurship."

Hercules has clearly been imaginative, versatile, and venturesome in the introduction of new products, even at times going into production on a small scale before any market for a particular product was clearly evident; at the same time it has been cautious and conservative in entering new and alien fields of technology. It has been willing to venture extensive funds in speculative research in new fields; it has been unwilling to move into production and invest in plant and equipment in new fields before it had established a research base of its own. And it has been conservative in the methods chosen for entering new fields. For example, it was long after petrochemicals had become an important and growing aspect of the field of industrial chemistry that Hercules decided to enter in a significant way, and then it moved cautiously, relying largely on production processes the firm itself had developed. Another firm, technologically less conservative, might have entered much earlier and through extensive acquisition; Hercules has tended to emphasize the importance of establishing a technological position based on some specialty arising from its own experience. On the other hand, once the firm has become "basic" in a field, as some of the officials of the firm like to put it, this conservatism largely disappears and the variety and quantity of product is expanded as rapidly as developing technology and markets will permit.

This means, in effect, that the growth of the firm is fundamentally constrained by the knowledge and experience of its existing personnel. Hercules has apparently been loath to go into new fields of activity except through the relatively slow process of building up its internal technical resources. New people are continually being brought into the firm and trained in the processes and methods of the firm; new ideas are eagerly sought from the outside, particularly from abroad, and incorporated into the firm's research program. But new *bases* are not acquired "ready-made," so to speak, through extensive and rapid absorption of new people in new fields that are not easily integrated with some existing and internally developed unit in the firm.

The profitability of opportunities for expansion is examined not only in the light of the expected market for certain products or types of products, but largely in the light of how Hercules, with its existing resources and types of operation, could take advantage of and develop them. If the growth of the firm has been restrained by a "lack" of profitable opportunities for expansion, this merely reflects the lack of entrepreneurial confidence in the profitability *for Hercules* of areas of activity with which the officials of the firm are insufficiently familiar. Since a "technological base" consists not of buildings, kettles, and tubes, but of the experience and know-how of personnel, the basic restriction comes down to the services available from existing personnel; the problem of entrepreneurial confidence is fundamentally a problem of building up an experienced managerial and technical team in new fields of activity. Here, again, we can see the nature of the market as a restraining influence on expansion. To the extent that limited opportunities in existing fields force firms to go into new ones, the rate of growth is retarded by the need for developing new bases and by the difficulties of expanding as a coordinated unit. The speed with which firms *try* to move, however, is to a large extent a question of the nature of their "entrepreneurship."

The above interpretation of the growth of Hercules is based on a study of past history and of recent attitudes. It is clear that entrepreneurial attitudes, the "firm's conception of itself," have had a pervasive influence not only on its direction of growth but also on the method of growth and on the rate of growth. Whether these attitudes will persist depends on the way in which the entrepreneurial resources of the firm change as time goes on. Hercules takes pride in the long service of its people and in the fact that its board of directors is not only a "working board" but is also drawn from men who have spent a great part of their working life within the firm. The first president of the firm served in that capacity for 26 years, was chairman of the finance committee until 1952, and only retired from the board in 1956; of the 15 members of the board in 1950 all but 2 had been with the firm at least 25 years. As the men who built up the firm and carried it through its first few decades retire, it remains to be seen whether the growth of Hercules will be shaped in the future by the same considerations as it has in the past, for in spite of the importance of technological and market considerations, the entrepreneurship of a firm will largely determine how imaginatively and how rapidly it exploits its potentialities.

GENERAL MOTORS—CREATING THE GENERAL OFFICE

Alfred D. Chandler, Jr.

By the end of 1921, most of [Alfred P.] Sloan's [1] proposals had been carried out. Now the general office was much more than the personal headquarters of the President. Now the new general officers, assisted by the staff specialists, had more time to coordinate, appraise, and make policy for the different divisions and for the corporation as a whole. The new and explicit definition of the role of the general office and of the autonomous operating units and of the relations between them made it possible, for the first time, to integrate effectively the resources—managerial and technical as well as physical—of the agglomeration of producing, assembling, marketing, and engineering facilities and personnel that Durant [2] had assembled. Yet the corporation's leaders were still to have a great deal more work to do before the Sloan plan resulted in a smooth-running organization. Not until 1925 did Sloan and his associates feel convinced that they had an efficient and integrated administrative structure at General Motors.

Putting the New Structure into Operation

As the senior executives at General Motors put the new structure into operation during the four years following 1921, they had to devote constant careful thought to three areas: the definition of divisional activities

---

[1] Sloan began to direct GM's reorganization in 1920; in 1923 he became president of the company.—LG

[2] William C. Durant, founder of General Motors.—LG

REPRINTED with permission from Alfred D. Chandler, Jr., "General Motors—Creating the General Office," *Strategy and Structure: Chapters in the History of the Industrial Enterprise*, Cambridge, Mass.: M.I.T. Press, 1962, pp. 142–61. Copyright 1962 by The M.I.T. Press.

so that the work of each division would more effectively complement that of the others; the development of accurate and effective information to flow through the new structure; and the building of further channels of communication which would bring together more efficiently the efforts of the general staff and the operating executives. In carrying out this work, Sloan with his only superior officer, Pierre du Pont, and his two closest associates, Donaldson Brown and John Lee Pratt, revealed a continuing dispassionate, rational, calculating, and essentially pragmatic approach to the problems of management.

DEFINING DIVISIONAL BOUNDARIES

The first of these broad problems, that of defining the boundaries for the activities of each division, was closely related to market strategy. Concerned primarily with expanding output, Durant had made little attempt to develop a rational product line. The different divisions competed with one another. The corporation as yet had really no low-price car, for Chevrolet was still priced well above Ford.[3] In 1919, Chevrolet sold only 132,170 passenger cars, or 7 per cent of the total market; while Ford's output was 664,482 or 40 per cent of the total.[4] In 1921, the figures were 4 per cent for Chevrolet and 55 per cent for Ford. Buick, a more expensive car, was obviously as much the mainstay of the General Motors line in 1921 as it had been in 1908. In 1921, more Buicks than Chevrolets were sold. Cadillac, while producing the lowest number of cars of the five major divisions, made the most expensive product. It indicated its strength by the relatively small decline in output during the postwar recession. On the other hand, the production of both Olds and Oakland fell in 1921 to less than 1 per cent of the automobiles marketed.

The initial step, then, was to bring the quality of the products of other divisions up to those of Buick and Cadillac and, at the same time, to place the offerings of the different divisions in some kind of rational relationship. This second step was done by formulating a policy of bracketing the market, that is, of having each division produce for a specific price market. As the 1923 Annual Report recorded: "In 1921 a definite policy was adopted. The Corporation should establish a complete line of motor cars from the lowest to the highest price that would justify quantity production."[5] . . .

The same Annual Report noted that by 1923 the product line had been "realigned and adjusted and competition which heretofore existed

---

[3] A. P. Sloan, Direct Testimony, pp. 970–71 and 987, and *Annual Report of General Motors Corporation for 1923*, Mar. 24, 1924, p. 6. For prices see Kennedy, *Automobile Industry*, pp. 130–32.

[4] The figures for cars sold in 1919 and 1921 are given in Seltzer, *Financial History*, p. 213; Federal Trade Commission, *Report on Motor Vehicle Industry* (Washington, 1939), pp. 29, 31; and "General Motors Corporation—Comparison of Numbers and Proportion of Motor Vehicles (Passenger and Truck) Sold by Ford, General Motors and Other Manufacturers, 1921," DE GM 35. A. P. Sloan (Direct Testimony, pp. 970–71) succinctly described the quality of the corporation's different cars in 1920.

[5] *Annual Report of General Motors Corporation for 1923*, Mar. 24, 1924, p. 6.

within the car manufacturing divisions has been largely eliminated. Such a policy makes possible coordination not otherwise practical, in engineering, manufacturing, and particularly in distribution." [6]

The place of the divisions was now pretty well defined. Cadillac sold in the highest-priced position, Buick the next, followed by Oakland and then Olds, with Chevrolet in the largest-volume, lowest-price market. To protect its position and because of "an enormous potential market for a car of quality at a price between that of the Chevrolet and the Oldsmobile," the corporation in 1925 brought out the six-cylinder Pontiac.[7] With the development of the Pontiac, the General Motors basic line was essentially completed. The enterprise was approaching its goal of including in its line "a car for every purse and purpose."

The new management paid close attention to the supporting as well as the front line divisions. By early 1921, it became convinced that General Motors should not extend the old Durant strategy of vertical integration to include ownership or control of sources of the more basic supplies and materials. The Annual Report dated March 26, 1921 put it this way:

> Thus: a comparatively small portion of the total tires produced are consumed by the automobile manufacturer, the larger percentage being sold directly to users of cars for replacement purposes; the greater part of the production of sheets and other forms of steel is consumed by trades other than the automotive industry, therefore investment in these fields has not been made. By the pursuit of this policy, General Motors Corporation has become firmly entrenched in lines that relate directly to the construction of the car, truck or tractor, but has not invested in general industries of which a comparatively small part of the products is consumed in the manufacture of cars.[8]

General Motors explicitly decided not to imitate the strategy Henry Ford was developing, that is, to control and make nearly everything that went into the Model T. There would be no great plant at General Motors comparable to the one then rising on the River Rouge.

Next, a policy on interdivisional billing was established. Whether the products of a division went to other General Motors divisions or outside, they were sold at the going market price. No longer were prices between divisions to be negotiated; insiders would pay the same as outsiders. "Where there are no substantial sales outside," Donaldson Brown pointed out in 1927, "such as would establish a competitive basis, the buying division determines the competitive picture—at times partial requirements are actually purchased from outside sources so as to perfect

---

[6] *Annual Report of General Motors Corporation for 1923*, p. 6; *Printers Ink*, 116:3 (Sept. 29, 1921), 125:17–19 (Dec. 13, 1923).

[7] *Annual Report of General Motors Corporation for 1925*, Feb. 24, 1926, p. 7. The Oakland Division marketed and sold the Pontiac and in time dropped the Oakland and concentrated wholly on the Pontiac.

[8] *Annual Report of General Motors Corporation for 1920*, Mar. 26, 1921, p. 8.

the competitive situation."[9] Unless such competitive conditions existed, he continued, it would be difficult to evaluate the performance of the parts and accessories divisions. If the price which one division charged another was higher than the price in the open market, it suggested that the selling division was inefficient or that it was increasing its profit at the expense of the buying division. In the latter case, the financial record in terms of return on investment—the basic criterion in appraising divisional performance—would not reflect accurately the use of the resources of either division. As a further check, the Executive Committee as early as October, 1921, asked each division to make a detailed report of its reasons for making outside purchases of items which could have been bought within the corporation.[10]

THE DEVELOPMENT OF STATISTICAL AND FINANCIAL CONTROLS

Such refinements in the appraisal of divisional performance could only come, however, after the corporation had solved one of its toughest challenges—the development of accurate, uniform data on costs, production, income, and so forth. The man most responsible for mastering this challenge was Donaldson Brown, the former Treasurer of the du Pont Company whom Pierre du Pont had brought with him to General Motors. The builder of many of du Pont's basic financial and statistical controls, Brown in 1921 was probably as well versed as anyone in the United States in the development and use of these new administrative tools. His pioneering achievements at General Motors thus provide a useful illustration of the critical part that reporting and statistical procedures play in the design by which complex, modern industrial enterprises have become administered.

Brown and his general financial staff carried out their work in two stages. In 1921 and 1922, these executives concentrated on developing data and procedures essential to the general office if it was to obtain some sort of administrative surveillance over the many divisions. The lack of such information in both the general office and the divisions had been one cause for the 1920 crises.[11] To restore order and at the same time to prevent similar dangers in the future, Brown and his assistants began by building informational procedures to control the purchasing and production schedules of each division. Next, they devised methods for the more systematic allocation of capital and other resources and for the more effective use of existing supplies of cash. During this first stage,

[9] Donaldson Brown describes interdivisional price and policies in "Decentralized Operations and Responsibilities with Coordinated Control," American Management Association, *Annual Convention Series*, No. 57 (Feb., 1927), p. 10.
[10] "Extracts from Executive Committee Minutes, March 30, 1926," GE 903. At the meeting the Committee modified the older policy by requiring the approval of the Group Executives before making outside purchases.
[11] A sharp recession caught General Motors with huge inventories which had been purchased at inflated prices; the resulting crisis led to Sloan's reorganization of the company.—LG

they were also working actively to institute uniform accounting procedures.

After 1922, the financial staff concentrated more on refining their data and on perfecting their information and methods. During this second stage, they paid more and more attention to the development of data and controls dealing with anticipated conditions rather than to past or current performance. The coordination of product flow from the purchase of supplies to the final sale to the customer, the allocation of resources, the formulation of other policies, and even the appraisal of the performance of the divisions and the corporation as a whole, all rested increasingly on information about estimated or forecasted conditions. General Motors moved from basing administrative decisions and actions on present or past performance to making them on data concerning anticipated conditions in order to integrate its internal activities with changing market and other external conditions with more certainty.

Because an inventory crisis had precipitated the calamities of 1920, Brown's initial move was to improve controls over purchasing and production schedules and to coordinate these more closely with market demand. Even before he and Pierre du Pont had moved to General Motors, steps had been taken to regain control over the inventories. In October, 1920, after the market had disintegrated and when cash supplies of the corporation were becoming dangerously low, John Lee Pratt had been placed in charge of an Inventories Committee.[12] He was given broad powers. His committee was to examine the inventories of all divisions, and if it found any unit with a surplus of goods, that unit was to make no more purchases without the Committee's approval. Pratt had the same authority over payrolls. "The corporation was running short of cash," Pratt later testified, "and we were trying to preserve the cash."

One of Pierre's very first acts after taking the presidency was to enlarge the membership and the duties of Pratt's committee.[13] With Brown and M. L. Prenskey, the General Motors Treasurer, as new members, the Committee was to compute the write-down of existing inventory and to adjust the existing schedules so that each division would purchase only what was immediately necessary. Finally, the Committee was to receive from each division an estimate of sales for the next four months and to review all these estimates each month. These forecasts soon provided the information with which control over inventory could be maintained. This, in turn, permitted the dissolving of Pratt's committee in April, 1921.[14]

Such forecasts, systematically developed, became the basis for a large part of the statistical controls at General Motors. The divisions esti-

[12] J. L. Pratt, Direct Testimony, pp. 1404–05. The following quotation is from p. 1405.
[13] The Committee's new duties are described in the "Excerpts from Memorandum re Meeting between President and Plant Managers, December 1, 1920 (GMC)," DE GM 196, and J. L. Pratt, Direct Testimony, p. 1414.
[14] Ibid., pp. 1416–17.

mated the sales for each of the next four months and the volume of production and probable expenditures for goods and labor needed to meet these schedules. Only after the general office approved the forecast could the division purchase the necessary supplies. The actual estimating, selection of supplies, and purchasing, like the planning of flow and allocation of stock, remained the responsibility of the division managers. By 1923, these forecasts submitted on the 25th of each month, covering the current month and the succeeding three, had come to include "the amount of investment at the end of each month in plant and in capital working items," [15] as well as the estimates of inventory, output, and necessary purchases. To supplement these reports, the divisions were soon submitting others monthly which covered current financial performance.[16]

During these same months, the top executives at General Motors finally put into effect systematic procedures for the allocation of capital funds.[17] Appropriation requests now, as earlier in the du Pont Company, had to include detailed plans of the buildings, equipment, and materials required, the amount of capital needed for, and the estimated savings to be achieved by the request. A General Manager's signature was sufficient authorization for a request below a certain amount. Above that sum the signature of the Group Executive and President as well as the Manager was required. Larger amounts still called for the approval of the Execu-

[15] Donaldson Brown, "Pricing Policy in Relation to Financial Control," *Management and Administration,* 7:196 (Feb., 1924), and C. S. Mott, "Organizing a Great Industrial," *Management and Administration,* 7:527 (May, 1924). Mott wrote:

Inventory, production, and sales forecasts are presented every 30 days, on a blank which covers a period of 90 days. In the case of a report made on October 25, 1923, for example, the blank shows actual inventory at October 1, with estimates for November 1, December 1 and January 1, which of course include commitments already made or to be made within the period. Production and sales forecasts are given in the same manner and all of the information given as of October 25 is compared with similar information given as of the 25th, one, two, and three months previous. The actual results are compared automatically with previous forecasts; and this tends to secure accuracy in forecasting.

These data are given for the vehicle divisions and for the intercompany parts group as well. On another portion of the blank are set down actual production by months for November and December, 1923, and January and February, 1924. Data are also furnished, showing the total estimated for four months, in all vehicles and parts plants, both in the United States and Canada. Each month, therefore, opportunity is given to the executives to observe the closeness of relation between forecasts and actual results. The figures as they stand are reported by the president to the Executive Committee. The report in the form outlined brings clearly forward the conditions of the individual plant, inventories, and so on.

The detailed working-out of purchasing and the use and day-to-day control of inventory are well described in E. Carl Wennerlund, "Quality Control of Inventories —Physical Regulation Contrasted with Mere Financial Information," *Management and Administration,* 7:677–82 (June, 1924). Wennerlund was the head of the Factory Organization Section, formerly the Manufacturing Section, of the advisory staff.
[16] Pratt mentions "ten-day reports" as being worked out in early 1921. They were probably operating reports (J. L. Pratt, Direct Testimony, p. 1416).
[17] These procedures are carefully described in Mott, "Organizing a Great Industrial," pp. 526–27.

tive Committee and even greater ones that of the Finance Committee. All the large projects were first subject to review by an Appropriations Committee, the direct descendant, undoubtedly, of the Appropriation Committee that Durant had asked Pratt to chair when the latter first came to General Motors. In coming to final decisions, the Appropriations Committee and the general office relied on constantly improved forecasts of the over-all financial and economic situation.

With renewed control over long-term and short-term expenditures came a similar control of the corporation's cash resources. Instead of each division handling its own cash, as it had done before 1921, it now placed incoming receipts in one of more than a hundred banks in which the corporation had placed depository accounts in various parts of the country.[18] The divisions had no control over the depository accounts, and all disbursements from them were handled by the Financial Staff in the general office. Under such a system, the transfer of funds from one part of the corporation and the country to another was extremely easy and almost automatic. Whenever deposits in one bank exceeded a set maximum, the surplus was automatically transferred by telegraph to one of several banks selected to hold these surplus accounts, and whenever a division needed funds it would notify the general office, which would then telegraph a transfer from one of these reserve or surplus accounts. Such a system had several advantages, but the most important was the constant availability of a large pool of cash. At the same time, interdivisional billing was made much easier. One division billed another on a white slip, which the selling division sent to the Comptroller, who charged the buyer and credited the seller. This permitted settlement without any exchange of cash.

The crisis made possible one further advance toward systematic general supervision. At last, uniform accounting procedures were instituted in all parts of the corporation. A Divisional Comptroller, while reporting to his General Manager on routine matters, now followed the guidance of the financial officers in the general office on standards, procedures, and methods.[19] After 1921, the new Cost Accounting Section drew up accounting procedures for all divisions. Data from these procedures gave the division managers as well as the general office a relatively realistic picture of just what were costs and therefore profits. Now, for the first time, the general office had the basic information necessary for determining whether costs were in line with market prices and whether each unit was making a satisfactory return on its investment.[20]

[18] These procedures are described in Alfred H. Swayne, "Mobilization of Cash Reserves," *Management and Administration*, 7:21–23 (Jan., 1924). The system had such additional advantages as those of making available more bank credit to General Motors and of rendering it possible to invest excess cash so that it earned interest.

[19] General Motors Corporation organization chart, Jan. 3, 1921, GE 178. Sloan describes the financial organization of a division in his Deposition, Apr. 28, 1952, pp. 48–50.

[20] These procedures are indicated in Thomas B. Fordham and Edward H. Tingley, "Applying the Budget to Industrial Operations—Control through Organization and

But accurate accounting with its realistic evaluation of profit and loss required more than uniform procedures and improved data. In the automobile industry, with its high volume, its relatively high unit price, and its great plant capacity, the cost of a single unit varied directly with volume of output. Until full capacity was reached, the more cars produced, the lower the unit costs; while the lower the volume, the higher the costs. Costs, and therefore price and profit, were directly tied in with volume. Volume, in turn, was directly related to the demand for automobiles, which fluctuated widely from season to season, and from year to year.

To determine costs in the face of fluctuating demand, Brown used the concept of standard volume or, in his words, "the establishment of a percentage representing an assumed normal average rate of plant operation," over a long period of time.[21]

> This determines [Brown commented early in 1924] the so-called standard volume which is accepted as the basis upon which costs will be measured, and upon which the margin of profit is determined as necessary to afford a given average rate of return on capital employed. The established percentage must reflect the unavoidable fluctuations of business which render an even rate of production impossible, and, as far as practicable, should represent the economic situation of the industry, rather than any abnormal situation which might be recognized as pertaining to a given plant.

At General Motors, Brown continued, standard volume was set at 80 per cent of plant capacity. Manufacturing costs or "standard factory burden," and here the critical costs were those that varied partially with size of output, could be estimated at standard volume. If actual volume was below standard, costs would then be charged against profits as unabsorbed burden. . . . With costs for a standard volume of production and a standard allowance for commercial purposes, Brown and his associates were able to determine for each product a "standard" or "base" price by which to see whether costs were in line with the actual going market price.

Volume affected costs and profits in still another way. It altered the rate of turnover on invested capital. If sales were high, the capital used in the production of each unit could be turned over more rapidly than if the dealers were having difficulties in moving their products. The over-all rate of return depended, as Brown had realized much earlier at du Pont, on both the ratio of sales to profits and the ratio of sales to investment.[22] In figuring probable income, an accurate estimate of sales had become all important.

Budget," *Management and Administration*, 7:57–62, 205–08, and 291 (Jan., Feb., and Apr., 1924), and in the articles by Donaldson Brown in the same volume of *Management and Administration*, especially pp. 283–86.
[21] This and the following quotation are from Donaldson Brown, "Pricing Policy in Relation to Financial Control," p. 283.
[22] See particularly *ibid.*, pp. 417–22.

Since the planning of financial requirements (the allocation of funds for working and capital expenditures) depended on anticipated income, these factors, like the setting of production schedules, labor needs, the purchasing of supplies, and the allocation of other resources, had come to depend on accurate and long-term forecasting. In early 1924, the long-term estimates at General Motors were still calculated with little precision. Brown described the method in this way in one of a series of articles on the administration of General Motors that he and other executives wrote in 1924 in the periodical, *Management and Administration:*

> In December of every year, each division is required to present an outline of its view of probable operations for the succeeding year, embodying estimates of sales, earnings, and capital requirements. These outlines are in three forms, i.e.: "pessimistic," representing a minimum expectation, "conservative," representing what is considered a likely condition, and "optimistic," representing what the name implies, with production and sales capacity as a limitation.[23]

As the Vice-President in charge of Finances stressed, these annual, like the short-term four months' forecasts, were

> scrutinized by the central office and compared with current and past performance, attention of the proper officials being called to any abnormalities or marked deviations from what might be deemed a conservative sales expectation. Experience has led to the establishment of standards or working capital requirements in relation to volume of business and the forecasted investment in receivables and inventory are carefully checked against such standards, allowance being made for seasonal fluctuations. The tendencies of manufacturing costs and of selling and administrative expenses are observed, and profits are analyzed, with reference to the pricing policy laid down as governing the operations of a given division.

At the very time that Brown was writing his articles, in which the tremendous importance of accurate estimating was emphasized, an unexpected slump in the automobile market indicated a critical weakness in the corporation's forecasting methods. In the spring and summer of 1924, car production dropped off, and more for General Motors than for most companies. The first half of 1923 had witnessed, the corporation's Annual Report for 1924 explained, "an unprecedented demand for the Corporation's products and an inability to meet this demand. This resulted in the loss of sales and some dissatisfaction on the part of the Corporation's dealer organization on account of failure to make adequate delivery."[24] So output was kept high, and sales for 1923 were the largest in General Motors' history. In anticipation of a large spring demand, production was maintained at capacity during the first quarter of 1924.

[23] This and the following quotation are from *ibid.*, p. 196.
[24] *Annual Report of the General Motors Corporation for 1924*, Mar. 23, 1925, p. 8. Figures on production are in Seltzer, *Financial History*, pp. 212–16, and F.T.C., *Motor Vehicle Industry*, pp. 22–24.

As the second quarter passed, Sloan began to suspect that supply was beginning to exceed demand. In May, he decided to investigate by taking a trip west. Crowded dealer lots in St. Louis and then in Kansas City convinced him, and he ordered immediate cuts in production.[25]

The failure to anticipate a drop in demand and then to act quickly on it, a failure threateningly reminiscent of the fall of 1920, brought swift action. On July 2, after reporting on his trip west to a meeting of General Motors purchasing agents, Sloan told them that "machinery is being set up to have the production schedules properly controlled and control insisted upon." [26] The new policy called for ten-day reports from all the corporation's dealers. From these reports, existing forecasts could be quickly appraised and production adjusted to any sudden changes in demand. Sloan provided a further check on the actual performance of the market by obtaining periodic reports from R. L. Polk and Company on new car registrations.[27] By providing registration figures on all makes of new cars, these reports presented a clear picture of just what share of its market each of the different General Motors divisions enjoyed and if and how this share was changing.

. . .

Now the general office began to pay closer attention to the validity and accuracy of the long-term divisional forecasts, and to make up indices for the corporation as a whole. By 1925, the divisional and general office staffs were drawing up comprehensive over-all plans for all operating units, plans based on carefully thought-out, long-term forecasts. These annual "Price Studies" soon became one of the most effective ways by which the general office could oversee and check the activities of the division managers without seriously impinging on the latter's authority and responsibility. . . .[28]

As Bradley pointed out the estimate of the year's domestic sales, on which the price studies rested, depended on at least four major factors —the growth of the industry, seasonal variation, the conditions of general business, and activities of competitors. With these factors in mind, the initial sales estimate depended on "the number of cars which are likely to be sold to the public by the entire automotive industry" and this figure was "based primarily upon actual experience for the last three years, after giving careful consideration to the probable number of automobiles needed to replace those which will be worn out or otherwise destroyed during the coming year, and an appraisal of the general business

25 Dale ("Contributions to Administration," p. 45) describes Sloan's trip west.
26 "Excerpts—General Purchasing Committee re Production Schedule Forecasts from Minutes of Committee for April 18, July 2, Sept. 5, 1924, and Feb. 6, 1925," DE GM 125.
27 Testimony of A. P. Sloan, p. 988.
28 This quotation is from [Bradley, "Setting up a Forecasting Program,"] pp. 6–7, and the two following are from pp. 12–13. By this time the Financial Staff had begun, as Bradley indicated, to use more sophisticated methods in computing selling costs than Donaldson Brown had used two years earlier, pp. 8–9.

situation for the coming year." Then, from this forecast, a "Divisional Index" was drawn up based on the expectations for each division, taking into consideration the total amount of business available within its respective price group and the competitive situation. Thus, Bradley expected that:

> A forecasting program should serve two separate and quite distinct general purposes. In its broadest aspects, the forecast affords a means of gauging an operating program in terms of the fundamental policy of the Corporation regarding the rate of return on capital investment, as related to the pricing of the product, and the conditions under which additional capital will be provided for expansion. The second, and the more frequent, use of a forecast is as a tool for control of current operations.[29]

Because of the heavy investment in inventory, because of the several stages involved in the over-all manufacturing and selling of the mass-produced automobile, and because of the relatively large investment in plant, equipment, and personnel at each stage, scheduling and other decisions concerning the coordination of product flow at General Motors came to rest on anticipated rather than on present conditions, while the actual flow came to be adjusted every ten days to actual market demand. By the same token, the long-term allocation of resources as well as their current use was increasingly set by an estimate of the future situation. Forecasts, therefore, became essential to strategic planning and, at the same time, provided the general office, and the divisional executives, too, with a means to appraise operating activities.

In this way then, between 1921 and 1925, General Motors had worked out highly rational and systematic procedures that permitted it, on the one hand, to coordinate and appraise the operating divisions and to plan policy for the corporation as a whole, and, on the other hand, to assure a smooth product flow from supplier to consumer and a fairly steady use of plants, facilities, and personnel in an industry where the market fluctuated rapidly. Each division's actual costs and profits could be viewed against a standard or average cost and profit, and, with truly comparable figures, the performance of one division could be accurately measured with that of another. Thus the general office was provided with objective criteria by which to evaluate and appraise the work of their division managers. Similarly, as Brown and Bradley indicated, the detailed reports from the divisions, which made possible accurate analyses of the critical revenue and cost factors determining the rate of return on investment, permitted the executives at the top offices to locate sources of strengths and weaknesses of a division. As long as there was a constant flow of such information, there was little need for the general officers to be concerned with the specific detailed work within the divisions.

Beside providing essential data for supervision and appraisal, the new fiscal and financial procedures facilitated forward planning and pol-

[29] *Ibid.*, p. 3.

icy formulation. From this same information the general officers could determine, in broad terms, the price ranges and production schedules within which each division could operate. Of greater significance, a more rational allocation of funds for capital expenditures was made possible, and decisions as to where the corporation should expand, contract, or maintain its activities were made easier.

Finally, these synchronized procedures, by assuring a close coordination of flow from purchasing through production to marketing, helped to increase operating efficiencies. By keeping its varied activities tied together closely and related directly to day-to-day changes in market demand, the corporation was able to make a real reduction in costs. Manufacturing, plant, and sales facilities could be utilized at a fairly even and regular capacity. Both the manufacturing and sales force were assured of steadier employment. Outside suppliers, too, could keep their plants operating more evenly.[30] By reducing the amount of inventory needed, this careful coordination cut down the cost of working capital, lowered expenses of storing, carrying charges, and so forth. It is hard to see how expenses could not have been reduced by such rational control or how, without it, costs could only have increased.

. . .

Statistical and financial data and procedure alone, however, did not assure administrative control and coordination. If Sloan and Brown needed any reminder of this fact, the overproduction in the spring of 1924 provided it. The corporation's general officers soon came to spend much time on the road, visiting plants, seeing suppliers, and most of all talking to dealers.[31] Even so Sloan and the other general executives came in time to rely as much on the general staff as on the financial and statistical reports and visits to the field to provide them with essential information. The Advisory Staff played a critical role in permitting the general office to administer the separate divisions and the corporation as a whole.

DEFINING THE ROLE OF THE ADVISORY STAFF

The role of the Advisory Staff like that of the Financial Staff was to help coordinate, appraise, and plan policy. The staff carried out these duties

[30] The buyers at General Motors realized that the leveling of demand would please their suppliers, so that the General Purchasing Committee "agreed that a letter from Mr. Sloan dealing with the plan for controlling production which manifestly would control the demand upon suppliers for their products and materials, which our Purchasing Agents could refer to in conversation on negotiations with suppliers, might strengthen our buying position by conveying to the suppliers our efforts toward scientifically preventing wide fluctuations in demand resulting from drastic adjustments of Schedules," Minutes of General Purchasing Committee, Sept. 25, 1924, DE GM 125. For figures on improvement in steadying seasonal fluctuations in employment and on the improvement in the turnover of productive inventory, see Bradley, "Setting up a Forecasting Program," pp. 15–18, and Dale, "Contributions to Administration," pp. 51–52.
[31] Ibid., p. 47.

partly by providing the division managers and the general officers with expert advice and assistance which was used to improve current operations and to formulate future plans. [Charles P.] Kettering's research section worked on improved engines, parts, bodies, fuels, and other technical improvements to better automotive comfort and efficiency.[32] Hawkins' sales unit planned broad advertising campaigns, retail selling programs, showroom displays, and so on. The Factory Section developed and tested new methods of production, cost analysis, waste prevention, salvage, factory layout, design, and so forth. The Purchasing Section advised on work contracts that involved more than one division, assisted in interdivisional buying, and encouraged cooperation between the purchasing departments of the many operating units. In carrying out their advisory duties, the advisory staff was also able to keep a check on the divisions, to suggest ways to improve current methods, and to see how various policies were being followed. In this way they provided the general office with a steady flow of information on operating activities which, like statistical data provided by Brown's financial staff, was relatively free of any divisional bias.

Along with planning and checking activities, staff executives were expected to help coordinate programs and procedures so that the various functional departments in the divisions could perform their routines in approximately the same way. Essentially this meant that the staff assured an exchange of information on sales, production, accounting, engineering, and research, beside often providing data and working up plans to assist the division managers and general officers in outlining more general procedures. By spreading ideas and innovations of both the staff and line executives throughout the organization, Sloan hoped to exploit what might be called the administrative economies of scale—to make the most effective use of the talents and training of this large body of executive and supervisory personnel.

Very soon, Sloan, as Operating Vice-President, found that the staff was having difficulty in carrying out its advisory role effectively. The operating executives often looked on the staff men as interfering outsiders and theorists. For example, Kettering's most important project was the development of a radically new type of engine. According to the 1922 Annual Report, the motor was "cooled by means of copper fins brazed directly to the cylinder walls, thus doing away with radiator, water pump, and water jacket."[33] Not being subject to freezing or overheat-

[32] The role of Kettering's section is indicated in Boyd, *Professional Amateur,* pp. 117–26, and "Meeting of Car Division Managers with Executive Committee December 1, 1921," DE GM 104. The work of the Sales and Factory Sections is indicated in Mott, "Organizing a Great Industrial," pp. 524–26, in *Printers Ink,* 116:3 ff. (Sept. 29, 1921), 125:17–19 (Dec. 13, 1923). The initial duties of the Purchasing Section are spelled out in a letter from A. P. Sloan to all General Officers and General Managers of Divisions, Jan. 25, 1921, DE GM 43. As this letter stressed: "The use of such general contracts [are] to be entirely at the option of the Operating Divisions and, when used, all dealings to be directly between the Seller and the Purchasing Division."

[33] *Annual Report of General Motors Corporation for 1922,* pp. 15–16. The story

Alfred D. Chandler, Jr.   439

ing, it was lighter, more powerful, and used less fuel than a conventional motor. The operating divisions were far more skeptical about this engine than were Kettering's sanguine staff men. Its introduction would mean production headaches that they preferred to avoid. After millions of dollars had been spent on it, the project was abandoned. Kettering blamed the failure wholly on the resistance of the divisional engineers and production men who failed to see the potentialities of the new design. As Kettering's response suggests, the lines of communication between the staff and operating executives had broken down.

By the time of the rejection of the copper-cooled engine in the summer of 1923, Sloan had begun work on a scheme to reform the lines of communication so that the staff might fulfill its role more effectively. To assure closer contact between line and staff and between divisions themselves, he settled on the interdivisional committee. Like some of the first statistical and financial controls, this committee did not emerge from a long-range plan but rather resulted from the need for meeting immediate problems.

The genesis of the plan was the problem of purchasing, and the first interdivisional committee dealt with that function. When Sloan reviewed the activities of that committee in 1924, he wrote:

It has shown the way or what I believe to be the way of co-ordinating to the stockholder's benefit the functional activities of our different Operating Divisions without in any sense taking away from those Divisions the responsibility of their individual activities. In other words, expressed otherwise, I feel that in all our functional activities like purchasing, manufacturing, engineering, and sales, a great deal can be accomplished by proper co-ordination and, in my judgment, it is only a question of time when the development of the automotive industry will force us, due to the economics of the future picture, into just such things. The General Purchasing Committee has, I believe, shown the way and has demonstrated that those responsible for each functional activity can work together to their own profit and to the profit of the stockholders at the same time, and such a plan of co-ordination is far better from every standpoint than trying to inject it into the operations from some central activity.[34]

Sloan first turned to the interdivisional committee as a means of improving communication and coordination in the spring of 1922 when the division managers were expressing their skepticism about his suggestion for more centralized purchasing. He believed that the company could save from $5,000,000 to $10,000,000 annually if the purchasing staff in the general office drew up contracts on items that were widely used by

of the copper-cooled engine and the resulting line-and-staff conflict is briefly covered in Boyd, *Professional Amateur*, pp. 119–23. See also *Automotive Industries*, 48:1253 (June 7, 1923).
[34] "Memorandum dated December 1, 1924 from Alfred P. Sloan, Jr. to Members of General Purchasing Committee," DE GM 65.

the corporation as a whole.[35] The division managers offered many objections.[36] Some feared it would tend to cancel a division's long experience in buying for its particular needs. Others emphasized the diverse requirements of the various operating units. Still others thought that the loss of control over purchasing would seriously infringe on the authority and responsibility of the manager.

As a result of these objections, Sloan proposed that the contracts be drawn by a committee of purchasing agents representing the different divisions.[37] Besides writing specifications, the committee was expected to define broader buying policies and procedures. It had a permanent secretary with an office of his own. His job was to prepare lists and agenda for the meetings and to make detailed studies and reports. The actual specifications of the contracts and their wording were left to the purchasing office at headquarters.

After the discontinuance of the copper-cooled program had made clear the need for better line-and-staff coordination in other areas, Sloan formed a General Technical Committee to coordinate engineering and other technical activities, a Committee for Institutional Advertising, and then a General Sales Committee.[38] Shortly afterward, he added a Works Manager and a Power and Maintenance Committee.

. . .

General officers sat with staff specialists and operating executives on the interdivisional committees. Sloan, who had become President in May 1923, was on all the committees and was at different times Chairman of the General Technical, the Works Managers as well as the Purchasing Committee.[39] At least one member of the Executive Committee besides

[35] A. P. Sloan, Letter No. 25 to General Managers of Divisions and other Officers, May 8, 1922, and attached memorandum entitled "Proposal for Coordination of General Motors Purchases," DE GM 49. See also A. P. Sloan to J. H. Main, Feb. 9, 1922, DE GM 48, A. P. Sloan, Direct Testimony, p. 1032, and "Meeting of Car Division Managers with Executive Committee, Nov. 3, 1921," DE GM 45.

[36] The replies of the General Managers and their purchasing agents are given in several exhibits in the General Motors-du Pont Antitrust Suit, DE GM 50–60.

[37] A. P. Sloan to Division Managers and other Officers, Nov. 28 and 29, 1922, DE GM 61 and 62. A. P. Sloan to J. Lynch (Feb. 6, 1923, DE GM 328) shows that Sloan was Chairman and Lynch Secretary of the Committee.

[38] Memorandum from A. P. Sloan to P. S. du Pont, J. Raskob, C. F. Kettering, and Fred B. Fisher, August 6, 1923, GE 904 (D.C.). At General Purchasing Committee meeting on August 2, 1923, Sloan outlined the functions of a "proposed Works Engineers Committee." This is possibly what became of the General Technical Committee, General Purchasing Committee Minutes, Aug. 2, 1923, DE GM 152. The committees are described in Mott, "Organizing a Great Industrial," p. 526; Donaldson Brown, "Decentralized Operations and Responsibilities with Co-ordinated Control," p. 15; and A. P. Sloan, Direct Testimony, p. 994, and indicated in "Chart showing General Motors Corporation Organization, January, 1925," DE GM 2. The make-up of the General Technical Committee is given in *Automotive Industries*, 51:531–32 (Sept. 18, 1924).

[39] [General Motors Corporation—Organization Charts, Jan. 1925 and Apr. 1927, DE GM 2 and 3;] and Donaldson Brown, "Decentralized Operations and Responsibilities with Co-ordinated Control," pp. 15–16.

Sloan sat on each committee. Brown chaired the General Sales Committee, and Pratt came to head the General Purchasing. The committees, therefore, provided a systematic and regular means by which the line, staff, and general officers could meet monthly or even more often to exchange information and to consider common problems. . . .[40]

THE ROLE OF THE EXECUTIVE COMMITTEE

The interdivisional committees' most important functions were to make recommendations to the Executive Committee and to propose new policies and procedures or revisions and modifications of old ones in their major functional area.[41] Except for the Purchasing Committee, none of the committees made final decisions, which were left to the division managers or to the Executive Committee.[42] As individual members of the Executive Committee were also on the interdivisional committees, they took part in the discussions leading to these recommendations and so were able to present the proposals and the reasons for them to their fellow members when decisions were required.

The Executive Committee thus remained the governing body at General Motors. Only on matters of very broad operating policy, particularly if major expenditures were involved, did the decisions of this Committee need the approval of the Finance Committee or of the Board itself. Once the crisis had been surmounted, Pierre had enlarged the small, emergency Executive Committee that he had created in late 1920. Then, after Sloan became President and Pierre, Chairman of the Board, in May, 1923, still other executives were added to the Committee. In 1925, it included ten members.[43] By 1924, the other senior committee—the Operations Committee, consisting of the major operating divisions and staff departments—had been reduced to include only the general man-

[40] A. P. Sloan to C. F. Kettering, July 25, 1924, GE 666.
[41] For example, the General Sales Committee, in a meeting in May, 1925, defined the corporation's policy on trade-in and resale of used cars. The members agreed that Ford's policy of insisting that the dealers make a profit on used cars was unrealistic. The basic aim of the dealer should be to sell as many new cars as possible and to profit on the over-all transaction rather than merely make a profit on the used car sales. Then on Oct. 8, 1925, the Committee spelled out in detail just what the corporation's policy for all divisions would be on used cars, F.T.C., *Motor Vehicle Industry*, pp. 215–16. The Federal Trade Commission's report, quoting from the General Sales Committee Minutes, then describes later modifications and adjustments of the policy. On pp. 255–58, the report cites the Minutes of the Committee on the formulation of the corporation's policy concerning exclusive dealerships.
[42] Donaldson Brown, "Decentralized Operations and Responsibilities with Co-ordinated Control," p. 16. The General Purchasing Committee also set up standards and specifications for parts and equipment for all divisions. (Minutes of General Purchasing Committee, DE GM 152, and A. P. Sloan, Direct Testimony, p. 994.)
[43] *Annual Report of General Motors Corporation for 1922*, p. 3; *Annual Report of General Motors Corporation for 1924*, Mar. 23, 1925, p. 3; and General Motors Organization Charts, Jan., 1925, and Apr., 1927, DE GM 2 and 3.

agers of the car divisions.[44] Its function appears to have been little more than the discussion of common problems and the exchanging of information. The Executive Committee clearly made the significant entrepreneurial and strategic decisions.

The members of this committee had the time and psychological commitment as well as the necessary information to concentrate on broad strategic matters. Unlike the committee during Durant's regime, nearly all its members were now general officers without any detailed operating duties. Possibly recalling the experience of the Durant period and realizing what had happened at du Pont after he had left the company, Donaldson Brown undoubtedly expressed the feeling of General Motors' top executives when he commented in 1924 on the dangers of management by operating chiefs. Although such committee management did allow the general managers to have a say in basic policy formulation, Brown pointed out that for this very reason the resulting policy was likely to be a compromise between interested parties. Such Executive Committee members could not view problems impartially nor probably look at them in the interests of the corporation as a whole. "Policies should be dealt with from an impartial understanding of the operating aspect," Brown wrote, "and in the exercise of the dual function [as division head and member of the Committee] it is difficult for the individual to divorce himself from the departmental viewpoint." [45] Although there were some exceptions, general officers rather than division managers carried on the basic entrepreneurial activities at General Motors.[46]

THE FINISHED STRUCTURE

By 1925 then, the structure, initially designed by Sloan before the crisis of 1920 and put into effect early in 1921, had been worked out so as to assure effective administration of the many and varied industrial resources that Durant had collected. . . . The organization builders at General Motors had placed the divisions in logical relation to one another. They had instituted a large over-all administrative office with general executives assisted by staff specialists to coordinate, appraise, and set policies for the multifunction autonomous operating divisions. The lines of authority and communication between the general office and the divisions had been carefully defined and then supplemented by the formation of the Interdivisional Committees. Finally, a mass of accurate data, both on internal performance and external conditions, had been developed to flow through these communication channels. Nearly all ac-

[44] The initial make-up of the Operations Committee is indicated in the chart showing the organization of the company, Jan. 3, 1921, GE 178. Its later make-up is indicated in Mott, "Organizing a Great Industrial," p. 526.
[45] Donaldson Brown, "Pricing Policy in Relation to Financial Control," p. 195, and A. P. Sloan, Direct Testimony, p. 997.
[46] In 1925 Harry H. Bassett, General Manager of Buick, was on the Committee as was Lawrence P. Fisher, head of Cadillac, in 1927, General Motors Organization Charts, Jan., 1925, and Apr., 1927, DE GM 2 and 3.

tivities of General Motors had become keyed to forecasted market demand and estimated financial and economic conditions. Such data, compiled regularly by the divisions and then checked and supplemented by the general office, made unnecessary Sloan's original suggestion for a special staff office devoted to interdivisional scheduling.

The new organizational structure served General Motors well. From 1924 to 1927, the Corporation's share of the motor vehicle market rose from 18.8 per cent to 43.3.[47] In the following year, its profits stood at an impressive $276,468,000.[48] From then on, General Motors has maintained the leading position in the industry. The clearly and rationally defined structure became increasingly valuable as the demand for automobiles leveled off and competition intensified. The industry had sold 1.5 million passenger cars in 1921.[49] By 1925, the new passenger cars produced in a year reached 3.7 million, and for the next four years the demand for new cars averaged somewhat under four million a year. Then, with the depression, the call for new cars declined rapidly. While the saturation of the market had relatively little impact on General Motors' profits, it proved disastrous for Henry Ford, Sloan's major competitor and an empire builder who in his later years rarely thought in terms of structure or even strategy. Ford's share of the market plummeted from 55.5 per cent in 1921 to 18.9 per cent in 1940 when his sales were far behind Chrysler's 23.7 per cent of the market and General Motors' 47.5 per cent.[50] And after 1926, Ford's profit record was indeed dismal.

Because of General Motors' success, its underlying structure remained relatively unchanged. However, Alfred Sloan, President until 1937 and Chairman of the Board until 1956, was constantly adjusting and modifying the organization. The relations between operating, staff, and general officers were adjusted primarily to meet changing market conditions, particularly during the depression and after World War II. In the middle of the depression, for example, General Motors temporarily combined Buick, Olds, and Pontiac into one division in order to cut down administrative costs.[51] But the multidivisional "decentralized" structure remained intact.

Probably the most significant structural change after 1925 came in the mid-1930's with the abolition of the Interdivisional Committees and the formation shortly thereafter of the Policy Groups consisting of general and staff executives in the general office.[52] Through these groups,

[47] F.T.C., *Motor Vehicle Industry*, pp. 29–31. This rapid rise was partly because of the Ford shift from the "T" to the "A," but in 1931 General Motors' share was 41.8 per cent.
[48] Kennedy, *Automobile Industry*, p. 211, claims that this was the largest net profit yet made by an American corporation.
[49] F.T.C., *Motor Vehicle Industry*, p. 29.
[50] Edward L. Allen, *Economics of American Manufacturing* (New York, 1952), p. 293.
[51] *Automotive Industries*, 69:532 and 536–37 (Oct. 28, 1933).
[52] *Fortune*, 17:73 ff. (Apr. 19, 1938); *Annual Report of the General Motors Corporation for 1937*, Mar. 31, 1938, pp. 37–38; "Report to the Stockholders of General

the general office became even more explicitly responsible for strategic decisions and the divisions for tactical ones. . . .

The administrative changes at General Motors between 1920 and 1925 had an importance beyond their contribution to the successful management of the automobile company, for the innovators advertised their accomplishments. Proud of what they had achieved, they described their new organizational methods and techniques in articles appearing in professional journals and in papers delivered at the meetings of the American Management Association. In these essays, they also set forth the new "principles" or "philosophy" of management that they believed their experiences to demonstrate. Donaldson Brown made the most precise statement of this new philosophy of decentralization in a paper on "Decentralized Operations and Responsibilities with Coordinated Control" that he read before the American Management Association in 1927. Here Brown made the distinction between "policy and administrative control." [53] The Executive Committee assisted by a general staff was responsible for setting the long-range policies within which the divisions operated. The heads of the autonomous divisions, responsible for the making and selling of automobiles and other products, enjoyed "administrative control." Brown's statement on the nature of decentralized operating responsibilities and centralized policy formulation marks the real beginning in the United States of the publication of many articles, books, and pamphlets about administrative decentralization. Just because General Motors' executives described so enthusiastically the structure they had built, the corporation became, more than that of any other company, the model for similar structural changes in other large American industrial enterprises.

.   .   .

Motors Corporation, May 17, 1937," pp. 2–5; and testimony and exhibits in the du Pont Antitrust Suit. F.T.C., *Motor Vehicle Industry* (pp. 527–29), indicates that the General Sales Committee lasted until September, 1933.

[53] Donaldson Brown, "Decentralized Operations and Responsibilities with Co-ordinated Control," pp. 7–8. Most of the other articles by senior General Motors executives have been cited earlier in this chapter.

THE THEORY OF COUNTERVAILING
POWER *John Kenneth Galbraith*

I

On the night of November 2, 1907, the elder Morgan played solitaire in his library while the panic gripped Wall Street. Then, when the other bankers had divided up the cost of saving the tottering Trust Company of America, he presided at the signing of the agreement, authorized the purchase of the Tennessee Coal & Iron Company by the Steel Corporation to encourage the market, cleared the transaction with President Roosevelt and the panic was over. There, as legend has preserved and doubtless improved the story, was a man with power a self-respecting man could fear.

A mere two decades later, in the crash of 1929, it was evident that the Wall Street bankers were as helpless as everyone else. Their effort in the autumn of that year to check the collapse in the market is now re-called as an amusing anecdote; the heads of the New York Stock Exchange and the National City Bank fell into the toils of the law and the first went to prison; the son of the Great Morgan went to a Congressional hearing in Washington and acquired fame, not for his authority, but for his embarrassment when a circus midget was placed on his knee.

As the banker, as a symbol of economic power, passed into the shadows his place was taken by the giant industrial corporation. The substitute was much more plausible. The association of power with the banker had always depended on the somewhat tenuous belief in a "money trust"—on the notion that the means for financing the initiation and expansion of business enterprises was concentrated in the hands of a few men. The ancestry of this idea was in Marx's doctrine of finance capital; it was not susceptible to statistical or other empirical verification at least in the United States.

REPRINTED with permission from John Kenneth Galbraith, "The Theory of Countervailing Power," *American Capitalism*, Boston: Houghton Mifflin, 1952, pp. 108–23.

By contrast, the fact that a substantial proportion of all production was concentrated in the hands of a relatively small number of huge firms was readily verified. That three or four giant firms in an industry might exercise power analogous to that of a monopoly, and not different in consequences, was an idea that had come to have the most respectable of ancestry in classical economics. So as the J. P. Morgan Company left the stage, it was replaced by the two hundred largest corporations—giant devils in company strength. Here was economic power identified by the greatest and most conservative tradition in economic theory. Here was power to control the prices the citizen paid, the wages he received, and which interposed the most formidable of obstacles of size and experience to the aspiring new firm. What more might it accomplish were it to turn its vast resources to corrupting politics and controlling access to public opinion?

Yet, as was so dramatically revealed to be the case with the omnipotence of the banker in 1929, there are considerable gaps between the myth and the fact. The comparative importance of a small number of great corporations in the American economy cannot be denied except by those who have a singular immunity to statistical evidence or striking capacity to manipulate it. In principle the American is controlled, livelihood and soul, by the large corporation; in practice he seems not to be completely enslaved. Once again the danger is in the future; the present seems still tolerable. Once again there may be lessons from the present which, if learned, will save us in the future.

II

As with social efficiency and its neglect of technical dynamics, the paradox of the unexercised power of the large corporation begins with an important oversight in the underlying economic theory. In the competitive model—the economy of many sellers each with a small share of the total market—the restraint on the private exercise of economic power was provided by other firms on the same side of the market. It was the eagerness of competitors to sell, not the complaints of buyers, that saved the latter from spoliation. It was assumed, no doubt accurately, that the nineteenth-century textile manufacturer who overcharged for his product would promptly lose his market to another manufacturer who did not. If all manufacturers found themselves in a position where they could exploit a strong demand, and mark up their prices accordingly, there would soon be an inflow of new competitors. The resulting increase in supply would bring prices and profits back to normal.

As with the seller who was tempted to use his economic power against the customer, so with the buyer who was tempted to use it against his labor or suppliers. The man who paid less than prevailing wage would lose his labor force to those who paid the worker his full (marginal) contribution to the earnings of the firm. In all cases the incentive to socially desirable behavior was provided by the competitor. It was to the same side of the market—the restraint of sellers by other sellers and of buyers by other buyers, in other words to competition—that economists came to look for the self-regulatory mechanism of the economy.

They also came to look to competition exclusively and in formal theory still do. The notion that there might be another regulatory mechanism in the economy has been almost completely excluded from economic thought. Thus, with the widespread disappearance of competition in its classical form and its replacement by the small group of firms if not in overt, at least in conventional or tacit collusion, it was easy to suppose that since competition had disappeared, all effective restraint on private power had disappeared. Indeed this conclusion was all but inevitable if no search was made for other restraints and so complete was the preoccupation with competition that none was made.

In fact, new restraints on private power did appear to replace competition. They were nurtured by the same process of concentration which impaired or destroyed competition. But they appeared not on the same side of the market but on the opposite side, not with competitors but with customers or suppliers. It will be convenient to have a name for this counterpart of competition and I shall call it *countervailing power*.[1]

To begin with a broad and somewhat too dogmatically stated proposition, private economic power is held in check by the countervailing power of those who are subject to it. The first begets the second. The long trend toward concentration of industrial enterprise in the hands of a relatively few firms has brought into existence not only strong sellers, as economists have supposed, but also strong buyers, as they have failed to see. The two develop together, not in precise step but in such manner that there can be no doubt that the one is in response to the other.

The fact that a seller enjoys a measure of monopoly power, and is reaping a measure of monopoly return as a result, means that there is an inducement to those firms from whom he buys or those to whom he sells to develop the power with which they can defend themselves against exploitation. It means also that there is a reward to them, in the form of a share of the gains of their opponents' market power, if they are able to do so. In this way the existence of market power creates an incentive to the organization of another position of power that neutralizes it.

The contention I am here making is a formidable one. It comes to this: Competition which, at least since the time of Adam Smith, has been viewed as the autonomous regulator of economic activity and as the only available regulatory mechanism apart from the state, has, in fact, been superseded. Not entirely, to be sure. I should like to be explicit on this point. Competition still plays a role. There are still important markets where the power of the firm as (say) a seller is checked or circumscribed by those who provide a similar or a substitute product or service. This, in

[1] I have been tempted to coin a new word for this which would have the same convenience as the term competition and had I done so my choice would have been "countervailence." However, the phrase "countervailing power" is more descriptive and does not have the raw sound of any newly fabricated word.

the broadest sense that can be meaningful, is the meaning of competition. The role of the buyer, on the other side of such markets, is essentially a passive one. It consists in looking for, perhaps asking for, and responding to the best bargain. The active restraint is provided by the competitor who offers, or threatens to offer, a better bargain. However, this is not the only or even the typical restraint on the exercise of economic power. In the typical modern market of few sellers, the active restraint is provided not by competitors but from the other side of the market by strong buyers. Given the convention against price competition, it is the role of the competitor that becomes passive in these markets.

It was always one of the basic presuppositions of competition that market power exercised in its absence would invite competitors who would eliminate such exercise of power. The profits of a monopoly position inspired competitors to try for a share. In other words competition was regarded as a *self-generating* regulatory force. The doubt whether this was in fact so after a market had been pre-empted by a few large sellers, after entry of new firms had become difficult and after existing firms had accepted a convention against price competition, was what destroyed the faith in competition as a regulatory mechanism. Countervailing power is also a self-generating force and this is a matter of great importance. Something, although not very much, could be claimed for the regulatory role of the strong buyer in relation to the market power of sellers, did it happen that, as an accident of economic development, such strong buyers were frequently juxtaposed to strong sellers. However the tendency of power to be organized in response to a given position of power is the vital characteristic of the phenomenon I am here identifying. As noted, power on one side of a market creates both the need for, and the prospect of reward to, the exercise of countervailing power from the other side. This means that, as a common rule, we can rely on countervailing power to appear as a curb on economic power. There are also, it should be added, circumstances in which it does not appear or is effectively prevented from appearing. To these I shall return. For some reason, critics of the theory have seized with particular avidity on these exceptions to deny the existence of the phenomenon itself. It is plain that by a similar line of argument one could deny the existence of competition by finding one monopoly.

In the market of small numbers or oligopoly, the practical barriers to entry and the convention against price competition have eliminated the self-generating capacity of competition. The self-generating tendency of countervailing power, by contrast, is readily assimilated to the common sense of the situation and its existence, once we have learned to look for it, is readily subject to empirical observation.

Market power can be exercised by strong buyers against weak sellers as well as by strong sellers against weak buyers. In the competitive model, competition acted as a restraint on both kinds of exercise of power. This is also the case with countervailing power. In turning to its practical manifestations, it will be convenient, in fact, to begin with a case where it is exercised by weak sellers against strong buyers.

III

The operation of countervailing power is to be seen with the greatest clarity in the labor market where it is also most fully developed. Because of his comparative immobility, the individual worker has long been highly vulnerable to private economic power. The customer of any particular steel mill, at the turn of the century, could always take himself elsewhere if he felt he was being overcharged. Or he could exercise his sovereign privilege of not buying steel at all. The worker had no comparable freedom if he felt he was being underpaid. Normally he could not move and he had to have work. Not often has the power of one man over another been used more callously than in the American labor market after the rise of the large corporation. As late as the early twenties, the steel industry worked a twelve-hour day and seventy-two-hour week with an incredible twenty-four-hour stint every fortnight when the shift changed.

No such power is exercised today and for the reason that its earlier exercise stimulated the counteraction that brought it to an end. In the ultimate sense it was the power of the steel industry, not the organizing abilities of John L. Lewis and Philip Murray, that brought the United Steel Workers into being. The economic power that the worker faced in the sale of his labor—the competition of many sellers dealing with few buyers—made it necessary that he organize for his own protection. There were rewards to the power of the steel companies in which, when he had successfully developed countervailing power, he could share.

As a general though not invariable rule one finds the strongest unions in the United States where markets are served by strong corporations. And it is not an accident that the large automobile, steel, electrical, rubber, farm-machinery and non-ferrous metal-mining and smelting companies all bargain with powerful unions. Not only has the strength of the corporations in these industries made it necessary for workers to develop the protection of countervailing power; it has provided unions with the opportunity for getting something more as well. If successful they could share in the fruits of the corporation's market power. By contrast there is not a single union of any consequence in American agriculture, the country's closest approach to the competitive model. The reason lies not in the difficulties in organization; these are considerable, but greater difficulties in organization have been overcome. The reason is that the farmer has not possessed any power over his labor force, and at least until recent times has not had any rewards from market power which it was worth the while of a union to seek. As an interesting verification of the point, in the Great Valley of California, the large farmers of that area have had considerable power vis-à-vis their labor force. Almost uniquely in the United States, that region has been marked by persistent attempts at organization by farm workers.

Elsewhere in industries which approach the competition of the model one typically finds weaker or less comprehensive unions. The textile industry,[2] boot and shoe manufacture, lumbering and other forest industries in most parts of the country, and smaller wholesale and retail enterprises, are all cases in point. I do not, of course, advance the theory of countervailing power as a monolithic explanation of trade-union organization. No such complex social phenomenon is likely to have any single, simple explanation. American trade unions developed in the face of the implacable hostility, not alone of employers, but often of the community as well. In this environment organization of the skilled crafts was much easier than the average, which undoubtedly explains the earlier appearance of durable unions here. In the modern bituminous coal-mining and more clearly in the clothing industry, unions have another explanation. They have emerged as a supplement to the weak market position of the operators and manufacturers. They have assumed price- and market-regulating functions that are the normal functions of managements, and on which the latter, because of the competitive character of the industry, have been forced to default. Nevertheless, as an explanation of the incidence of trade-union strength in the American economy, the theory of countervailing power clearly fits the broad contours of experience. There is, I venture, no other so satisfactory explanation of the great dynamic of labor organization in the modern capitalist community and none which so sensibly integrates the union into the theory of that society.

IV

The labor market serves admirably to illustrate the incentives to the development of countervailing power and it is of great importance in this market. However, its development, in response to positions of market power, is pervasive in the economy. As a regulatory device one of its most important manifestations is in the relation of the large retailer to the firms from which it buys. The way in which countervailing power operates in these markets is worth examining in some detail.

One of the seemingly harmless simplifications of formal economic theory has been the assumption that producers of consumers' goods sell their products directly to consumers. All business units are held, for this reason, to have broadly parallel interests. Each buys labor and materials, combines them and passes them along to the public at prices that, over some period of time, maximize returns. It is recognized that this is, indeed, a simplification; courses in marketing in the universities deal with

2 It is important, as I have been reminded by the objections of English friends, to bear in mind that market power must always be viewed in relative terms. In the last century unions developed in the British textile industry and this industry in turn conformed broadly to the competition of the model. However, as buyers of labor the mill proprietors enjoyed a far stronger market position, the result of their greater resources and respect for their group interest, than did the individual workers.

what is excluded by this assumption. Yet it has long been supposed that the assumption does no appreciable violence to reality.

Did the real world correspond to the assumed one, the lot of the consumer would be an unhappy one. In fact goods pass to consumers by way of retailers and other intermediaries and this is a circumstance of first importance. Retailers are required by their situation to develop countervailing power on the consumer's behalf.

As I have previously observed, retailing remains one of the industries to which entry is characteristically free. It takes small capital and no very rare talent to set up as a seller of goods. Through history there have always been an ample supply of men with both and with access to something to sell. The small man can provide convenience and intimacy of service and can give an attention to detail, all of which allow him to coexist with larger competitors.

The advantage of the larger competitor ordinarily lies in its lower prices. It lives constantly under the threat of an erosion of its business by the more rapid growth of rivals and by the appearance of new firms. This loss of volume, in turn, destroys the chance for the lower costs and lower prices on which the firm depends. This means that the larger retailer is extraordinarily sensitive to higher prices by its suppliers. It means also that it is strongly rewarded if it can develop the market power which permits it to force lower prices.

The opportunity to exercise such power exists only when the suppliers are enjoying something that can be taken away; i.e., when they are enjoying the fruits of market power from which they can be separated. Thus, as in the labor market, we find the mass retailer, from a position across the market, with both a protective and a profit incentive to develop countervailing power when the firm with which it is doing business is in possession of market power. Critics have suggested that these are possibly important but certainly disparate phenomena. This may be so, but only if all similarity between social phenomena be denied. In the present instance the market context is the same. The motivating incentives are identical. The fact that it has characteristics in common has been what has caused people to call competition competition when they encountered it, say, in agriculture and then again in the laundry business.

Countervailing power in the retail business is identified with the large and powerful retail enterprises. Its practical manifestation, over the last half-century, has been the rise of the food chains, the variety chains, the mail-order houses (now graduated into chain stores), the department-store chains, and the co-operative buying organizations of the surviving independent department and food stores.

This development was the countervailing response to previously established positions of power. The gains from invading these positions have been considerable and in some instances even spectacular. The rubber tire industry is a fairly commonplace example of oligopoly. Four large firms are dominant in the market. In the thirties, Sears, Roebuck &

Co. was able, by exploiting its role as a large and indispensable customer, to procure tires from Goodyear Tire & Rubber Company at a price from twenty-nine to forty per cent lower than the going market. These it resold to thrifty motorists for from a fifth to a quarter less than the same tires carrying the regular Goodyear brand.

As a partial consequence of the failure of the government to recognize the role of countervailing power many hundreds of pages of court records have detailed the exercise of this power by the Great Atlantic & Pacific Tea Company. There is little doubt that this firm, at least in its uninhibited days, used the countervailing power it had developed with considerable artistry. In 1937, a survey by the company indicated that, for an investment of $175,000, it could supply itself with corn flakes. Assuming that it charged itself the price it was then paying to one of the three companies manufacturing this delicacy, it could earn a modest sixty-eight per cent on the outlay. Armed with this information, and the threat to go into the business which its power could readily make effective, it had no difficulty in bringing down the price by approximately ten per cent.[3] Such gains from the exercise of countervailing power, it will be clear, could only occur where there is an exercise of original market power with which to contend. The A & P could have reaped no comparable gains in buying staple products from the farmer. Committed as he is to the competition of the competitive model, the farmer has no gains to surrender. Provided, as he is, with the opportunity of selling all he produces at the impersonally determined market price, he has not the slightest incentive to make a special price to A & P at least beyond that which might in some circumstances be associated with the simple economies of bulk sale.

The examples of the exercise of countervailing power by Sears, Roebuck and A & P just cited show how this power is deployed in its most dramatic form. The day-to-day exercise of the buyer's power is a good deal less spectacular but also a good deal more significant. At the end of virtually every channel by which consumers' goods reach the public there is, in practice, a layer of powerful buyers. In the food market there are the great food chains; in clothing there are the department stores, the chain department stores and the department store buying organizations; in appliances there are Sears, Roebuck and Montgomery Ward and the department stores; these latter firms are also important outlets for furniture and other house furnishings; the drug and cosmetic manufacturer has to seek part of his market through the large drug chains and the department stores; a vast miscellany of consumers' goods pass to the public through Woolworth's, Kresge's and other variety chains.

The buyers of all these firms deal directly with the manufacturer and there are few of the latter who, in setting prices, do not have to reckon with the attitude and reaction of their powerful customers. The retail buyers have a variety of weapons at their disposal to use against

[3] I am indebted to my friend Professor M. A. Adelman of the Massachusetts Institute of Technology for these details.

the market power of their suppliers. Their ultimate sanction is to develop their own source of supply as the food chains, Sears, Roebuck and Montgomery Ward have extensively done. They can also concentrate their entire patronage on a single supplier and, in return for a lower price, give him security in his volume and relieve him of selling and advertising costs. This policy has been widely followed and there have also been numerous complaints of the leverage it gives the retailer on his source of supply.

The more commonplace but more important tactic in the exercise of countervailing power consists, merely, in keeping the seller in a state of uncertainty as to the intentions of a buyer who is indispensable to him. The larger of the retail buying organizations place orders around which the production schedules and occasionally the investment of even the largest manufacturers become organized. A shift in this custom imposes prompt and heavy loss. The threat or even the fear of this sanction is enough to cause the supplier to surrender some or all of the rewards of his market power. He must frequently, in addition, make a partial surrender to less potent buyers if he is not to be more than ever in the power of his large customers. It will be clear that in this operation there are rare opportunities for playing one supplier off against another.

A measure of the importance which large retailing organizations attach to the deployment of their countervailing power is the prestige they accord to their buyers. These men (and women) are the key employees of the modern large retail organization; they are highly paid and they are among the most intelligent and resourceful people to be found anywhere in business. In the everyday course of business, they may be considerably better known and command rather more respect than the salesmen from whom they buy. This is a not unimportant index of the power they wield.

There are producers of consumers' goods who have protected themselves from exercise of countervailing power. Some, like the automobile and the oil industry, have done so by integrating their distribution through to the consumer—a strategy which attests the importance of the use of countervailing power by retailers. Others have found it possible to maintain dominance over an organization of small and dependent and therefore fairly powerless dealers. It seems probable that in a few industries, tobacco manufacture for example, the members are ordinarily strong enough and have sufficient solidarity to withstand any pressure applied to them by the most powerful buyer. However, even the tobacco manufacturers, under conditions that were especially favorable to the exercise of countervailing power in the thirties, were forced to make liberal price concessions, in the form of advertising allowances, to the A & P [4] and possibly also to other large customers. When the comprehensive representation of large retailers in the various fields of consumers' goods distribution is considered, it is reasonable to conclude—the reader is

[4] Richard B. Tennant, *The American Cigarette Industry* (New Haven: Yale University Press, 1950), p. 312.

warned that this is an important generalization—that most positions of market power in the production of consumers' goods are covered by positions of countervailing power. As noted, there are exceptions and, as between markets, countervailing power is exercised with varying strength and effectiveness. The existence of exceptions does not impair the significance of the regulatory phenomenon here described. To its devotees the virtues of competition were great but few if any ever held its reign to be universal.

Countervailing power also manifests itself, although less visibly, in producers' goods markets. For many years the power of the automobile companies, as purchasers of steel, has sharply curbed the power of the steel mills as sellers. Detroit is the only city where the historic basing-point system was not used to price steel. Under the basing-point system, all producers regardless of location quoted the same price at any particular point of delivery. This obviously minimized the opportunity of a strong buyer to play one seller off against the other. The large firms in the automobile industry had developed the countervailing power which enabled them to do precisely this. They were not disposed to tolerate any limitations on their exercise of such power. In explaining the quotation of "arbitrary prices" on Detroit steel, a leading student of the basing-point system some years ago recognized, implicitly but accurately, the role of countervailing power by observing that "it is difficult to apply high cartel prices to particularly large and strong customers such as the automobile manufactures in Detroit." [5]

The more normal operation of countervailing power in producers' goods markets has, as its point of departure, the relatively small number of customers which firms in these industries typically have. Where the cigarette or soap manufacturer numbers his retail outlets by the hundreds of thousands and his final consumers by the millions, the machinery or equipment manufacturer counts his customers by the hundreds or thousands and, very often, his important ones by the dozen. But here, as elsewhere, the market pays a premium to those who develop power as buyers that is equivalent to the market power of those from whom they buy.

[5] Fritz Machlup, *The Basing Point System* (Philadelphia: Blakiston Co., 1949), p. 115.

.　.　.

Seven ⌐ *The Labor Union as Innovator*

THE AUTOMOBILE INDUSTRY
Walter Galenson

The conflict between the AFL and CIO during the years preceding the [second world] war centered about a number of issues and took place at several levels:

Internal constitutional issues. The question was whether the AFL could "give away" the jurisdictional claims of its affiliates, with the dominant craft unions maintaining staunchly that it could not, and the industrial unions asserting that paper jurisdictions should not be permitted to stand in the way of organizing the mass production industries. A second major constitutional issue was the right of the AFL Executive Council to suspend an affiliated union, an issue which was resolved by the council itself under the spur of a threatened deadlock between the craft and industrial union forces.

Organizing strategy. Lewis [1] and his associates insisted that industrial unions were required in the light of new technology and of great corporate power. The craft proponents preferred to rely instead on the

---

[1] John L. Lewis was president of the United Mine Workers and a leader in the formation of the Committee for Industrial Organization. The CIO (1935) became the Congress of Industrial Organizations in 1938.—LG

REPRINTED with permission from Walter Galenson, "The Automobile Industry," *The CIO Challenge to the AFL,* Cambridge, Mass.: Harvard University Press. Copyright 1960 by The President and Fellows of Harvard College.

method of the federal labor local, which could then be partitioned among the claimant crafts, or joined together with other federal locals in a new international union, as the circumstances required. The Lewis group was also more prone to use the government for its purposes, as against the traditional AFL view that "what the government gives, it can take away."

The struggle for leadership. John L. Lewis was undoubtedly desirous of becoming the acknowledged leader of American labor. The way to the top within the AFL was barred, for Lewis had long demonstrated his lack of regularity, for example, by running against Gompers for the AFL presidency in 1921 (William Green had nominated him for the office). A dual federation provided another road, one which might have proved more successful if Lewis had been able to curb his overweening ambition at crucial junctures.

The conflict of generations. The AFL in 1936 was controlled by men who were of advanced age, and who had been at the helm for a good many years. While the original CIO leaders were not young men, the new industrial unions were led largely by men in their twenties and thirties. Some of them had come from the AFL, but there was little sense among the new crop of leaders of the historical development of the AFL, of its slow growth in the face of intense employer opposition, or of its traditions, particularly with respect to jurisdiction. They could not understand the hesitation of the "old guard" to embrace the opportunities for organization that offered themselves, and they were impatient at the eternal quibbling over outmoded lines of demarcation. The AFL moguls, on the other hand, had little confidence in the staying power of the industrial workers and their young leadership. They had gone through the organizing boom of the period after the first World War, and had seen the complete collapse of efforts at industrial unionism. Lewis, for all his faults, had the genius to bridge the gap between the generations, and to put his experience as an AFL organizer and AFL international union president at the disposal of the forces which were thrusting the semi-skilled industrial worker to a place in the sun alongside the craftsmen.

．　．　．

The General Motors Strike

The strike called by the UAW[2] against General Motors at the end of 1936 ranks as the most critical labor conflict of the nineteen thirties. Up to this time, the UAW was a small, struggling organization, with great ambitions but few members. It emerged from the GM strike perhaps not yet a major power, but certainly a factor to be reckoned with in the industry. And it was able to capitalize upon its limited gains from the GM strike to consolidate its position into an impregnable one.

[2] The United Automobile Workers, a CIO union.—LG

As a prelude to the General Motors strike, employees of the Bendix Corporation of South Bend, Indiana, manufacturers of automobile accessories, engaged in a sit-down strike on November 17, 1936. The sit-down strike was a relatively new device. It had been employed on a large scale by French metal workers in May, 1936, and while instances of sit-downs are to be found in the United States even prior to this date, it was the Rubber Workers who first used it as a regular instrument of union policy. Between March 27 and June 13, 1936, there were 19 known sit-down strikes in the Goodyear Akron plant alone,[3] and one rubber concern in Akron reported having had over 50 quickie sit-down strikes lasting from several minutes to several hours.[4] The Bendix local of the UAW had been rebuffed a number of times over a period of years in its attempt to be recognized as the bargaining agent for the workers in the plant. In none of the previous sit-downs had the workers remained in the plant overnight, but the Bendix employees decided to remain until the company agreed to recognize the union. After staying in for nine days, the union won a contract calling for recognition as representative of its members, a bilateral grievance board, two-hours call-in pay, and a day's notice of layoffs.[5]

On November 25, the day the Bendix strike was settled, workers in the Midland Steel Frame Company in Detroit sat down. This plant manufactured automobile frames for Chrysler and Lincoln, and within a few days, one Ford and five Chrysler assembly plants were shut down for lack of frames.[6] At the end of a week, the company settled for a ten-cent-an-hour wage increase, seniority in layoff and rehiring, and time and a half for overtime, the most notable union victory to that date.[7]

Another important preparatory strike occurred at the Kelsey-Hayes Wheel Company in Detroit during December. The workers remained in for five days, and the strike was called off sooner than it might otherwise have been to make way for General Motors. In this strike, Walter Reuther for the first time demonstrated his leadership capacities.

The General Motors strike was not the result of any strategic master plan. It began inauspiciously when, on November 18, workers at the Fisher Body plant in Atlanta sat down for a day in protest against the discharge of an employee for union activity. On December 15, employees of the Fisher Body plant in Kansas City sat down for the same reason, and forced the Chevrolet assembly plant in that city to close for lack of bodies. At Homer Martin's request, a conference was held between him and GM officials, which resulted in the following statement by William S. Knudsen, then executive vice-president of General Motors:

A personal interview was granted Homer Martin, president of the United Automobile Workers, at which Mr. Martin presented various alleged dis-

[3] Louis Adamic, "Sitdown," *The Nation* (December 12, 1936), p. 702.
[4] *Monthly Labor Review*, May 1937, p. 1235.
[5] *United Automobile Worker*, December 10, 1936, p. 1.
[6] *The New York Times*, December 2, 1936.
[7] *United Automobile Worker*, December 10, 1936, p. 1.

crimination cases and grievances outlined in his published telegram and letter. Mr. Martin was advised to take the various matters up with the plant manager or, if necessary, the general manager having jurisdiction in the location involved, this being in conformity with a corporation operating policy.[8]

Following this rebuff to the union, the strike began in earnest. On December 28, a sit-down was commenced at the Fisher Body plant in Cleveland when the management postponed a conference with union representatives. The next day, the strike spread to the Fisher Body and Chevrolet plants in Flint, Michigan, which was to be the focus of events in the ensuing months. Actually, these strikes were premature. The top UAW leadership had planned no action until after January 1, 1937, when a Democratic administration under Governor Frank Murphy was installed in Lansing, the Michigan state capital. The workers at the Flint and Cleveland Fisher Body plants, key units in the General Motors system, jumped the gun in their impatience to have it out with the company. The importance of these plants has been described as follows:

These two plants were the major body manufacturing units of the corporation—"mother plants," according to GM terminology—being responsible for the fabrication of the greater portion of Chevrolet and other body parts which were then shipped in so-called "knock down" form to the assembly plants throughout the country. All the stampings for the national Chevy production were turned out in Cleveland. Fisher one [Flint] on the other hand manufactured irreplaceable parts for Buick, Oldsmobile, Pontiac and Cadillac. In particular the great dies and enormous presses needed to stamp out the mammoth simplified units of the new "turret top" bodies were concentrated in the Cleveland and Flint body plants. Possibly three-fourths or more of the corporation's production were consequently dependent on these two plants; an interlocking arrangement that was not unusual, moreover, in the highly specialized auto industry and especially among the leading corporations. There were perhaps a dozen other plants equally crucial to General Motors but in only the two designated was the union strong enough to halt production.[9]

During the following week, employees of the Guide Lamp Company in Anderson, Indiana, the Fisher Body and Chevrolet plants in Norwood, Ohio, the Chevrolet transmission plant, the Chevrolet and Fisher Body plants in Janesville, Wisconsin, and the Cadillac assembly plant in Detroit, were all struck. Slowly the tieup continued to spread through the vast General Motors system, and by early February almost all the 200,000 GM employees were idle, with the weekly production of cars down to 1,500 from the mid-December peak of 53,000.[10]

The first reaction of the GM management was one of shocked indig-

[8] *The New York Times*, December 23, 1936, p. 12.
[9] Henry Kraus, *The Many and the Few* (Los Angeles, 1947), pp. 78–79.
[10] Joel Seidman, *Sit-Down* (New York, 1937), p. 21.

nation. In reply to a letter from Homer Martin requesting a collective bargaining conference, Knudsen wrote:

> Sit-down strikes are strikes. Such strikers are clearly trespassers and violators of the law of the land. We cannot have bona fide collective bargaining with sit-down strikers in illegal possession of plants. Collective bargaining cannot be justified if one party, having seized the plant, holds a gun at the other party's head.[11]

In a prior interview, Knudsen reiterated his previously expressed position that all problems should be settled on a local basis with plant managers. "I cannot have all these matters come here," he said, "because that would concentrate too much authority in this office and I would be swamped." Martin retorted to this: "General Motors is an operating company, not a holding company. That is why we want a national conference. Policies are made here and cannot be changed by local or divisional representatives." [12]

On January 2, 1937, upon the company's petition, Judge Edward Black of the Genesee County circuit court issued an injunction restraining the union from continuing to remain in the Flint plant, from picketing, and from interfering in any manner with those who wished to enter the plant to work. When the sheriff read the injunction to the Flint strikers and asked them to leave voluntarily, he was laughed out of the plant. A few days later it was discovered that Judge Black held a block of GM stock with a current market value of $219,900, which served to discredit his action and in effect rendered the injunction of no practical import.

On January 5, the company posted on all its bulletin boards a message from Alfred P. Sloan, Jr., its president, stating it to be the firm and unalterable position of General Motors "not [to] recognize any union as the sole bargaining agency for its workers, to the exclusion of all others. General Motors will continue to recognize, for the purpose of collective bargaining, the representatives of its workers, whether union or non-union." It may be recalled that the National Labor Relations Act, which gave exclusive bargaining rights to the majority union, was in effect at the time, but the Supreme Court had not yet ruled upon it and there was widespread belief that it would be held unconstitutional.

As a condition for meeting with union representatives, GM insisted that the plants be evacuated. The union offered to do so, provided the company in turn would agree that all plants would remain closed, without movement of equipment or resumption of activities, until a national settlement was effected.[13] This proviso was unacceptable to GM, and the first efforts at conciliation collapsed.

The corporation then turned to a frontal attack, and Flint, Michigan, became the center of the stage. More than 50,000 Flint workers were employed in GM plants, and a back-to-work movement was started

[11] *The New York Times*, January 1, 1937, p. 10.
[12] *The New York Times*, January 3, 1937, p. 2.
[13] *The New York Times*, January 5, 1937, p. 14; January 10, 1937, p. 34.

under the sponsorship of the Flint Alliance, a new organization hastily formed in opposition to the UAW. The union claimed that the Alliance, the president of which was George Boysen, a former GM paymaster and at the time of the strike an independent business man, was company-sponsored, while industry pictured it as a spontaneous reaction on the part of loyal workers against a small minority of UAW strikers.[14] On January 11, the heat in Fisher Body Plant No. 2 was shut off and attempts were made by the company police to prevent food from being carried into the plant.[15] The sit-downers, faced with the possibility of being starved out, captured the plant gates from the company police to assure their source of food. At this point the city police attacked in an effort to recapture the plant gates. For hours the strikers battled the police, fighting clubs, tear gas, and riot guns with such improvised weapons as two-pound car door hinges and streams of water from fire hoses. The news of the riot spread, and the strikers were reinforced by thousands of supporters who poured into Flint. The battle ended with the strikers still in possession of the plant. Fourteen strikers suffered bullet wounds in this encounter, which became famous in union mythology as "The Battle of the Running Bulls." [16]

At this juncture there might well have been a prelude to the bloody events of the Little Steel Strike half a year later. The city was in a state of civil war, with the sit-downers determined to resist any further attempts at eviction. To prevent further bloodshed, Governor Frank Murphy of Michigan despatched 1,500 National Guardsmen to Flint, with instructions to maintain the *status quo*, that is, to prevent attempts at forcible eviction of the strikers. He summoned union and company representatives to meet him in the state capital at Lansing, and on January 15, a truce was arranged: the strikers agreed to leave the plants on January 17, and negotiations were to begin the following day. Plants in Detroit and Anderson, Indiana, were evacuated, but shortly before the Flint strikers were scheduled to leave, the UAW learned that General Motors had sent telegrams to workers in the Cadillac and Fleetwood plants in Detroit directing them to report for work, and also had agreed to bargain with the Flint Alliance as well, and refused consequently to carry out any further plant evacuations. A few days later the company admitted that it had agreed to meet with representatives of the Flint Alliance, but asserted that since the UAW represented not more than 5 per cent of its employees, "it would be the height of absurdity for it to try to represent the whole body of company workers." Besides, said the company, meetings with the Alliance had been scheduled for 9 A.M., while the UAW conferences were not to begin until 11 A.M., so that no conflict

[14] See Edward Levinson, *Labor on the March*, p. 155; and *Automotive Industries* (January 16, 1937), p. 73.
[15] Fisher Body No. 2 was a Chevrolet assembly plant without the key significance of Fisher Body No. 1. However, the union was less well established there, and the company apparently felt that its recapture would constitute a damaging blow to union morale.
[16] Levinson, *Labor on the March*, p. 157.

of scheduling was involved.[17] The union learned about the intention of General Motors to bargain with the Flint Alliance through William Lawrence, then a reporter for the United Press, who had secured this information from Knudsen, and asked the union about its attitude toward the company's policy. It is likely that the evacuation of the plants would have been carried out on schedule if not for this piece of information.

General Motors declined to enter into negotiations, and the truce collapsed. Attempts at conciliation then shifted to Washington, where Sloan and Knudsen agreed to meet with Secretary of Labor Frances Perkins at her request, but refused to see John L. Lewis. The latter, angered, made the following statement to the press:

> For six months during the presidential campaign the economic royalists represented by General Motors and the Du Ponts contributed their money and used their energy to drive this administration from power. The administration asked labor to help repel this attack and labor gave it. The same economic royalists now have their fangs in labor. The workers of this country expect the administration to help the strikers in every reasonable way.[18]

Sloan, in his turn annoyed at the turn of events, left Washington for New York, and upon receipt of a letter from the secretary of labor requesting him to return, replied: "we sincerely regret to have to say that we must decline to negotiate further with the union while its representatives continue to hold our plants unlawfully. We cannot see our way clear, therefore, to accept your invitation." [19]

At a press conference the next day, President Roosevelt expressed the view that Sloan's decision was a very unfortunate one, while Secretary Perkins went much further in her condemnation:

> an episode like this must make it clear to the American people why the workers have lost confidence in General Motors. I still think that General Motors have made a great mistake, perhaps the greatest mistake in their lives. The American people do not expect them to sulk in their tents because they feel the sit-down strike is illegal. There was a time when picketing was considered illegal, and before that strikes of any kind were illegal. The legality of the sit-down strike has yet to be determined.[20]

Faced with this pressure, Sloan returned to Washington and met with the secretary of labor, but to no avail. The corporation then prepared to take the offensive once more on the industrial front.

The UAW, fearing that GM might succeed in reopening enough plants to commence production, decided to extend the area of the sit-down. Secret plans were laid to capture the strategic Chevrolet No. 4 plant in Flint, where motors were assembled. To draw police away, a de-

---

[17] The New York Times, January 18, 1937, p. 2.
[18] Quoted in Howe and Widick, The UAW, p. 58.
[19] The New York Times, January 26, 1937, p. 1.
[20] The New York Times, January 27, 1937, p. 1.

tachment of men under Powers Hapgood and Roy Reuther made a feint at the nearby Chevrolet plant No. 9, thus permitting 400 workers to occupy Chevrolet No. 4 without difficulty.[21]

General Motors responded by securing an injunction from Judge Paul V. Gadola ordering the Fisher Body plants evacuated by February 3. Thousands of union supporters swarmed into Flint from other automobile centers, determined to prevent the forcible eviction of the strikers. All windows were barricaded with metal sheets, and defense squads were organized, as the 2,000 men now within the plant prepared to resist. The sheriff, however, declined to attempt enforcement of the injunction without assistance from the state, and Governor Murphy, anxious to avoid bloodshed, wired the sheriff to take no action pending further negotiations. He also prevented state troops, which had surrounded the plant, from taking any violent action. Thus the deadline passed quietly, and the union had won a significant victory.

The situation still remained explosive, however. Flint city authorities were reported to be arming vigilante groups. The chief of police was quoted as saying: "Unless John L. Lewis wants a repetition of the Herrin, Ill., massacres he had better call off his union men. The good citizens of Flint are getting pretty nearly out of hand. We are organizing fast and will have between 500 and 1,000 men ready for any emergency." [22] At the direct request of President Roosevelt, Knudsen finally agreed to meet with Lewis. Following is Lewis' description of his reception upon his arrival in Detroit:

> It is a matter of public knowledge now that the Governor of this State read me a formal letter in writing demanding that this action [evacuation of the plants] be taken by me, and my reply to the Governor of the State when he read that letter, with the knowledge of the President of the United States—and the approval—was this: "I do not doubt your ability to call out your soldiers and shoot the members of our union out of those plants, but let me say that when you issue that order I shall leave this conference and I shall enter one of those plants with my own people. And the militia will have the pleasure of shooting me out of the plants with them." The order was not executed.[23]

Although the negotiations came perilously close to rupture on several occasions, Governor Murphy succeeded in bringing about a truce on February 11, 1937.

· · ·

General Motors agreed to recognize the UAW as bargaining agent for its members only, a reduction of the original union demand of sole

[21] For an account of this episode by Robert Travis, in charge of organization at Flint, see *The United Automobile Worker,* February 25, 1937, p. 4. See also Henry Kraus, *The Many,* Chapters 10, 11.

[22] *Automotive Industries,* February 6, 1937, p. 171.

[23] United Automobile Workers, *Proceedings of the Fifth Annual Convention* (July 24–August 6, 1940), p. 104.

bargaining rights. Collective bargaining was to begin on February 16, and all court proceedings were to be withdrawn. To avoid a repetition of the incident which had ended the earlier truce, the corporation sent a letter to Murphy agreeing that for six months it would not bargain or enter into an agreement with any other union without securing his permission to do so. By this device, GM was spared the embarrassment of agreeing directly to bargain only with the UAW, while the latter was virtually assured of sole bargaining rights for at least six months. For its part, the UAW agreed to evacuate all GM plants which it was holding.[24] . . .

Sloan paid handsome tribute to Murphy for his role in bringing about the settlement: "The corporation, its workers and the public are indebted to the Hon. Frank Murphy, assisted by Federal Conciliator James F. Dewey, for his untiring and conscientious efforts, as well as the fairness with which he has handled a most difficult situation. Only his efforts have made it possible to resume work at this time." [25] The union, of course, was jubilant. A retrospective union evaluation of the significance of the strike had this to say about it: "The heads of the corporation were compelled, for the first time, to bargain with the spokesman of their employes, the officers of the UAW and the CIO. The end of the strike came on February 11, 1937, in a brilliant victory for the workers. . . . This was the greatest and most historic victory of the UAW. It broke the back of anti-unionism in the most powerful industry in the world." [26] A *New York Times* correspondent who followed the events closely wrote a few months later that "By entirely stopping production of all General Motors cars in January and February and obtaining recognition in the first written and signed agreement on a national scale which that great citadel of the open shop had ever granted to a labor union, the CIO . . . opened the way for the remarkable upsurge in sentiment for union organization which is now going on in many sections of the country. . . . Since the General Motors settlement, the union has been spreading its organization rapidly in General Motors plants, which were weakly organized at the time of the strike." [27]

The only dissenting note came from the American Federation of Labor. On January 7, John P. Frey, in his capacity as head of the AFL Metal Trades Department, wrote to General Motors stating that no other organization had authority to represent the skilled craftsmen in the automotive industry, and received a reply to the effect that no agreement would be considered which interfered with the legitimate jurisdiction of AFL unions. On January 11, Frey met with Anderson, Knudsen, and John Thomas Smith of GM, and indicated that the Metal Trades were

[24] *The New York Times*, February 12, 1937, p. 19; *Automotive Industries*, February 13, 1937, p. 209.
[25] *The New York Times*, February 12, 1937, p. 19.
[26] Edward Levinson, *Rise of the Auto Workers*, United Automobile Workers of America, p. 10.
[27] Russel B. Porter in *The New York Times*, April 4, 1937, IV, p. 10.

prepared at any time to sit down and bargain with them for the crafts-men, to which the conferees replied that the matter would be taken up with Sloan.[28]

Action was also taken with respect to the struck Fisher Body plant in Cleveland, where some AFL building tradesmen were employed. After consultation with Knudsen, four building trades unions sent a joint letter to the manager of the Cleveland plant in the following vein: "In behalf of our members who are employed in your plant, and who had no voice in this action on the part of an outlaw union in closing them, we request you to reopen the plants so they may return to their jobs, which they are out of through no fault of their own." [29] Frey went to Cleve-land to consult with the plant manager, but nothing came of this effort.

When, in late January and early February, the White House was putting pressure on GM to meet with Lewis, William Green twice met with President Roosevelt to protest the granting of exclusive bargaining rights to the UAW, but he received a noncommittal answer. . . .

An effort by Frey and some building trades leaders to see Roosevelt on this issue proved unavailing, and the best that could be arranged was a telephone conversation in which the president again refused to commit himself. On February 6, a few days before the UAW–GM agreement was concluded, Green, Frey, and Williams, the president of the Building Trades, addressed a joint telegram to Governor Murphy, warning him against exclusive UAW representation. Frey expressed himself as being "reasonably certain that not long after Governor Murphy received that telegram, he showed it to Mr. Lewis." [30]

In the light of these efforts, the following interview given by Wil-liam Green, the day after the signing of the UAW–GM pact, takes on a peculiar significance:

"The settlement represents a surrender in a very large way to the de-mands of General Motors management. We are not pleased at the defeat of any workers who have been engaged in a strike for forty days." . . . "You consider the settlement a defeat?" was the next query. "Well," said Mr. Green, "if you go on strike for one demand and press it for forty days and give up, what would you call it?" [31]

The demand to which Green was referring here was precisely that which the AFL was opposing so actively—exclusive bargaining rights. This episode served to exacerbate AFL–CIO relationships, and figured prominently in the fiasco attendant upon AFL entrance into the automo-bile industry several years later. It should be noted that the GM strike was supported by the Flint and Detroit central bodies of the AFL, as well as by John Reid, secretary of the Michigan State Federation of Labor.

[28] AFL Executive Council Minutes (February 8–19, 1937), p. 43.
[29] The New York Times, January 8, 1937, p. 2.
[30] [AFL Executive Council Minutes (February 8–19, 1937),] p. 43.
[31] The New York Times, February 12, 1937, p. 19.

The Sit-Down Strike in Retrospect

Scarcely any labor practice of the 1930's aroused as much animosity among employers, and public concern, as the sit-down strike, of which the General Motors strike was the most spectacular example. The sit-down strike trend, beginning late in 1936, rose to a peak in March 1937, when 170 such strikes, involving 167,000 workers, took place. In April, the month in which the Supreme Court upheld the constitutionality of the National Labor Relations Act, and in May, the number of strikes declined to 52 and 72 respectively. There was further tapering downward thereafter until by the end of the year the sit-down weapon had almost fallen into disuse.[32]

The principal argument in favor of the sit down, from the labor standpoint, was its effectiveness. With a minimum of organization, it proved possible for small groups of determined men to shut down indefinitely huge plants, and by concentrating upon strategic producing units from the standpoint of the flow of materials, to spread paralysis to plants with no organization. Some of the advantages of this form of action in distinction to a "normal" strike have been well summed up by a communist leader who was active in the automobile industry:

> Sit-down strikes give to the workers a greater feeling of strength and security because the strikers are inside the plants, in the solid confines of the factory, at the machines which are the sources of their livelihood, instead of away from the plant, moving around in "empty space," on the sidewalks surrounding the factories.
>
> Sit-down strikes give to the workers greater sureness that there are no scabs within the plant and no production is being carried on and makes it difficult to run in scabs. . . .
>
> The sit-down strike furthermore makes it difficult to resume operations even partially where scabs have gotten in because by holding down one section of the plant it is hard to begin operations.
>
> The sit-down strike affords strikers greater possibility of defending themselves against the violence of the police and company men. . . .
>
> The sit-down strike makes for a greater discipline, group consciousness and comradeship among the strikers because of the very position in which they find themselves and thereby enhances the militancy and fighting spirit of the workers.
>
> Finally, the sit-down strike arouses the widest sympathy and support among the working population because of the courage of the workers in taking "possession" of the factory and because of the self-sacrifice and hardship which such action entails.[33]

[32] See *Monthly Labor Review*, May 1939, p. 1130, for a tabulation of sit-down strikes for the years 1936 to 1938. In 1938 there were 52 sit-down strikes involving 28,700 workers, compared with 477 strikes and 398,000 workers in 1937.

[33] William Weinstone, *The Great Sit-Down Strike* (New York, 1937), pp. 29–32. Weinstone was at the time secretary of the Michigan district of the Communist Party.

From a moral point of view, UAW and other CIO leaders argued that the sit-down strike was merely a logical extension of the growth of worker property rights in their jobs. "Is it wrong," asked Wyndham Mortimer, a UAW vice-president, "for a worker to stay at his job? The laws of the state and nation recognize, in a hundred ways, that the worker has a definite claim upon his job; more fundamentally, it is recognized that every workman has a moral right to continue on his job unless some definite misconduct justifies his discharge. These sit-down strikers are staying at their work places; no one has a better right to be there than have these men themselves." [34] Francis J. Gorman, then president of the United Textile Workers of America, was quoted in much the same vein: "A sit-down strike is clearly the most effective and least costly way for the worker to insure himself against encroachment on his 'property right' to his job by company-hired strikebreakers." [35]

The national CIO, while somewhat more cautious than its young, enthusiastic affiliates, was inclined to take a pragmatic view of the sit-down, as evidenced by the following statement made by John Brophy, at the time organizational director of the CIO:

> We do not condemn sit-down strikes *per se*. We consider that various kinds of labor activity will be used to promote organization of workers and establish collective bargaining. Sit-down strikes, under some of these conditions, may be a very necessary and useful weapon. In the formative and promotional stage of unionism in a certain type of industry, the sit-down strike has real value.[36]

John L. Lewis took very much the same point of view: "The CIO stands for punctilious observance of contracts, but we are not losing any sleep about strikes where employers refuse to recognize the well-defined principles of collective bargaining. A CIO contract is adequate protection for any employer against sit-downs, lie-downs, or any other kind of strike." [37]

Despite the fact that AFL unions were involved in 100 of the 477 sit-down strikes that occurred in 1937,[38] the top AFL leadership disowned this strike technique from the first. In January 1937, the AFL Executive Council asked William Green to study the problem, and on March 28, he made public his findings, which read in part: "The sit-down strike has never been approved or supported by the American Federation of Labor because there is involved in its application grave implications detrimental to labor's interests. It must be disavowed by the thinking men and women of labor." He called the sit-down illegal and dangerous in the

[34] *The United Automobile Worker,* January 22, 1937, p. 3.
[35] National Association of Manufacturers, *Labor Relations Bulletin,* No. 18, March 21, 1937, p. 7.
[36] Louis Adamic, "Sit-Down," *The Nation,* p. 704.
[37] Quoted in Levinson, *Auto Worker,* p. 182.
[38] *Monthly Labor Review,* August 1938, p. 362. The CIO was involved in 293 of such strikes.

long run, and voiced the fear that its persistent use would result in the enactment of legislation inimical to the labor movement.

The press, business men, and legislators were with very few exceptions hostile to the sit-down strike. *The New York Times* condemned it as "a plain disregard of statutes forbidding the seizure of private property" and "essentially an act of lawlessness."[39] The *Christian Science Monitor* said that it placed "confiscation and seizure above law."[40] A group of Boston residents headed by A. Lawrence Lowell, president emeritus of Harvard University, wired Vice-President Garner on March 26, 1937, requesting that legislation be enacted to "establish the supremacy of constitutional government, law and order, national and state." Sit-down strikes were castigated in the following terms:

> Armed insurrection—defiance of law, order, and duly elected authority —is spreading like wild-fire. It is rapidly growing beyond control. . . . The issue is vital; it dwarfs any other issue now agitating the public mind; it attacks and undermines the very foundation of our political and social structure . . . freedom and liberty are at an end, government becomes a mockery, superseded by anarchy, mob rule and ruthless dictatorship.

The governors of Virginia, Texas, Mississippi, New Jersey, Illinois and California announced that they would not tolerate sit-down strikes in their states. The United States Senate, after considerable debate, passed on April 7, 1937, a resolution condemning the sit-down strike as illegal and against public policy, although it coupled with this a condemnation of industrial espionage and violations of the National Labor Relations Act.[41] Numerous anti-sit-down bills were introduced in state legislatures, and the State of Vermont enacted a law rendering a sit-down striker subject to imprisonment and heavy fine.

The courts were more directly involved than legislatures, and they almost uniformly declared sit downs illegal whenever called upon to enjoin strikers. On two separate occasions, as has already been noted, General Motors obtained equity injunctions, although in neither case was the order obeyed. The *coup de grâce* was eventually given the sit-down strike by the United States Supreme Court, which, in setting aside a National Labor Relations Board order that directed the Fansteel Metallurgical Corporation to reinstate sit-down strikers, declared: "It was an illegal seizure of the buildings in order to prevent their use by the employer in a lawful manner and thus, by acts of force and violence, to compel the employer to submit."[42] The Court also held in this case that sit-down strikers, by their lawless conduct, forfeited all rights under the National Labor Relations Act. However, the sit down as a union weapon for all practical purposes had been abandoned a year prior to the Supreme Court decision.

[39] *The New York Times*, March 29, 1937; April 3, 1937.
[40] Quoted in National Association of Manufacturers, p. 7.
[41] *The New York Times*, March 27, 1937; April 8, 1937.
[42] *N.L.R.B.* v. *Fansteel Metallurgical Corporation*, 306 U.S. 240 (1939).

In retrospect, the following may be said of the sit-down strike epidemic that occurred in 1937:

The strikes were clearly illegal, and there was little disposition on the part of anyone to take an opposite point of view. Although they would be unthinkable today, they were tolerated in 1937, and even received substantial public support, mainly because large segments of American industry refused to accept collective bargaining. Trade unions were the underdogs, and they were widely represented as merely attempting to secure in practice the rights that Congress had bestowed upon them as a matter of law. Senator Robert F. Wagner made this point forcibly in defending the sit-down strike in a Senate speech:

> The sit-down has been used only in protest against repeated violations of industrial liberties which Congress has recognized. The sit-down, even in the few cases where labor has used it effectively, has succeeded in winning for labor only such industrial liberties as both law and morals have long sanctioned. The sit-down has been provoked by the long-standing ruthless tactics of a few corporations who have hamstrung the National Labor Relations Board by invoking court actions . . . ; who have openly banded together to defy this law of Congress quite independently of any Court action . . . ; and who have systematically used spies and discharges and violence and terrorism to shatter the workers' liberties as defined by Congress.[43]

From an historical perspective, the sit-down era constituted an episode in the transition from one system of industrial relations to another; it hastened the replacement of untrammeled management prerogative in the disposition of labor by a system under which trade unions, as representatives of the workers, were to share in this function. It was perhaps inevitable that so violent a wrench with the past should have provoked management attitudes sharply antithetical to the new national labor policy. But by the same token, it is not surprising that industrial workers, having broken through on the legislative front, should seek to implement their hard won rights with whatever weapons were at hand, regardless of the law.

Despite all the public furor, the sit-down strike was actually a less costly weapon, in terms of human life and property, than for example, the traditional form of labor strife as exemplified in the Little Steel strikes of 1937. No deaths were directly attributable to the sit-down strikes, despite their quasi-military character. One of the industry's trade journals had this to say of property damage, when the rash of strikes had run its course:

> Damage at automobile plants caused by sitdown strikers appears to have been confined largely to non-essential materials with production machinery found unhurt after evacuation, a survey now shows. The losses were not insignificant, however. An insurance adjuster has made a guess

[43] *The New York Times,* April 1, 1937.

that the physical damage done to plants during all automobile plant strikes in Michigan would approximate $200,000. This is apart from losses due to deterioration of materials left outside plants.[44]

There is no inherent reason for the sit-down strikes to have followed this relatively peaceful course. Most contemporary observers, however, credited Governor Frank Murphy with having averted what might have been a very unfortunate development in insisting upon negotiation rather than in employing force to evict the strikers.

The most important aspect of the sit-down strike was that it paved the way for rapid unionization of the automobile industry. John Brophy has testified to the fact that in November and December 1936, UAW attempts at mass meetings were generally failures; few workers stopped to listen to speeches that he and Philip Murray made at plant gates.[45] It is impossible to ascertain what UAW membership was at the outset of the strikes, but certainly not more than a small fraction of the employees of General Motors had enlisted under its banner. Within six months of the beginning of the sit-down strikes, the UAW claimed a dues paying membership of 520,000,[46] and the first stage of organization had been completed for the entire industry, with the exception of Ford. It is not at all unlikely that General Motors and other manufacturers could have resisted the UAW more successfully if the union had confined itself to more orthodox weapons.

· · ·

[44] *Automotive Industries,* July 3, 1937, p. 4.
[45] Interview with John Brophy, March 19, 1955.
[46] United Automobile Workers of America, *Proceedings of the Second Annual Convention* (1937), p. 66. This was the claimed paid membership for June 1937.

INDUSTRIAL RELATIONS
IN THE CONSTRUCTION INDUSTRY:
THE NORTHERN CALIFORNIA
EXPERIENCE

Gordon W. Bertram and Sherman J. Maisel

The building trades in Northern California have had a long history of union organization. This century of experience, beginning in San Francisco in 1849, portrays the development, after two outstanding episodes of failures, of a successful system of industrial relations. The main concern of the brief review of labor relations undertaken . . . [here] is to show, to the exclusion of many other aspects, the importance of stabilization techniques in the absence of established collective bargaining, and to account for the delay in achieving collective bargaining. In the four decades preceding 1935, both the unions and the employers attempted to control San Francisco construction on a unilateral basis. Considering the many years of union organization, adequate collective bargaining was long delayed and did not develop until the mid-1930's.

The history of industrial relations can be usefully summarized by distinguishing four separate periods. The discussion is primarily concerned with San Francisco, the center of building trades unionism in California in the earlier years.

The first period of 1869 to 1896 has been identified as an era of unregulated competition in the building industry, which was injurious to employers, workers, and the public.[1] Efficient and scrupulous employers

[1] Frederick L. Ryan, *Industrial Relations in the San Francisco Building Trades* (2nd ed., revised, University of Oklahoma Press, 1936), p. 25. The summary of early labor history in San Francisco construction follows, in the main, the account given in this reference.

REPRINTED with permission from Gordon W. Bertram and Sherman J. Maisel, *Industrial Relations in the Construction Industry: The Northern California Experience*, Berkeley: University of California, Institute of Industrial Relations, 1955, pp. 14–26, 28–30, 55–59.

were penalized by the inefficient and unscrupulous. Working conditions and wages were unfavorable and hours were long, while constant strife between employers and workers contributed to higher construction costs to the public.

> The most notable event of the period was the searching by the worker for a way to introduce uniform rules into the market. All efforts to form a central labor body for the building crafts had failed, and yet the tendency was clearly in that direction. It was noteworthy, also, that the employers were slowly building up defences, in the form of associations, against the rigors of competition.[2]

UNION DOMINANCE AND STABILIZATION, 1896–1921

The formation of the Building Trades Council of San Francisco in 1896 marks the beginning of the second period.[3] This Council became one of the most powerful central labor organizations in the nation. Until the establishment of the open shop American Plan in San Francisco in 1921, the Council successfully imposed its will upon the building industry. It was during this period that building trades labor built their organizations in California construction. The San Francisco Council assisted in the organization of similar building trades councils in the San Francisco Bay Area, was the model for the county building trades council system in California, and from this system the State Building Trades Council of California developed.

In contrast, the employers during most of this period had no continuous central organization concerned with labor relations. The contractor associations which existed offered little effective opposition, and were incapable of presenting a united front to organized labor. Under the leadership of P. H. McCarthy, who was annually chosen president from 1898 to 1922, the Building Trades Council was able to impose an autocratic rule over affiliated crafts.

. . .

The result of . . . coercive techniques and controls was that one agency of great power, the San Francisco Building Trades Council, presented a single and disciplined organization, which successfully regulated important aspects of the industry. Through the use in part of the working card system, the Council enforced a closed shop, established the eight-hour day and high wage rates for all crafts, and secured extensive job control through working rules. Reflecting the attitude of the employers was the fact that San Francisco's superior conditions were won largely without recourse to strikes. But neither were they obtained through what is generally understood to be collective bargaining, for during the McCarthy period bargaining was collective only on the part

[2] *Loc. cit.*, p. 25.
[3] *Ibid.*, p. 26.

of the workers and primarily individual on the part of the many employers.[4] If the employers' associations did meet with the officers of the Council, it was only to raise objections to the position the Council had already taken. . . .

The basis of union strength in the building trades was actually closely interwoven with the development and growth of California and the city of San Francisco. Union dominance after the turn of the century can be attributed, in part, to the rapid increase in population and the consequent demand for construction. . . .

A further important reason for union success was the employers' slowness to establish effective counter organization. Such organization was delayed by policies of the Building Trades Council which operated, in some cases, in favor of the contractors. Concerning industrial relations in this period, Ryan states, ". . . probably the principal factor in the determination of these relations was the monopolistic agreement made between the Building Trades Council and the Mill Owners Association in 1901."[5] This agreement, renewed continuously for many years, was an important example of the collusive system which has been described as a ". . . labor barony, with the employer given protection on the condition of good behavior."[6] Competition from mills outside of San Francisco was eliminated by the condition that the affiliates of the Council would refuse to handle any material coming from a mill with less favorable conditions. Few other areas could, in fact, equal San Francisco conditions. The exclusive agreement, the basis of the closed shop in this period, was widely practiced.[7] These understandings existed even though actually opposed to the official policy of the Building Trades Council. They restrained competition by providing that members of a union would work only for members of a particular employers' association and obviously benefited certain established local contractors.

In addition to acceptance of the Building Trades Council's rule by the contractors in some trades who gained protection from competition, the Council was also recognized as an agency which brought some degree of certainty and stability to the industry. For example, Council policy required that prior notification of about three months be given to contractors regarding wage and hour changes. Once wages and other conditions were established they applied uniformly to all contractors, and competition founded on differences in wages and conditions was eliminated. In addition, the closed shop, among other results, established the unions as the source of skilled labor. Jurisdictional disputes resulting in work stoppages were controlled by the Council, and, therefore, interrupted construction work infrequently. In short, the unions exerted stabilizing influences, which were noted earlier as a distinguishing feature of

4 William Haber, *Industrial Relations in the Building Industry* (Cambridge: Harvard University Press, 1930), p. 407.
5 F. L. Ryan, *op. cit.*, p. 131.
6 [Selig] Perlman and [Philip] Taft, [*History of Labor in the United States, 1896–1932* (New York: Macmillan Co., 1935),] p. 78.
7 F. L. Ryan, *op. cit.*, p. 115.

the building trades unions. The Buildings Trades Council, in fact, ". . . claimed to represent not merely the workers, but all individuals and parties with an interest in the building industry. It particularly sought to impress upon the public the fact that the Council existed to encourage and improve the industry, not to destroy it." [8]

THE AMERICAN PLAN AND EMPLOYER STABILIZATION, 1921–1935

The period of union control of almost a quarter of a century developed under special conditions of expansion and growth in an area somewhat remote from a skilled supply of competing labor. The contractors, as a group, appeared content for some time to accept union control over most personnel decisions, as well as other aspects of the industry. The unions performed useful functions in the regulation of certain standards of competition, establishment of industrial peace and stability, and gave assurance that change would be orderly. At the same time, the structure was founded, in part, on collusive agreements of benefit to some contractor groups.

A third period from 1921 to 1935 brought a remarkable reversal in power. The Building Trades Council and union control were completely displaced by the open shop American Plan era.[9] The occasion for the introduction of the American Plan appeared to have centered around the reduction in construction activity, which confronted the contractors for a short time after World War I. With construction activity lagging and wage demands increasing with every rise in the cost of living, the contractors reacted with resistance to wage increases and criticism of the unions' control and work rules. By 1920, the Builders' Exchange, which had previously been a trade organization, assumed the functions of a central body of the employer association members. At the same time, the Exchange opened its membership to material supply houses and manufacturers of building materials. In retrospect, the Builders' Exchange might have become a permanent central bargaining organization of the contractors, for this was obviously needed. Instead, it became engulfed in the operation of an open shop drive, which was sponsored by interests quite remote from the construction industry. It appears that the building trades were diverted from a course of collective bargaining for a period of almost fifteen years by the activities of the American Plan.

[8] *Ibid.*, p. 117.
[9] The summary of the operation of the American Plan in San Francisco has relied upon the following sources in addition to interviews with union and contractor association officers:

F. L. Ryan, *op. cit.*, pp. 165–203.
Haber, *op. cit.*, pp. 409–41.
Employer's Associations and Collective Bargaining in California, Part II, Senate Committee on Education and Labor, 77th Congress, 2nd Session, Report No. 1150, Part 2, 1942, pp. 79–98.
Hearings on S 266, Industrial Association of San Francisco, Senate Sub-Committee on Education and Labor, San Francisco, Part 60, 74th Congress, pp. 21943–73.

The immediate circumstances of the introduction of the American Plan were the rejection by the Building Trades Council of an arbitration board award in 1921, which had lowered wages for most crafts. Declaring that the board had exceeded its authority, the Council took strike action. The San Francisco Chamber of Commerce pledged support to the contractors' Builders' Exchange, and threatened an open shop drive unless the Council accepted the award. But the unions delayed too long, for although the Council finally agreed to abide by the award, the Builders' Exchange already had begun to put the principles of the Plan into operation. To enforce the Plan in the building trades and to promote its adoption elsewhere, the Industrial Association of San Francisco was formed, with the support and substantial financing of part of the general business community. The Association successfully introduced a system under which uncooperative contractors, of whom there were a great many, were brought into line. Among the more important methods used to prevent contractor dealing with the unions were the reimbursement for losses incurred in strikes, and refusal of contractor access to building materials unless a permit was supplied by the Industrial Association. Workers were imported from other areas to act as strike-breakers.

The Association took the position that it was acting in the public interest, and that its policy was to maintain a balance of power between unions and employers. At the same time, however, it held that collective bargaining between contractors and unions was against the public interest. The Association did not directly attack the unions as such, but directed its public policy toward practices of the unions it regarded as untenable, such as the closed shop, inefficiency, collusive agreements, and suspension of management rights. The American Plan succeeded in displacing union power in practically all areas organized in California by the building trades unions. A notable exception was San Mateo County, bordering on the San Francisco Bay, where the unions were able to establish their own sources of building materials. Even though the construction industry enjoyed a building boom in the mid-1920's, the unions were unable to defeat the Industrial Association. With the advent of the depression in the early 1930's, the building trades were among those most severely affected by unemployment, and the unions were in no position to rebuild or even maintain their organizations.

· · ·

RELATION OF THE AMERICAN PLAN TO THE CONSTRUCTION INDUSTRY

If the building trades unions in fact contribute to the stability and successful operation of the construction industry, it is necessary to explain the sudden reversal of control in San Francisco and the subsequent fifteen years of employer domination. Contributing reasons for the reversal were the reaction to years of labor domination and internal conflict within the building trades unions. The central reason was the national campaign to establish the open shop. "The postwar drive (of the 1920's) to liquidate labor's war-time achievements was on the entire industrial front. In the highly organized trades wage deflation and weakening union control were its twin objectives." [10] The building trades in particular came in for attack since they represented a citadel of union strength. Moreover their practices often provided a ready target for criticism. In some large Eastern cities the attack came in the form of public or legislative investigations of graft or corruption. In San Francisco corruption was not an issue and the campaign came directly in the form of an open shop drive.

.   .   .

ESTABLISHMENT OF COLLECTIVE BARGAINING IN 1936 AND THE CONTEMPORARY PERIOD

Industrial relations founded upon collective bargaining was not established for the industry until 1936. Just prior to this fourth and contemporary period the collective bargaining provisions of the National Recovery Act assisted in establishing a number of agreements between the unions and some of the specialty contractor associations, but union agreements with the general contractors did not occur until 1936. The Bay Counties District Council of Carpenters in that year, for example, as a result of an arbitration award, entered its first agreement with the general contractors since 1920. With the introduction of legislation which made collective bargaining and union recognition a matter of public policy, the whole climate of industrial relations changed. The Industrial Association, which had continued its activities in other industries, dissolved in 1938 with the formation of the San Francisco Employers' Council, an organization functioning under entirely different principles of industrial relations. This new organization was not concerned with the construction industry, and the separate contractors' organizations assumed the responsibility of labor relations. Although labor legislation was paramount in ending the open shop period, steps to establish contractual relations were taken by both the unions and contractors. Differences in wages in this depressed period intensified the pressure of competition, while growing union strength brought work stoppages without a contractually recognized union to control them.

The latter part of the 1930's was a period of improving relations between the unions and the contractors. Just prior to World War II a new system of collective bargaining was begun with the general contractors and the basic trades employed by them which has become a main feature of contemporary labor relations.

THE ORGANIZATION OF COLLECTIVE BARGAINING

The outstanding feature of the collective bargaining experience in Northern California since 1940 has been the extensive regional system evolved

[10] Perlman and Taft, *op. cit.,* p. 511.

in certain of the trades. This new system is a departure from the more typical urban or metropolitan bargaining systems. One important achievement of this new method appears to be a closer approximation to equality of bargaining power between unions and general contractors than at any time in the history of Northern California construction. In itself this bargaining equality is an important factor in obtaining stable industrial relations. Further, in a genuine bargaining situation with relative equality, some of the disadvantages of the unions' close relationship to the industry are diminished. Equally important is the fact that the regional system of bargaining stabilizes construction operations over a very large geographical area. Since many of the larger general contractors engage in construction throughout Northern California, one master contract with each of the unions concerned reduces uncertainty for the period of the contract and facilitates competitive bidding over the whole area covered. In the trades using it, the regional system has meant the establishment of a single bargaining unit (with one exception) and a uniformity of wage scales and working conditions.

Under the current system, the State of California is divided into the 46 northern counties centered in San Francisco, and the 12 southern counties centered in Los Angeles.[11] Both union and contractor organizations generally separate their activities between these two bargaining areas. Over 100,000 construction workers and approximately 12,000 contractor employers are currently involved in the Northern California bargaining systems.[12] The workers—divided into 27 separate crafts plus laborers and helpers—are represented by the 19 A.F. of L. national or international building trades unions with several hundred locals in the area. Most of the different types of specialty contractors have formed associations which include contract negotiations with one or several of these locals as one of their functions.

The regional system is used by all five of the basic trades—the carpenters, construction laborers, operating engineers, cement masons, and construction teamsters—which are most frequently employed by the general contractor and the operative housebuilder.[13] The carpenters and laborers are the two largest building trades unions. One master contract, which covers all 46 counties of Northern California, is negotiated by the Associated General Contractors, with each of the unions in the basic

[11] For a description of construction bargaining in the 12 counties of Southern California, see Frank C. Pierson, "Building-Trades Bargaining Plan in Southern California," *Monthly Labor Review* (January, 1950), pp. 14–18.
[12] *California Employment and Payrolls, 1950*, California Department of Employment, computed from County Tables 1–25.
[13] The complete designations of these five unions are:
United Brotherhood of Carpenters and Joiners of America, AFL
International Hod Carriers, Building and Common Laborers Union of America, AFL
Operative Plasterers' and Cement Masons' International Association, AFL
International Union of Operating Engineers, AFL
International Brotherhood of Teamsters, Chauffeurs, Warehousemen, and Helpers of America, AFL

trades, excepting the carpenters. A carpenter contract covering 42 counties is also negotiated with the Associated General Contractors, but as noted previously, four Bay Area counties are covered by a strong metropolitan District Council of Carpenters which maintains its identity as a separate unit.

The region-wide bargaining of the basic trades has been accomplished on the part of the unions through the use of various types of organizational structure. One local of the Operating Engineers has jurisdiction over the entire 46 counties and it was the first basic trade to sign a master agreement with the Associated General Contractors. One District Council of Plasterers and Cement Masons represents all local unions of Cement Masons in contract negotiations in Northern California. Similarly a District Council of Building and Construction Laborers represents all locals of construction laborers in the 46 counties. Construction teamsters locals are represented through the Heavy Highway, Building and Construction Teamsters' Committee for Northern California. The Bay Counties District Council of Carpenters has jurisdiction over four Bay Area counties, and the Carpenters in the remaining 42 counties are represented by a committee brought together by the International Brotherhood which includes nine District Councils and a number of local unions without District Council affiliations.

Some other regional agreements also exist. The Piledrivers, an affiliate of the Brotherhood of Carpenters, negotiate a single uniform 46-county agreement with the Piledriving and Contractors Association and the two chapters of the Associated General Contractors. Since industrial pipe work is frequently done by general contractors engaging in the construction of oil refineries and chemical plants, several employers' groups representing both the general contractors and specialty contractors negotiated a 46-county agreement with the Northern California Council of local steamfitters' and plumbers' unions.

Since 1938 the Structural Ironworkers' Union locals have also conducted their negotiations on a 46-county basis. In some regions they are considered one of the basic trades, but in this area the Ironworkers Employers Association of Northern California, a specialty group of employers, negotiated with the Ironworkers' District Council to determine uniform conditions for the whole area.

For most of the specialty trades, on the other hand, collective bargaining is restricted to separate negotiations, involving one or a few counties, between a local union and a single contractor association. In these trades, there is a complicated craft union structure paralleling the organization of the specialty contractors. Seventeen of the 19 national unions have jurisdiction over the specialty trades, and within their jurisdictions are approximately 23 journeyman crafts plus additional helpers and hodcarriers. As a result, each locality may have from 20 to 30 separate local unions depending partly on the size of the construction labor force of a community. Since there are so many crafts, the membership of locals is necessarily small in most cases. Collective bargaining is conducted by craft rather than by union, and one union frequently has jurisdiction over more than one craft or type of worker. For example, both cement masons and plasterers are members of the same international union, yet bargain with different groups of employers, since the former are customarily employed by the general contractors while plasterers are hired by a specialty contractor. Similarly, the construction laborers, who bargain with the general contractors, are part of the same international union as the hodcarriers, who bargain with specialty contractors in the masonry trades.

While specialty trades unions generally have resisted the master agreement contract, in some the question of the merits of local versus regional bargaining is unsettled. District councils and other means of cooperative action do exist among the specialty trades unions, but they have not been widely used for bargaining purposes. However, in the metropolitan San Francisco Bay Area, the Painters and the Hodcarriers conduct negotiations on a multi-county basis. Six chapters of the Painting and Decorating Contractors of America negotiate a uniform six-county contract with three District Councils and four local unions of the Painters' union. The Masons' Hodcarriers in four Bay Area local unions have

TABLE 1

*Summary of Bargaining Systems in
Northern California Construction Industry*

Regional 46-County System

A. Single Contract
    Four Basic Trades:
        Construction Laborers
        Operating Engineers
        Cement Masons
        Construction Teamsters
    Two Related Trades:
        Pile Drivers
        Structural Ironworkers
B. A Bay Area Contract plus a 42-County Contract
    One Basic Trade:
        Carpenters

Local, City, and County Agreements

A. A Single Bay Area Contract with Others on a Locality Basis.
    Two Specialty Trades:
        Painters
        Masons' Hodcarriers
B. Primarily Local
        Nineteen Specialty Trades

formed a Conference to establish a uniform agreement with the Mason and Builders Association of California.

Even without single bargains, fairly uniform wage rates have been negotiated in the post-war period throughout the 46 counties in such cases as the electrical, painting, plumbing and heating, and roofing trades. In the other specialty crafts, the strong influence of the Bay Area unions on the pattern of wage scales in the remaining Northern California counties appears to have reduced the differentials between counties also. The bargaining arrangements discussed above may be seen more clearly in Table 1 [on the preceding page].

Where the 46-county system has been set up, there appears to have been some shifting of strength between the unions and employers. The metropolitan area of the San Francisco Bay has been the center of union strength. Within the heavily populated cities and counties of the Bay Area, a high degree of employer unity would be needed to match the highly successful building trades councils organizations developed by the unions. Since this employer unity does not exist, this matching is accomplished instead through regional bargaining which ties the metropolitan center of power of the building trades unions to the less organized outlying areas. This appears to diffuse the strength of the center and improve the position of the outlying areas. With a reduction in the strength of the union center, the position of the contractor has improved.

The use of a regional system has also shifted somewhat the influence of the building trades councils. As a group, the specialty trades are more closely related to the county building trades councils than are the basic trades. The councils continue in the specialty trades to play an important part in influencing and coordinating the economic policies of affiliated unions, in sanctioning or denying sanction of strike action, and in representing the general interest of construction labor in their area of jurisdiction. In the case of some of the smaller craft unions, officers of the building trades council may assist the local in the conduct of negotiations.

The five international unions in the basic trades operate independently in negotiations, without formal inter-union machinery. But in fact they are closely linked through common affiliations with the A. F. of L., the Building and Construction Trades Department, the California Building and Constructions Trades Council, and a network of affiliations of locals with the various county building trades councils in Northern California. On a regional level this inter-locking network of affiliations provides a basis for some agreement on common problems. It is difficult for any one union to follow a strictly independent policy. Since these crafts work on the job together or in related sequence, and often for the same general contractor, their interests are basically similar. Disturbance of accepted wage differentials between the crafts by entirely independent action would be regarded with some hostility by the other unions. Expiration dates of the negotiated contracts fall in the spring of the year, and provisions for two to three months notice of contract modifications mean in effect that negotiations for the basic trades all occur within the same period. If one of the unions takes strike action prior to the other unions' expiration dates, a sympathetic strike would be in violation of their contracts, but regardless of this, since the building trades unions would not cross picket lines of another craft in a sanctioned strike, the whole industry can be brought to a halt. For this system of cooperation to be effective, the objective of a particular international union must have the support of the other crafts, and this obviously gives the strike sanction great importance. One of the important functions of the county building trades councils has been to control the use of strike action within their jurisdiction. A policy which was not in harmony with the interests of the affiliated locals would not receive the support of the particular building trades council.

· · ·

Post-War Relations

The stabilizing influences and functions performed by the building trades unions are the most significant set of relationships determining the quality of industrial relations in the industry. However, the history of labor relations in Northern California demonstrated that also necessary and lacking in earlier periods was an equality of bargaining power. With the establishment of active employer associations and strong unions an approximation of equality, particularly through the extensive bargaining system of the basic trades, has been achieved in the post-war period. A further factor of considerable consequence has been the practically unabated prosperity of the construction industry for over a decade. Many problems have diminished in importance because of this prosperity.

As a result of the operation of these three factors, that is, stabilizing unionism, relative bargaining equality, and the industry's high level of activity, negotiations concerning new contracts in the post-war period have primarily been concerned with wage issues or economic issues rather than questions concerning the division of authority between management and labor. For example, the closed shop has not been an issue in this area since the end of the American Plan era. Even under the Taft-Hartley Act, as noted earlier, the closed shop has remained virtually unaltered in practice.

Strikes over contract determination when they have occurred have been over wage and related issues. While there have been a number of strikes among the specialty trades, few have been of any length in the post-war period. In many of the locals of certain crafts there has been a continuous no-strike record for well over a decade. In the basic trades, the only serious strike in the post-war period occurred in 1952. The occasion for this stoppage of over eight weeks which at first involved the Bay Counties Carpenters and the eight contractor associations, and eventually included all 46 county Carpenters, was the demand of the unions for a health and welfare provision in their basic trades. Fringe benefits had not been widely included in construction agreements in contrast to contracts in other industries in the post-war period and the unions interpreted this as an indication of their relative decline as a group in economic welfare.

In 1952, the Construction Industry Stabilization Commission, a Federal wage control agency, set a national pattern through their formulae establishing a maximum allowable hourly employer contribution to health and welfare funds. The maximums became the minimum union proposal. Inclusion in the agreements of a health and welfare plan undoubtedly was regarded by the employers as a first step to widen the whole subject matter of collective bargaining in construction. Acceptance of health and welfare plans in the Bay Counties Carpenters contract would have meant its ultimate extension to the other Northern California bargaining units. The other basic trades and some of the specialty crafts regarded the Carpenters' effort to establish a health and welfare plan as their own, and the cooperative machinery of the building trades unions, particularly the building trades councils, gave the strike their full support.

The result of this strike, in which the contractors finally conceded the issue, demonstrated the strength which a diverse craft structure could organize, and at the same time made evident the difficult problems of contractor unity. A basic difficulty among the multi-association contractor groups which resisted the Bay Counties Carpenters demands was that the pressures upon the homebuilders' associations and small general contractors to reach a settlement were much greater than those facing the large contractors.

As noted earlier each group faces different market and operating problems, since the majority of houses are built operatively by builders who have invested their own or borrowed capital in them, and delay seriously affects the homebuilders' position. On the other hand, the fixed costs of the larger general contractor are a relatively small part of their total costs. Work stoppages at the beginning of a construction season are serious, but less disastrous to the large contractor than to the homebuilder. The smallest general contractors' return is largely a wage income, and his fixed costs in a sense are the cost of his own support. For the smallest contractor, a lengthy strike is therefore difficult to weather. The result of these conflicting necessities among the general contractors, and particularly among the homebuilders, was to bring to an end employer resistance to the health and welfare demand. The conclusion appears evident that cooperation between operative homebuilders and all general contractors in collective bargaining may not always be possible when the employers adopt a policy of resistance to union demands. Although the development of regional bargaining has greatly increased contractor bargaining power, the post-war growth of a separate housing industry confronted with different economic necessities may seriously weaken the employer bargaining structure.

This lengthy dispute also indicated that if a strike does occur in the Northern California basic trade bargaining system, the effect is likely to be serious since the whole of the large area is involved. It is possible that under a more localized system of bargaining such as existed prior to the present system, the local contractors in the Bay Area might have conceded the union demand without a strike. But in the present case, the issue was region-wide from the beginning even though it began with the Bay Area carpenters.

It is difficult to place the general contractors' and homebuilders' long resistance to a health and welfare plan as primarily due to the increased cost it would entail. Since all competitors would share the increase equally, the incidence would ultimately fall upon the ultimate consumer or owner except in a period of declining demand. As indicated earlier, many considerations outside the level of wage rates determine the demand for investment in new structures. In addition the price effect of a wage increase should not be over emphasized. For example, in the housing industry in the Bay Area, the total labor costs of a typical house built by a medium sized builder were 25 per cent of all costs including land, materials, overhead and profit in 1949.[14] As a result, a 10 per cent increase in labor costs would increase the capital cost of the typical house by only 2.5 per cent. The labor costs referred to are the sum of all on-site labor costs incurred by both the homebuilder acting as general contractor and the subcontractors. Moreover, since the demand for new housing is, within certain limits, more a function of cost of monthly payments necessary to acquire ownership rather than of the capital cost of the structure itself, and since financing charges, taxes, and insurance make an important contribution to the monthly ownership payments, an increase in labor costs would have an even less direct effect on the price relevant to the consumer.

Even though the demand factors may make acceptance of wage demands by contractors in construction less difficult than in some industries, large general contractors still appear more determined than they have been in the past to resist union demands which they regard as excessive or unreasonable. The general contractors are conscious of their bargaining power, and while regarding the unions as important to the industry, they do bargain for acceptance of their own terms. Collective bargaining in the basic trades appears to be a genuine negotiation of demands involving compromise and concession.

14 [S. J.] Maisel [*Housebuilding in Transition* (Berkeley: University of California Press, 1953)], Table 50.

Nine ~ The Farm Organization as Lobbyist

SUCCESS *Grant McConnell*

In the early 'thirties the very survival of the American Farm Bureau Federation was threatened. Although the federation claimed to be "the voice of organized agriculture," [1] it remained but one of three general farm organizations. Despite unusual organizational advantages over its rivals, it had entered an almost disastrous stage of decline. The record of accomplishment after the spectacular days of the first congressional farm bloc was negligible. Its assault on the party system had been an admitted failure. Finally, and most seriously, the federation had compromised itself by collaboration in the Republican farm policy. It is doubtful whether the Farm Bureau could have refused to accept representation on the Hoover Farm Board without loss of prestige. Yet the facts remained that the Farm Bureau had participated and that the board was a failure.

By this time it had become clear that the American Farm Bureau Federation must find its place as a general farm organization. The rationale of its organization required that its function be broadly framed to appeal to different sections and different commodity groups. The early emphasis on cooperatives had not brought strong central organization. Instead, it had meant commodity particularism. Once the Sherman Act restraints on cooperative marketing had been removed, there was little to

---

[1] This slogan appeared monthly in *Bureau Farmer* (later renamed *Nation's Agriculture*), the principal publication of the national federation.

REPRINTED with permission from Grant McConnell, "Success," *The Decline of Agrarian Democracy*, Berkeley: University of California Press, 1953, pp. 66–83.

hold the various groups together. Moreover, the cooperatives already had their own federation. At best, cooperatives offered only the sort of auxiliary strength that friendly benefit systems give trade unions.

The sectional aspect of the problem was almost as apparent. The strength of the federation in 1930 lay overwhelmingly in the Middle West.[2] In commodity terms, its strength was corn-hog. The secondary focus was the South and cotton. Here, however, the power of the Farm Bureau was meager. Federation leaders had repeatedly noted that much of the opposition in Congress to the domestic allotment scheme supported by the Farm Bureau had come from the South.[3] There were outlying Farm Bureau strongholds in California and New York, with the dairy states of the Northwest perhaps also to be considered as outlying.

Thus the problem facing the Farm Bureau was fundamentally similar to that regularly before the major parties: to forge an intersectional alliance of two or more major regional interests and to pick up whatever outside incidental strength was consistent with the basic alliance. For the Farm Bureau, the basic alliance was obviously that between cotton South and corn-hog Middle West. The first step in framing it was taken when Edward A. O'Neal of Alabama was made president and Charles Hearst of Iowa vice-president.[4] The selection of O'Neal was not justified by the relative actualities of strength; it was, rather, a manifest of the policy to be followed in the future. The addition of Earl Smith of Illinois to the directorate somewhat later was perhaps a recognition that the primary center of Farm Bureau power must always be the corn belt.

This strategy, hardly more than an outline before the days of the New Deal, was laid down in 1931. It appeared at a moment when the crisis before the Farm Bureau was perhaps at its gravest. The membership figures reflected the first serious impact of the depression and the failure of Farm Bureau legislative policy. In 1931 there was a drop of 45,000, and eventually the size of the Farm Bureau was cut in half.[5]

The occasion which made the elevation of O'Neal to the presidency of the federation possible was the decision by the organization to support the Federal Farm Board. President Sam Thompson resigned as an officer of the Farm Bureau and joined the board at President Hoover's request. It meant recognition of the federation as a power in agricultural politics, something which the leadership may well have felt to be almost a necessity at the time, but the decision was hardly a pleasant one. As the Republican party substitute for farm legislation demanded by the federation and other organizations, the Federal Farm Board could not be presented as the achievement of the federation. Moreover, any hopes

[2] Cf. collection figures, American Farm Bureau Federation, *Annual Report*, 1930, 1931, 1932.
[3] Cf. O. M. Kile, *The Farm Bureau through Three Decades* (Baltimore, Waverly Press, 1948), p. 182.
[4] The element of "strategy" involved is suggested by the fact that neither O'Neal nor Hearst were opposed in the election. All other incumbent directors were returned. *Colorado Farm Bureau News*, January, 1932.
[5] For details see Appendix, table 1.

that had been pinned on the Farm Board as a means of raising agricultural prices were waning. The board chairman confessed that the job could not be accomplished without control of production.[6]

The situation of the Farm Bureau as one of numerous farm organizations was less than comfortable. Assuredly, however, the National Grange was no great threat. Its leadership had had a legislative program since the early 'twenties and had one now.[7] Yet there was little likelihood that the Grange would acquire, or even seek, any great increase of influence. The consistent conservatism of the Grange, secure in the belief that it had found a reliable basis of organizational survival, was stated by one of its presidents thus:

> The Grange has seen more than fifty farm organizations—State and National—rise and fall. It has gone through four great major depressions, and periods of boom and collapse, drought and bumper crops, and still moves forward because the soul of the Grange is its ritualistic side, and its emphasis is on moral and spiritual ideals.[8]

Such an organization might prove to be pallbearer to the Farm Bureau but never usurper.

The Farmers' Union was quite different. The Union had been through some of the same troubles which had plagued the Farm Bureau, particularly the conflict between cooperative and legislative emphasis. The legislative policy had won out in 1929. The stronghold of the Farmers' Union had been the wheat country of the Great Plains. However, there was a significant Farmers' Union in Iowa, which was first among Farm Bureau states in 1930.[9] The president of the Iowa Farmers' Union, Milo Reno, was also head of the Farmers' National Holiday Association, a group which sometimes became involved in incidents bordering on violence.[10] More alarming to the Farm Bureau than the dumping of milk upon the highway was the strong opposition to both the Farm Bureau and the Extension Service aroused by the Reno organizations, which organized a compaign to cut off public support for the county agents and to persuade Farm Bureau members to resign.[11] The farm holiday movement was perhaps the radical edge of the Farmers' Union in this period,

[6] Cf. remarks in Report to Congress, quoted in Russell Lord, *The Wallaces of Iowa* (Boston, Houghton Mifflin Co., 1941), p. 313.

[7] It consisted mainly of the export debenture device.

[8] From an interview with L. J. Taber, Master of the National Grange, in DeWitt C. Wing, "Trends in National Farm Organizations," U.S. Department of Agriculture, *Yearbook of Agriculture, 1940*, p. 950. Although this interview was apparently given at a later date, the point of view applies for the early 'thirties as well.

[9] The position of Iowa in the Farm Bureau has usually been second to Illinois. The 1930 data are drawn from figures on state collections by the national organization. Cf. American Farm Bureau Federation, *Annual Report, 1930*.

[10] For a description of such activities see Donald R. Murphy, "The Farmers Go on Strike," *New Republic*, vol. 72 (August 31, 1932), pp. 66–68.

[11] Cf. "Who and Why? The Opposition to the Farm Bureau," *Iowa Farm Bureau Messenger*, March, 1933, p. 9. See also Gladys Baker, *The County Agent* (University of Chicago Press, 1939), pp. 58, 59.

but it was not repudiated by the parent organization.[12] In fact, the leadership of the Farmers' Union conceived of the organization as still standing in the old Populist tradition, militant and aggressive.[13]

In this situation the most rankling taunt was that farm relief had failed because the farm organizations could not agree on what they wanted.[14] Aside from its obvious element of truth, it underlined the failure of the Farm Bureau to make good on its claim of being the unique spokesman for agriculture. Moreover, the increasingly widespread belief in the truth of the charge represented a peculiar threat to the Farm Bureau, since it, more than either the Grange or the Farmers' Union, was committed to the role of legislative agent to the farmer. Accordingly, the new O'Neal regime attempted to form a united front with the other general farm organizations. Three meetings were held in 1931.[15] These efforts bore fruit early in 1932, when the big three organizations reached agreement on a legislative program.[16] The agreement was vague on the crucial point, how to raise farm prices. However, it did call for anything —whether the debenture plan or the equalization fee—that would work to control surpluses. Beyond this, the program denounced the sales tax, an unequal tariff, and speculation; it favored money stabilization (i.e., inflation) and Philippine independence.

The leaders of the Farm Bureau Federation took credit for the new "unity." [17] In point of fact, the agreement was not much more than a façade. The Grange was lethargic and the Farmers' Union was suspicious. However, the Farm Bureau was encouraged to enlarge the scope of the movement at the head of which it had placed itself. Representatives of fourteen farm organizations met in October.[18] Whatever the differences among the various groups, the fact of the meetings was of the first importance. The Farm Bureau was quick to appropriate and exploit the advantage.

The structure thus built before the national election endured through the critical period when agricultural policy was being formulated for the

[12] John A. Simpson, national president of the Farmers' Union, announced himself as also representing the Farmers' National Holiday Association in 1933. Cf. Hearings on the Agricultural Emergency Act to Increase Farm Purchasing Power, Senate Committee on Agriculture and Forestry, 73d Cong., 1st sess., 1933, p. 104.

[13] For the full flavor of this, sample the collection of speeches by John A. Simpson, *The Militant Voice of Agriculture* (Oklahoma City, 1934). See also William P. Tucker, "Populism Up-to-Date: The Story of the Farmers' Union," *Agricultural History*, vol. 21 (October, 1947), pp. 198–207.

[14] This charge was echoed by, among others, the editors of *Fortune*. Cf. "Bounty," *Fortune*, vol. 7 (February, 1933), p. 118.

[15] *Bureau Farmer*, vol. 6 (October, 1931), p. 15.

[16] Unsigned article, "United We Stand," *Bureau Farmer*, vol. 7 (March, 1932), p. 4.

[17] American Farm Bureau Federation, *Annual Report, 1932*, p. 6.

[18] American Farm Bureau Federation, Farmers' Union, Grange, National Cooperative Milk Producers' Federation, American Cotton Association, Agricultural Press, National Live Stock Marketing Association, National Fruit and Vegetable Exchange, Mid-South Cotton Growers' Association, National Committee of Farm Organizations, Dairy and Poultry Cooperatives, Inc., Farmers' National Grain Corporation, National Wool Marketing Corporation, Pure Milk Association. *Ibid.*

New Deal era. Early in 1933 the organization of the National Agricultural Conference was completed. The effect for the Farm Bureau was to make its own leader, O'Neal, more conspicuous than before. Again in 1934 the conference met and drove for its common objectives, but this time the Farmers' Union was a discordant voice in the general harmony. Thereafter the conference usually went its way without the Union.

Nevertheless, the spokesmen of the Farm Bureau were able to rejoice over the successful passage through an exceedingly difficult time. It now mattered little that John Simpson was talking about "fake farm organizations"; [19] the claim of the Farm Bureau was good that "the organization stands at the pinnacle of its power and influence in national affairs. The advice and help of our leaders are sought in the highest councils of our nation. More and more the Farm Bureau is looked to for leadership as the spokesman of organized agriculture." [20] What the Farm Bureau had been unable to accomplish by direct organization among farmers it had managed by adroit manipulation of other organizations. That is to say, it had solved an immediate problem of its own internal life by action in its external affairs.

The first fruits of this external policy appeared even before inauguration of the new administration. Roosevelt sent Morgenthau, Tugwell, and W. I. Myers as his representatives to the conferences of the Farm Bureau in December, 1932.[21] Here was assurance that the "voice of agriculture" would have some kind of a say in measures to come.

More interesting (and more obscure) is the part that the Farm Bureau played in the selection of the new Secretary of Agriculture. According to the semiofficial historian of the organization, O'Neal exercised a veto on the plan to give the post to Morgenthau.[22] At any rate, the choice of Henry A. Wallace seems to have been thoroughly acceptable to the Farm Bureau. Wallace had been one of the witnesses summoned to Washington the previous year to testify on a measure sponsored by the organization.[23] Policies of the Farm Bureau had been supported by Wallace's editorial page, and the Wallace family was regarded, at least retrospectively, as a firm supporter of the Farm Bureau by the faction now in control.[24] Very early in the life of the new administration O'Neal announced, "I regard Secretary Wallace as the farmers' right bower in the Farm Bureau's program. He has cooperated with us 100 per cent . . . we believe he will continue his cooperation." [25]

The agricultural program that emerged early in 1933 was claimed by the Farm Bureau as its own. In one sense, the claim was justified. The Farm Bureau gave its support to the legislative program of the early

[19] Simpson, *op. cit.*, p. 52.
[20] American Farm Bureau Federation, *Annual Report, 1934.*
[21] *Bureau Farmer*, vol. 9 (April, 1934), p. 27.
[22] Kile, *op. cit.*, p. 194.
[23] *Wallaces' Farmer*, vol. 57 (May 28, 1932), p. 299.
[24] The elder Wallace had at one time been critical of the cooperative phase of Farm Bureau policy.
[25] *Bureau Farmer*, vol. 8 (April, 1933), p. 5.

New Deal in agriculture. In another sense, however, the claim was misleading. The previous convention of the federation had passed a set of
seventeen resolutions in the legislative area. The program ran from a
demand for "honest money" through the guaranty of bank deposits,
economy in government, and the St. Lawrence waterway. The resolution
on the agricultural surplus was far from definite.[26] The farm mortgage
problem and the monetary panacea seemed to loom larger in Farm Bureau concern at this time. Yet the general trend of future policy was already fairly clear. Roosevelt had favored the domestic allotment plan
during the campaign, and opportunism, if nothing else, would seem to
have suggested Farm Bureau support for this device.[27]

The evolution of the ideas that went into the scheme is usually
traced to W. J. Spillman, with contributions from John D. Black and
M. L. Wilson. In any assessment of the factors which determined Farm
Bureau policy, a large share of importance must be attributed to personal influence with the New Deal leadership. Certainly, M. L. Wilson
and Rexford Tugwell strongly supported the adaptation of the domestic
allotment idea to the legislative program of the new regime.[28] The other
fundamental idea in the evolving farm program, "equality for agriculture," with a base calculated on the years 1909 to 1914, came from
George N. Peek and Hugh S. Johnson.[29] Significantly, all but one of
these men had a part in the administrative history of the new farm program.

In the fluid time of 1933 this personal element was a source of uncertainty in the equations of power. The program that was coming out of
the actionist New Deal might well take surprising turns. The Farm Bureau had a measure of security in having supported the program outlined
by Roosevelt during the campaign and in having secured a degree of
commitment from the conference of farm organizations. Yet the Roosevelt farm contingent held divergent tendencies and the farm organizations were far from united. The latter fact was demonstrated first. In the
last session of the lame-duck Seventy-second Congress a bill was brought
up embodying the essentials of the later Agricultural Adjustment Act.
O'Neal, the first witness called, claimed to represent some fourteen farm
organizations, including the Grange and the Farmers' Union.[30] The
united front survived this claim, but the bill nevertheless failed. When
the new Congress met, the rift in the unity of the conference suddenly
became obvious. Taber of the Grange gave unqualified support to the

26 American Farm Bureau Federation, Resolutions, 1932 Convention.
27 *Wallaces' Farmer*, vol. 58 (October 1, 1932), p. 513. Russell Lord comments,
"The Farm Bureau was fronting for the domestic allotment measure, but many of
its leaders hated control of production quite as ardently and confusedly as George
Peek did." Lord, *op. cit.*, p. 330.
28 Lord, *op. cit.*, pp. 305–24.
29 Henry A. Wallace, *New Frontiers* (New York, Reynal and Hitchcock, 1934), p.
148.
30 Hearings on the Agricultural Adjustment Relief Plan, Senate Committee on Agriculture and Forestry, 72d Cong., 2d sess., 1933, p. 14.

program, but Simpson denounced it. Simpson's objections were not in themselves important except as they indicated a return by the Farmers' Union to insistence on its own particular variant.[31]

The Agricultural Adjustment Act passed in May.[32] The basic plan had been chosen. Production was to be restricted on a quota related to previous acreage planted. The inducements were subsidies drawn from a variety of processing and other taxes. Although the act itself was complex, the plan was simple—and little more than the plan had been decided. The conflicts of agricultural politics shifted to the more obscure fields of administration.

George N. Peek, the first administrator of the Agricultural Adjustment Administration (A.A.A.), has said, "The farm organizations had little to do with the program." [33] This statement by one of the main participants must carry some weight. However, the issues as seen by this effective but blunt and unperceptive man tended to revolve about the controversy within the Department of Agriculture between the "liberal" group and the "agrarian" group.[34] In no small degree, this controversy was a matter of personalities. The "liberal" group looked to Tugwell for leadership. The "agrarian" group was the older element which had come to look upon the department as its peculiar property. It would be difficult to single out any individual as its head. Perhaps Chester Davis came as close as any to the position of leadership.

Many of the differences between the two factions lay in the fact that the liberals were a city-bred group and lacked the homespun mannerisms of rural America. Anyone who has spent much time about the department is aware of the degree to which the protective coloration of rustic ways is cultivated in the offices of the vast buildings on the Mall. Failure to achieve this coloration is itself ground for suspicion.

The issues were finally reducible to the question of who was to receive the benefits of the A.A.A. program. Necessarily, they involved the structure of power which was essential to the Farm Bureau. The climax of the conflict came in the "purge" of 1935. The immediate issue was a

[31] The program of the Farmers' Union was based upon assurance to producers of cost of production, and was quite as much oriented to the commercial farmer as was the program of the Farm Bureau. The testimony reveals that the alliance strategy of the Farmers' Union was based upon cotton and wheat as against the Farm Bureau's cotton and corn. Cf. Hearings on the Agricultural Emergency Act . . . , Senate Committee on Agriculture and Forestry, 1933, pp. 104–08, 339.

[32] The close working relationship between the administration and the Farm Bureau is illustrated by the fact that the bill was drafted by the counsel of the Farm Bureau at the request of the Department of Agriculture. Cf. D. C. Blaisdell, Government and Agriculture (New York, Farrar and Rinehart, 1940), p. 42; American Farm Bureau Federation, Annual Report, 1935.

[33] G. N. Peek (with S. Crowther), Why Quit Our Own? (New York, D. Van Nostrand Co., 1936), p. 93.

[34] The tags "liberal" and "agrarian" are used by Russell Lord, The Agrarian Revival (New York, American Association for Adult Education, 1939), p. 158. The ideological diversity of the "liberal" group is indicated by the fact that it included points of view ranging from that of Victor Christgau to that of Lee Pressman.

legal interpretation relating to the share of tenants in A.A.A. payments.[35] The issue was genuine, but it was mingled with other genuine issues and with matters of personality. The picture, dramatic though it was, did not show the underlying problem of power and administrative structure.

To understand the part of the Farm Bureau in the A.A.A. program it is necessary to consider again the relationship between the Farm Bureau and the Extension Service. Although economy in government had repeatedly been favored by resolutions passed at Farm Bureau conventions, the saving was never envisioned as applying to the expenditures of the Extension Service. O'Neal "personally polled" the Senate Committee on Agriculture in 1931, attempting to gain increased appropriation for Extension.[36] A similar battle to fight cuts in Extension appropriations took place in 1932.[37] At the same time, the Farm Bureau was seeking to tighten the relationships between the colleges, the Farm Board, the Department of Agriculture, the Extension Service, and itself.[38] O'Neal and Charles Hearst of the Iowa Farm Bureau took Henry A. Wallace along with them to call on C. W. Warburton, director of Extension, to argue for the use of county agents in presenting to farmers "the way in which different types of economic policies affect agriculture." [39] To the Farm Bureau, an administrative structure which held so little place for the Extension Service was far from satisfactory. The trouble rested, in all probability, in the independent status of the Farm Board. Despite the presence on the board of a Farm Bureau representative, the board was insufficiently responsive. What was needed was a "complete coordination" of the board with the other agencies.[40] This implied a larger role for the Extension Service.

One of the most important Farm Bureau purposes in the legislative drive of 1933 was to correct the administrative structure of the previous era. An independent board had proved rather too susceptible to congressional influence.[41] The device for inaugurating the new program was at hand in the Extension system. O'Neal made this one of his points of emphasis in a visit to the White House with Wallace:

> Where is there an agency that is so close to the grass-roots, and that has so much influence with the real people? [i.e., as the Extension Service and the land grant colleges] . . . I was strongly against any political

[35] Russell Lord has told the story in some detail in The Wallaces of Iowa, pp. 393–409.
[36] Bureau Farmer, vol. 6 (September, 1931), p. 10.
[37] Cf. unsigned article, "No!" Bureau Farmer, vol. 8 (December, 1932), pp. 3–6.
[38] Cf. O'Neal speech reported in Wyoming Farm Journal, November 31, 1932, p. 9.
[39] Editorial note by Wallace in Wallaces' Farmer, vol. 57 (April 16, 1932), p. 221.
[40] Bureau Farmer, vol. 7 (January, 1932), p. 12; vol. 8 (January, 1933), p. 6.
[41] "The farm organizations sought to remove the administration of this bill [A.A.A.] as far as possible from the hands of Congress, endowing instead with dictatorial powers the incoming and then unknown Secretary of Agriculture." Lord, The Wallaces of Iowa, p. 312.

administration of the act. Anything savoring off such an administration would be fatal.[42]

O'Neal's distaste for "political administration" of the A.A.A. was paralleled by the desire of administrative heads to obtain extensive participation in the program. The latter derived in part from a fear that the price effects of the program would be limited by an inadequate response by producers. There was also, however, a genuine and widespread belief that local involvement of the farmers themselves in questions of administration was the essence of democracy. Accordingly, the administration developed an elaborate plan for consulting "the real people":

> First, after having studied the situation to determine how an adjustment for corn and hogs might affect incomes of farmers, the A.A.A. held a series of regional conferences participated in by representatives of agricultural colleges and by farm leaders in the present program. In these conferences, the various alternative directions which a program might take were discussed. The gains which farmers might expect to realize through the alternative plans were assessed, and the desirable adaptations of the plans to the particular conditions of different regions were considered. The farmers and state representatives at the conferences expressed themselves on all points involved freely as did the representatives of the A.A.A. and gave their opinions as to whether farmers in their regions wanted a program for 1935, and if so, what kind of a program they wanted.
>
> The second step was the referendum taken among corn and hog farmers, following discussions sponsored by the farmers' production control associations, and committees. In the actual voting, no record was kept of individual votes and no questions were asked as to how any farmer had voted.
>
> After the votes had been tabulated, and the majority will of the farmers was known, the third step was a meeting in Washington at which representatives of control associations, general farm organizations, the State colleges and the A.A.A. worked out the program in detail.[43]

The central feature of the plan was the county production control association. The local association had not only the duties outlined above, but the assigning of quotas and the checking of compliance through local committees as well. Obviously, all this required a staggering amount of organization work. For wheat producers alone, there were 1,450 of these associations.[44] By the end of 1934 there was a total of more than 4,200

---

[42] O'Neal speech to convention, Association of Land Grant Colleges and Universities, *Proceedings,* 1933 Convention, p. 87.
[43] H. R. Tolley, assistant administrator, A.A.A., "Agricultural Planning in a Democracy," Association of Land Grant Colleges and Universities, *Proceedings,* 1934 Convention, p. 64.
[44] George E. Farrell, "The County Production Control Association," *Extension Service Review,* vol. 5 (February, 1934), p. 23.

county associations.[45] In the first year of the A.A.A., 70,200 local farm leaders were trained.[46]

From the standpoint of the Department of Agriculture, only one agency could accomplish the task quickly—the Extension Service. Most of the educational activities of Extension were shelved, and agents were directed to turn their efforts to the organization of the A.A.A. program. The A.A.A. itself developed an organization, but this was confined principally to Washington.[47] The real reliance was upon the county agent. Many of the agents became secretaries of the local associations.[48]

The result for the Extension Service itself was a new lease on life. A new enthusiasm followed from the "enlarged field of service." [49] More tangibly, the A.A.A. provided the wherewithal for expansion of the agency. Funds were transferred to Extension and new personnel were employed. Geographically, the blank spaces in the map of the nation by counties were quickly filled.[50] The period of decline of the Extension Service had come to an end; it now maintained a genuine "action" program and, moreover, had gained an improved claim to leadership at the local level.[51]

The building of an administrative machine for the A.A.A. was not the accomplishment of the Extension Service alone, however. The officers of the Department of Agriculture recognized the farm organizations as

[45] "Agricultural Adjustment in 1934," U.S. Department of Agriculture, *Report of AAA* (1934), p. 219.
[46] "Serving American Agriculture," U.S. Department of Agriculture, *Report of Extension Work* (1933), p. 5.
[47] At the end of 1935, the A.A.A. had 6,511 employees, of whom 5,522 were in Washington. J. S. Davis, E. G. Nourse, and J. D. Black, *Three Years of the AAA* (Washington, D.C., The Brookings Institution, 1937), p. 50.
[48] *Ibid.*, pp. 71–77. Cf. also Baker, *op. cit.*, pp. 70–77; U.S. Department of Agriculture, *Report of Extension Work* (1933), p. 6.
[49] W. H. Brokaw, "Adjustment Program Influences Extension," *Extension Service Review*, vol. 5 (December, 1934), p. 179.
[50] The number of counties having agents (male) was as follows:

1929...2,323	1933...2,307	1937...2,876
1930...2,376	1934...2,814	1938...2,989
1931...2,447	1935...2,857	1939...2,990
1932...2,369	1936...2,922	

The number of counties taken as agricultural is 3,076. Since 1939, the figure of counties having agents has been quite stable. Data from annual reports of Extension Service, various titles.
[51] It is worth observing that during this period of expansion there was a steady undercurrent of criticism of Extension Service on the grounds that it was giving assistance only to prosperous farmers. In 1941 the Extension Service published a pamphlet written by M. C. Wilson, *How and to What Extent Is the Extension Service Reaching Low-Income Farm Families?* Extension Service Circular 375 (1941). Wilson concluded that, although the Extension Service is organized to give educational service in areas which are handicapped by a high concentration of "disadvantaging" conditions in comparison with other areas, in practice "Extension is reaching a somewhat larger proportion of those of higher socio-economic status." This condition was caused by "the limiting factor" of personnel (p. 20).

consultative organs in themselves. In addition, the Farm Bureau responded to the organizational desires of the department and joined the campaign. When the A.A.A. was first set up, the Farm Bureau sent word to the state federations to decide whom they wanted to administer the act in their own states. In many communities the local farm bureaus "literally took over" the task of organizing the A.A.A. committees.[52] Thus, by exploiting the sudden opportunity given by government willingness to act, the Farm Bureau succeeded in making the A.A.A. its own in administration as well as in policy. There was more than mere braggadocio in the statement that "the Farm Bureau and the A.A.A. are inseparable." [53]

A membership campaign was conducted by the Farm Bureau to parallel the intensive organization of farmers for the A.A.A.[54] The new vitality among county agents, the exhilaration of attaining favorable legislation, and the assurance of a benevolent attitude in the department combined to make the campaign a success. Membership rose both spectacularly and steadily through the years of the first A.A.A.[55] The organization of commercial producers in A.A.A. control associations almost necessarily redounded to the advantage of the Farm Bureau, not only because the bureau had been alert in capitalizing on its part in legislation and its close ties with the Extension Service, but also because the federation was an organization of commercial farmers.

This was most apparent in the South, where the Farm Bureau had a peculiarly pressing problem of organization. The very necessity which had brought O'Neal into the presidency—that of cementing a regional alliance between the Middle West and the South—required that the Farm Bureau display greater strength in the South. The membership of even the largest state Farm Bureau in the South was only about half that of the seventh largest state federation elsewhere in 1934.[56] The gravity of the problem undoubtedly helped to overcome the distaste of the national leadership for identification with the special commodity legislation for cotton and tobacco to supplement the A.A.A.[57] The federation was

[52] Admittedly, other farm groups grumbled. Kile, *op. cit.*, p. 205.
[53] *Iowa Farm Bureau Messenger,* April, 1934, p. 11.
[54] "Farmers have become organization-conscious. The situation appears more propitious for organizing agriculture than at any time for many years." American Farm Bureau Federation, *Annual Report, 1933;* also an unsigned article, "Signing 'Em Up," *Bureau Farmer,* vol. 9 (April, 1934), p. 5.
[55] From 163,246 in 1933 to 356,564 in 1936. See Appendix, table 1. Ralph Russell has plotted Farm Bureau membership against cash farm income. Although the comparison is interesting, income is only one element in a complex story. "Membership of the American Farm Bureau Federation, 1926–1935," *Rural Sociology,* vol. 2 (March, 1937), p. 33.
[56] The estimate is based on dues collected by the national federation. Alabama was the largest Southern federation. It was surpassed by Illinois, New York, Indiana, Iowa, California, Minnesota, and Ohio. American Farm Bureau Federation, *Annual Report, 1934.*
[57] These were the Bankhead and Kerr-Smith acts, which may be roughly described as special A.A.A.'s with compulsory features. Cf. testimony of O'Neal, Hearings on Amendments to the Agricultural Adjustment Act, House Committee on Agriculture, 74th Cong., 1st sess., 1935, p. 298.

already alive to the dangers of "commodityism," but the risks were worth the prospective gain in prestige for the organization in a key area.

The gains in the South came somewhat slowly, since a large amount of formative organization work was necessary. However, by the end of 1936 results became apparent. In that year the Southern region made the largest gain. A special organization department was set up and a mass campaign was directed throughout the South. County agents, who were generally freer in that region than elsewhere from legal restrictions on outside organization work, were stimulated to form farm bureaus and sign up the beneficiaries of the new government programs.[58] During this period some of the local farm bureaus became adjuncts of the county agents rather than the other way about, as in the normal situation.[59]

When the A.A.A. program went into operation in the South, some of the results of this organizational history became apparent. During the famous "plow-up" stage of the program, stories of fraud and influence by the Ku Klux Klan circulated. A system by which payment checks were diverted to creditors of actual farmers was openly arrived at in consultations between government officials and the local participants in this grass-roots democracy. Tenants were generally excluded from benefits paid from A.A.A. funds, despite their greater relative personal sacrifice to the program.[60] The explanation lay mainly in the fact that, as one group of observers noted, "the Agricultural Adjustment Administration organized its program under the direction of the planters themselves."[61] The county agents and the Farm Bureau were the means of organization.

[58] "A special procedure has been worked out for rebuilding Farm Bureau membership in the southern states and the basic outlines of this plan with appropriate adaptions have been applied successfully in Arkansas, North Carolina, Virginia, and Mississippi. A similar plan is being organized in Louisiana. Under this plan, an organization program is carefully worked out by representatives of the national organization, state organization, and the Extension Service, definitely allocating responsibilities, mapping out the steps to be taken, assigning membership quotas all the way along the line, and providing for a method of thorough preparation, a period of mass action with district mass meetings and leaders' conferences and a period of intensive follow-up work.
"The Extension Service in the Farm Bureau states in the southern region have been outstanding in the splendid cooperation and assistance which they have rendered in this organization movement." American Farm Bureau Federation, *Annual Report, 1936.*
[59] Cf. Baker, *op. cit.,* p. 141.
[60] For accounts of the injustices of the program see Webster Powell and Addison T. Cutler, "Tightening the Cotton Belt," *Harpers,* vol. 168 (February, 1934), pp. 312–13; C. S. Johnson, E. R. Embree, and W. W. Alexander, *The Collapse of Cotton Tenancy* (Chapel Hill, University of North Carolina Press, 1935); Minority Report of W. L. Blackstone of Southern Tenant Farmers' Union, Report of the President's Committee on Farm Tenancy, prepared under the auspices of the National Resources Committee, 1937, p. 21; Arthur F. Raper, *Preface to Peasantry* (Chapel Hill, University of North Carolina Press, 1936), p. 245; Davis, Nourse, and Black, *op. cit.,* pp. 120, 338, 346–48. See also quotation from unpublished study by Gunnar Lange in Gunnar Myrdal, *An American Dilemma* (New York, Harper and Bros., 1944), pp. 1247, 1248.
[61] Johnson, Embree, and Alexander, *op. cit.,* p. 51.

This was the essential background of the discord in the Department of Agriculture which erupted in the 1935 "purge." [62]

This, then, was the pattern established in the early years of the New Deal. The Farm Bureau had succeeded in identifying itself with the legislation. By the decision to use the Extension Service in administering the A.A.A. the department had helped to identify the Farm Bureau with the administration of the program. The results had been, on the one hand, a vast increase in the strength and influence of the Farm Bureau and, on the other hand, a great financial boon to the type of farmers who were the natural clientele of the Farm Bureau.

The A.A.A. was struck down in the Supreme Court on January 6, 1936.[63] The crisis thus precipitated affected not only the Department of Agriculture and the whole New Deal but the welfare of the Farm Bureau as well. On January 9 the national board of directors met in special session. On January 10 the Farm Bureau leaders presented a program to a conference of farm leaders summoned by Secretary Wallace. On January 11 the conference adopted a soil conservation plan embodying the essentials of the old A.A.A. On January 14 the executive committee of the Farm Bureau drafted a proposal to go before the National Agricultural Conference on the following day. Approval was obtained there, and in the short span of seven weeks the A.A.A. was legislated back into existence.[64]

. . .

Local administration was reorganized under the new substitute for the old A.A.A. Whereas previously the local control associations had been based on particular commodities and had numbered more than 4,000, now the local groups were consolidated into "county agricultural conservation associations." There were now only 2,711 of these.[65] This change represented a clear organizational gain for the Farm Bureau on three scores. First, administrative organization was now general and not broken along commodity lines. Second, it paralleled the local Farm Bureau structure. Third, it was more amenable to direction through the county agents. In the South the county agent automatically became secretary of the local association; elsewhere, "in most counties in nearly all States, county agents . . . [were] elected to this position." [66] The effectiveness of the system for Farm Bureau purposes was attested in the following summary:

[62] Tugwell is reported to have early identified the land grant college system, the state Extension directors, and the county agents "with the ruling caste of farmers, the most conservative Farm Bureau leaders, the cotton barons of the South, the emerging Associated Farmers of California, the banker-farmers of the Middle West." Lord, *The Wallaces of Iowa*, p. 381.
[63] *U.S. v. Butler*, 297 U.S. 1.
[64] Chronology is given in American Farm Bureau Federation, *Annual Report, 1936*. See also "A New Adjustment Pattern," *Nation's Agriculture*, vol. 11 (February, 1936), pp. 4, 5.
[65] U.S. Department of Agriculture, *Report of AAA* (1937), p. 60.
[66] *Ibid*.

Out of 169 members of the State Soil Conservation Committees, in states where the Farm Bureau is organized, a total of 117 are Farm Bureau members, and in a number of states, 90 per cent or more of the county and township committeemen are Farm Bureau members. This shows the extent to which the Farm Bureau is furnishing leadership of the Soil Conservation program.[67]

The distribution of financial benefits under the new act was not greatly unlike that under the old.[68]

The Soil Conservation and Domestic Allotment Act of 1936 was admittedly a stopgap. Despite Farm Bureau consultations with experts on constitutional law, there was much doubt in regard to the chances for the act in the Supreme Court. Moreover, an extensive series of problems had grown out of the existing system. Even the men who were strategically situated in the Department of Agriculture felt that restriction of production meant an "economy of scarcity" and was out of accord with the long-range goals of the New Deal. The soul searchings that went on at this time were at least in part the result of a desire to resolve the dilemma of restricting production of food when starvation was at large in the world.

In February, Secretary Wallace called a conference of farm organizations to help frame new "permanent" legislation.[69] Far more than the presentations of 1933 and 1936, this was a Farm Bureau undertaking. As O'Neal frankly explained to the Senate committee, "The farm organization leaders were asked to draw the bill and the Farm Bureau employed Mr. Lee and Mr. Lee worked with the Department and advised with experts and economists in the Department in order to work up this draft of the bill for the farm leaders." [70]

· · ·

The act which finally passed in 1938 incorporated most of what the Farm Bureau had asked, including soil conservation, acreage allotments (voluntary, with benefit payments), commodity credit loans, marketing quotas, crop insurance, and parity payments. The provision for marketing quotas incorporated the referenda device and storage loans in quota years. For practical purposes the loan system under the Commodity

[67] American Farm Bureau Federation, *Annual Report, 1936.*
[68] One check paid out under the new Soil Conservation and Domestic Allotment Act was for $60,388 (to the Delta Pine and Land Company of Bolivar County, Mississippi). Hearings on the Agricultural Adjustment Act of 1937, Senate Committee on Agriculture and Forestry, 75th Cong., 1st sess., 1937, pp. 105–106. In 1936 some 116 payees received, in benefits, more than $10,000 each under the program. Cf. U.S. Department of Agriculture, Production and Marketing Administration, *Agricultural Conservation Program, Statistical Summary, 1948* (1949), table 13, p. 73. This table gives the history of payments by size-of-payment groups. Unfortunately, it is less than revealing as it is drawn up.
[69] *Nation's Agriculture,* vol. 12 (March, 1937), p. 12.
[70] Hearings on the Agricultural Adjustment Act of 1937, Senate Committee on Agriculture and Forestry, 1937, p. 9.

Credit Corporation was the immediately important part of the act. It quickly became a legal fiction for direct subsidy of commercial producers. For the rest, the act was sufficiently complex to confuse those who had doubts in regard to its merit.[71]

With the passage of the 1938 act, the Farm Bureau had accomplished its basic legislative program. At the same time it had established itself in a position of preeminence among farm organizations. . . .

In the achievement of power during the 'thirties the Farm Bureau surmounted some obstacles so successfully that their existence tends to be overlooked. The most important of these was what O'Neal and others labeled "commodityism." In one sense it was the same difficulty that had been at issue in the conflict over cooperative marketing in the 'twenties. It was hoped that this problem would be solved by the elevation of O'Neal to the presidency. His selection set the seal, so to speak, on the long-desired interregional alliance. It is significant that the comment appeared soon after O'Neal's inauguration that, until the Farm Bureau's formation, agriculture had been bound by "sectionalism and commodityism." [72] The statement as it stands is untrue for the long term. The great historical agrarian movements had surmounted the difficulty. Yet for the period preceding the Farm Bureau's ascendancy it was true. The failure of the organization in the later 'twenties was the failure to gain the support of cotton producers.

"Commodityism" was not eradicated by any single measure of the Farm Bureau in the 'thirties. It continued as a recurrent problem. Its appearance in the supplementary acts for cotton and tobacco has already been noted. It appeared in the Marketing Agreements Act of 1937, which permitted "orderly marketing" of milk, fruits, and vegetables. The Farm Bureau supported all these measures for the simple reason that the commodity groups were too strong to be resisted and it was better to placate than to antagonize them. Perhaps there was an issue of "commodityism" in the addition of scattered crops to the A.A.A. list of seven "basic" commodities in 1934 and 1935. The additions brought the total to fifteen.[73] This was undoubtedly a continuation of the conflict among commodity groups which had appeared in the original conference called by Secretary Wallace in 1933.[74] An issue of "commodityism" involved the powerful milk cooperative group in the 1937 hearings on the "permanent" A.A.A.

The Farm Bureau repeatedly attempted to give assurance that it was the organization to represent all commercial groups.[75] The head of

[71] A convenient summary of the act appears in Blaisdell, op. cit., pp. 60–68.
[72] Unsigned article, "Where Agriculture Speaks," Bureau Farmer, vol. 8 (November, 1932), p. 2.
[73] See Davis, Nourse, and Black, op. cit., pp. 32–50.
[74] Wallace, New Frontiers, p. 163.
[75] "The Farm Bureau at Washington looks after them all . . . the cotton farmer in Alabama, and the dairy farmer in Minnesota, the sugar producers in cane regions, and the best farmers in many states . . ." Unsigned article, "Keeping Tab on Washington," Nation's Agriculture, vol. 12 (April, 1937), p. 6.

the Wyoming Farm Bureau told Western cattle and wool growers, who had stayed aloof from the Farm Bureau, that their own association alone could not get the results offered by the Farm Bureau.[76] It was much the same with various other groups. The argument was not wholly convincing, however. The narrowly focused commodity organizations had a peculiar strength deriving from their own narrowness of structure and purpose. To take an analogy from the world of labor, a small craft union of highly skilled workers can often make gains for its members through the craft organization that would be impossible if those particular workers were submerged in a large general union. . . .

A second although lesser problem appeared momentarily on the horizon in 1935. The A.A.A. and the Farm Bureau together had promoted the organization of farmers into local control associations. These were plainly intended as "public" associations, but the analogy to the origin of the Farm Bureau as a "public" auxiliary of the Extension Service was fairly obvious. O'Neal early warned that established farm organizations must be used in A.A.A. operations instead of creating new ones.[77] In May, 1935, the fears of Farm Bureau officials seemed to be in danger of realization. The secretary of a Texas control association issued a call for a convention of state organizations to be held in Washington. Although Wallace and Chester Davis took steps to head off the movement, some 4,500 farmers accompanied by 100 or so county agents did come to the capital. They made a protest against the current drive of processors to destroy the processing tax, and then dispersed. A memorandum from Davis ended the episode.[78]

The incident nicely symbolized the relationship which meshed the Department of Agriculture, the land grant colleges, the Extension Service, and the Farm Bureau. The county agent was made to play a political part, yet his activities were conducted at the end of a leash. The same control which was exerted over him extended in some degree to the other public bodies involved. Increasingly the control was vested in the Farm Bureau. The able leadership of the bureau was, in all likelihood, aware of the significance of the administrative structure. Use of the Extension Service in administration of "action" programs was one of the points which O'Neal took up with the President in 1933.[79] It was consistently a matter of high policy with the Farm Bureau throughout the formative years of the A.A.A.

At the same time, the Farm Bureau leadership was careful to ensure the continuance of its own influence with the Extension Service and the colleges. In 1933 O'Neal appeared, as he often did, before the convention of the colleges' association. He reminded his hearers that it was the

76 H. J. King, "Stockmen Need the Farm Bureau," *Nation's Agriculture*, vol. 12 (June, 1937), pp. 1–2.
77 *Bureau Farmer*, vol. 9 (January, 1934), p. 15.
78 "Officials of the A.A.A. acted quietly in numerous ways to discourage such a development" (i.e., the rise of a new farm organization). Davis, Nourse, and Black, *op. cit.*, pp. 271–73. Cf. also Lord, *The Wallaces of Iowa*, pp. 449–50.
79 Cf. American Farm Bureau Federation, *Annual Report, 1933*.

Farm Bureau that had really fought for their appropriations.[80] The provision of funds for the Extension Service from the A.A.A. was further evidence that cooperation with the organization program carried its rewards. The passage of the Bankhead-Jones Act of 1935 under Farm Bureau urgings was perhaps the best demonstration that the federation was the real source of this financial support for the colleges. This act authorized regular appropriations on an enlarged scale for research and Extension. The Farm Bureau could be counted on to fight for the authorized appropriations.

Although the benefits to the colleges were both substantial and assured, the costs of the act were heavy. Even in the crisis-ridden days of the early A.A.A., members of the association had misgivings. It was noted in 1934 that "the Agricultural Adjustment Act has imposed, at least for the time being, certain responsibilities which cannot, even with the most liberal classification, be termed educational." [81] Already new doubts were being voiced.[82]

Yet these were minority dissents. The relationship between the Farm Bureau, the colleges, and the Extension Service became closer rather than otherwise, and in 1936 the Farm Bureau reported that it was more intimate than ever before.[83] The bureau had enough assurance of this affinity to insist regularly upon "coordination" of all efforts in agricultural administration, with the Extension Service as the coordinating agent.[84] Inevitably, the bureau was violently opposed to the recommendations of the Brownlow Committee of 1937, which would have increased the conservation activities of the Department of the Interior.[85] More interestingly, the Farm Bureau opposed the Bailey and the Cooley bills of 1940 and 1941, which would have "decentralized" agricultural administration by placing it in the hands of the state directors of agriculture.[86] Although the bills would have given a token to the grass-roots theory

[80] Association of Land Grant Colleges and Universities, *Proceedings,* 1933 Convention, p. 89.

[81] H. J. C. Umberger, "The Relationship of the Land Grant Colleges to the A.A.A. Programs," Association of Land Grant Colleges and Universities, *Proceedings,* 1934 Convention, p. 108.

[82] I. O. Schaub, "Can Extension Continue an Educational Program and Administer Enforcement and Regulatory Measures?" Association of Land Grant Colleges and Universities, *Proceedings,* 1934 Convention, pp. 183–85.

[83] American Farm Bureau Federation, *Annual Report, 1936.*

[84] See, for example, the resolution on coordination, passed at the 1939 convention of the federation.

[85] The President's Committee on Administrative Management. For the reaction of the federation see *Nation's Agriculture,* vol. 13 (1938), p. 7; also the American Farm Bureau Federation, Resolutions, 1937 Convention.

[86] For example, the Bailey marketing bill, which would have made appropriations to state departments of agriculture for the encouragement of cooperative marketing by farmers, was opposed on the grounds that (1) the state departments of agriculture were primarily regulatory bodies, and (2) state directors of agriculture were political appointees in whose hands additional powers would prove "extremely dangerous." *Nation's Agriculture,* vol. 15 (September, 1940), p. 2. See also vol. 16 (May, 1941), p. 14.

which the Farm Bureau has sedulously advocated, the plain fact was that here the organizational interest of the Farm Bureau lay with the federal Extension Service rather than with the state agricultural departments.

As for the Extension Service itself, its leadership remained content with the fruits of its association with the Farm Bureau.[87] It is difficult to say whether the Extension heads continued to believe that their activities were primarily educational or whether they conceived that they actually shared in the political power which they had served to build. If the latter, the words of B. H. Crocheron should have come as a shock:

> During this and previous administrations it [Extension] has acted as chore-boy for the Federal Government and for the farmers' organizations. Those who believed this policy would bring to Extension vast resources and power have been mistaken. The nation has given the credit to the bureaus that have been helped and not to the great outstanding agency, Agricultural Extension, which has done the helping.[88]

What might have been added was that the power accrued to the Farm Bureau.

[87] "Government's relation to the American Farm Bureau Federation probably is a little closer than to any other farmers' organization, because of its origin and because of the fact that its county Farm Bureau units are organized primarily for the purpose of aiding the agricultural colleges and the Federal Department of Agriculture—to do the extension work assigned these two institutions in the National Agricultural Extension Act of 1914. No other farmers' organization has such a purpose. The A.F.B.F. has always backed extension legislation to the limit." C. B. Smith, director of Extension, "Farm Bureau and Extension," *Nation's Agriculture*, vol. 15, January, 1940, p. 9.

[88] B. H. Crocheron, "Re-defining the Extension Job and Field of Action," Association of Land Grant Colleges and Universities, *Proceedings*, 1941 Convention, p. 192. Crocheron was director of Agricultural Extension in California.

THE TECHNOLOGICAL
REVOLUTION *Edward Higbee*

Now that American agriculture has been invaded by the computer, radioactive elements, and the credit card it is somewhat unusual to find a farmer who plows with horses and thinks that one way to make money is not to spend it. Such a man, however, is Valentine Y. Byler of Pennsylvania who came to the attention of an Internal Revenue agent when he neglected to pay his Social Security assessments.[1] Mr. Byler is an Amishman of the Old Order faith, and Old Order Amishmen scorn the government's Social Security program because they feel it is the Lord's will that members of a family living on a family farm should care for one another to the end of their days. These thrifty folk are convinced that one way to keep farm and family together and to avoid public support is to rely upon horsepower which can be raised at home on home-grown hay. Store-bought tractors that run on store-bought gasoline are the devil's own temptation. These being his convictions, Mr. Byler was momentarily stymied when the Man-from-Washington flashed legal papers, attached his work horses, and sold them to pay up his federal retirement arrears. If at that point one more old-fashioned son of the soil had dropped out of agriculture no one would have been surprised. However, the Amishman, abetted by friendly members of his sect, borrowed another team, plowed his fields, and waited for the rains to reward him.

Talk with any Amishman and he will declare that his way of farming is a natural to beat the mounting pressures that today drive families of modest means off the land. Talk with a statistician who knows census data and he will say that the chances for survival of those who cling to old ideas and old methods are rather slim. Farming has become a high-speed business rather than a philosophy or a way of life. And it is no

---

[1] *Evening Bulletin*, Philadelphia, May 10, 1961.

REPRINTED with permission from Edward Higbee, "The Technological Revolution," *Farms and Farmers in an Urban Age*, New York: The Twentieth Century Fund, 1963, pp. 7–13, 24–30, 39–42.

longer a dependable social security institution. The farmer who expects to lead the pack has taken off his overalls to put on his business suit for a trip to Washington and a talk with his congressman.

Change

American agriculture is beyond the halfway mark in its second major technological revolution. During the first of these upheavals on the rural landscape, between 1850 and 1910, the Indians of the Great Plains were confined to reservations, Negro slavery was abolished, and the total of farms increased from 1.4 million to 6.4 million, most of them owned and operated by a single family.[2] These changes occurred during the revolution of the mule and the horse when animal power on a mass scale was harnessed to a marvelous assortment of tillage implements, and man in the United States was released from the hoe, the sickle, and the fear of hunger. Now agriculture is undergoing a second period of change— the revolution of science, mechanics, and heavy capital investment. While it has not as yet done away with the family farm it has gone a long way toward getting rid of the farm family.

In 1935 American farm units reached an all-time peak of 6.8 million. Since then there has been a precipitous drop in numbers. By 1961 there were left only 3.7 million. Within another decade or two this figure will very likely be cut back to 1.4 million. Since this was the starting point in 1850, the cycle will then be complete. Eventually, as the story is told of how this nation grew and changed, the era of the small family-homestead will appear brief. With its demise any influence which widespread security in land ownership may have had upon the American psyche will cease to exist. A hundred years ago, when there were only about 32 million people in the United States, about 65 per cent of them lived on farms. By 1980 probably less than 5 per cent of the people will live and work on the soil. Although most of the land will continue to be devoted to husbandry, the newer ways of rural life will bear little resemblance to those of the past. The culture, even more than the agriculture, of 185 million Americans is in flux.

In 1800, during the time of the sickle, an average of 56 hours of labor were required to produce an acre of wheat. By 1880, when the horse-drawn reaper was widely employed, it took 20 man-hours to grow and harvest an acre of wheat. Today on the Great Plains less than 2 hours of labor will do the job and do it better. A single mechanical cotton picker can gather as much fiber as forty pairs of human hands. Go into the country on a bright July day and there one man may be seen to bale and load 10 tons of hay in an hour while sitting down. Twenty years ago two men working with pitchforks could not have done that

2 *Historical Statistics of the United States—Colonial Times to 1957,* U.S. Department of Commerce, 1960, p. 278.

much in a whole afternoon. Just how many hours are saved by a modern harvester that tops and pulls an acre of radishes in an hour is any weekend gardener's guess. This is the machine which made the lowly radish one of the supermarket's best year-round buys. By 1910, when horse-drawn implements had taken over a substantial part of corn production, 147 man-hours were required to raise 100 bushels. This was quite an improvement over the 344 man-hours needed in the hand-hoe days of 1800, but today a few exceptional farmers in the corn belt raise 100 bushels of corn with less than 4 hours of labor.[3] Better seeds, pesticides, and more fertilizers, as well as machinery, have made this progress possible. The improved efficiency of modern agriculture is as fabulous as the conquest of outer space, and it is far more significant for the welfare of humankind.

The number of horses and mules on American farms reached a peak of almost 27 million in 1917. By 1960 the total had dropped to 3 million. In the same span of time the number of tractors increased from 51,000 to nearly 5 million.[4] Now aircraft are considered the most efficient spreaders of fertilizers and pesticides where large acreages require quick, uniform treatment. Because rice fields are often flooded, growers of this crop are particularly inclined to be airborne. They hire planes to seed, fertilize, and spray pesticides, and when the crop is about to ripen they hasten maturity by spraying hormones from the air. Rice growers have also discovered that planes are more effective than scarecrows at dispersing blackbirds; when birds become a problem a farmer may place a call to the nearest air service to buzz them. So many operations are done by commercial pilots on a custom basis that some people claim rice plantations are run by telephones rather than by farmers.

In 1961 the irrigated fields of southern California got a glimpse of the first self-propelled lettuce packers which cost over $20,000 each and pack 600 boxes of lettuce per hour right in the field. These mobile "factories" which lumber down the lush green rows like dinosaurs carry ten girls and a boxing crew. The girls wrap and seal each head of lettuce in a plastic cover while the boxing crews pack them for trucks that follow. The trucks carry the cartons to cooling plants at rail sidings and within a few hours the chilled lettuce is on its way across the continent.

For a long time it was thought that the culture of tree and bush fruits could not be mechanized but now there are dozens of operational models that prune and pick. Modern orchards look like giant hedgerows after they have been trimmed by buzz saws mounted on hydraulic beams transported by tractors. Some fruit growers have reduced field labor forces at harvest time to one-tenth of former requirements by using mechanical tree shakers and fruit catchers which are wrapped around the trees like firemen's life nets.

[3] *Yearbook of Agriculture, 1960*, U.S. Department of Agriculture, p. 169.
[4] *Historical Statistics of the United States—Colonial Times to 1957*, U.S. Department of Commerce, 1960, p. 285; *Statistical Abstract of the United States, 1962*, Bureau of the Census, p. 607.

Paradox

Mechanization in farming brings about the same economic and social changes that it does in industry. Already it has eliminated the need for cheap, illiterate hired labor in the production of corn and wheat and, to a considerable extent, cotton. Now mechanical devices are taking over jobs in fruit and vegetable production where some of the most primitive and degrading conditions for human living in rural America still prevail. While labor efficiency and living standards have improved more rapidly in agricultural areas than in cities in recent years, some of the nation's poorest people are yet to be found in rural districts where social and economic progress took a detour. It is ironic that within that very segment of the economy which suffers from the overproduction of food there are farmers and farmhands who suffer from malnutrition because they cannot afford to eat properly. For these persons more progress cannot come soon enough.

One of the strangest features of modern American agriculture is that farm income stagnated during years when technical efficiency made some of its greatest gains. In the decade 1948–57 production per man-hour on farms increased 48.6 per cent while the improvement in other industries was only 25.5 per cent. During the 1950's the average annual increase in production per worker was slightly above 6 per cent in agriculture. Outside of agriculture it was under 3 per cent. At the end of 1960 capital investment for each worker in agriculture was $21,300 compared with $15,900 for each worker in other industries. In 1960 one farmer produced enough food for 26 persons whereas in 1940 his efforts fed only 11 persons. In 1959 the average income of all farm families from agriculture was $2,875 while that of all urban families was $5,911. In that same year 18 per cent of all farm families had total incomes of less than $1,000 whereas only 3 per cent of all urban families had such inadequate incomes.[5]

Something must be wrong with this story. How could anything doing so well be so badly off? It does not make sense.

Two Extremes

The dreary picture developed by these statistics is both true and false. It is mathematically correct but it is deceptive because it lumps all farmers together, and it credits farm families with farm income only. If the non-farm earnings of farm operator families are included, then it turns out that their average net income for 1959 was $5,115. The fact is that quite a few tillers of the soil do extraordinarily well even without off-farm earnings. These are the big-spending, modernized, full-time, professional

[5] *Food and Agriculture: A Program for the 1960's,* U.S. Department of Agriculture, March, 1962, p. 8.

farmers. . . . Others at the tail end of the barnyard pecking order are called farmers only because the Bureau of the Census and the Department of Agriculture do not know exactly where to cut off a factory worker who is a part-time farmer or a farmer who is a part-time factory worker and just plain unemployed most of the time. In some rural sections underemployment and seasonal unemployment are as serious as joblessness in distressed urban areas. Yet tens of thousands of rural indigent are called farmers even though they cannot raise enough to feed themselves properly.

It is the great weight of poverty at the lower levels that makes all agriculture look sick in statistics when in reality the upper crust which produces most of the food could pass its physical any day in the week and be classified 1–A. In public discussions about the ills of husbandry a distinction seldom is made between what is a social problem of wider scope and what pertains strictly to the agricultural economy. Because coal mines are shut down in West Virginia the public does not assume that all industry is in a slump, yet similar deductions are made with respect to agriculture. In 1959, 2.2 million operators of 61 per cent of all American farms averaged *five times* more income from work away from their farms than they did from work on them. Most of these people did not earn much either place. Furthermore their marketed production was only 13 per cent of all farm output in 1959.[6] This being the case, the question might be raised whether these persons should be classified as farmers when the problems of agriculture are being considered.

There is widespread indigence in rural areas because many people called farmers are not financially able to meet the costs of technological improvement. This is not the fault of the people concerned. They have simply been by-passed by a technology too rich for their blood. While some operators can make it on credit cards others have to scrape along on money. The latter keep falling farther and farther behind. Most city factory workers long ago became reconciled to the fact that they could not own and operate their own shops. Now it is the farmer who faces the realities of an industrial age.

No reasonable headway can be made in reshaping national policy toward agriculture until it is recognized that the players at the top and the players at the bottom are not in the same league and the spread between them is getting wider. Eighty-seven per cent of the value of all farm products sold in 1959 was accounted for by 1.4 million farms, or 39 per cent of the total.[7] If the other 2.2 million farms were to go out of business by 1969 their output would not be missed. The big question is how will all these people who are not needed in agriculture find ways to make a living elsewhere? Already city slums harbor hundreds of thousands of rural refugees, many on welfare rolls.

.   .   .

[6] *Food and Agriculture: A Program for the 1960's,* U.S. Department of Agriculture, March, 1962, p. 50.
[7] *Ibid.*

Better Plants and Fertilizers

The technological revolution in agriculture, which has resulted in surplus production and in surplus farmers, is partly genetic and chemical. Better plants and better animals as well as advanced knowledge about feeding them both have made it profitable to use better machines. While the new machines may reduce unit costs by mass production, the mass itself is possible only because better germ plasm and better nutrition are also there. Plants as well as animals must be fed for maximum growth. There is a physiological limit to the increases in yields which can be obtained by work alone. This fact is well known by those in backward parts of the world who labor with machete and sickle. Good seed does not result in miracles of production unless the soil is fertilized. The achievements of modern agriculture are the consequence of a complex chain of scientific discoveries and technological advances. If a farmer disregards any link his crop may be a failure. That is why the example of American excellence in farming has not been copied widely elsewhere in the world. The agricultural achievement of this country, no less than its industrial ability, is the product of the total economic and social environment. It does not stand alone and cannot be exported as some diplomats have dreamed that it might be.

In 1949 the average yield of corn per acre in the United States was 38 bushels. By 1959 it was up to 51 bushels. In the corn belt average yields in 1961 were 67 bushels per acre. On specialized cash-grain farms the average yield was 86 bushels per acre. Now new hybrid seeds are coming out of university experimental plots which are superior to anything even dreamed of, except by the geneticists who breed them. A 100 bushel per acre average for the corn belt is a fair prospect for 1970. The new corns have a genetic potential for production which is between 25 and 50 bushels per acre above that of any corns known to the farmers of 1961. Present types of seed can utilize efficiently about 90 pounds per acre of the essential element nitrogen. The new varieties will efficiently convert 200 pounds of nitrogen per acre into plant tissue through more vigorous growth. If the American chemical industry could not supply cheap nitrogen in almost unlimited amounts, the farmer could not benefit as much by the remarkable advance in corn genetics.

On what is called "God's Little Acre" in Prentiss County, Mississippi, two teen-age boys, Lamar and Linden Ratliff, established a world corn production record of 304 bushels per acre in 1955. Since then the young Ratliffs have tried in vain to surpass their own achievement. In 1961 they came close with 283 bushels. That year they applied 38 tons of manure, a ton of concentrated 14–14–14 fertilizer,[8] and a ton of nitrate of ammonia to just that one acre of ground. They also irrigated it. The Ratliff corn is grown on the same plot that the boys' father first planted to

[8] 14–14–14 fertilizer is fertilizer which contains 14 per cent nitrogen (N), 14 per cent phosphorus (P_2O_5), and 14 per cent potassium (K_2O).

corn over thirty years ago. Every year until the boys were able to take care of it the father obtained higher and higher yields by giving it more and more fertilizer and attention. The field became a hobby. Now this one-acre plot has become the talk of farmers all over the country. Father Paul Ratliff once remarked, "I remember working this field and not getting a trailerful." In recent years his sons have harvested more than five trailerfuls from that single plot. In the past harvest day at "God's Little Acre" has been a county celebration. Folks have converged on the homestead from miles around. Mrs. Ratliff has provided a huge free meal and county farm agent W. T. Smith has acted as official weigher. Technicians at Mississippi State University have run moisture tests to make the yield official.[9] What surprises lie in store for Prentiss County when the young Ratliffs get hold of the new souped-up hybrids is anybody's guess.

What is happening to corn is happening to wheat, to peanuts, and to sugar cane; in fact it is happening to azaleas, roses, and practically every other economic plant. In humid areas where drought is not a limiting factor the growers of wheat thought they did well years ago when they harvested 20 bushels per acre. Today 40 and 50 bushel yields are common in the Midwest. Denmark led the world in 1959 with an average national harvest of 66 bushels. Now plant breeders at the University of Washington have produced an average of 140 bushels per acre and on one experimental plot they obtained 152 bushels per acre.[10] In 1960 the average yield of potatoes was 9 tons, but the champion potato grower of Pennsylvania had an average harvest of over 23 tons in 1961. Potato production has become such a highly specialized and highly concentrated operation that the major portion of the total United States crop is now supplied by 6,492 leading growers.[11]

Superior Animals

The livestock side of farming has been revolutionized by new concepts of breeding and feeding. The old notion that purebreds were tops has been assailed by hybrid vigor. Crosses are the fashion and performance testing through progeny now is the popular way to determine the superiority of an animal. The carcass at the packing house and the size of the feed bill are more important than appearance in the show ring. Conformation as a standard for judging the best of class is out of date except at pet shows and at Atlantic City. At one of Oklahoma State University's demonstration farms a Swine Evaluation Station, or "Hogs' Hall of Fame," has been established to test the caliber of boars through the performance of their progeny. Pigs in lots of six from different sows but

[9] *New York Times,* November 12, 1957.
[10] *Evening Bulletin,* Philadelphia, January 5, 1962.
[11] *United States Census of Agriculture, 1959,* Vol. II, Chapter 7, pp. 854–55.

sired by the same boar are compared with similar lots of pigs sired by other boars. The pigs are comfortably housed, fed the same prime ration, and given temperature-controlled water. All they have to do is enjoy life and grow. When they reach 201 pounds their careers as research assistants come to an end. Their carcasses are dressed and measured for quality of loins, hams, bacon, and the total amount of all lean cuts. Then days on feed are compared as well as the total amount of feed consumed. By analysis of the performance of the offspring the genetic influence of the father is determined. The best males get a chance to exercise their talents under the most encouraging circumstances, while the inferiors follow their progeny to the abattoir.[12] A similar research approach is used at many experiment stations with beef cattle, dairy cattle, sheep, swine, and poultry.

Broilers

Probably the most remarkable progress in animal breeding has been achieved with poultry. This is not surprising. Genetic improvement is the consequence of gradual progress generation by generation, and it is possible to get several generations of chickens into the record books in the same two years that it takes a single calf to grow from conception to a baby beef. Also, one hen can produce a lot more offspring for selection than a cow. Today leading producers employ their own geneticists and statisticians and they patent their private strains of birds.

As recently as 1955 a broiler chick required 3 pounds of feed to make 1 pound of gain. By 1960 there were commercial flocks that made 1 pound of gain on less than 2.5 pounds of feed. In a recent trial the University of Georgia produced a pen of eight broilers that averaged 4.28 pounds on 8 pounds of feed in eight weeks. Of course the feed is getting "hotter" and the broilers are becoming better converters with every step of progress. High-energy or "hot" feed is a mixture high in protein and high in fat, which results in rapid gain. This is important because the faster the chicks can be raised, the greater the number of flocks that can be handled in a year by given manpower and given facilities. Broiler houses are expensive. Some are three stories high. Some are 600 feet long. They house as many as 40,000 or 50,000 birds for every workman. Poultry growers, like metropolitan real estate syndicates, must secure maximum tenancy to make their accommodations profitable. To produce a 3 pound bird in twelve weeks was considered efficient a decade ago. Now a commercial flock should hit an average of 3.4 pounds in eight to nine weeks. Such a fast turnover cuts down overhead.

. . .

[12] *Farm and Ranch,* January, 1962.

Changes in Production and Marketing—Contract Farming

A combination of better germ plasm, better feeds, and a better technology have converted broiler production into a factory industry. Even the farmer has been revamped. No longer is he likely to be his own boss, even in his own chicken houses. The risks of market fluctuations and the heavy costs of thousands of birds and their feed have made him hedge. The average broiler grower chooses to be a piece worker under contract to some feed dealer or processor who takes the risk. An efficient broiler grower makes a good income for himself and his sponsor when he can market at two cents a pound over costs of production. In an industry as competitive as the broiler business is today this is one way for the little man without everything to find some security. Rather than try to lick the processors, he can join them. Of course that means they will boss and he will say yes, even on his own farm. If this is hard, so is life. The process of integration need not end with just a single tie-up between farm and processor. It can go the full distance from field and barn to the retail chain store, and those involved can all lean on one another. Whoever puts up most of the credit will issue the orders. The system is similar to that by which the "independent" service station operator joins the oil industry. The boom in contract farming in recent years is just one more indication of the industrial nature of modern agriculture.

The small operator can get credit more easily if he has an agreement with a processor which assures him of a fixed market price. Frequently it is the processor himself who grants or guarantees the credit. In return the farmer settles in advance for a margin of profit which will save him from disaster but seldom make him rich. In effect he accepts a wage in return for a reduced risk. Since he relies chiefly on someone else's capital or credit he could hardly expect more. In return for financial support the processor gets an assured supply of raw material at a low price. If the market is demolished by overproduction the processor takes a licking. He may even be liquidated and, if he is, the whole of his empire may collapse with him. If the market zooms, the bonanza is usually split between the processor and the farmer according to some prearranged formula. As a rule the checks and balances of competition and "fair trade" keep the market from either skidding or skyrocketing, but occasionally the big wheels try to roll over one another in a price war.

Contract farming is most highly developed in those branches of agriculture where turnover is fast and operating expenses exceed the value of farm real estate. Many freezing and canning crops are produced under such arrangements but poultry production is the prime example. Georgia leads all fifty states in this industry, yet Georgians were picking cotton rather than plucking broilers twenty-five years ago. In 1935 only a half million broilers were marketed in Georgia. In 1960, 320 million were sold there.[13]

. . .

[13] *Agricultural Statistics, 1961*, U.S. Department of Agriculture, p. 419.

Efficiency

As all segments of American agriculture have amply demonstrated, the surest way to prosper is not through artificially rigged bargaining power but through increased efficiency. When farmers integrate with processors, or when co-ops provide a medium for collective bargaining, the efficient producer ultimately reaps more benefit than the inefficient producer. A contract price which is favorable to the average producer will prove a balloon to the efficient and a sinker to the incompetent or under-capitalized. Efficiency on a mass scale is more profitable than efficiency on a small scale. Thus a good manager must have ample capital if he is to use his talents to their full extent. A good manager without capital is handicapped. It goes without saying that capital in the hands of an incompetent is wasted.

The recent course of evolution in the dairy industry confirms this general conclusion. What is particularly significant about dairying is the rapidity with which new adjustments are taking place. No major segment of American agriculture is now undergoing a more profound and accelerated shakedown. In 1950 there were 3.6 million farms with milk cows. By 1959 there were only 1.8 million. Nevertheless, depressed as the general market for dairy products appears to be, there are conditions under which it provides an incentive to those with capital to expand their operations. In 1950 there were 3,593 dairy farms in the United States with more than 100 cows. By 1959 the number of farms with over 100 cows had risen to 6,594, and there were at least 34 farms with over 1,000 milk cows each.[14]

Dream World

The tourist in southern Florida finds rich fare in a trip around the rim of Lake Okeechobee if he is fascinated by the wild swamps of the Everglades and the engineering techniques of modern reclamation. He sees landscapes of native flora that have changed little since the days of Spanish exploration. Almost alongside he observes some of the most advanced drainage and irrigation projects to be found anywhere. This is one of the nation's most prosperous winter farming districts, specializing in sugar cane, fresh vegetables, and intensive dairying. As the resort cities of Florida's coasts have boomed in population the inland rural districts have prospered.

North of the town of Okeechobee, where the flat landscape is accented by the feather-duster plumes of palm trees, the traveler comes suddenly upon the tidy, white-fenced domain of the McArthur Dairy. A sign tells him that he is welcome to enter. Thus he has an invitation to see for himself a 20th century bovine dream world unmatched for its

[14] *United States Census of Agriculture, 1959*, Vol. II, Chapter 6, Table 26.

scale anywhere in America. In 1928 the McArthur Dairy began operations with 20 cows in open country that was eventually to become part of Miami: 1928 is almost "ancient times" as the history of southern Florida is recounted. In subsequent years more people came into the area and built. Miami grew and the little dairy was forced to move farther into the country. It made several moves of this sort, retreating before the advance of the city only to be caught again. With each shift the market improved and the herd increased. By 1962 the enterprise had grown to 8,000 registered Jerseys—enough to stock 400 average Wisconsin dairy farms.

By 1962 the McArthur Dairy had transferred most of its operations to the wilderness north of Lake Okeechobee. There it had turned thousands of acres of wild land into productive year-round pastures sufficient to accommodate most of its herd. Plans have been made to consolidate the entire enterprise at Okeechobee. Already four giant milking barns have been constructed. These white barns are immaculate and each cow is given a scrubdown shower under a hose before milking. The milk itself goes directly from the milking machines to stainless steel refrigeration tanks. A fleet of refrigerated trucks hauls the milk to bottling plants. There are three small villages, each of about thirty houses, for the families of herdsmen and milkers. The homes for the workmen are new and the villages have palm-lined streets. Buses shuttle children to and from the public schools.

Eventually when all 8,000 Jerseys are assembled at Okeechobee there will be seven milking barns and around 150 families of permanent help. Construction is already underway. A number of the present milkers and herdsmen are former dairy farmers who sold their own properties to become a part of the McArthur team. Cows are milked on a round-the-clock schedule. The men work in shifts and the cows follow an equally precise routine which divides their life between pasture and barn. Not only is the scale of operations impressive but the orderliness and cleanliness of the whole establishment leaves the visitor with the conviction that milk could not be produced under more favorable conditions. It is an operation that could set the pace for the future dairy industry granted enough markets like that in southern Florida. There are farms similar to it in almost every state with a large urban population; they vary primarily in scale and in certain techniques that are appropriate to particular climates.

·   ·   ·

Specialization

All in all specialization and concentration are the principal trends throughout the economic structure of American agriculture. Only a comparative few out of many are able to cope with the financial and technical demands of modern farming. Lack of skill in bookkeeping and cost analysis can hurt a farmer today as much as a deficiency in the art of husbandry. The technology of management takes precedence over field or animal husbandry. A successful rancher with outfits in Montana and Wyoming came into his profession after having been vice-president of a transcontinental trucking company. Said he, as he sat comfortably in his living room before an exquisite picture-window view of the Big Horn Mountains: "If my cattle needed help in an emergency, I'd be the least useful person on this ranch. I employ a foreman for that." He had gone into ranching rather than into apartment investments in Los Angeles, he said, "First because I like country life better than city life. Secondly, I made a cost analysis just as I did before I went into the trucking business. I decided I could do better than the average." Any farmer today who cannot do better than the average is on his way out. Others are ready to replace him.

Impact

The technological revolution in agriculture has been more than a switch to new machines, better germ plasm, streamlined marketing systems, and more efficient management of capital. It has affected people more than it has affected the land, yet the influence upon the land has also been profound. Economic and social dislocations in rural areas have been harder to cope with than the new technology itself. While there are half as many people on the soil as there were twenty-five years ago, farmers are still a surplus commodity. The machine has been welcomed. Men without capital have been rejected. Less thought has been given to the problem of surplus men than to that of surplus crops. More anxiety has been expressed over price supports for milk than over how to get those surpluses consumed by people who need milk but cannot afford it. Abuses of acreage allotment privileges and scandalous grain storage operations have aroused public indignation, but the plight of disrupted lives has been accepted apathetically.

The way the farm problem has been dealt with resembles the way in which urban renewal has been tackled. Depreciated physical assets have been researched with the most scrupulous attention and generous subsidies have been granted to rehabilitate property. . . . The human problem has been swept under the rug. Surplus farmers continue to leave the occupation which once offered Americans the best opportunity to become "self-made." Now a man must "have it made" before he can farm.

· · ·

A 8
B 9
C 0
D 1
E 2
F 3
G 4
H 5
I 6
J 7

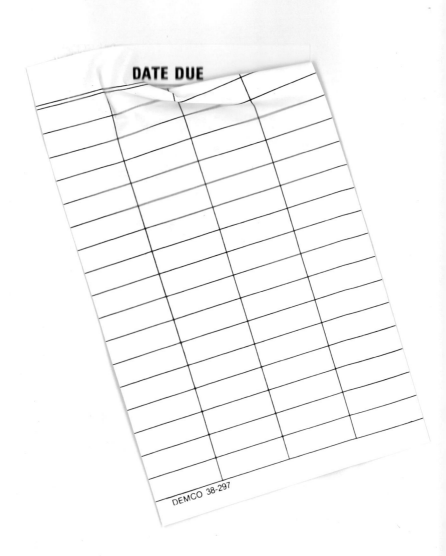